KU-736-211

THE
STONE
ROSES

AND THE RESURRECTION
OF BRITISH POP

BAINTE DEN STOC

WITHDRAWN FROM DÚN LAOGHAIRE RATHDOWN
COUNTY LIBRARY STOCK

D1327958

THE
STONE
ROSES

AND THE RESURRECTION
OF BRITISH POP

JOHN ROBB

DUN LAOGHAIRE- RATHDOWN LIBRARIES	
DLR20001001451	
BERTRAMS	03/07/2012
	£14.99
QA	

1 3 5 7 9 10 8 6 4 2

This edition published 2012
First published in 1997 by Ebury Press, an imprint of Ebury Publishing
A Random House Group company

Copyright © John Robb 2012

John Robb has asserted his right to be identified as the author of this Work in
accordance with the Copyright, Designs and Patents Act 1988

All rights reserved. No part of this publication may be reproduced, stored
in a retrieval system, or transmitted in any form or by any means, electronic,
mechanical, photocopying, recording or otherwise, without the
prior permission of the copyright owner

The Random House Group Limited Reg. No. 954009

Addresses for companies within the Random House Group can be found at
www.randomhouse.co.uk

A CIP catalogue record for this book is available from the British Library
The Random House Group Limited supports The Forest Stewardship Council
(FSC®), the leading international forest certification organisation. Our books
carrying the FSC label are printed on FSC® certified paper. FSC is the only
forest certification scheme endorsed by the leading environmental
organisations, including Greenpeace. Our paper procurement policy
can be found at www.randomhouse.co.uk/environment

MIX
Paper from
responsible sources
FSC® C016897

Designed and set by seagulls.net

Printed and bound by CPI Group (UK) Ltd, Croydon, CR0 4YY

ISBN 9780091948580

To buy books by your favourite authors and register for offers visit
www.randomhouse.co.uk

INTRODUCTION
The Resurrection and the Third Coming

The Stone Roses have become folk heroes, frozen in time. And their story, with roots in punk through post-punk, scooter boys, skinheads, Northern Soul, psychedelia, acid house and Madchester, is everything that is great about British street culture.

They astutely embraced it all, an encyclopaedia of British street smarts and British street style. They were at the heart of the post-punk tribal wars when you were defined by what you wore, and in 1989 they fronted the biggest and most important pop culture scene in the UK since punk itself. They operated outside the hipster elite and made music on their own terms. They took the past and created the future. They broke massive without anyone's permission and they defied the music business. They were out of control and never got on the album/tour treadmill. They imploded instead of taking the world. They could have been U2 but became the most influential and coolest band of their generation instead. They were their generation's equivalent of The Clash, the band that had everything and then gloriously threw it all away.

In the intervening years their myth has grown so much that there is hardly a British band that hasn't taken something of their spirit, energy, music, style and swagger, and run with it.

Their career seemed to have ended with a comma rather than a full stop. Unfinished business. Unlike most bands that fall apart, they still had plenty to offer. No wonder their comeback has been greeted with such excitement.

The Stone Roses reformation is one of the most shocking comebacks in pop history. In a year when arguments about retromania raged and every band you could think of had reformed, there was still one band that seemed like it would remain in the past. Like The Clash from the punk era, the band that had influenced so many seemed incapable of being part of the legacy that they had created.

When The Stone Roses announced they were reforming at that glorious, chaotic press conference on 18 October 2011, they created a wave of emotion that they could never have expected.

'The magic is back,' texted Ian Brown, adding, 'We gonna shake it up!'

A staggering 220,000 tickets for the three announced gigs at Manchester's Heaton Park sold out in 40 minutes, the internet was jammed and the country went into a rush of Roses mania. They became the fastest-selling tickets ever for a UK rock gig. It took everyone aback and underlined that in the modern, cynical UK we had simply run out of folk heroes. Bands were increasingly becoming something of the past and the pop culture played out on mainstream TV and in the tabloids had become a desperate world of *X Factor*'s boring soap opera and flimsy pop celebrity culture.

That The Stone Roses' comeback pushed this modern circus from the spotlight was some achievement. That a band who had released two albums and who had briefly flickered in the mainstream more than 20 years ago, were welcomed with such an outpouring of excitement was a measure of both their own innate genius and the desperation of music culture in the modern UK.

At the press conference there was a moment that underlined the band's status. Before they entered the room there were dark mutterings of 'they are only in it for the money', but then when the band sloped into the room they got a standing ovation. It was like Robin Hood had come back from the dead as Ian Brown led his merry men into the room.

It seems a long time since the last squelches of feedback and sound faded away at the band's gig at Glasgow Green on 9 June 1990, their last with the proper classic line-up. Unbeknown to everyone that night, Reni would never be on stage with the band again, although he stuck around long enough to record the *Second Coming* album in those fumbling, faltering years as the band dissipated the energy they had built up.

They fell apart in acrimony and that seemed to be that. Ian Brown had a successful solo career making records that traded little on his past, John Squire sold a lot of records with The Seahorses before putting down his guitar and becoming a successful artist. Mani became the greatest free transfer in rock'n'roll when he joined The Stone Roses' sister band, Primal Scream. And Reni? Well, Reni just slipped away to Whalley Range to recover from it all and bring up his kids.

The dream was over and the band became a retrospective and very big footnote in UK music history, a constant in those 'Greatest Album Of All Time' lists, still influencing young bands in garages everywhere.

When they re-emerged in 2011, the world was a different place. There were mobile phones and internet technology. The music scene was vastly different. In fact it was on the verge of collapse. The internet had changed everything and no one bought records any more. Celebrity pop was everywhere and yet nowhere. You could hear music wherever you turned but no one was paying for it. The recession was biting and capitalism seemed like it might be about to meet its end.

Ever wise to the importance of context and the challenge of keeping things relevant, Ian Brown wanted, at first, to announce the band's reformation the day after the UK summer riots of 2011, but they waited a few months. When asked how long they would carry on, he laughed. 'We will keep going till the wheels fall off.'

And no matter how long they do keep going, one thing is for sure – they'll have the masses following them. The band is, if anything, just as relevant today as they've ever been. They are the people's band.

I once asked Mani why they became so legendary. The affable bass player answered, 'People like the fact that we were like normal guys and the mandate was always, "If we can do it, then why can't you?" If you look at a lot of the bands who have come in our wake, a lot of them have got up after The Stone Roses because we kind of opened the door and showed people the way of doing things and then just let them get on with it, you know?'

They were part of their times, but they were also a catalyst for the future. They took trad guitar music and breathed new life into it and when they put out 'Fool's Gold' they virtually patented the perfect nineties pop record.

This was a book that had to be written. It's a book about the band, the lifestyle. It's written from the streets of Manchester, and shares the same rehearsal rooms and venues, even the claustrophobic tour bus during their slow rise to the top; it staggers around E'd out of its head at the climax, and it sits around waiting for something to happen in their five-year stretch of doing nothing very much. It tracks the last stand and the downfall; it enjoys their solo years and this special reunion edition is there for the comeback too.

It's there for the famous reformation press conference and it's there with John Squire and Ian Brown when they make their return to the stage in Manchester at the Ritz in December 2011.

It's basically there every step of the way, tracking the myth of The Stone Roses, feeling the force of a people's band as it's pushed into the mainstream and beyond.

It was a bastard difficult book to write, as looking at the past through a cloud of righteous partying had warped many minds. But in this fully updated and revised edition, I've elicited loads more new information, including nearly a hundred new interviews with band associates and members from over the years, and there are new chapters too. As always everyone remembers the story differently, everyone disputes each other, and new unheard details of legendary anecdotes have come to light. Like the band the story evolves and all of this new information combines to produce the most complete and detailed history of this seminal band. It's a good job that I was there and sharp as fuck, or this tale of pop perfection might have been lost in the mists of time.

John Robb

THE BIG DAY OUT

Blackpool, 1989

The eighties had been a let-down. So far. Mainstream pop had become stale and boring...Smashy and Nicey DJs playing to boring fluffy-haired groups of grinning fools. The low point had been Live Aid. Great cause – terrible music. Meanwhile the underground had been thriving with all manner of great music that only occasionally made itself heard via the likes of New Order or The Smiths. It's a measure of how lost music was that when The Stone Roses started writing their pure crystalline pop gems, the best they could hope for was cult underground status. But, as the decade drew to an end, the culture started shifting. Fast.

It's one of the truisms of pop culture that if you change the drugs you change everything. Ecstasy had arrived and acid house was scorching the minds of a new generation. It was everywhere; opening the doors to a drug binge that dwarfed that of the 1960s. Suddenly the music scene was moving in fast-forward. The feeling was that anything was possible: even the Iron Curtain was crumbling. A couple of years down the line Nirvana would make it, but even their breakthrough would not match the impact of the positive rush of E-fuelled optimism in the UK that came when the Roses (along with fellow home-town pop hooligans, Happy Mondays) gatecrashed the pop party.

The Roses album was released in the spring of '89 and had been a steady cult seller as they toured the country with audiences slowly building. Over the 40 gigs in the year before Blackpool the crowd had started looking different, dressing in loose-fitting clothes, and there was a new feeling in the air. Indie gigs stopped being dour and were now parties.

The Stone Roses were breaking out and people were starting to notice. On 12 August 1989 they played their masterstroke and sold out the 3,500-capacity Empress Ballroom in Blackpool's Winter Gardens.

Overnight, with this audacious gig, they became the most important band in the country. A band that went from playing the toilet circuit of 200-capacity venues was now selling out a big hall with a new sound and a new look. In a nod to rave culture, the gig wasn't just a gig, it was an EVENT, a hijacking of popular culture.

Several years later Ian Brown explained it all to me. 'We all wanted to do something special. I can't remember who came up with the idea originally. I would like to say it was us so I could say it wasn't Gareth [the band's manager],' he laughs. 'There was general talk amongst us that we didn't want to just do the circuit like other bands. We never played the Boardwalk in Manchester. We didn't want to play the traditional circuit. We'd played the warehouse parties in 1985 and wanted to take that further. We wanted to play our own thing, to keep it exciting, to keep it in line with that underground party atmosphere that was going on at the time. We wanted to play places where bands didn't play; that was our number one priority.'

That night in the teeming heat and euphoric atmosphere of the Empress Ballroom, the first rumblings that something new was about to enter the rock'n'roll mainstream were being felt. The ornate Victoriana of the hall was filled with mad fuckers, indie heads, stoners and house fiends looking for some rock'n'roll crossover.

Built in 1879, the Winter Gardens is a great venue. A collection of different venues under one roof, with the Empress being the biggest and the grandest. In the thirties and forties the great George Formby was a regular performer there when he was the biggest star in the UK, and dance orchestras played to packed dancefloors. The Rolling Stones had caused a riot there in 1964 that saw them banned from Blackpool for 35 years, and it was where the political parties held their conferences for decades until they got too snobby for the seaside. The Roses' timing was impeccable.

Suddenly The Smiths seemed to be a long time ago. In pop a few months can seem like a lifetime. Here were new gods for old, bowl cuts for quiffs, baggy cuts replacing indie styles. It was a guitar assimilation of the acid house vibe that was engulfing youth culture at the time. The Stone Roses were never acid house musically but they were immersed in the culture; they were pop culture junkies. They understood the new communal vibe. If post-punk indie music had spent years being elitist, this music was for everybody. Bands had spent years snubbing the mainstream, but here was a band who wanted to own it.

Acid house had arrived without the traditional music press/radio route. Raves were massive. They were, above all, a colourful fun celebration. The Roses at Blackpool was a trippy rave but with a different soundtrack.

In fact, it was the dawning of a new pop era. Manchester had been backing the Roses for several years but now it was time to go overground, to go beyond the cult underground status that had trapped every cool band of the last ten years.

The thousands of fans milling around the Blackpool streets with their fresh new flares, fresh faces and fresh Stone Roses T-shirts before the gig knew that they were at an historic event. The Stone Roses had seized the times and there was an air of pop revolt where things were changing fast and you were either on the bus or off it.

Ian Brown was thrilled to be at the centre of the pop culture shift. 'The idea of the gig was to make it a day out in Blackpool, like everyone loves doing, and go and see a band and because of that there was loads of kids waiting outside the venue.

'I remember being at the soundcheck at the gig and just being amazed by the number of kids who had flares and Reni hats and money shirts (as they became known) on. That amazed us. We never expected that. We wanted to look different from the other bands. We did wear semi flares back in 1986 but I was wearing full-blown flares by then. The others had big parallels on. We knew we looked different from all the other bands. We didn't realise or think the kids would start dressing like us, so it was a bit of a shock. When we got to the soundcheck thousands of kids were on the streets.

'We had toured since the album came out. We had done little shows in places like Chester and Portsmouth and this was the first big gig, the first time since the album was released that we had seen all the kids dressed up. It was a shock to us. We were laughing with joy; shit we didn't expect that. All these kids were not all Manchester kids, they were from Liverpool, St Helens, all the other towns, mainly all northern kids. A lot of them were so young, like it was their first gig; maybe we were the first band they got into.'

That youthfulness, that feeling that a new generation had arrived, was what Blackpool was all about. Old timers complained about the flares, a transgression of one of the sacred rules of the punk rock code, as the most important youth culture since punk was taking over.

Photographer Ian Tilton returned to the town he grew up in on The Stone Roses' tour bus and took a series of brilliant shots of the band that have defined them ever since. 'I wasn't actually commissioned by *Sounds* music paper, who I was working for, to do the Blackpool shots, I just asked the band if I could come along and they said "yeah sure" so I got on the tour bus in Manchester and we went over to Blackpool. It was a magic day.

'Hanging out with the band backstage there was just this lovely, loving confidence about them. Ian and [his close friend Steve] Cressa were like that [shows two fingers locked together]. There's a picture from that day with them both leaning on each other with their heads together fixing the yo-yo that Ian would take on stage later and that's how it was, great mates. There was a lot of love in the area and it was a beautiful thing to see.'

Ian snapped away as the band hung out backstage.

'As soon as we got to the Blackpool Empress Ballroom we saw the crew that were filming them – the people who filmed *The Tube* up in Newcastle – and they had set up the track for the dolly. The camera goes on the dolly so it can smoothly pan across the floor and Ian and John jumped on it and start zooming around the ballroom, with Ian pulling faces like he's riding a motorbike. I got some great shots of that. It was a fun day and those pictures sort of summed that up.

'There was also some messing around with my camera when the band picked it up and used it. That was their revenge for a *Sounds* photo session that I'd recently done with them. On the cover of the magazine, they had used individual shots of each member. Reni's picture was of him in his Reni hat with his chin slightly sticking out. When it was published he wasn't happy – but he was the one who pulled the face! He was angry at me for sending it off. Saying that, I thought it looked great and that's what happens sometimes.

'So they got back at me, didn't they? They pinched my camera when I was at the front of the tour bus, on the way to Blackpool, and took pictures of each other looking like this [sticks his big chin out comically]. And Alan Smith, their roadie, as well. Reni put it back in my bag without telling me they'd done it, so it was only when I developed them I saw that the cheeky fuckers had took my camera and wasted half my film on it!'

Tim Vigon was a young Roses fan who had followed them throughout the year and was making his own fanzine about the band, *Made of Paper*.

'The band's live plot had taken a huge turn. The seemingly endless list of gigs during 1989 came to an end and only one more was planned – a trip to the seaside in August to Blackpool Empress Ballroom. Suddenly, going to see the Roses wasn't just something we could do once or twice a week, it was six weeks away…six whole weeks…that was a fucking lifetime to us in those days. We talked about that gig and planned it for weeks, what we'd wear, getting there – what would they play? What would it be like? People who had laughed at us before for liking these bands with weird names were growing their hair and wearing flared jeans – they even wanted to go to the gig – things were changing…

'In the meantime I'd decided to write a fanzine. You just did that sort of thing then. Nowadays you'd write a blog, or just go on Twitter – but I had to DO something…I had buckets of energy fuelled by this band and the life we were living at the time, so I decided to write about it. There was no plan, aims or objectives, I didn't think anyone would care – if I sold 50 of them to like-minded nutcases and our travelling group grew some more then great. It was a typically teenage affair – a track by track (complete with marks out of ten) of the album, gig reviews, a 'feature' about how us hard-core fans were going to have to accept that the world was about to discover "our" band and they wouldn't be our little secret any more…I can't even look at it now…it's just an outpouring of young naive enthusiasm.'

Tim took the planned-out fanzine to Blackpool to show The Stone Roses.

'But of course I wanted the band to like it…so off to Blackpool I went complete with a ringbound file with all the planned pages for the fanzine in it, hoping to somehow get the band to see it. The day before I went into my mum's work and made hundreds of little photocopied flyers advertising the zine – "*Made Of Paper*; The Stone Roses Fanzine; On sale Monday in Piccadilly Records". They wouldn't mind, I'm sure…

'We got to Blackpool and there was no doubt about it, the whole thing stepped up a notch that day. Hundreds of people wandering around the golden mile, buying up what became known as "Reni hats" – the local traders couldn't believe their luck – selling out of sun hats that had probably sat on their shelves for a decade. People swarmed the town wearing approximations of the band's outfit on the album sleeve, a baggy army out in full force – it really was happening.'

After years of neglect everyone was now on the band's case. And it wasn't just *Sounds* now, Bob Stanley from *Melody Maker* was already head over heels in love with the Roses, describing them as 'four blokes from the Stretford End and four teenage Jesus Christs. Pop perfection'. *NME* called them 'the future, the resurrection'.

The swagger, the clothes and the anthems – in the summer of 1989 the Roses had the lot. It was a sea change in popular culture and here they were, the partying fans along the Blackpool Prom, a new youth army in way too much denim and attitude, fired by the Roses' bravura and great tunes. For the first time in years there was a genuine rock'n'roll phenom-enon coming off the streets. The Roses walked it like they talked it; they had a fanatical football-style following and it was here tonight that new reputations would get forged; a night that years later still seems legendary.

This was the perfect place for a pop coming-of-age. It was an audience who were ready for some kicks, a day out to the seaside with the greatest band of the coming pop generation at the helm.

For the Roses it was a million miles away from the perceived sneery hipness of London, where most bands play their breakthrough gig. Blackpool has its own magic and its own allure – for those from Manchester it was the number one holiday extension of their brute northernness; the place I grew up in is a tatty seaside town of long beery weekends, quick shags in seedy hotels, riding donkeys and throwing up after ten pints of weak booze. It was a rites-of-passage, windswept, full-frontal attack of pure undiluted bawdy British fun.

It was a glorious, gaudy, tacky place of illuminations on acid, amusements in the blustery rain and skid-row hedonism. A full-blown bacchanalian belch in the face of good taste…and it meant good times, cheap glamour and even cheaper thrills. For Mancs, Blackpool was only ever a swift train ride away, and today, to top it all, The Stone Roses, a band who had served a long and foul apprenticeship in the toilets and dungeons of the UK live circuit, were throwing a coming-out party. A band who had up till now only smouldered were now ready to ignite into their full pop splendour. All through the long warm months since the Roses' eponymous début album had been released that March there was a real feeling that something was happening.

The rave generation had bands now to listen to while chilling out after a long night in the city's clubs. The Beatles tapes were getting supplemented by the Roses and the Mondays – two bands that walked and talked the new jive, and who seemed to have soaked up some of the surrounding culture. Two bands that, even if they didn't play acid house, seemed to have the flavour, the atmosphere and the vibe of the times infused in their tunes. The Roses had the credibility – they may have had their roots in punk and post-punk glam, they may have steered a course through the fallout of the Jesus And Mary Chain and Creation Records – they may have been almost rock, but they had been affected by the times. They were the new breed. They had soaked up some of the new sounds, way ahead of the pack and although their début album was hardly acid house it was infused by the infectious optimistic spirit of the times. It just felt right – throughout that summer they had been the soundtrack of the multicoloured tidal wave of optimistic partying in Manchester. The band, totally ignored 'down south', might have been a big deal in 'the north' but now they were ready to flex their muscle on the big stage. This was a gig for the nation. Later, in the 1990s, Oasis made playing to 100,000 seem like a warm-up gig, but in 1989 even daring to play to a hall holding 4,000 people was considered madness, especially this early in a career. This was way out of order, too cocky, too arrogant; but the Roses had their fingers on the pulse and were armed with a stiff shot of self-belief.

This pop generation demanded big gestures, large communal gestures. It wanted its bands big, bolshy and yet from the street, it wanted big spaces to celebrate, large-scale parties and big-time fun. The new rock bands that were going to survive had learned a few tricks from acid house and rock gig as community event was back. 'The crowd is the star,' as singer Ian Brown said.

That day the band left Manchester early in high spirits. Their album had been selling consistently since its release in the spring and there was a clutch of singles gnawing at the back end of the charts. They weren't in the Top Ten yet but they were about to go silver, definitely on the up.

Ian Tilton enjoyed the band's camaraderie, and if there were any nerves about headlining a show ten times the size of most of their previous gigs, everyone involved believed they could make it work. 'The atmosphere on the coach was great. That was a time when they had really got it together. They had this ultra confidence. They were getting a really big following in Manchester. It's this family thing again, this roots thing that all the great Manchester bands have. They made people want to watch them. It was all down to word of mouth. Nobody outside Manchester knew this was happening even a few months previously. I phoned the live editor of *Sounds* about covering them and he thought it was too early to do anything and even at the Hacienda show six months before he was still uncertain before saying yes. None of the editors in London knew the phenomenon; outside Manchester people hadn't really heard of them.'

The audience building up at the Empress was a mixed bag: scene veterans, people who had followed the band from their roots in Manchester, fresh-faced pop virgins, freaks, dealers and baggy teens. This was the day when the band finally got the crossover crowd, from the council estates to the rock press readers. It was everything that had been worked on from the start – from manager Gareth Evans giving away tickets and T-shirts to kids who wouldn't normally be seen dead at shows for bands like these, and the disaffected former Smiths crowd looking for new heroes – and it was all coming together.

1989 was, for most people, the early days of ecstasy, when the drug symbolised good times: before the comedown, the breaking down of barriers and the chilling out of football thuggery, not the whipped-up tabloid death sentence of today.

In the late 1980s there was a new innocence, a new pop dawn, and a Victorian hall packed to the seams with pop kids ready to ignite was a big deal. It was a day of big gestures and grand partying, it was a day of drugs, booze, chemicals, cheap weed and headache-strewn hangovers in cheap Blackpool boarding rooms and hotels. It was an unstoppable surge of flappy flares and greasy hair towards the Winter Gardens and into the Empress Ballroom.

Pre-gig the band showed none of the tension you would expect for the big one, as Ian Tilton recalls. 'I remember Ian and John getting on really well, larking around…they were really laid back – quite happy to sign autographs for people. Outside the Winter Gardens there were loads of people waiting in the afternoon. The band were not at all rock star-ish and they seemed to be really happy. They also seemed to hold back just a bit, keep something in reserve, make sure there was something enigmatic about themselves.'

There were hundreds outside, many without a ticket and, seizing the moment, someone from the Roses' crew booted in the side doors of the venue allowing a joyous tide of humanity to surge into the hall. The atmosphere was one of celebration.

'We wanted to give people a big day to finish their summer,' Ian Brown claimed later. 'The gigs had not been packed outside Manchester till then. In March 1989 we played to 30 people in Liverpool, 50 in Leeds. It was on that tour that we played to 12 people in Cardiff and four of them were the Manic Street Preachers. We played in Brighton to about ten people. We didn't have a crowd outside Manchester till the album came out.'

The tension in the hall was cranked high, the way-over-capacity crowd surging forward as the opening ghostly bass of 'I Wanna Be Adored' rumbled through the building. Cool as fuck, the Roses sauntered on-stage, Ian Brown limbering, bouncing like Muhammad Ali, overflowing with the cool arrogance that was his trademark, high-fiving the stage, lolloping on with the now-legendary electric yo-yo, pimp rolling. He mumbled, 'Manchester in the area. International. Continental.'

Brown rode on the blast of adoration from the crowd, and the rest of the band threw ice-pops into the seriously over-heated audience.

'Manchester, Manchester,' the crowd roared, many of them from anywhere but. Brown stared and replied, 'Manchester, yeah yeah, I love you, cos I'm from Glasgow.'

The familiar chug of the bass sent shivers through the teeming mass, the deep throb being the opening hallmark to the Roses' live experience – the perfect opening. John Squire stood motionless, his guitar in an Apocalypse Now fog of feedback and squelching sounds before the delicious lick of the melody curled in.

Then Reni kicked in and the Empress was bopping. From the balcony it was an impressive sight, a celebration of youth, vigour and rock'n'roll. It was like watching the Stones in their pomp. A great British rock'n'roll band prepared to go the whole way, a massive enveloping wall of sound. 'You adore me,' Brown sang, half to himself and half to the crowd, who quite obviously did. The stark atmospheric feel of the song, half gloomy and ice-cold, and half celebratory, caught the mood of the moment; it was an exhilarating rush of rock'n'roll. He mooched the stage, inventing a whole new way to front a band, a break with the strutting, extrovert rock-god tradition. His moves and cool had already inspired the young Liam Gallagher the previous year on 30 May at the International 2 in Manchester when The Stone Roses supported James at the Campaign For Lesbian And Gay Equality gig.

Someone threw a pint of beer and he opened his mouth like a goldfish and pretended to catch it. Cool. A whole new generation was looking for a new messiah and Brown was there, prowling and hungry.

Brown stood there with his soon-to-be-legendary white shirt with the burning £ signs round the collar, maybe signifying that the days of indie paranoia over money-making were over. Brown walked on the spot, his head lolloping from side to side, a street cool take on the E-head mad fucker dance; everyone recognised the immaculate stoned moves.

Ian Brown smiles at the memory of the special night. 'The money shirt? I bought that in Paul Smith. It was the only one on the shelf and I thought, wow – that looks ace! At the time it was fifty quid which was a lot of money then but I thought no one else is going to pay fifty quid for that so I'll have it and no one else will. It was burning twenties and tenners around the collar; you could see the flames on the print. In the end I give it to a lad. I wish I hadn't now, I never took it off that year, I was either wearing that or the yellow shirt like on the album cover – I used to wear them two shirts in 1989.'

As Ian Brown surfed on the excitement, John Squire was playing brilliant guitar, his skanking intro to 'Elephant Stone', with the wah-wah cranked up bigger and more powerfully than was the norm, reinventing the then under-used pedal for a whole new generation. The wah-wah had been dissed by punk after reaching its peak with Hendrix, Sly and the early 1970s psychedelic soul kings. Its distinctive sound was part of some of the greatest music ever made: Funkadelic, 'Psychedelic Shack' by The Temptations, Hendrix, Miles Davis, Curtis Mayfield, Isaac Hayes – all the young kings. Squire, by tapping into that tradition, was reinvigorating the guitar and making it something primal, something funky, something sexy; a sound that would become synonymous with the new baggy generation.

Meanwhile Mani is holding the bass down, his contributions evermelodic – holding tight with Reni's drums; one of the greatest ever rhythm sections. By the time they cut loose with 'Waterfall' the Roses are coasting. 'Who's from Blackpool...anybody?' asks Brown. 'Waterfall' is a gas, likewise 'Sugar Spun Sister', rock-solid classics that years later would still be staples of indie discos nationwide.

'International, continental,' imparts Brown, obviously liking this line, as the band crashes into the anthemic 'Made Of Stone', that sliver of pure pop greatness. It never felt better than when it was delivered at Blackpool.

'I Am The Resurrection' has now moved a few more gears. Strung out, drawn out, cataclysmic, it's the Roses' grand finale, a huge song. Biblical and hypnotic, it's a moment of true and perfect empowering beautiful arrogance, a song of great guitar playing, every lick carrying a tune.

During the long instrumental section Brown picks up the bongos and again does the shamanic stoned rock messiah thing. Whether they actually add much to the sound is irrelevant – it's a cool manoeuvre.

After the show Vigon is one of a clutch of fans at the front of the stage desperate to get backstage and hang with the band that he's met briefly before on the small club tour. As usual the security aren't into making things easy and push the sweaty fans around. But the Roses are made of different stuff and are determined to be a people's band, as Vigon explains: 'Gareth kept promising an interview with the band, but on the night he said that I couldn't talk to them as they were too stoned after the gig. I just wanted to get backstage, I wanted them to approve of the fanzine. Security was saying that we couldn't go backstage while Steve Adge (the tour manager and sometimes neo manager of the band) was arguing with promoters – "Let these people back" – and he literally dragged us over barriers in defiance of the promoters and walked us into the after-show party. We had our cameras and snapped away; the band each looked over the fanzine and gave it their blessing. John Squire said it was very thorough and Reni said it was sound but don't be turning up on his doorstep and shit like that.

'At the party Ian was bouncing around. I've got a picture of him shaking hands with this big guy – I didn't know who he was at the time but later it turned out to be Martin Merchant from Audioweb and then whilst most in the room probably made it through the night with a cocktail of heady chemicals, we were back in the car heading for Macclesfield high pretty much solely on the events of the day.'

Returning home he put the fanzine together. But the power of Blackpool had had a greater effect than even Tim had expected...

'The fanzine wasn't ready for Monday...we had to get the photos developed – this was 1989 don't forget! And I had to get access to my mum's photocopier at work,' he continues. 'By Thursday I had it sorted and sauntered into Piccadilly Records with 30 fresh-maiden copies of *Made of Paper*. As usual I sought out my behind-the-counter friend Martin, and (somewhat belatedly) asked him if they'd sell my fanzine. "Of course," he replied. "What's it about?" When I told him, he shook his head and smiled a little half smile and went off to fetch the manager. The manager came out swearing his head off: "Where have you been, you little prick? We've had people bothering us about this fucking fanzine all week and we didn't even know about it?" I mumbled my apologies and said that it was all done now and I had it with me. "How many copies have you got?" I told him and his face turned purple. "FUCKING THIRTY? YOU'D BETTER GO AND GET PHOTOCOPYING, YOU LITTLE TWAT – WE'RE GOING TO NEED HUNDREDS OF THESE."

'That's what it was like with the Roses. It was like an exponential thing...unstoppable momentum and people wanted anything they could get their hands on that made them feel a part of it, and laughably and unwittingly, my photocopied nonsense had a bit of their default magic dust. Five hundred people had been in asking about the magazine. As it turned out I sold 3,000 of that first issue.

'That buzz of knowing that you're seeing something powerful and a bit magical that the world won't be able to ignore. I was in the right place at the right time, and I'll be forever grateful to the Roses and the City of Manchester for that incredible grounding and unforgettable experience that's pretty much shaped my life ever since. It's so rare, maybe even unrepeatable...but they made it feel so fucking natural.'

For the Roses and the Manchester scene it was the day when everything went off big time. Suddenly everyone had to agree that there was a new phenomenon. There was a new hunger in the air and there were new mainstream heroes to deal with. As Vigon remembers, 'It was the first day when everybody wore Reni hats, it was the first time people wore baggy tops and it was the day the Manchester scene started.'

THE BEGINNINGS: 1962–80

Ian Brown: Early Years

'I was born in Warrington and lived in Foster Street until I was about six...'

Ian Brown was born on the outside.

Warrington. Neither Liverpool nor Manchester. Bang in the middle. Right in between. Offering a tantalising glimpse of the big city on either side. Neither Manc nor Scouse, its lack of strong regional identity has provided some strange quirks. Rugby league not football is the sporting religion and British Telecom built a massive call centre in Warrington because it was found that the Warrington accent was the UK favourite. Warrington itself lies just over the Lancashire border in Cheshire; it's a big industrial working-class town surrounded by the richest county in the UK. A nether world of mixed affiliations.

Ian George Brown was born on 20 February 1963 to George, a local joiner, and Jean, a telephone receptionist at that massive call centre. The eldest in the family, he has a younger brother David and a sister Sharon.

He remembers his childhood as being relatively trouble-free, at least at home. He attributes his anti-establishment streak to his socialist, republican family. His father, according to Ian, was a 'sweet and shy' man and his mother an 'outspoken woman'.

He talked about his family to *Uncut* magazine. 'I grew up in Warrington, which was grim but fun. We were poor, down to earth. My father... looks like me, yeah.'

Foster Street is a classic northern terrace: no front gardens, two up, two down, back to back and all about community.

At school Ian Brown was already building up a reputation as a loudmouth, a troublemaker. Belligerent, unruly, headstrong, the young Brown was already locked into a path of stubborn self-determination.

In 1969 the Brown family left Warrington and moved to Timperley, a few miles from Manchester city centre. Timperley, also famous for the late, great surrealist comedian Frank Sidebottom, is caught between the never-ending sprawl of Europe's biggest housing estate, the very working-class Wythenshawe, and the comparatively leafier suburbs of Altrincham – two very different worlds pulling in opposite directions.

'We didn't have a garden in Warrington, just a back yard, and in Timperley we had a back lawn. Thanks to me dad for not being a smoker or massive boozer for that. It was great. It was on a train line and it was only six miles and only twelve minutes on the train from Manchester city centre so from the age of seven I was in town all the time.'

Not that Brown has ever abandoned Warrington; he still has a house in the area. 'I came back there because I was sick of living in Manchester. I was getting burgled far too often and I just wanted the quiet life back in Warrington. I found a nice little house to settle down, and I'm usually there about once a week.'

The move to Manchester was a fortuitous one. It's difficult to imagine Brown bumping into like-minded souls in Warrington, let alone his now near neighbour John Squire. (The legend has it they met in a sandpit.) Manchester in 1969 was a very different city to the Euro wine bar, glitzy, neon metropolis of the early twenty-first century. Back then it was yet to emerge from its dank, dark, Lowryesque cloth-cap cliché, still attempting to come to terms with post-industrial decline. In the nineteenth century it had been the second biggest city in Europe, an industrial powerhouse, but with the decline of the cotton industry it was looking for a new role.

Manchester was slowly beginning its long period of reinvention. It had its own beat scene, a post-Merseybeat rush of bands like The Hollies (occasionally quoted as an influence by the Roses), Freddy and The Dreamers and Herman's Hermits, who had been the biggest band in the world in 1965. Bigger, briefly, than The Beatles!

In football terms, in the sixties, the city was booming. It was the city of flash. Manchester United were not only the kings of Europe but they did it with swagger and style. Since the 1958 Munich air disaster when the 'Busby babes', potentially the greatest British football team of them all, were wiped out in an air crash, United had been building a legend and a footballing dynasty from the ruins. By 1969 Manchester United were in the ascendant; they had won the European Cup the year before and alongside local rivals City, were the superstars of British football.

George Best was the flash king of European football, stick insect thin with his El Beatle haircut, mesmerising skill and pop star swagger. Impossible to miss for a young United fan like Brown.

Pop and football dominate the north-west psyche and the next thirty years would see this reinforced.

So Young: Ian Brown Grows Up In Manchester...

Settling into Timperley, Brown was the loudmouth kid, the ringleader. On his new street he occasionally bumped into John, the shy, quiet, kid but they were not great friends. It would be a few more years before his friendship with John Squire would tighten up.

It was in Timperley that music started to have an effect on him. He started ploughing through records that were left lying around. 'My auntie gave me a pile of seven inches. 'It's Not Unusual', Tom Jones; 'Help!', 'I Feel Fine' by The Beatles; 'Satisfaction', 'Under My Thumb', 'Get Off My Cloud', by the Stones; 'The Happening' and 'Love Child' by The Supremes. I would have been seven or eight and I had a little Dansette. They were the first discs I had. I've still got them.'

The seven-inch single is still the classic pop salvo. Nowadays when the single has been reduced to a marketing tool, a free download, a YouTube viral, a boy band smirk or a way to promote an album, it's hard to remember that back then the single was king. The Beatles/Stones/Kinks/Motown – the glorious sixties pop single practitioners were banging out endless singles a year, each one a statement, each one capturing a slice of time for ever, each one a mini symphony.

The first record that Ian Brown bought was 'Metal Guru', T-Rex's classic 1972 number one – Marc Bolan, the inventor of glam and one of the greatest ever British pop stars, in his prime.

Pop music was part of the young Brown's life.

'When I was a kid, like everyone in the north, I was into The Beatles, then I heard T-Rex's "Metal Guru" and that was the first single I bought from the local market. When I was nine I was into Gary Glitter: "Rock-'n'Roll Part One" was a great record. I still think Slade are great – Noddy Holder was one of the best singers to ever come out of Britain. He had a voice like John Lennon He sung rough, out there, full on.

'Alice Cooper I liked as well. I didn't even know what an album was till 1976 when I got Alice Cooper's *Billion Dollar Babies* for Christmas; before then it was singles for me. My mum had *South Pacific* and Perry Como. I had Alice Cooper's 'School's Out', that was what I was into at 12 really. Then Bill Grundy was in the papers with the Sex Pistols and I got really into punk. I got the Sex Pistols and I heard The Adverts on Piccadilly Radio that March 1977 and got their single, 'One Chord Wonders'. I also heard The Clash on Piccadilly Radio when they played

'Career Opportunities' and 'Janie Jones' and I got half of each song on a cassette by taping them off the radio like you did in them days.

'They were playing the songs just before The Clash album came out, when they were previewing them.'

Another key flavour feeding in was Northern Soul. Wigan Casino was the epicentre of the hippest scene in the north-west, a scene that was influencing the way everyone dressed whether they were aware of it or not. Flared trousers, star jumpers and even feather cuts/suedeheads were arguably popularised by the seventies soul scene. All the hip kids in the schools were practising their backflips to the casino scene beat.

Phil Thornton, Runcorn's finest social commentator, succinctly and cynically sums up Northern Soul and the way it infused a patchwork of pop cultures of the north-west in the early seventies, a mish-mash of competing styles that built the foundations for the post northern pop scene.

'Northern Soul was a direct antecedent of today's hedonistic clubbing scene but the majority of those on the periphery of the scene were never real soul disciples, merely followers of fashion. By 1976 Northern Soul was mainstream with Wigan's Chosen Few appearing on Top of the Pops and reissues of tired old stompers diluting the passion for a crowd more interested in athletic showboating than a genuine appreciation of music. The youth clubs of the north-west were a melting pot of competing tribes in the late seventies – soulies, punks, mods, skins, Bowie freaks, even heavy rockers – each armed with their own supply of cherished 7 inches and LP tracks for the DJ to play.

'It was hard not to take in all these influences and construct your own eclectic canon of influences – this is how Madchester was made; not in the aloof arty playgrounds of the city's bohemian elite, but out there on the council estates youth centre dancefloors.

For Mani, dance is just part of Mancunian life. 'It's strange how Manchester always had that dance music thing going on,' he reflected years later. 'I think cos we were always kind of into dance music, and for me punk rock is dance music. We were always into like getting on the dancefloor up north. Drinking and dancing, these were the things you do when you were depressed and poor and we were all really good at it.'

Northern Soul's roots go back to the early sixties club scene of Manchester. In 1963 the Twisted Wheel opened its doors for the first time with Roger Eagle (who ended up booking bands at the International 1) as the house DJ. In the early sixties it was a popular blues/R&B venue.

In 1966, when it moved to its new home in Whitworth Street, its legend started to grow. Roger Eagle quit after getting fed up of being asked to play faster soul records for the speeding mods. He was replaced by DJs willing to pump up the speed of the tracks. A London journalist called Dave Godin came up to review the scene and, struck by the differences in sound from London, coined the term 'Northern Soul' to encompass the myriad upbeat soul records the Twisted Wheel regulars were dancing to, turning away from the psychedelic late sixties and creating a fashion all of their own, with stomping soul records, crisp raw sounds and a vicious backbeat.

Key singers from the States and frequent visitors to the Twisted Wheel included Ben E. King, J. J. Jackson, Oscar Toney Jr, The Vibrations and Junior Walker.

In backwater towns and cities across the north of England, in places like Wigan, Stoke, Stafford and Blackpool, obscure post-Motown soul releases were revered. The mods' love of one-upmanship, of the small label, of the hottest sounds was in its element here.

The Wigan Casino Soul Scene had come directly from this sixties uptempo soul basis and stuck to this sound quite rigidly for a long time. Blackpool Mecca (or more accurately the Highland Rooms) considered itself a soul club before a Northern Soul club and stuck to the black soul sound of the sixties while Wigan allowed the sound to broaden. Eventually, the Mecca started to play recent or newly released uptempo soul records, sometimes unknowingly and later deliberately. Over a couple of years the musical policy there shifted to the new sounds and then fragmented, allowing pure disco and funk.

Small independent labels in America pumping out attempts to emulate the success of Motown on a cheaper budget were ruling the roost. That their records were rawer, less polished and cranked full of energy was a huge plus mark. They may have sold jack shit in the States but to the youth of the north of England, wired on cheap speed, their records made a perfect backdrop to extrovert dancing. A whole subculture was born, a subculture that in the early seventies dominated school playgrounds in the north-west as kids learned the dance steps and wore the clothes that were coming out of the clubs. Northern Soul continued to gain popularity until the mid-seventies, when punk and disco stole its thunder. However, it never totally faded away.

Northern Soul provided the backdrop of cool in the early to mid seventies. It was about clothes, clubs like secret societies, an outsider culture with its own code, like the early acid house scene and the underground nature of rave culture, it was a big whispering cult held together by its own dress code (just check those flares!). Lines can be drawn with the Roses cult escape and the whole Manc baggy thing years later. In its very northernness and its own strict street cool, it was a whole new way of living 24 hours-a-day pop lifestyles.

Whilst the young Brown was navigating his way through the pop battlefield of the early seventies he was also choosing idols from other mass media. 'When I was a kid, there was no one bigger hero for me than Muhammad Ali. I can see that '74 Foreman fight in my mind as clear as a bell, and I got all the books. My walls were covered in Ali pictures, whilst later it would have been the Pistols.'

Ali was the man. His indomitable fighting spirit, his fierce intelligence, his utterly astonishing boxing skill and his powerful political and cultural presence made him a crucial and inspirational figure. Not only was he knocking them down in the ring, he was also knocking them dead outside the ring.

He stood for the downtrodden and his black power Muslim leanings made him a controversial figure in the straight-laced world. He refused to fight in the Vietnam war and stood up against racism. He had a radical political agenda and a bucketload of charm to explain it to middle England. At the time Ali was, perhaps, the greatest folk hero of them all.

His insolence and witty wordplay in the full glare of the world media, his uncrushable spirit and self-made determination all struck home with Brown like it did with millions of kids worldwide.

Brown picked up on Ali's never-ending self-confidence and his right-eous arrogance. It also turned him on to boxing and then on to martial arts – two disciplines that he still has a strong interest in to this day.

In 1973 Ali was joined by a new hero. Bruce Lee burst on to the scene and brought with him a revolution of interest in the martial arts. A revolution that would turn Brown's head. At school the myths about Bruce Lee would constantly circulate. When the double bill of his films *Fists of Fury* and *Enter the Dragon* was shown in Sale, Brown was there, although his favourite Lee film is *Big Boss*, also known as *Chinese Connection*.

Already entranced by Ali, it didn't take much of a leap for Brown to get into Lee, martial arts' first-ever popular culture superstar.

The acting and the stories in the films were, of course, pretty light-weight, but the fight scenes were something else. Here was a fighting form that not only seemed ruthlessly effective but was also graceful and had its own poetry and its own beauty. Brutality and beauty rolled into one, no wonder the young Brown was hooked.

Bruce Lee was on a fast track to becoming a superstar, fact and fiction becoming entwined in his mystical legend.

Lee popularised martial arts, his incredible physique and fighting skills became the unattainable dream of many young teens in the early seventies. Brown, bitten by the Lee bug, was involved in karate until teenage kicks of a different type began to take over his life.

For seven years karate was a single-minded obsession for him, an obsession that took a steely discipline and resolve a million miles away from standard teenage rebellion. He would cycle four miles to the Dojo after a day at his new school, Altrincham Grammar.

Brown quickly moved through several styles of karate till he found the one that suited him. In the local Dojos Brown first learned Wado-Ryu, a relatively modern form of Japanese martial arts founded by Hironori Ohtsuka Sensei in 1934. Developed from the Samurai martial art of Ju-jitsu and Shotokan it was a softer, more natural means of self protection. Even the very name Wado-Ryu means 'way of peace'. From this he specialised in Bujinkai, a modern form put together in the early seventies which mixed Wado-Ryu with the Shaolin praying mantis form.

'I was well into karate. I started when I was 11 and I did it till I was 18. I started with Bujinkai, it's the Okinawa police style. I was addicted to that. I did it seven days a week and was teaching it when I was 14. I would run a class on the Saturday. I got the brown belt and I was a few weeks from the black belt. I was reading a Bruce Lee book where he was saying, "Who are these people to grade me?", and that made me think.

'There was this kid, the cleverest kid in school. He was awesome, but he had his own mind. He wouldn't take his O levels and he wouldn't do his karate the way they told him. I sort of fell into that way of thinking as well. I guess it was a bit of a punk thing. The kid never got beyond his white belt. I think I took some of that attitude off him. Which is why I eventually left the club. I regret it now. It was a stupid thing to do. I was into punk rock by then, in 1978, though, and that was affecting me. I like to think I would have got my belt, it would have been great to have got it. I did it every night, one-on-one teaching sessions after school.'

The training, the physical and mental demands of the sport say a lot about Brown. This steely discipline is something that lurks in him, that gritty patience and resolve that typified the Roses and their endless rehearsals, whittling their tunes down to a black belt perfection.

Lee and Ali. These were role models and idols and part of the mid-seventies cultural backdrop. Superstars in the suburbs. And, like pop stars, unattainable idols.

In the real world of mid-seventies Britain, things were very different. It was a world of shortages, bleak winters and confusion. By 1975/76 the UK was at a cultural low point, the sixties rock stars had run out of songs. They looked awful – straggly long hair and bloated middle-aged faces. They would spend years in the studio fucking about instead of making records; they were out of touch and lost. They needed a kick, a one-inch punch to the taste zone. The talk was that pop had done everything it could. There was nowhere left to go.

For the teens growing up in the mid-seventies to be constantly told that they had missed the party, that the sixties was the greatest time ever wasn't just grating. It was getting really fucking annoying.

Every generation needs its own defining point. Its own soundtrack. Its own standard bearers. And just round the corner something was coming. Some big time trouble-making was about to be visited on the lazy smug world of pop…

'Right now.'

Every time you hear it, it still sends a shiver down the spine. Followed by that hideous cackle and the fattest guitar imaginable descending into a beautiful maelstrom of sound.

Fucking hell. This was more than a pop single. It was a music war…

It was 'Anarchy In The UK' by the Sex Pistols.

It was a generational calling card.

After this. Nothing. Would. Ever. Be. The. Same. Again!

Year Zero: Punk Hits the Suburbs

Punk was just waiting to happen.

To understand just how exciting punk was you have to understand how boring the mid-seventies really were. If the early seventies had provided some sort of action with the fab pop shakes of glam rock, the mid-seventies was one of those periods of cultural hiatus. Pop music had got fat and lazy.

It was quite possible to be a cabaret act and hog the charts; the album charts were full of long-haired buffoons in shabby denim with their dull anthems.

For the 14-year-old Ian Brown it was a call to arms, as he remembered to *Record Collector*.

'Punk changed everything. The band I most got into was the Sex Pistols. My mate had "Anarchy In The UK". He got it in Woolies for 29p 'cos after that *Bill Grundy Show*, they put the record in the bargain bin! I loved "I Wanna Be Me" on the other side – that lyric about "cover me in margarine" was great. Then I got 'God Save The Queen' the day it came out. I was fourteen. I remember thinking, "Oh wow, that Pistols record is gonna change the world. And it did, in a way.

'The next thing I heard was The Adverts' 'One Chord Wonders' on Piccadilly Radio in early '77.

'I went to gigs in the late seventies. I saw the Buzzcocks in the Mayflower [26 March 1978]. I remember a load of Teds came down because there was some Ted convention in Belle Vue and Buzzcocks were launching their album and Pete Shelley had to stop the fighting.

'Button badges were the thing then. We used to go to that weird underground shop on Peter Street, Savoy Books, where they sold all the old books and porn. It was all hippie counter culture books. We used to pretend to be tying our shoelaces and nick the badges. I've still got Buzzcocks and Pretty Vacant badges...

'Buzzcocks were the key band at the time. I remember seeing them on the telly on *So It Goes*, which was the programme that Tony Wilson used to do. It was really important. They were right on it. We would watch it even if it was Elvis Costello, although he was all right when he started. They had some great stuff on there like The Clash live, Belle Vue [at the Elizabethan rooms, Belle Vue, 15 November 1977]. They showed four songs on TV. Penetration were on as well. The Banshees before they were signed. Buzzcocks filmed at the Mayflower for two nights.

'Manchester was great in the punk days. We had our own bands like Slaughter And The Dogs, Buzzcocks, V2 – they were a big band to us. I saw the Drones supporting The Stranglers at the Apollo [13 October 1977]. The Drones album, *Temptations Of A White Collar Worker*, that was great; there was Ed Banger's "I Ain't Been To No Music School" single. The Drones were one of the first bands I saw. I also saw punk shows at the Apollo – The Clash, The Stranglers – and The Jam at Salford University.'

The band that made the biggest impression on the young Ian Brown, The Sex Pistols, have remained a constant in Ian Brown's affections. Even in 1985 he was telling journalist Paul Greenwood, 'If I could write a song as good as "Anarchy" I would be happy.'

The Sex Pistols' impact on the pop scene of 1977 can never be too exaggerated. Those that fell in love with the band then are still out there to this day, their whole mindset still fixed by the sheer power and pop brilliance of the band. Not only did they affect people with their killer songs and Steve Jones's awesome guitar sound, they threw up a whole mass of ideas that are still settling now in the pop hinterland.

From situationism to anarchy, from the clothes that you wear to the way you cut your hair, from telling the monarchy to fuck off, to questioning everything about Britain. They were sex, style and subversion rolled into one. Many of the questions they asked still remain unanswered. And for many teenagers at the time, like Ian Brown, they were a U-turn in their lives.

The acerbic individuality and stark-staring anger of Johnny Rotten is very much part of the Ian Brown psyche; the royalty-hating, rock-star-debunking, myth-destroying psyche is still there in his schtick. The Pistols set Brown on the way to becoming his own starman; they were a whole new template for what a rock star could be. They called for bands to form in their wake but not for copycat bands…like the Roses themselves would do ten years later.

Punk was not just about the music. The style was equally important and as confrontational.

'That spring I started dressing punk,' Ian remembers. 'It was not easy getting punk clothes. You used to have to hunt for your gear. I got a pair of tight cords from Stretford Arndale. They were the only tight pants you could find in the city. We found proper shit stoppers – like Max Wall pants. At the time everyone wore flares – businessmen, bus drivers, they were everywhere… You would get laughed at in the street all the time! I remember guys on our street encouraging their daughters to laugh at us, pointing their fingers laughing. Downstairs at Village Barbers there was a secondhand store where you could get paisley shirts and old sixties jackets with little lapels that would pass as punk jackets when you put pins in. To spike up my hair I used to have to put sugar and water in because there was no gel by the end of the night – it was running down your face – that was all part of it.'

There was also the risky business of buying the records. 'We would get the train into town looking for records. One of the places we would go to was the old Virgin Records shop. They used to have old train seats with headphones on them where you would listen to the new releases. We used to hang out there and in Discount Records in the underground market.'

It was here that the young punks would meet their older adversaries, the Teds.

'They would come into the shop. They seemed ancient even then, like big men from Belle Vue with drape suits on. There was a big Ted versus punk thing at the time. I always remember this big Ted coming in and taking The Clash album out at Discount Records and saying, "Shouldn't this be in the comedy section?", and all the punks looking at the floor!

'The Teds would chase you all over the place. I met Pete Garner [the first Stone Roses bass player] around this time – Pete was right on it even if he was only about 13. He had his mohair jumper, I remember that. The night before his exams he went to see The Clash and that fucked up his O levels.

'One night on Market Street in the city centre he had his brothel creepers on and these Teds came up and said, "Get those fucking brothel creepers off," and we went down to undo them. This woman went past with her pram and we jumped up over this pram and legged it.'

Punk wasn't like any form of rock'n'roll before. It had one foot in the star system but another on the street. The energy of the Pistols was a supreme catalyst that bounced around the whole country. They played Manchester twice in '76 and inspired a whole local rock'n'roll infrastructure. The whole Manchester myth from The Smiths to Factory onwards roots itself back to those Pistols shows.

The Pistols may have been the spark but the inspiration to get directly involved came from local Wythenshawe bootboy glamsters turned punk rock outfit Slaughter And The Dogs who had a big effect on Ian Brown.

'I was too young to go to the 1976 Sex Pistols Free Trade Hall shows at the time. We would look to the older ones on the scene who were 18, 19 and say, "He's a top punk." Next door to me, the fella who lived there would work with Mike Rossi from Slaughter And The Dogs' dad, so you would hear these stories about things going on.

'We went to see Slaughter And The Dogs at the Wythenshawe Forum with V2 [2 March 1978] and I always remember when we came out there were all these kids with belts out saying, "You're not at home now, you're in Wythenshawe," and we had to leg it home which luckily wasn't too far away. I never got battered but we would always get started on every week; we would come into town and get started on.

'I was hanging around Wythenshawe one day with my mate Steve Pugh and we saw Wayne Barrett, Slaughter And The Dogs' lead singer across the street, and we were looking over and he said, "Who the fuck are you looking at?" and we said, "You're Wayne Barrett!", and he said, "So fucking what, what you looking at? Fucking hell!"'

'We didn't know at the time that they were sped up glam. We were too young. They were great. They were also on the *Live At The Roxy* album, which was an important album. When they signed to Decca, that seemed really cool. They should have been massive.'

Suddenly punk didn't seem a million miles away. It was right on the doorstep in Wythenshawe! A wild riot going on, tantalising, just within reach. The message was, 'Anyone can do this, have a go'. It's perhaps one of the most powerful messages that music can give out.

And here was a band having a go round the corner and getting some sort of national recognition for it. The tales of Slaughter And The Dogs' wild gigs were hitting the teenage grapevine at Altrincham Grammar. Your very own Pistols on your doorstep. Now that's something.

They released a series of well-received singles which have since become collectors' treasures, including the early punk anthem, 'Where Have All the Boot Boys Gone'. They also had a single 'Cranked Up Really High', one of the first records produced by a young upcoming producer called Martin Hannett, a vital connection in years to come. It's an anthem to the cheap twin punk kicks of speed and booze, a celebration of the wild-eyed lifestyle even then getting sourced by Brown.

'They made some great records, 'Cranked Up Really High' is brilliant. They were really great, that's what made the Roses work with Martin Hannett, who produced them earlier on. The 'B' side of the single, "The Bitch", is brilliant.'

Running around town, the teenage punks were getting a crash course in late seventies Mancunian street culture.

'It was pretty violent in Manchester in the seventies. You would go to town on a Saturday afternoon in the punk days and see stuff like firemen hosing people down in the underground market. Perrys fighting punks, kids fighting in the bus station; at night-time there would be battles up and down the bus station in Piccadilly Gardens. It was pretty violent but it's exciting, innit,' Ian grins, adding, 'I didn't used to be involved in that although I did hang around with a gang of lads who got into scrapes but it wasn't for me.'

In the couple of years that followed punk, Brown would pick up on some of the rawer edges of the national musical fallout that came after punk. Groups like the tough psychobilly outfit The Meteors, whose cartoon image and tough guy stance camouflaged an amazing guitar player and, initially, a great band. There were bands on the edges of the 'Oi' scene like The Cockney Rejects and the under-rated socialist skinhead band from the north-east, The Angelic Upstarts.

Ian told *Record Collector*, 'I used to go watch The Angelic Upstarts! Mensi – top kid! I roadied for them a few times. I've seen them 15/20 times. Top band. The film that really captures those days was Shane Meadows' *This is England*. That was great. It was just like it was with the tie-dye jeans and that. It was brilliant. I was into scooters and Cockney Rejects and The Upstarts. I went to several Upstarts gigs. Rob Powell and me roadied for them; four gigs it was. Bolton was one of them. Mensi is a top bloke. The Cockney Rejects were great as well. I read their vocalist Stinky Turner's autobiography the other week. It was brilliant. It wasn't right, them getting tagged with being Nazis. The Upstarts got that as well, but Mensi was the opposite to all that. They got that because they are working class from the estates. People didn't understand them.'

Pete Garner recalls Ian Brown hanging out with the Upstarts.

'Ian went to loads of their gigs,' says Pete. 'He knew Mensi, their singer...we always knew Mensi's politics were cool; he was a great guy.'

The Angelic Upstarts, who were South Shields-based were inspired by The Clash and released a fantastic run of singles that were charged with a righteous street anger. Their vocalist Mensi, who brought a street politic and anti-Nazi flavour to the band's lyrics, remembers Ian Brown following the band in 1979/80. 'I remember Ian Brown being around at our gigs in the Manchester area. There was always a crew of people hanging around with us. In those days a lot would happen; we used to fight all the time with the fascists.

'One time the promoter didn't pay us so we went searching for him the next day. We kicked in the door of his office but he wasn't there. Then we were driving out of Manchester and we saw him in a car! So I ran out of the van and tried to punch his window through. He mounted the central reservation, turned and went the other way. We were in a Transit.

We crossed the central reservation as well and chased him. He got stuck at some traffic lights and we attacked his car with hammers and baseball bats. He drove onto the grass verge and got away.

'Ian Brown was at that gig but whether he was there for the bit afterwards I can't recall. But that was the sort of thing that would happen at gigs at the time. He was at a club in Manchester as well and helped me in with the gear. I think that's where I met him. It was a pretty modern community centre on a housing estate. I used to have to sit everybody down and have a plan of action in case we were attacked. I used to tell everybody what to look for; the badges and the Celtic crosses. I'm sure he was there that day.'

Punk may have been a rigidly defined musical code to some but it also threw open loads of possibilities to others. Even groups like the Upstarts, who could be considered a quintessential British punk band, were bringing music from their youth into the mix. All over the place there were hints of The Who, the Stones, even The Beatles, Northern Soul/ska/mod in the mass of punk bands who were fast emerging. The Year Zero of punk, that attitude of hating anything before 1977, was fading as the new rock'n'roll generation started looking at the roots of the new wave and rediscovering a whole canon of like-minded musics. People were re-evaluating Tamla Motown, Northern Soul, Ska and late sixties garage psychedelia, from Arthur Lee's Love to Iggy to The Doors to Hendrix to the Velvets – anyone who ever had any fire in their soul was reconsidered and honoured in a thousand teenage bedsits and bedrooms. Funk and a whole forgotten pile of great soul and R&B records were thrown back into the equation. It was a great melting pot of sound. With punk and its influences swimming around his head Brown was on the lookout for like-minded souls to share his new passion with. He didn't have to look far.

That shy kid hiding behind his fringe four doors down had recently been turned on to the three-minute revolution by Brown. Their friendship was now firmly bonded by punk.

'John lived up the same road. We started hanging out together about 13 or 14. In 1977 he was getting his head kicked in at school and I jumped in and helped him out. I knew he lived up our street but I didn't hang out with him then. That night, because I felt a bit sorry for him, I took some records round. I had recently bought "God Save The Queen". It was really exciting, and it must have been about then when I went round to John's house. I took round the first Clash LP and The Adverts' "One Chord Wonders" and knocked on his door. He had The Beatles' *Live At*

The Hollywood Bowl. He didn't have any proper LPs, just compilations – that one with the surfer on the front, The Beach Boys' *Golden Greats.* I played my stuff and he got it straightaway and he got really into The Clash. He bought their album and Sex Pistols' "God Save The Queen".

'When I met John he was really into art. He never used to do games; they let him do art instead. He used to do up school shirts with Clash-style stencils. I used to walk about in these shirts that he had stencilled up with tight pants and braces and baseball boots – that was our look – and a black jacket with pins on it. The shirts would have 'You Generation' from Generation X or Clash-style things sprayed on. We would see things and copy them and then make our own.'

Brown and Squire had actually met years before. Says Ian, 'There was a sandpit in the fields near our house. We may have met there when we were about five, I'm not sure. He remembers me being naked, playing in the sandpit.'

The legendary meeting of Brown and Squire is part and parcel of British pop mythology. The sandpit meeting in 1968 is a story that has marked similarities with a certain Mick and Keef meeting in a sandpit when they were toddlers only to meet again years later as teenagers and form the Rolling Stones. Coincidence, or just a good rock'n'roll mythology story?

Squire remembers his first brush with Ian Brown. 'I've vague memories of meeting him at his friend's house,' he says. 'It was like an arranged marriage! A parental thing. The school catchment area had a line that went down the street. He was on one side, I was on the other, but eventually we went to the same secondary school. I didn't really get to know him until punk. He was somebody locally who was into the same music. We'd swap records and things. At the time it felt like an illicit underworld.'

It was just another casual bonding through the new music. Another link forged in the molten heat of the punk fallout. All over the nation life-long acquaintances were being put together, bonding over precious punk rock vinyl, bonding over where to get non-flared trousers from. For those who dared to make the major jump from the mid-seventies mush to the brave new world of punk it was all about new relationships, new patterns of existence.

Brown also turned Squire on to Slaughter And The Dogs. Years later John still really rates 'Cranked Up Really High'. 'The single conjures up images of flailing fists and feet on Saturday night dancefloors in Manchester. It's a blistering track with the ultimate unintelligible vocal.'

Brown and Squire were chalk and cheese. 'We were total opposites,' Ian recalled. 'I was very outgoing, the kid that would stand on the table in front of the class doing impressions of the teachers. I was the class joker and he was the loner. He got out of sports so he could do art. I think he was the first kid in the school to play truant, and he did that by himself. But at 13, 14, we'd walk the streets together and sit in each other's bedrooms playing records. He got his guitar when he was 15. The first thing he learned to play was "Three Blind Mice". Then he'd play his guitar for me when I went round. He's a funny kid. I know he's really, really quiet and doesn't speak to no one, but when he was with me he'd never shut up. Everybody knows him as a man of few words, but in them days he was garrulous with me, definitely. I did spend a lot of my life and a lot of the Roses' life talking for the kid. I knew him so well that I'd finish his sentences off. And then in the end…that didn't happen.'

'It was definitely a case of opposites attract,' pointed out Squire. 'He was more popular, yeah. I was happy to be a loner. I prefer it. We hung about for a short period, then when we started the band it became more permanent.'

In the late seventies, as the two fourteen-year-olds hunched over the record player, a whole new world of possibilities was opening up. For Brown it was the exuberant nihilism of the Sex Pistols that fired his extro-vert rebellious streak.

The artier Squire was besotted with The Clash. He painted a mural of the band on his bedroom wall, wore the creepers repopularised by the band, tousled his hair like their guitar player Mick Jones. Another new friend, another local kid fired by punk who had started to hang around with the Sylvan Avenue boys, Pete Garner, remembers just how much John loved The Clash.

'John would play The Clash's first album every day. I remember one day he turned up with a guitar string instead of a shoelace in his brothel creeper. It turned out there was a picture of Joe Strummer in the music press with the same thing that week. But that's what it's like when you're really young, that's the sort of thing you do, isn't it?'

The music may have been the common bond but as people John and Ian couldn't be more different. They were filling the gaps in each others' personalities. Where John was quieter, more introspective, Brown was already more outgoing, rowdier. Chalk and Cheese, Brown and Squire…

So who was this shy quiet kid, the polar opposite who lived two doors down from Ian Brown?

John Squire: Early Days

John Thomas Squire was born on 28 November 1962 in Broadheath, Lancashire. He was brought up in Timperley, going to a different primary school to Ian Brown despite living across the road and four doors down from him.

Even at an early age he excelled at art. He was the quiet kid with the shy half stare from behind his floppy fringe, daydreaming his way through school. Contemporaries describe him as being withdrawn and 'in his own world' and being especially gifted at art.

When Squire was a kid he got an autograph from *Blue Peter*'s Biddy Baxter. 'I sent her a picture of me guinea pig having a bath in a kitchen bowl,' he says. 'I got a *Blue Peter* badge and a signed letter from Biddy Baxter, cos it went up on the pictures-of-your-pets board.'

Like Brown when he was growing up John was surrounded by music. His parents listened to Elvis and Peggy Lee but especially The Beatles. Remembers John, 'I always consider them almost other worldly, The Beatles. The fact that they grew up in a northern working-class environment and still made it. That showed that you didn't have to come from London, or you didn't have to come from America to make it.'

But it was punk that put all John's musical and art obsessions into focus. His curiosity in punk had been ignited by his new mate across the street and John Squire dived headlong into the exploding scene. It was a total inspiration.

'I think London punk bands had more of an effect on my motivation, than where I was from. The whole ethos of The Clash, Pistols, all that era, and the fact that they promoted themselves on the platform of "anyone can do it". I don't know if that was true, but it certainly made me think that maybe I could.'

And according to Squire, it was Strummer's impassioned example that was an inspiration. A chance quote from The Clash's vocalist on TV had fired him up.

'This wasn't personal advice, it was TV advice. Joe Strummer from The Clash turning to the camera in a very stoic move. He was asked if he had any advice for the kids out there and he said, "Believe in yourself, you can do anything you want." That one went in and stayed.'

John Squire loved The Clash; he 'liked their painted trousers', he once explained, referring to one of The Clash's earliest looks in 1976 when they splashed paint Pollock-like over their stage gear, an art school reference that can only have come from The Clash's artful bassist, Paul Simonon.

It was seeing The Clash at the Apollo in 1977 that turned John Squire's head. 'The Complete Control tour, I think it was called. It was the first gig I'd been to. I'd been listening to the band's music for about a year and was obsessed with them and it was the first time I'd seen them in the flesh. It was just the most exciting thing I'd ever experienced, being right down at the front and getting thrown over the barrier into the pit and being taken out by the side and being put back in again. I can remember feeling at the time, "This is where I want to be".'

It also can't have escaped the 14-year-old John Squire, hunched over his guitar, that The Clash's engine room was the best guitar player from the punk rock generation. Mick Jones. Looking like a starving Keef Richards, and armed with a Les Paul Junior and a cool sneer, the super-cool Jones was the link between the punk present and the rock'n'roll past.

The Pistols' Steve Jones and The New York Dolls' Johnny Thunders were also firing him.

'They were the only guys who were playing any sort of fast runs; every-one else just played chords,' 'John explains, adding 'There's a low note on "God Save The Queen", probably an A-string, just before the begin-ning of the second verse. Dowwww! Really fat and thick. One note…raw sex. I heard that…had to go to do it myself.'

Johnny Thunders was an incredible talent who burned out in a haze of hard drugs that eventually contributed to his untimely death. His ringing guitar sound was a big influence on the Pistols and, in turn, John Squire and the nearby Johnny Marr.

Squire worked hard at his guitar and even took a couple of lessons. 'I probably spent too long practising guitar on my own,' he muses. 'We didn't live in a musical street, and it wasn't until just before the first Roses album that I met another proper guitarist. This guy I used to work with used to go to a blues and folk guitar teacher in Rusholme; I went with him a couple of times and he taught me a lot. Apart from that, it all comes from books and cassettes. Plus I had the record player…' he explained to *Total Guitar* magazine.

Squire's industrious father wired up a train set transformer to the said record player, allowing, with a tilt of the dial, variable voltage. So not only could 45s be played at 33⅓, when the guitar parts got a bit tricky 33⅓s could be played at, ooh, 12⅙. 'It was so good when I got into Page, Hendrix and Clapton because I could slow everything down and pick out guitar lines. Very helpful.'

From here, Squire absorbed a smidgen of chord theory – 'I don't carry it up around here, though (taps head)' – and cherry-picked the best licks he could from a book called *Lead Guitar* by Harvey Vincent. 'It came with a flexi-disk and was all blues-based,' he remembers. 'That stuff just came easy to me. Dunno why…I just liked the sound. Still do.'

Squire's first guitars were the sort of cheapies everyone kicks off with. He swiftly moved on to a Höfner 335-style semi. A guitar that he still owns years later. 'I've still got it,' he grins. 'But I've, erm, painted it with a splash of household gloss.'

The Gretsch Country Gentleman pictured on the inside of The Stone Roses' 'lemon' album was a live favourite, but John Leckie vetoed its use for the album's recording.

'He said it was too woolly, and he was right. For a lot of the first album I hired in a pink sixties Stratocaster which I ended up buying because it sounded so good. The Gretsch went missing…'

Looking for a fatter sound on *Second Coming* Squire's main guitar was a Sunburst '59 Les Paul Standard which was previously owned by Cheap Trick's Rick Nielson. 'The neck looked unplayable at first,' recalls John. 'It was so chipped – like a map of the Swedish coast. But it sounded really nice. I don't know too much about guitars so I could easily be sold a fake – but I know when one sounds special.' When the Roses' business affairs were liquidated, the '59 Sunburst was sold as, strictly speaking, it was band property.

Quietly building up his guitar prowess, sat in his bedroom spending hours with his guitar and his painting, Squire was perfecting the twin skills that would dominate his life.

In the meantime he, like Ian, was in the final year of Altrincham Grammar and there were new horizons to look forward to.

During their last couple of years at Altrincham Grammar, Ian Brown and John Squire had bonded tight over punk rock. On the two-mile journey home to Sylvan Avenue they would talk their way through the usual burning topics of teen culture, football, television and music.

Another classmate at Altrincham Grammar was future Stone Roses drummer Si Wolstencroft.

'John and me were in the Latin set together at school. We didn't pay much attention to Latin though! I think Ian might have been in the wood-work set, I could be wrong. It was great. We did the minimum amount we had to do. We were not top of the class but Ian got a few O levels. I got half a dozen. John got the same as me. Ian is smart though. He's been managing himself the last few years. Ian was more a judge of character. He would talk to people to get the truth out of people, which you need to do in the music business.

'In Latin, me and John were sat at the back together and we would draw cartoons. I would draw a drum kit and he would draw all sorts of things like inventions and clockwork machines that do weird things – quite bizarre really! Basically John got off football because of his artistic talent, which they recognized, whilst me and Ian were out there scrapping on the pitch with everyone else. But we were all in the gang. Ian, he was more a show-off, a chatterbox – he would imitate all the teachers and he would have us all rolling about.

'We were not nasty at all, but naughty. Me and John were the first to get the cane for writing on the desks in the third year – six of the best from the headmaster who was a right bastard from Boston in Massachusetts. He was right strict. We would do stuff like playing peashooters with rolled up bits of paper which we would stick in our mouths and chew to make them sticky, and shoot them to the ceiling and they would stick there!'

Like many pre-punk teenagers it was glam rock that informed Si's musical tastes.

'When I first went to school The Sweet were my favourite group. I had pictures of The Sweet all over my bedroom wall. They were my favourite group till The Clash came along. With John it's hard to say what he was into – maybe Bowie obviously and perhaps Slade, maybe some heavier stuff but I'm not sure.'

Squire was still living the life of the mind, painting, making models and playing the guitar, while Brown was already mooching around the city centre, hanging out on the fringes of the hooligan skinhead and suedehead scene to a soundtrack of punk rock and Northern Soul. It wasn't always safe. Manchester is a rough city (then and now) but these were Brown's roots. His real roots, mixing the glam of T-Rex with the stomping bonding of Northern Soul, hanging with the gangs, the karate schools, Ali's sharp lyricism and neat arrogance…a melting pot of ideas that would mark him and, through him, a whole generation. These excursions up to the city centre were the first mini travels by Brown, the first of his wanderings, and he would relate these tales to John Squire, the sat-at-home art boy from across the road who was quite content to sit in his bedroom, drawing, painting and daydreaming.

The two friends followed the punk fallout through their last couple of years at Altrincham Grammar School. They grabbed a bunch of O levels and in the autumn of 1979 they started at South Trafford College (now Trafford College), a large tech college in Altrincham with a real crossover of kids from all the surrounding suburbs and a whole new bunch of faces to mix with.

College Days: From Altrincham Grammar to South Trafford College

It was the autumn of 1979 and, depressingly, Thatcher was about to beat Labour in the elections. The country was going through one of its bouts of turmoil where nothing worked and the whole system seemed to be collapsing. Punk was said to be dead and its energy was splintering into a mish-mash of youth cultures. There were gang wars between rockabillies, post-punk Peel heads, skinheads, 2 Toners, mods, punks and metalheads.

Some people swore allegiance wholly to one scene while others cherry-picked from all the different tribes. South Trafford College typified this fallout. A minority of kids were immersed totally 24/7 in youth culture, while the rest ignored it completely.

Pacing the corridors between lessons – the corridors were packed as 2,000 students sluggishly moved from one classroom to another. The new intake would size each other up. Most of the students were into nothing in particular so it didn't take long for those 20 or so kids that had been fired up by punk to find each other.

New boys Andy Couzens and Ian Brown noticed each other but it wasn't all bonding and record swapping at first.

In fact there was an element of tension. Says Andy, 'I'd seen them lot in there but I never really spoke to them. We just walked past each other in the corridors giving each other the eye…me and Ian. You know, "Who the fuck are you!!"

'Everyone had that horrible crossover look between Joy Division and punk with a bit of mod starting to creep in here and there…There was a bunch of us into it...about 2,000 students went there and there was 10 or 15 into punk/new wave...Ian Brown was getting into that mod thing proper with tonic suits and short hair with a sort of side parting...John Squire looked like Mick Jones – creepers, short leather bomber jacket, wrist band with studs...he called himself Johnny...Pete [Garner] wasn't at college there...I met Pete later...'

A year younger, Pete Garner was starting to hang around with the gang. The punk thing was bringing people together.

'I didn't go to college. I was at Burnage High School and they were at South Trafford College. I had a lot of work to do to keep in the gang. You just don't speak to people in the year below and from a totally different school but we bonded over the punk thing.'

Pete had bumped into Ian and John in the fields near where they all lived. There was a river and small nondescript bridge that became the focal point as he remembers.

'I met them at the bridge and all that...I'd seen 'em a couple of times before. I started chatting. There was a bit of piss taking going on! John was quiet, he didn't say much, he was really into The Clash whilst Ian was more Pistols and The Jam. John, for some reason, was never having The Jam...For me The Clash was always my number one, I love the Pistols too...but me and Ian really liked The Jam as well...'

The Bridge

In between Sale and Altrincham there's this bridge and for generations kids have hung out there. Every teen lout across small-town England knows of the sort of place – a landmark, a meeting point, a place to get stoned and pissed, a place to fuck about and fight – a focal point and a beacon for all sorts of crazed activity. For Pete Garner this was the place.

'The Bridge was like the meeting point, when everyone was ten or eleven they would hang out there and when they got to about fourteen – I guess they found something better to do and moved on,' he remembers.

Garner was hanging around there when he was an early teen. Just a casual young kid, making mischief. He thought he was the coolest person there. He was certainly the biggest and most of the other kids thought that he was the toughest. It was something to play on in the jostling for power that dominates those long empty evenings of adolescence.

Sometimes a clutch of kids would come over from Altrincham or Timperley, bored and looking for some lightweight trouble and some laughs. Ian Brown and John Squire were just two of many that drifted around and hung out.

It was pretty fucking boring in south Manchester in those far-off days. 'We thought that we were the king punks of the area. When Ian and John turned up we would give each other shit. I guess at some point there must have been some sort of mutual respect,' laughs Garner.

They started getting friendly when talk turned to what gigs they had been to, exaggerating into the evening, embellishing the classic punk shows they had attended up in Manchester. It was mostly braggadocio.

At the time, Garner was going to Burnage High School. It was there that by a bizarre coincidence he would also meet Aziz Ibrahim, the future Roses guitar player from the last stand at Reading Festival years later. 'He was a good lad. He would always have a guitar with him. He played it all the time whilst everyone watched him.'

Aziz himself remembers being in the same class as Pete.

'Burnage High School…top days! Great days…best times. It was an all-boys school, I was into sport there. Did really well at basketball…Pete was the school Goth! He was artistic, really into his artwork…We were mates because I played basketball and his mates were on the same team…'

While they were bonding at the Bridge there were the first stirrings of some musical action. John, who had become immersed in the whole Clash myth, was taking his Mick Jones fascination one stop further and earnestly copping the licks off The Clash records. By grafting away he had become a comparatively useful if rudimentary punk rock guitar player.

But the band's biggest Clash lover missed out on the greatest blag of the year and one of the best stories that surrounds the pre-Roses…the day they hung out with the band themselves!

Manchester's Pluto Studios was set up by Keith Hopkins, guitarist from Herman's Hermits, in 1968 in Stockport. The studio had moved to Granby Row in Manchester city centre in 1977 and it was where Brian and Michael had recorded the big 1977 hit 'Matchstick Men and Match-stick Cats and Dogs'.

It was also the scene of an unlikely recording session on 1 February 1980.

Ian Brown and Pete Garner had heard that The Clash were in town recording somewhere so they decided to see if they could find them.

Pete Garner: 'We got a train into town. We didn't know where they were going to be. Ian said it was in a studio somewhere in the city centre. It was pissing with rain. We had no idea The Clash were going to be in town, we just thought they might be! Pluto was the only studio we knew in town so we sat on the wall opposite the studio in the rain. We thought this was ridiculous and then this car pulled up and The Clash got out and invited us in, which was amazing! What other band would invite two kids in to hang out with them?'

Ian Browns remembers the famous day. 'We were in town in Granby Row, where Pluto Studios was. We heard these drums and it turned out it was The Clash doing "Bankrobber". So we knocked on the door, they let us in and we hung around for a day. They were nice, sound. Topper was just regular. Strummer was a bit of a weirdo! He sat under this grandfather clock, clicking his fingers in time with it.'

'I thought he was a bit fucking nuts,' says Pete. 'Until I went in a studio to record and realised about studio time!'

On The Clash's *Greatest Hits* compilation sleeve notes, written by Albert Transom (Joe Strummer's alter ego), there is a reference to 'these kids' in Manchester hanging out in the studio.

The Clash were also a reference point for another local schoolmate who had gone on to South Trafford College, a sharply bequiffed young drummer who lived a couple of miles away from Timperley in Altrincham, Si Wolstencroft.

'I met Ian and John at "Alty" Grammar School in the first year when I was 11 in 1974,' he recalls in a voice that has the same South Manchester burr as Ian Brown. 'I was in the same class as the pair of them. I gravitated towards John at first, I don't know why, but I was friends with both of them. They were like they are now. I forgot how withdrawn John is till I saw him at the 'Justice Tonight' gig in 2011. John and Si were Clash buddies who went on the road to follow the band.

'When the Clash album came out in April 1977 we were 14 and we became firm friends and talked about The Clash non-stop. John was neighbours with Ian in Timperley. Ian was also into the punk thing but more into the Sex Pistols and he really liked The Adverts. He might have gone to see The Adverts at the time. There were other bands as well like The Specials. We went to the 2 Tone tours at the Apollo in Manchester in 1979.

'The Specials' "Gangsters" came out in 1979 and we thought, "Fucking hell, that's amazing!" and bought into the whole thing. Me and Ian had the 2 Tone suits – cheap ones from Carnaby Street and loafers with the little tassels on them.

We had already seen The Specials on The Clash's *Out On Parole* tour because the tour support, Suicide, couldn't make it that night. This was in The Specials' early days, before "Ghost Town". Ian was into punkier gigs and the faster stuff like The Angelic Upstarts and the Oi bands as well. He was more of a skinhead, and then there would be the scooters as well, which helped to define him. John was not so much into that sort of thing. John kept his influences close to his chest after The Clash had come along. Ian had loved Motown as a kid and John had loved The Beatles and maybe even stuff like Santana.'

It was one afternoon at South Trafford College that they decided to get their own band together. The Patrol had been formed on a whim, as Si Wolstencroft remembers:

'The only reason I went to South Trafford College was because them two had done. We had started a group that summer for a laugh. I don't know who suggested getting a band together, it just seemed a natural thing to do, a bit of a rebellious thing to do. I don't know whose idea it was. I was already drumming by then. I learned by watching *Top of the Pops*, looking at Slade and The Sweet. I kind of knew what to do by myself already. I'm not sure when John Squire picked the guitar up but it didn't take him long to learn how to play.'

Ian Brown bought Si's Woolworths bass from him ('for fifty quid – that's how we started off,' explains Ian). They had formed a tight-knit core but there was still one ingredient missing…they needed a singer and someone mentioned the cool-looking kid in the right gear who had been skulking about the college.

The Fight Club!: Andy Couzens' Unusual Audition

Of course nowadays the singer is some sort of sensitive cove who builds a band around his mercurial talents. Or something. But this was the punk era and the rules were less well-defined. Messier.

The Brown/Squire/Wolstencroft bedroom band knew they needed a singer. But where could they find one?

It couldn't be just anyone. After all, there were already strong personalities at play here.

Punk rock bands required nutters to front them, not singers. Even Ian's hero Johnny Rotten, a contradictory sod at the best of times, covered up his shyness with a sneering tirade of hilarious and downright nasty put-downs. They needed someone to front their Clash riffing, someone with a bit of craziness about them.

Hanging around in the college canteen in late '79, Ian Brown and Si Wolstencroft had spotted a bit of a commotion. Never ones to avoid a bit of bother they moved closer. The short-haired hooligan they had seen around the college was pounding some other kid into the floor. The other kid was in tears. It was a nasty, brutal exchange and they were impressed.

Andy says, 'I had a fight in the canteen. Some fucking lad the night before had given my little brother a bit of a going over…so I laid him out. He was crying by the time I had finished. It was the first fight I'd had for ages…It was at lunchtime with a load of people watching. There was a bit of a stunned silence. You just didn't do that at college. It was supposed to be further education and beyond all that!'

The silence was deafening. The laid back world of further education had just witnessed an unlikely burst of aggro.

So Couzens is standing there pumped full of adrenaline. He's just pummelled this kid. The refectory has gone silent. He wanders off, gets a meal and sits down. He can feel the shocked looks of the rest of the college on his back. The confused silence that most people give off when they have been that close to some action fills the room.

He also notices two figures walking towards him.

It's that guy who's been giving him the eye since he came here and his sharp-looking mate. The one with The Clash style tight quiff and 'London Calling' era Clash gangster punk chic.

'I spoke to Ian first…Simon Wolstencroft was there as well,' Andy recalled. 'He was into the later Clash look, creepers, Crombies, quiff… neckerchiefs and all that "London Calling" look…I did this lad in and then I got myself a brew and some lunch and they asked me if I could sing! I always wanted to be in a band and I wasn't aware they had a band. I was always going to see punk bands but I couldn't play anything. They came over and said "Can you sing?" and I said "I'll have a go."'

Not that this is the way that Si Wolstencroft remembered how Andy joined the band. When interviewed by The Fall fanzine *Biggest Library Yet*, his take on Andy joining was very different.

'The Patrol was my first band formed with John Squire and Ian Brown in the last year at Altrincham Grammar School. Andy Couzens was asked to sing with us partly because his wealthy parents bought him an MG sports car when he went to South Trafford College. This was a big novelty at the time but we definitely noticed him. Ian and Andy were handy fighters. Of course, Ian used to do karate when he was younger.'

Si Wolstencroft explains: 'At the college we were seriously looking for someone to sing. We had spotted Andy Couzens and we liked the look of him. He had The Clash gear on and a spiky hair look with a Crombie. Also, he had a guitar as well and his mum and dad had bought him an MG Midget to go to the college. It was a tiny car but we could all squeeze into it if someone was squashed between the two front seats.'

The band now had a singer. He had agreed to come over and rehearse in the next few weeks. Andy Couzens, after drifting round school and being the outsider, now had a gang of like-minded people to hang with. At last he had somewhere he could really call home. And that home was now calling itself The Patrol.

Andy Couzens

Andy Couzens was born in Stockport in 1962. It's not a town for which he retains a lot of affection: 'Stockport's like a village, it's weird. I couldn't wait to get out. I finished school and went as far away as I could, which was…Altrincham!'

He had moved constantly through his youth. 'My parents moved every two years. Always within the Stockport area and then out to Macclesfield… I was always moving school which didn't make life easy."

His parents young being had one hidden bonus. It meant that he was surrounded by pop music, pop music that was not that far removed from his own generation. It was a great music education.

His father had a business to do with telephones in the days before privatisation and BT. His father had taken risks with the business and it wasn't till the early eighties that it had paid off.

Stephen Lea, who would later briefly become The Stone Roses' lawyer and was the Couzens' family lawyer, remembers Colin Couzens.

'His dad didn't have a pot to piss in when he was starting out. There was good and bad times. It wasn't as through Andy was driving around in flash cars all the time. His father wouldn't spoil him. Colin was quite young and quite switched on and believed in Andy and would do what he could to help him.'

Andy's parents' musical background was a key influence on him.

'My parents were into the Stones and hated The Beatles. They also liked loads of soul stuff like Wilson Pickett. My mum was 16 when she had me so she was almost like an elder sister.'

As the sixties turned into the seventies the parental soundtrack remained hip. 'My old fella got into Zep and Floyd and when you're a kid you pick up on what's around.'

It must have been frustrating – hip parents! But in the early seventies there was the first real generational shift in pop. As the sixties generation grew up into prog rock, the teenagers were busily finding their own sounds. While his father was getting into prog and hard rock, Andy was getting into glam.

Glam rock has been snootily dismissed by 'musical experts' and 'pundits' for generation after generation but it was one of the classic British musical moments, homemade stars with a machine gun run of great seven-inch singles. Couzens loved Slade and the rest of the glam bands but the band that he really fell for at the tender age of 11 was Bryan Ferry's Roxy Music.

'The first record I bought was 'Pyjamarama' by Roxy Music. I still love it now, it drags me straight back. It reminds me of kids hanging out doing fuck all...In '73/'74 I really liked Roxy, yeah, I also love glam, I loved Slade – ace band. Marc Bolan was great. "Metal Guru" is still one of my all-time favourites...'

T-Rex are one of the greatest British pop bands that ever existed. Bolan was the inventor of glam and put out a fantastic series of pop singles and albums that have influenced a whole cross-section of popstars ever since. Ian Brown, unbeknown to Andy, was also a big fan at the same time.

'He was a big Bolan fan...T-Rex was a great band, yeah! It's weird. I never got the sexuality side of it at all...I was too young really to notice if stuff was sexual or not...I liked Alice Cooper as well...That period had some great records, great singles.'

At school, being a new face as he moved from school to school, Andy was the target for bullying. The outsider just arriving in each school surrounded by kids who already knew each other inside out. It toughened him up. Fast. Kill or be killed. Andy had to fight back.

'When I was a lot younger I was quieter because I was moving often, so I was always the new face at school and you know what lads are like – wanna see how hard you are…so I learned to keep myself to myself…'

Already toughened up by his school experience and armed with a vicious temper and a keenness to fight, Couzens was drifting towards the ultimate male bonding world of football violence.

In the early seventies, football hooliganism was massive. It did a lot to define street culture; the decade was the high water mark of football violence with a whole subculture built around it.

The skinheads were a reaction to the hippies and had begun transforming into football hooligans. Their hair was growing out into feather cuts. They retained the cherry-red Doc Martens and parallel trousers (often bottle green), hitched up to show off their neatly polished boots. Every match went off big style. It was common to see hundreds of hooligans chasing each other all over the place on match day.

The appalling condition of most of the football stadiums and the way that the fans were herded round like sheep only added to the boiling pot of malevolence.

For Couzens it was escapism and male bonding and community all rolled into one. At last he felt like he belonged somewhere. 'When I got into my mid-teens, I got badly into football violence. I'd go and see Stockport County every Friday without fail. There was always a battle on every match. Always arranged at the tunnels at Stockport station.'

He dressed in regulation thug gear. 'Doc boots – cherry-reds, parallels…sheepskin donkey jacket…the feather cut started disappearing, getting shorter and shorter like becoming a suedehead. Then I went to the bigger games in Manchester…United was always too clean cut and regulated so I went to Maine Road instead and that was serious, nasty stuff…We were with a group of lads who went into Moss Side and met up with a bunch of guys called the Cool Cats, a bunch of black guy hooligans…and a few white guys…'

Andy Couzens was no shrinking violet when it went off. 'I've got a really bad temper, a really short fuse…The best thing about Maine Road was the Kippax, the police stood between the two massive high fences… and you could spit and throw things at them throughout the game. I got a right kick out of it. A bunch of us would go out on Friday night to Stockport and Saturday to City. The football was incidental, an excuse. I went to a lot of away games as well. It was good for a laugh on those seventies football specials. They didn't have a seat in them, the windows were plastic and we had a riot!'

This sort of life couldn't go on for ever and Couzens was no Neanderthal. He realised the violence was going to have to be tempered. He needed another outlet for his frustration and energy and one night in the summer of '77 when he was at home he flicked across the stations on the radio and was captivated by this fast snarling tune.

It was the first great pop record he had heard for years. Nothing had moved him since the glam heyday of three years before. The singer had a whining bratty voice but sounded sharp and intelligent.

He was hooked. The group was The Adverts, one of the seemingly endless parade of punk rock groups that seemed to be spiralling out, filling the vacuum after the Sex Pistols had exploded.

He suddenly started to notice that there was this whole new subculture going on. A new world, a new code, a new language and he was hooked. Greedily he started to soak up these new influences.

'I heard the tunes…I didn't read about it, I just heard the tunes…there had been a bit of a lull in music. I remember even buying an Abba album, ha! ha! ha! I remember buying a Wings album, which I never liked. Wings' *At The Speed Of Sound*. It was awful.'

At last there was a musical culture that felt like it belonged to you. 'No more Elvis, Beatles or The Rolling Stones,' crowed The Clash on '1977'. Fed up with being told that the pop party was over in the mid to late seventies, teenagers were now having their own party.

'I heard the music and you could tell there was something, the thing for me was that it sounded so angry. I related to that straight away. It was great…and then it opened my eyes. It changed everything for me. I started going to gigs. It was such a different world than my upbringing in Stockport. I was shocked, black people mixing with white people. Women on their own. A real eye opener. It changed the way I thought about everything. It buried my violence. Coming from where I come from all you aspire to is getting pissed on a Friday or Saturday, putting a suit on so you can get into pubs and being married by the time you're 21 with kids. Most of the people I went to school with did that.'

Manchester was great for punk rock. Outside London it was the second punk rock city. Every major band played there at the Electric Circus, and it even had its own scene, its own bands and Andy couldn't get enough of these groups.

'I saw The Clash at Electric Circus. I saw The Clash so many times, I always loved the Buzzcocks. It was all the sexual contradictions in their lyrics that always tickled me. The Pistols and The Clash were fantastic. The Adverts I liked but they let you down a bit, they didn't quite move you in the same way as the Pistols and The Clash and then the next thing that really hit me was Joy Division.'

By 1979 punk was becoming a straitjacket and although he still loved the simplistic rush of the three minute punk rock buzz for years to come, Andy was now fired by the new soundscape that groups like Manchester outfit Warsaw were carving from the punk template.

'I saw them when they were called Warsaw, playing in some fucking awful place at the arse end of Manchester, near the Northern Quarter. I'd follow them around a bit. Bands like that you could go and see and they actually meant it, which sounds so corny now. When they've really got some self belief and when you got an idea of their personalities from what they are doing, it's totally gripping…'

When Warsaw turned into Joy Division they really captured the post-punk paranoia, the bleakness of the times.

'All the best music does, doesn't it? I met Diggle and Shelley loads of times. I met The Clash a few times. They were everything you thought they were going to be.'

Meanwhile Couzens was now settling into some sort of school routine. 'I was still at school now in the fifth year. Bramhall High School which was a nice safe little environment. It was a little bubble. Mike Pickering, the DJ, went to my school and Gordon King who ended up in World of Twist went there as well. We were pretty good friends at school. He was always a bit more arty, with a bit more artistic flair, shall we say. He'd wear an Afghan coat and smoke draw and I was like more of a hooligan!'

Couzens surprised himself by sailing through his exams. 'I got O levels…about eight of the fucking things. The stupid thing is all that build-up to them. I never picked up the certificates. It was just a joke.'

He drifted into higher education. 'I then went to South Trafford College. I did A level maths, physics and electronics…It was a technical college and had an arts side to it as well, which is where John Squire was.'

And it was at college that he was to make some friendships that were to change his rock'n'roll life. As he entered South Trafford College in the autumn of 1979 he quickly noticed a handful of other punk rock nutters but they were from another part of town and remained distant. Couzens tried to keep his head down. Get some A levels and fuck off.

But that one slip, that one relapse to violence, that one moment of fury in the canteen, had put him into an unlikely musical situation and he was now the singer in The Patrol.

The band started rehearsing at Si's parents' house, where he had his kit set up. It made sense. An extension of the gang. Everyone who was touched by the hand of punk seemed to have some sort of band going now. Every bedroom, garage and youth club was rattling to punk riffs and spiky teenage energy. And this crew were no different.

Ian had picked up the bass. It was the easiest instrument to start on and the ultimate punk rock instrument. The coolest person in every punk band was the bass player so why not? From The Clash's Paul Simonon to The Stranglers' JJ Burnel – the bass had been elevated to the coolest instrument.

1980–81

The Patrol

Early 1980 John and Si went on the road for the first time for a tour that would dominate their musical thinking for the next few years. During January and February of 1980 they hitchhiked round the country to see The Clash at their peak on the legendary *16 Tons* tour.

Si recalls: 'The music we were starting to do with The Patrol was loosely based on The Clash. Squire and myself were massive fans at the time. I left college to follow them around the country on tour in early 1980. We went to Bridlington Spa, Bristol Locarno, Deeside Leisure Centre, London Lyceum, Hammersmith Palais. I had a part-time job and we were living at home – that's why we had spending money for National Express!

'We slept on stations a couple of times. We never slept on the band's hotel room floor – Joe Strummer was well known for that, looking after his fans. It was a very exciting time – a big learning curve. I'd always wanted to play drums since I was ten years old and miming to The Sweet and when I saw it for real I wanted to do it even more. I can't speak for Ian and John but I couldn't wait to get out of Timperley and Altrincham and play music.'

On the tour they were just two more fresh young faces in a sea of punk rock teenagers. The pair of them joined the ever-increasing pack of young waifs and strays who would hitchhike up and down the country checking out the greatest punk band of them all.

A whole generation of British rockers cut their teeth following The Clash from gig to gig, some of them crewing with the band, some blagging guest list places and some just turning up at soundchecks and getting looked after by the band.

It was a big deal with The Clash to have this bond with their fans. The adventure of following a band on the road was a key part of the punk rock experience. But perhaps, more than following bands around, the most powerful message from punk was 'do it yourself'. The whole notion, the whole inspirational idea was that anyone could have a go. All over the punk nation it seemed that everyone was at it, blagging, buying guitars, forcing mates into being drummers, getting hold of youth clubs and putting gigs on.

Every ragbag collection of mates were now forming themselves into rock'n'roll bands. And the Timperley boys were no exception. John Squire had been glued to his guitar, listening to those incendiary Clash records, copping those Mick Jones licks. Listening and learning. The Clash's artful and adrenalised take on punk rock appealing to his nature.

Si was honing down his drums by listening to The Clash's remarkable drummer Topper Headon. Meanwhile The Patrol was coming together.

Ian Brown remembers: 'We had started The Patrol in 1979. Andy Couzens was the singer because we were impressed with his bottle. We had seen him in this fight weighing into this kid, and because the other kid was bigger than him we thought, "Let's ask him to be the singer." He looked right as well: he was wearing winklepicker shoes, a long black Crombie and had a spiky haircut so we knew he was coming out of the same sort of thing that we were.

'He was better off than us. He had his own car and lived in a big house. Which was useful because we eventually rehearsed in the cellar of his house when we moved out of Si's. He had all the gear there, the amps and the drum kit. We got our own PA and sprayed it bright green because The Clash had one that was bright pink.

'I guess we were Clash copyists. That was what inspired us. I played bass in the band because it was the easiest thing to play. Even then, though, I must have been a frustrated singer because I used to write the words and do the backing vocals as well as introducing the songs when we eventually played live.'

Andy went for his first rehearsal with the band. 'I arranged to meet Ian just outside Timperley train station. I was driving by then. They rehearsed in the back bedroom at Si's house in Hale Barns. The first time I ever met John was at that rehearsal. I had seen him around at college. I thought, "There's that fucking Clash clone, ha!"'

Andy plugged his mic into John's guitar amp and shouted his way over the songs, finding his way over the three chord workouts. 'Si had a good kit and he could play. John was pretty good but it was all The Clash copy stuff. He played a bit of lead as well. He'd had proper guitar lessons. Ian was on bass and couldn't really play. He was a proper punk bass player. All fast strumming.'

There were also some tunes to work on. 'They had a couple of bits of music. They had had a few jams before I got there. John was the one who got it all together initially. They all went to Altrincham Grammar and had gone through discovering punk, all that sort of thing, so it grew from that really. No songs. Just jammed bits of music. John had brought some lyrics with him that he thought I might want to sing. It was a real Clash reggae type of thing called "Jail Of The Assassins". Pete has a tape of that some-where Years later we'd always joke that Pete was the Bill Wyman of the gang, hoarding all the stuff! Reni tried to keep stuff as well but could never concentrate long enough. In Sweden Reni kept a really detailed diary, came home and lost it.'

The rehearsals at Si Wolstencroft's mum and dad's place near Ian's and John's in Timperley were going well. They had scratched together some Clash-style punk rock tunes. John Squire was good enough on guitar to make the whole thing convincing and Si's drumming gave them a solid enough backbone.

Ian Brown remembers: 'We had a song called "Jail Of The Assassins" because we thought that was what Strummer had written on one of his stencilled shirts. I had known Si a long time even then; he was the first kid I met at school. He was the only person to have Docs on so I clicked with him straightaway. I have been mates with him since I was 11.

'After The Patrol he played on the original Smiths demo that got them the deal. He said, "They won't get anywhere with that weirdo on vocals!" He's a great drummer and great kid as well.'

The band's personalities were already at the fore in the tight confines of the hot bedroom. The distorted riffing through the cheap amps and Andy's coarse vocals were further muffled by the fact that his cheapo mic was jacked up through John's amp, which added to the distorted punk mêlée. As he shouted down the mic and attempted to put some punk rock life to John's lyrics, Andy had a good look at his new mates.

'Si was always quiet. John was dead serious, a lot of presence about him. Ian was cocky as fuck right from the word go – trying to vibe me out. I wasn't having any of it, I remember saying to him, "So you are a fucking mod, are you? What's all that about!" The thing I remember about John the most was that he was very typically artistically natured. Quiet and shy. He always had a fringe to hide behind. I remember thinking he was quite interesting, you know…'

From brawling madman in the college to lead singer in 24 hours.

Things were moving fast in DIY punk culture – the message of the times was of being involved, of doing something!

The band rehearsed hard. The work ethic was already ingrained. Recalls Andy, 'We started rehearsing a few times every week. That was one thing we always did. We rehearsed every night that we could. We never really had a night off. We would do it all the time, live and breathe it. It's the only way to get things done. I remember the songs were all real Clash-type things. "25 Rifles", "Too Many Tons" named after The Clash's *16 Tons* tour. There was also one called "H Block". I did a few lyrics but they were mainly John's. It was all punk rock nonsense really!'

The Clash legend looms large over the Roses and their early incarnations so you can imagine how cool it was when the feeling was reciprocated. Years later Pete caught The Clash on TV being interviewed.

'I saw Strummer getting interviewed on Snub TV just after I left the Roses. They asked him if he liked any bands and he said the Roses. I choked on my brew. I wanted to speak to John and say "Jesus!" Strummer had picked up on the Roses just when the album came out and they were still really underground. I'd love to have met him and tell him me and Ian had met him that time.'

Quickly the songs came together. Listening to a rehearsal tape from March 1980 you can hear a pretty competent band honing down its Clash chops. The songs charge past, raw vocals over the slashing riffs, 'London Night Out', '25 Rifles', 'Human Disease', 'Stepping Stone', which sounds more like a cover of the Pistols' cover of The Monkees' song than the original. There was a rudimentary run through of the Chuck Berry standard 'Johnny B Goode' and, changing the tempo, the attempt at The Clash reggae of 'Jail Of The Assassins'. There was 'Stars And Stripes' which was 'sort of our "I'm So Bored Of The USA",' remembers Pete, referencing The Clash's anti-Americana tirade.

Garner was sitting in with the band, hanging out at their rehearsals, part of the gang, pretending to be their roadie. They were surprisingly adept for a teenage punk band. Pete remembers how together they were.

'Si was into Topper. He was aspiring to that sort of level really. Ian's bass playing was pretty rudimentary – classic punk style, the guitar was really The Clash. One number was their sort of "Police And Thieves", a bit "Guns Of Brixton", not proper reggae by any stretch of the imagination, that was "Jail Of The Assassins…", there was also "Up On The Roof".'

Si can just about remember the songs they wrote.

'Ian played bass but there was also one where he sings and Andy played bass when Ian sang. Pete was a mate of ours at the time and would hang out with us. And, after I started to hang around with Johnny Marr, Pete moved in on the bass briefly. There were about five songs, I think. I remember "Too Many Tons", which was named after The Clash's "16 Tons" tour that me and John had been on. There was a song called "You're Laughing Now" and maybe a Generation X cover, which I think we performed live. Me, Squire and Ian were really into Generation X who we saw live. I think John gets lot of guitar technique from their guitar player, Derwood. Derwood's playing was like fireworks going off! It wasn't solos all the time but aggressive and cut through.'

Another musician who lived nearby had already befriended part of the crew, Pete Garner. Years later Johnny Marr himself remembers: 'I was working at Aladdin's Cave in town. I really liked this guy, he seemed pretty cool. Pete lived between me and my girlfriend. He was this great guy and there wasn't many of them around. He was working in the original Paperchase in town and I was in there all the time. He had dead long hair…he would talk through his hair. I was coming to town all the time because I was working there and getting a new band together rehearsing at Decibel Studios.'

Already the pre-Smiths and the pre-Roses were running in parallel. Both bands had so many crossovers, coming from the same musical areas, sharing influences and working in the same pool of musicians. Their careers would match up several times over the years.

The Patrol were bonding over their musical tastes. This was a crew that knew their music. Says Andy, 'We were into the same stuff. Generation X's first album was a big one with all of us. We listened to everything from glam, to skin, to punk. We all delved into Johnny Thunders and the New York Dolls separately from each other. It was a real meeting of minds. We all had a core of stuff we really liked. We branched off into our own stuff as well. I was into Joy Division when the others weren't, although I remember turning John on to some of the early Joy Division stuff. I had two copies of the first EP. I gave John one. He was bang into it.'

Even then, right from the start, the band were incredibly earnest about what they were doing. They rehearsed hard. There was no pottering about. As a result they swiftly tightened up. You can hear it on the rehearsal tapes, songs coming together quickly. Now they were ready to play live.

*

On Friday, 28 March 1980 they played their first gig. They had managed to get on to a punk rock bill at the Sale Annex Youth Club. It was a typical youth club affair. The felt-tipped and photocopied poster tells the whole story: for 30p you could see The Patrol supported by Stretford punks Suburban Chaos at the Youth Club 'behind Sale Town Hall!' screamed the missive, which also has the curious slogan 'roadies don't wear jips' scrawled along the bottom. Even now a bashful Pete Garner won't explain what this means!

Andy Couzens recalls this first gig, 'Our first gig was at Sale Annex, in some youth club in the middle of Sale, a really grotty youth club. A couple of other bands played. A punk band from Stretford, I can't remember their name, but they were a proper noisy punk band like Discharge. We went down pretty good, we were shocked! We had been rehearsing so much it was as good as that stuff was going to get. Ian was doing his thing, sucking in youth culture, that's what he's really good at. We were all looking more Clash like. Me and Ian had short hair. I was jumping around. John used to move around as well in a Mick Jones style.'

The Patrol watched the other band Suburban Chaos's set and were impressed by the band's fierce sound. Suburban Chaos were far closer to the full-on leather, bristles, studs and acne assault of Stoke's fast and furious Discharge, a band who took the three minute protest of classic punk and crushed it into splenetic rushes of dark and viscous sound.

They accompanied this with a fiercer look, leaning more towards the bleached spike hair and leather jackets stuffed full of studs. It was the start of the punk look that had become accepted by the media as the standard image for the movement and Discharge's influence can be felt to this day in US hardcore and speed metal.

'When we arrived at the gig I thought "Hang on, I know these guys,"' says Pete, 'and it turned out that a year before I was at some disco dancing to some punk records and these punks had piled in and kicked me in the face. I got up trying to sort them out and they just looked at me. There was loads of them so I left it at that! And it turns out that they had become Suburban Chaos!'

Despite this rather raw initial meeting with The Patrol's roadie, the bands got on well and planned some more gigs in the south Manchester hinterland.

For a first gig The Patrol were pretty good. Their Clash-inspired work-outs may have seemed tamer in comparison to Suburban Chaos's assault but the sheer brutal edge of their frontman and their bass player's berating of the crowd helped them through. They played a handful of songs and surfed on the adrenaline of being on stage for the first time. The small crowd were into it, after all it was punk and the buzzsaw attack was enough to pass the cred test. The bass player stared maniacally at the crowd and frantically assaulted his instrument and the drummer, hiding behind a tight quiff, held down the rat-a-tat punk rock beat.

The Patrol were now in the business of playing more gigs. Remembers Andy, 'We played a village hall out in Lymm and a youth club in Stretford to a bunch of punks. They ended up following us around, glueheads and punks – probably 15 to 30 people there but it felt full! We had about eight songs by then.'

On 15 May they played their second gig at the unlikely named Vortex in Lymm, out in Cheshire towards Warrington. Again Suburban Chaos were supporting. Says Pete, 'Suburban Chaos had a song called "Anarchy In The Suburbs" that was their anthem. They were all right. I mean everyone was sixteen at the time. We all became mates. They were Stretford lads, we were Sale lads. It was a bit like West Side Story!'

The next day The Patrol were on home turf with a show at South Trafford College.

The band also played Altrincham Precinct, Lostock Youth Club on Friday 11 July 1980 with two bands called Stray Dogs and Corrosive Youth, both from Stretford. It was 50p to get in. The Patrol's brief existence was made up of local gigs in south Manchester and surrounding towns, punk rock shows with local bands that people who went have mixed memories of.

Si's memory is fuzzy. 'There was a gig in Lostock. I don't remember that gig but I remember the punks from a Lostock pub called the Melville? There was a few of them – all pretty tasty guys at fighting. We used to hang out in that pub with them.'

The Patrol had now moved their rehearsals. 'We had written the early songs at my mum and dad's house near Altrincham football ground,' says Si. 'Then we moved to the scout hut on Bolton Road near where the Brooklands tram stop is now. We would all write the songs together; sometimes that's the best way to do things. I think Ian was writing all the lyrics but I'm not sure.'

Now with their own rehearsal room, Si remembers the band working hard.

'I can't remember whether we rehearsed during the day or if we took the stuff home in Andy's car. We had four or five of our own songs and did a cover of "Blockbuster" by The Sweet that Ian sang and Andy played bass on. We also did our own stuff as well as a couple of punk covers. The most memorable gig so far was to a really lively audience of Stretford punks. We did half a dozen gigs in the end; Dunham Massey village hall was another gig. We did Lymm Grammar School one Friday night. It was an end-of-term do.'

Dressed in the mixture of clothes from the post-punk period – black drainpipes with red piping down them, modish drainpipe jeans and pullovers, biker boots – the band, bolstered by their run of gigs and with a set of their own tunes, then decided to take the next step. That summer they were confident enough to cut their first demo, recorded on a four-track.

'We did a demo that was limited to a hundred copies,' recalls Ian Brown. 'But I don't have it any more. All my stuff got nicked years later so I don't even have a copy myself! We did our song "Jail Of The Assassins" and, "25 Rifles".'

Si Wolstencroft has a clearer memory of the recording. 'It was recorded above a restaurant called the Greenhouse on Great Western Street at the Rusholme end. We did it at night-time in the winter. We did "Jail Of Assassins", "Too Many Tons" and another one, maybe "25 Rifles". I seem to remember it was a hundred and twenty quid for a four-track studio – not eight-track – which was not cheap for the time when you think about it. The demo sounds not bad for our age; it even sounds half reasonable now. I think that was John's influence. John knocked the songs into shape, and me and Ian worked round what John did. I was aware it sounded very Clash-like when I got a cassette at the end of it. I was reasonably happy with it.'

Si ponders the Clash-influenced lyrics.

'I'm not sure what "Too Many Tons" was about. "Up On The Roof" – Ian sang that one, it was Clash-related, about Paul Simonon being prosecuted for shooting prize racing pigeons in London. The Clash came into everything we did in a big way.'

It was their one and only demo. 'We did that demo as The Patrol,' recalls Andy. 'The studio was where Mick Hucknall did a lot of stuff with his punk band the Frantic Elevators. The only reason I know this was because we met him in there.'

The demos show a band surprisingly adept. Far from being a youth-club bunch of chancers, there is a touch of musicality about the band. John Squire's guitar is already the stand-out; on 'Jail Of The Assassins' his choppy rhythm playing hints at a future dexterity. The guitar, of course, has The Clash stamped all over it, the same sort of slashing almost reggae copped grinding chops that defined The Clash. It gives the songs their edge, their distinct flavour.

Si's drums are excellent; his rhythms are far ahead of youth-club bands and solid proof of a couple of years' playing under his belt. The demo is very competent and the melodies are strong and stand the test of time.

Says Pete, 'Si was a massive Clash fan and was modelling his drumming on The Clash's Topper Headon, which is not a bad place to start to learn how to play drums!'

Headon was, perhaps, the best drummer to come out of punk. He had spent years pre-Clash playing with soul bands and had even done a stint with The Temptations. Adding this knowledge, this arsenal of soul-infused drum rolls to his rock solid rhythms, he gave The Clash a dynamic, powerful, backbeat. As young Si drummed along to Topper, he was unwittingly picking up a whole history of pop music drumming from the skinny Clash sticksman. It was also a door to the many other musics that lay just beyond punk, a hint at the power of soul or the freedom of funk, and would be a profound influence on his future drumming direction.

His partner in rhythm was Ian Brown, whose bass playing was a bit more than punk rock rudimentary with good Clash-style runs. Andy Couzens and Ian Brown's vocals have a youthful innocence but they suit the punkiness of the tunes.

After recording the demo there was another clutch of local gigs. Ian Brown remembers, 'We played about five youth clubs altogether with Corrosive Youth, a punk group from Stretford. I remember we played in Lostock.'

The Patrol's act was beginning to take shape over these shows. Inspired by the confrontational abrasiveness of punk, the band's more extrovert members were cranking up their punk schtick. Says Andy, 'Ian always had to have a microphone so he could shout at people. It was funny. It was good for a laugh. We played at the college and played the Portland bars in town as well…'

Andy remembers them supporting Seventeen, who eventually became The Alarm, at the Portland bars, although Pete denies this. 'Me and Ian had been to see them in a few places before,' says Andy. 'We just bothered the guy putting the gigs on there. He said he had Seventeen coming up and we grabbed it.'

Pete Garner can't remember The Patrol playing with Seventeen. 'I could swear they never played with Seventeen. We were aware of them but I'm sure we headlined at the Portland Bars with Corrosive Youth supporting.'

Andy later recalled, 'It was our first proper gig with a PA. It was total shock. I could hear myself…Seventeen were good guys. I liked the band but by 1981 they had turned into The Alarm. I was disgusted with them. One minute they were good and going in a certain direction, then they were all spiky hair and leather belts.'

Whether the gig was with Seventeen or not, it was their début in the city centre and was another big step forward for the band. Out of the youth clubs and on to proper stages. Things were starting to happen!

They also nearly replaced Adam And The Ants, just before their big chart breakthrough, at another Manchester venue, the New Osborne club in Miles Platting in the summer of 1980 (now closed, the Osborne would become the Thunderdome – one of the key acid house clubs in Mad-chester with a more street take on the house scene). This was a gig that Garner set up.

'I booked that for them. The Ants should have played the Osborne. I rang up to see what time they were playing and they hadn't made it. I said, "I know a band that could play; I'll get them down." Ian and Andy said, "Brilliant!" but we couldn't find John anywhere. It turns out that he was sat in a field being artistic! It would have been a bad idea anyway, they were too young, a bunch of 16-year-olds playing to an early Ants crowd. Big Mohican crazies…can't see it working!'

Si Wolstencroft remembers it slightly differently.

'The venue asked The Patrol to step in and play because Adam And The Ants had broken down on the motorway. Luckily we couldn't get hold of Andy Couzens so we couldn't do it.'

Ian Brown ponders on the band's lost potential biggest gig: 'One night we could have supported Adam And The Ants just before they got big but we couldn't find our van to get into town, no one had a motor and we couldn't find Andy that night so it was, "Fucking hell, we could have supported Adam And The Ants!" – they were not that big then but every-one knew them – they were a great band. "Xerox" is a top song.'

On 8 August, The Patrol were back in action at Dunham Massey village hall, again with Suburban Chaos and Corrosive Youth.

A couple of months later on 14 November The Patrol played their last show, again returning to South Trafford College with Scorched Earth and Strange Behaviour. It was a whole 50p to get in.

After the gig there was no set decision to stop. South Trafford College was never intended to be the band's last-ever gig. Within days of that gig they were back in the rehearsal room, working on tunes, looking for that elusive change in direction. There was a feeling that it was time to move on. Branch out a bit. Get the music to do something more than just follow The Clash route. Explore what else could be done. Andy Couzens explains.

'We decided we were going to change it all. We were still rehearsing after the last gig. We were all trying to push it forward. We weren't going to push it any further forward with what it was...'

As already hinted at the gig, the line-up was about to shuffle. The music they now wanted to make required more than a shouty singer who got the job because he beat the shit out of some kid in the canteen and the bass player was itching to step up to the mic. At the end of the set, when Ian Brown started to sing 'Blockbuster' (a song that Squire was still listing in his top ten favourite records years later), Pete Garner picked up the bass for the first time.

Garner remembers well his elevation from mate/roadie to getting on stage for the first time. 'I had never played bass before they showed me the riff to "Blockbuster" and I just got up and hammed my way through it! It was the last time I played bass for years!'

'Ian sang the song whilst Pete chugged away on his bass guitar. It was his first time on stage and a precursor of the Roses' eventual first line-up.

The End of The Patrol

They went back to the rehearsal room, keen to explore this new line-up's potential. They even felt confident enough to look outside their tightly-knit community to pull in another musician.

Says Andy, 'Before I moved to guitar we got another guitar player in. I can't remember his name. I had to sack him because John and Ian wouldn't dare. This guy was on rhythm guitar. I think this was before we got Ian to be the singer. I've a feeling he was called Neil, I'm not sure. He was a bit of a beer monster. One of those types. I said to John, "I can play the guitar instead, I can't sing!" I never could, I never professed to so I moved to guitar.'

It was the moment Andy had been waiting for. There were limitations in shouting over a punk racket. He preferred the guitar. It was more him. The Patrol were trying to change. The new influences were adding to their natural musical curiosity.

'We had done a few gigs. Towards the end the music had started to change slightly. It went away from The Clash thing, more rock'n'roll for want of a better phrase. We were getting into Johnny Thunders, really drifting that way. John was pushing it that way. It's funny how bands work, you feed off each other. Playing off each other's stuff, arguing, and something gets spat out. You might have a riff, but the other person can't play it, or someone starts singing along with it...'

In the weeks that followed the South Trafford College gig they carried on rehearsing, messing about with the formula. But it was getting less and less enthusiastic.

'So Ian went on vocals. I learned a few chords from John and Pete came in on bass,' says Andy. 'Just for a few rehearsals and then that fell to pieces again. By now we had a bit of a PA, turn it up and it feeds back. Everyone shouting at the guitar players: "Too loud!"

'We used to call round for John and he'd be in his what I would call pathetic slipper phase and his brother Matt would come out instead. Matt is just like John but a...laugh! John would be in his bedroom making models...You'd go round, he was one of those guys who would melt plastic cars so they would look like they had a crash. You think, how's he done that? They were all painted up afterwards...Fucking brilliant...'

Even as the band fell apart they remained friends.

As Andy Couzens points out, 'We were still mates. Because we continued to go out with each other and hang out one, two, or three of us... one night rehearsing, the next night not. I do remember Ian got a job working at the DHSS in Sale. Pete was working anyway in Paperchase in town. John was for a long time sat at home making models. Si had a job in a fish shop in Wilmslow, and he started doing stuff with Andy Rourke and Johnny Marr. He did those demos with them.'

Si had met Johnny Marr and was moving into a new orbit.

'A mate of mine, Dave Columbo, who used to drink in the Vine with Ian and John, said he knew a shit-hot guitar player who was looking for a drummer. I started smoking lots of weed and listening to lots of records.

I really got into the funk thing. That's probably where I got my nickname from. It was Johnny Marr who nicknamed me Funky Si because we were listening to funk through these huge great big speakers, Andy playing his bass along to it all. We were getting really stoned and I was getting really into the funk.

'I'd only see Ian and John occasionally after that – hearing about what they were doing musically while I was doing this new band Freak Party with Andy and Johnny. '

Freak Party had already recorded a demo, 'Crack Therapy', at Decibel studios in Ancoats when they'd started looking for a drummer who could push their funk-influenced band a bit further. The funkier chops employed by Freak Party made a change for Si from The Clash riffola of his previous outing, it was a new challenge. He remained in Freak Party for a year. They never gigged, preferring to hone down their sound with endless rehearsals. Their sound was the tough, clipped, curiously northern take on funk, the sort of dark-hearted wah-wah attack employed by the likes of A Certain Ratio. Si was now listening to Grandmaster Flash, broadening his musical horizons, getting funkier.

For the whole of '81 they rehearsed hard. But they could not find a damn singer, someone to front the outfit. They had some guy called Wade who could only do the John Lydon whine and was ejected only to become a male model. The band got even funkier, jamming hard, inspired by Marr's disco and funk records.

Johnny Marr remembers the band's early days: 'I was getting the band together. We had somewhere to rehearse because Andy Rourke's mum and dad had split up and his mum went to Spain and left four teenage boys in this great semi-detached house. So, I moved in with Andy and our equipment. The house was like the Beverly Hillbillies with these kids running around with guitars with no adults and lots and lots of pot.

'We basically listened to Joy Division's *Closer*, *Sextet* by A Certain Ratio and *Low* by David Bowie. You listen to *Sextet* and *Low* and you will get a little bit of the feel of how Andy Rourke was such an unusual bass player. He's a born musician anyway and a born artist. I was playing funky punk guitar and Andy playing tight bass lines. Me, Andy and Si were cooking up post-punk funk and considering getting in singers. I was making these tentative forays to the microphone but I was not that keen.'

For a brief moment Johnny Marr considered going back to The Patrol and seeing if their young charismatic singer/bass player was up for coming on board.

'That was when we got really tempted to go and personally talk to Ian Brown. I knew Ian Brown through Pete and Si. I knew John a bit. We were checking each other out, like you do. We would talk about records. But there was an understanding that Ian and John were a musical item, so that's what stopped me asking Ian. I always respected and liked John, they had a real good understanding of each other. So then I decided to go and see this guy who had been on the scene called Morrissey...'

Si didn't 'get' the new singer and left the band that would become The Smiths. But another of his ex-bandmates could see the appeal. To Ian Brown, The Smiths were an important band: 'We did love The Smiths and the fact they had come out of Manchester, and it was real and they made it, really gee'd us up. I got all the tapes of their early days. Pete lived opposite Melanie, who was going out with Andy at the time, and she gave Pete all the tapes of them rehearsing. I thought the first album was a bit disappointing, not produced too good, but "This Charming Man" is a great pop tune.

'Morrissey was a great pop star because he was so unlikely with his National Health glasses on. He was clever as fuck and his interviews were really funny. That was inspiring to us to be like ourselves – not that Morrissey was like us! But that you could do it. We saw that.'

And The Patrol?

It wasn't happening. There were not enough kicks involved in being in a band for Brown. He was looking at the road. Looking for some adventure and the pull of the mod scene towards the scooter clubs was proving too strong.

'I was already playing with Johnny Marr and they had got into the whole scooter thing, but I didn't,' Si remembers. 'My mother was a night nurse and saw the victims. She talked me out of it, but the rest of them got really into it. They had the parkas, the works.'

The rest of them would still go out, go round the south Manchester suburban sprawl, talk about life, punk rock, rock'n'roll, clothes and girls, the usual stuff.

'We even used to go in pubs, and none of us drank, just a couple of orange juices and a coke. We would go to house parties in Sale. It was full of women, young girls...great,' Andy recalls.

Si wasn't the only one to start shifting away from his punk/Clash roots in that summer of 1981. Things were changing. Even a bunch of Clash diehards were starting to feel the post-punk landscape shifting. The mod thing was affecting Ian Brown. Though he still loved punk, the skin/mod influences were now starting to cross-pollinate his tastes.

Andy Couzens saw the change in him: 'Ian was getting into all that mod stuff like…Secret Affair. He was bang into Madness, he loved Madness…ska. 2 Tone was his big thing – Sham 69, Cockney Rejects, The Upstarts, which I must admit I loved as well. He was hanging out with Mensi, roadying. I went as well. I got right into the skinhead end of mod as well. Sta-Prest, Ben Shermans. I remember seeing Jimmy Somerville with the skinhead look – Harrington, Levis and Doc shoes – and that killed it. Overnight every skin in the country was burning his clothes! He ruined it overnight!'

Ian was the first to lose interest in The Patrol. He was bored with being in a band. There were now new ways of getting on the road. New ways of getting out and about. A bit of adventure. A bit of bother. And they didn't involve hanging around and rehearsing. Ian Brown was about to enter a new phase of his life and a phase that would influence him and his friends for the next few years and beyond. He told *Record Collector*, 'It wasn't serious. I never really wanted to be in a group so I sold my bass and got a scooter with the money – £100.'

1982

Scooter Scene

Understanding the late seventies means understanding the proliferation of youth cults of the time. While punk itself had claimed that 1977 was year zero and that to listen to any other music was a crime, there were hints from the top that this just wasn't so.

John Lydon had mixed it up in the summer of 1977, playing his favourite records on the Tommy Vance show and name-checking an eclectic mix of dub, Can and Captain Beefheart. The Clash were soon embracing a whole host of styles and the strands of sheer brutal energy that had combined to make punk were unravelling fast.

There was a mod revival, a Ska revival (c/o 2 Tone), even a heavy-metal revival. For post-punk street teens like the Roses and their gang of mates there was plenty of action to choose from.

Whereas the media portrayed all the youth cults fighting each other, there was plenty of crossover, especially when common interests like girls, travel and getting out of your head were concerned. The itinerant Brown was bored with being in a band. He wanted to get on the road now; a punk with skin and mod leanings, he hooked up with the scooter clubs, a melting pot of restless spirits.

The scooter clubs were just one of the many strands of culture that the wreckage of the punk rock generation clung on to after the fallout but they had, in fact, been around for decades. Starting off in the late fifties when middle-class weekend rebels were more fascinated with the nuts and bolts of their bikes than any sort of youthful tearaway action, by the late seventies the scene had become a home for punks, skins and hooligans as well as mods and scooter boys. In the early eighties it had become a burgeoning culture all of its own, with its own soundtrack played out at festivals and meetings.

Mark Sergeant of *Scootering* magazine sighs as he picks up one snapshot of the time. 'There's a picture here of the Burnley scooter club. They had long hair, massive sideburns and flares and they were calling themselves mods.' It's fair to say that the scooter scene had wandered a long way from its hip suburban roots.

Mod is the youth culture that is at the roots of much of the malarkey in UK pop culture. The Pistols, The Clash and, especially, The Jam had quite definite mod roots. The coolest British bands have always been clothes, hair and drug obsessives, not being able to separate this from the music. In fact, many Americans sneer at the British, calling our bands 'haircut bands'. Style is all for the classic British band and the gang that's at its core. Mod was the starting point and the backbone to many cool bands and it was going through some sort of renaissance.

The massive success of The Jam in the punk era had definitely had some sort of knock-on effect. Less extreme than punk, it was far easier to become a mod and many took this option. *Quadrophenia* was to prove a massive turning point for the scene, putting it back into the centre of youth consciousness, and making mod and scooter culture fashionable again. Overnight Ben Shermans, Sta-Prest and suede shoes replaced battered Docs, as Pete Garner remembers: 'I was still the punk in the crowd and I was still hanging out with them but we would go to parties and they would be mod parties. People wouldn't let me in because of my punk clothes; it got to be a real drag.'

Looking the spit of Mick Jones, Pete felt like the last punk in town. Not that their social lives were totally modernised. People still remember Ian Brown turning up at Meteors gigs in town and going down to rockabilly punk nights like Chicken Shack at Devilles or Legends on a Thursday. Meanwhile, John Squire would go down to Pips with its legendary Bowie/Roxy nights. The multi-roomed layout of Pips meant it was like five clubs in one, different rooms playing Northern Soul and oldies. Youth cults may have been fairly tribal on paper but for most teenagers if music was fast, exciting and fucked up, then they were having a slice of it, criss-crossing scenes to get their kicks.

Ian Brown still liked his fast, exciting and funked up music, but even he couldn't deny change: 'Things were starting to change at the end of the seventies. Punk was going, it was changing into other things. We still liked some of the bands like The Jam and the Sex Pistols but they split up in 1979. I was getting into all the new punk groups that were coming out like The Angelic Upstarts whose "The Murder Of Liddle Towers" has just come out and was brilliant, and I liked a lot of that new raw punkier stuff like The Cockney Rejects' "Flares And Slippers". The big tunes were things like Sham 69's "Ulster", their first record, and their follow-up singles like "Borstal Breakout" and "Angels With Dirty Faces" – I was really into them and also the mod revival bands.

'I was going to the Russell Club in Manchester to watch bands. That's where I saw Secret Affair, Purple Hearts and the Chords all on the same night. I was really into The Specials as well and Madness – I saw their first-ever Manchester show.

'It was about this time, in 1978, that we started getting into scooters. We weren't mods. But that was OK because you didn't have to be a mod to be on the scooters. We didn't have mirrors on our scooters like the mods did. We would take the leg shields off and have them all boned down. I had a 2-Tone suit and I had a green parachute outfit.'

Clothes were still key to the ever hip to youth culture Brown.

'We used to go London to get 501s, you couldn't get 'em up here. We would get the first train down and last one back at night and you'd have the whole day in the Old Kent Road markets and the old mod shops, get Ben Shermans and button-downs, and buy secondhand paisley shirts, tonic pants, Sta-Prest pants, which would get taken in. We would wear Doc shoes and monkey boots as well. Back in '74, when I went to school and wanted a pair of Docs, my mother said, "You're not having a pair of bovver boy boots." You had to start on monkey boots, just like in the film *This Is England*.

'When you went to school in your Docs you would think you were ace! You'd think you're the boy. I had cherry-red Docs and would polish them up. We were not Perry Boys but we did wear Kickers as well and Lee jeans and Harringtons. Also, wicked Fruit of the Loom sweatshirts.'

The Perry Boys were a youth cult influenced by the mod/skin scene – Manchester's pre-scally scallies. Fred Perry tops and a neatly combed one-eye wedge were the keys to the look.

'We didn't have wedge haircuts so I suppose we were mod/skin/Perry Boys because of the way we looked although we used to fight with the Perry Boys when they came to Scarborough when we were on a run. A lot of the original punks in Collyhurst became Perry Boys in '78/'79. They were the first Perrys,' says Ian.

The scooter clubs were nominally clubs for scooter owners to take their machines out on runs but the mods hijacked the runs in the sixties and had hung on so that by the eighties it had become an underground scene in its own right. For a lot of kids they were another gang, another excuse to get out of town and a great way to hang out with like-minded souls from all over the country. Ian was one of those kids.

'My first scooter was a Lambretta J125 from '66. All over the north in the late seventies/early eighties, there were still loads of Northern Soul and scooter boys. East Manchester was heavy metal, but in the north of Manchester, it's Northern Soul. There were still loads of clubs to go to. We used to go to the Beehive in Eccles and the scooter boys used to fight with the lads from that area – where the Mondays were from, Swinton. So yeah, we used to fight them every week. Years later, we laughed about it.'

Andy remembers them all going out and buying their first scooters: 'I went with Ian to buy a Lambretta. He's one of those people who breaks everything! Ian can't wear a watch, or anything mechanical. He breaks anything when he goes near it. He bought this Lambretta and it never worked for him at all. It never went! He was completely incapable with it! The thing with Lambrettas is that they didn't fucking work. It's like owning an old motorbike. You had to take it apart and clean it. I could do that but he couldn't do it at all...So he went out and bought a Vespa. John bought a Lambretta. He didn't ride it that much, but spent a lot of time pulling it apart, painting it, getting everything copper plated. You could say each bike was a reflection of the owner's personality.'

Brown's next Lambretta has become legendary, like something out of *Easy Rider* and painted pink. It was built to attract attention, and he got stopped by the cops wherever he went. Says Ian, 'Yeah, that was a Lambretta GP200 – extended forks, banana seat, leg shields off. Sweet and Innocent, it was called. And I had a Vespa Rally 200 with "Angels With Dirty Faces" painted on the side. I had five or six over time. We went to all the rallies – Brighton, the Isle of Wight, Scotland, Great Yarmouth. Two years later, I got John into it. He had a GP200 that he made up himself.'

Ian took his scooter with him when he moved to Hulme in 1982, lugging it up the stairs to his William Kent Crescent flat. In those days, leaving it down on the street would have been asking for it to get swiped. Hulme was a notorious sprawling housing estate on the edge of the city centre of Manchester. Full of squats, it was a cheap (or free) place to live where you could experiment and be creative.

Ian Brown spent a couple of years in the concrete sprawl of Hulme. 'In 1981, I was 17 and staying in Withington at my girlfriend's but when I broke up with her I moved into William Kent Crescent in Hulme. I was in William Kent till 1984 and then in Charles Barry Crescent in early '84... I was at 313 and I remember The Fall's drummer Karl Burns was at 316. I had two and a half years in Hulme before I moved back to Withington in mid-'85.

'When I first moved into Hulme there were families still living there. You would get a house full of junkie rich kids from Alderley Edge living next to a bus driver with his family,' says Ian. 'It was them rich kids who brought the drugs into Moss Side, the class As and the heroin, not the people who lived there with their regular lives. It was all weed in Moss Side before that.'

The scooter bug was catching and all the crew were getting mobile. John's scooter had 'Too Chicken To Even Try It' – a line from The Clash's incendiary 'White Riot' – painted over his petrol tank. He remembers his scooter days with affection as he explained to Dave Simpson for an interview with *ID*: 'A Lambretta is a very desirable object. Ian wanted one. I got one. I did it up, painted it. I wanted to show it off to other people who had scooters.' And that's what they did, meeting up at the scooter club's favourite pub in Stockport. They would all stand around looking at each other's bikes.

The pair of them hooked up with the Stockport scooter crowd, but were never in the club, being too maverick to really be members. They had the bikes and dug the music and went out on runs, hooking up with a whole host of unlikely people like Steve Harrison, who went on to manage The Charlatans, and a whole network of like-minded characters.

It was a new network, a new chain of similar souls from the whole of the north of England, adrenalised post-punk youth with a pocket full of speed and high-octane adventure on their minds. It was an excuse to get trashed, get out of town and hit the road. It was running with a gang, a gang mentality that would eventually resurface in the Roses. They would go away on bank holidays to Brighton and seaside resorts all over Britain, their helmets resplendent with the rabbit's tail that hung from the back. 'The biggest run we ever went on was to Scarborough,' recounts Manchester photographer A.J. Wilkinson, a scooter boy at the time. 'There were thousands of us. It was all the different scooter clubs, like Wigan etc., all joining together. I remember there was some bother when we got there as well. This was about 1980 – it was well into the peak of the scooter club scene by then.'

Martin Merchant, who went on to front Audioweb, knew Ian Brown from this time. 'I knew Mani and Ian really well from that period. Mani went to an all-nighter Northern Soul mod night in Oldham. There could be a fight so we all had to stick together. Mani had the best flicker in the world.'

It was also through the scooter clubs that Mani would come into the orbit of Ian Brown. 'With the scooter clubs you would get to know lads from all over the city. I used to hang out with lads from Chorlton and Levvy, Longsight, Ardwick, Clayton, Wythenshawe,' says Brown. 'We also used to hook up with this crew from north Manchester, from Moston and Failsworth and that was when I first met Mani. We heard about this skinhead who was causing all this trouble – he was this kid up in Moston who had a swastika on his head. I don't think he was a proper skinhead because when we went up there he had a white school shirt and black school kecks on – he was just a fucking idiot. He was causing untold grief so the idea was that 15 of us were going to give it to him.

'So we went down from Chorlton to this council house in Moston... the idea was that we were all going to wade in and stop this kid and his bad habits but this kid said, "Let me run up the stairs, see if he's in." So he ran up the stairs and the next thing this skinhead comes rolling down the stairs with all his head mashed in. The lad had done him on his own and rolled him down the stairs! He was in a pile at the bottom of the stairs – job done! Mani was there; he's got a thick flying jacket on, one of those US bomber ones. I remember the first time I set eyes on him and I thought, he's not a fighter, he's a lover. He's just here for the cause, not the fighting.'

Ian Brown was travelling around for his musical fix. 'I used to go to Northern Soul all-nighters in Rhyl, Rotherham and Doncaster, very into it I was. All through the night till late in the morning,' he told *Q* magazine.

The former members of The Patrol had started to drift apart – Pete Garner was getting deeper into the roots of punk, digging the Dolls/Stooges/ MC5 axis while Ian got into Motown and Northern Soul.

Pete didn't see John Squire for months, believing that they didn't really have that much in common any more. Then one afternoon he bumped into him in Sale and with fuck all to do they checked out records in a local record shop. They picked up the first Dexys album, because they liked the sleeve and the whole intense gang aura around the outfit. The band as gang thing was scoured deep into their consciousness. Nervously, they took the record home. At the time there were so many false hopes because nothing ever seemed to match the power of The Clash. The Dexys did though.

The combination of vocalist Kevin Rowland's soul-wrenching vocals and the band's bittersweet horn section, plus their wild-hearted outsider gang stance, struck a chord with thousands of post-punk wanderers.

John Squire Keeps the Flame Burning!

After The Patrol fell apart the others took little interest in playing music for a long time, but John Squire was continually playing guitar, getting better and better, putting in the hours that would eventually make him one of the best guitar players of his generation.

While Ian was washing dishes in Friday's hotel in Northenden to finance his bohemian roving scooter club lifestyle, John started work at Cosgrove Hall in 1980, putting his art talents to good use.

Cosgrove Hall was a cartoon-making workshop in Chorlton that had made many an award-winning TV series. Barney from New Order also worked there. It was here that Squire worked on *Dangermouse* and the models for *The Wind in the Willows*. One of the stars of Cosgrove, it is even rumoured he was behind the design of Bertie Bassett, the Liquorice Allsorts man. It was at about this time that John bumped into Pete Garner who was still working in the city-centre Paperchase shop.

Manchester in the early eighties was hardly the bustling youth culture capital that it is now. Now there are heaps of shops dealing in hip fashion, cool records and all the driftwood of pop culture. But back in the fallout days of post-punk there were plenty of bands, few venues and very few places to buy all the associated pop paraphernalia. Paperchase was a rarity – downstairs, they sold greeting cards and every magazine and newspaper you could think of. Upstairs, you could find the weirdest collection of cool records and fanzines.

Garner worked behind the counter, ever the amiable host, chatting to punters and buying in small fanzines to sell over the counter. It was here that I met him in 1982/83 whilst I was peddling my fanzine *Rox* round Manchester. Pete was one of the few friendly faces on the circuit of shops and we would have great chats about punk rock.

One afternoon, John Squire walked into Paperchase and hooked up with his buddy from the Bridge and school days. They talked about making an animated film in Squire's down-time at the Cosgrove Hall. They even went as far as writing the first chapter for the story for which John would animate the models. They fucked around with the film for a few weeks and then shelved the idea, but no matter – contact was established and fate was moving its clammy hand.

John hadn't seen Ian for a while – Brown was off travelling or messing around with the scooter guys – but he had met Andy Couzens now and then and the pair of them had also occasionally discussed starting the band off again.

Andy and John Get Their Guitars Out Again

Ian Brown was still hooked on seeking adventure on the road. Better than being stuck in a rehearsal room. John was happier painting his scooter, but Pete really couldn't give a fuck. The New York Dolls and Iggy and the Stooges didn't ride around on little hairdryers! He was a rocker, not a mod.

It looked like the band was over. Thousands of teenage punk bands had flourished in the tail end of the punk explosion but by now guitars were being put back in cupboards and dreams getting put on hold. People were drifting off to jobs, to drugs or the next big thing.

Andy Couzens, though, was missing the creative buzz of being in a band and a few months after The Patrol had fizzled out he decided to go round and see John Squire and see if they could get something going again. 'We didn't see each other for what seemed like ages but it was probably six weeks. I remember going out with John one night. We went to a pub in Sale, which was weird because no one drank really, and decided to get something else going.'

By now Andy had left college, or rather had been asked to leave, his temper having once again got the better of him. 'I took a swing at a teacher and told the principal to go and fuck himself.'

Even as early as 1981 Andy had asked John if he was still up for a bit of playing and a loose project sort of got off the ground. 'John and I started another band up with a guy from Hale, a drummer – a good drummer who popped up in a few bands later on. His name was Guy, I think. Factory-ish type of stuff. Good looking guy. Me and John playing guitar. I went round and said, "Let's do something", 'cos I love it, the band thing. The Patrol was gone and I wanted to do something. Ian was off on his scooter.'

This loose outfit never had a name. If anything, it served as a vehicle for the two guitarists, a way of learning those chops that might provide the groundwork for some future action, as well as keeping the flame alive. Not that they treated it lightly. This was no bedroom jam; the band were keen, driving backwards and forwards 30 miles a time to get their tunes together.

Says Andy, 'The core was me and John rehearsing in Warrington. I haven't a clue why we went there. It's really vague this period. We rehearsed above the YMCA opposite the town hall gates. There was that lad from Hale on drums sometimes. There was also another guy later on called Walt from Lymm in there as well. He was a proper punk drummer but we were trying to do something a bit more together musically. We got into The Beach Boys, but still listened to stuff like Generation X. We liked the Beach Boys songs – they were a bit more musical than punk. We were just trying to get music going, nothing else. No one was singing.'

Built around the two guitar players, the pre-Roses band assembled, an ad hoc collection of any musicians they could get their hands on. Eventually, though, rehearsing in Warrington didn't help. It's bad enough having to set your gear up every time you jam without an hour drive before you get there.

However, a few months after they knocked the project on the head they would reconvene as the Fireside Chaps, an unlikely name and probably just a joke. The important thing is that their part-time jamming bass player would also come with them.

Gary Mounfield had spent the post-punk years floating around various north Manchester outfits but now he was moving into the tightly knit gang of south Manc suburb punks.

Mani had arrived.

Gary 'Mani' Mounfield was born on 16 November 1962, making him the oldest member of The Stone Roses by about two weeks.

He was born in Moston in north Manchester, the 'other' half of the city. More Lancashire grit than Cheshire market town, north Manchester is more working-class and much less student-orientated than the south. Mani had lived all over north Manchester, as he pointed out to *Reds* magazine. 'I'm a north Manchester boy, originally from Moston but I moved to Failsworth and Newton Heath in my early teens and I still go up there for a beer because that's where all my mates are.'

Football made a big impression on him from a very early age. 'I'm proud to be a Manc, proud to be a Red. My dad was a mad United fan. Nobby Stiles is part of my family – my auntie's cousin or something like that and I was born to be a Red. I would have had my ears boxed in if I'd dared to be a Blue. As for school, I went to Xaverian College and after there I tried my hardest not to get a job and sat in my bedroom learning to play a guitar.

My childhood hero was Georgie Best. My mam and dad were mates of him. I can remember waking up in the morning and him being downstairs in my house having a late drink when he shouldn't have been. I really had a thing for Gordon Hill too. Those were the days for me: Admiral shirts, Stepney, Jimmy Nicholl, Houston, Buchan, Albiston, Daly, Macari, Coppell, Pearson and the Greenhoffs. Good days going to United.'

Teenage Mani went through punk and then on to the scally/Perry Boy scene emerging in the suburbs. Following United would lead him to the fringes of bother. 'Going abroad with the scals, doing a bit of this and that, getting nice trainers and that. I very nearly caught the ferry to Holland which kicked off with West Ham in 1986 but ended up catching a later ferry, which was full of Everton. I had to keep my trap shut but I still made it to the Dam along with about a hundred others. I used to go to away games all the time with a lot of those heads from Salford. I can remember going to Luton when we were on that ten-game winning streak in '85. We met up at Salford Crescent, got in a van and went down to terrorise St Albans for the day. It's only in the past few years that I've had to cut down on going, home and away.

'When I was a kid, I used to get the number seven bus from Failsworth which used to drop you by the swing bridge. It cost 50p to go in the Stretford End and I used to take our Greg, sit him at the front on a barrier, give him his Wagon Wheels and crisps and then watch the match. When we were old enough we used to get the specials through the seventies and eighties. I didn't miss many matches.'

Mani told *Reds* magazine about his most embarrassing match moment. 'I got caught spitting on the TV by my mam at a United v Leeds game. She was disgusted and said, "There's nothing big or clever about spitting young Gary."'

Like nearly every kid in Britain, Mani dreamt of football as an escape route from the drudgery of real life. That Peter Pan world of soccer showbiz was quickly negated when he realised that he just wasn't good enough to be strutting around Old Trafford, leaving one well-trodden alternative. 'I knew from the age of eight that I wanted to be in a band. I was never good enough to be a footballer and I'm lucky that I make a living out of music.'

Inspired by the punk message that anyone can make their own dream, Mani drifted through a whole bunch of north Manc punk outfits, learning his bass.

'I used to play in mad little punk bands around north Manchester, just fucking about basically, you know like you do? I would come home from school and go in to some music shop in Manchester and nick the Clash songbook and the Pistols songbook and learn from there. I always kind of had the ability to listen and change and figure out what was going on there and then play them in a pretty basic way. I'd been in a few bands previously including a punk band from Failsworth called Urban Paranoia who used to play at the youth club.'

Mani remembers meeting Ian Brown: 'I was first introduced to Ian in '79, but I knew his face already. Ian has one of them faces, a really striking-looking guy, you know? He used to love *Planet of the Apes* and I thought, "Fucking hell, this guy is amazing," you know what I mean? He used to say I was like James Cagney – just mooching about on my own, you know, up to no good!

'When we used to go on the scooter runs we used to hang out and just cause general mayhem at the seaside which was great. I think we really bonded over a mutual love of Northern Soul, punk and psychedelic and garage music. It was always based around music.

'I met John in the legendary Pips nightclub in Manchester. He was quieter than us – more the big thinker – but it was great to meet people who are different, you know?

'We forged a great friendship pretty much straightaway from loving Woody Allen films and loving music and scooters.'

The Timperley mob quickly became mates with Mani. After all, he is famous for being easy-going and approachable. No one ever has a bad word for Mani. Getting picked up by Andy Couzens for those long drives to rehearsal formed his introduction to the tightly-knit musical world of the others. Once in, he became a permanent feature of their ad hoc line-ups and nights out in the city centre.

Mani liked The Fall, The Stranglers, The Clash and Elvis Costello, but, like all great bass players, also dug Northern Soul, drifting into the same twilight zone of scooters, mods and skins as Brown and Squire, and at the same time pioneering the classic scally look of wedge haircut, psychedelic shirt and dapper jeans.

Scallies were the precursor to the baggy scene, linking the youth culture of the late seventies punk explosion with the rough-and-ready obsession with training shoes and foreign sports clobber of the eighties football mob.

Says Mani: 'I was in that Perry Boy scene quite early, you know. You wanna see the Roses' Warehouse gig bootleg video from 1985 and there I am dressed like a Perry Boy. It was, kind of, like, for me, a real mod thing, you know. Initially it was about clothes and music and stuff like that and I was running with the Perry Boys, even though some of them were a bunch of mad fuckers who kicked the shit out of everybody in town. I wasn't really into that side of things – I was a lover not a fighter. Even though I hung about with some proper bad bastards, that side of things just didn't interest me.

'The Perry boys were a youth cult like mod. I think it was very similar – the fashions change quickly and there was a lot of stuff based around music, you know – a lot of Perry Boys dressed in the long overcoats and would go to Pips but they'd listen to early Roxy, the Bunnymen, Joy Division and The Teardrop Explodes and all that kind of stuff. Originally, it was very music based as well as fashion based and then everyone got into it and it lost its individuality.'

It was this Perry Boy/Scally look that he claims to have brought eventually to the nascent Roses, the final style ingredient that connected them with the mainstream. That and his extraordinary bass playing.

1982

The Waterfront

Down in the cellar. What a crew! A couple of Perry Boys, a couple of artsy south Mancs and whoever was up for drumming! Yet again Couzens and Squire were attempting to resurrect some sort of band. A creative spark should never be wasted, so the Warrington jamming band was put back together on a more serious footing. But this time no more mucking about in a proper rehearsal rooms miles away. It was going to mean a return to the cellars and garages of Manchester. Andy Couzens' parents' cellar in Macclesfield to be more exact. Less hassle all round.

And Mani!

Says Andy, 'Mani was just the same then as he is now…exactly the same guy. The one thing about being in a band is that you never have to grow up. If you make enough money you never have to do anything. You can be 17 or 18 for the rest of your life.'

At about this time Mani introduced John Squire to a fellow Failsworth scooter boy they knew from the runs, Kaiser.

Kaiser remembers being approached by the shy John Squire of all people. 'I was hanging around in punk clubs like Berlin and the punk room in Pips. There was me and Mani and some of the other lads from the scooter runs. It was John Squire that came over and started chatting. He said he was starting a band up and asked me if I wanted to be the singer.'

They bonded over music. 'At the time we all still liked the old punk stuff. Ian Brown, who was around but not in the band, was into Madness; he loved them. John Squire was much more arty, none of us had ever heard of the stuff he was into, very strange! He was a very special type of person, John, very artistic and he really put his mind to what he was doing whether it was playing guitar or painting.

'John had a really different outlook on things to the rest of us. He is the most talented person I have ever met; no matter what he put his hand to it was great, from art to music as well as his scooter, which he sprayed up himself and looked really great. He was very mild mannered but I do remember one night when we went into a club in Manchester and without saying a word he went up to a lad who was a so-called hard man and had been giving him some shit. John hit him round the head and never got shit again.

'As for Ian Brown – well, years ago my mum died and my dad lost the house; all I had was my Lambretta and a rucksack with my stuff in it. I was sleeping in empty houses and anywhere I could keep warm but Ian said to move in with him and his girlfriend until I got somewhere to stay. He wouldn't take any money off me. I was there for a bit until I got my own place, so I owe him so much for that.

'Ian and John and I went all around on scooter rallies. One time when it was red-hot, we all got into togas and rode all the way to Weston-super-Mare. We spent the weekend drinking in togas! Still, Ian always looked great whatever he was in!'

Kaiser was one of the first to adopt the scally/casual look of the Perry Boys. After meeting Squire and before The Waterfront coalesced, Kaiser hung out with the pre-Roses in the scooter clubs. He looks back on the scooter club days with great affection.

'The scooter clubs were great. They were like family. I knew Ian Brown from a long time back in the scooter days,' he remembers. Laughing, he adds, 'Ian Brown was a nutter then. Getting up to all sorts.'

It was Kaiser's scooter connection that stood him in good stead with his new bandmates. Says Andy, 'We sort of knew Kaiser 'cos we had been going out in town. He was part of our little drinking clique and a scooter boy as well. He had a scooter, a knackered old blue scooter with "I piss on Anderton's army" (reference to controversial eighties Manchester police chief James Anderton) painted on the side panels in white paint. I had A.C.A.B. on my helmet and we'd get such shit from the police! They would stop us all the time.'

The band was a right mixture of ruffians and dreamers: John Squire, Andy Couzens, Mani and Kaiser...all they needed now was a drummer. And, as ever, getting a drummer was a problem. Getting a drummer is always tough in a band. No one wants to play drums. All that lugging gear around only to disappear to the back of the stage. All work and no glory!

Again, it was Mani who bailed them out. He had another mate in Failsworth, Chris Goodwin, who was up for it.

Says Andy, 'We used to rehearse at my parents' house in Macclesfield. I used to go and pick up John in Chorlton and then go up to Failsworth to pick Mani and the rest of them up. Musicians are fucking lazy, aren't they? I was always picking people up. I was the organiser. Drive around, pick everyone up, then rehearse.'

The band perfectly captured the hotchpotch of post-punk looks and cultures all. John Squire was still in his post-punk Clash look, Andy had his nutter short hair and denims, and the three north Mancs had a look of their own. Remembers Andy, 'Mani's all into that flick look, Perry Boys, Echo and The Bunnymen were big in Failsworth as well.'

The name The Fireside Chaps was obviously not to be taken seriously. 'John Squire can be cringeworthy when it comes to names!' laughs Couzens, adding, 'I guess that the band was a continuation from the Warrington thing. That band might have stopped for a few weeks and then the new band started.'

And where was Ian Brown at this time? 'We didn't see much of Ian at the time. He was always away on scooter runs.'

They would jam, rehearse and fool about. Watch road movies such as *Two-Lane Blacktop* and *Vanishing Point* (the film that was to lend its name to the fantastic 1997 Primal Scream album – the first with Mani). They would piss themselves laughing at Mani's Woody Allen take-offs. The ad hoc collection of south Mancs post-punk scooter boys and north Manc hooligans were having a good time. It was like two different worlds meeting, as Kaiser points out.

'Andy came up to my house to pick me up in his BMW! You never got posh cars like that round our way. We practised in Andy's house in a big cellar. It was in a big house in Adlington, a big mansion. An unbelievable place with a swimming pool. It was a real big shock to me and Mani. We had a great time just going in the swimming pool and hanging out with Andy and his brother who's a good lad.'

Things were going all right. Already songs were coalescing – but then they hit their first hurdle: Chris Goodwin left. Three rehearsals was enough for him and he quit the cellar jams, leaving his drum kit moldering away in the corner.

Again they were without a drummer but they elected to carry on without drums, just writing songs, trying to get it together. As ever they rehearsed many times a week, long and hard. And at weekends they still socialised in town, as Andy remembers. 'The rest of us were going out into town a lot. I seem to remember going to the Cypress Tavern, places like that. We went down the Hacienda as soon as it opened. It was the only place to go. When you're the only club in Manchester it's easy to get members! We ran down there to join really early on in 1982.'

By now, a few months in, they decided it was time to get serious and get a proper name. They had booked a studio to record a couple of songs for a demo and the thought of recording them as The Fireside Chaps was just too ridiculous for the band.

Says Andy, 'One night, after rehearsing we sat down and watched Marlon Brando in *On The Waterfront*. We all thought Fireside Chaps was a funny name but when it came to the point of doing the demos we thought, fuck, we can't put that on a demo tape on the tape box. So thanks to Marlon we took The Waterfront for our name and went in and did the demos.'

The two-track demo was recorded at the tail end of 1982 in some long-forgotten East Manchester studio. 'The demo was recorded somewhere in the back end of Denton. Somewhere round Mani's way. In a little studio someone had set up,' adds Andy.

The two songs they laid down were surprisingly competent. Poppy, even. The guitar hints at the eventual classic melodic Roses more than the initial punkier Roses. You can hear shades of Orange Juice and Postcard Records and even the classic Roses are in there. Any lingering traces of three-chord Patrol punkarama have long since been shed, although the movement's energy and toughness can't help seeping in over the jangly guitars.

Mani's bass drives the song and puts paid to any lingering myth about his only learning his trade when he joined the Roses full time. The bass work is very strong and the guitar is classic Squire with riffs, licks and melodic work cutting in and out effectively with Andy Couzens.

Those guitars definitely hint at the 'sound of Young Scotland', and Orange Juice, fronted by Edwyn Collins, took the brittle jangly guitars and made them into a template for a whole host of post-punk bands to use. Orange Juice, even though camping it up in a tongue-in-cheek manner, had been adopted by a surprisingly large quotient of ex-punks and scallies who got off on their energised guitar pop. At the same time The Waterfront were digging Edwyn Collins's idiosyncratic outfit and so were Little Hulton's ramshackle gang of Dickensian hooligans, the Happy Mondays.

Even Kaiser's vocals are a surprise. His singing is pretty well spot on with the same sort of northern accent that Ian Brown would utilize in the Roses. The singing, for a first demo, is really good and the gruffness you might expect is not apparent.

Kaiser explains his lyrics for one of the songs, 'Normandy'. 'John wrote most of the songs and I wrote some of the lyrics… "Normandy" was about a trip that me and Mani made. We blagged our way to France jumping on trains, and we ended up in Normandy, walking down the beaches. We were just Moston lads and we were gobsmacked, walking down there and I wrote the song about that and how thousands had died on those same beaches on D-Day.'

The other tune on the demo, 'When The Wind Blows', is a faster affair dominated by a catchy whistled section and some late-period Clash-styled rhythm guitar from John Squire whose guitar playing is excellent – great chops and chiming leads breaks. Again it has the '88 period Roses feel to it (albeit a tad less subtle) but the melody is there and the interplay between the guitars, and the melodic bass from Mani, proving that he was already a very good bass player. There are definite hints of something greater here.

The band were pretty surprised with the demos – they sounded really good! Fuck they almost sounded like a proper band. And Ian Brown? Well, he wasn't oblivious to what his mates were up to, as he explained to *Record Collector*. 'The Waterfront were great. They were like Orange Juice. They had a song called "On The Beach In Normandy". The Patrol was a racket so I got into scooters but John's still doing his band. He played me a tape and it sounded really good. I was impressed because I knew somebody who could play with that quality. Since '78/'79 John hadn't done much except play his guitar.'

Brown was still in touch with The Waterfront, hanging out at the odd rehearsal and the two recorded tunes had knocked him out. Then John asked him if he wanted to join up as a singer. Ian was interested and was back down in the cellar sharing vocals with Kaiser. Hanging out with his old mates. Dreaming the dream and getting off on the banter.

1983–8

From The Waterfront to The Rose Garden – Hanging Around!

The beginning of 1983 saw the various would-be musicians who floated around the varying line-ups, further away from realising any kind of musical dream than at any time since they were first fired by the punk explosion.

Ian Brown was working in the dole office or cleaning dishes at TFI Fridays in Didsbury. John Squire was working on the *Chorlton and the Wheelies* TV series in Chorlton's Cosgrove Hall. Pete Garner was still selling magazines in Paperchase in the city centre, 'I remember Morrissey coming in with his James Dean book that he had written, asking if you could buy a book of lyrics for the New York Dolls' albums. I thought he must live in a dream world if he thought such a thing existed for such a small group...'

The band that Si hadn't joined, The Smiths, was fast-tracking its way to indie dominance and then to the grown-up charts beyond. And in Manchester itself New Order were critics' raves, and hitting the charts regularly, and The Chameleons were one of the biggest home-town draws.

The Boardwalk was yet to open and the Hacienda was either a cold, half-full warehouse for touring bands battling muffled acoustics, or a student disco playing safe indie hits for cheap lager hunters mixing with the handful of hipsters.

For anyone bitten by the bug of rock'n'roll, gaps like this are dull and frustrating, but for a desperado like Andy Couzens it was a desperate time. He remembers this hiatus with no affection. 'There is a gap between the bands [The Waterfront and The Stone Roses] because John was always going home making models. I remember taking John down in a car with a bunch of models to Cosgrove Hall, he just wanted to do that; make an animated cartoon with models...'

Musically, Couzens was still broadening his tastes and like the rest of his occasional bandmates he was digging deeper into psychedelia, getting rootsier, moving further and further away. 'I remember starting to get into The Misunderstood and stuff like that. It goes back to the picture on that single sleeve they lent me when I joined The Patrol, that kind of look. I started getting into all that. There never seemed to be much on until the International opened and loads of those bands came over. I remember it started having bands like Jason & the Scorchers, loads of stuff from the States. I went and they were crap – all rubbish. I hate all that Yank shit anyway.'

Couzens even started digging some of the post-punk pre-Goth outfits emerging in London who were trying to forge something different. 'Brigandage showed a bit of promise but fell apart. It was a really horrible period, nothing seemed to be happening. Manchester was really horrible then. It was shite...I still lived in Macclesfield at my parents' house.'

Apart from that, time was spent drifting around town at night getting into trouble. The Waterfront had stopped; the two-vocal thing had not saved the band. 'We were still hanging out after The Waterfront. I still saw Kaiser, Chris Goodwin, Mani. In fact, I last saw Kaiser a year ago on the way to a United match.'

Then there was the strange jamming session that Andy Couzens and Ian Brown had with Clint Boon, who remembers an ad hoc Manchester supergroup years ahead of its time.

'Ian Brown and Andy Couzens came down to the rehearsal room at the Mill with Mani and the idea was, "Let's all get together and make one big band." They came down in one of Andy's big American cars. It didn't really gel. Andy was a rockabilly guitarist and Ian was a more conventional singer, but I was into driving trucks over microphones as Mani was recording smashing bottles into bins. We were like a quiff electric 'Frankie Teardrop' Suicide crossed with Einstürzende Neubauten and sixties psyche. I've got it on tape somewhere. Mani played bass. I played the organ and sang. Chris Goodwin was on drums.'

Ian Brown recalls: 'I met Clint Boon through Mani. They had this band, The Hungry Socks. We went to meet them. I didn't want to sing. I didn't like the set-up when I got there so I pretended I didn't like the mic I was using and that I had never sung in my life before.'

It didn't work and after an hour or so Ian Brown and Andy Couzens went.

Back in town treading water, the crew would inevitably run into fights in the city centre. 'I remember us having fights in Piccadilly Gardens,' says Andy. 'Fights with beer monsters waiting for buses. I do remember John getting his nose broken. One night we were coming out of Club Tropicana on Oxford Road, you know the one with the palm trees inside? I remember coming out of there one night and we got a right hiding. We used to go to the Berlin club a lot. Our first demo as the Roses would eventually get played in there one night just after we finished it, which was a shock...'

And it was this subterranean world of dimly-lit clubs playing post-punk, proto-Goth and psychedelic rock that was far closer to the Roses' roots than the shiny new world of the Hacienda. Clubs like Berlin have, of course, been written out of the history of the Manchester music scene. It was hardly a media haunt. You wouldn't find all the local journos hanging out there and it wasn't run by any local industry bigwigs. Berlin was the first club to play the Roses' demos and records and they even put on some classic gigs there. I remember once seeing the Spacemen 3 supported by Inspiral Carpets down there. Another key club was the Playpen with DJ Dave Booth whose eclectic music policy was going to be so influential in the Manchester music story.

As they hung around town and slowly drifted in and out of the world of piss-ups and violence, that mind-numbing existence of weekend lads, it was almost inevitable that someone would gather the clan again for one last go at it.

It was into this aimless drifting existence that the Roses were finally born. Coming back from town, Andy would quite often cut along Stretford Road and into nearby Hulme. He would then go up to the Crescents that dominated the middle of the estate and round to Ian Brown's place in the now demolished Charles Barry Crescent, the wildest and most partied out of the four Crescents that lay at the heart of Hulme in the mid-eighties. Past the squats, through the bohemian sprawl that formed the nerve centre of the new Manchester underground right to the middle of Hulme where the four huge imposing concrete blocks that dominated the area sat stoically in the murky Manc weather.

Recalls Andy, 'I'd go round to Ian's quite a lot. He was living with Mitch, the eventual mother of his children, she was at college with us in South Trafford and she was working on *Brookside* at this time...I remember his wok! He loved his wok! He fancied himself as a bit of a cook.'

Couzens still wanted to make some rock'n'roll and he was determined to talk Ian into it. Usually he just went round to hang out and have a laugh. But today he was determined to talk his old bandmate into doing something. As he cut through the decaying sprawl of Hulme and up the piss-stained walkways he was dead set on getting yet another band together.

'I Wanna Be Adored': The Roses Finally Get Their Shit Together

Andy Couzens wanted to play music. And he knew who he wanted to play with. It was just a matter of doing some persuading. The spark came yet again from Andy's fists. 'I had all that shit from fighting again. I have one of those temperaments, some people have a short fuse, I don't have a fuse at all, bang and I'm gone. I just kept getting in trouble like that. I needed something. I had a court case coming up for fighting. I went to see Ian. I was hoping that he wanted to make some music again. I was keeping my fingers crossed. I said, "Let's get something going, 'cos if I don't I am going to go down, I was staring at a jail sentence. They told me I was going to get six months.'

He had decided that he needed to get something to focus his life on other than drifting around town fighting, something to occupy him, something, anything, to get his temper under control.

Ian Brown wasn't so sure. 'I'd given up rock'n'roll in one sense,' he claims. But he was soon to have a meeting that would change his life. One night when he was having a party at his flat for Mitch's 21st birthday, a guest arrived that no one was expecting.

Geno! Geno! Geno! Geno!

In the early eighties, Hulme was full of squats and cheap flats with endless parties, and only a quarter of an hour walk from the city centre. It was a tight community, probably the biggest bohemian drop-out zone in the UK, and at this time it was at its post-punk twenty-four-hour-party-people peak.

One night Ian Brown had a party in his flat and through the door came the unlikely figure of Geno Washington, one of the kings of Northern Soul, The Don, the man with the sweetest soul voice. The man who Dexys Midnight Runners had honoured in 'Geno', their biggest hit.

On the night of the party Brown's flat was already experiencing some mad behaviour, as he remembers. 'Woody was the bass player from The Worst. He slept at my house. He'd ripped me curtains down 'cos he was cold but when I go in, in the morning, he's leaned up against the wall and the bed has burnt right round his body like a silhouette where he fell asleep with a cigarette, and the mattress has melted – it's smouldering. And he was fine!'

The party was in full swing when Washington arrived, fresh from a gig at the nearby Manchester University. He was looking for the now-demolished Reno club in nearby Moss Side and was asking for directions. But on hooking up with the young Brown, he smoked some spliff and hung out.

Says Ian, 'I'm at my party in Hulme…my mate Gluebag Glen, who was a good friend of ours and was with the Roses early on roadying but is dead now, went to see Geno Washington play in Manchester. Glen and Slim, who would also eventually roadie for us, brought Geno and his band back. I had never heard of Geno Washington at the time. To me he was just this dead cool old black guy…

'Then he asked where to get a spliff so I took him to the Reno club in Moss Side. I always remember him smoking in the street and this copper coming up and saying, "What the fuck are you doing?" And he said, "I'm Geno Washington, I can do whatever I like!" and carried on smoking. I thought that was so cool and the cop said, "Go back in there and smoke it." He didn't even bust him!'

Geno Washington was a legend on the Northern Soul scene. His Ram Jam Band had been the soundtrack to some serious dancefloor action and he was still out on the circuit, rejuvenated by Dexys' paean to him and the whole of the scene in which he was such a key player.

Washington remembers the night well. 'After the gig I didn't want to go to the hotel and these guys in the dressing room took me to this party. The joint was jumping. I got there and ask Ian if he's got anything to smoke and he calls a friend up and he comes round and I got my mojo working, I got God in my stride. [Ian] was a very good-looking guy with a very good personality. He had the looks and he wasn't doing the playboy thing, just busy drinking with his mates, telling jokes. I said, "You made me happy giving me the blow so I want to do the payback and show that I'm not a hustler trying to use you. I wanna give you some knowledge you don't know about and it might change your life."'

Washington gave the young Ian Brown advice that would change his life. 'So we got talking and I said, "These girls are around you are like flies to honey and you're not taking no notice. You got the looks, you got the body, you're healthy, you're young – you ought to be a singer, man, you know what I'm staying? Get in the pop business." And he says, "Nah, man, I've never thought about that." I said, "Do you write songs?" He said, "Nah, I have done a bit of poetry in school that my teacher said was good." I said, "You're only one inch from writing songs. If you can write poetry, you can write songs. Write your poetry; get with a band who can write all the music. You have nothing to lose; you are a star. I have seen the way girls react round you. They love you, your mates love you. You can change your whole life. Practice makes perfect. How do you get to Carnegie Hall? Practice!"

'No one ever told him something like that; he was very grateful so we dropped the conversation and got into the party mood. He actually introduced me to a good piece of ass that night. It was a damn good night.

'I come back ten years later and I get a call – you know who's one of the biggest fucking stars in Europe? In a band called The Stone Roses? Ian Brown! In his interviews, he says if it wasn't for Geno Washington I wouldn't be doing this and I said, "Damn!"'

The conversation left Ian Brown thinking. A few days after that, John Squire rang – did he want another go at the band? Andy was also into giving it his best shot. 'So there I was with Ian in Hulme. I was saying, "Right, let's get something going again. We talked about it a bit, what the line-up should be. I wanted Si Wolstencroft in and I know we were thinking of bass players, but who could we get?'

Obviously it should have been Mani but he was otherwise engaged…

'After The Waterfront stopped, I took to going abroad and thieving with a vengeance, man!' he explains. 'We just used to go away – lads from Moston and Failsworth. We used to just jump on trains and travel round Europe without paying and line up opportunities to get clothing, anything! They were pretty naughty days, but when Thatcher backs you into a corner you have got to get out of it somehow, haven't you? It was like a Robin Hood vibe!'

Pete Garner? Pete was part of the gang and he went back a long way. Maybe they were just keeping things south Manchester. Back to their Patrol roots! Andy ponders the Mani question. 'He was someone you went out and had a laugh with. He was in that Failsworth gang. And we liked Pete. I always thought there was something about Pete. He's just a great bloke, Pete. Someone who is great to have around. Whether he could play or not was irrelevant…we just ended up getting The Patrol back together – the big reformation.'

Everyone was up for it; Pete Garner on bass, John and Andy on guitars and Ian on vocals. And with one more call Si Wolstencroft back on drums. After four years The Patrol were back together.

Back in Andy's parents' cellar in Macclesfield they picked up from where they kept leaving off. They put together 'Nowhere Fast'. It was a very productive first rehearsal.

Within a week they had added 'All Stitched Up' and 'I Can't Take It Any More'. Not bad going when you consider the bass player couldn't actually play a note! 'You've got to remember that the only bass line I knew was "Blockbuster" from that Patrol gig years ago,' says Pete. 'I couldn't play the bass at all! I had only played once at that gig! At our first rehearsal everyone strapped on guitars and I was stood there saying, "What the fuck do I do?"'

That first rehearsal must have been some scene. Plenty of chat. Plenty of fooling. Andy and John's guitars working together. And then John launching into the chords for 'Nowhere Fast', which initially had a different title, and Ian picking out some sort of space for his vocal melody. Good mates making music together. The gang back together. Top buzz!

It clicked. And, it clicked fast. John's guitar playing was already quite a few notches above just another run-of-the-mill garage band. They had Ian back on vocals, his self-belief and obvious charisma well up for the task, and even if his singing was initially rough, well they weren't that bothered. This was a gang and, anyhow, the singer had 'decided' to get himself some singing lessons.

Getting singing lessons is considered to be just about the least rock-'n'roll thing in the world. Guitar lessons? Maybe. But actually learning to sing? That's a weird one. And it's something that can be very nerve-wracking. Even for cocky upstarts like Ian Brown. But Johnny Rotten had had singing lessons and he was the anarchist!

As Ian told *Record Collector*, 'Yeah, we started a few rehearsals and I'm singing and everyone's like, fuck, we can't put up with that! You'll have to have singing lessons. So I went to this old woman over Victoria Station, Mrs Rhodes. She'd get me there at six o'clock, open the window, with everyone coming home from work. She'd have me wailing "After The Goldrush" or "Strawberry Fields" out the window. The crowds looking up and she's saying, if you can't do it, go home. So I thought, fuck it, I'll stick it out. So I did three weeks with her. She had an 80-year-old dear on the piano!"

It is one of the myths that has always hung around the Roses. The one that Brown can't sing. Sometimes his voice can sound rough but when he's on it, he has his own voice. It sounds like Ian Brown, and surely the prerequisite of any singer is to sound like yourself. The early punkier Roses material he holds together with a brattish whine and eventually as the band become more melodic he even sounds, linking in with Reni, angelic on the records. In many ways Brown's vocal gives the band their distinctive edge, his stark northern accent instantly placing them. Added to that he has the attitude and the communication skills that connect with a generation – that's singing.

A month in and it was coming together. They had a set worked out and the songs were moving on in leaps and bounds. They even had a name this time. A proper name, a name that didn't sound stupid and one that pretty well captured them as a band. John came up with The Stone Roses and out of all the suggestions it was the one that stuck. It captured their hard and soft edges, the lovelorn melodicism and punk-rock edge, the angelic melodies and the tough street stance; soft songs with dark hearts. It was perfect.

Says Andy, 'We had no name at first but quite quickly we were called The Stone Roses. John came up with it. There was a whole list of names written down. Fucked if I can remember them! We had all written loads of stuff down. It's off a book cover I think. The hard and soft thing was an explanation that was added later on.'

They never called themselves English Rose. It was The Stone Roses pure and simple.

'I don't know where that English Rose story came from,' says Ian. 'John thought up the name "Stone Roses" – something with a contrast, two words that went against each other.'

Johnny Marr was one of the first people to hear the band's new name: 'I was still seeing Pete around. We were getting the 99 bus back to Wythenshawe one night after working in our shops and he was trying to come up with a name for his new band. He knew I was a Stones freak and he got off a few stops after me. He was saying it's got to be as good as the Rolling Stones. The phone goes five minutes after I got home and it was Pete Garner and he says the band have decided to call themselves The Stone Roses? I said, "Nah, that's too obvious, Pete!" So that's my claim to fame.'

Back in the cellar the songs were coming on. Nothing was carried over from The Waterfront. This time it was going to be serious. This time they were going to try and break that ground that they had attempted after The Patrol, soak up all those new influences that they had been chewing on from the post-punk sounds of Postcard and some of the pre-punk neo-psychedelia that they had been listening to, mix it in with the punk rock they were still fired up on. They were really up for it.

And out there the music scene was changing. There was a mini revolution going on. A feedback-drenched psychedelic rock'n'roll riot was goin' on in London. With guitars!

That year The Jesus And Mary Chain were setting the indie scene on fire with their feedback-drenched pure pop, their sweet songs and riots. Hard and soft, like a stone and a rose, they were to have a profound influence on many upcoming bands on the scene and John Squire was listening. 'I loved the sonic action approach to the guitar overdubs and the endless permutations the brothers found for those three chords. It changed the way I thought about writing songs.'

After the Mary Chain there was Creation Records and Primal Scream, leather trousers and bowl cuts, sweet tunes and tough street poses. There was Alan McGee and his pop vision. It was a pop vision that kinda matched the Roses' vision.

Years later Alan McGee told me, 'The Stone Roses were a beautiful amalgamation of Mancunian pop and psychedelia. Borrowing from The Three O'Clock and Primal Scream they made great Manc pop. Ian Brown is, was and always will be, a superstar to me and a million others. The first LP is a classic. I love them loads and probably always will do.'

So there were plenty of influences. Plenty of ideas. Even if they didn't have a proper rehearsal room…

What a Bummer…We've Lost a Drummer!

In the cramped cellar of the Couzens in Macclesfield they started to work up tunes; a meticulously planned and worked-out set of songs played by a studious, hard-working bunch of players with discipline and self-belief.

They knew each other inside out so it was easy work; after all, this was the last line-up of The Patrol revived after a few years. Musicians who have played together for some time have an inbuilt advantage. They've grown up together, got pissed together, been through all the same shit, told the same jokes, shared their musical tastes. It makes songwriting fast.

Says Andy, 'It just felt good again you know. It felt right. We just kept writing. All that very early stuff like "Mission Impossible". There was also stuff that didn't make it from that period of songs.'

Other songs came quickly and the band had a sound. It was a step on from The Waterfront: the chiming guitars were still there but tougher, heavier and with effects; the songs were more anthemic and with great melodies.

A few months in, though, they were dealt a bombshell. Si was leaving. He had been drumming for years and through his various contacts he was a known face about town. After all he had turned The Smiths down! He was the most successful and known musician among them. Getting back into the cellar after being on the verge of joining the band that was now dominating the guitar pop scene was certainly something.

They knew that trying to keep hold of Si was going to be difficult. He had been auditioning for bigger bands for the past six months and he finally got a job in ex-Special Terry Hall's new outfit The Colourfield. Adds Si, 'I was in The Colourfield with Terry Hall for a while, along with Craig Gannon on guitar. (I also got Craig his job with The Smiths.) I appeared on *The Tube* with him performing three songs, including Kim Fowley's "The Trip".'

Si got The Colourfield job and then drifted round the local scene, eventually in 1986 playing drums with Manchester's hairdresser to the stars Andrew Berry (he used to cut everyone's hair in the basement of the Hacienda). Berry's band was The Weeds, who had a single, the great twisted post Smiths-rush of 'China Doll', on *In Tape*. The Weeds supported The Fall on tour in 1986 and Si was asked to join Mark Smith's outfit where he remained for a decade. The Weeds, despite their potential, sadly fell apart.

Si was still mates with the Roses and in fact turned up at the Alexandra Palace show years later, where I bumped into him during the soundcheck where he was buzzing on his former bandmates' mega success. In 2000 he rejoined Ian Brown for a bit of drumming, programming and the odd bit of songwriting.

Si's departure from the cellar was a pretty big blow for the band. In fact it was a disaster. Getting a drummer is so damn difficult. But by now, they were a driven unit. That inner confidence was being bolstered by the great tunes that they were writing without him. 'Misery Dictionary' was written in the weeks following Si's departure. But they still needed a drummer.

They put in a phone call to the north Manchester posse and pulled their ex-Waterfront buddy Chris Goodwin from his stints in various north Manc bands like T'Challa Grid and Asia Fields.

Goodwin came down, but it was obvious that he didn't have any intention of sticking around too long. Says Andy, 'We were still at my parents' place. We got Chris Goodwin in. He came down for one rehearsal and left his kit. It was like he was just looking for somewhere to store it.'

Stuck again, they continued to jam away drummerless while writing songs. 'We rehearsed for ages with no drums at all, which is ridiculous when you think about it,' Andy continues. 'These days you'd get a drum machine. But we were still writing. Either me or John would come up with a riff. A couple of songs didn't make it. We wrote stuff like "Mission Impossible" when I went to John's one night. John lived on Zetland Road in Chorlton. He had the top floor flat and we wrote there.'

Now two drummers down, they had run out of options from their immediate bunch of mates. So they decided to cast the net a little wider and advertise. 'The first person to answer was the ex-drummer from The Skeletal Family. He came down in his ginger Beetle. 'You only remember the funny ones, don't you?' laughs Andy.

Howard Daniels had been in The Skeletal Family for about a year, joining them in 1983 and leaving early in '84. The Yorkshire-based band were at the poppier end of the Goth scene. And the classic Goth style of drums was a tumbling rumble of post-tribal toms. It may have fitted perfectly into The Skeletal Family but for the Roses music it jarred. Badly.

Within seconds of Daniels walking into the rehearsal room in Andy Couzens cellar, with his fringed jacket and Goth-tinged look, both parties knew that this was not a happening situation, but in the etiquette of auditions they had to persevere anyway.

Daniels parked himself behind Chris Goodwin's dusty kit and they kicked off with 'Tragic Roundabout' and 'Mission Impossible'. Daniels' arms were pounding out incessant Goth-style tribal beats on the kit; powerful pounding rhythms but not what the Roses were looking for. At the end of the song there was an uncomfortable silence. Howard looked up and said, 'I'm not into this stuff. It's got no tunes.'

'He didn't seem to be enjoying himself, so he didn't get the job.' remembers Couzen.

Still drummerless, they kept writing and the music was changing, as Ian Brown points out, into something else.

'We came from punk but we were slowing it down. The two Joneses, Mick and Steve, were our heroes. Punk showed that you didn't have to be a virtuoso or a hippie to make music. I remember Johnny Thunders being a big thing mixed in with the Postcard stuff. Also Empire, who were the guitarist and drummer from Generation X's band, were big with us as well.'

They faithfully put the ads back up round town and waited for the next bunch of freaks and weirdoes to start ringing. What they actually got a couple of days later was a call from some extrovert-sounding kid with a funny name. A kid called Reni.

'Every Time He Played a Song He Played It Different and Every Time It Was Brilliant…' Reni Arrives!

In 1984 one of the best places for a musician to find a band was looking at the noticeboard in the now defunct A1 Music.

It was in there that one afternoon while the band were hammering away at their clutch of new songs in Macclesfield, a cocky young guy bounded into A1 and took a look at the advert.

The ad asked for a drummer into Gen X, The Clash and Empire – pointers to the way the Roses were thinking at the time – the last gang in town, at the glammier end of punk rock.

Empire occupy an odd footnote in music. Now semi-forgotten, at the time they were a big influence on the Washington DC hardcore punk scene of bands like Minor Threat, and also on the early Stone Roses. If you listen you can detect their influence in the reverbed vocals and chorused guitars.

Not that this meant much to Reni. He was into rock, with Van Halen's 'Jump' being his all-time favourite tune. He saw the card and knew he could bag the job. He even pulled the ad off the wall to stop anyone else getting it.

As he left A1 that May afternoon, 20-year-old Alan Wren knew he was good enough to be in any band in Manchester but there was something about this ad that intrigued him.

He went home to Gorton, picked up the phone and booked himself an audition with the gruff voice at the other end.

The band themselves had pooled their money and booked the city centre Decibel Rehearsal Studios for the audition. No more fannying around in the cellar. This had to be done properly. They had never rehearsed in the city centre before but this was important.

'We moved out of the Macclesfield cellar to Decibel,' remembers Andy. 'We put an advert in A1 and listed a load of influences that Reni read and obviously knew none of them! He rang up. We were called the Angry Young Teddy Bears or some load of bollocks that week. Something someone had made up to wind people up with.

On 31 May 1984 they had the rehearsal room booked. This time they were going to do it properly. They didn't want to make the mistake of missing out on another drummer. What if he was really good? He might not want to join a tinpot outfit. They had to look more pro!

Decibel Studios was in Manchester city centre. Nowadays it's better known as Beehive Mill, a club come rehearsal room complex just to the north of the city centre in what was then a pretty run-down area of town. Inside it was a threadbare old warehouse with a whole bunch of bands rehearsing in there.

Back then the area was a rubble-strewn deadzone. Ian hopped into Andy's car and they drove round to Reni's house in Gorton. When Reni answered the door they were in for a shock.

According to Andy, the drummer came to the door dressed in a pair of furry moonboots and too-tight jeans. 'He denies it now, but when Reni rang up he called himself Renée on the phone. Me and Ian went to pick him up. I seem to remember he looked mad. Big long coat on with these big furry moonboots. A pair of them awful stretch denim jeans. His dress sense was fucking terrible!'

He may well be exaggerating – when your author bumped into Reni a couple of months later he wasn't dressed that crazily.

'We loaded his gear into the car and went to the rehearsal room. We took the gear up three flights of stairs, it was such a pain in the arse!'

You can almost hear a crackle of expectation on the cassette of that very first rehearsal. The explosive excitement as he connects with the band straight away. They run through 'Nowhere Fast'. It's the simplest one to play. It's Reni's first-ever song with the band and there is a palpable buzz of excitement. Suddenly they sound like The Stone Roses – those drums are so distinctive, so Reni.

Pete Garner is still entranced by just how good Reni was at that first rehearsal: '"Nowhere Fast", "All Stitched Up", "I Can't Take It Any more", "Mission Impossible" were the songs Reni first rehearsed. We never discussed it, we knew he was in! He was fucking amazing! What a drummer…

'Fuck, you can hear it on the rehearsal tape. Reni explodes into the song. Even its complex structure is learned in about five minutes.

This is a find. What a player. You can feel the band buzzing. I mean Si was good. Really good. But this was special!'

Recalls Andy, 'When he started playing he was mad as a hatter. He played like Keith Moon. All those little things that he can do! Double hits! Unbelievable stuff, so fluent, no effort. He can actually do all that. Amazing…We wanted him in straight away, he was that fucking good. We weren't sure if he was going to have it! We weren't that good at all, pretty rough in fact…'

Why did he join? A drummer that good could have joined any band. A couple of months later he confided in Andy. 'He told me a while later that the thing that really struck him was how much we believed in ourselves. The sense of belief that he got from us all. He'd briefly been in [semi-successful local metal outfit] Tora Tora and if he hadn't joined us he would have ended up as a jobbing musician.'

On that first rehearsal tape you can hear Reni being unsure about the songs. He thought they might not be strong enough. Then they launch into 'Tragic Roundabout'. Now he gets it. Now he knows what they are capable of. He can hear this one. Remember Reni comes from the rock world, indie music means little to him. Where's the tune? Where's the song? This is a whole new discipline for the band and a good one.

'I'll bounce ideas off you,' he says. There is laughter and the band crash into 'Roundabout' again. Pete's stub-toed bass intro rumbles in yet again and again something magical happens. Reni's drums have the stamp of the Roses all over them, the loose Keith Moon rolls, the tricks, the gleeful unrestrained joy of playing and the unrestrained extrovert energy so rare in British musicians. It sounds like magic dust has been sprinkled all over the songs.

It's May 1984 and the Roses' sound is already fully formed: the stop start of the song, its clever structure, its overflow of melody and the twin guitar work of Andy and John's guitars cranked to max treble. You can hear the flavour of the Postcard bands in the guitars and the chiming brittle treble of Empire. The tunefulness is there, underlined by something darker and more sinister.

'Keep going, please keep going,' yelps Reni as the song stops. There is a lot of laughter as they try to explain to the new drummer where the song goes but his confidence is so outrageous he doesn't need to be told.

Reni knocks around with the Max Wall snare drum rat-a-tat. The band laugh and then launch into yet another version of the tune. After what seems like a million attempts, the band finally gets to a version that includes Squire's melting solo.

It's a nightmare song to audition anyone with: its endless parts, its continually evolving structure – it's hardly 1-2-3-4 and then one beat, but Reni's on it. 'We can do this, I know we can,' says Ian.

They have a break and Reni asks what's going on with the band.

'We got loads of chances of gigs, got to get on with it. We know GBH and we know Peter and the Test Tube Babies...and that's about it.' A voice, possibly Andy's, comes out of the gloom, name-checking more unlikely punk outfits. 'We like all kinds of music' it explains to the drummer. It is some sort of truism, because even though they are still wearing their punk roots firmly on their sleeve their music is a long way from the far more hardcore nature of where the punk underground has gone. This is back to the roots of punk, with garage psychedelic licks and the twin-guitar melodicism that roots back to the core of classic six-string pop. At the same time the FX-laden guitar gives them their own flavour. Only Manchester's own Chameleons operated anywhere near them.

Even from that first rehearsal with Reni you can hear all the hallmarks of the Roses sound that would captivate the upcoming generation five years later...

After that uplifting pep talk, they crash into a few bars of something that sounds like 'Coming Of Age'. 'I can't remember the tune,' laughs Ian as the song falls apart after a few bars.

'We're coming of age and you can't take it away,' intones Brown over a Who-style workout.

And then they dive back into 'Tragic Roundabout', the band's relief at actually being able to play along with a drummer after all these months is readily apparent. These songs have been waiting to be pushed by the drums. They are pretty well finished. Arranged. Ready to go. Getting anyone to drum on them must have been a buzz. But getting a drummer like this must have been quite a moment.

The songs are stuffed full of licks and the guitars peel off for mini solos and tuneful riffing. The song ends.

'That sounds really good, know what I mean...' enthuses Reni as 'Tragic Roundabout' clatters to a close, the tune being the only one that he actually really liked at that first rehearsal!

At the end of the rehearsal they huddle together. They want Reni in.

He thought about it and said 'Yes.' It wasn't so much for the music, he later claimed but the band's confidence, their total belief.

The allure of this fierce tightly knit crew appealed to him.

The Roses were ecstatic. They will always readily admit that the real turning point for them was when Reni joined the band. Now they had a foundation to build on. Says Ian, 'Finding Reni was crucial. John was a punk guitarist when we met Reni, but Reni could play anything. He'd been brought up in pubs, so he'd practised and practised on his kit and played with proper pub entertainers. He had a musical talent that none of us had then. We all had to graft and work, but he was born with it. Pete Townshend saw our first gig (Moonlight, 1984) and said he was the best drummer he'd seen since Keith Moon.'

Reni's metal angle was just another obtuse influence to add to the band's stockpile of sounds. Says Ian, 'We liked The New York Dolls, still do. John, Andy and Pete were very into Johnny Thunders, Reni was into Van Halen. He'd never heard reggae when we met him. He'd been brought up in east Manchester, which was more heavy metal. He was into Thin Lizzy and AC/DC. He was a proper rocker, used to go to Donington. We used to rip the piss out of him for his music. But we were very enthusiastic. We just wanted to make a noise.'

So just who was this manic drummer, this wise guy from east Manchester who would 'play every song completely differently and brilliantly every time'?

Jump! Reni

Alan 'Reni' Wren was born on 10 April 1964. He was a streetwise kid from the Ardwick/Gorton part of the ring of rough estates that surround the Manchester city centre before panning out to the cosseted suburbs.

Already famous in his area for being a cocky, confident character, he was also known as the kid with the drums. Even at a very young age he was thrashing around on drum kits set up in his parents' pub where a kit was permanently set up for pub bands to play on.

The local kids thought Reni was a freak because he was such an amazing drummer, a total natural. Reni didn't care. He was already jamming along to anything and anybody. Stepping in with bands in the pub, playing along with whoever was around or just by himself. Says Pete, 'When he joined us he was already in two other bands. He was checking out who was the best bet but he thought we looked interesting. We had something!'

Graduating from the pub, he was playing in mates' bands, just going-nowhere sort of stuff round Gorton. It was somewhere to sharpen up his act – get those drums tighter and meaner – but it wasn't enough; he knew how good he was.

By the early eighties it was time to break out and try his hand at something more serious. Maybe the spur was his close drumming mate getting a dream break. It had only been a few months before that one of his best mates, Simon Wright, had answered an ad ('drummer wanted must hit hard and heavy') to join AC/DC.

It had been a long shot but Wright had got in. Some scruff from the estate was in one of the biggest rock bands in the world at the peak of their powers. It was like a dream come true, a yob from the street playing the world's stadiums.

Adds Pete, 'He had a Man United shirt on TV playing with AC/DC. He was older than Reni – showed him some stuff...'

Seeing his mate in the stadiums must have been a spur to Reni. It must have sharpened his resolve to get hooked up in a band. Some say that he stepped into Wright's shoes in Tora Tora, a local Manchester rock band that his mate had drummed in before moving on to the awesome Aussie rock giants, but no one will confirm it.

So, wanting to breakout, Reni began to scour the ads around town. Next thing he was in the Roses.

The Three Rs…Write, Rehearse and Record – Summer of '84

During the summer of 1984 they rehearsed for a couple of months at Decibel, but the studios' grubby environs and some equipment going missing made them less than happy with that situation. So they moved a few blocks further into town, to Spirit Studios on Tariff Street, and it was here that the whole myth and legend of The Stone Roses really started to flower.

John Breakall, who ran Spirit Studios, remembers the band rehearsing down there: 'The first band down at Spirit on Tariff Street were The Smiths. I had befriended Dale Hibbert, who was the first Smiths bass player, when they were doing their first demo and they needed a rehearsal space so I found these premises owned by a church on Tariff Street and opened up some rooms. After The Smiths, Simply Red and the Happy Mondays were in there and then the Roses came down. Andy Couzens and Pete, the bass player, came to check us out.'

It was here, bang smack in the middle of the Manchester music scene, that the Roses started to make the right sort of contacts that would link them into the city's infrastructure instead of flogging away forgotten out in suburban cellars. They would swagger around the tight corridors of Spirit with their attitude turned up full.

'They did some basic recording at Spirit – very basic, because the studio was terrible,' says Breakall. 'A basic four-track in those days, and they did a cassette: "Misery Dictionary" and three other tracks.'

Now with a permanent home and a steady line-up coalescing, the band's songwriting began to hit top gear.

Andy Couzens remembers it as a prolific time. 'When someone joins and you get a new rehearsal room then loads of material seems to get written. If you dry up, then go to a new room and start again! The songs will come! In Decibel the songs we put together were "Mission Impossible" and "Nowhere Fast". In Spirit, the songs we started getting together were "Tragic Roundabout" and "So Young", "Tell Me", "Fall". We wrote a lot of the Hannett stuff there, nearly all of "Getting Plenty".'

They also rehearsed in Spirit's other rehearsal rooms out in Chorlton, flitting backwards and forwards from the city centre to the suburbs with fellow Spirit outfits like Carmel and The Membranes. The Chorlton studios were a two-room affair carpeted with a good vocal PA. They were spacious affairs and it made you feel like a proper band going down there.

As my band, The Membranes, rehearsed in one room we would wonder who the tough-looking bunch of short-hairs were in the neighbouring room. The music pounding through the rehearsal room walls sounded good. Anthemic powerful rock music, it had the spirit of The Clash but had gone somewhere else with affected chorused guitars and powerful drums. You could clearly hear Ian Brown giving it his all over the top.

One day I had to go next door and borrow some guitar strings off the band. It looked like it could be a bit heavy but I knew Pete from hanging out in Paperchase and Reni and I had met a few times. The Roses were affable, easy-going. In fact they helped us get our gear back to our west Didsbury bolthole in Andy's big white van. We had just seen Ian Brown moving in next door to us.

It was in Chorlton that the band entered the second phase of their songwriting. Andy Couzens remembers writing one of their most famous tracks. 'We wrote "I Wanna Be Adored" there. By this time Pete used to sit out a bit and I'd play the bass while we jammed basic things out, then I'd give the bass back and show him what I had been playing. Likewise John would do the same.'

Pete Garner says the song came naturally. '"I Wanna Be Adored" arrived. It was virtually the same as the final recorded version except the intro was a bit shorter. I remember at the time that we didn't fit in anywhere, we looked like we were in five different bands.'

While the Roses were toiling away in the rehearsal room, fellow Mancs and Spirit rehearsal-room neighbours The Smiths were in their ascendancy. Ian told *Record Collector*, 'I liked the fact that The Smiths came from our home town and I knew Andy Rourke when I was a kid, so I was happy for them. I liked "What Difference Does It Make?"'

Andy will admit, when pushed, to some respect for The Smiths. 'We said we hated them but had a secret adoration for them as well...'

There were musical parallels between the bands: there was a very English atmosphere that surrounded them both, and some of the Roses' early songwriting reflects a similar flavour. The two bands' careers had been running together from day one and there were many points when they were in the same place at the same time.

Spirit was not only the place where the Roses first really got their shit together and wrote nearly all of their early material, it was also the place where they began to infiltrate the Manchester music scene, coming in from the cellars and the suburbs into the city network.

The first important contact they made was Steve Adge. Steve 'the Adge' Atherton was helping to run the rabbit warren of rooms. He was a tough-looking ex-rockabilly who was a fistful of years older than the band, but with a similar musical background. All ruffians with a love for rock'n'roll, it was obvious that Steve Adge and the Roses would bond.

He hit it off with them immediately. Recalls Andy, 'Spirit was where we met Steve Adge – another nutter. We always seem to attract them! He's from Hyde and they are a bit strange out there! He was a lot older than us. We were in our early twenties. He was, like, in his thirties.'

Says Pete, 'He was playing in a band called Third Law with Mark, his younger brother. Third Law rehearsed down there. I bought my bass amp off Steve.'

But Ian Brown was already familiar with the man. 'I knew Steve Adge from before that. I'd met him one night at the poly disco…My mate had got six months for a robbery. He had come out of jail that day in '82 and we went to the poly. He went to the toilet and this skinhead in a big boiler suit went by and kicked my mate's drink over.' What ensues next was a bloody scene of skinheads brawling and swearing at each other, but Ian remembers clearly how it ended.

'My mate went up to the skinhead and demanded the money for his drink. Now he's pretty fierce looking – he was a skinhead too. But the kid tells him to fuck off, so my mate sticks his fingers up the kid's nose and bounces his head up and down and the kid fucked off.

'Five minutes later, through the crowd we see these bouncers and this kid with about five of these other kids looking over. Steve Adge walked over. I've never met him in my life and he said, "Are you in some bother?" I said, "Me and my mate are going to get leathered by these kids here." So Steve Adge walks over, takes off his belt and said, "Who wants it?" Nothing happened, but it did the trick. The bouncers threw the lads out. Then Steve turned around and said, "Hi, my name is Steve," and that is how I met him.'

The First Demo

On 26 August 1984, 12 weeks after Reni had joined, the Roses decided that they were ready to cut their first demo and shunted their gear down the narrow stairs of Spirit rehearsal studios. They booked two ten-hour sessions and recorded four songs: 'Tragic Roundabout', 'Misery Dictionary', 'Mission Impossible' and 'Nowhere Fast'.

John Breakall laughs as he remembers the band's bare-faced cheek. 'There is the infamous story, where they borrowed, stole, or whatever, the keys to Spirit. And they locked themselves in the studio overnight. I'm pretty sure that's later on when they did "Sally Cinnamon". I think Tim Oliver engineered it. They locked themselves in overnight – this would be '84, '85-ish. My secretary rang me up about ten o'clock in the morning – and basically my staff and students couldn't get into the studio because the Roses had locked themselves in and they wouldn't let any fucker in. I was still in bed and I didn't know who she was talking about so I asked, "Who are they? What do they look like?" So she gave me an explanation, said they've got a bit of an attitude, and I realised who she meant.'

Pete Garner believes that the demo captures the band perfectly: 'It sounds better than the Hannett album we recorded later on! A lot rawer. You can hear Reni's drums. I never thought that Hannett suited the band. Listen to our earlier stuff, that's what we really sounded like!'

Down in Spirit there is an eight-track round the back. Generations of Manchester engineers have learned their trade in there. For this session the Roses worked with Tim Oliver. They handed him a tape of their glam punk heroes Slaughter And The Dogs. 'We told him that's the sound that we were looking for,' laughs Andy Couzens. For these south Manchester lads, heads filled with glam and punk, the Wythenshawe-based punk band with their 'Where Have All The Bootboys Gone' anthem was the closest that they had to role models in the search for the perfect pop sound.

They commenced with the first of the two ten-hour sessions, recording 'Tragic Roundabout' and 'Misery Dictionary'. It was at this point that they decided to change the name of 'Misery Dictionary' to 'So Young' because the original sounded 'too Smithsy' and if there was one thing they didn't want, it was to get confused with those fast-rising superstars of the Manchester scene.

They then recorded 'Mission Impossible' and 'Nowhere Fast'. Anyone who has heard these demos will tell you that they are a lot more representative of what the band was about. You can still hear flashes of the poppier end of punk on the Buzzcocks rush of 'Nowhere Fast' (or 'Just A Little Bit' as it would become), 'Mission Impossible', and the bass-driven 'Tragic Roundabout'.

Ian Brown singing vocals in the studio for the first time since singing one of the three tracks on that Patrol demo sounds youthful, his double-tracked voice cutting clearly through the twin guitar attack that would dominate were it not for that explosive drummer.

'Reni never played the same thing twice,' laughs Pete admiringly, 'which was pretty mental when it came to recording!'

They copied up the demo onto a hundred cassettes and John did his first piece of Roses artwork, photocopying the band's hand-drawn logo stuck on to a paisley shirt. Armed with a demo and a proper set, it was time to get playing.

'We'd buy *Sounds* every week,' explains Pete Garner, adding, 'and Ian noticed an advert for a benefit gig in London with an address to send a demo to and, being the main hustler in the band, phoned up and sent a tape to this woman called Caroline Read who was promoting the show at the Moonlight. We didn't really expect to get a reply, but Ian told her that we were massive in Manchester. I guess that must have swung it.'

Ian remembers sending off the demo. 'The first Roses gig was at the Moonlight in Hampstead, an anti-heroin benefit that Pete Townshend put on. I'd seen an advert in *Sounds* saying they were looking for bands. Caroline Read, who managed this Welsh band Mercenary Skank, was putting on an anti-heroin benefit at the Moonlight club in London. I lived in Hulme, where everyone was on skag except me. So I wrote a letter saying, "I'm surrounded by skagheads, I wanna smash 'em. Can you give us a show?" And they did.'

23 October 1984: The Roses' Debut Gig

Ian Brown was once asked if he rehearsed his stage moves in front of a mirror. 'Well, when you do karate, you train in front of mirrors – so I'd always looked in mirrors. A few Ali moves but I never stood there with a tennis racquet,' he answered. In the earlier days the speed-driven band were riding on a surfeit of energy and Brown was a bug-eyed wildman diving around the stage. Their high-energy rock'n'roll demanded some sort of confrontational stage chops and Brown was ready to develop them.

They had rehearsed hard over that summer. The addition of Reni had made a massive difference. Suddenly they'd felt like a proper band…and now they finally had a gig. Not just a local circuit gig, either. A show with Pete fucking Townhsend!

The gig was a cause close to Brown's heart. His junkie neighbours in the Hulme high rises had got him down. Speed was OK for the early Roses but the sheer waste of time and life due to the heroin monster was something he disliked. Brown was always very anti-hard drugs, maybe a reflection of his martial arts background.

'On the top floor of Charles Barry Crescent where I was living there was an opera singer next to me and a dentist and all them heads were all junkies. I said I wanted to do something about that. They wrote back and asked us to play and that was our first gig.'

Pete Townshend! Of all the sixties bands, The Who were the closest to the Roses – a wild drummer, an introverted artistic guitar player, a dynamic frontman and a rock solid bass player: the same dynamic that sparked off both bands.

An anti-heroin gig at the Moonlight Club, London – what a start! Garner still has the poster to this day, a photocopied A3 with the Roses' name scrawled on in felt-tip alongside secret headliner Pete Townshend and the other support, Mercenary Skank.

Before the gig the whole band went down to London to meet Caroline Read and her then-boyfriend, Mercenary Skank frontman Mark 'Scratch' Downing. It was a measure of the band's gang-like determination.

The demo and Brown's gab on the phone had certainly done their job; Mercenary Skank were blown away by the songs. Not only had Read rung back with the go-ahead for the show, she also asked the band if they wanted her to manage them.

With nothing to lose, they piled into Andy's white Chevy van and went down to London to sort out some sort of management deal.

Mercenary Skank, at the time, were an up-and-coming punkier version of The Alarm from the same town, Rhyl. Downing now lives in Exeter where he restores antiques. When called upon to restore antique memories of the Roses he is keen to talk the band up: 'They did the anti-heroin benefit with us at the Moonlight Club in West Hampstead. The first impression of them was when they sent our management company a demo tape. We thought it was fantastic. We played it all the time. Being management we'd get the odd tape. The management was part of the band as well. At the time there was no one we really liked. The Stone Roses sounded like they had the same kind of bloodline, like The Clash and the Pistols and stuff like that. It was a really good tape. I remember "Misery Dictionary" ["So Young"] being really good. They had a surly, shitty attitude which we thought was great.'

The Stone Roses played on their confrontational, surly attitude.

'We all went down to London before the Moonlight gig,' says Pete. 'Always the whole band, everyone, went to everything. Loads of people said we seemed aggressive at the time. I didn't see it as aggression as I was in the bubble. People said that they were intimidated by us, they assumed everyone in the band was a wanker, because we were pretty arrogant.'

But this surliness didn't put Mark and Caroline off the band. 'We said that we liked them so much that we would like to help them. Caroline wanted to sign them to her company, Before the Storm Management. She asked them to do gigs with us. They seemed pretty keen to get involved.'

A couple of weeks later they returned for the gig. The band hopped into Andy's white Chevy van with Kaiser at the wheel. 'When the Roses started I used to help them out. I would drive the van and help set the gear up.'

They hit the motorway to London. None of them had been on stage since 1980. Four full years of rehearsing or hanging out, scootering or working, and at last they were about to get the adrenaline rush of being on stage again. Only this time they were armed with an amazing drummer, a drummer who had his own explosive way of playing. Pete Garner is still buzzing over Reni's playing.

'Reni never played the same thing twice. You'd do a song and then five minutes later when you played it again he played it completely differently. He was amazing. It was like having ten Keith Moons playing all at once.

'The Moonlight was interesting as we played the only full cover that we ever did. We did a version of Nazz's "Open My Eyes". Me and John were mad on Nazz. It was one of our favourite groups at the time. Pete Townshend told us we reminded him of the early Who so we had hard-ons all the way home!'

Nazz were built around Todd Rundgren (who also produced The New York Dolls) who formed the band in 1967 in the USA. 'Open My Eyes' was their first single but they fell apart by 1969 after a disastrous attempt to move into the teen market.

Nazz's sharp looks and clever songs made them a hit with John Squire and Pete Garner and 'Open My Eyes' was the only fully played serious cover the Roses ever did. Nazz have since slipped out of the pages of rock history but nonetheless in Manchester they had somehow retained two youthful fans.

The Roses exploded through the song: they just completely went for it, wired on adrenaline and cheap speed, and buzzing from getting out of the van after the long, dark journey down to London.

Normally in soundchecks the rest of the bands stand around looking bored. For most bands the soundcheck is a chore. But the Roses were going ape and the other bands stood there open-mouthed. After they finished the tune the assorted musicians clapped.

It was a supreme accolade and a pointer to just how good the Roses actually were after all those months of endless rehearsing. And the Nazz song was perfect for their warm-up.

Says Andy, 'That first gig at the Moonlight. In the soundcheck the song that we did was "Open My Eyes" by Nazz. The version we did was really tough. It's a great song live, really good and people were going, "Fucking hell". People were coming up and saying, "Where are you from?" We had had that much whizz by this point, that everything was very intense.'

Cowboy hat-wearing indie rockers High Noon played first and then the Roses hit the stage for their set. There were no nerves. Nothing. Just confidence. A speed-fried confidence. The supremely arrogant frontman gave the crowd his combative staring-eyes attack. The lanky bass player rocked out, his long black hair hanging over his face. One guitar player shuffled backwards and forwards, peeking out shyly from under his fringe; the other toughed it out with a tight quiff. They looked like a street gang, a right bunch of moochers.

The set was just about all the songs that they had managed to finish writing in the months since Reni had joined. 'Mission Impossible' opened the show, followed by 'Nowhere Fast', 'All Stripped Down', 'Tragic Round-about' (their song about Martin Luther King) and the set ended with 'Heart of Staves'. This was a band that was making no apologies for its presence.

Mind you, other factors were at work that night. Couzens laughs as he looks back on that awesome début show. 'Some of us were doing loads of speed that night. In those days we were massively into speed. We hardly ever drank and we never smoked dope. One person who never did any speed was Reni but he was such a natural speed head he didn't need any.'

Old mate and former Waterfront vocalist Kaiser drove them down to London. 'That time they played the first gig, the anti-drugs gig, they were out of their heads speeding!' But then the Roses, like most of the punk generation, didn't look on speed as a drug. Smack or dope were drugs. Hippy shit. Speed made you think. Fierce. Made you more aware. Crazier. It was sharp and dangerous. It didn't mong you out. Well, not for a few years anyway.

But of course, the real reason the Roses really flew that night was that they had worked their arses off for the show. 'We rehearsed like mad for that gig – we put everything into it,' recalls Andy. And not just musically: 'We worked out all our moves and what we were going to wear, every-thing. We knew that we were special, we knew that we were very good.'

The Roses had spent their whole post-punk lives living for this moment – this gig was everything that they had been dreaming about, waiting for.

For a northern band to début in London was always an experience of mixed fortunes. It was the big moment because the whole music business was for some reason based in the capital and every little band in the country had to come 'down sarf' and show themselves to the lazy A&R departments of the early eighties.

Pete Townshend was blown away. He couldn't wait to get the loose-limbed drummer kid up there for his encores.

Remembers Ian: 'Reni was made up – his first-ever gig and there he was doing "Pictures of Lily" and "Substitute" with Pete Townshend! We came off stage and Townshend was like, "You look really good up there and your drummer's great". Then he said, "As an end-of-the-night thing, I wanna play a couple of tunes. Do you want to do it?" Reni's like, "Yeah!"

'He tried to poach Reni for his solo album and Reni told him to fuck off. We were made up because it showed the belief Reni had in us – we had this megastar at our first-ever show and he was telling us we look good on stage and that and how great our drummer was and wanted to poach him, and he stayed.'

Pete Townshend may have been a rock legend but it didn't faze the young band. Couzens, like the rest of the band, acted as surly as possible. 'He had asked if he could borrow our drummer and we just pointed to this heap on the floor and said, "If you want him he's over there, just go and ask him."

'Everyone had a colossal ego in the band. I remember at the end of the set at those times Reni would collapse on to the floor. It was hard to tell whether he was putting it on or not, although he put so much into it, it could have conceivably been true.'

When Townshend played 'Substitute', Reni, who was a fan of sorts, but not a massive one, turned to Pete Garner and shouted 'How the fuck does it go?'

Says Pete, 'As if he was bothered, know what I mean, he could just drum to anything, he was a total natural.'

They followed it up with a last run through of 'Won't Get Fooled Again'. The rest of the band just stood there laughing. What a night.

The gig was a major success for the young band. They had impressed some of the most respected old-boy musicians, they had blown everyone away with their sheer raw power, they had drawn an instant offer of management by a London manager and to cap it all the music press was down at the gig in the form of Garry Johnson from the ever-perceptive (now sadly defunct) *Sounds*. He was there to review their first-ever gig and arrangements were swiftly made for an interview in the next few weeks.

Back in Manchester things were also moving. A music biz contact of Steve Adge's called Howard Jones asked him if he knew of any cool bands rehearsing in town and to keep a good look-out for anything out there. Steve was only too happy to oblige.

Late October 1984, Adge rang up Jones and said, 'Yeah, there's something here you may well be interested in looking at. They're called The Stone Roses.'

Howard Jones, a ginger-haired maverick music nut who had just left the Hacienda, where he was general manager, was a man with a mission. He wanted to prove to the Factory people that he could cut it on his own and wanted a band to manage. He made a few calls and prepared himself to check this band out.

The Stone Roses, meanwhile, had already played that début London show and, unbeknown to Jones, already had some sort of London management.

This unexpected London angle suited the band because the Roses had a plan. It wasn't a foolproof plan. But it was a plan. The band that had come together in the suburbs outside the city's hip inner circle had a complete contempt for the Manchester hipster music scene. This was the band that would write what some would say was the anti-Hacienda/Factory song 'Fall'.

Being punk/mod/scooterists, the Roses had their own definition of cool, a cool that was a long way from Factory's anti-rockist art-school version of events. While Factory were celebrating the whole morass of post-Joy Division outfits, the Roses were still sticking up for bands like Slaughter And The Dogs and banging on about Northern Soul. It was different versions of the same city.

They felt like outsiders in Manchester; the city's scene had developed a long way away from where they were going. They were on the outside looking in before they had even started.

So, fuck Manchester!

Let's go and play in London first.

Manchester can wait.

We are the Roses.

Says Andy: 'We didn't want anything to do with Manchester at all. We opposed all the raincoat-wearing Manchester Factory bands. All that cliquey elitism.'

And now things were up and running at the other end of the country. This was doing things differently and it appealed to them. They were going to do this from the outside. Fuck all that local band shit.

The Stone Roses seemed to have achieved more at their first-ever gig than most bands achieve in a year.

Still buzzing, they had climbed back into the white Chevy for the long haul back to Manchester. They had come down to London and blown everyone away. They knew that they were good. Maybe that inner confidence wasn't just bullshit, maybe they were a band that was going to tear it up, and tear it up quickly.

The gig also got them their first review of sorts. In the crowd was the lugubrious Mick Mercer – writer of the Goth manuals, some-time editor of the now-defunct *ZigZag* and all-round eccentric. Then writing for *Melody Maker*, his review appeared on 10 November. The band, press junkies at the time, scanned the review. They were mentioned in the list of bands at the top of the piece but Mick had neglected to mention them in the review itself.

'We came back to Manchester after that gig thinking that we were The Beatles and went to buy the paper and there was no mention at all,' laughs Garner.

Stop! Start! Stop! Start! – That's band life for you!

So it was back to Spirit with renewed vigour to attack the songs and wonder what to do next.

There was the *Sounds* interview to do and Caroline Read had offered them another couple of shows playing with Mercenary Skank on 21 and 22 November. There was somewhere in Exeter and another show in London at the Ad Lib club; a mini tour! Two dates on the road.

And Howard Jones wanted to meet them. He was talking about band management and record deals – were they interested? They decided to meet him.

They had already agreed to let Caroline Read manage them, but what the hell! More managers means more gigs. Let's see who can get the most, eh?

The Roses Get the Jones

Howard was buzzing. He could trust The Adge. The tip-off had got him thinking. Apparently there was a hot band in town right under his nose.

First, though, he had to get everything into place. What's the best way to show the Factory up about record labels! I'll form my own! And who better to do it with than another ex-mate of Factory, legendary producer and wildman Martin Hannett.

Before going to see the Roses, Jones rang up Martin Hannett, the maverick who had made his name with his imaginative production with Joy Division and a whole run of Factory acts.

The two met up. Hannett was looking for a new band to work with. He loosely decided to come in with Jones and get a new label together. On 12 November the pair of them met up with Tim Chambers and formed Thin Line records. Now he was ready to meet the band.

On 15 November Jones went to Spirit to meet the Roses. He was full of attitude as he entered Tariff Street. He had something to prove. 'It had become a bit of a thing for me to find a good band in Manchester. I went down to Spirit to check out the Roses and...'

Picks up Andy, 'Howard Jones came down. He had just lost his job as general manager of the Hacienda. He said he was setting something up with Martin Hannett.'

He went down the stairs into the tight warren of corridors and up to the rehearsal rooms. The dull thud of other bands rehearsing away, the confusing mush of sound that makes up the eternal din of rehearsal rooms worldwide greeted him. He then pushed the door open and apprehensively entered the room. The Roses were in there, looking young, tough and mean, but were also deceptively polite. The band started to play and at first Jones was very confused.

'They were absolutely fucking diabolical. It was a racket, but one of those kinds of rackets that are so exciting. They had songs there. I couldn't believe some of the actual lyrical content. It was brilliant. I'm into lyrics as well – I love Dylan – and Ian Brown's lyrics were great.

'I was thinking does Ian Brown realise how evocative his words were? They work on so many different levels. Does he understand how powerful these words are? I eventually got to know Ian and got to realise how deep a thinker he really is. There isn't a thing he doesn't think about. I thought this guy is a great songwriter.'

In the murk of the room and in the endless racket Jones started to notice more than the songs. He was instantly struck by the way the band hung together. There was no slacking here. This was a band that knew how to be a band. Says Howard, 'They looked great. Like a gang. Each one was different. Like a tall one, a thin one, a hard one, a soft-looking one, and John looked like if you said boo he would jump. Reni looked so young, I didn't realise he was so young. I couldn't believe it [he was 20 and they were 22–23].'

Despite the 'racket', despite everything, Jones had to think on his feet. There were decisions to be made. 'Everything is about instinct. I'd heard a lot of bands that were better than them and more ready musically, but I thought this band has got legs, this will go. I was full of it anyway. I was the big time Hacienda head honcho, Mr Manchester who didn't pay to get in anywhere!'

The rehearsal had made an impact, although they had been loose and ragged and very, very loud. Howard knew instinctively that here was a band that could set him up. Get this crew in the studio and some of those songs that are buried in the noise will leap out. Martin Hannett would make sure of that. There was potential there…

The next day he went back to another rehearsal and they talked it out. Quickly Howard found that there was some sort of rapport between him and the band. They definitely knew what they didn't like. 'They hated the way Hacienda and Factory dominated the Manc scene…They saw me as an insider until I gave them my spiel about how I was nothing to do with Factory any more.

'Steve Adge had warned me about this – about how they hated all that scene. I told them that I'm resigning from Factory and starting my own company. By this time I had spent a lot of time with Martin Hannett who was also pissed off with Factory. I told them that we're going to start a label and the first band I'll sign will be recorded by Martin. If you go with me now you will have product out within months.'

They agreed that Howard was now their manager. Says Ian, 'That was Howard Jones, the original manager of the Hacienda, who became our manager in 1984. He formed the label so we could release the single, rather than go for a full deal.'

The band now had a proper manager. For Andy Couzens it was an odd feeling.

Howard was like having your dad round. All of a sudden it stopped being a racket. It was a bit more serious. He said he couldn't make out the songs because it was so loud and distorted, but there was something in the self-belief and conviction that we had that made him think, 'yeah, these are great.'

Jones told the band that he wanted to sign them to this new label. He said it would rival Factory and they would be the first band on it. They would also be able to get loads of free studio time in Strawberry Studios, the major north-west studio in Stockport, because Hannett had some down-time owed to him there. They may all be night sessions but what the fuck, they were free!

They could record an album or at least demos for next to nothing with one of the hippest producers in the country. This was the man who had produced Joy Division and masterminded the whole Factory sound.

Big deal, thought the coolly sullen band. That meant nothing to them. But they remembered that Hannett was also the man responsible for Slaughter And The Dogs' crisp, neat and powerful production of the 'Cranked Up Really High' single and this impressed them so much more. When they eventually went to the studio this was the record they took, trying to get their melodic anthems crossed with the sheer visceral thrill of Slaughter And The Dogs' amphetamine rushes.

So the Roses had found themselves a manager – a manic sharp-looking geezer who seemed to appear from nowhere – a producer and a label. Things were moving very fast.

Howard liked what he saw but there was something rankling him. 'Your bass player's great but he needs a haircut,' was his summation of the situation.

'I thought, you cunt,' guffaws Garner. 'I told him to fuck off. I wasn't happy at all.'

But Jones still became the group's sole manager. Or so he thought. What they had neglected to tell Howard was that they already had a manager of sorts, having hustled themselves a loose arrangement with Caroline Read back in London.

Recalls Howard: 'I didn't know anything about Caroline Read. What happened was that she thought she was managing them and they never spoke to me about it! She was ringing Andy and he never told me. The first time I met her was four years later when I was going to Berlin with The Buzzcocks. I didn't know anything about Caroline.'

They also had their first piece of national press, in *Sounds*, thanks to Garry Johnson. The hard-working Ian Brown had singled Johnson out as the journo most likely to get behind the band. Johnson had joined *Sounds* with the help of his mate Garry Bushell, and Brown had posted him a cassette.

'I put Ian Brown's tape on in the office and it sounded brilliant,' Garry says. 'He had sent me a letter saying he had seen stuff I'd written in *Sounds* about other bands and thought that I would like it. I got in touch with him that night on the phone. I was so impressed. They'd made a cover for the cassette as well; it looked great. We had a few chats on the phone then I went to Manchester to meet them. They met me off the train and I spent the weekend up there.'

Avid music press reader Pete Garner was also aware of the journalist. 'That November Garry Johnson had rang up because Ian had sent him one of the August demos as well. We all read *Sounds* and Ian knew that Garry was the one writer who could be into us. He rang us up and came up to Manchester to interview us on 30 November.'

They whisked the journalist round to Andy's house. 'I met them at the station,' remembers Garry. 'Andy turned up in this big white van. I went round to his house in Manchester. It was like a mansion in the country with a snooker table, a really nice place. I stayed round there.'

Johnson was backing the band to the hilt. After the interview he had the band mentioned in *Sounds* every week.

'I got the band in the *Sounds* gossip column all the time. They would come down to London and I would take them to parties. There was a party on a roof garden. Spandau Ballet and Leee John from Imagination. Another time at the Cockney Pride pub Ian and Renee [as Garry calls the drummer] got on stage with Frankie Flame and sang football songs – that got in as well.'

Johnson started trying to get the band noticed. 'They would come down to London all the time and stayed round my flat in Hackney. I was a big Jam fan and mates with Bruce Foxton and there was talk of him producing them but nothing came of it. We went to meet him anyway.'

Johnson took it upon himself to do a campaign on behalf of the band. There was something that he liked about the group, making him the only journalist in London who was on their case, but even with contacts finding a record deal was no easy feat.

'I took them to every record company in London and they got turned down by all of them,' he explains. 'Pat Stead was a friend at Sony and I took a tape up to Hugh Gadson, who's now the co-manager of Madness and would also be the manager of EMF. I did everything I could to persuade him to like the band, but he had just signed Ring Of Roses and didn't want two bands called the Roses.

'So, I took them to see Joanna Burns at Phonogram and, also, Steve Tannebum. I went to Arista's Patsy Johnston…the band got thrown out of some labels because of the way they looked! At the time, they always had this little following of skinheads who would come up with them and were all different ages. One looked about 14, one about 20, a little mob – nice kids but looked dodgy.'

It seems there were plenty of kids on the street who could see something they liked, but there were no record labels snapping them up…just yet.

The band set out on the road again for the two other shows set up by Read. The first was supporting her other charges, Mercenary Skank, on 21 November at Exeter Labour Club. The Skank's Mark Downing remembers the show.

'The gig was put on by a fan of ours called Alf: there was hardly anyone there. They went on stage and made a racket…they were great, the gig really stands out in my memory. I haven't seen that many bands that are that good, particularly in the early days, 'cos it's so hard to do when you're not gig-tight…it was their image more than anything…

'They really reminded me of early Clash. For some reason I always remember John Squire having some sort of flares on. He always had his distortion pedal full on! I tried to tell him he didn't have to do that. Andy and Ian Brown would career about the stage. They also had a very glam, long-haired Gothy type in the band as well…and they might have had an attitude but they were really nice people as well, polite even.'

Joe Rebel, the legendary Clash fanatic from Exeter, was also at the gig. 'I was down the front for the Roses but all I can remember is Ian Brown had star quality even then, shuffling and staring out the audience (all 40 of 'em!). I don't think anyone then would have predicted the huge influence The Stone Roses had on a whole generation.

'A nifty poster for the gig ended up on a wall at my then-band's rehearsal space. Yonks before eBay and megabucks for rock'n'roll memorabilia – unfortunately the poster is no more – the place was flooded and was swept away up the River Exe.'

In their naivéte the Roses had set out on the long drive to Exeter, believing that this gig would be the same sort of thing as the Moonlight, the same story as London – an astounded crowd surfing on their sheer talent. This is how they saw it and it made the seven-hour drive rush past far quicker. Naturally it was a damp squib.

Welcome to the real world of the road.

Fuck, they were going to have to work a damned sight harder than they had figured. But that work didn't mean the usual thing of slogging around in Manchester like other bands, as Couzens points out.

'Manchester was a pit. There was nowhere to play. We just thought we may as well concentrate on London. Me and Ian would go down to London and do some hustling as well as the stuff that Caroline Read sorted for us.'

The day after Exeter they were back in London, playing with Mercenary Skank again at Kensington's Ad Lib club. This, according to witnesses at the time, was their best gig yet. It was billed as the Christmas punk extravaganza in an attempt to get some heads in the place. A curious venue tucked away in some posh looking Victorian blocks, the Ad Lib was a regular gigging venue in the mid-eighties, with people like Johnny Thunders playing there (what seemed like) all the time.

The Stone Roses Ad Lib gig was reviewed in *Sounds*, their first-ever proper piece of national music press before the *NME* and *Melody Maker*, and printed on 5 January 1985. The journalist was Robin Gibson, a firebrand Scot who loved his Stonesy glam punk as much as any of the band and knew what he was talking about. He never minced his words.

Gibson hated the Roses and slated the gig. Years later his hatred is just as strong. 'They were crap, man. I never understood the whole thing,' he says 20 years on. 'I just don't understand why they were so popular. I remember when they started taking off, years later, and Hall or Nothing (their press people) gave me 10 singles to hand out around the office and everyone went on about how crap they were. Weeks later there was a clamouring to write about them. I still didn't get it.'

Gibson stuck the boot in with the review, claiming the Roses were like Mercenary Skank before they got any good and that they were hindered by their singer. He did admit that they had the power but not the songs. He just wasn't having it at all.

An interesting footnote to the Ad Lib gig is the small shot on the inside of the *Garage Flower* album showing the band on stage at the venue. Ian and Andy look remarkably similar, in white kecks and short hair, while John and Pete hold up the glam end of the band. Already, though, they look like a band, a gang.

Their London manager Caroline Read was still enthralled by the band's young drummer. Says Mark Downing, 'Musically Reni was the main strength at the time and she was in total adulation of him. She tried to nick him for us. She wanted him to drum for Mercenary Skank and if she could have got him she would have.'

But Pete maintains that this could never have happened. 'By this point there was never any question of him joining anyone. We were locked in by then. It was the five musketeers and all that. Even if AC/DC had asked him he would have turned them down. You only get one chance with people your own age and you're all mates and we all knew it was our one chance to do it.'

The Ad Lib hadn't been the same sort of buzz as the gig last month at the Moonlight, but they still went down well and still got people talking.

They returned back to the north buzzing over their raids on London and ready to get a début northern show under their belts. They had a big crew of mates, c/o the scooter scene and Steve Adge's ready-made crew of muckers from Hyde, as well as the Failsworth connection with their mate Mani, and their own south Manc boys…mates who were starting to buzz on their tales of gigs in London, starting to buzz on the demo that was floating about. Everyone wanted to see the band play up north. They returned to their rehearsal room and carried on rehearsing till the end of the year. There was talk of gigs in January and February and that *Sounds* feature was to run just after Christmas.

Meanwhile Jones was getting organised. He blagged Hannett and some down-time at Strawberry for their first proper sessions in mid-January. The Roses were ready to record their début single and potential début album. 1984 was a good year. What would 1985 hold?

1985

January

Traditionally January has the music press tips for the upcoming year. Half the fun is just how spectacularly wrong these can be. Flicking through *Sounds*, the band were buzzing to see that they were tipped. Garry Johnson was now well on their case.

Over the years there have been several claimants to being the first journalist to get on The Stone Roses' case. Not even in Manchester had anyone picked up on them. They didn't hang out on the local media scene. They were outsiders. No one has ever mentioned Johnson who went on a one-man campaign for the band, dragging A&R down to their gigs, dropping their name off to all and sundry, really pumping them up.

He predicted great things for the Roses when he had to choose his bands for 1985. Printed on 29 December in *Sounds*, Garry Johnson's prediction stated that 'The Stone Roses will have a hit indie single and album in the next year...' His other tip was a long-lost band called Immaculate Fools. This was to be followed up with the full-page interview he had conducted a couple of months previously.

On 4 January 1985 the Roses had played their first headline show at the Fulham Greyhound by default. It was intended to be another support with Mercenary Skank but the Skank pulled out of the gig because Mark had laryngitis.

The Roses were supported by Doncaster's long-forgotten Last Party (raved about in *ZigZag* by Mick Mercer and an amiable outfit). The Roses played hard, driven by Reni's sweat-soaked Keith Moonisms. Garry Johnson was, yet again, on their case, dragging down A&R from Rough Trade – a label who a couple of years later would be embroiled in a battle to sign the band.

At Fulham they decided to close with 'Getting Plenty', a brand new song: a bruised love song in another great set of dark, cynical lyrics.

Up till now they had closed with 'Tell Me' because its extended instrumental sections gave Ian Brown the chance to wander into the crowd for his confrontation with the audience bit. This was his key move in the early period: walk into the crowd and sing into people's faces.

The only problem was that 'Getting Plenty' was too new and, typical of a new song getting its first gig, it fell apart. Not the climatic exit to the set that they were hoping for.

The following week they were back in London again. The ubiquitous Garry Johnson had managed to blag them tickets to another one of those showbiz parties where freebies were rained upon the celebs and the guest list was stuffed full of wannabees, ne'er do wells, chancers and attendant scum.

It was the day before the *Sounds* feature went in and Johnson also took them around a few more record companies with their demo. The band's London excursions seem to have been conducted without the knowledge of their other manager, Howard, who was still setting up his label in Manchester!

They first checked out CBS and then went down to Arista again. Sat around in the air-conditioned vacuum of Arista they were stunned to spot David Cassidy pacing around the offices. No one had heard of him for years and here he was on the verge of a comeback. They sat there staring at him, the young bucks versus the old guard – that's the showbiz way.

None of the labels were interested in the Roses, what the fuck? What do they know anyway?

The party was a spectacular rooftop garden do. Everyone, apart from the Roses, was famous. The place was crawling with mid eighties celebs, the Rolling Stones, Slade, Bananarama, Captain Sensible, The Cult and again David Cassidy.

Standing in the corners were Chris Quintin, star of *Coronation Street* and Tik and Tok (two New Romantic mime artists) and it slipped further downwards from there to hungry 'B'-list celebs. It made the front covers of all the next day's national press. Pumped with an endless supply of free food and beer, the Roses wandered around swigging free champagne out of bottles and lobbing the half empty bottles over the balcony.

The Roses must have felt totally out of place. All those months in the rehearsal room and now here they were in New Romantic London!

'We felt like impostors,' spits Pete Garner. 'But we met Captain Sensible and we were excited. We loved The Damned. We told him that we loved his song "Idiot Box" [obscure Damned track from their critically slaughtered second album that was one of the sole Sensible contributions to their canon and a way cool tune to boot], he couldn't believe it.'

Captain Sensible considered trying to sign the fledgling band: 'I remember The Stone Roses really early on. I had my own label called

Deltic in the late eighties. The idea behind it was we would put out good music when all the other labels were putting out shit. The idea was that one record would pay for the next one. We had a lovely secretary that worked there called Karen and her flatmate had a band called Trash. She kept badgering us to sign them.

'We wanted to do The Stone Roses because we thought they were phenomenal. They had sent us this 4-track cassette demo. We were so vibed up by it but we put the Trash record out and it bombed; it didn't sell one fucking copy…so we couldn't sign The Stone Roses.'

At the end of the party, The Roses capped the evening off by having their picture taken with Bruce Foxton of their beloved Jam, all except for Clash fan John Squire, who apparently hated the Woking trio.

The Roses kept travelling backwards and forwards to London. They would play gigs or just go and hang out and every week Garry Johnson would get a story into *Sounds* gossip column. He also kept taking them to parties and checking their gigs.

'The second time I saw them was at the Marquee on 7 January. I was blown away with it. My impression was that they blew Mercenary Skank off stage. The crowd were not there when they first came on but they got closer and closer and after they were really buzzing. I remember there was talk of Caroline Read managing them that night.

'They used to stay at mine. I used to supply them with sandwiches and flasks of drink if they were going to drive back to Manchester. Ian always had fruit and they would have marmalade and peanut butter sand-wiches too. Some nights we would hang out at McDonald's on Charing Cross because it was one of those rare places in them days that was open all night.'

'Flower Power': The First Feature

Garry Johnson had already done the interview in November and had trav-elled up to Manchester where he stayed at Andy's house and interviewed them in the greasy caff on Piccadilly; just by the bus station and under-neath the massive slab of concrete skyscraper that dominated and insulted the city centre at the time.

When the feature went into *Sounds* in mid-January, Johnson had even managed to get the Roses' name on to the front cover of the paper. Under the headline 'Flower Power' (the first of years of crap puns on the name), the picture of the group with the piece had them staring meanly at the camera. Ian and Andy's hair was slicked back, Pete had a Stooges/MC5 style black mop and Reni looked like a 14-year-old kid, whilst John was in glam punk mode. It was a variation of that shot that crops up every now and then when someone wants to call them Goths. They do look a bit of a hotchpotch mob, but they were quite definitely not Goths. Garry Johnson raved in the piece: 'The Stone Roses have an indie smash single and album inside them.'

Couzens is still bemused by this early burst of press activity. 'We were staggered. From then on we thought that Johnson was a really good contact and we thought, right, let's dig deep into this guy and see what he has got for us. We stayed at his house, me and Ian – a couple of head cases on speed – he was like a like-minded soul, he was a speed freak and he always wanted to be in a band – that was his whole thing, he'd put on The Small Faces' "Lazy Sunday Afternoon" and sing along to it.'

In the piece, The Stone Roses also fibbed to Johnson, claiming that they had coach loads of fans that followed them everywhere. It was a self-fulfilling prophecy as months later, when the Roses played Preston, the coach loads turned up – they were one of the first new generation bands to get that huge street following. Years later, the tradition would continue as the fans would cram buses and coaches and travel across Europe on a booze and drugs-fuelled binge to check out their heroes in another bout of incredible street decadence. It's a tradition that has roots right back in the scooter gang background of the Roses.

Garry Johnson was fascinated by the band's cross-section of influences: 'They talked about early Bowie, Mott The Hoople, Redskins, "Lean On Me". They liked The Jam as well. They liked the Pistols and obviously liked a lot of old glam and punk. It was street glam punk though – more Slaughter And The Dogs – not just raw street punk but the bands with an image and not just the sound.

'They talked about how they used to go to Manchester airport a lot; they'd smoke weed and go up there and chill out and watch the planes land.'

Getting a feature in the music press is a big deal for a new band. It's the first big break, serving the notice of something happening. This was fast. Rarely does a band get a full-page feature this early. They were three gigs old, unknown in their home town, unknown anywhere really.

They knew that they were on to something good but they didn't expect it to come together this fast. Usually a press agent hustles some press or there is a record out; there is a reason for the article.

Johnson was well on the case here even if it would be a few years till he was proved correct. This was the mid-eighties and this was *Sounds*. *Sounds* was always hot for new bands. Certain writers could just walk in and put bands into the paper this early.

The Stone Roses Record Their First Single

On 13 March the band decamped to Stockport's Strawberry Studios to record 'So Young' and 'Tell Me' with Martin Hannett. They informed Hannett that working with Joy Division was all well and good but it was that Slaughter And The Dogs sound they were really after. Fine sentiments but as a band they didn't really sound much like Slaughter. There was none of that incendiary speed-driven Wayne Rossi guitar going on here. Even on these two more up-tempo songs the Roses were dealing in effects-laden guitars and subtle dynamics. This was not relentless glam street punk but something else.

Hannett set about recording the band in his usual painstaking manner, adding effects all over the place, carving the sound into whatever landscapes he wanted. For this he was ably assisted by engineer Chris Nagle.

It was Hannett's status as a living legend that was useful for giving Howard Jones' Thin Line label credibility – more usefully they also managed to get the band four free days in Strawberry Studios and this was where they recorded the début single.

Andy Couzens' lawyer Stephen Lea, who would go on to help the band in the early days, remembers the sequence of events differently. 'Andy and his dad paid for the early recordings with Martin Hannett. It was before Howard Jones got involved and then Andy came to me and said they were to be managed by this guy who was running the Hacienda, Howard Jones – he and Martin and someone else would be involved in putting out some recordings and that's where Thin Line came from.'

Between 13 and 17 March the band trooped down to Strawberry Studios in Stockport to grab some of Hannett's down-time, to cut their début single, 'So Young'/'Tell Me'.

Named after The Beatles' 'Strawberry Fields Forever', Strawberry had been set up by Stockport-based band 10CC in the mid-seventies. At one time it was the best 'state of the art' studio outside London. By the mid-eighties it was still the premier studio in Manchester, with Hannett working on most of his classic productions there.

Hannett had invented his own sound over the years. He was behind the monumental, ground-breaking sound of Joy Division's two crucial albums as well as ACR, John Cooper Clarke, and a whole host of Mancunian tracks. His harsh, cold, futuristic style perfectly suited those groups. He was also a total legend as much for his excessive lifestyle as for his production techniques.

Couzens vividly remembers the experience of working with Martin Hannett. It was a key educational moment for the band.

'I loved it, even though he was a total mess. He was bad on something at that point. He kept going on about trying to destroy his ego. But whatever he did, he did it instinctively. The record was engineered by Chris Nagle, and Ian Brown just didn't get on with him. He kept saying that he couldn't get any response from him, so you've got that, and Martin asleep on the couch. It was a weird way to make a record.'

Working with Hannett was always an interesting experience. Making up his own techniques along the way, linking together chains of effects to create strange new sounds and textures. To some he was a genius and to others a drink and drug-addled, crazed wildman.

Sometimes in the studio he would be inspired and brilliant and sometimes he would fall asleep under the desk, leaving engineer Chris Nagle to mop up, do all the work.

Ian Brown was bemused by the working process: 'Martin Hannett was producing the sessions. He was losing it a bit by then. I would be doing my vocals and I would say, "Hang on, I've got to get a drink of water," and he would lean over to the studio intercom and say, "Ian [Curtis] used to say that." He would do loads of mad things, like he would shut himself in the control room and lock the door so we couldn't get in. He would fall asleep on the desk and all the faders were pushed up on the desk in the shape of his belly where he had been sat. His engineer Chris Nagle said, "Just leave it, that's 'the curve', that's the Hannett sound!" So we left it. The version of "So Young" was so trebly that when we went to play it in the car and turned it up, Reni's nose went "bang" like that!

'It was too loud and trebly and so extreme, more extreme than the Mary Chain. He had lost it. He used to play "Transmission" quarter-inch tapes. He would put them on and bask in it as if he was trying to remember how to do it and we would say we wanted to sound like Slaughter And The Dogs' "Cranked Up Really High".'

The unassuming Nagle, who was as talented in his way as Hannett, went on to produce the début number one albums for The Charlatans and the Inspiral Carpets. A lack of ego has made sure that he has never really got the credit that he deserves for helping to create several groups' sounds.

Howard Jones, after working in the jaw of the beast, was obsessed by Factory and fascinated by its corporate image and artwork. You can see it in the press releases he put out for the band at the time. They are blatant rip-offs of the in-house Factory style – all stark visuals and sharp lines. This didn't make the band too happy – at the time they were hardly massive fans of the Factory machine.

The plan for 'So Young' was for it to come out in three entirely different mixes – each with its own separate catalogue number like Factory mixes. Mix number one was the song proper, mix two was to be a DJ-only mix and mix three was, crazily enough for a small label on a tight budget, to be finished off in Nashville (yup, that's right, the country-and-western town – someone had a bit of a pipe dream obviously). The fact that none of these mixes ever happened shouldn't surprise anyone.

'Imagine trying to get Hannett in and out of the country,' laughs a well-known Manchester scenester. 'What a field day the Customs would have had with him!'

Both tracks released later that year showcase the Roses' early sound. All powerful rock bluster and imaginative powerful mid-eighties chorused guitars, but even at this early stage you can hear Brown's English, nasal almost folk melodies, rising above the guitars. It was a younger, more aggressive, speed-driven Roses that sits in the vinyl here. Both tracks are in-your-face, no-nonsense rock with more bluster than the band's eventual sound. Curiously they have stood the test of time and their powerful sound lands between Theatre Of Hate and The Chameleons but with their own distinctive style. They show a band feeling its way out of punk and into somewhere else.

Ian Brown, though, was not fond of them. 'I wouldn't give 20p for that single,' sniffed the lead singer a few years later.

Howard Jones Gets Things Moving

Now in the management hot seat, it was time for Howard to prove that he could pull a few things off. He began by shaking down a few local contacts. *City Life* was already sorted. Bob Dickinson had the demo.

'The first thing I knew about the band was the demos,' remembers Bob, adding, 'I've still got the demo's handwritten label with the Zetland Road address on it, which was John Squire's flat where I did that interview with them for *City Life*. I do remember seeing them around that time. They were interesting to see, not like other bands. They had obviously listened to a lot of stuff from the sixties – what is now called freak beat – that's what I thought anyway. I think I may have projected my idea of music onto them. They may not have seen it that way. I certainly thought they were an interesting proposition at the time. I went to a few early gigs. I went to the one at the International 1 on 19 May and the one at the university union later in the year.

'They were hugely entertaining to watch because Ian was very balletic. He used to throw himself around and jump around like a ballet dancer. He could do all these moves whilst Reni was a great drummer, a stunning drummer. They were just entertaining, they didn't care. They were hugely arrogant about themselves on stage but not in a horrible or malicious way. They kind of had a point. I came away from the interview liking them even though they pooh-poohed my ideas about them.'

At the same time the band made a valuable connection on local radio. Tony the Greek (Tony Michaelides) was the DJ on the main local indie radio show on Piccadilly Radio and he was slipped one of the hundred demos by Pete Garner. Liking what he heard, he put it straight on his show and on 3 and 10 February he played a couple of tracks from the tape.

Unusually, the songs caused an instant reaction with the listeners. There were phone calls. It seemed that the Roses tunes had something. Tony the Greek booked them in for a session.

Paula Greenwood worked at Piccadilly Radio at the time and was a big fan (she would later move into journalism before setting up Playtime Records, putting out the first records from the Inspiral Carpets and New Fast Automatic Daffodils). 'When the demo tracks went out we had quite a lot of people calling in saying how much they liked the band,' she recalls. 'They did have quite a few hardcore fans and mates who were probably calling in, but the reaction was really positive on the phones. There were definitely people calling in asking for tracks to be played again and that's why we got them in for a live session.'

Pete Garner was surprised by the response. 'Loads of people rang up and we were booked for a session on 24 March – at that point we hadn't even played in Manchester.'

Piccadilly Radio had been asked to put together a showcase of local bands at Dingwalls in London. The bill had already been fixed but Tony managed to get the Roses added on at the last minute. 'It was like *Five go to London*,' says Paula. 'A package of five upcoming, local Manchester bands we put together to play in London.'

Dingwalls has been the scene of many Manc triumphs over the years. The year or so before I had seen The Smiths' début headline London show there, when they played to a half-filled room and left a huge heap of gladioli on the floor as the curious looked on. Only a couple of years later the Manc baggy scene would be introduced to London via the venue as both the Mondays and the Roses played classic shows there.

The other Manc bands making the furtive run down to the city for the Piccadilly show included Glee Company, Communal Drop, Fictitious Names and Laugh, who eventually transmuted into Intastella. The hosts were Bob Dillinger, a local singer-songwriter-come-comedian, and Mark Radcliffe, who was working at Piccadilly at the time.

The idea of a Manchester showcase, pre-1989, was fairly meaningless. Since punk, the city had been banging out influential and important groups but there was no scene as such, there was nothing connecting these groups. It was assumed that Manchester would soon run out of groups. With the Piccadilly Radio session booked, Howard printed up a flyer in a neo-Factory artwork style to flood the city with, publicising the session and a couple of upcoming shows. I remember seeing them in piles around the Boardwalk rehearsal room.

The buzz, though, was building.

Of course, being the Roses, when they finally trouped up to Piccadilly to record the session they did things their way. Says Pete, 'There was some throwing of chairs in the studio – a pretty reckless thing to do! But it gave it an edge!'

For the session they recorded their newly written 'I Wanna Be Adored', giving the now legendary song its first public hearing, and they played a harder, slightly faster version of 'Heart On The Staves' and the anthemic 'Tell Me'.

The session has gone on to become one of the most sought-after early Roses bootlegs. But what the fans don't realise is that they may not be getting the actual session itself. Recalls Pete, 'The radio session we did live and it went pretty well. Then as we were about to take everything down and go home, the recording engineer came in and said I forgot to press record! He'd put it out live but he hadn't recorded it. We had to do three songs again and it wasn't half as good. They repeated it quite a few times after that, playing these not so good versions and these are the ones on bootlegs. All the versions I've heard are the shit ones. We'd done our work! Trying to be for real the second time just doesn't work.'

Paula Greenwood still buzzes about the session: 'At the end of the session ginger Howard Jones gave me a signed photo, which he had. We'd done various acoustic sessions and stuff but it was the first time we had a real live band in the studio making a bit of a racket so I guess for us it was a bit punk rock really – more psychedelic punk rock than punk rock!'

Adds Howard, 'It was the first live radio session on Piccadilly Radio for ten years. At first we were going to do it acoustic with just John and Ian but eventually we decided to do it with the whole band.'

This is not quite the way the band remembers it. Pete laughs, 'I've never heard of that. The only person who would have thought of that is Howard. It was never mentioned to us. I mean, why would you do it acoustic? It would be a total non-representation of the band and acoustic versions of songs that no one has heard anyway. Pointless!'

A band was starting to emerge that couldn't be shoehorned into the shiny new Manchester music scene. All their mates and their gang buddies were screaming for a hometown gig, so when plans for a gig in nearby Preston were announced it was an ideal opportunity for a show of strength from the Roses' fan posse.

White Riot, I Wanna Riot: The First Northern Show

After recording the single, The Stone Roses went back to the rehearsal room and carried on tightening up the band. Back in the Chorlton Spirit recording studios, the band were working hard.

You'd see them going in and out of there all the time. They would rehearse the same song over and over, honing it down, note perfect (curiously the early Oasis would be like this when they rehearsed next door at The Boardwalk, countless versions of 'I Am The Walrus', as Noel disciplined the band to perfection).

The Chorlton rooms were not your usual dank, mouldy, sweat-soaked semen-stained shit-holes – these were carpeted spaces with good PAs inside.

There was some more excitement in the camp when a phone number Ian Brown had picked up on a jaunt in Europe, during the summer of '84, turned out to be a good contact. Brown had met a Swedish gig promoter called Andreas Linkaard and blagged the geezer with tales of how big the Roses were. Linkaard told the singer that he would sort out a tour of Sweden for the band.

Ian shoved the number in his back pocket and forgot all about it till one day in early '85 he decided to give it to Jones. 'Ring him up and sort out a Swedish tour,' he gruffly asked his manager.

'I had gone travelling round Europe with my girl and we got to Berlin,' remembers Ian. 'I was sat at a table when I heard this bloke saying he promoted gigs in Sweden. I said, "I'm in the biggest band in Manchester, called The Stone Roses," and we had never even played Manchester at the time. I made sure I got on with him to get this thing sorted out. When I got back they had a call box in the flats I lived in, in Withington, and eventually I organised the tour on that, and in April '85 we went to Sweden.'

A European tour, total gonzoid fun to be had! Jones wasn't so sure. 'I thought it wasn't the best time to go away. We were just building things in Britain and then we would be away for three weeks. I was worried by that.'

But before they went to Sweden there was another British date to play. The band were booked for their first northern show: on 29 March, the Roses were booked into Preston Clouds. It might not have been Manchester but it was close enough. Down at Spirit, they told us they were playing Preston which was always a great town for playing gigs in. Our band The Membranes had played there a few months previously and there had been a kick-off with the security. The bouncers had got on stage and it had really gone off. We had to leave fast. We warned the Roses that it may be a bit lairy.

This was the outfit's first chance to play to their hometown crowd, who were already buzzed up on the reviews and rumours about the Roses' gigs in London.

Everyone was going up to the show. Manchester was buzzing. At the time Clouds was a big disco, the sort of place where during the week there would be a groin exchange to the thump clod of bad disco. On Fridays it was alternative, the biggest indie night outside the main cities in the north-west.

It was also staffed by some mean bouncers.

Being the first northern gig it meant that the Roses were going to be taking a huge crew of Mancs up there with them. The last few months had seen the band's legend spread in their hometown. All those London shows and all the press that had come their way had helped. Combined with the fact that they hadn't played a hometown gig intrigued their mates and the hometown pop kids. And the Roses had mates, lots of them – they had networked the whole city in their scooter and running-around-town days.

Says Andy Couzens, 'Steve Adge was the leader of the gang and there were all these punks, Goths and skins from Manchester there. Steve loved a rumble and that night with all the tension there was plenty of opportunity for that.'

Howard Jones recoils at the memory of the gig: 'There was some heavy types there, some skinheads. The Roses had Kaiser and some of his mates with him. It was always useful to have some big guys around. There were a couple of dodgy NF types around. I wasn't happy with that and had a word with them. I said I didn't want them at the gigs because the band wasn't about that sort of thing. I had already been around all that sort of thing with Factory and didn't want it again. There were also a couple of troublemakers, who were not political but who had been around the scooter gangs. I knew Ian had been in the scooter gangs and that had been wild but by the time I got involved he had changed a lot because he was living with Mitch, who was a really intelligent woman. He was a socialist.'

There were going to be some big handy crews going up there. Chris Griffiths and Phil Smith, who would eventually be the core of the band's crew, went up with them as well. They ended up pinning the drummer from another Manchester-based band to the wall after spotting him lobbing bottles at the band. Even before the band hit the stage it was tense.

Phil Smith tells the story of the night: 'Something had happened in the club, there was loads of us there. There must have been about 40 or 50 people who went from town mob-handed. Rob Hampson who nearly joined the band on bass had been thrown out of the venue for some reasons I can't remember, and they had to demand that he come back in.'

During the set just to add to the tension the Roses' gear decided to pack in, typically at a big show – the one where you get to show your mates the power and precision of your band – teething problems crept in.

Andy Couzens turned around aghast. After a lot of crackling, his lead packs in – he can't get anything out of his guitar. It's the ultimate nightmare for anybody in a band; total silence. Howard Jones leaped on to the stage and attempted to repair the lead – only to feel the power of Couzens' shoe leather booting him off again.

'That's why we always called him "the rhino",' laughs Andy. 'We would always give him shit and he would always come back for more.'

It took ten minutes of fumbling around to find another lead. A complete nightmare. When you've taken the stage you want to take it seriously, you want to own that stage, you want to make it your home turf. A one-minute gap can feel like a lifetime but a ten-minute gap lasts for ever. It's ten minutes of silence and tension. It's ten minutes of a fidgety crowd tanked up on watered-down booze and snide drugs. It's a loose match to the powder keg that has been building up all night.

In the lull in proceedings, in the dreadful silence that all bands fear, John Squire decided to kick into one of the rare covers that they had been knocking out in rehearsal for a laugh. To the shock of the few sober members of the audience and the amusement of the band he crashed into the space-age Eddie Cochran chug of Sigue Sigue Sputnik's classic 'Love Missile X1-11'.

The London-based glam shock outfit who had been built around ex-Generation X member Tony James had burned a bright and fast trail in the sky, rather like the love missile itself in the video of the song.

Sputnik were a brilliant group, a way-over-the-top dress sense – like a skyscraper New York Dolls on angel dust – and played a pulsating rock-'n'roll disco rush of songs that had grabbed them a massive deal and a fistful of hype. They had burned bright and they burned fast and then disappeared but their back catalogue is well worth checking. Their glam riffing was an instant hit with the glam-punk-digging Squire.

Finally a lead was found and the band kicked back into action. The atmosphere was hot and some of the negative energy got turned into the white heat of adrenaline excitement, but then more problems occurred halfway through the set. Pete Garner's bass string snapped. It's the E – the thick one – the one that never breaks – the one that some bass players have on their bass for years, especially if they dig the dead sound. Another yawning gap occurs as the band stand around aghast. It's a total disaster.

Garner fixes on another E string – he's as aware as anyone that the tension is building. His hands shake with adrenaline but the damned string is now on, only now the tuner is bust and he can't get the damn thing into tune. Fuck, when will this nightmare end? This is a total fuck-up, he tunes by ear and the band kicks off again.

It's stop – start – stop – start.

'Trust A Fox' – a song with quite brilliant lyrics – goes out of time as the band, normally so tight, is knocked clean off its tracks by all the mishaps. They soldier on to 'Tell Me' and then Reni, sensing the frustration and fucked off with all the disasters, kicks his kit over and Andy smashes his guitar up. It's absolute chaos, bottles and fists are flying – the atmosphere is ugly.

'The thing about Ian being a kick boxer is that he can look after himself in those situations. He didn't feel frightened and neither did Andy because Andy is quite rough and tumble but John and Pete in particular are not fighters and they were terrified. It was going off all over the club, Manchester versus Preston, then everyone against the bouncers,' recalled Howard.

The Preston riot was the first big myth in the Roses canon. The moment when they realised the power of rock'n'roll, the way it could release some loose energy into a building. It hadn't been pretty but it was a buzz and everyone was talking about it. It also meant that the regional stringers who were reviewing the show for the national music press were left distinctly unhappy with what they had seen.

Says Pete, 'Ro Newton from *Melody Maker* came backstage and tried to do an interview. "Do you condone any of that violence that has gone on?" She was trying to get Ian to do the "Oh yeah it's a terrible thing", but he wouldn't do it...so she went totally against us at that point. I was glad I wasn't in the audience. It was a really lairy load of Mancs who came down...fighting with people from Preston. All I remember was that when we were playing there was tension in the air beforehand. We went on and it erupted into a Wild West salon thing... It was pretty naughty!'

Howard Jones used the bad review in the band's favour: 'Ro Newton slagged the gig off in the *Melody Maker* but we took the line "the sound is painful" from the review and used it in our press.'

Mani staggered, pissed, into the dressing room and was asked to leave. He turned around shouting, 'I thought we were meant to be mates.' He would later apologise for the incident, just another part of the chaos.

One piece of Roses history had been made though. Scruffy and falling apart, marred by bad sound, a band just about holding it together – 'I Wanna Be Adored' made its live début.

The band were starting to get to grips with dynamics, pacing and great songwriting and it's a sign that they are getting confident enough to create deceptively simple songs.

Two days after the Preston riot, Piccadilly repeated their session and a week later they packed their bags for Sweden. In between, on 5 April, there was to have been a gig at Oldham Oddies, but the plug was pulled on that. 'It was a good job as well,' a Manchester scenester notes. 'That was ripe for a riot, that was a rough old venue and the Roses were now getting a bit of a reputation.'

Maybe it was a good time to go to Scandinavia

'We Were Like Animals': Sweden

Sweden was the Roses' Hamburg, that pre-fame stint in Europe that moulded The Beatles, that jaunt away from home in harsh conditions with a string of gigs that tightened the band musically and as a unit. Says Andy, 'It was our first big proper break. It was where we went serious. We made John give up his day job. We got him on the phone in Sweden and made him do it. Ian was signing on and stopped.'

Sweden moulded the Roses. Continues Andy, 'I don't think we played anywhere in Manchester till after we had been to Sweden. Even John Squire reckons that was the best time for the band. That was where the band first became a proper band and gelled…We were there for a month, but it seemed like forever! In Sweden the gigs varied. It's not difficult to make it big in Stockholm. It's only a small music scene, especially if you're going out every night causing the mayhem we did. We were all over the papers, women chasing after us…We didn't know how long we were going for when we went.'

When, during his Euro jaunt, Ian Brown bragged to Andreas Linkaard, the stranger on a train in Germany, about his band, he wasn't really expecting a tour. After all there was no proof that his band even existed, let alone that they were massive in the north of England. If massive meant one fucked up gig in Preston and a handful of supports in London then maybe he was telling the truth, but that was the mark of the man, he could be utterly convincing if he needed to be.

But then north Europe back in the mid-eighties wasn't really like Britain. It was far richer and had far fewer bands – plenty of bored kids who love music and loads of disposable cash. Add to that a traditional interest in just what those rowdy Brits are up to.

Whatever Brown said, it had been enough to bend the ear of the Swede who arranged the gigs with the help of his father (who was a concert promoter). After Howard Jones's follow-up call he promised the band a couple of shows that March. It may not have been a whole European tour, in fact it wasn't even enough gigs to justify a trip, but no one was thinking about the details. This was the Roses, right! And this was a band that was going to the top. Music press, London gigs and now a European tour (of sorts). Smart.

Here was a chance to go on holiday – bum around Sweden and get the band super-tight – this was going to be a great experience. Two weeks after the Preston gig they set off in Andy's van. Says Howard, 'Me, the band and the roadie, Gluepot Glen, went on the trip. As usual Andy wouldn't let anybody drive his white Chevy – so he drove all the way there! We were all crammed in the back with the gear. Thank God they only had small amps! John and Andy had small Roland amps and we all sat on those.'

Like any party of rock'n'roll droogs on their first tour, the band partied hard. It was a triumphant vibe. It always is when you're on the car ferry. The dullest of environments, a floating motorway service station on a ten-hour ride can be turned into a superb jaunt…adrenaline, high jinks and a rare drinking spree for the band combined to make this a memorable trip.

Arriving in Sweden the next morning the band were a little the worse for wear. Even with spring on the horizon Sweden is a fucking cold place and a desperate place for a vanload of pissed-up musicians with no petrol and a very vague plan of action. It slowly began to occur to them that the tour organisation was a tad suspect. Howard laughs, 'We didn't know what gigs there were, where we were staying, or how much money we were getting. We were due to meet Andreas at 8 o'clock on 9 April at Stockholm Railway Station, that was the only plan that we had! I often wondered what would have happened if he hadn't been there. We would have been fucked! We didn't have his phone number or anything!'

Even getting to Stockholm seemed fraught with danger.

'We arrived in Sweden with no money at all. We needed some Swedish cash to get petrol. We had got off the ferry in Sweden. We couldn't get petrol. We suddenly realised that there's only twenty quid in the kitty! We were stuck in this blizzard with no petrol and the engine turned off and no heat in the van. We could have frozen to death! We sat there in the cold getting colder, hung over from alcohol. And then in the blizzard a car pulls up, it was the first one in an hour. I jumped out and banged on the car window. The Swedish guy inside opens the window. I said, "Look I've got no money, help!" He just pulled his wallet out and just gave it to me. It had about a hundred and fifty quid in Swedish money in it and he just drove off. I must have looked like some sort of lunatic mugger appearing out of the snow. With a vanload of lunatics behind me in the van.'

Eventually they arrived in Stockholm and hooked up with Linkaard. After 24 hours on the road, Pete Garner remembers them gratefully dossing down in his flat. 'We had driven for a day, we got to his flat at six and Andy slept till teatime the next day!'

Two days later on 10 April they played their first gig at the Big Bang Club in Linkopping, a Swedish logging town. Ian's mate, Andreas Linkaard, not only booked the shows but had previewed the band in the local papers and eventually reviewed the shows as well – a one-man music biz machine – it was all part of the service, Swedish style.

Ian Brown, though, wasn't about to reciprocate this charity – remembering John Lydon's combative band/audience stance he opened the début show with 'You're all Swedish twats', a phrase that he had managed to pick up in Swedish. That's the Brits abroad for you – taking a massive interest in local customs and languages and learning key phrases to share with the locals. After that scene-setting salvo, the band crashed into 'Mission Impossible'.

Despite Brown's obvious disdain for the audience, the Roses went down well and their resistance to doing encores finally crumbled. When the baying crowd hauled them back to play another song from the set, they, like all young bands, simply didn't have enough material. They had to dip into the set and replay tunes.

The review of the gig describes a band buzzing with full confrontational powers, stating 'singer Ian runs around like he has rabies'. It also points out that 'he rolls around on the floor'. He also likes The Stone Roses music, 'because it is violent and has a close connection to punk', and then indeed describes the music as psychedelic punk.

There were more encores at The Olympia in Norrköping. Spring was in the air, it had been a few months since that début gig and now they were touring abroad and struggling along with life on the road and all that entails.

The band had never encountered anything like this before and had no idea of tour finances – after all they had stumbled into their tour van with a handful of money cashed from their giros. In Sweden they were flabbergasted by the high cost of living – reeling at having to pay £4.50 for a pint of lager – they were totally skint already.

There were plenty of long and frustrating gaps in the touring schedule, time for broke band members to starve and where inter-band tension could thrive.

Fortunately they met the manager of a local supermarket who stole food for them – even then they fought like dogs over the scraps. It was the real rock bottom tough life – the sort of backs-to-the-wall situation that shapes up a band.

Andy Couzens recounts the struggle. 'On the road it was horrible. We were so broke we became like animals, we fought over food and we fought over money, we took it all out on Howard – he became the band punch-bag.'

The manager had to put up with all kinds of pranks – some of them fairly amusing in a typically dumb, bored, on the road sort of way. Unless you were Howard Jones, who bore the brunt of all the jokes. 'One place where we stayed we took all the slats out of his bed and it collapsed when he went to bed in it…I guess it's funny the first night but we did it every night,' laughs Couzens, who also remembers Reni putting slabs of bacon in Jones's bed.

At one point relations between the band and their manager slumped to an all-time low point, with Jones being kicked out of the van in a freezing late-night foul storm and left on the roadside.

'It was about minus 20 outside,' says Couzens, 'there was a row as usual over someone sitting on the bench in the van. I opened the door and kicked him out and left him in the middle of nowhere. He had to walk for an hour and a half before he got back to where we were staying.'

The Roses were tasting rock'n'roll stardom in Stockholm. It may have been low-level stardom but they were flouncing round the Stockholm bars, living it up.

The rest of April they swaggered around the city, partying like kings and living like pigs. They also managed to cram in a few more gigs travelling out of town to Boras (where they didn't bother to play – 'the venue was a shed,' laughs Pete, 'so we didn't play and then we found out that people travelled for miles to see bands there and it was one of the main venues in Sweden!') and Vastertores, then back to Stockholm on 23 and 25 April for two unlikely shows, one supporting the Go Betweens and one headlining at the Studion.

At one Swedish gig it kicked off and there was a riot – the police came down and arrested the whole crowd. This sounds like ace fun – any rock'n'roll band worth its salt enjoys a good riot and the cops raiding a venue is an adrenaline rush worth a million.

On 30 April they played the last of two shows at Lidingo and then got back on the ferry to the UK. It had been just over three weeks since they came to Sweden. They had done their rock'n'roll rite of passage.

The Swedish experience tightened the band up. It also taught them the rules of the road, the mean and tough existence of living with no money in a strange land. They generally played to few people, they had a run-in with the cops, they fought with each other, they returned to Manchester worn out but with valuable lessons learned.

Now they were ready to take on the toughest gig of their career so far.

The hometown show in Manchester. But where could they play? After all, they were no mere local band.

First Night in Manchester!

Before they had gone to Sweden, Howard had booked them a gig at Manchester International 1's 800-capacity hall. Not a bad size of venue for a band who had only played a handful of gigs.

It was the Roses' debut hometown gig at the venue, which was the biggest venue a local band is going to get for a showcase event.

Phil Smith remembers a small crowd turned out. 'It was always the same people at first who went to see them. We thought they had just formed to do the tour in Sweden!'

The band were watched intently by International owner Gareth Evans. 'The first time I saw the band was at the It's Immaterial support gig they did that Howard Jones promoted in 1985 and there was no one there. I thought the charisma of John Squire just standing there doing nothing was really powerful. It reminded me of the bass player from Booker T and the MGs. The bass player had a circle drawn around him, in his contract, he wasn't allowed to move out of this. John Squire just stood there. Ian Brown – I just loved the voice because I was always pissed off with these people going to stage school and just learning to sing. Pop is about your own distinctive voice.

'Howard Jones had put an Easter festival on at the International and I watched the whole gig; there was hardly anyone in the audience.'

The band were in fine swagger. Their intro tape is the hilarious Tom Jones full-on sex anthem, part ironic and part of their background, 'It's Not Unusual'. Brown hit the stage oozing arrogance.

'Hey, why don't you over there come here?' he yells at the crowd. 'You might learn something.' The voice is deadpan, arrogant. Spat out like John Lydon. The band play 'Mission Impossible', 'Adored' purrs in over a chuntering Joy Division very Manc slice of gloom, Garner's bass the backbone. 'I Wanna Be Adored' sounds virtually the same as it would do when it became the anthem of the baggy generation, a blissed out rolling tune that captures a future summer lost in an ecstatic daze. Back in '85 the context is very different, but the song already sticks out from the rest of the set.

The two guitars are phlanged, heavy effects dominate. The band are in full rock mode. The sound has the punk aggression and anger. It's got an eighties psychedelic tinge added to with the cheapo guitar effects that were flooding the market at the time. The songs already have the twisting and turning structures that dominate the classic Roses work: drop downs, stop and starts, long build-ups and explosive choruses, hook laden guitar licks and frantic Keith Moon drumming, false endings and a hint of eighties stadium big soundscapes dominate the sound. There is even the coldness of the sort of soundscape that dominate the parallel Goth scene, not that the Roses are a Goth band by any measure.

Brown's vocals have an anger and arrogance. There are the deadpan northern vowels all over them and, typically Manc, no effort or concession is made to singing 'nicely' or 'properly'. It's like a celebration of all that is brilliantly unmusical in the northern voice, a 'like it or lump it' attitude that dominate the areas' great vocalists from The Fall's Mark Smith through to New Order's Barney. Even the rising star of Morrissey has one of those voices, albeit a lot nicer…

The band are tight. That month in Sweden had done them a power of good. Even if they are getting a good reaction Brown is still skulking on the stage. 'Stop talking fucker,' shouts Brown, sounding angry. The anger sparks the song into life and Brown sings the song furiously.

'Ian was really good in small venues,' explains Paula Greenwood. 'He could be quite menacing. He would walk into the crowd and go into people's faces.'

They end with 'Tell Me', Brown spitting: 'This is your last chance to dance, anyone who is anyone already knows it...'. He takes his long mic lead for a walk into the crowd as the song ends: 'I am the garage flower,' he spits over the 'Thanks for everyone who came, a pitiful display...' And he throws his mic on the floor.

Years later Liam Gallagher's sneering vocals will have Ian Brown stamped all over them; the manic speed-driven Roses singer is already the role model for all those nineties Brit vocalists...

The First Warehouse Party

After a couple of months' break they returned to London on 4 July, supporting Dr And The Medics of all people at the unlikely Croydon Underground. It was another weird show, more treading water while waiting for the single to get pressed up.

'I remembered the girls in Dr And The Medics putting their wigs on in the dressing room and thinking it was pretty funny,' smiles Pete Garner. 'It looks like a weird gig now but it was a gig...at the time we would play anywhere but not in a pub.'

Just when it seemed the band were wandering around with nowhere to go, Steve Adge came up with another masterstroke, a masterstroke that would truly define the way they operated as a band. One afternoon in Spirit he asked them if they were up for playing a warehouse party that he was arranging.

Bob Dickinson was one of the people who went to the gig: 'I went to a warehouse party round the back of Piccadilly railway station under some archways. People told us about this gig coming up, a secret gig. You had to turn up at a certain place at a certain time. You went down a tiny back alley to the big derelict goods station no one uses any more. The Stone Roses were the main attraction.'

They needed something to give them that mystique, that edge. Something to take them beyond the local band support treadmill. They had a few fans and the thuggish-mate following, they had the numbers, they were worth more than a few mediocre supports.

The warehouse parties were a stroke of genius. In 1985, years before the acid house scene made them the norm, the thought of grabbing a warehouse and putting on a party was pretty novel. Inspired by his trip to London, the Adge was working out the logistics of an all-nighter in Manchester.

Ian Brown credits Steve Adge with the idea: 'It was Steve who started the warehouse parties. He put the three warehouse shows on which started everything. He said, "I got the place in Fairfield Street behind Piccadilly train station, I was thinking of doing a party. It's called 'The Flower Show' and I want a band to play, are you up for it?"

'Not only was it a great party but it got us known really quick in Manchester. On the Friday we went out putting up posters for everyone that was coming out of the clubs for the warehouse gig, but we were covering up all the posters that had been put up by the gangsters who ran the poster mafia in Manchester...the posters were saying "Gig on tonight, Stone Roses onstage at 4". Later on, I was in somewhere like Corbieres in town and a guy came up. He said, "You know, I should really be breaking your knees...You've been putting posters over my patch tonight – guys get their knee caps broken for less!" He let us off – he knew our intentions were good. At the time I didn't have a clue what he was on about!'

The whole idea of the gigs was to have a powerful effect on The Stone Roses and the way they operated in the future. It sparked the belief that they could be a powerful force and play outside the established music business network. It would feed into the way that they promoted their own shows at Spike Island and the tent gigs. It could even be said that this staunch outsider policy was their eventual downfall. But when they were burning brightly, their very independence and unpredictability was one of their most powerful strengths.

Every classic band has mythological moments and the Roses have certainly had plenty of these built into their career. Like The Clash and the whole lineage of 'great British bands' they were certainly very astute at peppering their career with defining moments.

Already they had played the classic début gig in London, done their 'Hamburg' in Sweden, had their very own personal 'white riot' in Preston and recorded the first live radio session for years for the local radio station that was getting plenty of street talk in the town. They were working with one of the hippest producers in the UK, a man who had almost single-handedly built up the Factory sound.

A special band doesn't bother itself with chugging round the local circuit. There's always a mountain of other local bands to clamber over, all mini versions of whatever's going on. It's a rat race. And a band like the Roses, who by now had been playing music for five years in various guises, was above all that sort of 'three local bands for one quid' nights.

Steve Adge had been meaning to put on a warehouse party for ages. It wasn't going to be easy. A small city means the cops can sniff out some sort of party action pretty damn fast and in the mid-eighties the cops were busting to get involved. After all, these were the days of Anderton's barmy army, with James Anderton, the iron-fisted, big-bearded God's cop who was already making his presence known in Manchester's club land with raids and strange biblical proclamations, hardly being a big fan of a gig like this.

Being a master blagger Adge phoned British Rail and hired a railway arch on Fairfield Street just behind Piccadilly Station. He didn't exactly tell British Rail what he was hiring the arch for. He paid the money, hired in the PA and kept schtum.

Pete Garner explains the covert nature of the gigs: 'He booked it and secretly photocopied directions of how to get there. People bought tickets without knowing how to find it. He'd been to London, buzzing about a warehouse party he'd been to. He'd sold all these tickets which told you to ring Spirit and find out where the gig was. He rented the arch knowing that if they found out about the gig they would pull it. "The only dress restrictions is no blue uniforms" was handwritten on it.'

It was just like going to a rave would be three years later. Armed with a handwritten scrawl and a hand-drawn map, the punter walked past Piccadilly Station and then the first road past the Star and Garter pub and then down a bleak and uninviting-looking alley.

It was all very well worked out, a military operation. Manchester's first-ever warehouse party was under way.

The tickets screamed 'Blackmail Records presents Manchester's first warehouse party', adding 'Warehouse 1 The Flower Show with special guests The Stone Roses'.

The party was on 20 July. After the soundcheck the band went round to Ian Brown's Hulme flat on Charles Barry Crescent to hang out and get through the long wait to stage time in a bit more comfort than in a damp old peeling red brick warehouse in the city centre. No one knew what to expect.

One of the faces around at the flat was Steve Cressa. 'We met him down in the Berlin club. He was always like a young kid in there, running around being pretty sharp,' recalls Couzens, adding, 'I spoke to him and he sort of joined the gang. He was one of the few people that we let into the rehearsals and hang around. There was always loads of people that wanted to come down and watch us rehearse but we couldn't really allow it. It would have been really horrible.'

For Brown, Cressa was a soul mate and an inspiration as Couzens recalls. 'He was a real culture vulture, always taking things from people, Ian looked to Cressa as some sort of entertainments manager.'

Then wallowing in the rotten hulk of the Hulme flats, Brown and his inner coterie of mates and gang members were living the rock'n'roll dream, careless and carefree. These people knew that they were destined for big things, and tonight's show was just another peg up the ladder.

When they eventually hopped into the car and left for the gig, though, they were apprehensive: maybe no one would show up, maybe no one would find the place.

When they arrived at about 11 o'clock ready to play the show, they were shocked by the number of people wandering around. They sat in the car wondering what the fuck all these people were doing hanging around Fairfield Street – till they realised that they were down for the show.

Inside the pop kids were buying raffle tickets for their beer – another Adge wheeze, who figured that if the police raided the joint then they couldn't get done for selling beer. It was a wheeze that the house generation would pull off at countless warehouse parties themselves three years later. The band sat around ready to play, but unlike a normal gig there was no set time to hit the stage.

They had to wait around till about 1.30 am before they played. Another myth about the party was its 'pumping acid house soundtrack' as attempts have been made to put it up as some part of the eventual rave scene of the late eighties.

'The music was nothing like that,' remembers Pete. 'It was nothing to do with dance music.'

Mike Joyce from The Smiths was there. 'I saw The Stone Roses at Fairfield Street. There was a danger aspect about going to see them at the time, you know, "Come on, let's have a big fight!"'

The gig starts off with loads of feedback...loads of 'woo woo's' from Ian Brown...Again Reni's amazing drumming powers the set, it's very rock'n'roll sounding. Ian Brown's vocals are shouty and angry; they sound strong, sound good.

Decked out in black, they had hit on yet another image. This one really worked. It gave them a sinister edge, an almost Joy Division angular scowling presence, a dark-hearted street gang look. They looked like a unit. A clockwork orange dressed in black. And it was all encapsulated by their frontman with his slicked-back hair and his pinched scowl and charisma.

Brown dead-eyed the audience, his stark staring eyes looking right through the packed throng, a throng buzzing on excitement on the band's post-Preston reputation. It was a crowd made up of mates from the scooter club days, local music scene drifters and word of mouth hipsters.

Two girls at the front had home-made Stone Roses shirts on, complete with a rose hand-drawn on the back. The band was now building a following.

After all the electric gunk of guitars being picked up and the loose feedback of gear waiting for action, they had crashed into their set. A gang of young punks, full of testosterone and energy. Ian is in and out of the crowd, standing on the monitors, his long mic lead clutched in his fist. Total attitude. Andy Couzens zigzags the stage slashing the chords on his guitar and Pete Garner swings his bass about, his raven black hair flapping in his face, looking studied rock'n'roll cool whilst copping shapes from Johnny Thunders, Mick Jones and the whole pantheon of post-Keef dyed-black-hair punk rockers.

John Squire is stood still letting his guitar do the talking whilst Reni is stripped down. Topless, his wiry frame in a pair of Adidas tracksuit bottoms, he's just a blur of sweatshod energy. His drumming is remarkable; it makes a mockery of every other British drummer on the scene, his constant rhythm barrage driving the band on to a different plane.

The early Roses are a special band. The raw power and belligerent energy of this set makes you wonder what would have happened if they had ever recorded this stuff properly, with a more sympathetic producer, one that understood the classic British rock'n'roll sound that they were honing down here, a sound that fits into the lineage of prime-time Who, The Clash, the Pistols – a different line than the one they eventually chose to pursue (although flashes of this fearsome rock'n'roll power would flash up occasionally in the years to come, like their last-ever Reni show at Glasgow Green).

This is no early version of a band fumbling around with the keys of greatness but a fully-fledged, fully formed band complete with its kick-ass sound.

Ian Brown remembers: 'At the gig we had all our mates lined up to DJ and at about three in the morning this big Rasta turns up and says, "I'm the DJ!" He DJ'd reggae all night, which was great. The warehouse parties gave us an underground vibe. They were the first warehouse parties in Manchester. We did three. Mint.

'We had the place done out with car tyres hanging from the ceiling. When the police turned up there must have been loads of people in there and we were saying, "What are you going to do?" This was before there were flats in the city centre. It's not like we were going to disturb anyone.'

John Breakall sees the warehouse parties as a defining moment. 'The first hint that I can think of when I thought there could be something special with the Roses was the warehouse parties…the parties were illegal, so it had to be secret. You had to ring Spirit's telephone number and go down to Spirit to get directions.

'We had all the beer stored down at Spirit and Steve Adge and me used to do runs every twenty minutes. We had to pile the money on top of the fuckin' desk down there at Spirit.

'The police turned up, at the party, as they do, and Steve, thinking on his feet – and Steve was fantastic at this – said it was a video shoot. Hence, that's why we paid everybody a penny…you walked in there, you got paid a penny and it was a video shoot! So they went away.

'It was a Friday night, not sure if it was warehouse party one or two, and at 11 o'clock there was a mad exodus from the Hacienda all the way down to Fairfield Street. The Roses were going on stage and somebody had nicked the generator! I think Reni and Ian, it was definitely Reni and somebody else, chased these bastards down. They had started and launched into "I Wanna Be Adored", and all the power went after 30 seconds because somebody had nicked the generators, so it all kicked off.'

Andy McQueen was one of The Stone Roses' earliest and most eloquent fans: 'I remember the warehouse parties being really cold…they were pretty shambolic to be honest with you, pushing the equipment on a cart to one of the warehouse gigs. And I'm sure a generator broke down at the other one, but again for everybody who was there it was kind of exciting because we'd never experienced those kind of gigs. They were in a way quite new in Manchester – well, they were to me.

'We were all kids and it was pretty exciting being a part of something quite new and fresh, you know; there was something about them that was pretty shambolic yet exciting, Ian was very enigmatic and yet quite menacing as well. There was a lot of very bolshy attitude and Ian was always pretty good at getting off the stage and getting close to the crowds which I thought was pretty exciting at the time – a lot of bands wanted to be sort of Joy Division, being sort of miserable.'

It was this night that the legend of the Roses in Manchester was truly born. The band was talked about on the grapevine for weeks afterwards. They hit the stage and blew the place apart. Couzens remembers certain band members really going for it.

'Reni never took speed normally but that night he was really buzzing. Normally he's fast enough as it is but at this gig he was like a hyper version of Keith Moon.'

For Couzens the warehouse parties were the peak of his career with the band. 'They were the best two gigs that I ever played with them. There was nearly 400 at the second one, it really felt like a major event. It was brilliant,' he enthuses.

For The Stone Roses it was their first Manchester triumph; for Steve Adge it was something to work on. He would be the warehouse party promoter. He went on to promote A Certain Ratio in similar circumstances soon after and the Roses again on 30 November. From then on he gradually moved into the band's tight inner circle, ending up as their virtual manager in later years.

That début warehouse party meant a lot to the band. It meant that The Stone Roses had finally arrived in their hometown and on their own terms, setting a precedent for future off-the-wall gigs. A perfect frame of mind to go in and record their songs

Recording the Début Album That Never Was

During the summer of 1985 The Stone Roses began to record what could have been their début album. The tracks, which eventually came out as the *Garage Flower* compilation years later, captured the band at their hard rock peak. Their so-called eponymous début in 1989 was, in some ways, their second album.

The band's harder edged rock'n'roll is mixed with Hannett's cold, hard, electronic edge. It sounds like a very different band, but there are hints of what's to come, especially since two future classics, 'I Wanna Be Adored' and 'This Is The One', are recorded.

Fortunately it never got the release, leaving them time to put together what would be the eventual début album four years later. An album this early into their career would have been too soon.

Howard Jones was keen to get on with the album. The single was ready for release now and they needed something to follow it up with. They booked Strawberry Studios from 3 to 26 August, plenty of time to get their live set down on tape.

First there was another London show at the legendary Marquee, and the Roses, like most bands with a bit of fire in their souls, had managed to get themselves banned. They were added to an ever-lengthening list of outfits blacklisted from the club after Ian ran foul of the management of the Marquee. He had taken his Lydonesque stage act thing a touch too far and shoved a mic stand through a monitor at the front of the stage. Ever confrontational, the wiry frontman was rubbing people up the wrong way.

Back in the studio they recorded nearly everything that they had. They put down the live set and a few extras: 'Getting Plenty', 'Here It Comes', 'Trust A Fox', 'Tragic Roundabout', 'All I Want', 'Heart On The Staves', 'I Wanna Be Adored', 'This Is The One', 'Fall', 'So Young', 'Tell Me', 'Just A Little Bit' (formally 'Nowhere Fast'), 'Mission Impossible' and another track ('Haddock' is a loose bit of feedback that was never a song and which was run backwards and put on to the *Garage Flower* album by compiler Andy Couzens in the nineties).

They were getting studio time on the drip. The decision to record with Hannett at this time may well have been a financial one as well as a creative one, Hannett having plenty of down-time owed from his never-ending sessions in the studio.

They were also changing as a band. Typically when a band hits the studio to record a set of songs they are already moving in a different direction. Even while they were spending long night hours in Strawberry working away at the tunes the Roses were instinctively moving away from their rockier roots.

Listen to *Garage Flower* now though and the songs sound a lot better than people will lead you to believe. Their anthemic quality, their inherent rousing rock'n'roll power and their inspirational anthemic vocals may not have been the soundtrack for the hipsters but there are some great moments going down here and for some this was the Roses' best period.

There were already flashes of the inspirational redemptive songwriting that would eventually make them the key band a few years down the road. 'I Wanna Be Adored' was recorded by Hannett and is a slightly faster, heavier version. But it was 'This Is The One', written after Martin Hannett locked the band into the studio and told them to write another tune, that saw the band make the first of several creative leaps forward into the next few years.

'This Is The One' was a triumph. Built around Garner's pumping bass, the song, which is still many people's favourite Roses tune, builds and builds till it hits that soaring climactic chorus. It really is the bridge between the two Roses, the anthemic punky version of early years with Ian's exhilarating, almost shouted, vocal and the crystalline pop of classic Roses.

'This Is The One' has the same sort of soaring shouting chorus that marks out 'So Young' and 'Tell Me'. It also, even in this earlier slightly faster rockier version, has some of the amazing guitar interplay that would become the hallmark of the classic Roses sound.

Perhaps one of the greatest songs of their career, 'This Is The One' is a surging, monumental anthem. It would be the high point of their set for years and one of the key tracks of the eventual début album.

Couzens remembers the moment with pride. 'At the time we had two classics, "All I Want" and "I Wanna Be Adored".' Now we had three.'

The band was never happy with the final recordings. They felt that Martin Hannett had somehow suffocated them and it's true – Reni's drums lose that swing that is so key to his style. This didn't stop the late Scott Piering, the top indie record plugger in the country at the time, who was having a lot of success with The Smiths, representing Rough Trade in London, from attempting to set up a deal to release the record.

Couzens believes that the album's non-release was a blessing in disguise. 'It's probably a good job that it didn't come out at the time, because like most bands in the studio for the first time, we weren't quite sure of what we were doing. We were all really fucked up, the sessions would go on all night. It was difficult to record, but I think that it was worth bringing out years later as a document of what we were like in the early days. Despite the mayhem, Martin taught us one thing – he taught us how to write.'

Martin Hannett's soundscapes have made some bands, enhanced others and merely got in the way of some. Add on to this the fact that the Roses just weren't ready to record an album. The songs were good but the band had only played live about twenty times. They hadn't gelled as a live unit in that deep sort of way that really makes a band. The trip to Sweden may have bonded them as a live unit, it may have been their Hamburg, but The Beatles spent four years going backwards and forwards to Hamburg.

Towards the end of the session they came up with a couple of tunes that pretty well signposted the direction ahead and put the brakes on the album and its release.

While Martin Hannett was sleeping, burnt out by his crazed chemical surge through the rock'n'roll lifestyle, the band took him up on it; they decided to lock themselves into the studio until they came up with something.

According to Couzens, the Roses were about to go into creative over-drive. Whilst '"Here It Comes" came from a riff that John had, "Sally Cinnamon" was influenced by The Walker Brothers. 'We would jam stuff out for hours on end. Reni was crucial for us at this point. He was brilliant to jam with.'

For a gang of south Manc ex-punks coming out of football violence, petty hooliganism and punk rock modernism, they were going through big changes. The Roses were now starting to listen to music a long way away from their punk roots; they were checking out stuff that had been classed as hippy music.

'I wish I had heard Jimi Hendrix earlier, I wish I had heard his records when I was 12,' Ian Brown once told the press.

'The Jesus And Mary Chain were a really important band in many respects,' Couzens recalls. 'They opened a lot of doors for people like us. Before them you weren't really allowed to listen to loads of groups but they turned people on to a lot of great bands. From that point we started listening to Stones, Beatles, Byrds, Misunderstood and sixties garage bands. The flavour of our songwriting started to change.'

Crucial changes were afoot in the Roses camp. Pre-Hannett they were dealing with rock with a punk edge, it was cruising along in one dynamic, and had very little variation in its style. After Hannett, after the Mary

Chain, they were dealing with a lot of new flavours, and it was at about this point that John Squire's guitar would really start moving to the fore.

Hot from the studio they played Manchester's Hacienda that August, a gig recorded on eight-track by Martin Hannett who was also mixing the sound that night. With hair greased back and in white kecks, Ian Brown was now the consummate frontman. They were supported by Playne Jayne, a swap gig with the London-based psychedelic outfit that was played at the Marquee in London the week before.

'We played with Playne Jayne,' recalls Ian Brown. 'There was a psyche garage scene in London at the time but we were not part of that. Bands like The Prisoners – never really liked them. I suppose I should have done! It was about that time that I discovered Jimi Hendrix and Love. Paul Gambaccini used to play Love and that's where I got into them. We based our Roses album on Love. "Waterfall" is pure Love. I got into Love and Jimi Hendrix after discovering LSD in 1985. I then rediscovered The Beatles. Suddenly you're tripping and "Strawberry Fields" sounds, like, wow! And you're getting into *The White Album* and *Abbey Road*, them sort of albums now.'

In the murky acoustics of the Hacienda's muffled acoustics, Martin Hannett was in overdrive. 'He did amazing things to the sound of John's guitar. It was brilliant. Everyone was gob-smacked,' says Pete Garner.

For the band it must have been interesting to hit the stage of the venue that, at the time, represented most things they didn't like about the Manchester music scene.

At the gig Brown was as wired as ever. At one point he jumped into the crowd for his walkabout. The Hacienda dancefloor froze with fear. No one wants to be that near a singer at a gig!

Garner reminisces, 'During the encore Ian jumped in the crowd and everyone went mad. We thought he was gone for, we thought that he was going to get killed!'

'So Young'! – September 1985, The Roses Release Their First Single

At last, after all those years of being in and out of bands the Roses had some vinyl to shout about.

The début double 'A' side single produced by Martin Hannett was a two-song salvo that perfectly captured the younger, rockier, speed-driven Roses, a Roses fronted by a manic, crop-haired, paisley-shirted madman who would dive into the crowd with his mic on a long lead trying to get a reaction, trying to get a confrontation.

You can hear it on these tunes. The songs tap into one of those Manchester sounds that is never really written about, the chorused guitar, raw power that made and still makes The Chameleons one of the city's most popular bands. It's a sound that younger bands like Puressence would pick up on years later.

'So Young' is Brown shouting 'c'mon get up!' from his Hulme balcony at the dope-stained bohemian community. Brown was appalled by the wasting away culture in Hulme. It grated against his work ethic (although, it must be said, it's a charge that could easily be levelled against the Roses themselves in years to come!).

Says Ian, 'Mainly the lyrics are about personal experiences, about my friends or about how I feel. The single "So Young" is about when I lived in Hulme, everyone who lived there seemed to think it was great to stay in bed until teatime. It's just a waste of life. I'm saying you've got to get out of bed today. They could be doing something more worthwhile with their time.'

It's unfair to say that Hulme was completely an area where people did nothing with their lives. Meshed in with the drug culture and the twenty-four-hour-party-people scene there was a lot of creativity, a lot of cutting-edge ideas, it was, and to a certain extent still is, the area that gives Manchester a rare bohemian flavour.

'Tell Me' is Brown adopting his Lydonesque drop-dead stare and co-opting the Pistols frontman's lyrical arrogance. With its 'you can't tell me anything' and 'I love only me' howls, it could be something off Lydon's first Public Image album, it has that same sort of stark poetic belligerence.

On 9 September the single finally came out on 12 inch only. The Happy Mondays also released their début single, the 12 inch of 'Delightful' on the same day. At the time, though, both bands were bands out of their time. Eventually their careers would intertwine for their two-pronged attack on the UK music scene.

'Soon after, in 1986/87, we would go to a lot of their shows in London and when we played they would be in our dressing rooms,' says Ian about the Mondays. 'The Dingwalls shows and when they played the Astoria and

LSE, we would be there. This was two years before anyone really knew about us in the rest of the country. We were encouraging each other, getting a buzz off each other's bands.'

The single was big locally but trying to get any national attention was going to be difficult. The Roses were one of those bands that would fall between two stools, too polished and too rock for the indie sector and too raw for the mainstream. They were too northern and also too rock for most of the music press and there was very little potential radio play outside the playlist in the mid-eighties, and the great John Peel was not a fan.

In effect they would have to rely on a strong live following to sell a single. It was too early, but maybe Thin Line thought they could bludgeon the band through, maybe use the single to get the gigs to build up the live following outside Manchester.

The first review of the record was in local music paper *Muze* by Paula Greenwood. Paula was now writing as well as working with Piccadilly Radio. She was a big fan of the Roses and would support them in local papers.

She wrote, 'Every gig is an event and this, the long awaited début single, is big, loud and beautiful. They have certainly matured since their demo and with the help of Martin Hannett they have become smooth and hard.'

Paula Greenwood explains: 'I wrote for that really awful magazine called *Muze*. I interviewed The Stone Roses for them and another magazine called *Avanti* because nobody else liked them at the magazine. I interviewed them in one of the cafes in Piccadilly next to where Piccadilly Records used to be. Reni, Ian and John turned up. It was my first interview and I was pretty naïve so the questions were pretty basic!'

Locally, the single was selling strongly. They found themselves at number two in the Piccadilly Record Shop charts – a good sign as this was the key indie shop in the city. The demo had been getting played a lot in local clubs and so did the single.

ZigZag, a key underground music magazine at the time, commented that the record 'had a good production that brings the best from a tested song', while *City Life* claimed that it was 'very un-Manchester'. The Roses had a strong local following in a city that traditionally supported its home-grown bands enthusiastically.

That was not the problem, the problem was getting known nationally. An idiosyncratic well-supported local scene like Manchester was great for creating new bands but a band could get stuck – ending up like James,

The Chameleons and a host of other groups, who at the time were home-town superstars with little fan base south of the Mersey.

Compared to The Smiths it was nothing, but the Roses were now off the mark. A couple of weeks later the Paula Greenwood interview was published in *Muze*. Ian was in full Ali-inspired flow – firing off quotes with an arrogance and self-belief way beyond the band's current size. He claimed that the reason that the band had played comparatively few gigs in Manchester was that venues were 'too small-time' and, fired up by the warehouse shows, that they were into playing gigs that had 'no bouncers, no law – where everyone can have a good time'.

When he played he liked to see 'rows of blank faces or jaws dropping when we go berserk'. He finished with 'we just want to do it and do it big and once it's done it's done.' Telling words for the future – especially underlined with the following quote: 'We'll either be massive or fizzle out, there is no in-between for this band.' Brown was obviously already working to his own itinerary.

The Happy Mondays' 'Delightful' was confusing people even more and even with the backing of the much bigger Factory label, it was hardly flying out. The Mondays were currently too raw and too strange while the Roses had yet to fuse their rock with the molten melodies that would get them the lift-off. The two bands, though, were aware of each other at the time with Cressa hanging out with both groups.

The Mondays were the real deal, they didn't give a toss about notions like credibility. They were out to get what they could. They didn't have any sort of conventional pop look, they looked rough as fuck. At the time they looked like a mad bunch of fucked-up thieves more than a band, but they played weird left-field rock with a fab funky bounce, mainly provided by Paul Ryder's Northern Soul fused bass lines. The surrealism was punched in by Shaun Ryder's brilliant stream-of-unconsciousness lyrics.

Paul Ryder definitely left an impression on Pete Garner. 'I knew he was a shit-hot bass player. Everyone in Manchester was raving about him being the best thing in the Mondays. We thought that we were going to be the band that broke out of Manchester and yet here was this other band that really looked like they were going to do it as well.' Garner looks up. 'After we heard the Mondays we knew that there we were not going to be alone.'

The Happy Mondays' whole demeanour, their pimp roll, easy-rolling natural vibe was to have a big effect on the Roses.

Just two days after the single was released on 11 September, The Stone Roses were back down in London playing a launch party for photographer Dennis Morris who was releasing a photo book of the Sex Pistols at the Embassy club in London. They were supporting The Chiefs of Relief who featured the former guitar player from Bow Wow Wow, the late Matthew Ashman, and, on drums, the legendary ex-Pistol Paul Cook whom the Roses, being avowed Pistols fans, were pretty excited to meet.

On 26 October the band took yet another trip down to London to play another show in the capital. They played their twenty-third gig at a rock week at the Riverside studios.

The week of gigs featured headliners like Mighty Lemon Drops, The Membranes, The Shop Assistants. It was a series of gigs showcasing the best upcoming UK bands of the time. Many of these bands would never break big but in the eighties the indie scene was far more underground than it would be later on.

At the Riverside the Roses supported That Petrol Emotion, the Irish band formed from the ashes of the Undertones, that was dealing some great music coupled with sharp political comment, especially on the Irish question.

First on were Banjo Fury and then The Stone Roses played to a sparse audience. They copped another review in the *Melody Maker* but it was getting pretty clear that, apart from Garry Johnson, no one was really going for the band.

The *Melody Maker* sharpened its claws and went in, Ian Brown copping the brunt of the attack. 'What's this whirling torso, an undiplomatic spunky splash of energy...' they wrote, adding something about the 'wretched state of the dire dirges'.

That left *Sounds* the only paper to support the young band. Garry Johnson says:

'Reni was like a young Keith Moon, a great personality at the time, always joking, like how you imagine a Keith Moon to be. Ian Brown had an aura about him. He knew he would do something but not in a big-headed sort of way but you thought he knew it.

'At that time they hadn't found what they were looking for. They had a bit of everything. To me they seemed completely different from anything else. I knew they were going to be big – they stuck out, they had the whole package on and off stage. They had the whole attitude.'

Johnson was the only journalist who really got the band at the time. The general consensus of the press was that they were too rocky. Music journalists have always veered closer to the indie end of music and The Stone Roses' music and attitude didn't sit too well with writers at the time, as Manchester DJ and journalist Dave Haslam explains.

'I didn't know them as people and I remember finding their early work just a bit more testosterone-fuelled than the music that I really liked. It may have just been my misapprehension but I just remember for some reason feeling that they were too Theatre Of Hate-ish, and maybe I was wrong but that was just my impression of them and seeing them live in the early days I felt that the crowd kind of reflected that in the sense that I thought the crowd was a bit macho. I saw them at the International and I went to a warehouse party. Later on I realised there was a progression, and quite a big progression from their early work, and I remember then becoming aware of them as people at the Hacienda and for example seeing them at gigs like when The Jesus And Mary Chain played at the Hacienda.'

Ian Brown ponders their dislocation from the mid-eighties media: 'We were not hip in 1985 with journalists. We got a slagging in *City Life* but they were all London boys who wrote for *City Life* and they were scared of us. Jazz funk was the scene then for the trendies; they didn't understand our kind of music.'

On 22 November they played another show in Manchester in the main hall of the university, a room that holds about eight hundred. When the band rolled up in their van they were surprised to see students helping carry the gear into the venue for them. This was the first time this had happened, strangers carrying the gear, the most hated chore in rock'n'roll. This was a pretty neat taste of the big time.

'It was the first gig where we got out of the van and people carried our gear in for us,' remembers Pete Garner. 'There were loads of students helping us to carry our stuff in. Slim was roadying for us with Gluepot Glen. It was an easy day for them.'

Slim was something of a legend on the Manchester scene. A big fuck-off guy, Slim has been crewing for bands for years. Garner knew him back from his school days.

'Slim had a go at me at school when I was in the second year in the playground,' Garner recounts. 'You just didn't wander into the big kids' playground but we were playing football and our ball went in there. I went in and got it. Just when I put my foot on the ball this fat guy ran up to me and smacked me in the face and I went straight down. After that, years later, I saw him at loads of punk gigs,' he recalls, adding, 'He was a trouble-maker! He was always standing on the balcony gobbing on people!'

Support that night were The Brigade, ironically a Clash style band reminiscent of The Patrol. They seemed to be on the circuit for years before fizzling out.

A week later, on 30 November, they played another warehouse party. People at the show remember that the warehouse was massive and that, being November, it was really cold. This time the Roses told British Rail that they were filming a video.

'It was at a different place…fucking freezing again,' recalls Pete. 'We hired a massive room. It was not as intimate as the first one, there was a dead high ceiling. I remember doing the soundcheck with gloves on. We played these songs all day every day. It wasn't a big deal that Ian didn't go to the soundcheck. Andy sang in the soundcheck. I've got that on video, that's funny!'

This time there were even more people at the show than the one before. It was obvious that as far as Manchester was concerned the Roses were getting to be a cool band to be into. The two warehouse parties had served the band well. They gave them an outlaw edge, an underground dangerous vibe, an added hipness that took them out beyond the ruck of local bands slogging around the circuit.

Kevin Cummings, the fast-rising local photographer who would even-tually take some of the classic Roses shots, took pictures that night.

The set also featured a new song, the melodic jangling 'Boy on a Pedestal', a tune pointing the band in a different direction. Unfortunately the song had only been written the day before and fell apart.

The gig was reviewed by local face and DJ, Auss, who has been a fringe member of the Manchester scene for years DJing and hanging out. He noted that the gig was the first time for a long time that people had been seen to be enjoying themselves. Garner remembers things a touch more earthily. 'There was some woman pissing in the street,' he recalls.

The set hung together well, despite the logistical difficulties of putting a show on in such awkward circumstances. It wasn't until 'Getting Plenty' that the generator, which had been humming almost as loud as the band's set, blew up, ending the gig. Karen Ablaze, who put together the cool Ablaze fanzine and was one of the eventual key players in the inspirational Riot Grrrl scene, was there.

'I remember at the end of the show Reni leant back and smashed the window at the back of the warehouse. It was really freezing. The band were great that night. They were much better in the early days. I really liked the sort of stuff that they were doing then, it was much more soulful, it was much more them.'

In November the *NME* finally reviewed the single. Mat Snow weighed in with 'the great lost Martin Hannett produced this and a right silk purse it is too, pure post-punk apocalypse, even that won't persuade me to play it again.'

Bob Dickinson followed this up with a 28 November review in *City Life*. 'The sound leaps violently out, The Stone Roses are truly teenage,' he wrote, despite the fact most of the band were now in their very early twenties. He also noted that they were 'pretty self confident.'

Bob interviewed them for the magazine. 'In the interview they talked about this question of whether they were a psyche band or not. They didn't want to admit to it. I know a lot of people thought at that time that they were a Goth band but I can't imagine why, apart from strange photos at the time which suggest Goth band haircuts for a brief moment.

'They had a combined attitude when lots of bands don't. Lots of bands don't know how to talk to journalists but they definitely had an idea about themselves and had come up with a way of handling journalists that was very professional.

'I would be going to those gigs on my own. I don't remember there being huge audiences for them. They had some fans of their own but the university gig was very sparsely attended. There was a big hole in the middle of the floor, people were standing round the edges of the room and nobody was standing at the front of the stage. I can't define what their followers were like. It was a bit of a mixed bag.'

The only other band in Manchester remotely like The Stone Roses were The Chameleons and they had just been picked up by Geffen Records. There is even a weird story that still goes round that Geffen was sent over to Manchester to sign this new rock band doing the rounds in the city. Apparently the A&R on the track of the Roses stumbled across The Chameleons and signed them instead.

As 1985 drew to an end and 1986 kicked off, the Roses entered a period of inertia. The first 18 months had been a buzz, they seem to be heading somewhere, but the album was just not right. Already they weren't happy with Howard Jones' management. Something was going to have to give.

Smeared! The Graffiti Controversy

The band were not liked by the hipsters in Manchester who were forever pushing their own agenda, which got ignored by everyone else. Their attitude and music didn't fit into the trendy inner circle. Tony Wilson mislabelled them Goths and their rockier music was rubbing these people up the wrong way.

One night, if an Ian Brown interview in *Record Collector* is to be believed, he and Reni were going to distance themselves even further from these people. Ian told the magazine: 'Me and Reni decided we'd been ignored for long enough. We'll cover the city with "Stone Roses". So we sprayed everywhere at about seven/eight o'clock at night. Reni was spraying the front of a library and there was a copper stood just around the corner – but the copper couldn't see him!'

The graffiti campaign was to mire them in a controversy that hung round their necks for years. The first time that the Roses came to most people's attention in Manchester was with this much-copied campaign. It gave a stick to those that wanted to beat them and cemented their thuggish image with the scene hipsters.

All the way from Burton Road in Didsbury to the city centre, and especially on the walls of the circular library building, their name was sprayed. The band always claimed that it was an over-zealous fan, while graffiti experts pointed out that the graffiti went all the way from their current bedsit HQ in West Didsbury and along the bus route into town.

Whatever and whoever, someone seemed to have graffitied the whole city.

Looking back years later, Couzens is hardly ashamed of the campaign. 'Ian and Reni did the graffiti. We used to go and watch Seventeen who were a great power pop mod band who eventually became The Alarm, and wherever they went they sprayed their name. We thought that this was a really cool idea.'

This version of events is still disputed by others close to the band. 'It was a fucking fan that did it right, for fuck's sake, they were not that sort of band,' gruffly recalls an unnamed associate.

The campaign by the band or 'over-zealous fan' had a dual effect on the band's Manchester profile. It made them instantly notorious. It pissed off the bookish wing of the Manchester scene – like The Smiths-loving south siders.

The band were instantly ostracised by *City Life* and the *Manchester Evening News*, even the local Granada TV news felt obliged to jump on the self-righteous bandwagon. If anything it helped to make them feel more like romantic rebel outsiders and may have affected the way that they perceived the press and media for years to come.

Muze magazine was one of the first to lay into the band, screaming 'It's own up time, who's responsible for the graffiti? The band themselves deny involvement because "it's too tacky",' they screeched.

It seemed as if everyone on the city's music scene was outraged – a combination of sudden civic pride and an inevitable backlash on the spotty new brats on the block was biting deep. It's hardly like Manchester is the world's most beautiful city. The city trades off its pop heritage. The same self-righteous denouncers of the graffiti were the very ones living in the shadows of the bands that were using any means necessary to project themselves on to the public.

Couzens is still amused at the repercussions of the campaign. 'It finished us off in Manchester. We could get no gigs, no press. Tony Wilson was slagging us off and made moves to make sure that we couldn't do anything. We tried for a rehearsal room at the Boardwalk and they wouldn't let us in there as well. We were outsiders, we had total notoriety.'

The graffiti made the front pages of the *Manchester Evening News* and the letters pages were filled with annoyed missives. In one way the spray painting had worked – it had made the Roses notorious.

The Roses were the talking point of a city music scene suddenly overcome with self-righteousness. Graffiti and rock'n'roll are hardly new bedfellows. Most band's music is aural graffiti and all the better for it. Pop is not meant to be respectable. At the time Norman Tebbit was handing out awards at pop ceremonies and the eighties, post Live Aid, saw pop become horribly sanitised.

It was a burning controversy that took years to calm down. While everyone raged and got on their high horses Pete Garner took a trip to town with his mother. He passed some of the spray can work and cringed with embarrassment waiting for the inevitable dusting down, but was surprised at her reaction.

'Someone has sprayed your band's name on the wall over there,' she gushed in awe, adding, 'You must be getting famous.'

And even in the daft world of rock'n'roll Mum knows best.

1986

Boys Seeking a Pedestal: The Roses in Limbo

The band had got as far as they could and they were now outgrowing their style. It was time for a change. A new broom. A new direction.

The tracks they had recorded with Martin Hannett had pissed them off; they felt that they had better songs, a better sound. The recording had inspired them to retreat back to Spirit.

John Breakall was impressed with the band's work ethic: 'The band were very focused. They knew what they wanted and they were going for it and nothing was gonna get in their way. Nothing. I wouldn't say they were aggressive to reach that goal – they were just very focused. They would rehearse eight days a week if they could. They were full-on.'

In the sessions, almost as a reaction to their recordings, they had come up with 'Sally Cinnamon', a big jump forward in their capabilities. Pure shining, shimmering pop, 'Sally Cinnamon' opened the door to a new Roses style, also audible on 'Here It Comes'.

'We wanted to move as far away from "So Young" as possible,' says Brown. Howard Jones was now out of the picture as well, as Andy Couzens explains: 'We weren't sure what he was doing. He had brought in Tim Oliver to help out. We didn't even know who was managing us.'

Ian Brown was happy to move on: 'Howard Jones was now gone. We had done the ten songs with Hannett. We had gone to record the demos in some down-time – it was not an album and they were talking about releasing an album.

'With Hannett it didn't sound right. He was a lovely fellow but he was so far out of it then, he didn't know where he was. He was sat under the mixing desk cross-legged like Buddha. We found him once in the tape room in a bit of a mess. It was sad. He went massive in size and would wear a big black kimono. He was a dead intelligent head who lost it because he was too intelligent.'

The band knew they were already going somewhere else musically. So all plans were shelved, sketchy plans that included the album and the two follow-up singles to 'So Young' – 'I Wanna Be Adored' (which had even gone as far as apparently having a sleeve designed for it by John Squire, a sleeve that would eventually be used for the cover of *Garage Flower*) and the single after that, 'This Is The One'.

They had pulled the brakes on. Then the Roses scrapped the album. The band's swagger needed a proper soundtrack, a new soundtrack. They could do better than this. They sat and listened to the tapes. There was something not quite right. They felt that they were in the studio recording an album far too early into their career. It could still have come out but they binned it. No wonder the Roses' eventual début album sounded so accomplished! For a band stuck on the dole to scrap an album takes some discipline. Takes some guts. But they were perfectionists.

They had done something very rare in bands. They had put their foot down. They turned their back on the record deal, the album, the whole fucking schedule.

Not for the first time in their career The Stone Roses took matters into their own hands. It was time for some proper songwriting. Time to let the music really talk. Instead of getting bogged down in gigs they retreated to the rehearsal room, disappeared from the scene and started writing songs. Proper songs.

They changed the way that they wrote – no more working up riffs and making them into songs. They started to relearn the whole creative process and learned how to write songs.

This also saw a slight shift in the band politics. Instead of mainly John throwing riffs into the rehearsal room and Ian huddled in the corner putting his words to them, Ian and John worked together on the tunes round at John's flat.

Listening to a rehearsal tape from March 1986 you can hear a different band beginning to emerge from the 1985 one. The guitars are turned down. They are janglier. More melodic. More thought out. There are dynamics getting applied. Quiet bits. Loud bits. Bits where Ian Brown can sing instead of shout. A bit of tension and then a chorus. Melody is the key. There is less thrashing and more finesse. Reni is still a powerhouse but the complex song structures are letting him toy with the rhythms even more.

In these tunes you can pretty well hear the classic Roses sound getting put together. Here is the rough template finally being moulded; the sound of '89 is getting stumbled on early in 1986 in Spirit recording studios in city-centre Manchester.

By the time they got back on the boards to play a gig on 5 March after a break of four months they were a different band. Back on stage at the

King George's Hall in Blackburn they were faced with a rather bored crowd waiting for Paul Cook and Matthew Ashman's (ex Bow Wow Wow) Chiefs Of Relief to come on stage. That night they débuted new songs 'Sally Cinnamon' and 'All Across The Sands' – an innocuous song with a typically dark lyric.

The 'crowd' though were in no mood for such double-edged songs and stood there bored and listless. The Preston Riot was in no danger of getting repeated here.

The band had had enough and as a wind-up the Roses dredged up their Sigue Sigue Sputnik cover from Preston Clouds the year before. This time they played 'Love Missile' four times in a row and left the stage snickering.

Sweet revenge.

It had been a long time since the Roses had done anything. It is a tough time for a band when the initial promise seems to fade. The surge of gigs, press and music biz attention sometimes comes to nothing – at this point many bands fold. They see the dream is an empty dream, that there is nothing worth pursuing and pack it all in, going back to their normal lives.

The Stone Roses were already dug in too deep to believe this. There was a massive emotional investment to the gang and they really did believe that they were going to get somewhere.

'So Young' had hardly set the world alight. Typically for a new Manchester band it had sold well in the hometown and done nothing anywhere else. Manchester, as ever, was supporting its bands like football teams.

There was already a big Manchester scene early in 1986. It was starting to get its own look, its own idea of what it was about. The Hacienda, although often empty, was looked on with pride. It was a prestigious club to have in a city of this size. There were Manchester bands like The Smiths and New Order who were big ground-breaking bands, the city was hip and there was a feeling in the grass roots that there was something else going to break.

But the Mondays and the Roses? You have to be kidding mate! The Mondays were a bunch of hooligans that had puzzled people by blagging a deal with Factory. They sold no records at all and their prospects of a breakthrough looked very dim.

And the Roses – even worse! They were just a rock band with a penchant for spraying buildings with graffiti. Just thugs whose pride in what they did meant that they would dash off bad-tempered letters if journalists slagged them off. Journalists like Paul Lloyd who reviewed them for the Poly arts mag *Pulp* and received a hatful of angry mail from Ian Brown as a result of a rather negative piece.

The graffiti campaign, the rowdy following, the press photo with the leather trousers, John Squire's bandana and Pete's long New York Dolls hair had seen them wrongly labelled as Goths by the city's fashionistas, hamstrung by their terror of rock.

'We wore the leather pants because they were rock'n'roll but we tried not to be a rock'n'roll band,' explains Ian Brown. 'Not in that kind of corny way. The Beatles had worn them in Hamburg, Rotten had worn them in the Sex Pistols and Sid Vicious and Steve Jones. I've read an interview with John saying he was a big fan of the Mary Chain but I don't remember wearing leather pants because of the Mary Chain.'

Paula Greenwood was just as confused by the Goth association. 'Everyone says that they were a Goth band but I never thought that. They didn't come on stage dressed in black, singing miserable songs. Everything about them was positive. They were optimists and they had something that no other band had at the time.'

The pundits' money at the time was on a whole host of no-mark outfits. Everyone was looking for the new Smiths. It would take acid house, ecstasy and the end of the student dominance of the city's music scene to mark the next key shift and that was a good few years off yet.

It had been 18 months since their *Sounds* feature, but without a press agent they hadn't really followed this up. Bands in the modern era know the whole system and go with its dictates. At the time, though, bands would be shocked at getting in the papers and then would disappear for ages, bemused at their lucky break.

On 25 March they played their first Midlands gig at Warwick University supporting Love and Rockets, the remnants of ultimate Goth band, the great Bauhaus. Love and Rockets would eventually go on to have a number two hit in the States.

Recalls Pete, 'I was a big Bauhaus fan but they would not talk to any of us. They didn't want to associate with us. We must have been like little kids to them.'

By now, the Roses were always ending the set with 'This Is The One' instead of 'Tell Me'. This brilliant song was an effective and all-defining full stop on a set that was slowly but surely moving away from the rock kernel of its roots and into something more flowery and more melodic.

The band were moving from speed to marijuana and acid. Like all pop culture, you change the drugs and you change the music.

Slowly evolving, moving on up towards the sugar spun pop...All they needed now was some sort of human dynamo to point this new pop nous in the right direction.

Maybe this ad that someone had spotted in the paper from a local manager looking for a band could be the answer. It was from the bloke that ran the International 1. He must know some people.

Enter Gareth Evans

Sometimes a band's manager is a quiet figure, plotting and scheming away, someone like Oasis's Marcus Russell with his low-key approach, doing the deals and just getting on with the business. And sometimes the band's manager is a larger-than-life character who just can't help getting to be almost as famous as his charges.

Gareth Evans is such an ebullient character, and while the Roses were going through their initial growing pains he was making his own moves on the city's music scene by buying the two International clubs and becoming a hands-on promoter who fussed around the touring bands and always looked after the musicians in town, which made him great company for people like your author, who spent hundreds of nights in his clubs.

Evans' own history in the music business went back to the sixties.

'I was a mod and started working at the Jigsaw club in Manchester in 1968. They trusted me with the takings and I didn't rip them off so they gave me the keys and said, "Run the place."'

Gareth started booking bands like The Yardbirds or Long John Baldry with Rod Stewart on vocals, and helping make a name for the club.

'The Jigsaw was in Cromford Court where the Arndale is now, opposite the Cromford Court Casino where the Krays were thrown out and taken back to Piccadilly Station. When I closed the Jigsaw at night I would go in the casino. I went in there with Martha And The Vandellas, after they would only sing two numbers because [the Jigsaw] was rat-infested – they were quite correct but my apparent charm in those days got Martha to play more! Then we went in the casino after and we gambled – the girls in there used to give me free food.'

Gareth Evans is the most controversial character in The Stone Roses' story. Rogue or genius, vagabond or visionary – everyone has a different opinion; sometimes the same person has opposing opinions. Armed with considerable charm and also a disarming way of pretending to know nothing, he was always scheming, always playing chess with the situation.

'I had the best mohair suits, off-the-racks double vents. My trademark was a long yellow suede coat. A lot of the mods used to take pride in having Gareth on the back of their scooters!' he boasts. In the seventies he drifted down to Cornwall and then to London where he learnt to cut hair with Sassoon; returning home, he opened his own chain of hair-dressers in Manchester.

Gareth talks non-stop as he lays out his life. It weaves and twists around the decades in a flow: mod, croupier, hairdresser, before becoming the owner of 20 hair salons.

'I was also into gold bullion in the seventies. With the gold bullion I got into finance and then I heard that the Oceans 11 club was for sale and I bought it and made that the Internationals,' he adds.

Swiftly the two clubs turned into rock venues and a whole host of bands would pass through their doors. They were archetypical rock spaces: plastic glasses, beer-stained floors, shabby interiors and great nights of cool bands. The International 1 was the smaller of the two, aimed at bands that were coming through, while 2 was for more established stars chugging around the circuit.

Jenx, who worked there, remembers those early days: 'The International could be quite chaotic. Originally there were four owners, not two. The four were Gareth Evans, Mathew Cummins, Dougie James and John Bagnall. The smartest thing they did was bring Roger Eagle in to book the bands.'

At the International 1 Evans would often be on the door, letting in local musicians for free and stopping some journalists from getting in just for fun. It was here that one night he stopped Yasmin Le Bon from getting in to see Duran Duran play a low-key secret gig. 'I don't care who you are, love, get to the back of the queue,' he snapped at her. It was the measure of the man, no airs and graces, eccentric – no matter how loaded he became he would always travel second-class on the train, hating the whole concept of first-class.

Evans was a hustler, looking out for the main chance, but he also loved rock'n'roll, and when he finally hooked up with the Roses he totally believed in the band, using his money and the power of the Internationals to back them to the hilt.

'Simply Red rehearsed at the International a few times and I apparently managed them for a few months,' Gareth claims. 'Elliot Rashman and Andy Booth asked me in to help and they asked me a lot of questions. I never saw them after that but they said I was part of the team!'

Jenx laughs. 'When I worked there I never spoke to Gareth. There was no point – he doesn't operate on the same planet as the rest of us! I lived for music then.'

Gareth Evans suddenly found himself the focal point of young bands. 'Let me tell you that bands were coming to me for management because I had the International and they liked the way I talked. I had a full meeting with the Happy Mondays about managing them once.

'The story is I put an advert in the paper looking for bands but I deny this. There was a girl called Helen helping me and she said she wanted to manage bands working from the office and I said, "As long as you help do stuff in the office that's OK," so she put the ad in.'

Others, though, say that Gareth was looking for a band to manage – as ever it's all a bit blurred. 'The Stone Roses saw the advert and came in to the office in Andy Couzens' big American car. They all came up and pushed their way into the office trying to be rock stars but I wasn't impressed with that. Then we started talking to each other. I started saying things. Maybe I like talking.'

A year after The Stone Roses met Gareth at their very first Manchester gig at International 1, here they were in his office, the cocky young band and the ball of energy that was Gareth Evans in one of the more bizarre meetings in rock'n'roll history. It was a crucial coupling and one that really helped the band break through.

'We had seen the ad saying that they were looking for demos of new bands and the address was for the International. So we drove down there and burst into his office and demanded a meeting,' says Andy Couzens.

The Roses' impetuousness must have impressed Evans, a man who would have probably done the same thing in the same circumstances. It may have been a measure of their desperation though, as they had lost interest in the Hannett album and relations with Howard Jones were getting strained as Ian Brown points out. 'We didn't think that Howard was the man for the job. We argued with his ideas. We never signed a contract with him.'

The Roses felt that they weren't really getting anywhere and needed a new input, a new push. In a situation like this it's either change the band or change the manager.

For the time being they would settle for the latter. Ian Brown grins as he remembers the meeting: 'At the meeting he pulled out a big fucking wedge, ten grand, casually slapped it on his desk and we were thinking, of course you got money – you run a nightclub. It worked – he was a bit of a gangster, a rubbish gangster, but it's good to have a manager who is a bit of a gangster...you need someone like that. He was an outsider and he believed in us.'

The office at the International was a small place across the road from the club. When the Roses entered it must have been quite a sight, the arch hustler and the young band crammed into a tight space, each party wary but doing the hard sell, as Garner remembers: 'We launched into a massive spiel at him. We were dead cocky. "You will be our manager," we told him.'

Evans instantly recognised that this was a band that he could work with. He decided to show them some of his hard-sell skills. At the time he was flogging novelty underpants.

'He told us that he could sell anything to anybody. He was just going through this spiel when he dropped his pants and showed us his underwear; he told us that he was selling those as well. He tried to sell us a pair of pants!' says Pete Garner.

Maybe they didn't buy his pants but they bought his spiel. 'It was at that moment that we knew that he was the right man for the job,' adds Garner.

Gareth Evans laughs: 'That story is true. I did take my pants down and show them some knickers. I had got some machines and was making clothes – the underwear samples were made by real professionals, people made them in Rochdale and the hems were dead thick.

'I think the Roses wanted to play me some music but I said, "I don't want to know, my job is to get you known, full stop." I started doing crazy things, giving away tickets. Noel Gallagher said I gave 5,000 comps away when they played and it was rammed although we did sell a lot of tickets as well.'

The band also liked the fact that they could now rehearse at the International, get into his club for free and get complimentary drinks at the bar all night. This was more like it, the rock'n'roll lifestyle on the dole.

Ever the flash man, Evans took the starving band out to a spaghetti house a week later and signed the management deal with them in front of Paula Greenwood, the still loyal journalist.

They screeched down Burton Road in West Didsbury in two flash cars, and I bumped into them. It was all high spirits and high jinks at that point, and the meal ended up with them throwing spaghetti around the restaurant.

When Evans produced the contract that would later cause so much grief, he stated that he would sign them for ten years to which the band joked, 'Make it twenty, Gareth!'

Evans looked up, and without a trace of irony he stared back at them. 'Can I?' he answered.

Riot Part Two! The Dublin Disaster and the Simmering Tension Between Gareth and Andy

Three weeks with Gareth at the helm and the Roses now slowly entered a new phase. They moved rehearsal rooms from the cramped Spirit rooms to the stage at International 1. A proper full-on stage to get it together. Bliss! No wonder they started to sound like a big band. With a full PA to work their tunes they further developed their subtleties in their daily rehearsal regime. Says Pete, 'We would rehearse every day. Well you would wouldn't you? It's your job.'

Ian and John were starting to bring proper songs in and behind the scenes Gareth was in hyper-drive. Constant phone calls to record labels and local media. This was a one-man campaign. A promotional whirlwind.

The Roses demo tapes were getting mailed out everywhere. The follow-up phone calls were in place, a blitz of enthusiasm and self-belief that would even take the band aback!

The band's internal dynamic was also beginning to change. Gareth was meddling with the chemistry. He had his own idea of how this band worked. And to him it was the Squire/Brown axis.

Andy Couzens saw the cracks appearing: 'In those few weeks me and Gareth never got on. We had screaming rows. He would go on at me about loads of things. It was starting to get a bit frustrating.'

The tensions were beginning to show. Evans was concentrating on Squire and Brown. And there were mutterings in rehearsals. The allegiances in the band were always shifting. They always do in bands, but now with the change in style, the change in emphasis in sound, the noisier town-guitar thing was, perhaps, not working.

The first cracks had begun when Ian and John had started to draw together, becoming the band's inner core. Andy instantly felt frozen out; he wasn't a no-hoper tagging along for the ride. He could write tunes and organise a band as well and he would later prove this when he formed The High who nearly made it themselves a few years later.

As Brown and Squire gelled creatively the die was cast. All the great bands, the pair reasoned, had a songwriting duo at the core. Lennon and McCartney, Jagger and Richards, Strummer and Jones, it was all two-man songwriting teams playing off each other.

The Roses now had a songwriting machine with no extra space. Up until now things had been cool; they would still split the money five ways. After all they were still mates and they still believed in equality and all that.

But the main two songwriters were beginning to see things differently – they felt they did all the work, they wrote all the material. They were in effect the band. It's the conundrum that has ripped apart many great bands. There are no easy answers and both methods of splitting the royalties have good arguments going for them.

Brown and Squire decided that they would come clean and tell the rest of the band where they stood.

On the day Ian and John walked into rehearsals, the rest of the band could instantly tell that there was something going on. The pair of them made the announcement that as things were getting serious and they wrote all the songs they would not only take the credits on the record, they would take the publishing too.

The rest of the band would earn mechanical royalties etc, but the bulk of the band's money would be going to the main pair and that, as the songwriters realised, was the largest proposition of money that any band ever earns.

The rest of the group were aghast. Andy Couzens and Reni left instantly. The Roses as a gang was torn apart. They had always been more than just about making money – they were a gang, a united front, they were there for each other. Or so they had thought. It was a salutary lesson, but the ever-loyal Garner decided to stick it out with what was left of the group.

Couzens was livid but soon calmed down. Reni, though, realised that this was the best band he was ever likely to get in and returned. Says Andy,

'The argument at that point was about songwriting royalties. But at first it was more the aesthetic thing of having two names on the labels like Lennon/McCartney etc. It looked good. But the reason I eventually left the band had nothing to do with money.'

The remaining outfit was relieved, as you could be the best songwriting duo in the world but without a drummer, and especially one of Reni's clout and class, you were never going get anywhere. The fact that Reni was also starting to provide all of the harmonies on the band's songs and had the sweet voice of an angel had not gone unnoticed by his colleagues.

Pete Garner still purrs at the day when Reni first started doing vocals: 'I remember one day at the International, Reni said he wanted to put backing vocals on the songs and set a mic up. We thought it would be normal backing vocals but he did all this amazing stuff.'

The band returned to some sort of normality but as an effective unit they were shattered. It could never be the same again. They still had some gigs pencilled in, including a trip to Ireland for a gig at McGonagles on 31 May that Gareth had booked within days of managing them.

It wasn't all doom and gloom as they boarded the ferry to Dublin. For Manchester bands there was always something exciting about playing Dublin. The city had a vaguely exotic air of a hip and happening bohemian town – it was also rough as fuck with some of the meanest estates this side of Europe, but that meant nothing after living in Manchester.

The place the Roses were to play was McGonagles, a subterranean city-centre dive with a roof that looked like it was spat-out papier-mâché. A small venue, it was also the spot where most biggish touring bands made their Irish début. Normally a prestigious gig, someone had ballsed up big time when the Roses arrived. They had been booked on a heavy rock night.

The soundcheck went swimmingly and they went for a walk around the late spring Dublin streets, which is always a great experience, full of life and good vibes. When they returned to the venue they were appalled to find it packed with what they termed 'stinkers', rockers who were in no mood for a band like this.

The band's stagewear didn't help matters, either. Brown and Squire, along with Couzens, Garner and Reni, were decked out in matching Beach Boy shirts which John had made. They looked more like a bright and breezy clean-cut pop team than the rawhide leather and beer-swilling troupe that the rockers wanted.

There was an air of expectant trouble when they shuffled on to the stage, the sort of air that Ian Brown always thrived upon. Squire played it funny, making out that the band were a cabaret band.

The audience naturally didn't really get the joke and were braying and howling insults from 'Fuck off you English bastards', which was about as polite as it got, to threats of violence. They weren't even barracking for fun; this was undiluted hatred. The promoter was either a prize buffoon who couldn't tell his demo tapes apart or someone with a mean sense of humour. It was going to be a testing night.

Halfway through the set Squire decided to liven things up a little, and between songs he started to hunker out the stub-toed riff that was the totem, the alpha riff for the grease boys, 'Smoke On The Water', and as it rang out the place erupted. The band was taking the piss!

This time the violence was going to be more than a few beer-stained insults – it was going to be blood. It was sacrilegious to even tamper with the holy heritage of dandruff, and Squire had just put a dainty hoof in there.

The band retreated to the dressing-room where they had to barricade themselves in as the venue exploded. The promoter burst in through a back door and was livid. 'I'm not paying you fuckers for that,' he screamed.

He was met by a typical Roses response. 'You either pay us or we go out there and the place gets trashed,' they stated as cold as ice, prepared to go all the way with either option.

They stayed where they were while the bad-tempered crowd slowly dispersed.

Years later Garner met a girl who was at the concert, who claimed that it was the most frightening night of her life and that she had to shelter from the smashing glasses that were flying around everywhere.

After the gig the band got ready to return to Manchester. Whilst they got in the van, Andy Couzens went to the airport to catch a flight back to Manchester paid for by himself. It seemed a fairly innocuous move but it was one of the last straws. 'The gig was booked at short notice and I had arranged to see my girlfriend and I had to go to work the next day, so I was in a rush to get back.'

Andy's flight back from Dublin was just the sort of lever that Gareth was looking for. As he sat on the plane over the Irish Sea, Andy was flying home from his last-ever gig as a Stone Rose.

'Bands always make artistic decisions. I don't make artistic decisions,' says Gareth. 'With Andy the band never asked him back. It was a band decision; they could have asked me. The band wanted him out and the reason they gave was that he took a flight back from Dublin and in my world you don't desert your pals.'

Stephen Lea, Andy Couzens' lawyer, who had been helping the band out with their legal stuff, went to the meeting that was called to sort out the contracts just before the shit hit the fan. The meeting was held at the Eighth Day and Howard was there too: 'The band said to Howard, "You are the record company and manager. You can't be both," and I thought that was right,' he says. 'There was too much conflict between the two. So I prepared a letter from the band to Howard and went to the meeting at Eighth Day in the city centre.'

According to Lea, Howard tried to protest, but it was to no avail.

'Howard came to the meeting to collect the letter and Gareth blew him out with his first breath saying, "Whatever you have done for this lot, forget it."' Then Lea says the focus was on Andy. It was decided to adjourn to Gareth's office at the International and the argument continued.

'I didn't know about the flying back from the gig in Dublin at that point I don't think Gareth liked Andy and what he represented. Andy said, "Fuck this," and walked.

'I sat there a few more minutes and Gareth had a go at me. I sat there thinking, "Why am I here? This is a complete waste of time." So, I got up and walked out.

'I thought the rest of the band could have stuck up for Andy a bit more. I had been helping the band and had awful rows with Martin about getting paid. I had done a lot for them.'

For Andy Couzens the following years have been filled with frustration. Hooking up again with Howard Jones as manager, Couzens formed The High in 1989, whose classic guitar pop got the big launch the year after the baggy summer. They had the best press agent in London, Jeff Barrett, and with London Records pushing them, they all but fell short of the top thirty.

From five members to four, the Roses were about to kick-start a new era, but without the twin-guitar attack, they would need John Squire to up the ante. And the quiet guitarist was definitely about to do that.

From Five To Four

The first gig without Couzens could have been disastrous. The four-piece Roses worked hard – they only had a couple of days till their next gig at Leeds Warehouse on 6 June.

Andy had been a driving rhythm guitarist; his hard riffing had given them that rock edge that had helped grab all the attention so far. In pictures he very much looked like a member of the gang, sharing the same sort of slicked-back hair as Brown and the same sort of angular demeanour.

The band debated whether to replace him but it was obvious that John Squire was more than adequate at taking over and playing all the guitars – this was what they had wanted. He was fast becoming the best guitar player on the scene; his artiness, his depth of pop knowledge and all those hours of hard work were paying off.

The Leeds gig, though, was too soon after the rupture and they were left wanting. They went back to the rehearsal room and rebuilt their sound, the four of them utilising the new-found space and taking advantage of it.

John Squire's guitar playing was becoming phenomenal and the band was finally moving in another direction, away from the amphetamine-driven rock and into the dope-smoke haze of the more psychedelic pop. The Roses were already enjoying a surge of confidence that often comes after a band sheds a member, that tightening up, and like a football team with a player sent off who then raise their game, the band were starting to gear up to write the classics that would turn around their career. And how.

But still no one outside of Manchester was taking much notice. The band had gone through its first crisis and it was ages since the début single, but there was nothing on the horizon. Only Gareth Evans' persistent buzzing and hustling and the band's strong resolve kept things going through this frustrating period. In many ways that summer of 1986 was a real low point for the band. They played the Three Crowns pub in London in July and were poorly received. Brown sat on a stool in the middle of the set looking bored, and that night it must have seemed that it was going to be impossible to ever break out of their trap.

A couple of days later on 7 July they played the Monday night gig at the Ritz in Manchester (Mondays had been the Goth/student night for years) with The Flesh Puppets supporting. It was their first hometown show without Andy Couzens, and they had to put up with people asking where he was. But the new four-piece Roses were now looking and sounding good, and John Squire was more than comfortable in the rearranged songs. The set had been pruned for the four-piece and it's noticeable that 'I Wanna Be Adored', one of their oldest songs, was still not back in and would not return for another year.

At the tail end of August they played the Mardi Gras in Liverpool supported by The Danny Boys. It was almost like they were starting from scratch again, playing low-key shows. The year was nearly over and they were getting nowhere, and the odd gigs, combined with a massive gap between records, were leaving the band floundering. The local press was down on them after the graffiti campaign, and they were perceived as hooligans while the literary pop stomp of The Smiths was in its ascendancy. At that point the Roses were seen as throwbacks, no-hopers, just one of those Manchester rock/pop bands with an intensely loyal small local following, and that was all.

But at the heart and soul of the band things were very different. Phase two was kicking in, and with the air cleared, they were writing a phenomenal amount of songs. It was the greatest writing period of their career and that summer they revamped their set. In came 'Sugar Spun Sister' and 'The Sun Still Shines' – joining 'Sally Cinnamon' as wonderful bitter-sweet pop. Catching the Roses that summer would have been a glimpse into the future, with nearly half the set now made up of songs that would become classics to the just emerging new pop generation. Things were moving on; the old songs seemed dated and they were getting fed up with playing them.

Fan Sharon Bampton was at the show in Liverpool: 'I hadn't really heard of them; there weren't that many people there. It's all a bit of a blur now. I remember that they weren't as "Goth" as people were saying. There were moments when they seemed quite poppy. I remember Ian Brown really staring out at the crowd, he was quite fearsome in those days.'

A very different band was now emerging. Maybe in public there was little sign of any activity but this was the year when they started putting together the proper début album that would shake the British pop scene. Rehearsing away, learning their craft and fired by influences like The Jesus And Mary Chain and Primal Scream, they were coming up with real nuggets, drop-dead classics that would define a later pop generation.

Ian Brown was the positive force that drove the band through the low points: 'We had early versions of "This Is The One" and "I Wanna Be Adored" in 1985. We were ready from the start. We had the belief all the way. It probably came from me. I can remember being in my flat with my chips and beans and nothing else and I knew we were going to do it. I just knew it. I had faith in the rest of them. I had faith in Reni, and John was so good on guitar.'

Pete Garner was noting the new developments: 'John had just bought his first wah-wah pedal and written "Elephant Stone". It was a move forward. We thought that we were ahead of the pack again, when we heard the Happy Mondays' "Freaky Dancing" and realised that they were there as well.'

The two bands were moving symbiotically again. Their 1960s-fused pop hinted at a myriad new influences and fused punk rock with the sixties like The Jesus and Mary Chain and Primal Scream had done; bands who had the look, the rock'n'roll cool and the gang thing that also scored heavily with the style-obsessed south Manchester group.

The Roses were wearing paisley shirts and leather pants; they had bowl haircuts and roll-necked pullovers. It was a northern street take on the Creation leather look of the time. Creation Records, the label set up by Alan McGee, was the original home of The Jesus And Mary Chain and the current home of Primal Scream, and in the mid 1980s the whole label was decked out in a pimp leather crossed with a classic 1960s look.

John had the bowl cut and Brown was sporting a short rude shock of gelled spikes, Garner had the psychedelic pants and Reni, well, he had his own thing going. For many bands at the time, the Mary Chain were the alpha group.

The Jesus And Mary Chain were sullen biker leather and beautiful arrogance. Their gigs would collapse into skulking semi-riots, and their huge warm enveloping wall of pop and feedback seemed revolutionary – a mixture of 1960s girl groups, battered 'Nuggets' garage-track compilation LPs, garage rock and British psych freaks. They had simple but killer bruised melodies, they sang softly and sweetly of darkness, despair and love. This rang a chord with The Stone Roses. Their drummer, Bobby Gillespie, was so cool that he left to concentrate on Primal Scream, the band that he had started off before the Mary Chain, two key bands in one.

Kicking off as a metal percussion wind-up landing between Public Image Limited and Einstürzende Neubauten, Primal Scream soon incorporated Bobby's love of pristine pop. When he eventually got the band going good and proper they quickly became renowned for songs that seemed to last for seconds and were shots of pure melody. Again they were tough guys singing soft songs, love songs dripping in sentiment and sung with a stone-cold sneer. It was that classic clash of opposites that a band like the Stone Roses could appreciate.

Music press photographer Ian Tilton remembers an early Primal Scream photo session that tells all about the band: 'I was out in the hills near Glasgow doing some pictures of them and they were all about this melodic pop music, almost sentimental in a way – when along flies a butterfly and lands on the guitarist's shoulder. One minute they are all looking at the camera and the next he claps his hands and splatters the butterfly all over the place…that summed them up brilliantly.'

The Primals as well, even though they were included on the very indie C86 compilation, thought bigger and wanted bigger. They believed that they were a classic band. They had a song called 'Velocity Girl', that was ninety seconds of killer crystalline pop and collapsing chord changes. It struck a bullseye in many hearts, especially with The Stone Roses who would make a rare trip into town and see the Primals, hearing echoes of their beloved Love.

In fact The Stone Roses loved 'Velocity Girl' so much that they half-inched the chord sequence for 'Made of Stone', and took the Primals' song one step further and turned it into a bona fide classic. That's what pop is all about – influencing, changing and altering. If you like it, you have it; take the original and improve.

Bobby Gillespie knew this: 'Aye, people have mentioned that they took "Velocity Girl" over the years. But if they did, they made it better, much better – "Made of Stone" is a classic.'

And Bobby, the astute professor of pop, is a man who knows.

That December the Roses recorded their first demo as a four-piece in the basement flat of a house in Chorlton, Manchester. During the session they recorded 'Sugar Spun Sister', 'Going Down', 'Sun Still Shines' and 'Elephant Stone'. 'Sun Still Shines' featured the odd mono mix of all the bass and drums on one side and the guitar and vocals on the other.

The disconcerting sixties style sound mix was provided by Garner, who'd managed to get his hands on the controls. This demo was the first time that they had started to take an interest in what they sounded like as a band and not just their own parts. The demo is the point where the band started to take control of their sound, a control that leads directly to the début album. The tunes drip melody and a summery pop feel. They are so close to the 'Lemon' album sound and yet three years away from its release.

Manchester radio DJ Alison Bell lived in the flat above the demo space. 'I lived in a rented room in a house on Stockton Road, Chorlton. The landlord, Russ, was in a band called Playing At Trains. He was friends with the woman who ran a shop called Magic Balloons at the end of the road [where Stockton Road met Beech Road]. It was a kind of fancy dress hire shop/party shop etc. Reni used to work for her from time to time and that's how Russ knew him, I think.

'Russ had a 16-track recording studio in the cellar/basement – the room below mine. The Roses recorded a demo there in about 1986. It had "Elephant Stone", "Going Down", "Sugar Spun Sister" and an un-released track called "Sun Still Shines".'

At least creatively 1986 was ending on a high note!

1987

Cat and Mouse – Evans Plays the Waiting Game

As 1987 kicked off the Gareth Evans machine was kicking in. Full on. Behind the scenes he was spending hours on the phone. Hustling. Hoping. His self-belief was outrageous.

On paper the Roses were in a desperate position. Way out of sync with whatever crap fashion or dumb cool was knocking about, they were a couple of years down the line and still getting nowhere. Their original crew of fans had dwindled – confused by the new melodic direction the band had undertaken. Slowly their replacements were beginning to appear, new recruits and new faces previously not sure of the band's reputation who were getting hooked into their new style.

On 30 January they played Manchester International 1, yet another crossover gig for the band. The new Roses audience was slowly appearing and making up the majority of the crowd, the last demos had floated around town and new faces were now checking them out. The pop kids were appearing, the word was out the Roses were not so much the hooligans of yore, the whisper was that they were actually, possibly the best songwriters in the city since The Smiths! They were writing pop tunes that were dripping classic guitar-pop licks.

John Brice was a big fan of the band from the early days. 'I remember Ian came out on a scooter at one gig at the International. He would always find an interesting entrance. Ian always had that star thing.'

Gareth Scores a Record Deal

Gareth was mailing that demo everywhere. And there was very little reaction. The only record label that were even returning Gareth's calls were the Wolverhampton-based Revolver FM. A curious label to be interested in the melodic guitar pop that the Roses were playing, but a label none the less.

Gareth quickly found out that getting a deal was not going to be so easy: 'The Roses had been hawked by Howard Jones around everywhere and I didn't realise this. I had to get them a deal. There were not many independent labels, a real alternative scene. I talked to a few people. I needed someone who could distribute it. I'd spoken to London Records. They were great to me and said, "Get another band and we will give you a deal."

'They came to see the band at the International; the place was packed and everyone was going crazy over the Roses and then there was trouble at the front. This girl who was later in bands came from the front to the bar. She said, "I'm having a great time," but unfortunately there was blood pouring from her eye and London said we don't want any of this. The only label that was interested was this small label in the Midlands called Revolver.'

Revolver FM had been releasing low-cost glam metal/rock CDs and selling them into the lucrative Japanese market, as well as releases from the UK Subs and The Vibrators. The label's boss was Paul Birch who ran the operation from his house just outside Wolverhampton or from a Mayfair hotel room. His partner was Dave Roberts who had played in Silverwing, a glam/metal outfit from Macclesfield. Roberts had freelanced for *Sounds* before getting involved in running a record label and then pooling his resources with Birch.

The initial contact with Revolver had come from local booker Sandy Gort. Sandy managed the Macc Lads who had been signed to Revolver and he put Gareth in touch with the label. Revolver's number two, Dave Roberts, would be at the International reviewing bands for *Sounds* and Gareth, as was his wont, would always look after journalists.

One night Gareth cornered Dave Roberts in the International and told him he would have a permanent place on the guest list if he could get his boss to finally release the Roses on his label.

A few days later label boss Paul Birch relented and signed the band on a reverse deal (the band are the ones to provide something on signature, not the company).

Gareth recalls, 'I got this guy called Dave who used to come down to the Internationals to review bands and I persuaded him to open this label called "Black" on Revolver – an independent label. We hassled the guy who owned Revolver and got this label. He got the record out and it got in the indie charts.'

Gareth was looking for a one-off deal to get the Roses into the indie charts, up their profile and hopefully score a proper big-time deal. A meeting was arranged. Jumping in Gareth's Jeep they made the ninety-minute journey down to Wolverhampton. It was two worlds colliding – Paul Birch with his long flowing hair was very much the boss of a label that put out rock and glam records, whilst the Roses had a street Manc cool. Birch preferred the band's earlier rockier stuff; he could smell the glam influences that were in the band's music – the touch of The Clash, the hint of New York Dolls, a whiff of Empire! They had now moved on from these earlier influences, moving in a different direction. The new jangle pop was about cool, a studied cool.

But it was a marriage of convenience: the band desperately needed a release and Paul Birch was astute enough to hear the pop potential of 'Sally Cinnamon'. One of the oddest deals in the history of the Manchester music scene was done. The Stone Roses had a one-off single release on a Midlands metal label.

On the way home, as if to exorcise the past, Gareth, a man of wild gestures, threw the last remaining boxes of 'So Young' in the road and reversed his Jeep over them. The band looked on smirking and surprised. 'That's the ghost of Howard Jones removed forever,' their manager shouted, adding, 'the new era starts now!'

A week later Gareth looked through the contract and signed it. There was no time to fuck about, there was also no leeway to manoeuvre. In hindsight the Roses, with their now-legendary status, signing goofy deals seems crazy but you have to realise how tough it was at the time to get anyone interested.

For Revolver, signing the band may have been a favour but it was one that gives the label an odd footnote in the history of rock'n'roll.

Says Ian Brown, 'Mick Middles was writing things in the *Evening News* saying, "Have they not made it yet?" and then we got that deal with Revolver.'

'That Revolver single helped a lot,' states Gareth Evans. 'Our biggest break then was The Smiths breaking up because that was our space. We had the songs definitely.'

As the calls intensified between Manchester and Wolverhampton while the Revolver deal was being done, Gareth was working on building the Roses' profile up in Manchester.

Owning the two International venues left him well placed to do this. He would put the band on at the smaller International 1 and knock down the ticket price, give away tickets, anything to get the crowd in. In the past two years the band's audience had been changing, the word was getting out. The Roses were appealing to a whole new audience with their jangle pop thrills.

Gareth had been handing free tickets out around town. One of these tickets ended up in the hands of a young Noel Gallagher, who mooched down to the International for his first sighting of The Stone Roses.

'I was walking through town, carrying a guitar. It was the Lord Mayor's parade – we have mayors in Manchester, 'cos it's out in the sticks and that – and this fellow walked up to us in the street and gave us a big bunch of tickets. The Stone Roses were playing at International 1 and he said, "Have these and bring all your mates." So we were like, "What the fucks's all that about?" It subsequently turns out that the fellow that handed us the tickets was Gareth Evans, who used to do this quite regularly in town – he used to go round all the people who looked like scallies and he'd give them all tickets. So I went down to the gig with this bird. It was a Saturday night and we were round our way with nothing to do, so we all bolted down there. The gig was full of students, so we went to the bar.

'It was when they were still a five-piece. The Roses were in mid-Goth, early scally period then with Andy Couzens on guitar and the long-haired bass player. Ian Brown had this harlequin shirt on and a walking stick and slicked-back hair, like Dracula. They definitely had something about them. I bought "Sally Cinnamon" at the gig, I love that song but that version is the best. They had such a weird image, though. The song is not what they looked like: they were hard looking and the drummer was topless – going bananas.'

Noel Gallagher became one of the band's early fans of their second phase.

'Next I started to find out about them. In those days you could go into Afflecks Palace and get bootleg cassettes of the Roses and other bands. Every time we went to see them 50 more people would be there, and another new song I'd not heard of would get played. You can just tell with bands like that that it's going to happen.

'There were 50 people who went to every gig in Manchester like Clint Boon or you and I was the 51st. There was something about them that spoke to me. It was melodic guitar pop, great songs; the missing piece of the jigsaw was the way they looked. When The Stone Roses appeared to the rest of the country, everyone thought they came up with that look but they were virtually the last people into dress like that, God bless them. People think it's the other way round but apart from Mani, when they dressed like that that's when it happened. Those are the magical times in every band's existence when you are virtually the same age and have the same circumstances as your audience. When you are scraping forty quid a week to have a good time and you are not yet a rock star and you can relate in the most special way and that's magic.'

The Stone Roses played several shows at the International.

'Gareth would always put the Roses on to support bands that were totally inappropriate, which used to drive Roger Eagle nuts,' recalls Jenx. 'Or a band would turn up to set up and the Roses would be practising in the club. I am pretty sure they practised mostly at the International 1 as there were sound problems with 2 as it was a residential area. Roger liked the Roses as people but was tainted towards them due to Gareth and, don't forget, they didn't shine for a long time and I must class them as one of the bands that Roger missed seeing. I think most people missed their potential if they knew them early on in their career. I certainly did!'

Gareth Evans had concentrated on utilising the International 1 to showcase them to A&R, giving out free tickets to students and indie heads – filling the venues up – giving the impression that the Roses were far bigger than they actually were.

Now armed with tunes that were backing up their grandiose claims, the Roses would spend '87 frustratingly on the slow curve towards ascendancy. They were getting bigger and bigger in Manchester, this was the year that they became a proper big draw in the hometown. Elsewhere they were still ignored. But they were still powered by that enormous belief, a belief now being translated into great songs.

Self-belief, though, doesn't pay the bills. They were so broke at the time that Reni was apparently working as a kissogram. It was a measure of the poverty under which they were living.

But at least they had a home for their second single and that May they released 'Sally Cinnamon'.

'Sally Cinnamon'

The Roses' sound was now changing. Pulling back from the amphetamine assaults of their earlier years, they were discovering a more melodic side to their music, a less angry uptight sound. It's a difficult transition to make and one that plenty of bands should never make. But the new melody-soaked Roses seemed to suit the band. They retained some of the earlier flavours of the songwriting, the anthemic huge choruses and the inspirational rallying-call songs, but this time they were more dynamic, more subtle. They were learning about songwriting and finding out that it really suited them.

Ian Brown explained the new Roses sound to *Record Collector* who asked about the oft quoted Byrds influence and the painstaking songwriting process the band now set out upon.

'The Byrds came later. John got into them around early '88 but I've never owned a Byrds record. No, the influence was a nice tune. We never deliberately tried to copy anyone. We ended up writing tunes that sounded like The Beatles. We'd have 'I Feel Fine' or 'Day Tripper' but with different lyrics, accidental. So we'd drop them. Me and John went to Italy once just to write and we slept rough – we took an acoustic guitar and sleeping bags. We came back with three or four tunes. Wow, this is great. Well, no, they're like The Beatles!'

And evidence of this new Roses sound was stamped all over their upcoming 'Sally Cinnamon' single. Even its title was telling a different story.

One night in the International 1 an excited Gareth Evans ushered me into the office. He handed over a 12 inch single. It was a pre-release of the 'Roses' second single and the manager was positively exploding with excitement.

Released on 28 May, 'Sally Cinnamon', flipped with 'Here It Comes' and 'All Across The Sands', is pure unadulterated pop. It was bagged in a black-and-white sleeve photo (taken by John's brother Matt) of sweet dispensers outside a shop.

Recorded in Wolverhampton, it's as about as far away from their rock as they could go. Says Pete, 'We produced "Sally Cinnamon" ourselves with Simon who was our soundman at the time. He did the Happy Mondays as well.'

It offended some of their old fans like Karen Ablaze who told Ian Brown of her worries. 'He wasn't happy about that. He got really angry. I didn't like the new direction that they were taking. I really liked the older stuff like "Heart On The Staves", it was also more soulful.'

Karen was now in a minority. The Roses were starting to attract a whole new host of fans; disaffected pop kids and indie fans bored of the charisma-bypass indie shufflers were all starting to buy into the band. So far these were hometown indie fans only, the rest of the UK still wasn't getting it.

Liam Gallagher told me that this was the first Stone Roses song he heard. 'Our kid came home with the single and I thought it sounded great. At the time my older brother liked The Jam and Noel liked The Smiths and this sounded like something else.' He didn't have much choice. He was sharing a bedroom with Noel, who points out, 'I'd been into the Roses for a while and we shared a bedroom at that point and I played the single a lot.'

'Sally Cinnamon' hints at all those dynamic chops and changes in tempo that would be the band's trademark, along with the non-stop rush of melody, when they finally released their début album. The flipside 'Here It Comes' and 'All Across the Sand' followed suit; here was a band steeped in sweet tunes and a band, in '87, totally out of sync with the times.

'Here It Comes' is a typical piece of homespun Brown philosophy, an anti-celebrity sneer, a swaggering plea that directly bonds with the audience. It's yet another song that's a bridge between their punkier initial phase and already burgeoning new melodicism. Live in the early days it was an aggressive workout and had recently been dropped as the Roses' subtle change of direction had made the aggressive side of the band more and more redundant.

The single came out and didn't even get in the indie chart, but in Manchester it sold by the bucketload, aided no doubt by non-stop radio play on Tony Michaelides' key *Last Record Show*.

Andy McQueen, perhaps The Stone Roses' biggest fan of the time, remembers going out to buy the record the day that it was released. 'I went into Virgin Records to see if it was there and it wasn't. I met Ian Brown in Virgin and we were both disappointed that you couldn't buy it there.'

It seemed like the mainstream was a long way off. They sold out the 1,000-pressing of the single; it was enough to prove that somewhere someone loved them but it was hardly going to guarantee any chart action.

At the time the single got no national air play and no national press reviews. The local writers writing for the national press were frothing at the mouth, pointing at the Roses' now big hometown following and the classic pop that they were by now effortlessly parading, but it was going to be some time before London got it. Live-reviews editors on the national music press were just not having it.

'I rang up about covering the band,' says one journalist, 'and they told me that there was no way a band could be that popular in the north if no one in London liked them!'

If there was one thing that the Roses managed to achieve when they finally broke massive, it was that no one would get ignored again just because they didn't go drinking in Camden.

Slowly but surely and by word of mouth, The Stone Roses were starting to make an impact.

Four Become Three

In June they were back out on the road. Around this time Pete Garner told them that he wanted to leave the band for good.

'We realised that Pete was not that great on bass when we were tripping,' says Ian Brown. 'We could hear he wasn't on it and we thought, "Oh fuck, what are we going to do? Pete's a really good mate." But Pete saved us that job when he said, "I've got the feeling you're going to be massive but I've got to pull out as I'm not made for it." That was a tough time; there was just the three of us. We used to hang around all the time at Reni's house in Gorton, me, Johnny and Reni.'

It was a difficult decision for Pete. He felt that something had been lost in the band – the core bonding friendship had been broken since the money row the year before – but he mainly felt that he was holding the band back, and walked.

He said he would carry on playing gigs for them until they found a new bass player. His last Manchester show was at the International 1 and that was the night The Stone Roses met Paul Ryder from the Happy Mondays properly.

The gig had been the first sign that the new Roses were picking up a good crowd for their new sound. After the gig Gareth ordered the band home to create a mystique.

'I remember John Squire's face when I told him they should go home and not mingle after the gig,' he reveals. 'I said, "Don't go out front and talk to your buddies, go out the side door and disappear." They were dead sick because they had to go back round to Reni's house whilst I was having a great time.'

Paul Ryder, the Happy Mondays' bass player, went back with them. 'The first time I saw The Stone Roses was at the old International, the little original one. Cressa told me they were playing and said, "Why don't you come with me and watch them?"

'After the gig everybody went back to a house in Belle Vue, I think it was Reni's house. They got straight off stage and left. We knew each other through Cressa. He was a big instigator in getting people to meet up. I don't remember leaving the house so it must have been a really good party. There were plenty of girls in there. I remember thinking, "Wow they know loads of girls." We didn't have any girls at the time.'

There were a few more shows and Pete continued to fill in. On 26 June they played the International 1, a gig Gareth Evans invited the music business to, and really papered the house with free tickets. He shouldn't have worried though, as the band were by now pulling in a solid following.

They had been rehearsing in the International, and the advantage of playing on a large stage through a big PA was starting to tell on the group. They now sounded like a big-stage band. Instead of being crammed into some vile rehearsal room squashing their sound down they could experiment with space in their music, letting it grow, feel big.

The day after, on 27 June, by one of those weird quirks of fate, the Primals played the same venue. In many ways Glasgow's Primals were the sister band to the Roses; both bands were from tough cities and both bands had a deep love for the underground pop classic tunes that they fused with their own post-punk outlook, and created melody-strewn sensitive pop. The Primals would be one of the few bands that the Roses would check out when they played in town, although they always denied this.

In mid-July the Roses travelled over to Sheffield to play the Take Two club, and the set had now been radically shaken up: 'Elephant Stone', 'The Hardest Thing In The World', 'Sugar Spun Sister', 'Here It Comes', 'Sally Cinnamon', 'Where Angels Play', and 'Your Time Will Come' (the last being one that they never recorded and which is still one of superfan Andy McQueen's favourites), 'She Bangs The Drums', 'The Sun Still Shines', 'Mersey Paradise' and 'This Is The One'. The set was now taking shape.

Ever the political animal, Brown hated flags and all the heavyweight symbolism they carried with them. The support band's girlfriends were waving a Confederate flag at him, and this was a red rag to a steaming bull, as Andy McQueen remembers: 'Ian stopped the gig and went into a speech about the flag and how it represented slavery, white supremacy and racism.'

Then it kicked off again. 'There were these rock-chick girls, friends of the band, who were heckling the Roses. Ian, during "Sugar Spun Sister", said something back and one of the girls threw a pint at him. He went back, had a swig of water and spat water at this rocker bloke. Then everyone jumped in and told him to calm down.'

The Roses also played Liverpool at the legendary Planet X on 17 July, only their third gig in that year of transformation, to about 15 people. The band's music was developing but Brown was still into his confrontational stage bit. Prowling around the venue with his long mic lead, shorn hair and a thousand-yard stare he would go right up to people at the bar and stare them in the eyes, demanding attention.

Between the few gigs the band was now in creative overdrive. Ian Brown could be spotted walking down Burton Road in west Didsbury, lugging a set of keyboards over to John's in Chorlton. 'They are better for writing melodies on,' he would smile. Never was their creative partnership as strong as in this period.

At the time John said, 'The amount of songs me and Ian have to reject! We want perfect songs. We've got loads that aren't quite good enough. We want to be like The Beatles...they could change their style as much as they wanted, yet they were still undeniable as their songs were so good.'

On 11 August, the Roses played Larks In The Park, a mini festival that took place every year in Liverpool's Sefton Park, the large green space next to the crumble of Toxteth.

Days before, Brown had threatened to pull out of the gig if it was raining, remembering the Happy Mondays' recent balls-up in Manchester's Platt Fields where only thirty people turned up in the rain-sodden mid-summer afternoon.

Eventually he relented and the turnout was far better than expected. In 1987 Larks In The Park was the usual collection of local outfits but with a couple of pointers to the future. Liverpool's The La's, who had been working the bars and pubs of Liverpool and had built up quite a following with their skiffle pop, were in the same boat as the Roses, pure pop with no national audience. They were the main event along with the Roses themselves, and quite a few fans travelled from Manchester that hot August afternoon.

The Stone Roses played on the stage surrounded by the grassy slopes with loads of stoners sitting back and getting smashed in the summer sun. The band played next to an ornate pond which Ian Brown ended up jumping into, probably wrecking his leather trousers.

John Power was playing with The La's that day. 'At that time I think The La's had just been signed...I remember it was a very sunny day, absolutely roasting, but to be honest I don't remember the Roses being that great.

'I'd never really heard of The Stone Roses at the time and I don't think Lee [Mavers] had either when they played that day. What I gathered was they were kinda overcoat, a bit more kind of Bunnymen in their look. To be honest I don't think we really noticed them and I don't mean that in a bad way. I did take a lot of notice when the album come out though.

'I think when they played Larks In The Park they were coming out of whatever scene they'd been into. They were not so much the working-class urban kind of northern thing at the time but...there comes a time when a band finds who they are and they don't have to pretend and that's something The La's had and Cast had, what the Roses had.'

John Power captures the moment the Roses were closing a chapter; after this it was all going to change. And fast.

For many pundits it was headliners The La's that seemed ready to lead the charge of new northern bands that were waiting in the wings, but an idiosyncratic pace of work and an erratic recording schedule put paid to that. Lee Mavers's band had to virtually succeed on the coat-tails of their Mancunian neighbours before burning out; The La's blew it in a way that the Roses could only dream about.

Another chapter was about to close for the Roses; Larks In The Park was Pete Garner's last gig for the band. He went on to manage a record shop and be one of the cool heads hanging around town. Eminently like-able, it seems that everyone has a good word for him. He was never bitter about the band and would even carry on going down to rehearsals for a good stretch into the future. He remembers watching a rehearsal a few months after leaving and they played him 'I Am The Resurrection'. He was stunned. He knew that the band were moving forward fast.

He remained good friends with them and was recently spotted dusting down his bass guitar for a long-awaited return. An under-rated bass player, he was never the Goth of legend, and his melodic bass runs contributed enormously to the band's burgeoning new sound. He left right on the edge of their success, the great lost member of The Stone Roses.

The line-up crisis had re-emerged after one year. Where do you find someone who could slot into the gang, the tight-knit unit that was the Roses? Ian and John were knocked for six. Sure they knew that Pete was leaving, but they hoped that it wouldn't actually happen. They would spend the next couple of months in the doldrums. They even got another bass player in for two weeks, Rob Hampson – Pete came down and showed him the bass lines and he appeared in an Ian Tilton photo shoot for the band and then left.

Back to three.

The Perfect Wedge...The Return of Mani!

It wasn't easy for a band as close as this to get a new member who would fit into the ranks. They didn't really deal with outsiders that easily. So when Pete made his decision and the new bass didn't fit, it was a very dejected-looking John Squire and Ian Brown who bumped into Clint Boon, who had now formed the Inspiral Carpets, down at the Boardwalk one night.

'They said that they were looking for a bass player and did I know anybody,' says Boon. 'At the time we had Scott Carey in the Inspiral Carpets. Scott went on to form The Paris Angels, but he was a massive Roses fan. I could have suggested him, but that would have broken the band up, so I told them that I would think about it and left it at that.'

While Clint is keen to point out that he doesn't want any credit for this vital last cog being put into place for The Stone Roses, he did bump into Mani's brother Greg in Manchester city centre the next day and told him what was happening.

'The next day I saw Mani's brother Greg in Manchester,' recalls Clint, 'and I said, "I was with Ian and John last night and they need a bass player." Mani was working at the Opera House doing lights and I said [to Greg], "Get your brother in there quick."

Phil Smith remembers: 'At first when they needed a bass player they couldn't find Mani because he wasn't really about. He lived over in north Manchester and they must have sort of forgotten about him. I think he kept going to France, he was bumming around in Europe. I think when it didn't work out with Rob one of them bumped into Greg, Mani's brother, and that reminded them. Whichever one of them it was that bumped into him thought, "Fuckin' hell, what about Mani?"

'Manchester is not full of musicians like Liverpool is, where you can whistle and another guitarist pops out. While this was going on there was a gap. Even then they used to take a long time to do anything anyway, they'd only do the odd gig here and there and then sit around and plan for years. We were always waiting for them.'

Mani returned from the European jaunt a wanted man: 'I came from Europe and was hanging round town when my brother told me that he had bumped into Clint Boon who had told him that the Roses were looking for a bass player. Clint had, in turn, met John and Ian who had just gone and put an advert up in A1 or somewhere in town.

'I think my brother said, "Oh Mani's doing nothing," and then I got a call from John later that evening and he said, "Come down." They had been persevering with Rob Hampton, who had been in the band for about a week after Pete had left. Rob was a good mate of the band but for some reason it just didn't click. I just went, "I'll give it a shot."'

Mani had been there from the start. He was the obvious choice.

'I was always a fan of the band, I always looked for them and always used to go and watch them back when they were doing the more kind of punky/psyche kind of gear and I always knew they had something because I knew I would always end up with them anyway. It was just a feeling that I would be there at some point in time.

'So I went to meet them and it was just like "Let's see what happens" basically. I just started going to stay at John's house in Chorlton and chatting through things and I remember being up late at night with Ian. Gradually, I came up to speed playing-wise and then the confidence was there to just start taking risks and trying things with the music and just pulling each other along really, you know?'

For Ian Brown, Mani joining the band was the moment. 'Everyone who came to see the Roses at that point said that Mani was the final piece of the jigsaw. He looked great and could really play well.

'"Elephant Stone" was the first song we wrote with him and he changed the way we played, he added a groove. Mani was into smoking weed and reggae and playing the bass. He was great. We used to think he had a little monkey face! He looked like the actor Hywel Bennett.'

Mani, from the day he joined the band, was like a bolt of enthusiasm, and the garrulous wide-boy joy at being up there on the big stage was infectious. The man of the people who'd got the big break was the final piece of the jigsaw.

'It was always pretty much on a catch-up job,' Mani says. 'The rest of the guys had been together for a lot longer than I had and I came into it later, but at a good time. I took what was there and put my own stamp on it in a way. It was good, you know, a great learning curve. I had to learn fast. I always felt I was looking over my shoulder for approval because it was John and Ian's songs…

'People say that when I joined the band, that's when they became the band, and that's heart-warming, it gets me buzzing…I did feel we became more unified, even though I probably wasn't as talented as the other guys but I think I brought something to the party in a spiritual kind of way. I don't want to get all hippy about it but there was kind of a loyalty, determination and a good-vibe spirit that came with me as well.'

It was an enthusiasm that he would always bring to any situation. Mani was the rogue Rose. Mani's début gig was at the International 1 on 13 November 1987. I remember the gig and how young and fresh-faced he looked. He fitted in instantly, and as he'd always been a fringe member of the gang he knew the moves. He walked the walk, he talked the talk, he was a Rose before he was even in the band.

The legendary line-up was now complete, and now it was time to go and collect. The show at the International was a triumph and the set they played was: 'Sally Cinnamon', 'Elephant Stone', 'Here It Comes', 'I Wanna Be Adored' (now back in the set), 'Mersey Paradise', 'Going Down', 'Your Time Has Come', 'The Hardest Thing In The World', 'Waterfall', 'She Bangs The Drums', and 'This Is The One'.

Long-term fan and mate of the band Swinny saw the gig. 'One night I saw Mani and he mentioned he'd joined the Roses. He gave me a tape with some demos on that was rough but interesting. We all piled down to his first [gig] at the International and you could tell when they came out, introduced him as the new bassist and started up that this was going to be something a bit special. Each time we went to see them play they were getting bigger and bigger, and of course you know the rest.'

They were supported by The Waltones, another guitar-based pop band who at the time seemed omnipresent but just couldn't survive the great pop sea change that was looming on the horizon, although their guitar player Rob Collins would eventually join The Charlatans.

1987 Burns Out…

'Sally Cinnamon' was massive in Manchester. Gareth's policy of handing out tapes of the song around Afflecks Palace, the city-centre clothing emporium, was beginning to pay off. The plan was to get the student/music-paper readers into the band and then the normal kids.

The story still goes round of Gareth driving down Blackpool prom handing out Roses shirts to the coolest-looking people he could find, a bizarre old-school method of management. It was this belief in working from the grass roots up that would eventually hit paydirt two years later.

The Smiths were at the tail end of their career and something new was needed, something similar but with a more street edge. The times were toughening up and more attitude was required. The Roses and the Mondays were getting really good at just the right time, and there was something in the air, something was going to blow.

In mid 1987 small clubs were playing house music and the word was on the street about E; the hip were out looking for this wonder drug, a new way to blow your mind.

Around Manchester raincoats and long faces were getting put into cupboards. A city wrongly long associated with glum serious music was about to throw a massive party, and all were welcome.

It was to be a tantalising and fascinating turnaround in a city's pop culture and it was a turning point too in the fortunes of many people.

Gareth Evans was creating an air of mystery around the band, and A&R men would scuttle up to Manchester and see the band play the busy local shows that were becoming more the norm and less reliant on free tickets.

The Roses were dressing more street, the leathers gone. Now they had bowl cuts, Mani's wedge, long leather coats, stripy shirts, a neo-mod look with psychedelic touches, a bit more street but also distinctive with Squire's Pollocked artwork dripping off the guitars and the drum kit. They were now finally looking like a classic pop group. At the shows you could sense that something was happening, and that after all the toil they were becoming very much a contender.

Stephen Kingston wrote in a *Sounds* live review, 'Ian Brown fancies himself as a bit of a star', but added that he liked the songs as 'somehow they suck you in'. I was also writing about them in *Sounds* and another *Sounds* writer raved about the 'Man-United-style terrace ovation that greets the band. The Roses are to the Stones what The Smiths are to The Beatles,' while Penny Kiley raved about their show in Sefton Park in *Melody Maker*. The northern journalists were convinced, they were on the shop floor, and they knew that despite or because of Gareth's wheeling and dealing, combined with the Roses' now total brilliance, that this was a band that was bursting through.

At the time though, even with the rush starting to happen, it seemed hard to believe that Britain could go for songs as melodic and sweet as these. It seemed that classic rock'n'roll bands would be permanently fated to fall outside the mainstream.

Just getting to the edge of success, the 1,000-capacity halls and the back-end of the top 40 was about as far as it was feasible to go. It was going to have to take something really special to break out of the rut. The 1980s had all but killed classic pop music. The Roses were by now fighting a battle with an uninterested national media and a sceptical music industry, a battle that most bands that followed through their slipstream in the 1990s wouldn't have to contend with.

After The Stone Roses dramatically burst through, a totally different media and business machinery was in place. The national press, having ignored the Manchester breakthrough, have never since missed a band. The journalists have been on the case – chasing every lead up and down the country – powered by enthusiasm and excitement. The labels are there as well.

In the mid to late 1980s there was a massive scepticism about anything that rocked the boat; rock was of course 'dead', most pundits claimed, and nothing was ever going to change again.

They, of course, didn't count on acid house, the Manchester boom or Kurt Cobain, three totally different sources of a new pop revolution that beautifully upset the apple cart and set up the 1990s.

A few months into band management and Gareth Evans, realising he did not know anyone in the music business, decided that he may need some help. The two-man management of Evans and his partner Matthew Cummins was about to get a new addition – Lindsay Reade. Once married to Tony Wilson and a key player in the early Factory days, Reade was still managing bands when she first became aware of The Stone Roses.

'My first connection with The Stone Roses was when I managed 52nd Street, and they practised in a rehearsal room next to ours in Chorlton in 1984. I thought they were fucking awful. Well, let's just say it didn't appeal to me. Gareth always used to nab me when I went to the International and he told me he'd got this band, The Stone Roses: "Do you want to hear them?" So he set up this private gig at the International just for me to listen to them.'

It was an eye-opening experience and Lindsay was convinced. 'Gareth didn't have any contacts in the music business and obviously with my Factory background, I did. I think he knew he'd got something but he didn't know where to take it. So he needed support and asked me to co-manage them. I said I'd love to. I couldn't believe how good they were now.'

The relationship between them was interesting.

'For me Gareth was a bit of a wide boy, that's the polite way to describe him,' says Lindsay. 'He did have this charisma that was quite appealing.'

Lindsay worked fast and by the tail end of 1987 had got both Geoff Travis from Rough Trade and Roddy McKenna from Zomba interested in the band.

Whilst Geoff Travis was already an indie legend, the man who signed The Smiths and the head of the coolest indie label in the country, the younger McKenna was on the look-out for bands for the unfancied Zomba label. He was a firebrand Glaswegian who was starting himself a good reputation on the music scene and had close connections in Manchester.

McKenna had worked in Manchester as a researcher in TV and had met Lindsay at the time before moving to London to work in A&R.

'Lindsay Reade used to come down to London to play me the new Kalima, Jazz Defektors, and I would have meetings with her,' he explains. 'One day I was asked by my bosses to go and check out some band in Wales. Just before that Lindsay had been on the phone and said, "You have got to listen to this new band called The Stone Roses." So Lindsay sent the demo to me. I put it in the bunch of tapes I was going to listen to as I'm going to see this dodgy band.

'As I'm driving back in the middle of the night I put on The Stone Roses and I'm hooked. There is one track, "Here It Comes", that I have on repeat all the way back to London because, fucking hell, there was something about the way he was singing – the attitude and style and the cleverness of the lyric. I thought it was brilliant, like an anthem.'

Swiftly, Roddy went to Manchester to see the band.

'I went to Manchester straightaway to a gig at International 1 on 13 November and met Gareth and Matthew. I saw the band play and was really knocked out by them. Unbeknown to Roddy, Geoff Travis was also at the gig. It was the beginning of the big race to get them signed...'

1988

Here it Comes: The Deal, the Album, Everything!

Early in 1988, on 23 January, The Stone Roses played Dingwalls, returning to the venue where three years before they had played as part of a Manchester package.

The night was to prove key to their story. In the audience were both Zomba Records and Rough Trade. Whilst Gareth was chatting up Roddy, Lindsay was working on a deal with Geoff Travis.

It was also Mani's first London show with the band. This time they were headlining to a sparse crowd of devotees, mainly made up of fans who had come all the way down from Manchester to see them. I caught the gig as well and it was obvious the band had moved on from the Liverpool gig of the summer.

Not that the band were the slightest bit phased in the cold venue. Ian Brown bounded into the venue like a champion, and when they played the show later on, they oozed their guitar pop. Ian had finally toned down his aggressive long-lead forays into the room and the classic king monkey moves were now in place; a new frontman had replaced the speed-driven confrontational Brown of before. The new guise stood there challenging the audience to do something, to do anything. It was a pose that would be adopted by Liam Gallagher and a whole generation of British frontmen with varying degrees of success in the next decade – a frozen drop-dead cool that many of the frontmen didn't have and left them looking like a sack of potatoes left out on the stage.

For Brown it worked perfectly.

The band were now picking up on the street scally look, their new bass player with his Perry Boy fringe perhaps instrumental in the new-look Roses. This was less rock'n'roll, more casual. Maybe Cressa's influence was also coming to the fore, but for a band immersed in pop culture, dressing smart and dressing street was something that had been part of their schtick from punk to scooter boys and onwards.

John Squire had applied his love of Jackson Pollock's paint dripping technique to his own paintings and then, drip drip drip, allowed the paint to decorate the drums, the guitars and even some of their clothes. It was a neat pop and art connection. The band were quickly evolving into their final stage. The songs were there, the look was there and they still had their own idiosyncratic twist and if the audience wasn't there, then hey! they will be there soon enough!

Things were now moving on the label front and it was at this gig that the two labels who were chasing them came head to head.

'They were just brilliant, they were an absolutely fantastic group, fully formed, great songs, everything that had been written about them was true,' says Geoff Travis. 'The thing that was really wonderful was that the rhythm section was such an elastic dancing creature, which very few great rock'n'roll bands ever seem to be able to achieve. That's always one of the secrets to making a great band. If a rock'n'roll band can make you dance you are in a really good place, I think, and it happens too rarely. They really understood dance music but without aping someone else's genre; it just seemed to seamlessly work for them.'

About halfway through the first song, the moment Lindsay had been hoping for, hustling for, came.

'Geoff turned to me and said he wanted to sign them. I thought, "Bloody fantastic! That's it, we've got a deal, this is what we wanted. All that work's paid off." After the gig Roddy said he liked them but didn't have the power to sign them.

'I went into the dressing-room and said to the guys, dead excited, "We got a deal with Geoff Travis." They all looked absolutely vacant; John Squire didn't even smile. I said, "Are you not pleased, do you not think this is good?" They didn't appreciate it. I'd been trawling round London for six months, knocking on doors, getting it shut in my face. They were like, "So what?"'

Geoff Travis was just as excited and put the wheels into motion. 'We started talking to them about a contract, and in the interim period they came down to London. It was just me and the band, not Gareth,' he remembers. 'I met them at Euston and we walked across the road to the pub. We sat in the pub for two or three hours and just talked about music...about Arthur Lee's Love, dance music and hip-hop and we talked about the importance of rhythm. It was a good talk like you would have with some friends.

'It was very easy and convivial and we all got on fine. We had an understanding that we were going to work together and they got back on the train.'

Plans were put into place for their first record. The band had told
Gareth they wanted to record at Strawberry and do 'Elephant Stone'. It
all sounded good to Geoff.

'Peter Hook wanted to produce them, he'd been angling to do it for a
while,' he remembers, 'so we thought we would give him a try and booked
the studio and even visited them whilst they were recording.

'That's pretty much Rough Trade practice, like with The Smiths. We
thought, "We love these tracks, let's cut the single and let's get on with
it." That's how you build a relationship with the artist. We're not gonna
say, "We're not doing anything until you sign a contract, sonny." That's
not the indie way.'

Meanwhile another record label was making plans too. Roddy remembers the sequence of events quite differently. He starts at the Dingwalls gig…

'This story now gets told in many different ways: what I remember was
that when the band came off stage, I went backstage and I said, "Let's get
this deal done." Some people say I was holding the door shut so Geoff
Travis was locked out of speaking to the band.

'So we have this situation where I'm getting on really well with Gareth
and the band, and Lindsay was speaking to Geoff Travis at the same time.
It came to the stage where Gareth admitted Geoff Travis wanted to put
out a single and had paid up front for some services without a contract.

'This is what Geoff and the independents used to do – before they
signed a band they would send a photographer up to take photographs
and pay a wee bit of money for the rehearsal and potential record
producer, so psychologically the band think they were with that label.'

Geoff did put his hand in his pocket for a single and when it was
recorded, he had mixed feelings about the result.

'The band had recorded the single; it was good but the mix wasn't
right. Peter Hook in a way didn't finish the job. If he had finished the job
it might have been a different story…They wanted to remix it. I can't
remember why they went to Zomba Studios, but whilst they were there
doing the remix [what I heard was that] the engineer alerted his bosses at
Zomba that there was something really great happening in the studio and
they should know about it.

'This is where things went bad from the Rough Trade point of view.
This was at a time when there was some internal animosity at Rough
Trade. I've always thought, there was some conspiracy theory in my mind,
that someone didn't send the contract out on purpose. There were
rumours going around that Rough Trade made a crappy offer and Zomba

offered much more, but that wasn't the case: we were prepared to make a decent offer. So I don't think that contract ever arrived.'

Lindsay continues her story: 'I was in regular contact with the band and with Gareth, then they all went quiet on me for a couple of days. So I rang Reni. He said, "We've been to London with Gareth." He said they went into Rough Trade for this marketing meeting and then they came out of there, went straight round to Zomba and signed the contract.'

Lindsay was enraged and got on the phone to Gareth immediately. '"What was all that about?" I asked. "Not even telling me...I want you out of my life, I don't want you anywhere near me. It's finished, over. I'm not working with you any more."'

Lindsay wasn't the only one who was upset about the turn of events. The emotion of it all is still fresh to Geoff Travis. 'The proof that we were gonna do The Stone Roses is on my wall,' he says. 'I have the sleeve of "Elephant Stone" that John sent down to me. It's one of his Jackson Pollock imitations. It's on my wall and it's a John Squire original. I've got it on my wall to remind me of the error of my ways and never to allow a band like that to slip through my fingers ever again. I couldn't have been dreaming it because that artwork makes it all real. That is the single most heartbreaking thing that's ever happened to me.'

Every war has a victor. Geoff and Lindsay were upset, but Roddy and Gareth were happy with their lot.

'Roddy McKenna would come down the club. He was dead cool so I eventually signed the deal with Zomba. I knew it was a bad deal but because I knew about the Employment Act, I knew you couldn't sign people for life. I knew I could get out of it eventually,' Gareth says.

And Roddy now had the band he coveted and he had a better deal than he ever anticipated.

'A contract was printed off the machine with lots of clauses on it to be renegotiated. It's called a red line contract. It's a well-known process in the music industry...Basically the record company put stuff in knowing it will get negotiated out, so they are not forced to give away something really important for the contract.

'The band must take proper legal advice with someone who understands the terminology of a music contract. That was clearly marked on the contract sent to Gareth and Matthew...'

Roddy met up with the band, Gareth and Matthew in the bar of the Britannia Hotel. He took the head of business affairs from Zomba, Mark Furman.

'Gareth and his side agreed to sign and as we came out of the meeting the lawyer says, "You're not going to believe this but the band have not changed anything in the contract." Zomba even put in things like they had a percentage of the merchandise and they left that in, stuff like that, that was commonly taken out. We got back to London and I had got the band I wanted, brilliant. The lawyer, though, was saying the contract was a bit one-sided.'

Roddy reassured himself that once the band had proved themselves they would get improved terms, as commonly happened. But the deal wasn't completely done yet. There was one last panic to come.

'I go to the MD of Zomba Records at that time, Steven Howard, and he said, "What did you spend on the band?" It was like your mum sending you out for messages and you'd spent too much! Because, and this is a classic, because we had overspent by five grand or so, he says he doesn't want to sign the deal. This guy was saying after all that effort he was going to pull the deal. He didn't believe in the band. I was flabbergasted. I was saying, "They are the best thing I have ever seen."'

In the end Roddy managed to get his excitement across and finally got his boss's signature. With one last wipe of his brow, he could finally celebrate and the band could too.

Somehow it had happened. The band had got a deal. They were to be the first band to sign to Zomba's new imprint Silvertone, headed by the renowned A&R man Andrew Lauder. And, in the next few years, he was going to find out how difficult a band and a maverick manager really could be.

May 30: The Anti-Clause 28 Gig – Arguably One of the Most Important Gigs in Manchester Music History

Record Collector: 'Didn't you also headline a double bill with James?'
Ian Brown: 'Yeah, we did an anti-Clause 28 benefit gig – remember that thing about homosexual literature in schools?'

The anti-Clause 28 benefit was special, a call to arms against the Tory party's oppressive new piece of policy, which decided to put a clamp on the homosexual community as well as a host of others not considered to be in the mainstream of society.

In times to come Ian Brown would claim that this was 'a perfect Stone Roses gig'. He was at the height of his crowd confrontation phase and that night was pushing it as hard as he could.

Dave Haslam was the promoter of the gig. 'Paul Cons at the Hacienda was quite active in AIDS awareness at that time. He didn't know any bands so he asked me if I could put on a couple of gigs to raise some money for anti-Clause 28. They wanted to set up an office in Manchester to co-ordinate the campaign up here. The shows were the Roses with James at the International 2 and The Brilliant Corners at the Hacienda. I knew James would be up for a cause like that. And I thought maybe the Roses would be up for it. I had noticed a change in their attitude from aggressive to allowing a bit of femininity into their lives. I liked that mix of hardness and sensitivity in a band.'

The gig was a major triumph for The Stone Roses, who were supporting James. 'I knew James and was amazed when I came into the venue,' recalls Roddy McKenna. 'It was not just a James audience, there was something different in there, a different energy, and it was not just a "Sit Down" James audience.'

Over the years there has been a lot of talk about the Roses delaying their stage time to aggravate the headliners.

Some claim the whole show was an attempt by the Roses to move up the musical ladder. This is not the way Dave Haslam saw things.

'Around that gig there is a lot of myth making. Some say that there was an attempt to scupper James...that there were various power plays going on,' he says. 'I remember having to fit both bands on the bill. Both bands had pretty big followings in Manchester at that time. I needed them both to get on before curfew. I wasn't aware that they were trying to hold back to piss off James. Everyone knew that both bands were capable of being headline bands that night. At the time James were more established so they got to headline the show. Afterwards it seemed the Roses were saying we did this and that...'

Gareth is on record detailing all the strokes the band pulled that night. The posters round town with their name as headliners, delaying their stage time to play at the headline time. James were furious at the delaying tactics.

Dave Haslam points out: 'More importantly it was great that they were so up for doing the gig. I realized they weren't being cynical about the show when I talked to Ian about it. He also went on the anti-Clause 28 march a couple of weeks later round Albert Square. Ian was in the crowd.

He'd gone as a normal punter. He didn't use it as a place to be seen. He understood the cause. Ian Brown genuinely understood what was going on. I was quite impressed by that…'

Eventually, though, the band made it to the stage and the wait was worth it…

'Clang, clang, clang, went the bell, clang, clang, clang.' Ian Brown crossed the stage clanking a huge bell, ringing time's up for the old Manchester and ready for the new.

This is the one.

In 1988 Ian Brown was skinny attitude on legs with a crop of gelatined spikes, a tuff fringe crossed with a scally mop, while his shirts were Jackson Pollocked psychedelic slashes. This was an angry young tripped-out punk with a burning intensity taking on an audience that was split between the Roses crowd and James's audience.

But this old-skool, Lydonesque-attitude Brown was slowly being super-seded by the stoner-mystic Manc Brown. This gig was the bridge between the two.

Eileen Mulligan, one of the Roses' original fans, remembers the gig. 'Steve Adge was always really cool to us. He would always get us in, all the fans that followed them…The Roses always looked after their fans.'

At the International 2, the Roses seized their opportunity with a high-profile gig and a big hometown crowd. It was a gig that demanded a special attitude and Brown was taking no prisoners, as Andy McQueen pointed out. 'Ian Brown walked a tightrope at that gig.'

Alison Bell remembers it as one of the pivotal moments for the band. 'I remember clearly standing at the back at the base of the stairs with Steve Lamacq and various other London-based journos, all completely taken aback by the gig and the response from the crowd to the Roses,' she says. 'A few of us were doing the "I told you" kind of thing. Literally overnight, they all went back and started writing and talking about the Roses. Before that night, their fan base was confined to Greater Manchester.'

The benefit was a chance for the Roses to gather the clans, to break out from their fiercely passionate audience.

That afternoon the band cruised into the venue and soundchecked with 'I Am The Resurrection' on the stage they would sometimes rehearse on. The song, that only months before Pete Garner had been stunned to hear in the rehearsal, was fast becoming their anthem. Fleshing itself out, it transcended its influences and turned itself into a sprawling monster that a year later, when released, would become one of the anthems of that long and wild summer of '89.

The Stone Roses sounded good and sounded ready.

Due on at nine o'clock, they didn't hit the stage till later, building the tension up in the hall, making sure that when things started to happen they really would happen and also making sure that they got to play to the maximum crowd.

For the first time ever they opened with 'I Wanna Be Adored'. It was a smart move, the perfect opening, building with the sonorous bass line that for years would be the spine-tingling call to arms, letting John coax the guitar in before kicking off big style.

Ian Brown stalked the stage, clanking the bell, oozing cool, looking like trouble. A scuffle broke out at the front during 'I Wanna Be Adored' and he stared into the space. 'It's kicking off.' He sounded dispassionate and cold, shades of Johnny Rotten again.

When the crowd clapped with excitement he answered with a mock clap. He was giving nothing back except for attitude.

'I never set out to be a singer, I'm an exhibitionist and a lyricist,' he once told Paula Greenwood.

They ended the set with 'This Is The One', Brown sitting on the drum riser, staring out at the crowd – echoes of Lydon at San Francisco ten years earlier as the Pistols crumbled. That defiant not-playing-the-game front man role – sulky and dangerous. It was pure pop art. Instead of putting a downer on things, it made the music seem more aggressive and dangerous, a pivotal display.

It was an exercise in 'stillism' that Oasis would make into an art form nearly ten years later, and it was this gig that fired the 16-year-old Liam Gallagher and made him want to sing in the first place.

Liam was in the crowd that night and witnessed Brown's mesmeric anti-performance. 'It was doing my head in,' he explained. 'That was my favourite gig of all time, it killed me dead, changed me fucking life. If I hadn't gone that night, I'd probably be sitting in some pub in Levens-hulme for the rest of my life. I went there on my own because all my mates were into dance music, and stood outside. I didn't have a ticket and had to buy one from a tout. About half an hour before stage time I saw Ian Brown and Mani walk in the stage door. When the band came on stage it was a great moment. They came on to "I Wanna Be Adored" and Ian

Brown had that mayor's bell that he was ringing, he looked great. He may not be the best singer in the world but he had this total presence which changed my life. He just had it but the rest of the band looked great, they looked proper, formed – they looked like a real band.

'The year before Noel had come home with the "Sally Cinnamon" single that he had bought at a gig at the International and I was into that – Noel was into The Smiths and Paul my older brother was into The Jam but The Stone Roses were my band. When I saw them play what I liked was that they were lads like us. Like lads who used to run around Burnage. I couldn't relate to Morrissey but I could relate to Ian Brown. They look like normal lads not all-in-black types.'

As inspired by Brown's stage presence as the band's music that night, Liam vowed to front a band.

'The first time music ever did anything for me was when I heard The Smiths and then that night when I saw the Roses I thought, "Yes! That's here today, in my face, I can go with that." Morrissey was a bit weird for me, but Ian Brown was more of a lad. Him and John Squire were just lads, straight off the street, making this incredible music, and it really appealed to me. Everything just felt right that night and I went home and dreamt of being in my own band.'

His brother Noel was there too, celebrating his birthday.

'It was the anti-Clause 28 gig at the International with James and The Stone Roses. It was just at the point where the Roses were starting to break through. I'd seen them loads before that.

'At this Stone Roses anti-Clause 28 gig I see a guy on the balcony and he's got a little tape recorder, the red light's on and he's obviously boot-legging the gig, so I go up to him and ask for a tape and I give him my address and he asks me what other bands I'm into and I said, "I like The Waltones, Happy Mondays, the Inspiral Carpets," and he said, "I'm in the Inspiral Carpets!" I went, "Oh wow!" We kept in touch.

'We chatted away and we kept in contact through this and at the next Inspirals gig, I seen him and it turned out to be their last gig with their singer Stephen Holt. They rang me up and asked me to come and audition and that's how it all started for me.'

The Inspiral Carpets at the time looked like the next band to break out. They had just released their début 'Plane Crash' EP with 'Garage Full Of Flowers' one of the four tracks – the old Ian Brown lyric that they had turned into their tribute to the Roses.

*

At the time Ian Brown was asked by Andy McQueen for the now-defunct *M62* magazine if he prepared his mood before a gig. 'No I can't, because I don't know what the crowd is going to be like, because I never go out and have a look before we go on. I just like to walk on, you know, not knowing whether it's full or not. Just walk on and see what happens.'

'You always seem so disappointed with your audience,' McQueen continued.

'No, that's not true.'

'What about the gig at the International 2?'

'That's just how you saw me. I wasn't upset. That's just how you decided I was. I was dissatisfied with the lack of movement on the balconies. I'd sooner look out at the crowd and get excited watching people get into it. Not people just stood there leaning on a balcony watching me, I just want people to watch us and participate. Why should we do all the work? Why should I do all the work? That's what I think.'

'Did you actually enjoy the gig?' asked Andy.

'I think the anti-Clause 28 gig was a perfect Stone Roses gig, because you had all the people down the front who were so obviously lost in it all. And then you had the people on the balcony who either couldn't understand it, or wanted to drag themselves away because they were guilty watching the group thinking, "Oh I shouldn't like this group", but they couldn't drag themselves away.'

Andy might not have thought it but that gig did mean a lot to Brown. 'When I came on with the bell, it felt like the city was behind us, they wanted us to go and make it. They wanted us to go and become massive,' he says. 'I could feel them willing us on. We were the same as them but we were in a band.'

Manchester's International 2 saw the band poised.

Bass Viking at the Controls: The Stone Roses Record 'Elephant Stone' with the Legendary Hooky!

In the middle of all the label posturing, The Stone Roses had been into Strawberry Studios in Stockport to begin work on their third single, 'Elephant Stone'. In the studio Peter Hook was amazed by the band's musicianship. 'They were great players. We tracked up loads of guitars whilst I bored the band with my anecdotes. Gareth was always popping in like a wildman. One day he turned up dressed as Mani holding a bass! He always had loads of cash on him and would pay for anything the band needed. He really looked after them. If someone's hi-fi was broken he would go and buy another one.'

A two-inch tape of the session eventually sat in Hooky's own Suite 16 studios for years, discarded, forgotten about, lying on a shelf with a mountain of local bands. We used to get it down when we were in the studio and remix it for fun.

Shan Hira, the owner of the legendary, now-closed Suite 16 studio in Rochdale, remembers his then business partner Hooky giving him a desperate ring during the sessions.

'He asked me if I could come down to the studios and sort something out. They had a problem, they needed some hi-hats overdubbing on to the track, and Reni had gone missing. They couldn't find him anywhere.'

Hooky asked Hira, who was once the drummer in the seminal Factory band Stockholm Monsters, the Factory-signed act who were the first gang of funked-up lads pre-Happy Mondays, to put some hi-hats on the track.

'I wasn't happy about doing it at all. I sat there in the studio putting down the part when in walked Reni. His face was icy, it was a really bad situation. I felt really awful about it and got out of there as soon as possible.'

Hooky remembers this well. 'For some reason Reni wouldn't play this hi-hat part so I got Shan to do it. It was Christmas Eve and I thought no one was around and then in walked Reni and he was pretty pissed off!'

He also notes that the Roses' drummer was a powerhouse player. 'Singing drummers, eh? Reni wanted to do everything, he wanted to be the lead singer of the band, he was always coming up with vocal parts. I had to stop him!'

Peter Hook, himself no stranger to the pratfalls of rock'n'roll, muses over the Roses' eventual career. 'They could have been massive, couldn't they? They really had it. It reminded me of Joy Division really. We would have been massive in America like they would have been if we had just got there at the right time, but we lost a singer and the Roses wouldn't go because Gareth [jokingly] told the record label he wanted screaming girls at the airport like The Beatles or he wasn't going to go!'

The single's flipside 'Full Fathom Five' was the Roses' first venture into running their songs backwards. Flipping the two-inch of 'Elephant Stone' over, the band got off on the trippy wash of backwards sounds. It was just like The Beatles!

It was the beginning of a Roses tradition.

Mani was enjoying his time in the studio with his new bandmates too. 'The rest of 'em were amazing players, unreal, man. It's just some of the best players ever, you know. Reni was phenomenal – I learnt a lot from him. He was a great teacher. He told me a lot about rhythm. He turned me on to things which I probably wouldn't have listened to that much. Reni got me listening to a bit of Coltrane and stuff like that.

'He was an amazing drummer. He was that good, he could fucking do anything. He's done gigs with one arm, hasn't he? I mean he played with one arm as fucking good as two! The guy is a total genius, that guy is a proper fucking one-off, you know? You know it was really educational to be around all of them because there was a lot of different kinds of mixtures of styles of stuff that people liked that were getting thrown into the pot, you know? I think that's what made a pretty unique sound because it had bits of everything in there.'

The sessions were over and 'Elephant Stone' was in the can, where it sat for most of that year, waiting for whichever label was going to release it to come forward and do the job. White labels were pressed up and were floating around Manchester that summer where again the hipsters dismissed the band for being out of date. But the fans were buzzing. It sounded like another step forward, another classic single from Manchester's best-kept secret.

'I was asked to do the album. But I had to go and record a New Order one instead, so I was out of the frame,' says Hooky.

Instead it was John Leckie who got the job and, as if to rub salt into the wounds, the first person to suggest his name was now part of the Stone Roses' past.

'John Leckie was Geoff Travis's idea,' says Ian Brown. 'Zomba bought the "Elephant Stone" single off Rough Trade, and Geoff Travis sent me a postcard saying "I think you've made the wrong decision, but I'd still use John Leckie as your producer." Mani had the Dukes Of Stratosphear album that John Leckie had produced, so we all went to Mani's and listened to the album and agreed that whoever came up with an album like that had to be a genius because it sounded like pure sixties psychedelia but modern. It had a good range of sounds – a clever mind that's made it. So, he obviously had some knowledge of equipment.'

Mani couldn't contain himself at the thought of John producing their debut album.

THE STONE ROSES • 207

'John Leckie was really good at finding great sounds and the guy had a bit of a track record...I was particularly getting off on that Dukes Of Stratosphear album that he had done because there are some great sounds on there. It's XTC doing a sixties psychedelic record. It's just fucking amazing. With that I fell in love with John Leckie and his style.'

Gareth Evans recalls, in a mixture of truth and tales, getting John Leckie on board. 'One of the most important factors was convincing John Leckie that the youth of the country were dancing differently – believe it or not they weren't jumping up and down like at rock gigs, they were dancing on ecstasy at the Internationals and in London at various clubs and the movement was all different, and John Leckie made the decision to go with the Roses because I convinced him there was a change and plus I promised him a boat in Barbados if he'd do it!'

The suggestion of Leckie as producer had struck Roddy McKenna as a brilliant idea as well. Leckie's history, dating back through two decades of great music from being the tea boy on Pink Floyd and Beatles records to producing some of the cutting-edge, post-punk bands and those authentic psychedelic Dukes Of Stratosphear records, stood him in good stead to work with the Roses. John was invited up to a rehearsal and a gig so he could get to know the material.

When asked in 1990 what he thought of the band then, he replied, 'They were a bit of a shambles the first time I saw them. I got the impression that Reni was the star of the show and that a lot of people had just come to hear him drum. These days he's not trying to be Cozy Powell so much! I'm not sure why they wanted me...I know we went for some pizza in Stockport and Reni was saying, "What's your favourite record of all time?" And I just came out with Love "Forever Changes". They all fell about and said, "Oh, that's one of our favourite records!" So that could be the reason.

'That and the Dukes Of Stratosphear album that I had produced and they really liked. Ian was a big fan of The Adverts who I had produced in the punk era.'

John Leckie was to become a key figure in the band's story. Although they had toyed with getting Sly and Robbie in to do the album, Leckie passed the litmus test.

When they met him they, for some reason, asked him about his interest in Buddhism and he replied, 'Don't give away your possessions and never live on a commune.' Stark advice from a man who had been there and a reply that scored with the band.

Ian was suitably impressed. 'When we met John Leckie his brief was that he wanted to get each song sounding like it's the ultimate live version but with a twist,' he says. 'He'd done Pink Floyd, Lennon, George Harrison. He'd done the Adverts' LP as well, and I'd won that album in a *Manchester Evening News* competition in 1977 where you had to name their first single. I knew that because The Adverts' "One Chord Wonders" was the first punk single I had bought – so I won the album.

'John Leckie is dead laid back. He had a pseudonym – Swami Anand Nagara – which is his Sannyasin name by appointment of Bhagwan Shree. He'd been in the communes in the late sixties and we used to call him Swami. He's a cool guy.'

The band and the management had found a producer they were happy to work with. The stage was now set for some classic rock'n'roll action.

The Duke of the Stratosphear Himself...John Leckie

John Leckie has one hell of a track record. Post-Roses he has become one of the top British producers, an award-winning name to drop, the Roses' album finally pushing him into the mainstream of hip producers.

Leckie himself is an easy-going dude. Every year I bump into him at Glastonbury, soaking up the sun and the vibes. And it's the sixties vibe that is his roots. He started his career at Abbey Road in February 1967, joining straight from school. He had originally intended getting into the ACTT and then into the film industry. Straight into the deep end – he was the tea boy on Procol Harum's 1969 *A Salty Dog* album; the next day he was working with George Martin and Ringo Starr on Ringo's *Sentimental Journey* album; it was like a tour of rock legends because the following day it was again making tea, this time for Pink Floyd working on their 1970 *Atom Heart Mother* album.

It was a hell of a first three days but then Abbey Road was the pop mecca of the world. It was where The Beatles had recorded virtually all of their hits, the epicentre of pop culture.

Within a couple of months he started making all the usual studio promotions first as tape op, starting with Phil Spector and George Harrison's classic 'All Things Must Pass'. This was an incredible grounding and his reputation swiftly grew working with the Floyd or cult heroes BeBop Deluxe.

A contemporary of Martin Rushent and Trevor Horn, Leckie was one of the producers who came out of the punk era enhanced before moving into the eighties' new angular pop scene. His production debut was on XTC's *White Noise* debut album as well as working on The Adverts, and then in the eighties XTC's perfect pastiche of psychedelia – The Dukes Of Stratosphear – which typically of all band jokes backfired and outsold the master group.

Always a music man, Leckie told *International Musician*, 'Try playing The Beatles' *Revolver* or some of Captain Beefheart's albums and they really stand up. Technically maybe they don't quite match the records made nowadays. But the melodies, the quality of singing and the overall construction of the songs are classic. You can't beat a good combination of a good tune, a good rhythm, a good sound and a good arrangement.'

He pointed out that The Beatles and Jimi Hendrix were pretty much required listening in the Roses camp, although Leckie was surprised by how they didn't like Pink Floyd.

Pink Floyd were still a no-no for the scooter boys. After all, it was only two years ago that they were asking Martin Hannett to recreate his Slaughter And The Dogs production!

Leckie had a good honest approach to production. 'I think that my job as a producer is to make a record which showcases the band. That's certainly true of the way I work with The Stone Roses. I think their record should sound like their best gig. And so I try to get them into that sort of mood and that sort of frame of mind when we're recording. It's the same with the mix – I think it's good to highlight everyone's little bit.'

Looking back at the Roses' début, Leckie recalls, 'As an album *The Stone Roses* was quite difficult to record because we set ourselves a very high standard and scrapped a lot of songs. I was specific that they should play as a unit. They didn't want to sound like they sounded live but at the same time they wanted to have a band sound. Which meant the drums and the bass had to be real. We pushed ourselves hard to make sure we got good live takes with no session players so they could reproduce them live.'

International Musician asked him what made the Roses' demos really stand out from the heaps of stuff that he was sent to listen to.

'Commitment, of course. What struck me most when I first heard The Stone Roses' demos was immediately how much more commitment they had than most bands you hear.

'Plus they have a crazy manager in Gareth Evans which is always a big help in my book. People take more notice of a crazy manager than a sane and sensible one. If he's crazy and bolshy, he'll get noticed more by the record company and the press.

'People really do respond to total belief. Gareth forces it upon you endlessly. Even after years he would still phone me up and chew my ear about how great The Stone Roses are. My wife always says there is more to life than The Stone Roses, but you wouldn't believe it the way Gareth talks.'

The great guitar sounds generated by John Leckie's production can't have escaped the ear of John Squire, a man who was always looking for some way to fuck around with his sound and make his pop symphonies sound even greater.

Where Legends Are Made: Recording the Debut Album

By the spring of 1988 the band was ready to record. With Mani gelled perfectly into the ranks and the songs in perfect condition, the Roses were not just going to record any old album. They were going to record one of the classic all-time British rock'n'roll records. Fuck, even Gareth with his wild eyes and crazed enthusiasm can't have seen this coming!

With John Leckie in place, the band started work. The producer came up to Manchester and started to help shape the record.

'The band were well tight by this point,' says Ian Brown. 'We were rehearsing in the International 2 non-stop – that was the big advantage of having Gareth as our manager, owning them clubs. We used to watch all the soundchecks for the bands coming in to play that night in the club...except Duran Duran who wouldn't let us in! That was the night Gareth wouldn't let Yasmin Le Bon into the Duran Duran gig. He was like, "Not tonight, love," and shut the door on her! He always stopped the liggers coming in but he'd always let the kids from the estates in for free.'

By the time they made it into the studio the band knew exactly what was going on the album. 'We always knew the songs were strong, and we pretty much had it all worked out,' continues Brown. 'We did a week in Coconut Grove with John Leckie where he instilled the "work out your endings and your beginnings" in us. The last chord on "Sugar Spun Sister" is like a Pistols ending – every detail like that, we worked it all out before we went in. Every tiny detail. We spent five years writing the record. It was all sorted.'

The album was largely recorded in down-time in London's Battery Studios, which were part of the Zomba group who also owned the Roses' label Silvertone, which was in the same building across the courtyard.

Surrounded by ten-foot walls and behind automatic gates, Battery is almost like a mini version of Abbey Road, but with a scaled-down glamour. Hidden away from the suburban surroundings of Willesden, Battery is a great studio.

Roddy McKenna talks about the studios they used: 'They worked in a combination of studios, Battery and Konk. I remember going up to Konk and walking in, looking around. It was a wee bit surreal. John Leckie was in there with Paul Schroeder [recording engineer], who was important to the studio mix. John Squire was in the wee vocal booth with his guitar, smoking a joint, with a wee four-track machine, playing his guitar in the vocal booth. The other guys were in the studio. Ian, Mani and Reni were playing pool.

'And you got Mani listening to dub reggae, someone in the band was playing deep house, John Squire a guitar indie thing – it was a cacophony of wonderfulness. I was listening to this whole mish-mash of ingredients and this was one of the reasons I wanted John Leckie working with a young engineer. I wanted John Leckie to be the "Studio Godfather", but I also wanted someone who could understand sonically the music the band was listening to and that was the engineer Paul Schroeder.'

Paul Schroeder's role in the album was vital. He was the connection with the acid house scene some of the band were into. If the Roses were never directly acid house, it was this sonic coating of reverbs and flavours of acid house that Paul Schroeder provided that tinged their music with a futuristic edge.

'The band said they wanted to work with Leckie as a producer but as an engineer they wanted someone who knew dance music, so I was brought in,' explains the engineer. 'It worked pretty well, the mixing was good fun,' he says. 'We used lots of reverbs and set up the outboard equipment as one would do to mix a dance record.

'I wasn't necessarily adding dance stuff to the music, it was more just knowing the music and feeling it the way that one would feel dance music...Mani would always ask me if the bass lines were working properly in a dance way.'

The ingredients were all there – a band with five years already on its clock and songs that had been worked on for a long time ready to cook, a producer with years of experience who could link them directly to the sixties classics but also with a foot in the eighties. This was a band at the peak of its powers. They had been around long enough to perfect their muse but not so long as to get bored of it.

It was a mouthwatering prospect, and the Roses worked hard and meticulously slowly, piecing together the record. Soaking up the current pop scene, the Roses listened to a lot of house music and John Leckie remembers them playing it in the studio all the time. Ian Brown noted, speaking to local DJ, Dave Haslam, the following year, 'We're always getting fans coming backstage and hearing tapes we're listening to and going "How can you get it like this?" and we'd tell them to listen again.

'It's never true that if you are a guitar group then all you listen to is guitar music. In this group we can't get enough music. The first music I listened to was The Beatles and one of the first records I bought was "Pretty Vacant". Music had a pretty lean period in the eighties – that's why hip-hop and house have made such a huge impact.'

Leckie was impressed by the meticulous way the band worked. 'There was no discernible musical leader. Each member of the band was equally important. They hardly ever drank. Ian Brown didn't even drink any beer. That impressed me.'

The producer recalls the initial sessions for the album. 'I have actually looked at a diary and got the chronology. I didn't mix "Elephant Stone" first. We actually went in and recorded "I Wanna Be Adored", "She Bangs The Drums" and "Waterfall" and one other song that I can't remember. We did four songs and then I mixed "Elephant Stone" which Peter Hook had recorded with them before.

'All the time the band were trying to get out of Battery to go to Rock-field or go to somewhere a bit more comfortable than living in a bed and breakfast in Kilburn next to Battery, but we had to stay there because the record company owned the studio. The deal was because it was a new band and we would get cheap studio time so we didn't have a lot of time. We only had five days or something like five, maybe eight, days to do four songs, which we did, finished and complete.

'There were no other bands in the building. It was all programmers and producers and girl singers; you know, Samantha Fox was always hanging around. The hours were long; we started at seven in the evening and went on to about seven or eight in the morning. Then we had to drive through the traffic to where we were staying at like nine in the morning.'

Ian Brown looks back on those nights fondly. 'The sessions for the album were all-night sessions, 7pm to 7am. We had a lot of fatigued humour going on. We shared a rented house in Kensal Rise with this businessman called Jonathan. So we'd be getting in stoned out of our faces just as he'd be eating his breakfast with his suit on going off to do a day's work. It was pretty funny.'

Working hard, they got 'I Wanna Be Adored' down on tape. There was the killer new song, 'Made of Stone', with its amazing chorus and Mani's signature bass run and some awesome guitar from John Squire. There was the pure pop shakes of 'She Bangs The Drums' and the falling arpeggios of 'Waterfall'. No wonder the band were buzzing. No wonder the mood was good. Four drop-dead rock'n'roll classics and this was just for starters.

For the second session the band had moved across London to Konk studios, set up by The Kinks' main man Ray Davies. Konk is another great-sounding studio, mainly used for mixing but with a neat live room that potentially records a cracking drum sound. I have produced some stuff there and can vouch for the place – you even got to see Ray Davies in there sometimes.

Here they recorded 'Bye Bye Badman', 'Shoot You Down', 'I Am The Resurrection', and 'This Is The One', the anthems, the long extended jams, the amazing playing, less the straight three minute pop anthems, more the band showing just what they were capable of. Guitar, bass and drums as magical as it gets. And then they started to fuck with stuff, run things backwards.

Ian pointed out to *Record Collector*, "Waterfall" may have sounded like a Simon and Garfunkel song, "April Come She Will ". But we've never consciously stolen or copied anything.'

The track 'Don't Stop' was one of Ian's favourites. 'It was accidental. We got a tape of "Waterfall" on the Portastudio, which plays both sides. It sounded great backwards. We could hear lyrics coming out, words suggesting themselves. We went back into the studio, turned the tape over, put the vocal down and then put a forward drum over it. That's my favourite thing on the first LP. There's twenty seconds at the end that's a killer, the little rhythm that comes in.'

And 'Resurrection'? '"I Am The Resurrection" had a Motown kind of beat. It reminded me of "You're Ready Now" by Slaughter And The Dogs.'

Reni recalls how they wrote 'Resurrection': '"I Am The Resurrection" started out as a reverse bass pisstake of Paul McCartney on "Taxman". Mani used to play that riff every day, I'd come in and John would doodle some Fender over the top and we'd do it for a laugh at soundchecks. Finally we said, "Let's do it properly – this joke song actually sounds really good!"'

John explained to *Total Guitar*, 'I also like the fortuitous ending of "I Am The Resurrection". We had some bits left over on tape which we just dropped in at exactly the right points – that little rhythm guitar bit at the end. Also the acoustic jangly stuff on the end section, too; I'd recorded it on this little Philips ghettoblaster and I got the engineer to drop it in. It's a bit out of time, because we were just pressing Play to try and get it in sync. I think we only tried it twice, so it's a bit out of time. I like it, though.

'The low point on the album? I'd have done less overdubs, had stronger main guitar parts.'

Over the 55 days of recording spread out over the back-end of that year, the record itself was shaping up to be guitar pop perfection. Demo tapes that were leaked out set tongues wagging. There was some serious business going on in that studio.

Despite the fact that the album was sounding amazing, the band themselves have never been happy with the sound of the record. John Squire sums it up in one word: 'Twee.' Adding, 'I think it was mainly the production. We saw there being a huge gulf between the live sound of The Stone Roses and that first album. It was mostly recorded on an SSL desk, and it just didn't sound fat or hard enough. From a guitar point of view I see my approach as the main failing; I completely deconstructed what I played live and rewrote everything for the studio. That just seems a bit simple, and the switch from chordal to solo stuff just doesn't seem to work. The album just doesn't have the stamp of a real guitar player to me, apart from a couple of the solos. It sounds like a two guitar band, which we weren't.'

But there were creative high points that even the perfectionist Squire enjoyed. 'But I do like the guitar playing on "Bye Bye Badman". I worked through the guitar parts for that in this little breeze-blocked room at the back of the studio where all the air conditioning and mains switches were. I was just sat there with my little Portastudio sitting on top of its cardboard box; we were getting right down to the wire in terms of time, and when I went in to record I still didn't really know the part. I really enjoyed doing that.

'I like "Don't Stop" a lot too. It's the tape of "Waterfall" backwards, with the bass drum triggered, and the only real overdubs are the vocals and a bit of cowbell. I wrote the lyrics by listening to "Waterfall" back-wards and writing down what was suggested, what the vocal might have been. It's good fun doing that, because you sort of remove your involve-ment from the song, you don't really know what's going to come next.'

Mani enthuses: 'The album's different moods is the sign of a brilliant lyricist being able to relay the message, isn't it? If the music lures people into a false sense of security with one mood then you can change it all lyrically and Ian was great, you know – his lyrics are amazing…some guy! You don't meet many people that just don't write about fucking normal stuff like what they have had for their tea or something. Ian writes songs about fucking history and stuff that he felt. He's a deep thinker and a deep feeler and he's in touch with his spiritual side! I love his voice because it's from the fucking heart, man – great talent can't be taught, mate, it's got to be felt and he's still there and he's still doing it, man!'

Despite certain reservations, despite the band being worried about the record's 'monochrome' sound, they knew that they were sat on a classic record – very few bands ever like the sound of their recordings and John Leckie had done a great job.

When they moved over to Rockfield in Wales to finish it off and mix it down the vibe in the camp was positively upbeat.

Rockfield was a wheeze as well, set in beautiful countryside. The band chilled out and finished off the record; they loved the place so much that it would virtually become their musical headquarters for the next few years.

'Elephant Stone' Gets the Release

Finally released that October by Silvertone, 'Elephant Stone', now remixed by John Leckie, was another move forward, another hint at the golden groove that the band were about to hit. The song was pumped full of tunes and had those chops and changes that would eventually become a total feature of their sound. Riding on Squire's choppy wah-wah, it was a fast-paced rush through classic guitar pop. Ian Brown's sugar-sweet vocals were dripping an unlikely innocence.

The 'B' side, 'Full Fathom Five', rushed backwards with Ian Brown's reversed vocals sounding like some Byzantine monk singing in a spooky Far Eastern chapel as the crazed slurping rush of guitars scorched past him.

'The Hardest Thing In The World' was one of their older songs, but it was obviously picked because it was not one of the 'rock ones', it was a pure blast of melody. Listening to this makes nonsense of the claims that Brown couldn't sing. The solo is crystalline Squire. A non-macho guitar hero, John could dash off the greatest licks that were just total pop. The song was a medium-paced, dark-hearted ballad showing the emerging introspection of a band that was daring to admit to more than full-on rock and in-your-face speed psychosis.

The single was was also the first single to feature Squire's Jackson Pollock-styled artwork that would become the signature for the band. 'Elephant Stone' only managed to scrape into the indie charts at number twenty-seven. What the fuck were they going to have to do to get this pure pop to the people?

Andy McQueen was disappointed. 'Ian Brown phoned and said that he had a copy of "Elephant Stone" for me. I cycled over, the record sounded very disappointing – slovenly, scrappy and "live"…John later told me that he couldn't bear to listen to that version. Ruined it.'

The press reviewed the record this time. *NME*'s Edwyn Pouncey said that readers should listen to The Velvet Underground's 'Sister Ray' instead – a bizarre suggestion. *Record Mirror* told them that there was more to life than 'Lollipops, psychedelia and flakey grey skin' (just wait till next year!) and the radio ignored it.

Sounds dutifully interviewed the band. Ian Tilton again did the photo session, noticing that the band dynamic had changed with the addition of Mani.

'I got a great shot of them all lined up together at my studio, all real tight in with each other and they looked cool as fuck with like S-shaped bends to their collective image.

'John had his own idea with the Pollock stuff – like the sheet of glass that he covered in Pollock-style paint, which the band stood behind. That was done down at Gareth's farm. So yeah, he was inspired but he had his own visions of how he wanted the band to look. I remember Reni kinda changed because at first he was really up for it but then just lost interest and wasn't bothered any more later on. There was something that didn't twig for him and he seemed to get bored of photography, but the other lads were fine. Ian was the one I communicated mostly with and the others just used to fit in, including John. Most of the time he was very laid back and there was always a shyness with him; he didn't go out much and would stay in playing his guitar. Ian was a lot more outgoing and very easy to hang about with.'

At the tail end of 1988 they started to tour for the first time. On 26 November they played the St Helens Citadel. Back in the days when bands toured through St Helens, the Citadel was the circuit venue, a cool, well organised place; everyone went through there. It was the beginning of a long nine-month haul by the Roses through the small clubs of the UK, playing to gradually filling venues even after the album came out until word of mouth caught them up in such a spectacular manner.

Andy McQueen was there and was asked by Ian Brown to make up the set list for the night. It's an honour for a fan to get this close to the machinations of the gig. With trepidation he lined up the following: 'Here It Comes'/'Elephant Stone'/'Mersey Paradise', 'I Wanna Be Adored'/ 'Waterfall'/ 'Sally Cinnamon'/ 'Made of Stone'/'Sugar Spun Sister'/ 'Shoot You Down'/'She Bangs The Drums'/ 'I Am The Resurrection'.

'It wasn't that good a gig actually,' McQueen remembers, adding, 'Gareth drove me home in the really thick fog and asked me if I had ever had "some of this E". I said no and he asked, "Why not?" We stopped off at the International 1 and he gave me a copy of "Sally Cinnamon" and "So Young".'

Ecstasy was, by that autumn, a big craze. All that summer acid house parties had been kicking off all over the UK, all of a sudden bands and gigs seemed dated, very old-fashioned, like clumsy dinosaurs compared to an all-nighter in a field or warehouse.

Sometimes thousands of people would turn out for a night of rampant hedonism. This sure beat standing in a dank, mouldy venue with a few pints and a half-assed band as entertainment.

The rush of ecstasy was extraordinary, it was the greatest feeling and the music seemed to match perfectly. You couldn't stop moving, grooving on the music. Touching other people was a thrill, it was an incredibly tactile drug, it made the user feel warm and horny, the love vibe was high! It changed people's lives and ruined some others.

Tied in with the big warm bass end-beats and hi-speed gallop of acid house it was a perfect combination.

The camaraderie and the outlaw nature of the raves pissed all over the respectable indie scene. Going to see an indie band was like going to the library, it suddenly seemed sensible, boring and dull. It was tied by convention and rules. You paid your money, came in, stood about checking the band and went home. Where was the wild looseness that you demanded from rock'n'roll? It was as staid and sensible as DIY, just not sexy.

The first rave you went to was a wild carnal experience. Off your head on drugs and lost in this new alien music, the clothes were loose and bright and the vibe was a massive rush of positive joy.

No wonder the government was coming down hard on it, people can't have that much fun! They came down hard on ecstasy which, of course, fucks you up, but nowhere near as much as cigarettes and alcohol.

It was one of those sudden generation gaps that appears in pop.

The coolest bands would be the ones that took acid house on and let it influence their moves. Ian Brown, ever the culture vulture, was checking things out; he and the Roses would almost instinctively use some of the trappings of the house culture and fuse it with what they were doing. It was mainly the approach they were interested in, and oh, the drugs as well.

Back in the indie world they took one of their occasional trips down to London to play what was a desultory affair, supporting The Chameleons' off-shoot Sun And The Moon in a tiny room at a polytechnic in London. It was a shoddy gig, watched by a tiny pocket of punters. The band's innate self-belief was mistaken for arrogance and Ian Brown was looked on as being 'narcissistic' and they left gaps between the songs, chatting to mates.

The reviews were downbeat – the press were not getting the band yet. They didn't understand the band's baggy style, their self-belief and their music. It seemed like the band was going nowhere. But they still retained that steely resolve. They had come a long way and there was no turning back now. And they had that album ready.

On Tuesday 29 November they played at Olives in Chester. Again they were supported by 'some crap metal band'. Jo Taylor, who went to a lot of indie gigs in the late eighties, first saw the Roses at Chester and was blown away. 'They were just about there when I saw them. Friends in Manchester had been going on about how good they were as a band so I went to check them out. They sounded like the band that broke through the year after. It seemed odd at the time that there wasn't more people but you knew then that it was only a matter of time before they broke through.'

On 2 December they played the London School of Economics. The support was from a young band who had gone through the scooter club circuit themselves, The Charlatans. Martin Blunt remembers the gig.

'Steve Harrison, our manager, who had been on scooter runs with The Stone Roses years before, got us the support through Gareth. They were great, all the parts just clicked, there was something that I just hadn't heard in years, you know? Something that really did strike a chord – it was a bit like an epiphany.

'We had the scooter club rallies in common, and the mixture of music that was played at these, like your staple Northern and your bit of ska/reggae – nobody was averse to playing a bit of Echo And The Bunnymen and New Order – that kind of thing. Then The Smiths, which I think they took in. After the LSE we got a run of about four supports with them. Steve knew Gareth, 'cos Gareth used to come and collect the ticket money from the shop [Steve's record shop, Omega Music] and they used to get talking about a lot of things. Steve very much knew what was going on and it just felt like there was some kind of groundswell, especially with the music that was being made round that part of the north-west. The LSE was quite sparsely attended but you could see there was a few movers and shakers in the audience that night down in London. We then played at the International 1 in Manchester with them. We got pretty well received but when The Stone Roses came on it was absolutely rammed to the rafters. We got there and they'd sometimes still be soundchecking and it was, nothing was left to chance, Ian and Reni with the harmonies, just getting it right with the monitors. They were a cool bunch; it was the first time in many, many years I'd seen something that I went, "Wow – this is, this really is gonna happen." Beyond the realms of just a cult thing, as I think after that we did Trent Poly with them and there you could see the news had sort of spilled out and it were word of mouth.'

On 11 December they played the Edinburgh Venue. It was their first trip to Scotland. Andrew McDermid, who would go on to manage Stone Roses fanatics Whiteout (the band that Oasis would later support on their first national tour) remembers getting into the Roses at about this time. This was the first gig he saw them at. He was promoting bands over in Greenock; it meant that he was always hip to what was coming out.

'I had booked the Mondays from that Manchester agent, what's his name, aye, Brian Turner and he sent us "Elephant Stone" as well. We were all Primal Scream fans so we were hooked immediately, deffo.'

McDermid went to The Venue and was blown away. He'd also, by now, booked them for his own club, Ricos, in Greenock. It was the first thing that he was genuinely excited about for ages.

'I was booking stuff like James Taylor, The Chills and The Weather Prophets – all that indie guitar stuff was not happening, that was the size of the groups I would put into Ricos. We had the Roses booked for Monday, 12 December, and then they cancelled. We were told Ian had tonsillitis. Imagine how gutted I was, already I was a massive fan.'

Glasgow and especially the cluster of towns to the west of the great Scottish city would become a stronghold for the band.

That Début TV Appearance

The Roses also recorded their first TV towards the tail end of the year, appearing on Granada on one of Tony Wilson's arts and entertainment guides. They played 'Waterfall' and the session became part of their legend due to Ian Tilton's photos of the band which eventually became the pictures on the inner sleeve of the album.

Says Ian Brown, 'We did "Waterfall". Tony Wilson did the Hacienda and our manager did the Internationals and they were rivals so Tony Wilson never used to give us any space. The only reason we got on was because Paul Ryder told Tony Wilson we should be on his show.'

Another band had dropped out and The Stone Roses were a last-minute replacement. It's an iconic TV moment. Tony Wilson introduces the band, not looking too sure about them, and they start to play, looking cool and arrogant. Ian is angular in his modish clothes and Reni is wearing the white hat that will become so famous in the following year. They sound great framed by the old-style cameras and the studio's white backdrop – it's classic rock'n'roll TV.

Ian Tilton's black and white pictures capture the band right on the cusp. Stark images of a sharp and angular group, dressed in clean-cut mod gear, a band on the verge of the baggy revolution.

Ian Tilton: 'It was all pretty casual really. The manager Gareth rang me up and said, "Can you get to Granada Studios to shoot the band because they're off on Tony Wilson's TV show, *The Other Side of Midnight*?" When I got there the band were real excited that they were getting TV and I was chuffed for them.

'I took the shots, then later on John would choose which to use. I would send him the roll of all the pictures, a contact sheet, and he would ring me with the order for which shots he wanted. Then I would print them off and get them round to his house where he would cut them up, literally cut and paste the album layout together. So it was totally John who designed the album cover and what shots they used for it.'

Tony Wilson famously didn't like the band initially. He branded them Goths and hated their graffiti campaign. Tony being Tony was a man of strong opinions, but he was also prepared to admit he was wrong.

'At first I hated The Stone Roses then one night I was at home, about to crash out in front of the TV, and the Mondays were playing Chester in the small basement of a pub. I had the strange feeling that they were about to break; I don't know why because we were releasing the third version of "Wrote For Luck", but I thought this might be the last time they played a small gig, and indeed it was. Anyway, I went into the dressing-room and the drummer Gaz Whelen goes, "Hey, Tone, listen to this," and put something in the cassette player, and the cassette plays and I'm like, "Fuck, that's fantastic, what is it?" The whole group go, "Nyah, it's the Roses," because they all knew I hated the Roses.

'But I was always extremely flattered that even though they knew I hated them, they used a photo of their TV performance on *The Other Side of Midnight* for the sleeve of the great first album.'

The year 1988 had been one of patience. They had signed the deal and meticulously assembled the album. If the gigs outside Manchester were still empty, they knew that it was now only a matter of time. The necessary bedrock had been built. For the first time in their career they had a proper record label behind them and as the year closed they also had a brilliant début album under their belts. The Roses had their sensual, tripped out new pop sound together.

All that long work in the studio was beginning to pay off.

If 1988 had promised, 1989 was finally going to deliver.

1989

At Last! The 1980s Come Alive

'Sometimes the best band in the country is the biggest band in the country.' James Brown, *Loaded* magazine

Every now and then pop, culture and the times coincide with a ferocious force to create a whirlpool of excitement. Think 1956 and Elvis putting sex into the mainstream, think 1963 and The Beatles and the Stones copping the high-energy rush of optimism of the 1960s, think 1977 and the punk revolution, and think 1989 for the year that the crap 1980s music scene finally got trashed.

When 1989 began it didn't really feel that there was a revolution about to start. Rock, terrified of the rave culture, seemed even more conservative. As The Stone Roses took to the circuit they were playing to handfuls of people in backwater towns, and it was hard to believe that within eight months they would be selling out the Empress Ballroom in Blackpool.

Things were about to change.

All over Eastern Europe, the Communist old guard and their vile, cranky leaders were being overthrown by the people. Years of repression were coming to an end. Maybe it was time for the repression in pop to be overthrown by a new generation of bands hip to what was really going on out on the streets.

Ecstasy was massive now; every week more and more people were dressing baggy, looking all glazed and ranting on about house music. The clubs were packed. The Hacienda, the club started by Factory Records, had spent 1988 becoming party central, with DJ Mike Pickering pioneering acid house and packing the place out. Manchester was the fulcrum of this new culture. Remarkably, it had re-invented itself as the dance capital, and all thoughts of The Smiths had been briefly banished.

Ecstasy was one powerful drug.

Ian Brown remembers the year when everything changed: 'I went out through 1988 and 1989. It was a great time with the clubs. The Hacienda was magical, everyone loved each other. It was so different from the early days when there would be three people in there watching *Tron* on the main screen. When the Hacienda first opened I was a kitchen porter in Didsbury and my mate Stuart was the cellarman of the Hacienda bar. Another mate was the receptionist when it first opened in 1983 so I did go down there all the time. It was easy to get to as I lived in Hulme just up the road so I would walk there.

'I never joined as a member but I would get signed in because my girlfriend was a member. I used to go to the Nude nights DJ'd by Mike Pickering. But, I stopped going out at the end of '89 because I had to talk about the band every time I went out, people chewing my ears off about the band. It was boring me really.'

Ian Brown witnessed the sea change in the Hacienda first hand.

'Mike Pickering was the first one to play house music. He used to play house music – just piano, bass and drum – Chicago house a year and a half before the acid house thing. Mike Pickering doesn't take the credit but he was the first to play it, him and little Martin. Little Martin used to DJ at the Berlin in the early eighties and that was another big club for us. I was into house before the Es because Howard Jones played it as he got tapes off Mike Pickering. Cressa also had a couple of tapes at the time. I thought it was ace, just a piano and a beat. Dead simple. There wasn't much vocals attached to it.

'The Hacienda was changing the culture of the city. It was really exciting, everyone was dropping Es, that's what changed everything.'

And Ian was riding high on the crest of this wave of change, embracing a whole new culture. 'My first E was amazing. We had been into tripping on acid in '84/'85 and we'd been out tripping but never where there had been 2,000 people tripping! When you were tripping you would never get chucked out of anywhere for laughing at a squirrel or something. But not everyone was tripping then. It was windowpane acid and there was only a few of us into it. With Ecstasy though everyone was on it. It was wild and amazing.

'It was amazing when acid house took off and everyone was your best mate. It was beautiful, wasn't it? There were thousands of us and more and more each week. I thought we were going to change the world with this; Ecstasy was going to change the world. With the Es football violence stopped, violence stopped, there was a different atmosphere. You could bang into people and it was a laugh not a fight.

'Here were all the guys who had an edge to them and they didn't have an edge to them any more; the kids with glasses could feel OK; it made you feel sexy, it made you want to have sex, it was powerful, it was *en masse*. There was so many at it in the club, then back to someone else's house or the Kitchen in Hulme. We went to all the clubs, like Konspiracy. I went there when it was Pips and to Thunderdome a couple of times – that was a different vibe even if it was all Es, it was more north Manchester. A different atmosphere to the Hacienda – north Manchester gangster.'

As ever hip to the pop culture shift, Ian was bringing the acid house flavour back to The Stone Roses.

The band were looking looser and baggier. Ian Brown now wore those famous green cord flares that he had got from Steve Cressa. The rest of the band wore parallels, they looked great – one step in and one step out of fashion – cool on their own terms – the way pop bands should be.

Let the Tour Commence

The Stone Roses 1989 tour has become legendary. Playing small venues it was, initially, a culture shock. During February they confronted shocked indie fans at Warrington Legends and Sheffield University, looking like aliens compared to the staid wardrobe of the punters, their loose cuts directly opposed to the rigidity of the indie scene.

The band now had their own following, a coterie of fans from Manchester who dressed like them and helped to make an impression as they went from town to town. They had discovered the band in '87/'88 and were now a regular crew that followed them round these gigs.

Eileen Mulligan was one of them. 'The first time I saw them was at the International. I first heard them before that because my brother had bought "So Young" when it came out. I don't even know where he got it from, it was hard to find. He probably couldn't even remember. I keep telling him he should sell it on eBay!

'It was 1988. We liked them so much we went to Sheffield the next night.'

Another new fan, Mike Farnell, was there as well.

'My friend Andy McQueen had been raving about this new single and since we both shared a love for Primal Scream we shared a new delight in The Stone Roses. We went over to Sheffield and by the time I got to the gig I knew all the words to "Sally Cinnamon" – thanks to Andy singing the song all the way there in the car.' On arriving it was obvious there was a dodgy vibe. It transpired that the Roses had lost a flip of a coin and were to play support to the other band – The Prowlers – a sort of Black Crowes-meet-Hanoi Rocks outfit from Bradford. The Roses mood was darkened not so much by their billing as The Prowlers' backdrop – a huge Confederate flag. The Roses had confronted the band about the flag and pointed out that it is a symbol of slavery.

'Partway through the gig, The Prowlers' girlfriends were starting to barrack the band and eventually one stepped forward and threw her drink over Ian. He coolly mimed as if showering then stepped down from the stage and cockily walked around them singing at them close up and face to face. It felt as though things would go up a notch but The Prowlers and crew sloped off and I knew I'd just found my favourite band...'

The Stone Roses were bringing a very different vibe to the music scene, musically, stylistically and attitude wise.

'In retrospect the atmosphere was just like something new,' Eileen continues. 'It was different. It was like, "What's this?" It was something you hadn't felt or heard before. Before I had been listening to your sort of student indie like The Primitives. But this was different. Also it was homegrown. It was nice to have something that you could kind of have and be proud of being Mancunian.

'Musically I just thought, "Oh, I've not heard this before" too. 'It was a mixture of a new sixties thing and all sorts of everything. I liked the sound of it and that was it. I didn't know, "This is gonna be one of the seminal bands of a lifetime". I was very young and there were a few of us going to the gigs. You met people and we all liked it together. It was something we could share.'

For Eileen and it her mates it was as simple as that. Here was a band that they liked. But there were other people doing just the same. The word began to spread and the group began to swell...

'We just met pockets of people that were doing the same thing. You'd see them at gigs, so we gradually became like a little tribe...Our group expanded and expanded. Sometimes it was like 20 of us or more and we were quite protective, like, "This is ours." You want to keep it to yourself, you don't want anyone else to know. 'We all felt strongly about the music, all the energy...and we just became lifelong friends.

'The clothes were important. Looking back at pictures, it was very androgynous and you could tell who liked The Stone Roses from the way they dressed. It was very tribal. It's not like that any more, is it?'

*

On 23 February they played Middlesex Polytechnic. Sally Williams helped to promote the show: 'We put them on in the canteen. We had spent the whole term putting on really small bands, we had no money and we couldn't afford any bigger groups. But we thought that we should do well with this one. But only thirty people turned up – I couldn't believe it. I think it was the next night they were playing the Hacienda and they were going to get three thousand quid. They had this really massive fan that followed them around everywhere called Little Julia. She had Jimi Hendrix Experience written down one arm of her jacket. She was mentioned in Bob Stanley's *Melody Maker* review. They both stayed over at my house that night...I think she ended up following Dr. Phibes around the country after the Roses. That night The Stone Roses were brilliant. The next time I saw them was at Dingwalls in May and there was a big queue outside and then after that it was at Ally Pally...all in the space of a few months. It was astonishing how quickly they finally took off.'

The set they played that night at Middlesex Poly was: 'I Wanna Be Adored', 'Standing Here', 'Made of Stone', 'Waterfall', 'Sugar Spun Sister', 'Elephant Stone', 'Where Angels Play', 'Shoot You Down', 'She Bangs The Drums', 'Sally Cinnamon' and 'I Am The Resurrection'. It was pretty well the same set they played on this seminal tour.

This was the first time that Bob Stanley, the mastermind behind Saint Etienne and at the time a journalist for *Melody Maker*, had seen the band. He was the first London based journalist to get it since Garry Johnson in 1985, and he reviewed the gig: 'They sound like someone has sneaked a tab into your Tizer, they sound like the best thing I've ever heard. The Stone Roses. Jesus Christ...' Bob was on a rush, and from then on he was campaigning strictly on behalf of the band, eventually getting journalist Everett True into the group, and bringing *Melody Maker* on board.

As it moved into March it was clear that the rest of the nation was still lagging behind Manchester in its support of the Roses. But not for long.

On 1 March they played Bradford's Club Rio, the next day Cardiff's Venue and then Dudley's JBs, circuit gigs that were ill attended but which kept the band's soul fire burning. The 1989 tour was a gradual roller-coaster and the word of mouth was beginning to spread that here was a band coming through fast that captured the spirit of the times, playing a pop so pure, that it seemed remarkable that they had been ignored for so long.

On March 15 they played the long-shut-down Powerhaus venue in Islington in London. It was the first time that Creation boss Alan McGee had seen the band.

'The first time I heard the Roses was when my mate in Manchester, Debbie Turner, told me about them. I then saw them on TV on *The Other Side of Midnight*. They must have been one of the few bands I missed at that time between 1988 and 1992, when, with Creation we signed everybody that mattered. For some reason I didn't know about them till the record deal had been done. Debbie told me The La's and the Roses were both brilliant; she played me the seven-inch singles of The La's and the Roses and they were fucking brilliant. The first time I saw the Roses was at the Powerhaus in 1989. I believe it was not a very good sound, in fact it was shocking, I didn't know if it was a good gig or bad gig!'

Creation itself had been a big influence on The Stone Roses. There was the same basic concept of combining sixties psychedelia and punk rock. This was the label that released Primal Scream – the band closest to the Roses in spirit and sound. There was also The Jesus And Mary Chain, who released their first single on Creation – another influence on the Roses and the whole Creation look and aesthetic.

McGee scratches his head. 'It's hard for me to be dead straight about the influence Creation had on them. I heard they were at Primal Scream in Manchester and into *Sixteen Tambourine*, the 1983 album from The Three O'Clock. John Squire was into the Mary Chain and I heard he was into Santana as well but I don't know if that's true. They certainly dressed like a Creation band in 1985/'86. When I met them in 1989 they were lovely to me. Ian Brown was pumping the air with a black panther salute. Mani did threaten to shoot me years later when I had been managing Primal Scream for three hours! It was because of royalties not paid to the band before I looked after them. I had to point out that I had only managed the band for three hours. I never worry if a Manc threatens to shoot me! It's only when it's a scouser! Ever since then he's been an absolute gentleman.'

It was at Dudley's JBs that they were supported for the second time by The Charlatans (they had already done the Warrington show last month) still in their earlier Baz Ketley fronted phase.

The two bands got on. They were both plying a colourful guitar pop. But as the Roses effortlessly hit first gear it became obvious to the support band that they would have to do something if they were ever actually going to catch up with their near northern contemporaries. A line-up shuffle and a slight overhaul in style and The Charlatans would be there when the Roses had finally kicked the barn doors open.

What the Roses needed now was the single to break through. 'Made of Stone' was days away from release, and they had new radio pluggers, Beer Davies, on the case, who said that they were getting good reactions down at Radio 1. The mainstream resistance was finally wearing down.

Gareth Davies, who worked for Beer Davies, recalls how they got involved with the band.

'We had worked with Andrew Lauder when he was at Demon Records. Music labels were becoming more and more run by accountants, not by people interested in music. Zomba had tried to get Andrew to set up a label himself, under their funding, to get something about the music back. Andrew thought up the name Silvertone Records and set up in that little cottage opposite the Zomba offices.

'Andrew said, "We have got this band and we need a radio plugger – do you want to go and see them?" So I got a train to Manchester and was met by, I don't remember his name actually, a very tall guy that looked after the band at the time. He had a scar on his face that came from a dog that had bit him, which obviously set the scene. He drove me to this old church where the band was rehearsing and I went in with him and just stood there. They finished playing the song and I remember there was this little kid there with glasses on. As I'd been a school kid with glasses myself I knew his problem but he had a plaster on both arms of his glasses and one on the nose piece in the middle, which is an extraordinary trio to have! He must have been about nine or ten. The band finished this number and Reni said, "Give us a towel, will ya?" This little kid ran up to him with a towel to mop his face. Then they all came over and shook my hand. Reni lobbed this kid this towel and said, "There you go, you can have a go now."

Gareth assumed the kid must have been someone's little brother, but the truth was far more touching.

'We went outside and I introduced myself,' the radio plugger continues. 'I could hear seven bells being knocked out of these drums from inside the church as we were standing in the car park. I said, "Who's the kid? Is he a younger brother of yours then?" and they looked at each other and said, "No, we don't really know his name. We've been rehearsing for a week and he walked past and wondered what the noise was. He's just been coming in every night on his way home from school."

'When they went back in they said to him, "Think you better go back home now, you've been here a while and your parents will be wondering where you are." It was amazing really. They asked him if he wanted any orange juice to take home and gave him a couple of cartons.

'Then I heard them play some more. I went back to Andrew and said, "They're amazing." Not just because they sounded good but because they were so rounded, so level-headed. They could really play and there was something really genuine there.'

Single No. 4!: 'Made Of Stone'

'Made Of Stone' is a classic single. A perfect shimmer of guitar pop that is both melancholic and euphoric like all the great songs.

Somehow *Melody Maker* compared it unfavourably to Spear Of Destiny whilst I made it single of the week in *Sounds*, and *Record Mirror* was buzzing.

Richard Skinner, who was then hosting the early-evening slot on Radio One, picked up on the record and suddenly the word was out. In the middle of a music scene that was beginning to trip on the Es, a modern psychedelic record with a flavour of the Rolling Stones' 'Paint It Black' and Primal Scream's 'Velocity Girl', but transcending both of these with its own genius, was released.

A brilliant record, 'Made Of Stone', had all the effortless cool of The Stone Roses at their peak. Intro-ing with a shimmering guitar arpeggio before the bass enters, nailing down the minor-key melody, the song rips molten melody. The verse intoned by Brown is icy observation just waiting for the tug of the chugging guitars to lead up to the crescendo of the chorus. The chorus itself, when it comes in, seems to shift a gear. It's a beautiful and tragic piece of music, uplifting, dark and scary – pure pop but with a black soul.

On release its dark heart and shimmering psychedelic edge hinted at the oncoming summer. It was the 1960s, but with a definite late-1980s edge. 'Stone' was ice-cold and yet it melted the heart; it boasted one of the greatest uplifting choruses of any pop song ever released and it still sounds like a masterpiece today.

Their first total classic, 'Made of Stone', remains to this day one of the Roses' five greatest songs and one of the best singles released in the 1980s. From the first demos right through to the final release it sent shivers up the spine.

The record captures Manchester's teeming rain and restlessness, cold-hearted streets and casual nihilism. Ian Brown's vocals are perfect – the deadpan hushed crooning is at once menacing and celebratory – the arrangement is perfect and it boasts a soaring solo from John Squire.

Joining 'Going Down' the band's ode to oral sex, the single's 'B' side on the 12 inch, was 'Guernica', another chance for the Roses to stretch their sound out and another chance to run the 'A' side tapes backwards and put the vocals on forwards. Named after Picasso's awe-inspiring painting inspired by the savagery of Franco's army crushing the socialist-anarchist resistance in the Spanish civil war. Amazingly 'I Wanna Be Adored' was mooted for the 'B' side before being held back for the album.

The freak-out section was inspired, according to Ian Brown, by jets taking off at Manchester airport, the all-night café that overlooks the runway now being one of the band's favourite haunts.

Brown told *Melody Maker*'s Bob Stanley about 'Guernica': 'We go to Manchester airport and watch the planes land and take off. Your eardrums feel like they are shredding with the volume of the engines. And the fire coming out of the back – it's an awesome sight, being thirty feet from a plane. We want to get that sound on to the record.'

If there was a single moment when The Stone Roses broke out then this was it.

Simon Williams made it single of the week in *NME*, calling the Roses 'macabre Monkees, dreamers haunted by their own shadows'.

'Made of Stone' was a marker of things to come, a signpost on the road to the big time. Surely it would only be a matter of months now until the big breakthrough.

'Made of Stone' began doing the business, and instead of having a battle to get the band known Silvertone were suddenly sat on a mini indie goldmine. The single crashed into the indie charts at number four, and made a brief excursion into the top 100 of the main charts. There was now a small but hungry national fan base to start complementing the huge Manchester one.

Gareth Davies was working hard to get the song on the radio.

'When the single came out I would always have Gareth [Evans] on the phone to me. He knew I would get into the office between half past six and seven o'clock in the morning and he used to regularly call at seven – just ranting, maniacal rants, but some good things would come out of it.

'I remember him banging on about bumping into New Order and they would tell him they were on the football. Then he would rant for like ten minutes and I'd say, "Actually, it's a World Cup song, Gareth," and he'd say get The Stone Roses on there. I did go to the sports people on TV, which people didn't do at the time, and got them to use the instrumental versions of the songs. So we actually picked up a lot of coverage on sports programmes. We were the only people at that time who invited the sport producers to gigs and that really worked.'

The real battle for Gareth was getting the band primetime national airplay.

'There were people who were interested in playing the band, but trying to get on Radio 1 was hard. Kenton Allen, who is a big TV producer now, said, "You're six months ahead of everything else." So I said, "What's the problem with that for Radio 1?" and he said, "If we play it now people will just not like it." But he knew they were going to get there in six months. The band were ahead of the pack.

'The buzz had been growing about them. They'd done their first interviews and I remember they'd done a TV interview with this presenter Rachel Davies in London. They were very affable guys and had no sort of airs and graces about them or anything like that but as soon as the interview started the answers became very yes or no.

'So the interviewer, Rachel Davies, afterwards said, "God, did I do something to offend them or something? What's wrong?" I explained they weren't used to it and quite shy. But then the TV session finished and the band helped the crew load up all their stuff, hump all their gear out to the truck, which was not normally what bands do. It was really funny because I got a call afterwards saying, "We'll do a really nice piece, they're nice blokes," and stuff like that. The interview was on *Music Box*.'

Gareth Davies tried to explain radio to the band. 'I said, "When you do radio you've got to be quick with the answers because it's just dead air." So we went through all this and they had a Johnnie Walker interview for BBC London next...Reni sat in the middle and Ian and John either side of him. Johnnie said, "This is your first gig in London," and Ian nodded his head enthusiastically straightaway, but of course to the radio listeners it was dead air. They just weren't used to it. It sounded like a difficult interview but I remember Johnnie Walker was fine because he could see what was happening.

'Next, we set up was a *News Beat* interview on the radio and I remember Ian and John turned up with two sheets of A4 paper on which they'd scribbled down some notes. We went to this pub and I asked, "What's with the notes of paper?" and they said, "Oh, we thought you were really upset about the Johnnie Walker interview so we thought we'd have some ideas and we could talk about them."

'So they did the *News Beat* interview and they were the usual questions and answers then the guy said, "Have you got anything you'd like to bring up?" I thought they'd look at the paper but they said, "No, not really."

'I went up to the bloke afterwards and said, "I'm very sorry about that," and he said, "I was told this could be difficult but what lovely blokes." They were the friendliest blokes you could possibly meet but to most people they were distant and difficult, and all the rest of it, but it was nothing like reality.'

The band's interview silence effectively added to their mystique. In many ways it was a cunningly effective trick, and their dry sense of humour is always there.

One DJ who would noticeably not pick up on the band was John Peel.

'There were always people who would pick up on it but the one person who didn't and never ever played a track was John Peel and I remember him saying to me once, "Sorry, Gareth, my wife likes it, the children like it, but I just cannot get The Stone Roses." He just couldn't get it. It could be annoying but that was the point of John Peel: if he couldn't see it himself, it wouldn't be played, that was the charm of him.'

The word, though, was out as people were raving about this new band from Manchester, and their friends and their friends' friends were beginning to take notice. As April melted into May the venues the Roses played that had once been empty began to fill up; hey, they were now nearly half full!

As the summer started to kick in and it seemed like everyone was blissed-out on E, this shaggy pop group from Manchester were walking the new walk and talking the new talk. Along with the Happy Mondays, they seemed to be the harbinger of a new working-class psychedelic, acid casual, (un)consciousness that contrasted so sharply with the far more middle-class 1960s phenomenon.

This time the hallucinogenics were in very different hands, and this time they would be in the bloodstream of new crews of crazed drug outlaws, scallydelics and acid casuals as the press misnamed them at the time.

And it all seemed to be coming from Manchester. The city became synonymous with drugs and good times. It was going to be one hell of a summer. It seemed like a never-ending E-fuelled trip through some of the craziest pop scenes for years. Acid house had sparked a cultural revolution and now the guitar bands, after assimilating the new culture, were ready to reply...And what a reply! Hot on the heels of 'Made of Stone' The Stone Roses were about to release their début album, which captured the flavour of the times like no other record.

'We wrote them songs before acid house, and we recorded them in the summer,' says Ian Brown. 'We hadn't took Es when we made those songs, it come in at the same time. We weren't acid house, we were guitars and sixties melodies. Maybe Reni had the beat, but it was connected. The music is up and we were about the up, we were about community and the up positivity – the "nothing can stop us, we can do what we want" feeling of acid house. We were innocent...

'We used to freak journalists out because we used to have acid house on in interviews and they'd say, "What's that you're listening to?" They weren't into it but we genuinely were, playing it in cars and in coaches on the way to gigs. It must have been parallel because most of those songs were written and recorded before acid house. When we played Blackpool it was like a rave; everyone was on E except for us and my mum and dad!

'Gareth didn't understand acid house, did he 'eck! He was always pissed off that we went to the Hacienda because he thought that International 2 was in competition with the Hacienda and concerned with what Tony thought. He was pissed off that we went there because he thought that he had the club but they were all good places.'

On Monday 27 February, The Stone Roses finally broke into the media mainstream. They played the Hacienda; the club that Ian Brown had once hated so much in his youth but became a regular at soon after. It was now the hippest space in England.

The gig was a master stroke, the Roses were now coming in from the suburb clubs like the Internationals and into the city centre, they were a band about to break in a city that was by now seeking the twenty-four-hour party. They looked right, they felt right and they sold the place out.

Meanwhile publicists Hall Or Nothing organised the first big press for the band, and all the papers were there to review the show. It was make or break for the Roses and the triumphant gig was crucial to their eventual ascendancy.

The Roses' career had been going up in steps in Manchester, from the warehouse gigs to the Internationals, last year's bash with James at the International 2. It was time to move on up, raid the fashion palaces, get a foot into the door of the trendy. Filmed for *Snub* (a BBC2 music programme), this was the gig that started the media rush.

The Hacienda was going through something of a renaissance. It had originally been a live venue, a big, cold, modern barn with a dripping ceiling and a dreaded sound system. It had struggled to make ends meet until acid house and the likes of Graeme Park and Mike Pickering had made it the hippest club in the UK. It was the nerve centre for acid house – reputations were forged on the dancefloor, hushed rumours went round that the first-ever Es in the city were sold by Bez in the dark corners of the club, the erstwhile Mondays' percussionist/dancer hot-rodding a cranky old van up and down the M6 supplying the new drug generation with their pills.

In the last 18 months the club had become very hot indeed. It was the key place in the city and everything revolved round it.

But for a guitar band it was still looked on as a difficult gig, as the Roses had found out when they last played there three years ago.

Now was the perfect moment; this was the moment when acid house and rock were going to fucking get together and the Roses were one of the two bands, along with the Happy Mondays, who had the swagger and the nous and the understanding of the street culture to pull it off.

Andy McQueen was buzzing. 'I got down to the Hacienda at quarter to six just before the soundcheck, and there was a real sense that an event was about to take place. Ubiquitous baldies and longhairs stalked about and the gigantic PA just boomed the *Vanishing Point* soundtrack. It sounded crystal clear and very loud. The band arrived in dribs and drabs, all clearly excited, especially Mani, who was leaping about and slapping hands with everybody. I was very excited.'

The excitement was tangible all evening. Playing the Hacienda then was a very big deal, and was as big as you got if you were cool; long before your G-Mexes, long before Britpop and the big aircraft hangers, this was it. There was nowhere else to go; if you could just get on that stage and play, you seemed like you were a massive band. Fuck the rubbish sound system and the barmy acoustics, this was the big time. Bands yearned for the chance to hit that stage.

The Roses felt that they were on to something here.

In the soundcheck they attempted to play a new song, 'Where Angels Play'. Andy McQueen was simply stunned. 'It was gorgeous, really catchy, just classic pop.'

Even Andy felt that no one could have the audacity to be writing such great guitar pop in the late 1980s.

'I had that familiar feeling; the tune was so great I felt it was a cover, it sounded so perfect.'

This kind of guitar pop was something that the British were traditionally brilliant at and yet it was something that, at the time, almost sounded avant garde. The Stone Roses were neither indie or mainstream; instead they were heading for that dead zone, caught between two fanatical polar-opposite worlds.

And that was the beauty of the Roses: they, more than anybody else, destroyed that barrier for once and for all and unleashed a tidal wave of guitar pop that had been pent up for a decade, apart from The Smiths, back into the chart. For the first time since punk rock everyone felt included in the pop process. They got the council estate kids interested in being in bands again, but they didn't exclude the students. This, by accident or design, was their singular key contribution to UK pop culture.

McQueen hung around the soundcheck spellbound. 'Here they were mooching around in their outdoor coats making such beautiful music. It was what was so great about the band, it was like they made no attempt and yet they were effortlessly making brilliant music.'

The soundcheck, typically, took ages. There were lots of details to take in. A lot of texture to be honed. Ian sang all the versus of 'Resurrection' and they went on to play 'Where Angels Play' again, 'Shoot You Down', 'Sally Cinnamon' and repeated half of 'Resurrection', before diving into the drawn-out bluesy ending of 'Resurrection' separately. Ian leant down and played the tom-toms, detached.

Later that night the band took the stage and pop became a celebration instead of a chore. Guitars suddenly seemed modern again, effortless, the band were coasting, cool. The *NME* and *Sounds* raved, and suddenly the Roses were finally in favour. The press were thrilled; here was a band that could replace The Smiths and it was from The Smiths that the Roses got most of their audience.

The sound was spot-on, miraculously crystal clear; again 'Adored' kicked off the set and again Ian was taunting the crowd, mouth gaping, eyes staring, the king monkey moves apparent. Total attitude was required and delivered.

'Here It Comes', 'Waterfall', the new single, 'Made of Stone', segued into 'Shoot You Down', 'Elephant Stone' – it was becoming a legendary roll call – 'Sally Cinnamon', 'Sugar Spun Sister', a rush of pure pop, and the full stop. No encore.

'These brightest of sparks actually do merit your adoration,' enthused Andrew Collins in the *NME*.

After five years The Stone Roses were the hottest new band in Britain and the press had finally caught up with them.

Meanwhile, Back in the Real World

The tour continued on 28 February, travelling all the way down south to Brighton. In total contrast to the Hacienda, the gig at the Escape Club had 52 people paying £3 each to enter the upstairs room of a well-kept pub with a tight, small stage and a lop-sided bar. The Roses obviously didn't like it at all – they played four songs and left the stage, walking into the crowd and down the stairs as there was no exit on the stage itself. The last song of the set was 'Sally Cinnamon', and Ian Brown never even bothered to sing; he just sat there playing the bongos like a kid with a new toy, dispassionate, bored. He cold-shouldered the 'crowd'; 'Aren't you people polite clapping like that,' he sneered at the smattering of between-song applause.

John Brice muses on the band not catching on in the rest of the UK: 'I remember going to see them in Brighton. There was 20 people there. The vibe had not got to those places yet. They were staying in bed and breakfasts, hanging out smoking weed. It was interesting seeing them in close quarters – they were big in Manchester but there was a weird transition period when the rest of the country hadn't caught on.

'It hit me what an amazing harmoniser Reni was when you really watched the band – at the International, bouncing around with the crowd and singing along, you wouldn't notice that.'

It was in Brighton that they went to the dolphinarium and checked out the dolphins. Ian Brown let his tough street pose drop in an interview. 'We went to see a dolphin in Brighton. It was really sad because it was in a tiny little pool. None of us said anything for about half an hour. We just stared at it. It kept going past and turning its head and smiling. There was a load of people standing around the pool and it only jumped up when it saw us.'

They may have been sympathetic with the dolphins but with the press they could often be antagonistic. The band would test the journalists as Mr Spencer, who interviewed them for *Sounds* in 1989, points out.

'Interviewing them was mildly menacing. They had charisma and attitude; they were funny, but their jokes were in-jokes; it felt very much like
I was the southern softie being given the once-over by a close-knit Manc
gang, who could've made it a nightmare for me if they'd wanted to, but
happily, somehow, after having matches flicked at me by Squire (as I recall)
I won them over…'

In the article, Mr Spencer astutely points out that the Roses shared
with The Beatles 'a number of useful attributes – delightfully precise
backing vocals, catchy titles, irresistible choruses and a crafty cosmic
undertow. Psychotic, revolutionary, inscrutable, piss-taking bastards they
may be. But The Stone Roses know a few things about pop music.
Tonight's gig is a revelation, ending with a long, instrumental freak-out
that sends their itinerant Manchester following into a total go-go frenzy.

'They leave me flushed by that early matchstick bombardment, but
convinced by the rowdiest guitar rampage I've witnessed in weeks. They'll
go far…'

The tour continued; the band had never toured like this before. But from
that first gig, a show in Ian's birthplace of Warrington at the Legends club,
on 17 February they were pretty well on the road for the rest of that year.
Playing to increasing crowds, the Roses were one step ahead of the audience,
but this seminal tour, one of the classic tours, was taking a whole new culture
to a new generation and when the kids got it, they got it en masse.

'Twisting the Lemon, Man…' – The Stone Roses' Début Album Released at Last: May 1989

It may not have been a huge record when it came out but the Roses' début
is now acknowledged as one of the most important British albums ever
released.

Their début is up there with all the classic British rock'n'roll records
and proved that a British band could easily throw off the yoke of The
Beatles and the other heavyweight classics that mostly crush the spirit out
of any upcoming band. This record is as good as if not better than most
of those so-called classics.

The album opens, like their best gigs, with 'I Wanna Be Adored', with
the bass chugging in, lulling the listener into a strange unease as the crystalline guitar announces itself with a series of cascading lines before the

chords slash in. There is no other way you could start this album. 'Adored', once planned to be the Roses' follow-up single to 'So Young', then a 'B' side to 'Made Of Stone', had found its perfect place – opening up the perfect album.

Soon it would be the anthem to a new pop generation. The song, Brown's third person paean to sin and craving for adoration, neatly uncoils itself. The beauty of 'Adored' is the way it is so easily misunderstood – in the context of an arrogant singer intoning the lyrics in front of the adoring faithful it took on a meaning quite different from what Brown intended. But then that's the beauty of pop, misinterpretation, making the song mean whatever you want.

Riding in on that bass line, the song, written almost right back at the beginning of the Roses' career, finally finds its home, at the front of the album and, finally, at the beginning of their live set after spending four years floating around in the middle of the set list since its début in Sweden.

What the song and the album had was this huge sense of space. If guitar music had sounded muted and claustrophobic in the eighties, the best stuff scurrying into the underground, the Roses made music that, like acid house, sounded massive. It sounded like it could fill a whole city with its euphoric passion, a euphoria that tapped into the rush of E and the optimistic atmosphere at the end of the eighties, when so much seemed possible.

The other single pulled from the album, 'She Bangs The Drums', was pop as innocent as The Monkees, a saccharine blast of guitar pop that seemed to change tune with every twist of its fluctuating structure. It also showed a band that were oozing a cool confidence. Most groups would have built a whole song around one of these riffs. The Roses would almost discard them instantly before moving on to the next one. They were the new young kings of total pop.

'She Bangs The Drums' was the song that eventually gave the band their first Top Forty hit later that year, in July. Every twist and turn of the song seems to be crammed with another riff, another hook; hooks that sound at once so familiar and yet you can't quite place where you heard them before. The Roses having the imagination to twist pop into new shapes. Great lyrics as well from the songwriting duo, with Ian's uplifting swagger bounding along on the edge of pure arrogance.

John weighs in with the lyrics to the chorus planting a seed of self-doubt in the song, but all that is lost in the music. The Roses literally swagger their uplifting pop out of the grooves of the record. Two songs in and we're already celebrating a classic record.

'Waterfall' rides in on that burning arpeggio. A spooked figure, it shimmers with that updated psychedelic that the band were now so adept at. When the acoustic guitar drops in near the end it shifts another gear, you sit back and wait for one of those glorious churning endings that the Roses specialised in, but it tantalisingly goes to a fadeout.

'Waterfall' is further evidence of the sheer talent of Squire's guitar playing. It seems like every trick he's got up his sleeve is at play here, from the trademark wah-wah to spine-tingling acoustics – the non-macho guitar hero! There is a total sensitivity at play here.

The lyrics are, according to Ian, 'about a girl who sees all the bullshit, drops a trip and goes to Dover. She's tripping, she's about to get on this boat and she feels free.' Ian sings softly. It's a long way from 'So Young' and Reni's backing vocal perfectly complements the song. The deep, resonating dub bass is closing in on that Jah Wobble sound (amazing bassist from John Lydon's post-Pistols band, Public Image Limited. Wobble's bowel-rattling deep dub bass was PIL's signature. If you're a fan of Mani's bass sound, then check out Public Image's *Metal Box* album).

And now the going gets weird. As if to prove that pure pop is too pathetically easy, the Roses flip the two-inch for 'Waterfall' over for one of their backwards tracks 'Don't Stop' (they did four altogether). By now this backwards thing is rapidly becoming one of their trademarks, every release must have one!

In the sixties The Beatles had run the odd guitar or cymbal backwards but the Roses were not stopping there! For some fans this track is the low point of the album, an annoying break from the rush of pop perfection, but it neatly slaps the listener across the face – a trip, a break from the melodic easy listening, a neat reminder of just what we are dealing with here.

Plus it fucking works. It's not a lazy filler. The vocals, some of which are the original words slurring backwards with new added ones written by John, are equally bizarre. John always claimed they were just what was suggested to him by the track running backwards. For some listeners they drip some sort of hidden meaning. For me it's just great to hear the word 'imbecile' in a 'pop' song!

'Bye Bye Badman' is all brisk, frothy and light on the surface and is a classic case of the Roses being soft on the surface and tough on the message (underneath the sand the paving stones, perhaps!). For many a love song, it was actually about the '68 student riots in Paris, a time when pop radicalism nearly brought down a government, a time that must have been dear to Ian Brown's heart. A rock'n'roll romantic, Brown believed in the power of revolt and was fascinated by the situationists.

Ian Brown: 'If you go home and listen to "Bye Bye Badman" and then imagine it's someone singing to a riot policeman on the barricades in Paris '68 you'll get a picture of what we're about. The song is a call to insurrection.'

The song's theme continued to the cover of the album. The cover painting by John Squire (his best sleeve for any Roses record), is also called *Bye Bye Badman*, and the painting is littered with references to the song, from the daubed tricoleur down one side, to the lemons. (Ian Brown had read that the students in 1968 used to squirt lemons in the air to negate the effects of the CS gas fired by the cops.)

Says John, 'The lemons aren't a part of the picture, they're real lemons, nailed on because it was photographed on the wall – the photographer didn't have a rostrum camera. It ties in with the lyrics of "Bye Bye Badman", to do with the Paris student uprisings in May 1968. Me and Ian saw a documentary on it and liked the clothes: there was a guy, chucking stones, with a really nice jacket and desert boots. The students used to suck on lemons to nullify the effects of the tear gas. That's why the tricoleur is there. The green is inspired by the water at the Giant's Causeway in Ireland, where we went before a gig at Coleraine University.'

It was another neat twist in the Roses' mythology, another hint that there was something far deeper going on just underneath the surface.

There is something far more disturbing, something far more dangerous and political to the Roses than most people perceived.

'It's important to retain your aggression as you get older,' Brown told Simon Reynolds of the *Observer*. 'People like Tony Benn and Michael Foot do. The current Labour leadership can't compare with them. Labour's outdated and gone. It's been left behind, it's served its purpose. If you read the Crossman diaries or books about Harold Wilson they tell you that when Labour does get in it can't actually change the country, that's just the way, it's set up.'

And it was this radicalism that is much less subtly stated on the next track. 'Elizabeth My Dear', with the melody borrowed from 'Scarborough Fair', was Ian Brown intoning an anti-royal paean; the short track ends with a gunshot. These boys were not in the hunt for MBEs.

At the time the song, which quite specifically calls for the end of the monarchy, was put into sharper focus when Brown said he would be the man to suffocate the Queen Mother. This set off a bit of a shit storm in the tabloids.

Written in late 1986, 'Sugar Spun Sister' is one of the older songs on the album and one that they had already demoed. That original demo displayed a poppier touch than this final recorded version. It's hard to grasp just what the song is about. In a rush of lyrical images, the song could be about love, it could be about tripping, some say it's about a prostitute. There's a disdain for the hypocrisy of politics underlined in the great line, 'Every member of parliament sniffs on glue'.

'Made of Stone', released as a single the previous month, makes even more sense in the context of the album, another atmospheric rush of great melody in a breathless surge of pop.

John Squire, talking to the *NME* cryptically, attempted to explain just what the rush of the song meant to him. 'It's about making a wish and watching it happen – like scoring the winning goal in a cup final, on a Harley, electroglide, dressed as Spiderman…' Well, that explains it then.

'Shoot You Down' has the fingerprints of the guitar genius, Jimi Hendrix, all over it. Jimi had been fast becoming a major influence in the Roses camp; obviously with John's guitar playing, there's no way you're going to go near a wah-wah and not think about Jimi, but it goes deeper than that. The spiritual soulfulness of prime-time Jimi seems to have rubbed off on most of these tunes and the man's music – its loose-limbed funkiness and melodic riffology – is also key in the Roses' creative canon. With only the ending of 'I Am The Resurrection' to be added on, this was virtually the last song to be recorded in the album sessions. Brown's sinister vocal is a great counterpoint to the song's almost mellow groove. Again there is something nasty, something dark, hovering just below the surface; the contradiction in the name Stone Roses is still being used as a creative yardstick by the band.

'This Is The One' is another of the songs that stretches back to the band's beginning, when it was punkier and faster. A massive anthem and as euphoric as the band got, it's no wonder it's played at Old Trafford, being the perfect uplifting rabble rouser. The lyrics drip with religious references just like the closing track, 'I Am The Resurrection', which manages the almost-impossible and tops the euphoria of the previous song. The album's closer is the band at their most musical. The playing is fantastic and the coda is one of the greatest pieces of musicianship from any British band ever; the band lock into a groove and they are hypnotic in their brilliance.

When you finish an album you want that last track to be a bit special, something that really stretches the band, something that takes you somewhere else. And with 'I Am The Resurrection' the Roses perfectly fit that bill.

'I Am The Resurrection', one of the Roses' finest moments, was a song that ended their set for years, a rousing anthemic song that captured that euphoric rush of rock'n'roll adrenaline in a spiritual manner. The musicianship is incredible. All those hours in the rehearsal room were paying off big style! The stop/start and false ending, the tease of the song's climax...Awesome stuff. In 1989 it seemed to be on forever in every club that you went to in town. The anthem of a never-ending summer! A summer that many will never forget...

Alan McGee, the ex-Creation Records boss, is still stunned by the musical brilliance of the album.

'I defy anyone to find a better breakdown than in "I Am The Resurrection". It's better than the Rolling Stones' "Monkey Man"! Mani and Reni together – what a rhythm section! Ian Brown said he would pay money to watch Reni play the drums and I agree. He could play drums for two hours and you would not get bored. John Squire is great, Mani is great, Ian is the great communicator – he's up here yet. He's Ian Brown, he invented a lot of things, he invented being a Manc! Reni is the man, though, for me – the über-musician in that band.'

Gary Aspden, a Blackburn-born Manchester scenester and pop culture freak and now key player in Adidas, remembers the impact the album had.

'It's the greatest début of all time along with the Sex Pistols. It took me 15 years to realise that. I couldn't put it into the context of musical history when it came out. There are a lot of parallels between the two bands: both released two inspirational albums that inspired generations of musicians and both had managers that were difficult, but the Roses were better musically than the Pistols.

'In 1989/'90 we believed we could change the world and the Roses believed that as well.'

Emily Eavis, who runs Glastonbury festival with her father Michael, also felt the profound impact of the album.

'One of the best albums of all time and for a moment the greatest band in the world. No one else could touch the Roses and there is still something mysterious about them.'

Jon Savage, the legendary music journalist, muses over the album's impact. 'The first album, it's the great one, isn't it? I think that John Leckie must have caught them just at the right time.

'To be honest I think the great thing about the record is that it captures the moment, and it captures a pop cultural moment of great optimism, with the Berlin Wall coming down and the end of the Cold War. The eighties had been pretty grim and the record marked the end of the eighties.'

Mani remains proud of the album.

'I will still play the album out when I DJ and I will still listen to it for pleasure, you know? Which is strange as you get a lot of people in bands who just hate to go back and listen to their record, don't they? It still sounds fucking brilliant to me. It doesn't sound dated in any way shape or form.

'I think it still stands up and I think it's still very relevant. People remain interested 20 years down the line. It's sort of like become one of them "rite of passage" LPs. Like, everyone got into *Dark Side of the Moon* before; now it's the Roses – there are just certain rite of passage LPs in people's lives and I think we are in that category now. How the fuck we managed to get that together I don't know!

'It was a lot of hard work. No one ever gave us anything on a silver plate. There were always things conspiring against us and stuff like that but I think it's just the unity we had together as mates and as a band – the confidence that we had just made it. There was nothing better than being in each other's company every day and sitting in that old Spirit lock-up in Chorlton and kicking ideas about.'

Kevin Cummins, the top photographer who took the classic paint-spattered image of the band for the *NME* cover, looks at the album in the context of the band coming together through all those years in Manchester.

'When Howard Jones managed them they didn't seem like they were going to get anywhere. Then there was the paint incident when they sprayed their name in town, which didn't help, then they changed line-up and Mani joined and it was like it suddenly fell into place and the band was perfect.

'When I did the famous picture of them covered in paint I had already photographed them for an on-the-road feature for the *NME* where we went to Paris to do them. In those days they would play Paris and the whole crowd would go crazy and you would think they were getting big in France till you realised that most of the crowd had come from Manchester!

'I remember the gig in Paris. I met Gareth Evans backstage and he opened a briefcase with what must have had about a hundred grand in various currencies in it; it made you laugh really. Gareth was always really fond of the grand gesture!

'Usually for an *NME* on-the-road feature we would have the band live or posed on the road somewhere but this was something different – at the time everyone was so swept up in the excitement of The Stone Roses and it was really exciting, so we decided that we could do something different, so I came up with the idea of covering them with paint like one of John's sleeves.

'The album was perfect, every song is perfect and the sequencing of the tracks is also flawless…it's one of those few records that sounds perfect all the way through and you don't just listen to a couple of tracks but the whole album. The record was really timeless…a great record is about having a good producer and, like Joy Division, they had someone who saw the whole picture and captured the band. It's one of the great British albums. At the time you would hear it everywhere. As we liked to say at the time at the *NME* – it captured the zeitgeist.'

For John Leckie the album still really stands the test of time.

'I still think it's one of my favourite records because I can play it now and really enjoy it and still feel rather good about it. I'm amazed at how it holds together really, you know. It's like a unified album, you know, it's not a collection of tracks. There's no weak points in it, and how musical it is, it's totally about the music really. More than anything else on that record, it's the whole thing – the music and the playing, the melodies and things, even when I went back to the demos, which I just dug out, you can hear that on there. It's kind of not really what I did to it; it's really the tunes, you know? "Shoot You Down" and "Bye Bye Badman" and those sort of tunes are really nice.'

While Clint Boon sees it as a huge turning point in music that would change everything for good. 'At the time it was nice because obviously being Mancunians we had seen the build-up. We played gigs with The Stone Roses in the early days. We knew there was an album imminent and were looking forward to it so when it came I think in some ways it sort of spoilt the surprise because there was that familiarity with it.

'But in other ways we all realised it was a milestone in terms of the quality of the production, which was beautiful, and it was perfect for what the Roses were because it had that psychedelic edge and the melodies that were a big part of what they did.

'John Leckie's production was perfect; it could not have been a better production job. John Leckie provided the perfect blend, bringing out the softness a bit…they always reminded me of Simon and Garfunkel, in a complimentary way, because you know I'm a fan of that mellow end of the psychedelic spectrum; it always appealed to me.

'You could hear The Byrds in it and at the same time you could hear John Squire was into his Led Zep and it was just the perfect blend – it was not too much of any one thing.

'The extremes between "Elizabeth My Dear" and "I Am The Resurrection" are amazing – you could not imagine one band doing that since the psychedelic era. It was not something that rock bands did in the eighties, so for me it was a total knockback in the direction of the psychedelic years, which I liked.

'We were seeing history being made with what they were doing, like with Reni's approach as a drummer. There were just so many fucking elements of the story that made it a piece of musical history. But at the time I never realised it.'

John Niven, who wrote the hilarious and definitive book about the nineties music biz, *Kill Your Friends*, spent a year immersed in the album.

'When I was touring in an indie band in '87/early '88, you'd go to Manchester and see posters saying "THE STONE ROSES" and they'd be playing the International, where the big bands played. You'd think, "Who are these fucking cunts?" A year later we weren't listening to much else: the whole of that summer of '89 was just the first Roses album back-to-back. Like everyone in a standard-issue jangly indie group, I was stunned at the virtuosity of the playing. Much later, when I met Mani for the first time – on a Heavenly Records Thames boat trip in the summer of '97 – I made the mistake of telling him that the first time I ever took E I wound up Cossack dancing to the first Roses record. Every time I saw him after that he'd give a little burst of Cossack jigging, which was hugely endearing.'

Mike Joyce from The Smiths still celebrates the band.

'The album is mind blowing, really; they are one of those bands that you hear something and you think, "What's that? What is that? What genre is that? What exactly, where are their heads at?" Which I guess must have been the same when people heard The Smiths for the first time.

'With the Roses they heard something so fresh and so different and it had that arrogance, the level of arrogance that you can hear it when they are playing. I think there is always that fine line you have got to understand if you are in a band – you have got to feel like you are the best band that's ever been, otherwise what's the point of being in a band? You can't think, "Well, we're all right." You have got to be good – you have got to be great and you have got to be the best and you have got to have that level of confidence and swagger but coupled with talent…You have got to be able to back it up, and they did. Brilliantly.'

Noel Gallagher puts it all down to time. The right band at the right time. 'The album is obviously their finest ever moment. I think if anyone in a band, including me, had recorded only two albums and one of them was that début, I would be fucking pleased with that.

'Timing is everything in music…The Stone Roses album came out bang on midday on the right day in the right year in the right decade – unbelievable timing. It was just something about the way the music sounded.

'That album is so well executed, it's the exact expression of what that group was about. It was retro but it was so fucking on the money, it was so now, that album, it could have been recorded tomorrow morning.

'We used to go and see them all the time and I thought, "I want to see that set list recorded as a record so I can play it at home, so it was kind of a relief – it was so long in the making – we'd been waiting five years for it!

'The album is like a sense of relief for just having it right. It was something to play to people and tell them, "What the fuck have I been going on about for the last five years?" When it came out I just thought, "At last!"

'It's just one of those albums. I don't know anybody who doesn't like it. Without a doubt I don't know one person who doesn't like that album. I've never met a person when you put it on has said, "Turn that shit off."

'If you want to know what British pop music sounded like in 1989, you put that album on, and if you wanna know what great classic British pop music is all about, you put that on as well. It's an amazing feat to capture the time of the late eighties and then 20 years later you can still put it on and, fucking wow, it still says what's great about British music.'

Ian Brown himself still listens to the album now and then, as he told me in 2009.

'It just hits me how lean it is and well played it is, and listening to the instrumentals, just how tight it is. Everyone's got a part but it's fluid in the space at the same time. There's loads going on. The playing is brilliant.

And on every track the drums sound brilliant, they get you every time. Reni had some skill. He should have carried on after we split. He'd have been like Gene Krupa or Buddy Rich. He'd fill the Apollo up now if he just set up his drum kit in there and played.

'I never wanted it to be seen as me as the frontman – we wanted it to be seen as a four-piece band like The Beatles. I always refused to do pictures on my own for the press – that wasn't the idea of the band. We spent a lot of energy making out we was a four-piece and not a lead singer and a band.

'When the album came out, the label told us not to expect a chart position. They were like, "You won't get in the charts with this, you're an independent guitar band and it won't happen," and we were like, "Yeah, we will. We've done loads of gigs and 300 or so people would come to each one in each town, so we will" – bands now who sound like us will go straight into the Top Ten! But then it was different, but after our album came out things changed. That summer everywhere I went I'd hear the album coming out of cars, houses, pubs, bedsits… everywhere. The record sold itself.'

The album means many things to many people. But most will agree that this is one of the most powerful albums to have ever been made. It dripped religious references that added to its mystic allure and its sense of spiritual power.

'We saw "I Am the Resurrection, I Am the Light" on a church notice-board,' John Squire said to the *NME*, while Ian Brown told Simon Williams of the same paper, 'I believe in God. There must be some substance in Christ, because the myth has lasted so long. Like 2,000 years, but it's convenient because you don't have to make your mind up till you get to the gates.'

If the guitar gives the record its musical edge, Brown personalises the record, singing in his home-town accent, spitting out the vengeful lyrics with their shades of prime-time Bob Dylan or singing like a fallen angel, contrasting neatly with the euphoric rush of music that surrounds the voice, making it a valid platform for rock'n'roll. Apart from Manchester underground band, The Fall, Brown was the most northern voice you'd heard on a record at that point. It gave the Roses a particular identity, adding to the almost folky melodies. He gives the album its very British edge.

Lyrically the record hints at something far deeper and darker. Broadly speaking Brown and Squire's lyrics were biblical tracts and revolutionary rhetoric with love songs mixed with LSD visions mixed with cynical cutting shots. Both lyricists were on burning form for the début, with a dark humour fusing the anti-establishment love songs at every corner.

The package was completed with a bunch of great black and white shots taken by Ian Tilton from the 1988 Granada TV appearance that captured the band at their coolest. John hunches over his guitar deep in concentration, his long slender fingers doing something complicated to the arpeggio on 'Waterfall'; Ian Brown looks angelic and surly, oozing a menace and a danger. Mani looks like the scally that got the big break, his Pollocked bass looks too big for him.

In the background, behind Squire's Fender amp, Cressa is caught between dancing and changing the guitar player's bank of effects.

Reni has got the drums and the super harmonies down. He too, oozes a malevolent innocence. It just all looks so effortless, a band naturally stalking its domain, months before the peak of their powers. The shots captured a band that was totally in its stride. Pre flares, in parallels, the band look cool, like any rock'n'roll band at the moment when it all clicks.

The album was released in May. I gave it a rave review in *Sounds*, and *Melody Maker* covered it favourably. The *NME* was a bit unsure. In the next few weeks it sold steadily, a cult record, gradually getting a head of steam.

'I Wanna Be Adored': A Self-Fulfilling Prophecy

Maybe there is a point in your life when it all comes together. You've got the talent, the team is together, the times have changed and you're in the right place at the right time. For the Roses the release of their début album was perfection itself.

Squire's astonishing guitar talent was finally getting the space to shine, and the last 12-month surge of songwriting added to a stockpile of drop-dead classic songs that were left over from early days. After all, this was a band that had been going for five years, a band that wasn't short of talent.

In some ways this was their second album, the shelved Hannett album being their real début. Astute to the last, at the time they had prevented its release, instinctively realising that they weren't ready to put an album out. Whereas their proper début defined a generation.

The key record of its times, *The Stone Roses* set the agenda for nineties British guitar pop. It easily stands the test of time; from the vast range of tunes, the complex song structures, the superb arrangements and the lyrics that hint at a mystery, intelligence and depth that the band weren't giving away in interviews.

It's the moment when British music finally got to be in touch with roots rock'n'roll, taking on board Hendrix, Love, The Doors, Simon and Garfunkel, punk rock, psychedelia, etc. The Roses took retro into the future and weren't ashamed to wear their influences on their sleeves because they could remould them into something totally original. It was this moment, for some, when pop stopped going forward and swallowed its own history.

The sheer spaciousness and scale of sound of *The Stone Roses* perfectly matched the hunger of the house generation. Anthemic songs that were perfect for the new large crowd vibe that was sweeping Britain after years of huddling in the underground.

It was also a great pop album, at once exhilarating and dark. Sugar-sweet melodies cloaked dark lyrics and tracks that were a stupendous rush of adrenalised playing and anthemic choruses.

Stunning in its scope and its playing, it was a massive jump forward for the band who had only 18 months previously been tied to rock. They sounded like an outfit greedy for change, and had a huge swaggering confidence about making those moves.

The Stone Roses were the first British guitar band who were post-indie.

As Ian Brown pointed out to Mat Smith of *Melody Maker* a couple of months after the album's release, 'I don't like us being thought of as an indie band, cos I can't think of any good indie bands. Independent music hasn't thrown up much in the last ten years, has it? Maybe a couple of good records, "Psychocandy" and one or two Smiths records, but the other stuff I just wouldn't entertain.'

This was Brown's line: the Roses were a proper classic rock'n'roll band. There were no apologies from his band. The Roses wanted it large and they weren't going to stop now.

In the same *Melody Maker* interview Brown broke another taboo when he claimed the band's ambition was to be on *Top of the Pops.* 'I want to be on that show. I watched it last week and it was like *Junior Showtime.* I wanna shake them all up. We've got as far as we can by being stubborn and arrogant and unfashionable, and eventually it all comes around.'

It's that clear-cut. Things were different. The music scene was changing fast, making one of its occasional leaps forward.

'We've been bored with rock music for the last five years. Everyone I know has always liked rock music, dance music, punk and Northern Soul. I don't think it's unusual for our fans to be into dance music. Those dividing lines aren't there any more,' noted Ian Brown, in the unlikely environment of *Loving* magazine.

He also told *Rolling Stone* at the same time, 'I think pop music was saved by the advent of acid house and rap because whites have done nothing for ten years.'

Shocked, the American music paper asked what the last good white record was.

'The Sex Pistols' first LP.'

In the same interview John Squire was asked why The Stone Roses were needed.

'People want to listen to music. They like to dance, but they are tired of that machine noise. I mean, the songs sound like they were written by a computer virus. I suppose that a lot of acid house music is guilty of the same thing, of being completely cold and devoid of any human touch, and that is what we are trying to put back,' said Squire negating a lot of the indie dance connection.

Squire also explained the band's roots. 'The Beatles were the first band everyone I knew was into, even if they were born in 1970. But the Sex Pistols were the first band we could actually go and see. They were the group that made us want to be in a group.'

Not that the Roses had actually gone to see the Sex Pistols. The Pistols' two shows in Manchester in 1976 were ill attended but witnessed by the originators of the Manchester punk rock scene, a scene which provided the very pillars for the whole Manc musical establishment years later. The power and the nihilism of the Pistols, combined with the exhilaration of their playing and the sheer bravado of their music, scored with a whole generation. At the time considered to be non-players, the Pistols have become, over the years, one of the key influential bands in British rock – along with The Beatles – whose down-to-earth approach to everything from mysticism to rock'n'roll combined with an incredible talent, saw them survive the pratfalls of fashion and become almost over-bearingly hip in the 1990s.

Of course Oasis would take the fusion of these two groups one step further and almost join them together. With The Stone Roses there were plenty of other musical factors at play.

Ian Brown was bemused by a lot of the band's comparisons. 'Everyone likes to describe us as psychedelic and say we're inspired by sixties music, but in truth, we'd never actually heard most of those sixties bands until we'd read the reviews making comparisons to us. People like Arthur Lee and Love, when we read that we were meant to sound like them, we went out and got an album and were surprised to find a common thread. Hendrix, though, is the biggest influence – John loves him.'

Jimi Hendrix was something else, everything great in rock'n'roll – flash, sexy, cool as fuck and a genius guitar player. Hendrix, with a smoking-gun voice, was also one of the great rock vocalists. He wore proper rock-star clothes and had the swagger down perfectly. On his first three albums he pushed the guitar into a thousand different directions; it was a template that a lot of people have hideously abused. Squire, though, managed to pick up his sensitivity and sensuality in his playing.

Tony Wilson once said Manchester had the best record collections. Whether it's true or not, the Roses certainly were pupils of the new eclectic.

'We're all into different things. Reni is really into Sly And The Family Stone, Mani is really into reggae and acid house. We've all got different influences but we all meet at The Beatles, the Rolling Stones and Hendrix.'

Much, over the years, has been made of the eclecticism of the Manchester scene bands, and it's true that many UK groups have an incredibly narrow range of influences. Manchester groups, though, have tantalisingly ridiculous record collections, spanning a myriad styles from house to Latin, from punk to funk to metal to pop to kitsch to crap and back again.

It was this diversity, and a hunger for new sounds and experiences, that came to an unlikely roost in Manchester, and fuelled the creativity of a wonderful and crazed bunch of home-town action.

For Brown, as he once astutely told an American magazine, 'We are striving to be part of a new movement in rock, like The Beatles were to the 1960s and the Sex Pistols to the 1970s. We've got it.' When asked just what the 'it' was, Brown replied, 'It's something indefinable, it's an X-factor. I just want you to understand that we aren't being egotistical about this. We're just trying to show our potential.'

It would be the closest he ever got to defining his own role in the Roses.

The media were generally with the Roses now. 'Made of Stone' was an acknowledged cool record and the Hacienda gig had done them plenty of favours. It seemed like the Roses were about to ride a wave of good press for the album.

Fresh-faced Roses Mark One, out and about in London in 1985 with The Jam's Bruce Foxton and *Sounds* journo Garry Johnson. (GARRY JOHNSON)

Ian Brown in classic front man action
as the Stone Roses take over. [IAN TILTON]

1988. Poses stolen from The Clash. The Roses had the same strong gang identity as the influential British punk band. (IAN TILTON)

Granada Studios late '88. The Roses were never that good at getting told what to do by 'the man'. [IAN TILTON]

A pop band just about to break; young, lean and mean, sharp and angular. Note Cressa helping John with his effects. [IAN TILTON]

Pollocked! The Roses. [IAN TILTON]

At the height of the 'baggy wars' – the money shirt, flares, attitude and hair. Ian Brown is 'the Skull' giving it the malevolent pretty boy look that still echoes through most British guitar bands. [IAN TILTON]

Cressa the vibemaster in action! [IAN TILTON]

The classic mic pose. Ian Brown as the full-on 'King Monkey', pro-active and oozing self-belief with Mani at the 'One Love' video shoot, 4 May 1990. [PENNIE SMITH]

'F minor 7 dim/G flat major – sod it.' The first non-macho guitar hero in action. [IAN TILTON]

'No, listen, it's a number one!' The fact is, Reni can play guitar almost as well as he plays drums. (PENNIE SMITH)

Robbie Maddix – he came, he saw, he conquered. He had to do the impossible and fill in for Reni, the greatest drummer of his generation. By the time of the last stand he seemed to be running the band. (PENNIE SMITH)

'They went that way!' (PENNIE SMITH)

'No, this way!' (PENNIE SMITH)

1990 TV studio, Wembley. A lot has happened since Ian Tilton's original Granada studio shots, barely two years earlier. [PENNIE SMITH]

Still riding high as the gang, the Roses were by now full-on rock 'n' roll outlaws hiding in cornfields from the grind of the music business machine. [PENNIE SMITH]

Ian Brown, new soul warrior, stands proud as the band prepares to disappear for five years. (PENNIE SMITH)

The 'Rogue Rose' prepares for the acoustic section of the comeback tour. Madrid was one of the finest performances the band ever gave according to eye witnesses. (PENNIE SMITH)

'Come out with your hands up and bring the album with you!' [PENNIE SMITH]

'Can you lend me a fiver...?' The press conference kicks
off with a question from your author. [KEN MCKAY/REX FEATURES]

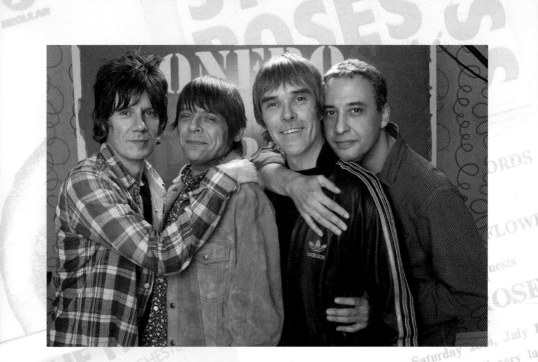

'About fookin' time...' Older, wiser and with a touching naive joy about being the Roses again. The band's first photo session since the reformation 2011.
[DAVE J HOGAN/GETTY IMAGES]

Justice Tonight! John Squire and Ian Brown join Mick Jones, The Farm and Pete Wylie in Dec 2011 at the Manchester Ritz – their first stage appearance since December 1995. (MATT SQUIRE/REX FEATURES)

Robin Denselow in the *Guardian* noted that 'Elizabeth My Dear' had 'dodgy' lyrics, but he also said, 'There are some good musicians at work here; they have the ability to swiftly move on when they are becoming dull. If they are this good live they should be well worth seeing.' He added, 'Back in Johnny Marr's old stomping ground there is a new northern psychedelic scene (flared jeans and all) which has led to a batch of new bands. The Stone Roses seem to be the first to swap their massive cult following for international success.'

Jack Barron grabbed the album for the *NME*, and gave it seven out of ten. He liked it but he was hedging his bets: 'This is an aural Big Mac laced with a psychedelic drill. This comes from Manchester and is made by people who think that Levenshulme is a suburb of San Francisco. This is The Byrds after they've flown the coop, this is living proof that acid is good for you. Just.'

Everyone was just warming up to the fact that there was something really good here and then, bang, they went massive.

Bob Stanley at *Melody Maker* went mad for the album. He thought the album was God and was everything that Bobby Gillespie had been talking up for years with Primal Scream.

US mag *Billboard* took an overview on the record: 'The Stone Roses are an English quartet that crossbreeds a thick gloom rock-derived sound with more than a hint of old-time psychedelia.'

The truth is The Stone Roses became massive without anyone's permission; they became massive because this was a great album, an album that friends played to friends and raved about in a breathless whisper.

There was still a lot of resentment about a band coming from the north, a cultural misunderstanding. Bob Dickinson, the journalist who first picked up on them in *City Life* a few years before, was now working in TV, booking bands in London. He remembers how the band were received by the media there.

'I went away to work in London for a while and when their first album was about to come out I tried to book them onto a Channel 4 programme I was working on called *Big World Café*, a sort of follow-up to *The Tube*. I had a huge row with Channel 4. He had a copy of the cassette of the album and he just did not get it at all. From the reaction in Manchester it was obvious it was going to be huge but he was really against it. I had this horrible row with him in front of the whole production team and I walked out on him. It was very exasperating. The sort of thing he wanted was U2 and Simple Minds – appalling eighties stadium bands. There was a very anti-Manchester feeling at Channel 4 at that time. We booked New Order and the production team hated the idea of them coming to London with their fans. They thought the audience would be thugs and football fans who would smash the place up.'

The Take Over

On 4 May the Roses played Liverpool Polytechnic, and witnesses remember that there were definitely far more people there than there had been before. The Stone Roses, now, had their own small brand of fanatics in each town. In Liverpool, though, they had broken through.

Keith Curtis, now the bass player in Goldblade, was there: 'I got in just as they started the first song and it was packed. You could tell that there was something going on. The crowd was really into it. There was a definite atmosphere.'

The promoter was Sean Morgan, who would go on to Manchester University and build it up to be the best venue in the country. He remembers the gig.

'"Elephant Stone" had been a big record round here and it was a fantastic gig, there was loads of people there. What I remember is that all the big-money, big-label bands who were getting all the push in the media couldn't sell tickets but here was this band who had this big crowd without any of that. I remember them getting there early and sitting in the bar, totally unfazed by the way things were starting to happen for them. I made a poster for the gig using the four heads from the *Sounds* front cover and the band liked it so much they used it for other gigs and sold it on tour.'

Fanzine producer Tim Vigon was there as well. 'The first time we saw the band live, it was at Liverpool Polytechnic in May 1988 – part of a marathon UK tour of shitholes that they did up to and around the release of the album. It was two days after the release. The music press had raved about the record, but really the pebble had just been thrown into the lake and the ripples were yet to really turn into waves. The band had already, as was their promise, become the biggest "in their street" and were selling out big rooms in the city to adoring audiences.

'But outside of town it was different. We didn't have a clue, we thought the whole world already knew – surely – so we got to Liverpool early, expecting the same sort of throng, but the gig was maybe half full, mainly with travelling Mancunians and a few curious locals. Scouse stalwarts The Real People supported (wearing waistcoats, by the way – they'd turn up a few months later in full baggy regalia with their mini indie-dance classic "Window Pane") and it felt like any other gig, but we were about to see the Roses...and once their road crew started to set up (even they looked as cool as the band) the mood in the room changed. Those present huddled forward and you could definitely sense the expectation. Cressa wandered out, we all squeezed forward...the band shuffled on like they owned the place. And they did. The bassline to "I Wanna Be Adored" rumbled forth. Those who KNEW began to move, a strange mixture of jumping and dancing en masse...and when the guitar kicked in, it was fucking bedlam. Tapes of the band's demos and works-in-progress on the album had floated around Manchester, so we knew the tunes, but we had no real idea what it SOUNDED like in the room right there. But it didn't matter; everyone was just right there. In it.'

Two days later in Manchester, Ian Brown walked onstage on a balmy night for a triumphant homecoming gig, ringing a bell – it was another of those moments, and there seemed to be so many with this band, and the room grooved as one with the band. Unbelievable stuff.

Tim continues, 'After that night we resolved to go everywhere and anywhere we could to see the band on this tour, which took in big cities and satellite towns alike. For every Manchester and Birmingham there was a Warrington, St Helens, Middlesbrough, Preston – they literally went everywhere. We headed to Shrewsbury, to see them in a club called Park Lane (every bit as neon and cheesy as it sounds). Now no one came to Shrewsbury, least of all a band who was starting to cause a stir, and this band was special. The promoters, security and everyone didn't know what had hit them. Even at this point, in a ritzy club in Shrewsbury, the crowd treated these four lads like returning rock stars. What a gig.

'As we wandered out, a bloke we recognised from always being side of stage with the band came up to us and said to us in full Mancunian glory, "All right mate, do you fuckers want to meet the lads?" We thought he was taking the piss, but full of adrenaline and youth we followed to see where we ended up, and unbelievably two minutes later we were stood in the Roses' dressing room. The band sat unmoved, smoking, chatting – things just happened around them. We couldn't believe it – we got our set lists signed, uttered gestures of adoration at our heroes and generally didn't know what the fuck was going on.'

The band took pride in being close to their fans.

'The fella who took us in was a gentleman called Steve Atherton, better known as Adge, and a bona fide Mancunian musical legend. He was the band's tour manager at the time. I'm not sure what Adge's motivations were, but his move was genius. The gaggle of fans in the dressing room must have made the band feel like every night of the tour brought new people and buzz, made them feel like stars, wherever and whenever. Perhaps this helped them to play that part so well – or maybe he was locking in people like us that he recognised from following the band around, knowing that the hardcore would spread the word like mini John the Baptists.'

The album was spreading, the media were picking up on it, but the band and the people around them were building an army of fans that loved this band like no other – and that was a smart, and powerful, move. In Walsall, at the salubrious Junction 10 a few days later, Adge recognised Tim and again let him go backstage, this time bearing that day's *Melody Maker*, the band's first-ever front cover, to be signed along with T-shirts, drumsticks and anything else they could get their hands on.

'There's no doubt about it, we felt part of something and it was something that was growing and growing, and there was no way anything could stop it, it all seemed so inevitable. Being so young we had absolutely zero sense of perspective. As I keep saying, this just seemed so natural and normal, we couldn't imagine things being any other way; we thought we'd just hitched a ride at a fairly early part of the journey and felt excited to be there, and each day anything could happen.

'The tour snaked on throughout May and June whilst plaudits for the album grew and "Madchester" became a media phenomenon. As the tour came to a close "She Bangs The Drums" was released and charted at number 36. The same week, the Happy Mondays' "Madchester" EP charted and both of "our" bands were going to be on *Top of the Pops* – fucking pop stars, but we always knew that – still, 20 of us gathered at my house to watch it and re-watch it over and over again on video.'

The 1989 tour is looked on by the hardcore fans as the band at its very best. Oozing the magic that would make them soar, they were a catalytic force, and all over the country amazed indie fans saw that there was a new way to be. Bands were springing up in their wake.

They were still only getting fifty to a hundred people at most out-of-town shows, but the grapevine was well and truly buzzing and the audience was building.

One of the myths about The Stone Roses was that they were hyped by the press, but this isn't true. By spring 1989 the word was out and they were going to happen anyway. The press could only hitch along for the ride and report this whole new pop scene that seemed to explode from nowhere.

The day after Liverpool they played the now sadly demolished Queens Hall in Widnes. This was a large Victorian hall in a chemical town bang smack between Manchester and Liverpool. If the Roses were going to really mean anything then this was the kind of place where they were going to have to cut it. In the surrounding towns, though, the story was out: people were hungry for the Roses, and the gig was yet another example of how far the story was starting to spread.

By now the band were in the middle of a press storm, grabbing plaudits by the handful after years of being treated as outsiders. The graffiti-spraying thugs, the Goths, the rock band, the ignorant boors smashing The Smiths' party – it was all getting swiftly forgotten. They were suddenly being feted and, not surprisingly, they were a tad bitter, so when asked if this press was enough by *Uptown* magazine while standing on the steps outside Widnes's Queens Hall, they just stared back and deadpanned, 'It's never enough, is it? We're disappointed that we haven't had more.'

What's it like to be big in Manchester?

'We're not massive in Manchester,' replied John Squire, adding, 'There are a million and a half people in Manchester and we only get two thousand.'

Confounded, the journalist asked them why they were so arrogant with the press.

'We're not arrogant, we are real. What do you want? A bunch of fakes with prepared answers?'

They were then asked about the 1960s comparisons.

'People who say that have no knowledge of music,' said Ian Brown. 'I don't know of any record in the 1960s that sounds like ours.' Which was true. He looked up and added, 'We don't have to sell ourselves. The music will sell itself.'

With Widnes and Liverpool buzzing, the Roses were on a roll, and it was now time, on 6 May, to play their home town again. This time they would move up another level.

The headline International 2 show was their biggest yet and, for many fans, their best yet. A sold-out crowd was at fever pitch as they hit the stage. Chants of 'Manchester la la la' filled the hall; there was a real pride about the scene, about the town. Suddenly everyone felt that Manchester meant something, that this 'grim' northern city had its own new music scene, a music scene that meant something and could take London on its own terms.

The stage was bathed in stark ultra-violet light and a slide of a Pollocked Union Jack was ripped across the back. The atmosphere was electric. The album, not even out yet, was already making massive inroads into the listening of the city, and everyone seemed to know the words.

The Roses played it straight and aloof – no more leaping into the crowd with a long mic lead for Ian Brown, who was working on the pimp roll now. Swaying and swaggering in his own world, stoned instead of speeding, floating about two foot off the floor, he stared vacantly at the crowd. There was still the menace of the Lydon-influenced young punk but crossed with a mystic stoner Manc guru.

He didn't speak to the crowd, there were no encores, they sloped off and left the hall rapturous. They didn't communicate a single bloody thing, except for total cool.

At the time it was what Manchester demanded and got.

The night was a celebration.

Manchester was now party central and clubs were opening up all over the city. Last year's Smiths fans were dropping Es, clothes were getting looser, accents were getting stronger and hair was getting longer. Uptight no longer seemed to exist, and there were mad parties in fucked-up flats all over the city. From Saturday nights in the Kitchen in Hulme, to the Hacienda's explosions of dance solidarity, to rambling houses in Whalley Range, grubby cellars in Rusholme – everywhere was booming to the big bad bass drum of acid house. And everywhere there were the pills: in pubs in West Didsbury you could buy them over the counter, in dark corners of the sudden plethora of clubs playing acid house you could score a handful, 'In The Area' revellers yelled, nonsensical slang was becoming codified, and crazy handshakes with freaked weirdos in clandestine deals in the bogs of nightclubs was the norm. It was a drug heaven. Strung out, cabbaged, whacked and plain weird was the mental currency of a city gone completely off its axis, and in the middle was Ian Brown.

'Whenever I would go round to Ian's place he would usually have a house full of people,' recalls Ian Tilton. 'I remember seeing Alfonso Buller

who Ian really liked having about. Alfonso was a DJ and would also organise nights and warehouse parties where he would go by the name MVITA
("Manchester Vibes in the Area"). Well, Alfonso was a little bit cheeky
but cool with it; he had the walk and the talk and all that and was like the
cocky one out of the whole gang.'

Sometimes pop is so powerful that overnight everyone seems to have
shifted a gear. In Manchester Afflecks Palace buzzed and Identity boomed
as a T-shirt store – its 'On the 7th day God created Manchester' T-shirt
became a design classic.

Eastern Bloc stopped being a stall that sold punk records and became
a booming dealer in indie and then dance. Piccadilly Records became one
of the main indie record shops in the UK.

House music seeped from every pore of the city. The powerful boom
of the bass drum was the keynote; guitar music like the psychedelic 1960s
pop of The Beatles and the Stones, the Mondays and the Roses, was for
chilling out post-rave, post-E; it was music to come down to.

The Roses themselves were missing a lot of this Manchester euphoria as
they were still on the road. The tour was starting to turn into a triumphant
victory celebration; on 7 May they were back at Sheffield University, and
the day after they were in Leeds at the Warehouse, where scenes of un-
bridled enthusiasm were reported.

Dave Simpson from *Melody Maker* was at that Leeds show: 'The whole
thing was just kicking off. I'd only just heard of them. I'd heard them on
Richard Skinner of all places, he had played "Made Of Stone" and it just
got me straightaway. It was so brilliant. The Roses were coming up to play
in Leeds and to tell you the truth the reason that I was going was to see
The Hollow Men, who were like a local Leeds band that I was really into
and were the support that night.'

Getting to the Warehouse, the main venue for up-and-coming bands in
Leeds at the time, Simpson was struck by a curious thing. 'The place was
absolutely packed with Mancs. It was really strange; all these people had
come over to see the band. That sort of thing never happened in those days.
It was like a football support thing. My mate who was driving me wanted
to leave pretty fast but I persuaded him to give the Roses 15 minutes.

'I remember John Squire coming on with his paint-spattered guitar
and they started playing "Elephant Stone", and the place kicked off. The
atmosphere was absolutely brilliant; people were dancing on tables. It was

the best atmosphere at a gig I could ever remember. There was a lot of Leeds chants going up. Ian Brown went up to the mic, looked at the crowd, and said, "Yeah, that's right, this is Leeds," really cool and confident. Everything seemed so colourful after gigs being so dark for ages. It was a turning point really.'

Overnight Simpson was a total fan; he rang up Silvertone the next day and blagged a pre-release of the album to review for his fanzine *Avanti*. His reaction to the record was typical of the thousands who were about to be caught in the euphoria for the band. 'I loved the album. I couldn't stop listening to it. I remember going down to the chip shop and I had to go back home because I just needed to listen to the record again. It was the spring going into the summer and the weather was great. It just seemed to capture the mood of the time perfectly.'

A month later the Roses returned to Leeds to play at the much larger polytechnic venue. In the last four weeks things had really shifted yet another gear as Dave Simpson remembers: 'I'd arranged to put them on the cover of my fanzine and I went along to the show to do an interview and even though it was a much larger venue it was really packed. I remember that there were loads of kids stuck outside who couldn't get in. That was definitely a rare sight in those days.

'I went backstage to get an interview and for some reason I was told to go and ask for Cressa and this skinhead with baggy trousers comes to the door. He then goes back in to find the band – it was all a bit farcical really. We did the interview in the bar and before the tape recorder was on they were really chatty and matey. As soon as the tape went on they went schtum and difficult. Normally if you interview a band that you like everyone is really matey and chatty, but this was different. I don't know why they did that; maybe it was Gareth's idea to make them seem more enigmatic. If that was the case it certainly worked.'

It would become the Roses' interview schtick for years on end, stony silence and off-hand answers, but at first it did really work, giving the band menace and mystique. There were some classic moments as Ian Brown would stonewall eager journalists, staring back with his large glacial brown eyes at their festering attempts to nail the band down. It was always done in a polite and civil and charming way, really unsettling for a journalist.

Simpson thinks, though, that it may have all blown up in their faces later on. 'At first it was really effective, it was a really cool thing, but eventually it seemed to get a bit nasty. It was like a schoolboy being really proud that he could really piss people off in the end. It was like they had started to lose sight of who they really were.'

Simpson spoke to Brown and Mani. 'John Squire came along to the interview and sat about three feet away saying nothing at all. Ian was really bolshy, turning all the questions around – like I was asking them how massive they wanted to be, like as big as New Order who were about the biggest an indie band could get. He turned the question around and started talking about what massive really was, and decided in the end that Michael Jackson was massive and the size that they wanted to be.'

Simpson loved the Roses because of Reni. 'I was a drummer and that made me listen to Reni; his drumming was incredible. They were saying that he learned his drums in the cellar of his parents' pub drumming along to jazz records. He was really exciting, unbelievable, the best drummer on the scene. I thought that A Certain Ratio's drummer, Donald Johnson, was unmatchable, but this was a different league altogether.'

The Roses' gigs were becoming events; even on the toilet circuit in the UK, where dreams are broken and countless bands are burned out by the sheer cruel drudgery of the venues, the Roses were putting on a very different show.

When *The Stone Roses* album eventually started its long haul in the album charts, it entered at 39 and crawled up to 19 before settling in somewhere between 50 and 60 for weeks on end, selling steadily. Repacked every now and then, it would go in the Top Ten for a week. *The Stone Roses* was a steady seller, a cult word-of-mouth release.

But it was spreading.

John Harris, the pop culture writer, was at school when the Roses finally broke. 'I remember at school everyone seemed to be into The Stone Roses, everyone seemed to have the album on vinyl. It was the same when I went to college in the south – they seemed to be the most popular T-shirt there. Later on everyone went out and bought "Fool's Gold" the day it was released. I think people found them a lot easier to get into than the Happy Mondays, who didn't seem to get that massive until *Pills 'N' Thrills And Bellyaches* came out. I remember every club in Manchester used to play the Roses album – places like Devilles seemed to play the whole album in one night. They were religious about it.'

Religious – that word again. The album's iconography was feeding back into the band's own myth. Their optimism and the rush of their music added to the E rush and the up vibe of the time. When clubs played 'I Am The Resurrection' everyone had their hands in the air like a religious experience.

Get in the Van...

That summer The Stone Roses were back on the touring circuit. This time, at last, they were packing places out everywhere and not just in Manchester. This time it was getting serious – the word was out and the wires were buzzing with the news.

Sat in the van with the Roses was Cressa pumping up the sound system, blasting out a cool and eclectic mix of music. The stereo was hammering the Rolling Stones, Hendrix, Burning Spear, PIL, hip-hop and house, a cool bitch's brew to burn away those miles of tarmac.

Also in the van for a few gigs was Jack Barron, the *NME* writer who was now most definitely on their case since reviewing the album. Jack was one of the key writers of the period, switching from underground American noisenik music to acid house and the Mancs bands in an E-fuelled Paul-on-the-road-to-Damascus-style U-turn.

Ian Brown was laying down the law on one of his key influences, John Lydon. 'I sneaked into a PIL gig when I was 14 and went backstage and cadged a cigarette off John Lydon and I found out that he wasn't the nasty bastard that he was portrayed as. That was very influential on me.'

They were also explaining to Jack the Stones' support story. Some parts of the Roses' story are so shrouded in mythology that it's hard to know whether Gareth Evans spun a yarn or they actually happened, but one of the great tales of 1989 is how they turned down The Rolling Stones' support slots in Canada. While it seems likely that the Stones could have wanted some hip indie cred by inviting them out on to the road with them, it sometimes seems difficult to believe that the gnarled old troupers could possibly be that hip to what was happening on the streets in the UK.

'We were told that we had some support slots with the Stones if we wanted them in Canada but, fucking hell, we're not opening up for them. They should open up for us! It's obscene that they are even touring – they lost it years ago. It's a shame that they haven't got any friends who're willing to tell them when to quit,' spat out Brown.

Barron then asked the vocalist, who was getting a stream of comparisons to the youthful Jagger, what he would do if he met the man.

'I'd want to punch him out, really. There was a time for three or four years when the Stones were red-hot. They looked good, sounded good, and meant what they were playing. Nothing could stop them. Now they are nothing but a money-machine. Sad really.'

Spoken like a true punk. Brown shared his generation's loss of faith in the Stones, once the world's number one bad-ass band but now considered by some a sad parody of former greatness and a sitting-duck target for hot new singers to take pot-shots at.

Barron was worrying whether the Roses were just another rock'n'roll band, and backstage, among the dope fumes and the brandy, there certainly seemed to be very little difference. Brown, though, realised, like many others at that time, that the fact that pop stars took drugs simply wasn't an issue any more. Everyone else was now taking drugs and lived far crazier lifestyles than any musician.

'I don't see us being in a rock'n'roll tradition at all. You go to a reggae gig or a punk gig or an artist's party or maybe just up to Alderley Edge to look out over Manchester, and you'll find people getting into spliffs and brandy. All kinds. That doesn't make them rock'n'roll. In fact I don't like rock'n'roll – the attitude and leather jacket. It's old hat. It's redneck.'

Britain was changing, and changing fast – the seismic shift caused by acid house was having repercussions. The story of 1990s pop culture would be the gradual intertwining of the two cultures of guitar music and dance culture, sometimes under its ugly title of indie/dance, with people going from one scene to the other and back again.

The Stone Roses were at the forefront of all this, either as a rock band canny enough to see where the scene was going, or as people who had always been into dance music, whether it be Northern Soul or ska.

Ian Brown related to Barron, 'I'd rather go to a club and dance, than go to a live gig because there just aren't that many exciting bands about. I hate that indie-rock-guitar mentality that people have where they won't even consider listening to dance music, which is some of the most exciting stuff around at the moment. Most of the indie rock scene is blinkered and fucked up by its own narrow-mindedness.'

The tour continued for The Stone Roses. There was to be no Oasis-style fast rise to megastardom. For the first half of 1989 the rise was slow but it was happening. From Tunbridge Wells' Angel Centre to Birmingham's Edwards Number Eight, from Shrewsbury's Fridge, to Aberystwyth University. They were grinding it out on the circuit.

On 15 May they played London's prestigious ICA venue and the now uber-fan Simon Kelly was there.

'The gig was an epiphany. There was a complete London Transport shutdown – no buses, trains or Tubes, but it doesn't deter us – we get cabs to and from the ICA...I think a lot of people didn't bother (I bet they wished they had) and my first sight of all things Stone Rose was roadie, Chris the Piss, selling T-shirts – I want one of those but I didn't have the money. I was taken in by a lot of the crowd singing along in northern accents: "I'd love to do it, and you know you've always had it coming". I was hooked. A week on, temperatures in the high 20s, the summer of love has begun and the Roses are playing Camden Dingwalls – completely mad, a sold-out gig with water dripping off of the walls and ceiling in that tunnel-like sweat box. Ian swinging on the pipes above the stage. Hooked...'

They were turning young minds all over the country. Typical of the new fans was Andy Bell, ex-Ride member and eventual Oasis and Beady Eye bass player. He caught the Roses that May at Oxford Polytechnic and was blown away.

Recalls Andy, 'The first Stone Roses record I heard was "Made of Stone". I was 18, I'd just started art school and Ride had formed just a few weeks before. I'd bought it because I liked the sleeve. I'd never heard the band, I think I'd seen some press.

'When I played the single, I liked the 'B' side more at the time, "Going Down", for the lyrics about Jackson Pollock and Ambre Solaire and the Byrdsy tune. Of course "Made of Stone" is more of a heavyweight tune in the long run. To an ex-Smiths fan, John Squire made a perfect follow-up for Johnny Marr as a guitar teacher. The Roses had a better image as well.

It wasn't just the music that was captivating, it was the whole package. There was a brilliant early picture of them taken from the ground up with all the flares intertwined. Cool clothes, fantastic haircuts, proper shoes. I started cutting out all their press and saving it. Never did that before or since with a band – I just liked the way it all looked.'

The Roses were to have a profound effect on a generation of musicians who were affected like Bell. 'The members of Ride had all just moved into a house together when the Roses' début album came out. You heard it and felt sad because it was so good you knew they wouldn't be "your own" secret for long. The jam at the end of "I Am The Resurrection" got me and Loz Colbert really into jamming together, guitar and drums, which had quite a big effect on the Ride sound I guess.

'We were really into Young MC's track "Know How" so when John Squire namechecked it, it was good to know we were on the same wavelength. They played Oxford Poly bar, early 1989. The place held about 200 people. It was a really good time for gigs there, I remember seeing Spacemen 3, The House of Love, My Bloody Valentine all around the same period as the Roses played.'

The gig was an event. The young musicians got there early. Very early. Continues Andy, 'Me and Loz went early to watch them soundcheck. Unbelievable charisma is all I can really say. We were sitting at this table round the corner from the stage and Ian Brown came and sat with us for a bit. They looked exactly how they did on the pictures from the album sleeve. Reni's drums were all painted different, a real hotch-potch. Seeing him free-forming around the kit to soundcheck the drums was fantastic.

John Squire came out after a bit and without any of those amateurish "amp-starting-up/tuning up" noises started playing dead cool Hendrix-y phrases. It was all so casually done but in another way a total performance. It must have been obvious to them that there was a little group of us checking them out.'

And then there was the gig itself. 'The gig was incredible, they were on top form. I remember it in freeze frames. Mani's face gurning as he swung round to catch Reni laughing his head off in the middle of a tune. Ian in his element, head nodding as he sings in front of a sea of bodies losing it. Seeing Loz's mad head as we flew around the moshpit singing along with "I Am The Resurrection". I went home mindblown, clutching a T-shirt.'

Andy was so inspired that he popped down to see them in Reading on 6 June.

'I saw them again a few days later at Reading Majestic. Even the crew looked like the band. The next one I saw was Alexandra Palace. When you'd meet people out and about, the first question would always be if they liked The Stone Roses, and everyone was saying that the Empress Ballroom had been the one, and this was next, so we couldn't miss it. When we arrived at the venue I remember everyone buzzing about the records being played by the DJ. There were big cheers for the tunes like "Voodoo Ray" and anything by the Mondays. But the place was so big that the sound when the band played was really swampy, a disappointment.'

The results of this excitement fed into Ride, one of the best British guitar pop bands from that era and a band that neatly straddled the so-called shoe-gazing and baggy scenes without being bogged down in the clichés of both. Ride released a series of cool records and were one of the new vanguard of bands on the Creation label.

'By this time Ride had a deal with Creation, and our first single had been recorded. We hadn't known about the Roses when Ride started (as a band we were primarily into Sonic Youth, the Valentines and The Spacemen 3) but I was totally having it as soon as I discovered them. They were a huge influence on Ride. The early themed sleeves that Ride did were a nod to the Roses and The Smiths. The sense of occasion in everything they did led us to play the Daytripper weekend with The Charlatans. The influence kind of got in everywhere.'

Multiply this influential excitement by about, ooh, 10,000 and you've got an idea of what was rippling through the UK's guitar pop rehearsal rooms that summer!

Also at the Oxford gig was Simon Kelly.

'I told all my mates in Oxford that they have to see this band on Wednesday 24 May 1989 and I made my way down to Oxford Poly...It seemed like quite a few Camden scene mates are down there and don't want to miss out either. Apparently Mark Gardener and Andy Bell were there too. It's my first meeting with the band. I am ushered backstage after the gig...Mani in joke crazy-eyes spring specs! All members affable and approachable, they seemed just like you and me.'

Single No. Five!: 'She Bangs The Drums'

On 15 July 1989 'the second summer of love' was burning bright. The term referred to the summers of 1988 and 1989 and captured the essence of the time: the free parties, ecstasy, the colourful clothes, the loose fit, acid house and the new tripped-out music of the Madchester bands. It was one of the hottest summers since 1976, a curious heat which always lets loose the crazed party animal just under the skin of the Brit, drying out the dampness of the national melancholia.

In the middle of this the band released a re-mixed version of 'She Bangs The Drums' that took the hi-hats off the intro and cranked up the guitar. Flipped with another set of 'B' sides that could have been singles in their own right, 'Standing Here', 'Mersey Paradise' and 'Simone', the single also came with another great John Squire paint-spattered sleeve and a free postcard of one of his paintings.

'That was a detail of a larger picture that was also used later on "I Wanna Be Adored", says Squire. 'We just homed in on one section of it. We were running out of time, and I didn't have time to work on it properly.'

'Mersey Paradise', casually tossed on to the 'B' side along with 'Simone', is the Roses at their most effortless with the now obligatory twisted lyric. Brown is singing about something dark and the vocal is tinged with an hallucinogenic vision – there could be a murder, there could be a suicide, there is the stench of death and it's all happening in the Mersey that flowed about ten minutes' walk away from his West Didsbury flat. It's a classic piece of shimmering Beach Boy-esque pop that transposes the subject matter from sunny California to the banks of the Mersey running through Manchester and Liverpool.

Not content with this, they put another potential 'A' side, 'Standing Here', on the flipside as well. 'Standing Here' is one of the last guitar pop anthems the Roses wrote before their tentative swing into the more groove-orientated stuff. For some this single represents the creative high water mark of the Roses. The 'A' side arrives riding roughshod over a pop riff which recalled the pop genius of The Monkees

'She Bangs The Drums' was a big fat slice of guitar pop. It was pure pop. It sounded like it was from an age that oozed far more innocence. That was until Ian Brown croaked in with the classic John Squire lines about the heady summer when pop went mad and it had the perfect kiss-off.

The single was their biggest hit so far, and their first to make the Top Forty, but still only managed number thirty-six. The group were unhappy as they could see from the long and winding tour that they had just been out on that they were getting bigger than this polite back-end-of-the-chart messing around. Something was afoot – maybe Silvertone just wasn't big enough to assure them of a definite big smash, and they would have to seek a larger label to fulfil their real potential.

Ian Brown told *Melody Maker* that he would be severely disappointed if they didn't have a number one by the end of 1989.

In hindsight number thirty-six does seem like a joke. Here was a group that within weeks would be selling out the 4,000-capacity Empress ballroom in Blackpool. Maybe at that time the pop charts just weren't capable of registering a very northern phenomenon.

The Stone Roses had moved a long way from the indie scene. They were getting the Fleet Street mentions and they were getting offers from massive bands desperate to boost their credibility, and audience, by getting the band as support. As well as the aforementioned Rolling Stones, Pixies (the American group who redesigned the rock song with the quiet verse and loud chorus that Nirvana took into the major arena) were one bizarre outfit to offer the Roses a support. But by now the Manchester band were far, far bigger than their American rivals in the UK.

New Order also offered more of a helping hand to their fellow Mancs, not that Ian Brown was impressed: 'New Order isn't massive. Michael Jackson is massive. That's what we are aiming for.'

They had their own agenda now, and a trip to Japan set them up as enormous stars there. They loved the country and the love was reciprocated. Japan was always a highlight for the Roses and a place where they were always big time.

Lifestyle '89

The whole myth of The Stone Roses as a dance band mushroomed throughout the late 1980s. It seems odd, now, to listen to those records and think that they were once included in many long-winded articles about acid house, with their picture adorning the attempts to describe this new phenomenon.

True, their gigs featured a barrage of house cuts, and they even went so far as having a home-made piece of techno featuring wailing sirens as their walk-on tape to the stage, but they were, musically, firm traditionalists.

Living in Manchester, the Roses were party to a huge mushrooming of dance culture which affected everyone in the city culturally, and totally changed the way it looks today. Walking around Manchester in the new millennium you are struck by the seemingly endless explosion of Continental-style chrome-and-glass bars, some of them sprouting out of run-down old Victorian red-brick warehouses, and all of them teeming with nightlife.

Years before any other city in the UK, Manchester was opening these places. It was a part of the city's culture almost from the off in the house era, booming sound systems and flash bars full of ravers, students and gangsters. It was the rough meeting the smooth that so typified the city culture.

The atmosphere around the clubs, fired by hedonism and great music, was electric. All of a sudden the city dressed looser – hair grew longer, people staggered down the street looking dazed, and everyone kept asking about this wonder-drug called E: just what was it all about? The post-punk generation were instantly suspicious of E, and it became a sink or swim thing. Those that took it discovered the ups and downs of a whole new way of life that transformed some people and ruined some others.

Ecstasy totally changed the pop and cultural landscape of the UK.

Utilising Reni's incredible loose drum patterns the band freed up the rhythm section, putting a funkier free-flowing undertow to their more traditional song structure. Fusing this with an understanding of the times they started to dress accordingly and The Stone Roses were suddenly the key band.

Ian Brown, at 26, was just young enough to get away with looking like 'every lad', and in the next few years he would become the totem, the iconic presence with the looks and the attitude that matched the new pop generation.

The Stone Roses embraced the new house-styled generation and became its rock'n'roll figureheads.

As Ian Brown once related to the press, 'Everyone is talking about indie and dance coming together. But everyone I know has always gone into each other's scene and had dance records since they were little kids. It's not a sudden thing that has happened. It's just that it took time to be presented, packaged and made palatable for the listener. You either get a good feel off a record or you don't – and there are as many bad house records as there are good rock records.'

The Roses had grown up through an intermingling of style from punk. They travelled through soul and ska, two of the greatest forms of dance music ever made. They flirted with funk, and they always dug the Stones who are perhaps the most danced-to group of all time. Ian Brown had travelled to Northern Soul all-nighters, the natural precursors to the house scene, and the band innately understood the drugs, clothes and music combination that fires all the classic pop periods.

To split music into two camps of rock and dance was always a flat-footed conceit, and to claim that rock had some sort of intellectual superiority over dance was totally laughable. The Stone Roses knew this and they duly profited from their lack of small-mindedness.

'Like Trouser, Like Brain': Flares!

The biggest culture shock somehow was the wearing of flared trousers. For the band it was a minor detail, an interest in clothes and styles that got bizarrely exaggerated out of all proportion. To a generation reared on tight-trousered orthodoxy, it was an outrage, especially as the Roses were from that cut of cloth, so to speak.

The history of the return of flares themselves is also a curious one. Phil Saxe, the original manager of the Happy Mondays, used to have a stall in the centre of Manchester in the early 1980s where he and his brother used to sell them; they bought up a load dirt-cheap, having no idea what sort of people would still be buying flares at this time.

Bizarrely enough kids interested in fashion started to pick up on them and soon the early Happy Mondays were swaggering around in flares. Cressa, to all intents and purposes the fifth member of The Stone Roses gang and the street-style expert, copped the look from the Mondays, giving Ian Brown a bottle-green pair of flared cords. They suited Brown immediately and appealed to his dual sense of street style and winding people up. This was more Lydon than Lydon!

The fact that they also totally suited his new, more dope-fuelled, shaggy mystic persona also added to the equation. He was quoted as saying, 'I've always been into clothes. When I was twelve I used to wear twenty-one-inch hipsters. Then I stopped wearing flares for a long time and now I'm wearing them again. Flares are really comfortable and they feel right. The main reason was because no one else was wearing them. We'll have to stop wearing them soon because everyone else is. Loads of people who come to see us are wearing flares and parallels. Some of them look better than me in flares! A lot of people don't cut it though, and they shouldn't wear them just because their favourite group does. They should wear what they look good in.'

He told the press a couple of years later, 'You get a buzz when people laugh at you because you aren't wearing the same pants. It's weird how something really simple like that can make you feel special. I remember years ago at school I got a pair of straight-legged trousers and was laughed out of town because everyone else was wearing flares.'

There were also some tips on how to wear your flares properly.

'With flares coming back people have to realise that you can't wear anything wider than twenty-one-inch bottoms. Anything more looks ridiculous. And they have to crumple. You just can't have half-mast trousers.'

Phil Saxe, the man whose stall was supplying the Happy Mondays with their flares and who would eventually manage the Mondays, remembers Cressa being around his stall more than the rest of the band.

'The Mondays knew Cressa. I remember seeing The Stone Roses around but for me they were not as much on the radar with what was going on as the Mondays and the Inspirals. The Stone Roses were more of a rock band, the Inspirals and Mondays were more Manchester scene and then the Roses took on the mantle. They started wearing the clothes the Mondays were wearing, not vice versa. I used to hear the demos for the album when I was working at Factory before they went in with John Leckie and I always thought that Leckie did a superb job. For me they were not up to much before that. He made a huge difference. At that time I sold them their first, well, they were not so much flares, more baggy parallels. I remember selling Ian and John baggy jeans and cords from the shop Somewear In Manchester. I didn't know them from the stall before that.'

For all this talk of flares, though, the picture of Brown on the inner sleeve of *The Stone Roses* captured in the Granada studios in 1988 by Ian Tilton shows him defiantly in straight-legs looking the sharp and angular neo-mod, all lean, mean and spitting attitude.

Flares were one of the main bones of contention during the Roses' reign – if there was one thing that really seemed to piss people off it was their trousers. They also caused the endless debate over who wore flares first.

During 1989, sales of flares rocketed. As a buyer from a UK chain of trouser shops reported, 'We tested them in four or five of our stores recently and they sold out in a few days. By April, whether you like it or not, you'll see a lot of kids wearing them.'

It was an accurate prediction. A lot of people did wear them and a lot of people did look fairly lumpen in them. Another buyer said, 'Flares offend the sensibilities of the older generation and that's why they are taking off. After a long period when father and son dressed the same and looked the same, things are going to change.'

The Roses and the Media Game

From the start of their roller-coaster ride to fame it was obvious The Stone Roses were no fools when it came to the media. They pulled their fair share of stunts (some of them were justified actions that didn't exactly harm their mythology): 'over the top' big gigs; inflammatory comments about royalty, other bands and politics; throwing paint around ex-record-company offices; made up mega gigs; pulling out of US tours – it was all great copy. One feature of the band's career had been their ability to stay on the news pages of the rock press almost permanently for years on end, from the earliest days with Garry Johnson at *Sounds*. And they did this by hardly saying anything at all.

Unlike The Manic Street Preachers, who seemed to come to every interview armed with a deadly machine-gun rattle of superb quotes, The Stone Roses would stonewall the journalist with shy guffaws, muttered asides, dispassionate staring, foot-shuffling silences and complete mind-numbing gaps, punctuated by the odd piece of incisive home-spun philosophy from Brown, who occasionally hinted at a well-read mind. There would be a complete silence from John Squire, witty banter from Reni, and Mani spouting off passionately if he let his guard drop.

They gave nothing away about themselves or their past, present or future; they set up a smokescreen, but with a lot of charm. They didn't lie, they just didn't say anything.

It's this enigmatic and yet disarmingly polite quality that helped to give them the aura that even now still cloaks them in a shroud of mystery.

Whether it was Gareth Evans who set up this smokescreen or the band themselves we'll never know. In real life they were nothing like their inter-views, apart from John Squire, who spoke little to people he didn't know.

'We hate tense people – you're only here once. It's not a rehearsal. The tense people are the twats who are only interested in making money and who ruin things for everybody else.'

When the *NME* asked Ian Brown why they didn't like getting interviewed he replied, 'I don't hate anything. It's just that sometimes the attitude of journalists and the questions they ask you can piss you off. But having said that, I don't expect anyone to get us right after meeting us for twenty minutes. Have you found us arrogant or difficult? I really don't think that we are. Too many groups feel like they have to play up to people all the time.'

The Roses never became part of the pop circus, and were hardly ever to be seen at any other gigs. Occasionally you would see Brown on his own at something like the Happy Mondays at G-Mex shuffling around at the back, unexpected and unrecognised, but for him and the rest of the band pop life was alien life.

For Brown his real heroes came from a very different world. 'Boxers are my heroes. I know it's a laddish thing to say, but it's true. It's the fact that they are putting themselves on the edge. They're amazing, you've got to be 100 per cent completely wised up all the way through,' he told the *NME* in 1989.

Stoned!

Drugs and rock'n'roll are completely inseparable; from Elvis speeding his way through his first tours to The Beatles bombed out of their brains from Hamburg onwards. Everyone is taking them, from coffee to heroin, and the ones that don't have to explain their clean agenda to non-believers.

Every new drug completely alters people's perception of pop music and culture. When ecstasy exploded across the UK, pop changed in a way that no one could possibly have predicted.

The Stone Roses' early years were dominated by speed. They were speed freaks. They drank little, looking down on alcohol (interestingly enough this tallies with the early house scene, where there was an E-fuelled disdain for booze).

In the late 1980s the Roses started smoking pot and there was an interest in LSD. Ian Brown was less the crazed-amphetamine-filled frontman and their whole look became shaggier, looser. By the time E hit the scene they had the shaggy E-monster look off pat.

Drugs, clothes and music – it's the triumvirate that dominates pop.

The E rave scene totally altered the make-up of cities. Manchester changed drastically, a direct result of the house daze of the late 1980s. It became a haven for students and one of the hippest music cities in the world, and all this came down to the rush of liberation which fell during the E explosion.

All week you could be buzzing on a Red And Black, a White Dove, some waxy pill, anything, and end up at some wild endless party. House music was the perfect soundtrack, booming across the city into the dawn hours, while rough kids, students, hooligans and music biz players were all freakin' in the crazed darkness, unopened cans of beer piled up at the side of the room as the big bass boom-boom-boom shattered the stiff upper lip, and people spilled out over the balconies.

The Stone Roses understood this, soundtracked it, paid lip service to it and indulged in it. It was that simple – they understood what was going on. In 1989 drugs were their making.

In the years that followed they were their undoing.

'Drugs and babies killed The Stone Roses,' John Squire noted later in his press interviews for The Seahorses, adding, 'Each member of the band was on a different drug. It made communication difficult.'

Inevitably it would scramble minds and help to lose the band's focus. Best to get high on life, kids!

Say It Loud! Say It Proud!

For a band that never said very much The Stone Roses said an awful lot, although they learned by the mistakes of previous generations, as John Squire pointed out: 'We were never into sloganeering like The Clash.'

Maybe not sloganeering but there was a hatred of the establishment. Ian Brown could always be counted on to have a potshot at the royals, 'We're all anti-royalist, anti-patriarch. When the ravens leave the tower, we want to be there shooting them,' he told *Melody Maker*.

As noted before, Brown was well read on the political trip, and now and then in interviews he would let slip his anarchistic leaning; in the lyrics as well there would be something hinted at, something revolutionary stirring in the soul of the protagonist. Everything was left vague, a blur of hints, a restlessness and a dissatisfaction with an archaic system.

The Roses never dealt in specifics – that was their strength. It was up to the listener to glean information from the tantalising tidbits.

From the 1968 student riots to anti-monarchy, pro-Tony Benn sentiments and a common touch, Brown had a restless soul and no set mandate.

Maybe that's the best way for pop – leave a trail of confusion and hint at greater possibilities, never sour the myth or the dream with the real sleaze of genuine politicians.

'Manchester – La La La!'

They were calling it the second summer of love or the third summer of love; it just depended on where your perspectives lay. The summer of 1967 can't have been as much fun though. When Manchester came alive in 1989, it had been through the heavy cloud of depression and had decided to party like crazy. The city began to transform itself on such a scale that even ten years later the echoes are still being felt. It was changing fast, the accents were becoming more marked, with everyone playing up their ruffian credentials. The Smiths seemed like an eternity ago. Everyone pretended that they knew a dealer, drugs were everywhere, people smoked dope on the bus, took acid in the pub and a few Es in the 'Hac'; and the dress style totally changed – flares, Kickers, Timberlands, long hair and goatee beards.

The Roses' gigs were peppered with chants of 'Manchester', but all this northern nationalism wasn't something that Ian Brown ever felt that comfortable with.

When Dave Haslam asked him about the 'Manchester north of England' shirts, he replied, 'Some of those T-shirts are bang out of order – "061 Cock Of The North" and "Born In The North, Die In The North" – to be so pro-Manchester is verging on something really dodgy. Being territorial like that is like being pro-English in miniature. Manchester is full of great people, but there are also a lot of twats here.'

Acid house was pumping out of the bars that were starting to appear across the city centre – it was the soundtrack interspersed with the Roses and the Mondays.

The clubs were packed, everyone bamboozled on E. It was several years before the sinister violence began to creep in and once the buzz of E had gone the buzz of fighting took its place.

But in 1989 fresh-faced kids danced crazier than Bez in back corners of clubs that had no regard for fire limits. Staggering down the streets on hot summer nights there were packs of people leaving clubs, eyes on stalks. Daft phrases started getting picked up – 'top', 'sound', and 'nice one' chased 'nish' and 'clish' and 'in the area' around the bars; jokey words and mad handshakes, daft whistles and shouts of 'Manchester In The Area' from loonies swinging off club and bar tables.

They were crazed times staggering from bar to club to club, chasing the scene, wallowing in its excess and fun. Suddenly a city outdid London and was the scene of pop action and all the bands basked in this new warm glow of hipness. Some better than others, of course; The Stone Roses and the Happy Mondays were better placed than the rest of the pack. Astute observers of pop culture and also riding in on the vanguard of the new way, they were seen as champions of the new lifestyle. Their music also captured the new flavour, subtly altering to capture the shimmer and the pulse of the times; the vacantness of the stoner's face and the sharp-dressed sense of the street punk were all neatly encapsulated in the Manc bands.

Very few of the bands actually took much musically from the acid house party that was bursting out everywhere across the city. 808 State were the closest musically and even they had their own idiosyncratic take on the new pulse; The Happy Mondays, with their natural funk, remixed their tracks and eventually got Paul Oakenfield in to produce their next album. The rest, though, were like James, who with an ear for a great pop tune finally made it after years in the wilderness. The same went for the Inspiral Carpets, who doggedly ploughed on with their treasure chest of great garage pop tunes and were rewarded with a run of pop hits.

Clint Boon enjoyed the camaraderie between the bands: 'We always had a healthy relationship with the Mondays and the Roses, the same with James, The Charlatans, Northside. There was a lot of camaraderie, not competition. Everyone was happy for each other. Every time we put a single out we would get a fax from Shaun Ryder saying, "Top single." There was a lot of friendships, obviously with me and Mani and many others. We were all rarely in Manchester at the time so would bump into each other rarely.'

The endless party spilt from the streets to the jails: Strangeways Prison rioted, and on the roofs of the ancient Victorian rotting hulk were dancing figures, the surrounding streets full of relations and zonked kids shouting up at the unlikely new heroes. They seemed to signify the new Manchester feel – desperadoes dancing in the grey, huddled against the night sky shouting and wailing tunelessly into the void. It was a bizarre entertainment.

It totally encapsulated the turn of the decade in the city.

Roses in Bloom! The Rest of '89

In August the Roses triumphantly capped their new-found success with the Blackpool Empress Ballroom gig which opens this book. This was the single moment when the band, at their pinnacle, burst through. For the core fans there never would be a better moment to savour than this; it was the greatest moment in their career. There would be bigger gigs, and some good times ahead, but The Stone Roses would never again seem as fresh and as exciting as at this moment in time.

Gareth Evans was well up for making the gigs an event: 'I wanted them to play different places, not run-of-the mill venues – the Winter Gardens, Ally Pally. I knew [the kids were] going to raves, the ordinary kids wanted to go to big events, to travel. Blackpool was perfect – it was the big day out. Manchester loves going to Blackpool.

'I wasn't nervous about Blackpool not selling out; promoter Simon Moran was working for me on this one.'

Local promoter Phil Jones was initially asked to promote the gig. 'Gareth said the band wanted to do a tour of seaside resorts so I booked this seaside town tour. Blackpool was the only one they ended up doing. I had all these gigs pencilled in in Southend, Brighton, Exeter, Bournemouth. I remember going round the country ringing up 1,500-capacity venues like Leas Cliff Pavilion in Southend, which was the only one that started selling tickets; he had sold six tickets before I pulled it early and concentrated on Blackpool.'

Blackpool was a risk but Jones felt confident.

'We felt it was the right time for the big gig; the papers were right behind them, there was such a buzz about it. We felt we could be cocky enough and do it and I think we bottled out of it by just doing the Blackpool gig, which was monumental. What they were good at was picking the right thing to do, and to be fair it was Gareth. I don't think the band had much to do with it. They had more say in Spike Island but not in where it was.'

Putting a big gig on in an unusual place brought its own problems, as Gareth Evans points out: 'What people don't realise is the effort going into Spike Island and all the big gigs. Before they happened I had to speak to councillors – in Blackpool it was a ballroom dancing place, a Labour party conference place. We booked the Savoy for the band to stay in but the police raided it and I was arrested for five minutes. They'd never seen anything like it.'

Blackpool was a triumph that is fondly remembered by the thousands that went.

Bruce Mitchell, the legendary Manchester music man, was a key player at all the gigs, bringing in the lighting rig: 'What impressed me about them was the way each of the guys was – you've got Mani banging the bottom end, Reni – great musician – playing what looked to me half a fucking drum kit, but always justifying Ian's vocals, singing that thirds apart thing that he always did. What a great ear that guy had, and John Squire's guitar chimed perfectly.

'I remember the sprung floor moved in the Empress Ballroom but we ratcheted the PA down, and the stage extension – bloody hell, we had to ratchet the stage extension down with five-ton lorry straps and we held onto the backs of the wigwam boxes as they swayed and the audience roared. It was sold out, it was an SJM gig. Steve Adge rented a big fuck-off bus to reflect the band's status and I think he pushed the driver out of the way to exit the gig, and I don't know if it was a mistake but he drove the bloody thing, with the band in it, down the tram tracks! I don't know if it was sheer bravado or incompetence! A great night, a fabulous night, that.'

Simon Kelly, who had been following the band on the road that year, made it to the gig: 'I was at Blackpool. The one-armed tout outside can't believe his luck as tickets are moving for shed-loads. Once in I hear Inner City's "Good Life" blasting out through a massive PA. Ian comes on stage playing with a yo-yo (that was apparently given to him by my now-mate Geoff), "Manchester Vibes In The Area, we're international, we're continental," he says down the mic. I'm standing at the back with journos John Robb and Bob Stanley and take in the whole scene. It's gone up a gear; everyone has caught on now and there's no way back.'

Stella Grundy, former member of Intastella and now a successful actress, had a very Blackpool experience: 'I remember being stuck in a car on a tramline. Somebody bumped into me recently and said they were in the car with me. I don't remember them, but I remember some guy off his head driving, and getting stuck on the tramline. So we were going round the tramlines – we couldn't get off these tramlines – we had to go all the way back, turn back. In the gig it was just bouncing, sweating, tripping. After the gig Cressa went a bit weird, he was doing lots and lots of bird whistling…Most of the audience were in the backstage bit; it wasn't for VIPs only. I would have said about a third of the audience were all backstage, it was that kind of feeling, a tribal feeling.'

Blackpool was the key gig of a generation. It was the moment. The live DVD is a pale imitation of the gig, which sounded amazing, and had the most intense atmosphere I have ever felt. After Blackpool nothing was the same again.

Vive La France!

Fired up by Blackpool and the rush of the big takeover, the band announced an even more daring gig – an autumn show at Alexandra Palace, in London, a larger and more ambitious show for the south of England. It seemed that there would be no stopping them now. Every wild-card scheme they planned to pull off was going to work – it was just part of the exuberant optimism of the era.

Before this, they set out for a European tour where they were a lot less well known. Simon Kelly joined them out there with his mate Stuart Deabill. 'We flew out to Hamburg and found the venue. It was a really small place with a massive barn door where you went in. We saw John Squire just round the corner of the door and he said, "Come in, come in." They seemed pleased to see us. Loads of fans went to the Paris show but only a few of us came to the dates before. They put this tape on post-soundcheck and blasted it out over the PA. At first we weren't sure what it was – it was well over eight minutes long and it sounded awesome. When Ian started singing we realised that it was a new Roses song. They came over and asked us what we thought of the new single. It blew us away. That was the first time I heard "Fool's Gold".'

Simon Kelly then went to Germany to see the band.

'At Hamburg I was at the front, taking photos with Mitsui – another Roses superfan at the time – and Stuart stood on a chair at the side of the stage shuffling from side to side along with the beat – trying to find the energy to keep swaying to an elongated "Resurrection" was never easy. We stayed on after the gig where we met up with a crazy English girl who put us up for the night. She was very proud of the fact that she'd let Clint Boon "sign her tit" when the Inspirals were over. After that me and Stu had a nervous sleep in her flat that night. Then it was off to Cologne on the train. The gig was memorable for Ian baiting the German crowd for being quiet. "Standing Here" and the guitar solo in "Made Of Stone" were immense, hairs on the back of neck stuff. It was Cressa's birthday, and I saw him being wheeled out, "passed out", after the gig on a trolley after drinking a bottle of brandy.'

In Rome Ian Brown had met the boxer Marvin Haggler in a club. He was a massive boxing fan and recognised him straight away. He just went up to him and started chatting to him.

'Amsterdam was the next stop – my first time there,' Simon continues. 'We had a day off before the gig, and Stuart decided to introduce me to Amsterdam's delights. Let's just say that by the next day I was feeling slightly yellow. We went to the soundcheck and Stu was skinning up for Brownie. The Cess Express had arrived and the 'Dam was awash with Reni-hatted, baggy-jeaned northerners. Backstage later, John was being grilled by a Dutch journalist: "Why do you think that you're the best band in the world?" "I don't know – ask him, he knows." He points to me – brilliant! Got hold of a girl I knew, who was over from Camden – capped a good night.'

Twenty-one years after the student riots that almost sent De Gaulle packing, the Roses arrived at Les Inrockuptibles Festival for their second gig that year in Paris on 12 October.

Put on by the French newspaper of the same name, the festival was showcasing current raved-about British bands. It would be an opportunity to see just how the Roses stood in comparison with their nearest rivals.

Fellow travellers, and two of the greatest lost bands of the era, The La's and Felt, also played but they were already being overtaken by the Manc four-piece. The La's had played with the Roses only two years before at Sefton Park in Liverpool and had seemed the band most likely to break.

It had been a couple of months since the Blackpool show but The Stone Roses were now well and truly a phenomenon. The Stone Roses were quite definitely a lifestyle. A gig in Paris was a great excuse for coach-loads of fans to dress in the latest wacky British street fashions and flood the streets of a bemused European capital.

The trip to Paris was one big beano. Coach-loads of crazy Englishmen in too much cloth, and with a scant regard for customs' position on drugs, were making the trip over the Channel for the Roses' first proper Euro-jaunt since those Swedish dates of a few years previously. The festival was being held in the brilliantly seedy La Cigalle, a venue that holds 1,200 people. The Roses fans made up well over half of the audience. It was home from home.

When the band hit the stage the chant of 'Manchester, Manchester' filled the air. This was regional pride as the northern boys asserted themselves in a hall that they totally dominated. It was a weird phenomenon. Could you imagine a regional band from France bringing hundreds of fans over to London dressed in some crazy pop fashion and chanting their home city's name? It was utterly bizarre.

Not that Ian Brown, a man noted for his distinct lack of interest in regionalism, was having any of it. 'Paris, Paris,' he sarcastically answered back, as he king-monkeyed around the stage. The atmosphere was truly tanked up; there was a ribald sense of celebration in the air that couldn't even be dampened by the CS canister that someone let off early in the set just before the band kicked off 'Waterfall'. Eyes were watering, people were running everywhere (should have brought some lemons!) – the band played on regardless, maybe unaware of the mayhem or getting off on the Paris '68 on the barricades' revolutionary vibe.

Simon Kelly remembers Paris as being the show that everyone seemed to have turned up for. 'You couldn't get near the band by then – the place was full of record company people and there seemed to be thousands of fans there. It was totally different from the shows on the rest of the tour.'

Back home, the talk in the press was now that the Roses were planning to release 'What The World Is Waiting For' backed by 'Fool's Gold' as the next single.

Ally Pally: Taking the New Vibe to the Capital

'It's not where you're from, it's where you're at...'

The legendary phrase (half-inched from Muhammad Ali's trainer in the late 1960s) was muttered by Ian Brown halfway through the Ally Pally gig when the 'Manchester la-la-las' were just getting too much.

After Blackpool and Europe, the Roses were in a buoyant mood. The mould was set, and this was a band who would attempt to go beyond the norm – think big, make gigs 'events', try and avoid the usual places and take their pop machine into different spheres of influence. It went with the ambition of the time, a new hunger, a belief that they could take this all the way. Gareth was looking for a big show in London and five months after Dingwalls they felt they were ready for something big!

Casting around for the next big one, Manchester promoter Phil Jones had hit upon the idea of Alexandra Palace, the large ornate hall in north London that held 7,000 people. Ally Pally was more suited to putting on antique fairs and exhibitions than rock'n'roll shows. But in terms of creating 'the legend', here was a spot which would suit them perfectly.

The 1960s happenings at Ally Pally had included the '14 Hour Technicolor Dream' in the spring before the summer of love of 1967. During the fourteen hours, Pink Floyd and Soft Machine thrilled the masses at a fundraiser for the fucked-up-by-litigation hippy newspaper, *International Times*.

There is also footage of a rather stoned-looking John Lennon showing off his walrus moustache and Afghan coat. The Ally Pally happenings had had that curiously English psychedelic vibe, a psychedelia that had one foot in music hall and the other on super-stoned drug turf.

On this 18 November 1989 evening, a huge army in pristine baggy were getting stoned on the hill on the way to the Alexandra Palace. Simon Kelly was one of them: 'The word on the street is that the whole thing is going ballistic. My Camden scenester mates, who can usually blag it onto most guest lists, realise that this is out of control, and that we'd better buy some tickets for the upcoming dates: the Mondays at the Town and Country Club (now the Forum), followed the following November Saturday by the Roses at the Alexandra Palace. I went up to Ally Pally to buy the tickets on a day off, just as they went on sale. I was quietly amazed by the venue, right on top of a hill in north London – it looked very grand and massive. The girl in the box office was quite surprised to see me – "We haven't sold many yet." The onslaught was yet to begin.'

Ian Brown, still harking back to the rush of the Manchester warehouse shows four years previously, explained to *Q* magazine the reason why they chose the venue. 'Originally we wanted to play somewhere different. So we tried to get a warehouse, but with all the parties it would have been difficult, and this was the only place that we could find that wasn't a rock-'n'roll gaff. The best legal alternative.'

Ally Pally was perfect for a band attempting to grab the moment. Surrounded by huge sprawling gardens, the opulent venue was in sharp contrast to the sort of dive in which most fans were expected to check out guitar music in the 1980s. It was a bold and beautiful gesture and the band went for it.

There was new power in the air. The Roses were caught up in the amazing sea change that was happening. It was a time when borders fell, people were freed and pop music became the people's music again. Brown felt that the 1990s were promising to be a hell of a decade: 'Anything is possible when people come together, like East Germany. I'm talking about people who are constantly being had over, sold short, misled, had the wool pulled over their eyes. Eventually they'll say that they are not having it any more…'

If only.

At the soundcheck of the big one, the hall seemed massive, almost too big. The band were on stage jamming and playing for ages, the loosest, funkiest, sassiest shit that they ever played. For much of the soundcheck they were a three-piece with Reni on vocals. Gareth Evans wandered around backstage in a knitted cardigan with a huge butterfly design on the back, grinning like a madman, vindicated that his eccentric vision was coming together.

The place was buzzing with stage crews building up the PAs and rigging the stage. The huge Victorian hall echoed with the clank of working crews. Watching the soundcheck was Si Wolstencroft, who was hanging out. The ex-Patrol drummer, now employed by The Fall, looked proud: his former band and school mates were the biggest band in the country. It had been a long and strange five years for both parties.

The soundcheck was a dream, and the sound was stunning. Reni sang a whole bunch of vocals and they jammed out the songs. The band was fluid. The vibe was well and truly up, and there was an air of excited expectancy.

As the crowds began to drift up the hill towards the venue, it was noticeable that there was a marked change in the make-up of the punters. Whereas Blackpool had seen the hip kids, by October it was a show where everyone who wanted a slice of the Roses was turning up.

Even though there was still a massive contingent of Mancs, there were also a lot of very new and very clean-looking flares and long-sleeved T-shirts and Reni bucket hats in the crowd.

This was not the hippy audience of the past. This was a generation that dug football, rock'n'roll, lager and getting stoned.

Despite the much-mooted link between the house and the rock scene, most of the crowd looked confused as the DJs filled the auditorium with house music. They waited for the band to come on. Ally Pally hardly captured the burning energy of a rave, and when the band hit the stage, the crowd seemed relieved that there was a rock'n'roll band to watch.

For many people in London, this show was the one when it hit them that something really was happening.

Fan Dave Norman had never seen the Roses before. 'I didn't know that they were that popular! And all the clothes that everyone was wearing. It was totally different to any other show that I had been to – it seemed like the north had its own look. In London the indie crowd just didn't dress in flares or baggy gear – that was more of a rave look. That night the two scenes completely crossed over. It seemed like after Alexandra Palace everyone loosened up.'

This was a feature of the times: when there was a dance-orientated band on people didn't dance like they were in clubs as some promoters naively expected, but stood there and stared at the stage, just like they always had done.

After all the buzz that had gone round after Blackpool there were plenty of new faces ready to make the journey to Muswell Hill.

There was an electric anticipation, which the Roses played on, coming onstage as late as possible, cranking the atmosphere. As ever there was no support; this show was about The Stone Roses.

When they finally hit the stage there was a massive rush of excitement which rode over the sound, which was now really shoddy compared with what it had been at the soundcheck. While the band played their set several things became obvious pretty quickly. The sound was awful in the foggy drone-filled cavernous hall. The atmosphere remained ebullient despite the sound – the Roses meant so much to so many people. They were a special band. Muddy sound? No problem, pal, this band is too special, they already soundtracked people's lives.

The fans were in a celebratory mood, as fan Geoff Hague points out: 'The sound was a bit muffled, but it was never as bad as anyone made out. I must admit that we were pretty well out of it. We spent a few hours getting stoned in the park before we got in. The total rush when the band came on seemed to last for the whole show. I'd been to loads of gigs before that and it was the first time I'd been to a gig where the atmosphere was like that. They were easily the coolest band in the world at the time.'

Here was a band that in six months had become a legend, and this gig was a celebration of the fact. They played all the usual songs, ending with a climatic version of 'I Am The Resurrection'; Ian Brown sat down playing his bongos, detached in his own world. The duff sound and dodgy venue weren't dampening this crowd.

'I was off me head that night, and I had to sleep on the station,' remembers fan Jay Nielson, 'but it was an amazing buzz, I felt like I was part of pop history.'

The reviews were, as ever, mixed. Mandi James, writing for the NME, noted how excited she felt about going to the gig. 'It was like going to see a band for the first time,' she raved, getting into the euphoria of the night, and as astute as ever, she pointed out the shortcomings, but was still besotted enough by the power of pop to get caught up in the sheer exhilaration of the event, writing about wide-eyed fans still grooving hours later – you could just tell that Mandi spent the night dancing with the spirit of the times.

Steve Sutherland, at the time writing for Melody Maker, was in no mood for this new pop regime. While admitting that the Roses were a 'goodish band' he was at pains to point out that he felt that the whole thing was a hype that had got out of hand. He felt that there was a conspiracy to make the band massive and that we were all falling for it. He decided that the crap sound of the Ally Pally made it very difficult for him to tell whether the band was actually any cop or not.

The *Morning Star* was confused, detecting a magic in the air, although the band just didn't seem to be able to grasp it. 'It was often grabbed for a while but they never held it,' claimed the generally upbeat review.

As 'I Am The Resurrection' ended in a climactic thud, the crowd were up for more and they got the shock of their lives when the Roses changed the no encore rule and kicked straight into an extended work-out of 'Fool's Gold' – a song no one had heard yet.

It was several minutes of fretwork from Squire, staggering a long way from the shots of pure pop that they were casually dealing out, almost into free-form seventies Miles Davis, Can avante funk, adding to the sheer groove of 'Fool's Gold' and Reni's mighty drumming that saw him take it up a few more levels than was normally possible.

By the end of the song, the band sounded as if they'd had enough. "It's not where you're from, mate, it's where you're at," chimed Ian, after the statutory 'Manchester-la-la-la' chants.

The Roses never really played encores. The Roses had no interest in giving too much away about themselves. They were working on the enigma, the enigma that was the key. There was no kowtowing to the audience.

Ian Brown explained to me. 'The vibe was similar to Blackpool; till showtime the vibe was amazing. Kids travelled from all over the country to go to the gig. It was massive; 8,000 people. It looked massive at the soundcheck when it was empty. We had a quadraphonic sound system; we wanted to get it right.

'We met all these kids from all over the country who were all dressed like us; it was amazing. By this time we felt like The Beatles – the band of the time.

'It felt like a big deal because we were from the north and there were 8,000 people there in London at this place where the psychedelic happenings had happened in the sixties. No one else [had] played it since then. The atmosphere was fantastic; the soundcheck was amazing. I've seen the clip from Granada of us walking down to the stage from the dressing room and I would love to see all of that.

'The actual show wasn't that great because of the sound. There was delay from the back of the hall to the stage; what we put out was coming back a couple of seconds later and I don't know if we were out of time.

We were so tight because were so rehearsed and the sound ruined that. I don't think we enjoyed the gig on a musical level. I remember coming out with John afterwards to get in the car to go to the hotel and we were pretty long faced because we didn't enjoy the night.'

Later on that night there was a party in a fucked-up old nightclub space in north London. The partygoers all sat there waiting for the dawn and for the drugs to wear off. Publicist Philip Hall sat at the table with me and some of the hardcore Roses fans. Brian Cannon, who went on to design all the Oasis sleeves, was down there along with several other people, Manchester faces, scenesters and hustlers enjoying the big night out in London. In the murk and the mush of the party, one thing was agreed on: it was a great night, despite the rough sound. It was a top buzz, it was a great party. It was pop history in the making.

Single No. Six!: 'Fool's Gold'

On 1 November, the Roses decided to get all incendiary themselves, and released their best-ever record and their breakthrough big hit single.

With a seven-inch clocking in at 4 minutes 15 seconds and a twelve-inch at 9 minutes 53 seconds, the band were obviously about to break out of the tight formats dictated by verse/chorus guitar pop, and utilise all their strengths. After a couple of years listening to dance, checking out clubs and nailing the Es, they were also about to deliver their take on the new dance-conscious youth of the UK.

The single was going to be their first serious new track since they broke massive over the summer and would be their first shot at the Top Five.

'Fool's Gold' was one of the Roses' finest moments, an alchemy of everything that was strong about the band. The Roses' awesome rhythm section had combined a great breakbeat, a killer simple bass line from Mani, and John Squire's funky bad-ass wah-wah licks on top. Ian Brown intoned a husky, menacing vocal, as ever, part homely and part preacherman, with the original mystic scally dope-shot voice. It was simple, sexy and funky as fuck. It was one of the musical high water marks of their career and an escape route that meant they had a choice of styles to play with.

The original loop was from a breakbeat album that John and Ian had. Commonly known as the 'Hot Pants' break, it is originally from Bobby

Byrd's 'Hot Pants – I'm Coming, I'm Coming, I'm Coming'. It was a breakbeat that has been used a lot but maybe never as effectively as this. Initially they took the breakbeat and John played guitar on it and Ian intoned the vocal, stretching out and finding a new direction.

The bass line was influenced by 'Know How' by Young MC, which is a sample from the *Shaft* theme song, performed by Isaac Hayes. Reni spent hours building his drums around the breakbeat – it was the perfect synthesis of the Roses' talents.

Amazingly, 'Fool's Gold' was also originally mooted as the 'B' side of the single with 'What The World Is Waiting For' as the 'A' side.

Roddy McKenna was among the many who thought it should have been the other way around. 'I flew back from the States, it was late night and I'm in Battery Studios, Willesden, London and Paul Schroeder is in there, back from Sawmills with the multitrack tapes on. He played the new single, which I liked but I was not completely knocked out by it. Then there's a track blaring out of the speakers. I said, "What the fuck is that?" Paul says, "Don't worry, this is just the 'B' side!" I said, "Paul, you don't understand, this is a smash hit record, this is brilliant.'

Paul Schroeder picks the story up. 'The album wasn't actually selling that well and it was the success of "Fool's Gold" that relaunched the album to be this huge thing that it is now. I was surprised it got to number 20 actually. It kept on growing and with the success of "Fool's Gold", with that smash quality, the album really started to take off. I knew as soon as I'd heard "Fool's Gold" that it was a smash.

'I don't think Leckie necessarily heard it, I think he was surprised that it got all the revere that it deserved. When they brought it in it was pretty fully formed as a song. It had the loop, and it had the guitar bass line. A little bit of John's wah noodling on top. The vocals were there, the actual song structure was pretty much there. We made it longer and bigger and better but the actual core of it was pretty much there.

'When we first started, Leckie wanted to get rid of the loop. I went, "Hang on, John, this is actually a huge hook, you can't get rid of it, it will ruin the song if you do." So we spent time with Reni adding to the loop to make it sound super fresh. We got the loop and we looped it round in an uneven number of bars so it would keep on tripping around and it would never really be the same each time round.

'Then added percussion and put some keyboards on. I actually played keyboards on that, which Leckie failed to tell anyone about. I could have made a fucking fortune out of that song! As a result I got fuck all. I didn't even get my name on it. I collared Clive Calder, the boss of Zomba, and said to him, "You have to check this out, this is brilliant!" So he had a listen to it and said, "Paul, you are absolutely right, this is a number one song. It just needs a remix.' And so he got Leckie to do it.'

Radio plugger Gareth Davies believes he may have had a hand in the decision over the 'A' side as well.

'We were working a white label pre-release of the single around TV companies and we biked it over to *Rapido* and *The Late Show* people. All they would go on about was this great bass riff on the track. I didn't have a clue what they were talking about until I turned the record over and noticed that they must have been going on about "Fool's Gold". It occurred to me straightaway the single was the wrong way round. The bass riff that everyone liked so much is the one that Mani plays on "Fool's Gold". I phoned Andrew Lauder at Silvertone straightaway and he agreed. That's the beauty of working with a small record company – decisions can be made very quickly.'

On release 'Fool's Gold' provided The Stone Roses with their first Top Ten hit, entering the charts at number 14 and then going to number eight. It also provided them with their first bona fide daytime radio record. Davies looks back at this crucial moment. 'I remember ringing the band up when the record was getting its first daytime plays and they were very excited.'

In Manchester there had been an interest in rock and dance that traced its roots back to Northern Soul and clubs like Legends in the early 1980s, when DJs like Greg Wilson were pumping out New York electro sounds years ahead of any other towns, inspiring A Certain Ratio and New Order to lose their raincoat shackles and funk up their rainy-city grooves.

The Roses were now pushing the boundaries further. They now had the tuff groove of funk, and they then crossed this with the open space repetition of Krautrock kings Can. It was an audacious and bold record and, along with the Happy Mondays, they were cutting pop that defined the times perfectly.

In a simple stroke The Stone Roses were looking forwards and not backwards. Here was the synthesis of dance and rock that everyone had been writing about; rhythm was king and melody was along for the ride.

If the second album had been put down there and then, it could have been grooves combined with sinister vocals that were half spoken and half rapped, interspersed with tripped-out guitar pop gems and some of the rock, because Reni and John would not have wanted to go totally down the groove road – played by a band that were so tight that they could lock into a groove and milk it, a band that were tight as friends as well as musicians, all buzzing off each other's talents and skills. For many pundits this was the great lost moment. If only they could have gone down this road what a genius album they would have made!

At the time producer John Leckie spoke to *NME*. When asked about the Roses' indie dance connection Leckie was a tad confused: 'I'm too busy to follow dance music. If someone takes me to a club then I hear it occasionally. If I like a track I'll buy it. I'm not really known as a dance producer. It's not my forte. It's a bit like me asking your opinions on classical music.'

Well, so much for the bridge between dance and rock then. Leckie was as confused as most people by this endless connection, although he did put it into perspective. 'At the time we were listening to a lot of dance music in our recreation period in the studio, so that probably leaked into the recording by osmosis so to speak. One of the reasons that "Fool's Gold" crossed over was because it was a song. A lot of dance stuff is great but there's no song. A good track is something you can strum on an acoustic guitar or play on the piano. That's the bottom line. It seems like a natural progression for us; all this categorising of music makes no sense to me.'

The Roses, at this point, were fucking with their template, attempting to move forward, as Ian Brown explained to Dave Haslam in 1989: 'We need to be constantly changing. You've always got to change. When you realise it's not there any more, then you're chasing your tail. Then you stop. You can't degrade yourself in public and ride on the back of an old reputation. We're concentrating more on rhythm now. On the first LP it was a matter of making the melodies sound good. Now we're trying to get the rhythms to sound better. "Fool's Gold" is the most different thing that we have done for ages. It's based on a continuous bass riff. All I know is that we never intended to sound like a 1960s group.'

TV was now calling. The Roses were booked to play on the late-night BBC2 arts programme *The Late Show* on 21 November.

Gareth had been thinking about broadening the band's media profile. An arts programme was perfect. He sent 'What The World Is Waiting For'/'Fool's Gold' to *The Late Show*, one of the last bastions of art on TV at the time. It was a smart move. He figured the Hampstead arts mob would like a bit of rough on their show.

He was still surprised when the programme's researchers phoned back and said they were keen to have the band on the programme! And, hey, they loved that funky 'B' side.

By now 'Fool's Gold' was in the charts, the Roses' biggest hit yet, and when they arrived in the studio for the runthrough that afternoon they were not a band that was going to get pushed around by a bunch of artsy fartsy TV people. Every time they got some sort of instruction, they stared back impassively. This was not a band that was interested in kow-towing to anybody else's idea of what a rock'n'roll band should do.

When it came to filming, the atmosphere was already fairly tense and when the band's cranked amps blew the BBC's noise limiters one minute into their live rendition of 'Made Of Stone', it was pretty well over.

Ian Brown spat into the mic, 'Amateurs, amateurs…we're wasting our time here lads,' as the group skulked away in the background.

The Late Show presenter Tracey MacLeod attempted to salvage the situation, ad libbing through the tension.

The incident grabbed the band a whole bunch of press coverage and got them pretty well blanked by the BBC, apart from the odd appearance, when it came to TV coverage.

In the years that followed, Gareth tried to claim that the whole incident was planned, that it was an attempt at national shit-stirring on the scale of the Sex Pistols.

'We'd arrived in the late morning I think and it all seemed fine although there was a technical problem with their auto cut out…this machine wasn't working properly and [was] cutting out before ten seconds. We knew that before the programme started really. So I was stood at the side and the sound cut out, I think because it was too loud. But it tripped out early.

'I was watching the monitor and in a bizarre way you think there's something wrong with the monitor and they weren't moving either. So then Ian was very clever, he walked behind the presenter Tracey MacLeod and he didn't swear at all so it was all left on. In fact my sister was at home watching and thought he was looking for me but he ducked down – that was just to make sure he was on the monitors because he could see them off stage…and did his little rant.

'The band went off and they were leaving. I said, "Ian, there's something I got to ask you," and he turned to me and looked at me to say, "Yeah?" I said, "Are you staying for the next number?" and his words were, "Who do you think I am? Mickey Mouse?" and off he went. They ripped me for ages afterwards because they thought I set it all up, because as soon as it happened the crew knew this was great TV. They all learnt really fast like that.'

Phil Smith was by now part of the band's road crew.

'*The Late Show* was hilarious. The Roses had said we will only do *The Late Show* if we can play live, and *The Late Show* thought they meant if it *goes out* live. They used to film it as live, but during the day. So they changed the schedule to put it out live, and they just meant they wanted to play live! While the band was on we had to wait around. We just sat about five foot away from the presenters and they were all really nervous. I think they thought we were gonna smash it up or something. We just thought it was hilarious.

'We were just nipping round the back to have a spliff, then coming back and carrying on laughing at them. The media in London didn't have a clue what it was all about or how to handle them. They were just scared or worried; they didn't know how to handle it. They just didn't know who these weird types from up north were.'

A Top Ten hit meant *Top of the Pops*, and they were booked to appear on 23 November. Normally an appearance on Britain's premier pop show was taken with good humour or great excitement. No matter how corny or how naff it was perceived as, it was also the best pop programme ever on British TV. There was something about its chart-heavy and simple format that worked beautifully. It was also the pinnacle in any promotion campaign and a crowning moment for the pluggers to get the band on to the show.

Of course things were different with this band.

'I had many proper sleepless nights over this one,' remembers Davies. 'I normally sleep like a log but the Roses on *Top of the Pops* was a cause of major concern for me.'

It turned out that the band didn't want to be on *Top of the Pops*; maybe like their heroes The Clash or Led Zeppelin they believed that the show would demean their work or, even cannier, they believed that the enigma that was sucking everyone in would be ruined by flouncing around on the show.

'They were certainly very smart like that. They were hardly what you would call over-exposed. It's like the only people to ever really see them perform were their true fans. It was very difficult for the casual observer to see The Stone Roses, and that became part of their allure,' admires Davies.

But *Top of the Pops* meant a whole new stack of logistical problems for the normally unflappable Davies.

'They didn't want to do it. They were staying at the YMCA hotel just off Tottenham Court Road, which was typical of them. You couldn't get further away from the rock'n'roll circus than that. I went over there to persuade them to do it. They didn't want to be seen miming: they wanted the amps onstage to make it look right. I got in touch with *Top of the Pops* producer Stan Appel, asking if they could use their amps. He said, "Why are this band so difficult? We have no problems with proper stars like Barry Manilow and Liza Minnelli."

'When they arrived in the taxi at the studio they told the driver to keep the cab running as they may leave at any minute. They didn't trust the programme, they didn't care, they would have just walked back out of there again. The roadies set up the gear and we waited. Gareth Evans was in a real flap. The Mondays were also on the show, and before the Roses went on he was trying to keep the two bands apart in case the Mondays spiked their drinks.'

Eventually it all went ahead smoothly. It went down as one of the legendary 'Top of the Pops', far more legendary than Barry Manilow appearing on the show.

'*Top of the Pops* was a good laugh because the Mondays were on,' recalls Davies. 'It was miming anyway and obviously because the Mondays were on as well there was chaos going on in the dressing rooms. In the sound-check some of the Roses did the Mondays and some of the Mondays did the Roses. *Top of the Pops* didn't have a clue who they were anyway. It was far less amenable to hip cool bands in those days than it was towards the end, so that was good fun.'

Ian Brown had a whale of a time. 'It was absolutely fantastic. We shared a dressing room with the Happy Mondays. Me and Shaun were sat in the make-up room and Shaun was asking if he could have my make-up, saying, "He's a good-looking fucker, look at my big hooter – give me his make-up!" [laughs] When we did the warm-up, Mani went on the kit and Gary Whelan from the Mondays went on the bass. We were going to swap and change about on the actual take. It was Tony Wilson who persuaded us not to do it because outside Manchester no one would know who we were. Mani was going to be Shaun and Shaun was going to be Reni. We got on ace with the Mondays. It was ace that we were getting this attention with another bunch of lads from the same city on the same path. We shared a lot.'

1989

At Last! The End of the Eighties!: Face-off with The Face

As another decade came to an end, 1989 had given the band a superb impetus. Not only were they the band of the year, their début album was already being talked about in hushed whispers as a rock classic. They were now being treated as one of *the* bands of the eighties.

That January, the first month of the new decade saw the Roses basking in the glow of warm press. The only dark cloud was the notorious Nick Kent feature that appeared in *The Face*.

It was a piece on the Happy Mondays and The Stone Roses and it left no one very happy with its content and its condescending manner.

Kent, a journalist, was a product of the mid-seventies rock star scene. He had cut his rock'n'roll teeth writing about Iggy Pop, Keef Richards, Sid Vicious and their ilk and was naturally suspicious of these two new bands hanging out at rock'n'roll central.

There was a whole new drugs and rock'n'roll party and he wasn't invited. Kent, a veteran of the drug wars, felt that it was his professional duty to take some ecstasy as research for the article, something that he trumpeted in his preview for it on *The Face*'s contents page.

'It would be pretty unprofessional if I wrote about these two groups without ever trying it – trying to look in from the outside.' The biggest shock was that he must have been one of the only hipsters in the country to have taken E.

He went down to the Mondays' and the Roses' joint *Top of the Pops* appearance, perhaps the pop moment of the year. It was a cultural and generational clash.

Kent painted the bands in a not particularly flattering light. The Roses' quotes were written out in northern accents that made them sound nothing like themselves (ever met anyone who says 'fookin'? He also seemed to think that the Roses' drummer was called 'Rhemmi').

The tabloids were now on the band's case as well. Brown's anti-royal stance was the sort of sensationalist guff that they thrived upon. *The Sun* went down to Sylvan Avenue to find out what neighbours thought of the vocalist's 'controversial' stance. They were gruffly rebuked.

Attention-seeking Tory MP losers like Geoffrey Dickens had tried to get the group banned from *Top of the Pops* because of the same stance. He urged viewers to switch off while the band was playing.

Paint Job: The Stone Roses Get into the Painting and Redecorating Business

With the band's big breakthrough it was almost inevitable that their recent past would catch up with them. FM Revolver had recently re-released their 1987 single 'Sally Cinnamon' without their consent and put together a promotional video for the single that the band was not happy with.

They managed to chart the single at number 46.

The Roses were fuming. They wanted revenge.

On 30 January after a band meeting at the International, the band set off to Rockfield Studios in Wales to work on their next single, 'One Love'.

During the meeting they had decided to visit FM Revolver label MD Paul Birch and his girlfriend Olivia Darling in his Wolverhampton office, which they promptly redecorated with coloured paint. Ian Brown then slipped outside and smashed the rear window of Birch's twenty-five-grand Mercedes with a brick and Reni gave the car a respray, a respray that was hardly likely to add value to the vehicle.

'The video was insulting,' Brown said at the time. 'Blokes selling fruit, a few pigeons, some black woman holding a baby, a picture of me on the front of *The Face*, a few people in flares…So we went and painted him.'

Paul Birch has a level-headed take on the fallout: 'There's two ways of telling the story and I'm happy to go along with the public relations story, which is the group turned up at the door, threw paint all over Paul Birch – "Well, you know, the bastard had it coming" – and that's the end of it. The group are the ones with the fans, not me. I don't want fans; I do want the group to have fans.

'They are a great band, they are an incredible influence and they have been served unjustly in my opinion. I'm pleased to say that when it came to The Stone Roses I believe that we did the right thing by The Stone

Roses at every level. We never held them back when we could have. Someone wound them up and put them in the right direction as it were. I'm not here to give them a bad name. I remain a fan.'

Birch remembers the reason behind the incident. 'We had re-released the single because we still owned it at that point. *The Chart Show* was on TV, produced by Keith Macmillan, and both Keith Macmillan and MTV said to us, "We need a video of The Stone Roses...we would like to play it on our shows but we can't just play a soundtrack – we need a video."

'[Several years later] we were up at Manchester, at In The City, and I was with a group of people at the bar. I'm sitting there with a group of people drinking, [then] everyone went silent. One said to me, "Oooh, that's Mani behind you, Paul." I think they thought, "Ohhhh, there's Mani and there's Paul Birch, something is gonna kick off." (I've never, by the way, in all the years, even had an argument with the group after everything that's happened.) And so I went up to Mani and said, "Mani, my name is Paul Birch, I am from Revolver Records, please don't hit me." He is a very nice man and I didn't think for a moment that he would. I said, "Please listen to what I have to say to you because it's really important and I've never ever had the opportunity to speak to any of the group and tell them what I am about to tell you now."

The whole incident itself had been strange from the start.

'In those days we used to have a staff of 40 and we had, during the day of the incident, several phone calls from the *NME* asking if The Stone Roses had been round. So it was a bit of a strange question.

'In fact it was only about 7.30 that evening, after everyone had left, that the band turned up at the door. Our accountant was working in the back office. I used to have an office upstairs. My wife went to the door (she was my girlfriend at the time); the band were there. She came upstairs and said, "The Stone Roses are downstairs." Five minutes later she came back and said, "Are you going to see them?" I said, "I thought you were joking when you said The Stone Roses are downstairs. Tickle me with a bloody feather, what do you mean The Stone Roses are downstairs?" I went downstairs and that's when it all kicked off.'

Birch was, understandably, less than pleased and even as the band were arriving at Rockfield Studios covered in paint, making it easy for the police to spot who they were, he was starting proceedings against them for wilful damage.

The band and Steve Adge were arrested. Ian Brown, John Squire and Reni were arrested in their hotel near the studio. Mani and Steve walked into Monmouth police station to give themselves up. They were taken to Wolverhampton where Steve Adge was released without charge.

The band put an injunction on the label and prevented them from showing the video. During February with the Revolver case rumbling on, Silvertone re-released 'Elephant Stone' on 19 February (it was The Stone Roses' second Top Ten hit, crashing in at number 8) and 'Made of Stone' a week later (surprisingly less of a hit at number 20). On the back of this 'She Bangs The Drums' re-entered the back end of the Top 40.

The Roses' past was now up for sale and there were plenty of takers.

They appeared in Wolverhampton Crown Court that March, where there was a disagreement over the amount of damage caused. Revolver claimed £22,000 and the band's representatives £8,000. The case was postponed, finally coming to fruition the following autumn.

I went down and covered the case for *Sounds*, sitting in court soaking up the near carnival atmosphere. While they were getting their wrists slapped, T-shirts with 'Ian Brown Is Innocent' emblazoned across the front were being flogged outside.

The band pleaded guilty to the charges and were fined £3,000 each plus £95 costs. The judge said that their actions were 'immature to the point of childishness'. The Roses sauntered into the court smirking.

This was a proper laugh. The band were convinced that they were totally justified in their action and they knew that the fine, although a tidy sum of money, would hardly break their piggy-banks.

After the trial they stood on the steps of the court looking cool as fuck, bad-ass rock stars in old Wolverhampton fooling with the system. They posed for pictures, laughing like guilty schoolboys, savouring every moment of the drama.

They may have been fined but they felt like they had won as they dashed to the waiting cars parked round the corner.

Fellow Musicians React to the New Pop Kings

The Roses' ascendancy hadn't gone unnoticed by some of the creaking rock royalty. *20/20* magazine quoted Pink Floyd man Roger Waters that spring: 'The Stone Roses reminded me of us twenty-five years ago.

They've got loads of bollocks and arrogance and won't take any shit. John Leckie produced the album and he engineered bits of *The Dark Side Of The Moon* and *Wish You Were Here*. I see they've got a Jackson Pollock paint-splashed Rickenbacker bass – the first guitar I spent all my grant on – I got a friend of mine to paint mine. I like that kind of open guitar sound and it doesn't sound like there is any machinery around. They wear flares, and why not? This kind of identity seeking in late adolescence is very crucial and will be till the end of time. Anyway people don't grow up – they just get older.'

Albeit pretty stuffy, but oddly perceptive.

Post-1989, the whole scene was opening up in the UK. There were hordes of new bands fired by the Roses and some older heads were turning. Spacemen 3, who had been dabbling in psychedelics for a long time, were hooking into the whole vibe. They had played several shows in Manchester over the years and had been pretty influential on several of the up and coming local bands. The Inspiral Carpets had supported them and the Happy Mondays had checked them out, as their guitar player Sonic Boom recalls. 'After a gig a couple of smoothies came up to me and I thought that they were going to hit me,' is how he remembers his first meeting with the Happy Mondays, adding, 'What you've got with the Mondays and the Roses is really accessible music, combined with a really cool attitude.'

Ian Brown noted at the same time that there was definitely something up on the streets. 'Everyone's dressing up again – 1986 seems like a lifetime ago. A few skins have been shed since then,' he was quoted in *Sounds* that spring.

Loose drugs and looser clothes were the order of the era.

The Stone Roses were currently at their catalytic best, central to the new art riot. Rumours of a massive show that summer were starting to surface. It would be the big one that would galvanise the imagination of the new pop generation.

There was talk of a strange place called 'Spike Island'.

Police and Thieves

In mid-May Ian Brown was caught up in a bizarre incident at the International 2. One that was a pointer for what the Manchester of the next few years was going to be like once the party was over.

The sinister gangster thing was starting to kick off as the drugs trade was far too profitable to be left to a few manky old hippies dealing out dope. The sharp street kids wanted in. There was a new generation of gangsters hustling for some action.

The city had become more and more tense. The so-called vibe seemed to disappear and the drug dealers looked rougher and rougher. Moss Side became synonymous with gangs, and Cheetham Hill, Moss Side and Salford fought out a drugs war in the city's clubs. Pundits reckoned that the whole drug business in Manchester was worth millions per year and there were plenty of takers.

The gunmen were starting to encroach on the music scene. Brown was watching local reggae band Ini Kamoze at the International club, when a gunman charged into the club and people went flying as bullets were shot into the roof; moments later the cops burst in and the whole place calmed down again.

It was to be like that in Manchester as the party gradually drew to a halt, as the comedown from E kicked in. The surly attitude of the pop stars was getting handed down to the streets as a licence for macho posturing. Drugs which had sent the scene through the roof two years before were also contributing to its downfall.

Manchester was going to be in for a couple of rough and ready years.

Spike Island

So there they were at the top of their game.

The Stone Roses had been the band of 1989, they had put out one of the greatest début albums ever, toured consistently, played the most iconic gigs of their generation, inspired a whole raft of musicians and changed popular culture.

They had the whole world in their hands and yet now, within six months, they were going to disappear from the limelight. How could everything unwind so quickly?

First though there was Spike Island, The Stone Roses' own festival and the logical conclusion to the band's own gigs, on their own terms.

What better way of capping Alexandra Palace than by putting your own festival on? When you've burned Blackpool, set your stall at Ally Pally and you're a dreamer, you may as well go for broke.

In 1989–90 it seemed like anything could happen, that was the vibe. Self-belief, boosted by ecstasy and the acid house boom (which promoted community, large crowds and loadsamoney for unscrupulous promoters), were all coming together and affecting the rock scene.

During the back-end of 1989 Gareth and his business partner Matthew, along with promoter Phil Jones, had been scouring the country looking for a suitable venue for a mega gig. All sorts of suggestions were thrown their way – disused caravan parks, old quarries, even the site from the legendary Bickershawe festival in 1972 where the Grateful Dead made their UK début.

People were hungry for big spaces and big ideas. At the time festivals were just getting themselves sorted out after dipping into a 1980s malaise of leather jackets and stale lager-fuelled crap bills. No cool band would be seen dead at a festival, let alone put one on themselves. But The Stone Roses were rewriting the rule book and if acid house was about the communal rush of the rave then why couldn't rock'n'roll replicate this?

On 21 December 1989 Evans had applied to Hatton Borough Council for a licence. The site, on a bleak piece of land next to the Mersey near Widnes, with a backdrop of chemical factories, was usually used for a local carnival and wouldn't be a problem for a concert.

All year rumours had been going round about proposed big Roses shows and the band, who were attempting to operate outside the rock 'n'roll circuit, were trying to pull off the big one, flouting conventions yet again.

There is a certain circuit that a band is meant to complete before selling out Wembley Stadium at the peak of its career. Now that every local band seemed to be playing G-Mex in Manchester, a 14,000-capacity hall, as if it was a small local gig, imagination was called for.

The festival was going to be the band's first British date of 1990. There had been some crazy rumours going round. One was about a show at Buckingham Palace or in one of the Royal Parks nearby. 'We want to do it. We're in negotiation with Buckingham Palace at the moment,' the Roses chortled.

It would have been a great moment as the anti-monarchist Roses pulled 40,000 stoners into central London, outside the grim old palace for a rowdy evening's mayhem.

Unfortunately it was a scam.

*

The idea for Spike Island was to place a gig somewhere between Liverpool and Manchester, a symbolic link between the two cities that were at each other's throats in football hooligan terms, but now, armed with their own music scenes, were rivalling London as the hippest corner of the UK.

Phil Jones had searched the UK for sites: 'We drove round the country looking for these weird places to put them on. There was a motorbike dirt track in Essex. I remember meeting these gypsy guys who lived there and they asked for too much money. Gareth lived near Spike Island and he heard that they did this annual small-town festival there. He went to have a look at it and met the council and signed up immediately. We wanted it to be in the north. It was a home gig of sorts. We were looking at doing two or three of that scale. I remember being in Essex for a good day and a half and we were thinking of one up north and one down south near London.

'Matthew somehow researched all the places – the more obscure the better. The deal was it had to be somewhere no one had done a gig before. Gareth and Matthew were from the outside of the music industry and were trying to do different things, and they pulled it off because they had the right band to do it with. Gareth went against the forces of the music industry. He made things up, like them supporting the Rolling Stones. He realised because of who he was and what he was talking about that he had the right band to do it. He was well known before for being a bit of a fantasy guy but he made it work.'

Gareth Evans batted off local objections. 'I had a lot of meetings with committees. The residents were not keen; there was a march through Widnes. People had banners saying "Go back to London" but I said, "I live down the road near Northwich." I got lucky when a girl wrote an article in the *Widnes Weekly* about the gas being made at Spike Island being for Saddam Hussein. She was interviewed by the Special Branch and she was in big trouble, but she got behind me for the gig. There was these women round Spike Island saying there would be needles everywhere but we said, "We have not even been there yet!"

'I had to put some pressure on the council to get the gig. I got to councillors but I won't tell you how I got to them.'

Once they found the site, they got to work.

The plan was to flood the semi-rivers around the island and build bridges, creating a natural barrier in and out of the gig. Everyone knew what a bunch of blaggers lived in the north-west; Manc guest lists were always ridiculous. Now here was a chance to blag the biggest party of the year. Anyone without a ticket or an approved blag was going to have to swim the Mersey to get in, and you can't get any more foolproof than that.

Spike Island was going to be the big one. It was the gathering of the clans. If Blackpool had been the moment when the Roses had proved that there was something special going on, then Spike Island, with the movers and shakers from all over the UK turning up, was an unprecedented show of strength for a group that had burst onto the scene only a year before.

Warming up for Spike Island, the Roses did a short tour of Scandinavia, returning for the first time since their poverty-stricken 'Beatles In Hamburg' bonding tour of Sweden five years before. This time it was different, as with hits under their belt the Roses were stars in Scandinavia.

Sweden and the surrounding countries had always dug British groups – they were in the UK pop sphere of influence and the bands had always been well-supported over there.

The début in Copenhagen on 15 May wasn't one of their best, and the next show, in a small venue in Lund in Sweden, had seen a crowd with some mad, ribald punk rockers spitting at the band.

But on 17 May in Stockholm the 1,500 punters crammed into the venue went mad. The Roses were big-time now in Sweden and the crowd went mental for the 'Adored'/'Elephant'/'Drums' opening salvo. The tour also saw the début of 'One Love', which *Melody Maker's* Bob Stanley points out is far closer to pop radio than the dancefloor. Stanley also records that they played 'Elizabeth My Dear', a rarely played live song, as well as débuting 'Something's Burning', the 'B' side of the upcoming single.

Post-show they got on the tour bus and headed for town to see what action there was. The sound system pumped 'Jumping Jack Flash', The Misunderstood, The Beatles' 'Nowhere Man', The Byrds – all trad rock fare. They got caned in a club called Melody, arriving through the door the moment the DJ put 'Fool's Gold' on to the turntable – it was perfect timing. Right then the Roses couldn't put a foot wrong.

Simon Kelly was back on the road following the band around: 'Me and Stuart decided to go to the first date in Copenhagen...I buy the flight tickets off of a mate of a mate, who worked for a small travel agency in the centre of London. Come the day of the gig, he hasn't sent the tickets. A mate of mine is going to drive us to Gatwick for the flight. He arrives at mine (slightly late). We drive to central London, eventually pick up the tickets, fly down the Westway to pick Stu up, only to find ten minutes later that he's left his passport at home. Foot to the floor all the way down the M25, M23, only to find that we're too late for the 3pm, but there is a 5pm from Heathrow. We get there and there's only one seat. So, we toss a coin, and I win.

'It's only three hours before the gig. I arrive and get a cab to the venue. I see that it's about £20 to get in and decide that after paying £190 for the flight, I wasn't paying another £20. I asked for the tour manager. Five minutes later Steve Adge arrives and exclaims, 'What are you doing here?' He invites me in. It's not a great warm-up; the band are quite rusty and you can tell they haven't played for a while. It's a bit quiet and Ian has a go at the crowd. "Shoot You Down" is all over the place. We do get a first hearing of "One Love", which breaks down, and "Something's Burning" in an elongated set list which includes "Don't Stop" and "Elizabeth My Dear", but Ian's vocals and harmonies are all over the place, a precursor of what was to come.

'After the gig, I wait around (I've got no hotel). I go to a bar next door with the band. Reni tries to pair me off with some more Danish lovelies, but I'm not in the band. End up back at their hotel late on, Ian Brown chewing my ear off, "Eh, I want you to tell me all about yourself." I'm almost dead after the day's exploits and just want to go to sleep, but he wants to talk. Eventually he lets me be. I get some kip on Alan the roadie's floor.'

In Stockholm the band were buzzing about the new single 'One Love' to journalists. They were about to go back into the studio and remix it. The cut hadn't been perfect and they needed more bottom end. The choice was now between the Adrian Sherwood version or the John Leckie version. Getting the bottom end right was always something the Roses, a band that listened to their reggae and dub, were keen on.

Mani's bass had the heavy undertow with resonations of deep dub and Public Image Ltd's great bass player Jah Wobble in its sound. It wouldn't be until Mani laid down some great bass lines for Primal Scream that his bass would get the fully bang-on sound that he had been looking for.

Back in the UK, tickets for Spike Island had sold out. Warm-up tour completed and new single ready, the scene was set for The Stone Roses' biggest gig.

The world's press flew into Manchester and the band were going to have a press conference.

A band that played the mystique card and the world's press who were not going to get it.

Now this looked like fun.

The Ultimate Media Stand-Off: The Spike Island Press Conference

By the spring of 1990, for the first time since punk, a whole series of street bands were hitting the charts. The flavour of UK pop had changed and things were getting brilliantly out of hand. Not only were the Roses planning to play to 30,000 people in the middle of an industrial belt in Cheshire, but they were going to have a full-on proper press conference as well.

No one interesting had done that in pop for years.

This was a chance for the band who didn't really communicate with the media to talk to the world's music press. This was an opportunity for the still generally cynical media to lock horns with the UK's latest music sensation.

The press conference was an odd and controversial occasion that was probably the brainchild of Gareth Evans, who spent the stand-off standing just to the side of the band with a grin slapped across his face.

Late afternoon on that midsummer day across Manchester city centre the press, the pundits and the blaggers started filing into the Piccadilly Hotel foyer. A curious building, the Piccadilly Hotel is the slab of concrete in the centre of Manchester that looks like it was donated from some fucked-up industrial town in deep Eastern Europe. At the time the huge neon signs on the side, the shitty chip shops on the ground floor and the ugly concrete of Manchester's second-tallest building dominated the city centre, making it seem far more grim than it really is.

Most rock'n'roll bands would have used the Midland Hotel round the corner, it being one of the famous haunts, but for some reason the Roses went for the Piccadilly.

Swigging beer and looking across the tramp-strewn wasteland of Piccadilly Gardens and on to the smog-filled mess of the bus station, the press pack were curiously less rowdy than usual. No one really knew what to expect. It wasn't going to be an easy ride.

I stood there and watched a whole clutch of Manchester scenesters and pop fiends mingled with the high and mighty and the self-appointed guardians of the new cool.

Late, as usual, The Stone Roses mooched into the room. The atmosphere got tenser and there was a curious silence as the band sat down.

'Why don't you ask summat? You've flown here from all over the world,' sneered Ian Brown at the not-so-merry throng. There was plenty of foot shuffling. Most of the press seemed to be stood at the back of the room, apprehensive about coming down the front. No one really felt like being the first to talk in such a hostile atmosphere.

'Tune in, turn off, but don't drop out,' added the singer enigmatically, leaning forward staring at the crowd with his big eyes doing the vacant John Lydon stare.

The questions that followed were the usual banal, unprepared pieces that always seemed to be the feature of these events, everyone always hoping that someone else asks something smart for them to steal for their own copy.

Journalist: 'When are you coming to America?'

'When you send us the ticket,' replied Mani, the Rose who seemed most affable.

Indignant journalist: 'Answer the question.'

Stone Rose: 'We are.'

Journalist: 'Are you guys prepared for this press conference?'

Reni: 'We're not a political manifesto. We never went to a school for press conferences.'

Journalist: 'How do you think Americans will appreciate Manchester sarcasm?'

Ian Brown: 'With an American accent.'

There were shades of The Beatles at Kennedy Airport in 1964 trying to be cute, fending off the more banal questions, only this time it was nastier and armed with a more 1990s brutish northern wit.

Unlike with The Beatles, the press didn't like what they were hearing.

Journalist: 'Do you like The Charlatans?' referring to the Northwich-based outfit who had supported the Roses earlier in their career and who were now making inroads into the mainstream with their Roses-influenced Hammond-driven garage pop.

Roses: 'We've never heard of them.'

Journalist: 'Would you play in a bullfight arena?'

Reni: 'It's just not on, is it? We wouldn't watch it on TV, so why should we endorse it.'

The questions were starting to get dumb.

Journalist: 'What did your parents do?'

Ian Brown: 'My father was a joiner and he told me to never work on a building site, and that's what I have done.'

Someone piped up and asked about the Strangeways Prison riots that had recently dominated the news, when prisoners had kept the guards at bay for several weeks from the Victorian Manchester city-centre jail.

Ian Brown perked up. 'It was great. It was like five lads keeping the whole of England at bay,' he stated, not realising that he could have been talking about the Roses themselves. 'It took a lot of strength. Anyone who has a go is a folk hero in Manchester.'

The tabloids, represented by the *Daily Star*, decided that it was time to get things on to home territory, and asked about sex, drugs and rock 'n'roll.

Ian Brown, feigning intense boredom, stared glumly out at the audience. The room was crackling with tension.

There was finally a question about Spike Island itself.

'We asked our manager Gareth to find us somewhere near loads of people and he found us Spike Island,' Brown deadpanned, referring to the considerable complaints that had come from the local residents about the gig. He added, 'We're not getting any money out of it. It cost us 400 grand to put on and we're getting nish.'

Someone asked if the band had any rivalries with any other local outfits. This was obviously not someone from the city because the bands, although disparate in style, were always pretty tightly knit. The whole nature of the band scene was always close, most bands cheering on their so-called rivals.

'It's not a contest is it?' replied Brown, with an icy stare. 'We don't have a grudge against anyone apart from Nick Kent.'

Journalist: 'Hello, I am from a national paper in Spain. I want to know when your recordings on Silvertone will be available all over the world.'

Brown: 'The people to ask are standing at the back.'

The Silvertone people at the back shuffled uncomfortably. No one likes to be made to speak in a full room of people, especially a room full of press determined for a story. Luckily a drunk grabbed the mic and started talking in late 1980s gibberish Manc-speak, 'Roses in the area. Spike Island got fuck all in the area aaaaaaiieeeee!'

Journalist: 'John, are you ever going to speak?'

John: 'No.'

Journalist: 'Do you think you are the best guitarist in the world?'

John: 'Yeah!'

The madman: 'Aaaaaaiieeeeee!'

Journalist: 'Do you think that you are the new Rolling Stones?'

Brown: 'This is 1990 innit? So I say to you the Rolling Who?' (Cheers and applause.)

Journalist: 'What do you think you'll be doing in five years' time?'

Brown: 'What a stupid question, how the fuck do I know?' (Indeed it was a stupid question and one that everyone always gets asked at these sort of things. Does anyone in music ever actually have a five-year plan?)

Journalist: 'You're being compared to some of the biggest bands in the world. How do you feel about it?'

Brown: 'Excited, bored – I'm waiting for someone to make me laugh.'

Photographer (to the gathered press): 'What I want to know is why the fuck are you all here? Why are you all so afraid to ask the band any questions?'

Brown: 'It's because we don't answer them.' (Nervous giggling and uncomfortable fidgeting.)

Journalist: 'Do you guys always bear a grudge? You've invited all these people here and you won't answer any questions.'

Brown: 'I've answered all the questions…except the stupid ones.' (Mumblings, atmosphere is increasingly tense and uncomfortable.)

Journalist: 'Since it's inevitable you guys are coming to America, you're obviously gonna have to do a lot of press. They'll want to ask about your private life. What are your backgrounds?'

Brown: 'I'm not telling you.' (A long gap of silence and shuffling.)

Madman: 'Wooooooagh in the area!'

Brown (belches): 'Urgh 'scuse, anyone want a cig?'

Journalist: 'Yeah, want some of this?' (Hands Brown a spliff.)

Brown: 'Who has come from the other side of the world? Hands up, you're being paid to ask the questions.' (Angry rumblings from the floor.)

Journalist: 'I paid my own fare, so fuck you, man!'

Brown: 'Ooooh.' (A row starts between two journalists and one of them turns on the Roses.)

At this point Frank Owen from *Details* magazine got to the front of the queue and, attempting to shout over a drunk mate of the band, he yelled, 'This is fucking bullshit! I'm from Manchester. I live in New York and this is bullshit. You're treating these people like fucking shit. [Another bloke starts telling him to shut up.] No, you shut up, you fucking dickhead.' (They start pushing each other.)

Brown: 'Hey, ease off, we're not treating anyone like anything.'

Owen: 'Don't give me that. I'm from here. I know when you're fucking winding people up!'

Brown: 'Sort your head out, man.'

Owen, now visibly annoyed, weighed in: 'I'm from Manchester and I know when you're winding people up. Why are you coming out with this anti-American shit?'

The Roses were momentarily startled by Owen and let him continue.

Owen: 'You're behaving like pigs to these people. Why are you dissing all these people here?'

The drunk loon made menacing steps towards him and it looked like the whole press conference may kick off with some real physical aggro. Everyone in the room tensed, expecting some hooligan action, but the drunk seemed to lack the focus necessary for the job and backed off.

Owen continued: 'It's the whole Manchester sarcasm shit. Why won't you answer the question?'

The band looked back baffled. 'What question?' they quietly replied.

Ian Brown looked up with another one of his vacant stares and blanked back with one of his odd phrases that could have come from his grandmother. 'I think you've got the right stick but at the wrong end.'

This was the high tension point where all the frustration and misunderstanding between the two sides kicked in. Gareth stood to the side, his face full of glee; it was this sort of confrontation that he loved.

Journalist: 'Have you seen tapes of when the Stones came to America? Does this remind you of that?'

Brown: 'No. [To aggrieved bloke.] You still upset?'

Owen: 'Yeah. I'm fucking still upset. These people come all this way and you won't answer the questions properly.' (Everyone on the floor starts arguing and shouting at each other.)

Brown: 'What are you complaining about? You've got a free trip over to England and you're going to see a great band tomorrow. Hands up who's paid to come from the other side of the world out of their own pockets.'

A photographer went down to the front and grabbed hold of one of the Roses' mics.

'You haven't asked goddamn shit,' he snarled, 'you lot haven't asked shit for questions.' It was probably the truest comment of the night.

A member of the band's management then grabbed the mic. 'How the fuck do you think the band feel sat up there in complete silence with all you bastards staring at them, asking them fuck all! You come all this way. Drink all the free beer and you haven't asked fucking shit! You're a bunch of fucking wankers in whatever language you speak. If I was them I'd fuck off now!'

The press conference was pure punk rock theatre. A pop art stand-off. No bands ever take on the media. It created a lot of enemies for the band but it was great to see their pure attitude.

As the press conference ended the journalists and everyone else drifted out into the still Manchester air. Gareth Evans took the opportunity to show me the contents of his car boot downstairs in the car park, stacked full of T-shirts. He was rubbing his hands with joy. He was going to be minted from flogging these the next day. It was the beginning of the serious merchandise era and the smart bands were getting the T-shirts out.

After the press conference the band were shocked at the antagonism that they had kicked up, but not too displeased. A bit of controversy was always to the Roses' taste. It was their punk roots showing through.

The press conference was the culmination of the Roses' odd affair with the press. At the start the press had feted them with that Garry Johnson feature in *Sounds* from their first-ever gig, and then there had been a two-year gap until I started writing for *Sounds* and pushed them, and the rest of the press started to arrive.

From then on the press themselves covered the Roses quite faithfully, cranking a gear when it was clear that the pop zeitgeist had suddenly sided with these northerners. The Roses gave very little back, blanking interviewers but with a disarming charm.

It was a confused and bizarre situation, and one that still pervades to this day, when northerners are quoted as saying 'fookin' instead of 'fucking', whereas southern bands naturally speak in perfect grammar. The northern bands are perceived as being simple oiks and the southerners as college boys, a gross simplification of reality.

No wonder John Squire virtually always kept his trap shut. Apart from one thing: when asked by the throng who his favourite painter was, he replied, 'Ronnie Wood.'

Now that's funny.

Off We Go to Widnes!

The Spike Island site itself was unusual. Surrounded by cooling towers and hideous factories, it was, perhaps, the ugliest festival site of all time. There was going to have to be a massive attempt to create some magic in the filthy backdrop of the north-west landscape. The brutality of the surroundings made no apologies: this was stark, this was real. Spike Island was no Glastonbury, there was no spiritual vibe here, maaaan – this was the real raw deal.

The attempt to create some magic wasn't happening on-site either. Only two beer tents and a few burger stalls dealt with a crowd that would have dwarfed most premier league football clubs. Backstage a mêlée of journalists tried to grab what little free beer there was, and got very impatient in the process. The fans, meanwhile, took it easy, despite all the handicaps. Their brand-new flares flapped in the breeze and the mood was for a party.

They got stoned and they waited.

Noel Gallagher remembers one of his future band mates making the trip to Spike Island. 'Bonehead used to be a plasterer, and he had a white Transit van done up with splattered paint just like the Roses' Jackson Pollock stuff, and he went to Spike Island in that – about ten of them all went at eight in the morning. They watched the gig from right at the back on the top of this Transit van, and the van looked fucking amazing. I always told him he should have kept that van. It would have been a fair sight seeing these ten plasterers sat on top of this van at Spike Island.'

John Harris, ex-editor of *Select*, remembers arriving at the site. 'I had a great time at Spike Island – despite Gareth's droogs taking my lager off me and my mates when we arrived at the gate. This meant that we had to go and buy more beer at the tiny stalls. All the journalists hated it just because the backstage bar shut down early. At the time we could sense that people had it in for the Roses. For us it was a great day out.'

In the background the huge cooling towers that shrouded the never-ending ICI factories on the banks of the Mersey formed the backdrop and the air was stale with industrial filth being pumped into the air. In some ways it was the perfect setting, a challenge. Could great rock'n'roll be created in such disgusting surroundings?

Spike Island was organised on a shoestring. It also nearly didn't go ahead. Danny MacIntosh, one of Manchester's best sound engineers who went on to manage the early Snow Patrol, was earning a wedge that week before the show helping to set up the stage. He remembers the nail-biting tension as the company he worked for waited for Gareth and Matthew to pay up the money that they were owed.

'Three days before the show they were still owed thirty grand and they weren't happy. They said that they wouldn't put up the stage if they didn't get paid. They still hadn't been paid even the night before, so I was sent up in an XR2 from Bedford, where the company was, to Widnes to pick up the money. They had left several ansaphone messages about me picking the money up. So I was already pretty nervous about the meeting. It was like something out of a gangster film. I had to meet Matthew [Cummins, Gareth Evans's partner] at a bus stop in Widnes, and I had never met the guy before in my life. He just gave me the bag of cash, thirty grand in a plastic bag! And I drove all the way back to Bedford at about 140 miles an hour. I was totally shitting myself. I thought that I was going to get done over!'

The last-minute nature of the festival affected its efficiency, but on the day, as it creaked and groaned into place, there was a definite air of excitement, as the new generation of pop fans waited for deliverance.

Of course putting a major rock festival on in Widnes was not going to be without its difficulties and it's to Jones's credit that he made the whole thing happen. The problems seemed insurmountable. The local council were strictly monitoring sound levels and the road crew setting up the stage complained of weird blisters caused by the chemical ooze being pumped out by the factories across the river.

On the day it felt like there were more than the 29,500 punters who had tickets on the island. The guest list alone was five thousand strong. Outside the stench of burgers and cheap merchandise, cheap blow and warm booze, the atmosphere was excellent. The baggy boom had now gone mainstream way beyond the cool kids. It was now for everyone and Ian Brown wanted to make sure it stayed that way...

'When we talked about the show we didn't want the tickets to be too expensive, just to cover the cost of the stage and PA,' he says. 'A few weeks later we found that hadn't happened and they had made this money and people had had their butties taken off them at the gate so they had to buy burgers. Things like that spoiled it for us.

'On the night the PA wasn't the best PA in the world. We should have had a bigger rig. Again it was important to us that we could find somewhere that wasn't rock'n'roll, somewhere that no one had played before. The site was in the middle of a big industrial estate in Widnes and we got 30,000 people there. There were kids from all over the country and that was massive for us to get them to a chemical estate in the middle of nowhere. There was loads of mad stories. Some kid tried to sneak in and left his balls on the railings. Some other kids tried to get over the moat. Matthew came in the helicopter and we came in the back of a Transit van with no windows in it. We were buzzing off that; we could see all the kids through the windscreen.'

Backstage there was a weird tension as the London set descended upon this grubby corner of the north-west. The usual crew of Manc ruffians hung out with middling indie bands and soap opera stars. The free beer, of course, ran out quickly, until someone climbed in behind the tent and switched on the beer pumps, freaking out the beer company.

The oddball support bill included the excellent African musician Thomas Mapfumo and his drum orchestra and then the On U Sound System with Jah Wobble on his heavy duty dub bass (the very same Wobble who was a loose influence on Mani's bass sound). Cranked through the On-U sound system Wobble's bass was going way over everyone's heads. Shame, as he was dealing some great music that afternoon.

Minutes before show time, the Roses mounted the huge stage, clambering up the stairs and the ramps at the back of the stage. I stood there at the side of the stage with Sonic Boom from Spacemen 3 and we watched the four matchstick figures as they walked out to the enormous roar of the restless audience.

Most of them were at their first-ever rock festival, let alone 'rave', and went berserk. For thousands of people it was their first chance to see a band that had played to barely fifty people in their local town just a year before.

As the set kicked off with 'I Wanna Be Adored' the atmosphere was cranked despite the sound seeming delayed. Enigmatic as ever, Brown did the pimp roll, walking on-stage holding a blown-up plastic globe. The symbolism was obvious – the singer had the whole world in his hands. He was wearing the same white top that he had worn for the press conference the day before. Brown was dealing the lolloping chimp moves that only he could stamp any sort of cool over. Keeping almost schtum for the whole show, all he could say was, 'The time…the time is now. Do it now, do it now.'

More Brown philosophy, more simple-speak that made perfect sense – grabbing the positive rush of the times and riding it hard. The night before, Brown had claimed that the crowd was the star and that anyone could have it. These were words that would echo through the UK's rehearsal rooms as legions of pop kids traded in their flares for guitars and started to rebuild the UK pop scene in the wake of the Roses' magnificent putsch, a putsch powered by their musical talent and Brown's charisma.

Whether he was carrying the large plastic globe around like he did at Spike or playing the bongos, Brown was doing the rock-star cool thing with a consummate ease. A Jim Morrison from the DHSS, every move was legendary.

For the fans it was a great day out. Carl, who was twenty-one at the time, still remembers it clearly: 'It was like a giant party, man. We felt free, at ease in the field. Me and some mates from Preston just went down there and we got totally stoned. We were out of it. The Roses were amazing that day. I don't care what anyone says, but that was such a great day out.'

Simon Kelly had made it to the gig: 'Spike Island has gone down in folklore as the culmination of the "Summers of Love". 27,000 tripped-out people on an island in the Mersey estuary. I went up with a van-load of mates from the Camden scene, and we didn't get there till 6.30. Quite luckily really. We met Stu and he'd been there since midday, sunburned and dehydrated.

'Everybody was "on one" and house music was blaring out from the main stage. I do remember Gary Clail singing "Beef (How Low Can You Go?)", and wasn't sure if he performed it, or was DJing. There was no beer, the queue was a mile long – I got backstage and it was the same there, everybody looking for booze or other substances.

'Much has been written of this gig, and you HAD to be there. [It was] a good band performance, but in truth the sound was shocking, blown about all over the place. We stood way back and I don't remember much, apart from coming up when the fireworks went off and then being off it all the way back on the long journey back to London – ha!'

Jenny, who was 18 at the time, says, 'It was a real hassle getting a drink, but Spike Island really meant something. It felt like our generation had its own thing. We just sat in the sun and got really out of it and when the

Roses came on we just danced like mad. Their songs were amazing. It just felt like you had known those tunes all your life.'

Phil Smith, the band's affable crew member, points out that 'Spike Island was great; as Noel always says it did its job just by getting everybody there. It really made a mark on the whole country. There weren't many bands that did arenas back then. If you're a Manchester band you are not going to be coming on through flaming hoops and make a spectacle, are you? You're just gonna amble on stage and play your tunes and that's it.'

For some it was a disappointment. On fan looks back less fondly: 'The sound was crap – you couldn't hear a thing, it was really muffled and there was all these poseurs who turned up – people who you had never seen before, in their Reni hats and flares. Blackpool was miles better. That was the one for us. That was the one that really counted.'

Remarkably there were only four arrests at Spike Island. There were two warnings about the volume (apparently a third one would have meant that the show would have been shut down by Widnes Council, though what they would have done with 30,000 pretty irate punters if it had been shut down halfway through is difficult to imagine).

The night ended with a fireworks display which cost over five grand. Some of the more stoned members of the audience stared into the sky, not sure if it was their heads exploding or the heavens.

Then for us it was a fast car back to Manchester for the very low-key post-show shindig at the International 1, where, for a couple of hours, aptly enough, attempts were made to get the sound system up and running to play some records. A bunch of people waiting for the comedown stood around, got bored and then fucked off home.

Coming Down: Glasgow Green

On 9 June the Roses got their big 7,000-capacity tent out and played Glasgow Green, a show that was, for many, perhaps their finest-ever live performance. Two days before the tent had been in Belfast where they had gone down a storm. The gigs were meant to be the first of many big-top gigs.

In another attempt to break out of the touring circuit and away from the traditional venues, the Roses and Gareth had gone for the idea of a touring circus tent. As it turned out, Glasgow was their last show for five years and the last time that Reni ever played drums on stage with the band, until the reformation (22 years later!), which is pretty fucking tragic.

The big top idea was perfection. The Roses wouldn't come to town and play the normal venue. They would bring the venue with them! Each show would be an event. They would bring their own bands, their own DJs – even their own crowd, dammit.

At the time of Glasgow Green, there were plans to bring the tent to London and there was talk of the Roses headlining on the Isle of Wight – mad rumours, insane ideas, some true and some made up by Gareth!

The tickets for the show were for sale in Scotland only and sold out like a shot. It was the Roses' first Scottish date since the 1989 club tour, when they had played Rooftops on June 22 1989.

Since then Glasgow had really gone for the 'Manchester' thing in a big way. You really noticed it when you arrived there that weekend – the city was awash with kids decked out in Manc baggy clobber. It was flares a go-go. The kids were dressed up like Mancs all over the city and even years later the clubs still do 'Manchester' nights.

In return many Mancs felt an affinity with Glasgow – a tough working-class city with a tradition of arty bohemianism and socialist politics. Both cities were hammered by the powers-that-be in London but refused to buckle down to the Tories. The same went for Belfast. The show there on the 7th at the Maysfield Leisure Centre had been great. When we arrived at the Glasgow big top just before the soundcheck the road crew were buzzing about the Irish gig. The band were hot. Spike Island has been painted as the point where it all started to unravel for the Roses but these two shows saw the band hitting a top gear, really exploring all the possibilities of that quintessential line-up.

If Belfast had been the band hitting a laid-back chillin' groove, Glasgow was fierce, full on rock'n'roll.

Mani has said in interviews since that this was their favourite ever gig. 'When we were on stage that day, we all looked at each other, and then it just went up another level.'

The show itself was a killer. The sound problems of Spike Island were ironed out – it was blistering and it was loud. Squire's guitar, cranked, massive and hard, was fuzzing at the edges, almost like the Sex Pistols. It nearly sounded like Oasis, years early. The gig was the missing link, sound-wise, between the two bands except the Roses were making some transcendental rock'n'roll, as opposed to Noel Gallagher's genius for writing anthemic songs.

Ian's voice was great, in total command, uplifting, perfect. 'Adored' sent the tent up several notches of excitement. The crowd sang along throughout the set, even on 'Elizabeth My Dear', and by the time 'Resurrection' is going through its chops you know that you are at one of the best rock'n'roll gigs you will ever go to.

The tent was sweltering hot, sweat dripped off the roof back on to the kids who were rammed in there. The atmosphere was electric, buzzing. Wandering round the venue you'd see some of the same faces that travelled all over the country to see the band, as well as a whole new never-ending stream of spotty young kids who were getting transported by the first proper band they would see in their lives.

And what an introduction!

Simon Kelly was at the gig: 'We drove up to Glasgow Green and arrived seven hours later and parked up by Celtic Park and walked up to the Green. I was on one by now, and saw the big top at the other end, and a big queue snaking its way down from there. We walked up past the queue of Breaker-drinking Scots in Reni hats and baggies, and look out for Spike (from Seemore Travel) who is getting us in. He arrives with Steve Adge and gives us our passes. It's a long way to go till kick-off on a beautiful, warm summer's night.

'Dave Booth is DJing in the tent, and the sun finally goes down. The opening chords to "I Wanna Be Adored" break out just after 10pm, and 7,000 mad Scots go mental. The band are on top form, the sound is fantastic AND LOUD! Condensation is dripping from the roof and raining on us. "Resurrection" seems to go on for hours, and then it's all over. Out of the tent, and backstage – the band holed up in a Portakabin. We see Spike, and he's talking to his mate Gareth Evans – I ask Gareth, "Why did John's guitar go all over the place in 'She Bangs the Drums'?" (something to do with his effects pedals, I believe), and Gareth laughed and said, "That's John Squire for you!"

It was the only low point in an earth-shattering display from four mates at the top of their game – little did we know that this would be the last time that these four members, the "classic" line-up, would play together in public for 22 years!

'And the night wasn't over yet – we were told to head for the Sub Club for the after-party. We got in easily with our passes. The Roses arrived at the club, and I remember Ian Brown walking around saying "Thanks for coming" and shaking hands. I remember getting my arse pinched by a group of Glaswegian lasses! Then we came out, and the sun was coming up. Stu decided to sleep in the car, as he had to wait for the AA to arrive and sort out an oil leak. I went off with John Robb and photographer Ian Tilton and a couple of their mates, and got my head down on someone's floor for a few hours in Glasgow's West End. We did manage to get home the next day, despite a few mishaps on the way, but we were exhilarated. Little did we know that it would never be this way ever again (well, until June 2012 anyway!).'

'Resurrection' clattered to a halt and Reni left the stage for the last time. If the Roses had not blown out the American tour two weeks after this show, if the Roses had just kept gigs like this coming, the pop landscape would have been so different. The second raters who grabbed their crown would have had to wait in line. There was so much great rock'n'roll left in this line-up. But barely one year after they hit the UK big time they were about to grind to a frustrating halt.

After the gig, at a curiously empty backstage, the band sat drained and quietly polite in a small caravan. The atmosphere was hardly celebratory but the awesome rush of playing to so many people must have taken its toll. The Roses really meant something to this audience and they had given everything that they had to fire them and it.

We had all piled down to the Sub Club, the hippest house club in Glasgow where everyone got totally blasted till the wee small hours. It was a night of mega strong E and endless drinking, beautiful girls, mad dancing and a large contingent of Mancs getting down with the Glaswegians. Somewhere in the blur, Mani was bouncing around – the affable party man – while the rest of the Roses crew held court in a corner of the club. It was a night of so much sweat that I had to throw my sweat-soaked socks and shirt out through Ian Tilton's car window the next day, on the drive back to Manchester in the glorious sunshine.

Even Ian Brown says it's the best gig he's ever been to. 'Glasgow Green was another idea to do something different with the big tops. Years later when Radiohead did the big-top tour, the agent told me they took the idea from Glasgow Green, which was the ultimate Roses gig. It was so hot in there; sweat pouring off the ceiling, it was like rain. Everyone was E'd up. The band was smoking that day.

'After Glasgow the vibe in the band was electric,' he continues. 'We thought we were going to be bigger than The Beatles. All we had to do was keep writing great songs. We were still writing at this point. We were still writing together. There are four or five songs that we've never done anything with. I wish we had a better chorus for "One Love". I think it's great but we rewrote it four or five times and it was never quite right. We went to Cornwall. We went to the Lake District. We went to west Wales on writing sessions.

'Shame that what happened there was that we discovered that we had to make the next album and we realised that this record company had us by the balls. Our solicitor said, "I think you can get out of it," and this was when we were about to make the second album, which would have been a funkier sound, which is where we was going. It would have been amazing but we never got there because of the court case.'

After Glasgow the band were caught in mid-air, trapped by court cases, record deals and trying to write the second album.

'We slowed down after that, didn't we? We caught Gareth with his hand in the cookie jar and we had all these court cases we had to do,' he says. 'A lot came out in the court case. We were keen not to blow it and stayed hungry. We had been on the dole for years so we paid ourselves sixty quid a week and when "Fool's Gold" came out we paid ourselves a hundred quid a week. We were still not lording it and we were saying to Gareth, "You look after the money and we'll sort it out later." Little things started happening with the management side that we found out in court. Then we had to wait for the appeal. Because of that, writing music was on and off at that time.'

But all that was in the future. After Glasgow Green it still seemed like The Stone Roses were invincible, an unstoppable force, a band that touched people's hearts and souls. They had the tunes and the attitude. They seemed to understand the pop culture codes and they had that indefinable X-factor that struck home with countless people from all walks of life. They had that street thing nailed down tight. Versed in pop culture they had a rough understanding of what was happening and just rode with it.

If they had managed to keep running from this point in then they could have had it all. Large.

In reality Glasgow Green was the last gig the band played in Britain for five years.

Turns Into Stone

On 25 June the Roses' new single 'One Love' finally got its release. A final delay was caused by a bizarre and unintentional glitch in the artwork.

The layout of the latest John Squire sleeve had looked like a swastika when viewed from certain angles. Squire himself noticed it first when he was checking the proofs of the sleeve. Shocked, he recalled the artwork and cut it all up and rearranged it as a collage.

'We don't want some kid to get attacked in a bar in somewhere like Barcelona because he's got that design on a T-shirt,' reasoned Ian Brown. Indeed one of the band's own roadies was stopped from going into the Hacienda wearing a 'swastika' T-shirt.

The sleeve design brings up the whole Nazi thing yet again. There have always been unsubstantiated rumours about the Roses' past in gangs with some more right-wing members.

There were some very confused ideas knocking about in the early eighties. NF skinheads dancing to the Jamaican folk music of ska, a post-punk right-wing confusion that had more to do with violence than politics. If you grew up in that era like I did, you would have seen people having their heads turned by the hate politics of the right. The Roses would have seen this as well, but how far would someone like Ian Brown with his Bruce Lee and Muhammad Ali fixation and socialist parents get into that kind of mess? Seems more than unlikely to me.

All this contrasts sharply with the sentiments behind the 'One Love' single and its music, which oozes the prime-time swing of the blackest of musics, funk.

'One Love' was the sound of a band moving on. Attempting to ride a fusion between Can and pure pop, it was under-rated at the time. Taking the formula of 'Fool's Gold' and stretching it out over several minutes, the song was funky loose chops and a neat spiralling wah-wah guitar. Brown went for the sinister whispered vocal, giving the song a menacing air. 'One Love' was mean, sinuous and funky, flipping over into a chorus that was anthemic as well as massive.

'One Love' was yet another example of the much mooted 'new direction' of the post 'Fool's Gold' groove, the sound of a band playing inside out itself, Brown again doing the drop-an-octave-mystic-scally bit, intoning some kinda street wisdom over the band's workout. The main let-down was the chorus – it sounded hasty and glued on. Says Ian, 'We were trying too hard to write an anthem.'

If you want the real business then flip the record over for 'Something's Burning'. This is where the Roses of 1990 were really cooking, visiting Can's vibe and fleshing it out with a jazzy xylophone or vibes. It was a sultry, smoking record and both tracks boded well for the second album. In a song littered with biblical references and dealing with morality and loyalty, they seemed to be moving away from the crystalline pop and towards a more groove-orientated sound, utilising the shit-hot drums of Reni and really combining the rock and the dance. They were getting fluid, losing their British skin, getting funky, getting black, getting to the roots of what this whole rock'n'roll thing was really about.

Where the 'A' side is merely competent, this is the band stalking seventies Miles Davis territory, bringing the voodoo down (if you like this kinda feel then go out and buy Miles's *Bitches Brew* right now!), effortless and awesome and with added xylophone. Brown intones the biblical morality over the top, ancient wisdom copped from the good book, digging deeper into the bible for inspiration.

When it was finally released the single crashed into the charts at number four.

All the delaying tactics before the release had many wondering if they were building up the advance orders – looking for a number one. Even at their peak, they just didn't have enough fans to knock Elton John off the top, or to push fatty Pavarotti or the *Neighbours* 'star' Craig McLachlan out of the way, leaving them stuck at number four.

That week's chart also included the Soup Dragons' 'I'm Free', the latest in a long line of baggy bands. The Soup Dragons were a Glasgow indie band who had gone 'indie/dance' and were now coining it worldwide with their own hit, a cover of The Rolling Stones' oldie. It was a perfectly executed pop trick and was selling a stack load in the Roses' wake. They were typical of a whole new generation of bands who were starting to crash in on the new pop scene, from Blur's Roses pastiche, 'There's No Other Way', to The Charlatans' sudden mass popularity on the back of a great pop album. There were a myriad different versions of the Roses wherever you looked.

The pop times were also changing. All round it was World Cup fever – New Order's 'World In Motion' was a big hit and everyone was getting into football after years of pretending to be bored with sport. The new 'lad' was starting to rear his beery head in the wake of 'E' culture. The Roses had unwittingly heralded a new era of blokedom, something that they never felt really comfortable with.

And then? And then it all went quiet.

Before 'One Love', before Spike Island, everything had seemed possible. Afterwards the band slowly came back down to earth.

TV Crimes: The Wogan Non-Appearance

As 'One Love' crashed into the charts, it opened up more TV opportunities for the band. Plugger Beer Davies was working the record hard. The band were now mainstream and were, in their plugger's eyes, ready for some teatime TV. At this level, *Top of the Pops* is a foregone conclusion, but what about mums' and dads' TV? What about Wogan?

If *The Late Show* was Beer Davies working overtime grabbing cool TV opportunities, getting the group onto the Wogan show was hustling beyond the call of duty. At the back-end of the eighties Terry Wogan had a nightly chat show. For years he'd been the housewives' choice on Radio Two, tucked away from the rest of the populace, but now you could hardly avoid him.

Persuading the researchers that having The Stone Roses on their show would be a really cool idea because it would get the younger generation into watching the show was the easy part. Getting the band to play by the rule book was going to be rather trickier. Gareth Davies remembers the latest set of TV problems.

'They insisted that they would have to be interviewed as well. Wogan's people were not too keen on this idea – they grumbled that there could be some sort of trouble planned. It was some time later that I found out that they actually planned to pull some kind of stunt on live TV. They understood the value of publicity, it would have ended their TV career, but they would have become really famous if they had pulled it off.'

It would have been a great TV moment, the humiliation of the pillar of the establishment by the band that didn't give a fuck. Wogan's people were right in their assumption and promptly blocked the group's appearance. There would be little TV left for the band; the enigma was still in place.

1991

Entering the Wilderness Years

Most bands who are at the top of the tree and powering a generation into hyperdrive take the bit between their teeth and go somewhere, but not The Stone Roses.

The wheels were beginning to come off. That deal with Silvertone, suspicions about the management, and a case of what seemed to be writer's block were all going to take their toll.

It was January 1991 and the band were just getting round to putting together rehearsal sessions to work on the new album. Nearly two years since the release of *The Stone Roses*, which had at once defined them and their generation, they were back together in an effort to start work on the follow-up.

On 13 January they decamped to Bluestone rehearsal studio in the beautiful wilds of Pembrokeshire. Bored in the country, the Roses soon started dossing around, doing anything to avoid getting down to the real business at hand. According to an *NME* report, they played baseball with pool cues, smashed windows, and threw aerosol cans into a bonfire, an ace laugh as pieces of burning red can exploded everywhere.

John Squire took an expensive set of Harrods carving knives and, as a special present for Doreen, the owner of the studio, built a giant cock-and-ball statue – a piece of artwork that went over the locals' heads – and they dubbed Doreen the 'old cock and ball', a nickname that stuck like dirt.

NME also claimed that all the band ate were chips, and when the studio served them baked potatoes they just threw them into the bonfire, pissing off the rehearsal space's cook, Pippa, whose culinary skills must have been put to a severe test in cooking the potatoes.

That's life in these country rehearsal spaces. There's nothing much to do but rehearse, and bands quickly find all sorts of school prankery to get up to instead. The vibe is that of a school trip and the most banal of practical jokes quickly becomes hilarious.

Rock'n'roll is an urban music and the buzz and the groove of the city is crucial to its formation. Country retreats were not right for the band.

Eventually in February a van came to pick them up, and all they had to show for their month's stay was a ragbag of stupid stories and a burning desire to escape. The snow drifts were so deep that a tractor was required to haul the van out of the mire.

It's almost a metaphor for the band themselves.

Maybe it served them right for trying to get their heads together in the country. There's something about urban rock'n'roll that just doesn't work when it's transported to the countryside. The fast-burning urban sex and pollution that is ingrained in all great rock'n'roll is so much part of all the coolest bands' early stories that the slacking off in the fields and wilderness that inevitably follows when they stretch out and enjoy their new wealth often means some truly crap music gets made.

Not that the Roses were going to make any crap music – it was just going to take them longer to rekindle the fire. In hindsight they should have hit the road, got the band feeling back again, and kept in touch with the street. The glory of the Roses was their anthems, their arrogance, their city music.

According to *NME*, when they signed the visitors' book on leaving the studios, John Squire, ever polite, promised that all damages would be paid for. The signatures themselves are probably the closest the band ever got to telling the truth about themselves at the time. Brown signed his name 'the laziest man in showbizness'; Reni with 'What Time Is It?', his calling card from spending the last month in a bored daze, and Mani, the court jester, wrote, 'Nothing off for good behaviour, vive la proletariat'. John Squire simply signed his name in introverted small letters.

Whilst the band were messing around in Wales, Gareth Evans was starting the process to get them out of the Silvertone contract.

Even in September 1989 there had been rumbles of the band leaving Silvertone. With all their new-found success they wanted to make changes to the contract that they had signed without scrubbing out some of the clauses.

After Spike Island Gareth firmly expected Silvertone to renegotiate, treat the band as the potential U2-size stadium outfit that they were on the fast track to becoming. Spike had been the pinnacle. It was obvious that this was a different sort of situation than in 1988.

John Brice, one of the band's original fans, was now working in the music business: 'When I was at CBS Gareth let me know he wanted to leave Silvertone and would we be interested. I felt weird because I knew

Roddy. I did meet with Gareth and Muff Winwood, who I was working for at CBS. Muff was pretty cool. He said, "We're here if you need us in the future." It was literally a five-minute meeting. I don't think the band knew about the meeting. Gareth was angling for other deals and big money, which they got in the end in America with Geffen.

'Gareth was a bit of a character. I had the same kind of feel of him as the Roses did. He was funny, he made me laugh and was a bit of a wide boy. He was good for the band at the start, giving away free tickets, making it seem bigger than it was. He absolutely backed the band and believed they would be the biggest band in the world. They were the first band to do that, to have that incredible self-belief.'

In the Roses camp there was also dissatisfaction with their chart placings for 'One Love', which had stalled at number four when they felt it should have been a number one. All this was eating into the band's relationship with Silvertone. They figured that with a bigger company they could get the mass audience that they felt was theirs.

Lob into this equation the eccentric management method of Gareth, the obstinate nature of the band and the fact that Roddy McKenna, the one link between the label and the band, was working in the US and you've got a very chaotic situation.

Technically the Roses' case held all the cards. The band were now massive, perhaps the biggest band in the UK, and were ripe for a bigger label to come in and snap them up.

A band in the Roses' position was worth big money. Their meteoric rise had not gone unnoticed; there were hints of spectacular money on the horizon. Could Zomba match this? Were they willing to take the chance?

Ironically it was this attempt to break out of the small deal that probably stymied the Roses' rise for good – the litigation, the arguments, the fallouts…The next few years the only headlines The Stone Roses got were boring ones, full of lawyers' names and details of record deals. Good business maybe, but fuck all to do with rock'n'roll.

Inevitably it all ended up in court as the band tried to get out of the Silvertone contract.

The *NME* quoted the Roses' lawyer John Kennedy talking about the injunction that prevented them from recording: 'It was agreed at the time that the group could go back to court and apply to have the injunction lifted if it was interfering with their career. Obviously the right to record and release an album is central to their career. Now the band want to record an LP so we will be making an appeal against the injunction in February.'

On 18–22 March the band appeared in the Law Courts in the Strand, London, to hear the testimony of Geoffrey Howard, their solicitor at the time of signing the Silvertone deal. Later in the week, the band's lawyer, John Kennedy, reported that they had been offered a deal with Geffen Records. Rumours of a Roses summer concert started.

On 23 March, the *Melody Maker* reported Ian Brown saying that if the case went against them the band would give up music and go on the dole. In the report The Stone Roses were quoted as saying 'Silvertone have got us for thirty-five years – we'd have only got ten for armed robbery.'

Silvertone were baffled by this unhappiness. They claimed that no one signed deals for thirty-five years and that the deal was based on the number of records released. There was a bit of posturing from both sides, squaring up for action. Silvertone, though, had no intention of losing the band and slapped an injunction on the Roses to prevent them from releasing any other records with anybody else until it was all settled in court.

Silvertone told the *Melody Maker*, 'We're fans as much as anyone else, we want them to make another record.'

On 25–26 March the band appeared in court in connection with the Silvertone contract – although Reni was ill and couldn't attend. The reasons behind the band's non-appearance on Wogan in July 1989 were discussed. It was revealed in court that Roses manager Gareth Evans's real name was Ian Bromley. He changed it while working at Vidal Sassoon's in the 1960s.

The press had been swiftly on the case of the band's label disruption. The first *NME* of the year had printed a huge story about the band taking Silvertone to court. The story claimed that the band would have to wait until November to get the case into court and the chance of getting material out seemed very slim.

The Roses' lawyer John Kennedy, who is considered to be one of the top music biz lawyers (and went on to represent Sony as an expert witness against George Michael in one of the other celebrated music biz cases of the nineties), prepared a 40-page document detailing why the contract that they had originally signed was not legally binding.

Gareth Evans seemed to love being in court; the drama and the tension was all fuel to him. Like a lot of rock'n'roll managers, he loved being on stage. They all dream of fronting a band or at least of fucking the lead singer. Gareth was definitely not interested in the latter and he had no chance of the former, so the court was his stage. You can imagine him being almost relieved that to get out of Silvertone would require a protracted court case that would have the music business sitting up and checking its procedures.

Silvertone were represented by Peter Prescott, QC, who kicked off by saying that The Stone Roses 'Can't now be heard to say "boo hoo I now want to get out of the contract".'

He also added, 'When The Stone Roses' career began to take off their success had been pretty modest. It is particularly galling for my clients that the group said that the contract is invalid and they are free to go off with another company.'

Silvertone were being aggressive but even they must have realised that they were on a hiding to nothing when the rumours started to appear that Gary Gersh, the leading A&R man at Geffen Records (and the man that signed Nirvana to Geffen) was on the Roses' case and was promising to pay all the legal fees (up to £300,000) and whatever it took to get them out of their contract. The big guns were lining up – the necessary finance was being made available and Silvertone were soon under the cosh.

Geffen were rightly hungry for the Roses. At this point in time if the band had kick-started their career again, they could have been one of the biggest bands in the world – they had the UK, they had Japan, Europe was getting interested and some hard touring would have sorted out the States.

Evans himself was lapping it up, staying in the posh Russell Hotel in London, walking around like a man possessed, giving journalists the runaround and grinning the shit-eating grin of managers who realise that their time has come.

When Geoffrey Howard, the brief who represented them when they signed to Silvertone in the first place, turned up in court to give evidence, the band turned up as well, looking suitably out of place at the proceedings.

They were there to hear Evans be described by the Roses' own QC Barbara Dohman as 'inexperienced in the music business'. These trial revelations would eventually prove to be the undoing of Gareth's grip on them as a manager.

It also emerged in court that one of the first major cracks that had appeared between the band and the record label was the group's lack of enthusiasm about appearing on the *Wogan* show to promote the 'One Love' single. They believed that the show was a touch naff. Ian Mill, counsel for the band and Gareth Evans, pointed this out to Silvertone in court.

'Terry Wogan is the housewife's choice and the people that appear on his show reflect that fact, do they not?'

Mr Jenkins, managing director of Zomba, replied: 'No, he has various musical guests – he has to have topical guests from all areas of music.'

Mr Mills replied: 'You do not think that there would be a perception among any part of the fan base of The Stone Roses that the group would be selling out by appearing on the *Wogan* show?'

Jenkins conceded that the band could have seen it that way before adding: 'I do not think so. It's one of those shows which is well established.'

It was these ridiculous snippets that kept the press well entertained throughout the spring of 1991 and showed just how banal the workings of pop really were.

On 27 March Evans backed up Ian Brown's story that the band had been paid poorly by Silvertone. They each earned £70 per week before tax, eventually rising to £200 per week as the hits started to come in, not bad if you can get it but laughable for a band in their position. Evans talked about why he had signed the deal in the first place.

'I knew Zomba were a hard company. I didn't want to rock the boat. I wanted to get on with the whole thing and relied on the prospect of a new contract as a reward. We built Silvertone up into what it is now.'

Asked why he had signed the band to a ten-year management deal, Evans replied, 'I wanted to be with this band for a long time. We'd been at it for five years and a lot of bands are following what we did.'

The case was helping to spell the end of Evans's tenure with the Roses. It also burst the bubble they had created as a band. Court always reduces everything to the black and white, exposing the workings and machinations of a group. It wrecked their aura. It ruined Silvertone's credibility. No one wins in these situations.

Meanwhile, outside the court room, the rumour mill was chewing over a story that the Roses were planning a huge comeback concert in the south-east of England. Like most of these rumours there was probably little more than wishful thinking involved in the story. It was the type of tale that would plague the news pages of the music papers for the next five years as the press looked for any tidbits of information on a band that at one moment had been everywhere and the next had completely disappeared. People were baffled by the way the band had seemingly turned its back on the big time, and the enigma fascinated everybody.

With April's usual blast of spring in the air, and not much to do, Ian Brown and Mani turned up at the typically protracted court proceedings and sat with thrilled fans. It was a Rolling Stones moment.

One of the classic images for many pop freaks is that of the Stones' court busts in the original summer of love, when the sharp-dressed dandies swaggered in and out of court and, apart from Brian Jones, got one over the stuffy establishment. There always seemed to be something romantic and swashbuckling and something very rock'n'roll about rolling in and out of court. Getting that rush of adrenaline, stalking across the Victorian portals of the ancient hallways and into the stuffy confines of the court itself. Heads turned, mouths were agape. It was like going on stage.

Brown paused from his big day in court to speak to the *Melody Maker*, relating how bored he was with the whole affair.

'It's more fun when there are witnesses because at least there's something to stare at. I'm getting a little bored with all these people pulling coloured flags from their mouths, but at least I'm beginning to understand their double speak.'

Meanwhile, back on the front line, Evans was under the hammer. Silvertone, in an attempt to loosen his control over his charges, revealed that he took a third of their money and had them signed to a ten-year deal – a shockingly long-term contract that is far far more than a manager normally takes. They also pointed out that he didn't give the band any accounts of his company 'Starscreen Management'.

In his favour, Evans claimed he had signed the ten-year deal because he was putting a lot of money into the band. He had a long-term vision for the Roses, a vision that was crucial to their success. His crazed ideas and his lack of knowledge about the way the music business actually worked were brilliant for the band.

Here was a man who dared to dream.

The case itself rumbled on. It was revealed that the contract had odd clauses, like the fact that the label wasn't obliged to release Roses products anywhere in the world and that the band would only get half the royalty rate from a greatest hits package. The tide was turning in the Roses' favour at last.

On 29 May the high court ruled that the Zomba contract was one-sided and the band were now free of its bindings. The band celebrated.

It had been an unusual case, as Roddy McKenna remembers: 'At one point it was surreal. I was going up to the high court and meeting Ian and Gareth for a coffee at the tube station at Embankment and then I'm going to the Zomba side in the court and they were in the other side.

'The court case was numbing for everybody. Zomba got their comeuppance and Gareth would get his comeuppance. You know what? Zomba thought they were going to win that case.'

On 29 May Judge Humphries found in favour of The Stone Roses' camp and the contract was annulled. The band were free. Instantly the press was full of talk over who was going to get the Roses' signature. There had been plenty of takers. Gareth himself had already been over in LA, flown out there by interested parties. He had been in talks with several labels.

It was on that trip in LA that David Geffen, head of the maverick major Geffen Records, got in touch with Evans. Alerted to the Roses by his head of A&R Gary Gersh, Geffen was fired up. In the past twenty years Geffen had built a fearsome reputation for himself, first as a manager before setting up Asylum, signing the likes of The Eagles. He then set up Geffen Records and had made big bucks out of Guns N' Roses and a whole host of big-time eighties outfits.

He had also masterminded, ironically, the John Lennon comeback of 1980 after a five-year hiatus.

Evans and David Geffen had struck up a series of eccentric meetings in LA where Evans' sales pitch was fascinating the big-bucks label boss.

Geffen paid a £350,000 advance to Evans as a good-faith handshake for the band. Gareth thought the label was just one of the options he had on the table, but Geffen told him that this was not the case; in their view Geffen now had the band.

It was about now that the management started to get out of its depth. The Stone Roses were swimming in deep waters.

The bidding war was coming to a head. That summer the Roses and Gareth convened at the Halcyon Hotel in Holland Park in London. There was a meeting with David Geffen that morning, ostensibly to sign the deal, then a break for lunch. Even this close to the wire there were four other major labels in the hotel hoping to persuade the Roses to sign to them, despite the advance Evans had already accepted from Geffen. The band were confused and Gareth was edgy.

For their new album they received a million-pound advance and would receive a further million when the record was released. Then each album onwards the advances would correlate to the success or failure of the previous records. It was a great record deal, the total opposite of the Silvertone one and one that reflected the band's current standing in the world of pop.

For the second album (the one after *Second Coming*) they would receive a minimum of $1.5 million, a maximum of $3 million; for the third $2–4 million; for the fourth $2.25–4.5 million; for the fifth $2.5–5 million, and on top of this a royalty rate of 29 per cent in all major world territories like the UK, the UK and Japan and 27 per cent elsewhere – the normal rates are between 12 and 18 per cent. It was a staggering deal; they were in the stratosphere; only major league superstars get to breathe this sort of moneyfied air.

By 1991 Geffen was hot. This was a big-money operation and was easily challenging the big boys. Breaking an outfit like The Stone Roses into the States would be great kudos as well as big money.

In Geffen's eyes the Roses were pretty well their band.

The final decision was to go with Geffen and for a wheeze they made the wacky snap decision to sign the contract on a bus, just like the Sex Pistols signing to A & M outside Buckingham Palace in 1977!

So dragging all the lawyers and the Geffen people out of the hotel they jumped on to a passing bus and ran upstairs sniggering. Briefcases were snapped open and the bizarre spectacle of a band signing a multi-million-pound contract on a bus unfurled itself.

Looking for a witness to the contract, they were going to get an old man who innocently sat near them to sign his name, but just before he had put his name to paper, the Roses' lawyer John Kennedy made Gareth put his name down as the witness. A momentous decision. For if the band would ever think of getting rid of Gareth, trying to claim that he had drifted away from the band prior to the signing of the Geffen deal, then what was his name doing at the bottom of the contract?

Not that the band were going to get shot of their manager – or were they?

The Geffen deal was potentially a big payer. Millions could be earned by the band as each album came out during the nineties. Now all they had to do was stop fucking about in court and get down to some serious song-writing. Get back to band business.

The Inertia Kicks in: Roses in 1991

The band themselves spent part of May in a house in north Manchester rehearsing new material, but the sessions crumbled when John Squire flew with his girlfriend Helen to Tenerife for a holiday. The rest of the band flew to Rotterdam to see Manchester United beat Barcelona 2–1 in the Cup Winners Cup Final, celebrating when Mark Hughes scored the winner.

At the time it was also reported in the *NME* that Reni was spending his time flying to most of United's games around the country. After years of struggle and poverty the band were enjoying lounging around like rock-star millionaires. Fun but fatal – the real work was still to be done.

Smarting from their court defeat and out of pocket from the result, Silvertone announced that they were to appeal against the verdict. Just when it seemed like the Roses might start functioning as a normal band again they were back against the wall. The appeal itself wouldn't happen for another nine months, stymieing the band's creative flow.

This was when the real rot set in. The Roses ceased to exist as a really full-on creative unit at this point and retreated into the wilderness years, spending most of their time playing and watching football.

On Tuesday nights down at the plastic turf at Man City's training ground in Platt Fields near Moss Side there was a football game – Reni started playing all the time. The game was tough and fast and a certain level of fitness was required to keep up. The standard was pretty high – some members of Yargo and A Certain Ratio also put in appearances and Ian Brown occasionally turned up as well.

Now and then when they felt like being a band again they phoned up publicist Philip Hall and filled him in on what was going on. The fact that they talked more about football was a giveaway to their current inertia.

It was deep into the summer and they still hadn't got down to the second album. Even if they recorded it this week they couldn't release it for another year. They were well and truly knackered by the music biz, a business that has little concern for people's dreams unless they can make plenty of big money cash out of them.

Reckoning that they were down £1 million from the Roses court cases etc., Silvertone decided that it was time to get some dosh back into the coffers. In August they released 'I Wanna Be Adored' as a single and reformatted the album in a gatefold package.

Bored, Reni started to get into trouble. His first case saw him in court on four charges. They included disorderly behaviour and illegal parking.

The court case revealed that he owned three houses in Manchester, including one of those funky little flats behind the Peveril Of The Peak pub near the G-Mex Centre in the city centre.

Reni was renting out his flats. It was also reported in the *NME* that his girlfriend, a paediatric doctor at St Mary's Hospital, had given birth to a son called Cody.

In September Reni's case finally came through – he was found guilty at Manchester Magistrates Court on charges of disorderly behaviour as well as two offences of parking in a no-waiting zone and causing an obstruction because he refused to move his car from the side of Burton Road, the bedsit bohemian high street of south Manchester in West Didsbury.

He also admitted two offences of parking in a no-waiting zone and causing an obstruction and was fined £50. Furious, Reni complained about the police. 'I have already lodged a complaint about the way I was physically abused by the police,' he stated in court.

He was not a happy bunny.

In September Ian Brown and Adge, noting the sudden rise in Roses bootleg tapes floating around Manchester, go down to Strawberry Studios to buy up the old master tapes of the Martin Hannett-produced album that was shelved years back. This was the album that Andy Couzens would stir up a shit storm in the mid nineties by releasing as *Garage Flowers*.

That October, Silvertone continued in their no-holds-barred getting-the money-back campaign when they released *The Stone Roses: Blackpool Live* video through Windsong.

Clocking in at just under an hour, the video was a pretty poorly-filmed document of the now two-year-old legendary Blackpool show. The ropey sound quality did the band few favours and it's difficult to grasp the sheer exhilaration and magic of what was already a piece of pop history. The previous month Silvertone had re-released the début album as two 45 rpm discs inside a gatefold sleeve while CDs and cassettes had 'Elephant Stone' added on as extra incentive for any collectors out there that needed mopping up. The sets were all numbered, with a limited edition getting pressed up for the vinyl version with a bunch of John Squire Pollock artwork and black-and-white pictures of the band thrown in for good measure.

On a more positive note that September, John Squire and his girlfriend announced that they had just had twins, a boy and a girl.

As 1991 ground to a close all the Roses had to show was a frustrating year of nothing. It was all court cases and attempts at writing material for the new album. An album that was already getting itself a high expectations rating from a hungry media and audience.

The advance from Geffen should have set the band up for an assault on the mainstream, but in fact the influx of money started the gradual split. Ian Brown bought a farm in North Wales and John Squire moved from Chorlton to Morecambe Bay. The other two band members stayed in Manchester.

The tightly-knit unit that was so vital to great rock'n'roll was already spreading out.

The band were in their late twenties, hardly hungry young bucks who were going to slog round the world. They had kids, their own lives and their own bank accounts…

'We won the case in March 1991,' says Ian Brown. 'They said do I want a bank account in the Co-op and I said, "I don't want a bank account. I want the money in cash." [They] said, "You got to get a bank account now," so I got this bank account at the Co-op…'

'The band were now moving away from Manchester so I bought a house in Wales, then John moved to the Lake District. We didn't know it then but we started moving apart.

'I had our Frankie in April '92 and John had a daughter at the end of '91 and that was another thing. We suddenly had gigs and responsibilities and it wasn't a gang any more. We had our own lives to think of.'

Despite the changes, the band themselves were working again. They had hired the Rolling Stones' Mobile Studio and were in Ewloe in North Wales near Ian Brown's new home. There were new songs. In all probability they just had 'Ten Storey Love Song' finished – a drop-dead gorgeous song.

But try as they might they couldn't quite ignite that old spark, that inspiration. It didn't seem to be the same any more. Spike Island had been where they had shot their wad, and now it was the morning after, the long hangover. Everything they had worked furiously for had been achieved. They had proved their point.

Money in the bank, objectives achieved, the Roses seemed to be slowly falling apart.

As Ian Brown points out: 'There was a pressure. It was a bit tainted because it was like we had written this masterpiece and now we had to follow it up. When you're writing, you should just write and write and at the end see what you got, but we liked editing. We went to Italy and spent two weeks there in 1990 and when we come back we had one tune that sounded like "Day Tripper" and another one that sounded like "Ticket To Ride" and we were, "Oh fuck it, they sound like The Beatles, we will have to sack them." Of course, years later Noel came along and he didn't care about stuff like that [laughs]. Then we got another batch of five/six songs. I got them on cassettes. There's one called "English Electric Lighting" or "Lightning" and one called "Mr Shy Talk", which was like shy talk or shite talk... "works his finger to the bone but never turns his mind on, he don't know... the children know him as Mr Shytalk, he wears a frown he wears you down".

'It was like bluegrass music and was probably about Gareth [laughs]. We had some tunes but that court case fucked us up big time because we had to do six weeks in court which was destroying and boring.'

The distractions of the band's situation were beginning to bite.

'We had to wait nine months for the appeal. We were stopped by the music business. If we had lost that case we wouldn't have been able to record and that would have been it, but we didn't care. We thought, "If we can't record what we will do is play gigs and play new songs at gigs and record gigs and sell them as bootlegs at the next show so the new songs will always be live versions. We won't be able to do any more recordings but fuck it." We thought it would be really ace to be this really well-known band whose songs were only on bootlegs. We were prepared for that and that case was either going to make us or break us. They were always going back to the eighteenth century in court, about how much of a man do you own, do you own his imagination? What a man owns of another man.'

The revelations in the court about the band's legal affairs were surprising for a band of this size.

'It turned out in the contract that we were not released in America and that was for perpetuity. The contract actually said the territory was "The solar system and all realms yet undiscovered". What the fuck was all that about? The guy we were up against ran the BPI the week they made the Pistols number two when they should have been number one with "God Save The Queen". We used to call him Lucifer Fruin. He was sat there in court. He was the one that did that to the Pistols and now we are up against him! At least we had David Geffen – John Lennon's mate – and he gave us £300,000 to fight the court case because that's what it cost to fight the case. "If you win it, you sign with me and if you lose it we will write that money off." We got out of the deal but in a way the deal still stood, in the way they paid us.'

1992

My God, It's 1992 Already!: The Wilderness Years Continued

With a whole year wasted in court and their fast-lane lives slowly returning to normal, the Roses realised that even at best they were not going to get any new material out till the autumn. The running jokes and gossip about where the fuck the band were had started to circulate.

Not only this but the band's creative edge was becoming decidedly blunted. Scurrilous rumours reported that John Squire had shown the band a bunch of new songs that he had written and they had turned them down. As a story it doesn't fit. What was starting to emerge was John's complete dominance of the music. The Brown/Squire songwriting partnership was effectively over. John was in creative hyperdrive, he was moving deeper into Led Zeppelin territory, moving away from the groove-based direction and pure pop that they had cut their reputation on.

John Leckie noticed at the session in Wales that there was a tension. The band was not as natural as it had been. Reni and John Squire were starting to become more distant. The talk was that the breakbeat in 'Fool's Gold' had started this. Some said that John didn't want to add drums to the track. The pair of them were still working together but there was a distance.

As the band sat there wallowing in Zep, Ian Brown was disgusted. 'What are you listening to them for, they haven't got what you've got,' he pleaded.

Brown knew in his guts that going the rock route was the wrong way. Of course it was playing safe and would possibly be the direct road to the mega-success that Geffen craved for the band, but this was the Roses! Where was the arrogance that made them stand out! Surely they weren't going to end up as just another band?

The rest of the band were gradually being frozen out. Brown was not called upon to work on the lyrics, there were more and more drum loops and Mani's bass was disappearing behind the guitars. This is no crime, of course, as Squire was a fantastic guitar player. It's just that the Roses' strength was accommodating each other's talents.

The band themselves had planned to get into the studio and record as soon as possible but they decided to get on with getting more tunes sorted out before they went in there. 'They realised they couldn't rely on hype,' insiders explained to the *NME*.

Early in 1992, a slightly concerned Geffen called a summit meeting with the Roses, and Gareth, in one of his last managerial roles, had straightened out a battle plan. Geffen had signed a band that was on the edge of the big breakthrough and now they had ground to a halt. They had realised that the band were no young bucks looking for never-ending world tours but they were seeing them as a band that could slot next to REM in the US market, a band for the maturing and vast indie guitar audience to grow up with.

Many musicians at this stage of the game are barely out of their teens. Life is a ball, they have nowhere to live so they live off the fruits of the road. Their idealism is not yet tainted and sex, drugs and rock'n'roll is still a golden ambition. For the slightly older Roses, they were dealing with pregnancies, kids and mortgages – all real-life stuff. They were also dealing with court cases and an indecisiveness about management.

Keeping the band together as a creative unit was becoming more and more difficult – not living in each other's pockets any more was not helping. Small differences can seem a lot bigger when bands start to live apart. Everyone grows up, the gang is no longer a gang but a collection of individuals.

Since the court case they had started wondering about Gareth. The revelations had surprised them and they began to think that maybe it was time for a change. That maybe he was not working in their favour.

Gareth had been the closest anyone had ever got to being in the gang. But he always realised the band would eventually need to move on. And now in early '92 the decision had been made.

The court case had taken its toll on their relationship. To lose Gareth was a traumatic decision but a vital one.

OK in theory, but getting shot of a wily character like Gareth was not going to be that easy.

It was going to cost them dearly in terms of time and money; Evans was a man who had already shown he loved a court battle and was not going to go without a fight.

Sometimes the bullshit piled up so high in the Stone Roses' camp that you needed wings to fly above it all.

Evans himself figured that the band should have kept him on for another six months. He was baffled when they turned down a series of big American shows, claiming that these gigs, with the full force of Geffen behind them, would have set up the Roses in the US. Personally he would have made damn sure those gigs had got played.

But now he was out of the picture and the band blew the gigs, pissing off the more sensitive American music business, a mistake that could well be costly in the long term. Or that was his side of the story...

Evans had been a key figure in the Roses' story and one of the most controversial, shapeshifting managers around. He was the last of the maverick managers; everyone you speak to will tell you different and completely contradictory things about him. Even those for whom he caused grief still tell you about his charm. He pretended he knew nothing about what he was doing, which could have been a ploy or the truth. His lack of conventional know-how allowed him to book Blackpool when no one cared about the band. He genuinely believed The Stone Roses would be massive when everyone else thought they were going-nowhere graffiti merchants. He was the last of the old-school, stop-at-nothing managers who would give away thousands of tickets like some sort of 1960s impresario. Some credit him with Spike Island, Alexandra Palace, the idea of not talking in interviews, Ian Brown's large blown-up globe onstage at Spike, even the paint-throwing incident at Revolver FM – each one a vital moment in the Stone Roses' career. When asked in the same article what he thought the Stone Roses' future was, the former manager replied, 'They will pull through, but they won't be massive. They aren't quite clever enough without me.'

And watching all this were several big American management teams, including Michael Jackson's heavyweight team. It seemed like every management team with an eye for the main chance was out there waiting.

So what did the Roses do? They went to ground. To North Wales to be exact – to Ian Brown's new place – to start work again on the new album.

Feeling more positive about their situation after taking the bold stroke of sacking Evans, the band finally decided to move into the studio and record the second album.

Now starts one of the weirdest periods in the history of any British rock'n'roll band – an immensely talented band caught in a bizarre creative and business limbo. In March they moved their operation up to Brown's place in North Wales – probably drawn by the beautiful countryside, and the quiet away-from-all-the-hassle vibes of the area. Geffen got excited and wanted to release the album in the late summer.

Scouring North Wales for suitable studios the Roses found out what most of the local Welsh bands already knew – the local studios were crap. But, hey, they were loaded. 'If Mohammed was not going to the mountain, let the mountain come to Mohammed' and they hired in the Rolling Stones' Mobile Studio, called John Leckie and parked it at the Old Brewery in Ewloe, a rehearsal studio with 12 bedrooms.

Again the lack of discipline began to bite immediately. The sessions would start very late afternoon and drag through the night.

Leckie noted that the band had six songs which they brought to the sessions and they began work on these amongst the usual tomfoolery of throwing eggs at each other and goofing about.

Brown kept himself fit and chased away the studio fug by skipping and boxing, Squire himself drank only a few glasses of wine and the Roses' rock 'n'roll reputation was left to Mani who was now calling himself the 'Rogue Rose', although this went no further than beer and a passion for the ladies.

Four years since they had started to record their début and things were very very different round the Roses camp. They had jettisoned their management, their record label, had become legends and were working in the shadow of that début album.

They were in the mobile for six weeks and shaped up some demos. However the pressure of the first album, an album that when it was released only got mixed reviews but was now slowly starting to get legendary status, was getting to them.

The Stone Roses was starting to become the blueprint to a whole host of new bands. It was getting mentioned all over the place; a massive sea change had happened in the British music scene and the Roses were not present to reap the reward. People were already saying that if the first album was so good the second album must be awesome. It was a hideous pressure for a band to be under and the longer they took to put the album together the worse the pressure was going to get.

In March it also became clear that the Roses were not going to be playing the massive outdoor Oxfam gig that had been rumoured months before. Unfortunately for the punters The Cure were chosen instead and the gig quickly lost any legendary status.

As the spring drifted into summer, it passed the three-year mark since the début album was released.

The Roses returned to the Old Brewery to work on some new material with John Leckie. They were in there for a month. They now had ten songs down. Some of these songs formed the eventual backbone of the *Second Coming* album, songs like 'Love Spreads', 'Tightrope', 'Breaking Into Heaven' and 'Driving South'.

Already there was a marked difference in the band's sound. Squire has upped the guitar ante – delving deeper into the blues and digging up whole heaps of filthy Zeppelin riffs. 'Love Spreads', in particular, zigzags on the dirtiest riff of them all.

The Roses were different now: they sounded like men compared to the boys on the first album. They had tired of the crystalline pop that dominated the début. The new songs were about broken love, sadness, personal pain. The lyrics were coming from John Squire, giving the record a very different flavour. The optimistic rush of the first album was replaced by the pain of growing up and an almost world-weary vibe descended upon the record.

Squire, feeling the pressure in the studio, the creative burden he was placing on his own shoulders, was resorting to cocaine to bolster his flimsy confidence. It was the first big wedge between him and Brown, who still preferred his marijuana. The different drugs at different times scenario was beginning to kick in.

And while John sweated on his Portastudio working on those overdubs and tunes, the rhythm section began a series of never-ending jams – Mani and Reni grooving to the loose funk that had dominated their creative peak. Fuck what would you pay to hear some of those tunes!

John Leckie was becoming increasingly frustrated with the band and their new songs. Some of the tunes were half finished and some of the others just didn't cut it.

A great producer, he did what producers must do in these situations and told the band that they simply didn't have the material to record an album. He told them to take time out and rest up, then write some new material.

Of course they ignored him and booked themselves into Square One in Bury for the New Year to continue work on the handful of songs. Astonishingly, so far no one from Geffen had turned up to check on their massive investment in the studio. They thought that this is how the Roses must work and they left the band to their own devices.

A band with no manager, an increasingly frustrated producer, bogged down in court cases and under increasing pressure...this would have been a good time for Geffen to come in and pull the band out of the mire.

Meanwhile, as The Stone Roses were wrestling with their difficult second album, the naffly titled baggy scene – of which they were meant to be the figurehead – had disappeared. Pop had moved on, bands that appeared in their slipstream like The Charlatans and the Inspiral Carpets were forging their own careers.

In the bowels of the Manchester Boardwalk rehearsal rooms, Noel Gallagher was working with his brother Liam's group and they were about to make pop history with a band that was modelled on the Roses. The vibe that the Roses and the Mondays had helped to create had disappeared and the gangsters had moved in. The clubs were racked with violence – the party was over.

The Happy Mondays were fading fast, after an interview in the *NME* with Stephen Wells where they went on about 'faggots', combined with a disappointing fourth album, had seen their last tour oozing with a sour atmosphere. The shows were dominated by support band Stereo MCs who were rising fast with a whiteboy, Brit hip-hop sound that somehow combined the swagger of the Roses and the street suss of the Mondays in a blistering street-pop package. It was ironic that they too would disappear into the nowhere land of attempting to record a follow-up.

In the pubs of Camden a new twist on the guitar scene that the Roses had kicked off was slowly moving into the music papers ready for a complete takeover…Britpop (a shitty term for a music scene which I made up as a joke in 1988 when reviewing the La's in *Sounds*).

As 1992 slid to a close there was very little activity in the Roses' camp – it was obvious that the album was not going to be ready till the following spring or even autumn. Geffen were still not panicking and the rock press busied itself with reports of the Roses getting spotted all over Manchester.

It seemed like they were doing absolutely fuck all, sitting around the Beech and the Horse and Jockey in Chorlton, chewing the fat or following the revived Manchester United all over the place. At one point they were spotted in Mantos on Canal Street celebrating United's Derby match victory over their less fortunate neighbours City.

It had been a long and frustrating year of false starts and dashed hopes, another year watching their crown slip.

1993

Still Nothing Going On: The Wilderness Years, Part 3

So roll on 1993 and with still no sign of any music at all, in fact no sign of anything – even the mooted sessions at Square One (sessions that saw the band delivered a pizza by the pre-Elbow Guy Garvey) – the still-managerless Stone Roses were starting to cause concern at Geffen Records. The multinational label had tried its hardest to be hip and modern and all nineties about the situation and left the band to their own concerns, but with this amount of money invested in the band, maybe it was time for them to sort something out.

Ian Brown remembers the optimism around these new sessions: 'In January '93 we went to Square One in Bury and rehearsed every night till about June '93 and we thought, "Shit, the songs are sounding great, let's stay here, leave the gear here and get Leckie to bring the mixing desk in here and try and record it."

'But then we thought, "Hang on, this is not going to work," so we decided to go to a big house in Marple...Reni didn't start getting up till tea time, at five/six o'clock at night, and it frustrated John Leckie because Leckie is a right grafter. It was frustrating, Reni not getting up, and he's saying, "My ankle is hurting, I've strained my ligaments." It was two/three months in that house.

'Reni was pretty grown up, more mature than us. He [had] the poorest background, he had been the most responsible. John Leckie said, "This is not working at all. Let's go to a proper studio." We went in July '93, went to Rockfield.

'Gareth had been sacked by now, we had gone through the court case with him, so it was now four chiefs and no Indians. We loved the fact that we had been on Geffen Records for two years and they had not heard a note...'

Geffen were wondering where the album was.

A&R man Gary Gersh came over and sat down with the band. He needed some answers. Like, just what the fuck was going on and have they managed to find a manager yet? It had been nearly a year since Gareth had been sacked and the band were virtually looking after themselves with Steve Adge taking on the managerial role.

There was talk of a summer single, just enough talk to get Geffen sent packing happy. It would have been a great time to put a single out; it may have been a long gap but the Roses were still massively popular and Oasis were yet to break and steal their thunder. This would have been the perfect time for the comeback.

The rest of the band arsed around at the football or popped over to Lanzarote for holidays. There was a distinct lack of action in the Roses' camp. It was more fun doing everything else apart from being in the studio. After all, after a decade of gloomy rehearsal rooms who wouldn't want to party?

Still, at some point the holiday had to end, the party had to be brought to a short, sharp stop, and as the fourth anniversary of the release of the début album loomed in March, Gary Gersh made one of his six-monthly visits to the band and their ersatz manager Steve Adge and insisted they recall John Leckie. Get something done. Get that summer single out!

They put in a surprise call to John Leckie and told him that they were ready to go into the studio and start recording.

Leckie, who hadn't worked with the band for almost six months, was puzzled by this unprecedented outbreak of activity and high-tailed it north.

There were nearly a dozen songs ready, with new tunes like the English folk-melody-drenched 'Your Star Will Shine', the driving 'Begging You' (written by Squire as he attempted to master computer programming and emulate the dense hypnotic backing tracks of Public Enemy with whom he had become obsessed – not quite the Zep freak of legend!) and the nearly completed 'Ten Storey Love Song' – a total classic that had John Leckie gasping. It screamed a hit. If only they could have got it together, got the record out for the summer of '93, it would have been a dead cert Top Five, a possible number one! In their absence the Roses legend was growing. An awesome tune like that would have been one fuck of a comeback.

With the band back in the studio Geffen sensed that there may just be some action on the horizon. What they needed to do was give the group a push, get their act together and start planning the campaign, the relaunch. What the Roses really needed was a manager, someone that they could deal with, so they went shopping for bosses.

They looked at Elliot Rashman, the very successful manager of Simply Red, and a figure widely respected in the music business for his ability to check huge egos.

Affable and straight-talking and a man who lived in Manchester, he seemed perfect for the job. Rashman, though, begged to differ. He was too tied up with Mick Hucknall and didn't feel that he was quite right. He suggested Nathan McGough, the fast-talking wheeler dealer ex-manager of the Happy Mondays, who was currently working in A&R at WEA.

Noticing that it was four years since that album got released, the *NME* travelled up to Bury to try and doorstep an interview with The Stone Roses. The band, seeing the journalist Gina Morris waiting to interview them, were as polite as ever but refused to be interviewed. They said 'Come back in a few months and we'll do a proper interview.'

Gina Morris was at the time a young freelancer: 'The *NME* in the early nineties was largely run by non-northern men in their mid- to late-twenties. I was 19, female and fresh off the train from Madchester. It was more that than my skill as a writer that got me a job. They thought I'd be able to track down the Roses when I sheepishly suggested it at the weekly ideas meeting. The plan was for me to write a funny little aside to a news-based article, which was never going to be a cover story.

'I wasn't cocky about it, just in case I couldn't find them, but I was confident enough. Having worked behind the bar at the Internationals 1 and 2, venues owned by the Roses' managers, I knew all the roadies. The same roadies that worked for, and were mates with, the band. It only took one trip to see Ian's old mate Slim and we had our lead.

'The "hunt" was thrilling all the same. I can still feel the churning nervousness I felt when I had to knock on the door of the rehearsal room, knowing one of them was behind it. These weren't the friendly blokes I once served free drinks to any more, they were The Stone Roses. I was starstruck. Sadly I was also now "the press" and though I knew Ian Brown would have happily chatted to us had their manager not got to him first, I had to accept and respect they weren't ready. Photographer Peter Walsh, a Manc who knew the band from way back, also respected their request not to be photographed. Instead the *NME* sent photographer Steve Double to take the "pap" shot of Ian outside the rehearsal room a few days later.

'The picture was pure *Sun* and they ran with the story on the cover... "GOTCHA!"'

A month or so into the session, producer John Leckie was beginning to feel weirded out by the strange vibe that surrounded the band, especially the way that nothing seemed to get done and their whole bizarre way of operating. Meanwhile Chris Griffiths and Phil Smith and the rest of the band's crew were starting to get itchy feet. Despite still being on the payroll they had nothing better to do than sit around in Phil's back garden playing chess. This was not what they had planned when they went on the road with The Stone Roses. It wouldn't be long before they upped sticks and went to work with the emergent Oasis, yet another lifeline between the two bands.

They hadn't meant to leave for good, as Phil Smith remembers.

'They had the time off because of the court cases but they had meant to play gigs but Silvertone cases got in the way. When I left to work with Oasis I had no idea that it was all falling apart.'

After twenty-six years of trying, Manchester United finally won the 1992/93 League championship and there were wild scenes in the city as thousands of fans hit the streets to party. Mani was spotted getting pissed in Leggets bar in Failsworth. Naturally things got out of hand and the police were called. Recalls Mani, 'That was a top buzz. It was rocking around the Pole in Failsworth. I remember we nipped off to the Broadway in Moston for a while and when we got back the riot police had Oldham Road completely blocked off. United won the League for the first time in twenty-six years and it's "kicking off" like revolution. The Old Bill were completely over the top that night, they must have all been gutted City fans.'

The Roses lost a link with Geffen when the A&R man who signed them, Gary Gersh, moved over to Capitol Records.

By now Geffen sensed the game was up. The Roses were fucking about. They would still be treated as a big act, but not a priority act. Time to cut losses and concentrate on other acts.

Finally in June the Roses checked into the Rockfield Studios for the first time since 1989, ostensibly to get the damned album recorded.

Rockfield itself is more than a studio, it's a legend. It had been set up by Kingsley Ward, whose kid brother owns Monnow Valley Studios just down the road. The two studios had built up some sort of rivalry over the years, to the point where they wouldn't lend each other microphones. The two brothers just did not get on.

Years before the pair of them had been in a band produced by the legendary Joe Meek. Lying around Rockfield were some of the compressors and Valve EQ equipment built by Meek himself who was born just up the road in Newent.

Kingsley Ward, an eccentric figure (he had recently been managing T' Pau) would pace the grounds with his yapping spaniels in tow and pretend to be bemused by what these musicians got up to. He had tales of Iggy and Bowie and every damned rock star you could name coming through the studios and their never-ending pranks.

Rockfield was actually two studios – one was in a coach house and one was in the stables. When you get there it doesn't even look that spectacular, not like, say, Abbey Road. Rockfield is cluttered with boxes and looks like the back room of a farm. It actually is a great-sounding room with all the warmth for a classic rock recording aided by a funky old Nieve desk – the perfect piece of equipment to harness what the Roses were looking for.

On 26 July John Leckie arrived at the studio to talk about the album. The Stone Roses were again locked into a bizarre studio timetable. It was as if no one wanted to grasp the nettle – maybe the pressure of the remarkable début was too much. Maybe nobody in the band wanted to take the lead and push the band on, maybe the power balance in the group had been disturbed again. The Squire/Brown axis had already been wobbled and now Squire was taking the lead.

Squire was now in creative overdrive – he may have not wanted to bull-doze the rest of the band but, on the other hand, because they were doshed up, smoking dope and sat in the rolling Welsh countryside, they were inevitably taking it easy.

Brown railed against John's cocaine use, but really it was just a thin veneer over the deeper problems in the band's relationships. Reni, too, was getting ostracised, getting out of the, ahem, loop.

There was talk of breakbeats replacing the drummer. Outrageous! But then, bumping into Reni one afternoon in Manchester, he seemed quite chirpy and even talked about how he was replacing himself with break-beats, how 'you've got to move on.' Perhaps he was being sardonic.

Of course this never happened in the end but wherever you looked the intense bond that had cemented the Roses was no more.

John Leckie wasn't sure about the direction the band were going in and, worn out by their slow work rate, quickly quit the sessions. He went on to work with The Verve and Radiohead and then on to Kula Shaker, becoming one of the main producers of the 1990s – another spin-off success from the energy released by the Roses' success.

Ian Brown had a novel approach to band business: 'I remember saying to the lads, "Let's fucking blow it all, let's go to the south of France and fly around in helicopters and fucking have a laugh." The four of us went on holiday in '92. We flew from Nice to Monte Carlo to San Tropez in a helicopter and spent ten grand in six days. We stayed in five-star hotels, which were about three hundred quid a night back then. John's girl was pregnant so he went home...It was a laugh really; a bit of a bonding thing as well. "Let's have a blow-out and then do some recording."

'Then we got to Rockfield...To me the second album still sounds good. They say it took us five years but it was really fifteen months in that studio...In September '94 we finally finished the album.'

The Roses had been happy with the sounds Leckie had got up in Wales. As they started at Rockfield, they told John Leckie that this was the kind of sound they were after for the rest of the album. As Ian told *Guitar* magazine, 'When it came time for the proper recording Leckie said he didn't think we had the songs. We'd given him three of the best tracks on the album! I thought "Daybreak" was fantastic as it was.'

After just one night at Rockfield, after being persuaded back into the studio by Geffen, Leckie decided that he had had enough of a project that he felt was suffering from under-rehearsal, lack of spirit and focus. Ian: 'When we first met John we were on the dole, and we'd go in and make a record in a day. Now it's different.'

There were still snatches of Leckie's production work that made the final cut, the atmospheric intro to 'Breaking Into Heaven', parts of 'How Do You Sleep' and some parts of 'Begging You'.

John was confused by the producer's departure. 'He was taking us aside one by one and waving bits of paper under our noses. He also started worrying more about the money, it seemed to me. It was good in a way 'cause it made us angry and you can really use anger.'

Squire, though, was looking for a warmer guitar sound, a more rock 'n'roll feel for his guitar than the 'monochrome' sound of their début. 'I'm not sure I like that saccharine and chrome-plated Leckie sound anyway,' says Squire. 'It sounded too neutered for the kind of record we wanted.'

John Leckie looks back on the album sessions wearily, as he told *Guitar* magazine, 'My role as producer is simply to capture that magic take. I'd tried, I really had, and contrary to what Ian says, I had no problems with the songs – they were great. John would come down from his bedroom, deliver them to the band and they'd be great, but I invested two years of my life in that record, on and off, and it seemed to be going nowhere. There was no discipline, no urgency and they just didn't have that magic in them at that point. It was a different band from the one that made "I Am The Resurrection".

'We'd had two sessions with the Stones' mobile and in the first four weeks we did three tracks and in the second six-week session we did just one, "Ten Storey Love Song". They just didn't have any life in them. I told them there's no point in hiring an expensive studio and coming out with demos so I said, "Go away, sort yourselves out and we'll try again." They were spending a grand a day and producing nothing! I was under contract to keep the album within budget, although I was never told what that budget was. If it had gone over budget I was liable personally for the costs. In the end it just got too much. There comes a point where you have to devote some time to your own life, other albums and projects.'

'We talked about me leaving the album for a while, in fact we had two or three big meetings about just that. I didn't want to go to Rockfield and I told them, but they managed to convince me it would work. I lasted one night.'

Leckie's parting shot was to, perhaps jokingly, suggest that the band get John Paul Jones, the Zeppelin bass player, to produce the album. The idea was never considered and they played on regardless. It was a definite pointer to the direction the music was going in.

The band decided to carry on at Rockfield and promote engineer Paul Schroeder to the production role in August. Engineers in most studio sessions do most of the dog work and have a perfectly good idea of what the producer was up to, so a promotion like this was never totally out of order. Local boy and tape-op Simon Dawson was moved up one rung to become the engineer.

Paul Schroeder was now the producer of the project. 'With *Second Coming*, it's almost like there isn't a five-year gap. It sounds like it came straight after the single "One Love". Silvertone released this compilation album with "Where Angels Play" and stuff [*Turns into Stone*]. I think it was going a bit more in that direction, but with more dancey looping and stuff.

'I think it would have reflected where they were at the time, which is very much in the dance area. Reni was really turning on big time. If they had made the album that year during "One Love" I reckon they would have become a different band. It would have been more Hendrix rather than Zeppelin.

'For *Second Coming*, I recorded about six or seven tunes from scratch. We kept parts of "Ten Storey Love Song"; we kept parts of a lot of things they'd already started. They had all these great intros to them…We used what bits had been recorded and if I thought that a certain thing was missing we'd do that bit. Like on "Ten Storey", we kept the guitars because they were lovely. We did vocals, drums, probably bass as well. I put on the intro and outro. There was lots already there when I turned up but we definitely recorded some stuff on about six or seven songs.' Schroeder was no stranger to the band's working methods. He had also worked on 'Fool's Gold' and 'Don't Stop'.

Listening through to what they had already recorded, the band decided to ditch a lot of recorded stuff, using it as demos, and start recording everything from scratch. In a studio that cost nearly a grand a day they were spending money like madmen…or rich men.

Starting to feel sluggish from the stuffy late-night environment of the studio, they began to take up mountain-bike riding. John Squire got heavily into it and would eventually spend hours cycling. It was a passion that he would come to share with his younger brother Matt. Squire also trashed nearly every rock'n'roll convention by taking up kite flying.

They also travelled beyond Monmouth and twenty miles down the road to Newport, to TJs – the great Welsh club looked on by many as the home of hardcore, a club where the likes of the Butthole Surfers, Hole etc. had cut their teeth in the UK and where Kurt Cobain had proposed to Courtney Love. TJs was a real dosshole in the best possible way and usually packed with wild, drinking, punk rock Welshmen up for a good time.

It's here that they become tight with a great local band called Novocaine who played a hard-assed but melodic pop punk. Brown's friendship with singer Steve eventually saw him writing a lyric for Novo-caine's song 'Brain'.

Back in the studio they were locked into the nocturnal rock'n'roll shift. Sessions often end just before breakfast time. It's bizarre how anyone can work these long shifts; past about two in the morning ears start getting wasted – you lose track of the treble end and start cranking the cutting-edge sounds, making things tinnier and thinner.

For recording, a late-night session is a nightmare but the Roses weren't even mixing yet. They were jamming endless all-night songs – hammering the tunes out, flexing the riffs, getting their fluidity back – working the chops, attempting to re-awaken the great band that had lain dormant for a good stretch of time.

John Squire would remain in his room for days on end writing songs and guitar licks and becoming more isolated from the rest of the band.

An easy atmosphere hung over the studio; they drew a crap cartoon with felt tips on the back of the studio door (it's still there), and local musicians popped by to hang with the Roses, especially the affable Reni and Ian Brown. They sat around getting stoned and laughing at the crap local TV. Ian Brown talked about anything that was going down, particularly John Lennon and Greek mythology. They joined their new-found buddies in drinking in downtown Monmouth, in the Nag's Head and the Bull.

Monmouth is a curious place, a small sleepy Welsh market town that thinks it's English. The town's youth were by now getting used to the influx of rock stars on to their patch. It was nothing to see a Stone Rose or eventually a member of Oasis in the Nag's Head. It caused a small stir, someone more funky to hang out with – some distant warrior from the rock'n'roll front line to doss around with. The town seemed to be able to accommodate these rock stars in its sleepy wake.

As the Roses gradually immersed themselves in the local culture, Mani began to get deeper and deeper into the local scene. Coming from north Manchester he'd seen friends fuck up badly on smack. He'd tired of city living and the bullshit that goes with it. He got his chance and he wanted to take it. Eventually he married a local girl and lived in Monmouth. The rest of the band abandoned him to his new country squire lifestyle – which included visiting a falconry centre in Cliffords Mesne.

John Squire seemed less interested in getting down with the locals and spent a lot of his time painting and playing his guitar, working out tunes on his Portastudio, locked in his room. Communication, as Led Zeppelin would say, was in breakdown. Band members would turn up at different times in the studio, but the gang had gone.

As the summer stretched into the autumn, the sessions went on and on, but again they seemed to lose interest. Taking time out for holidays, flying off to the football, spending their large advance and generally avoiding getting that second album together. With money coming out of their ears and no manager or record label to crack the whip, the Roses were again coming apart at the seams.

The former tight partnership between John and Ian was over. You can hear the tension on studio out-takes with John losing patience with Ian's attempts to sing 'Your Star Will Shine'.

Sessions were abandoned for a few weeks and ironically the band that slowly but surely seemed to be replacing them in the public's affections, The Charlatans, moved into the available studio space and started recording.

Finally in November the Roses got themselves back into the studio to get on with some more work. The year was nearly over and, apart from a heap of jamming sessions down on tape, there was nothing concrete to speak of.

Also in the studio were Lush, the affable, easy-going indie band fronted by Miki and Emma – two girls who know how to party. They became the latest band to get included in the Roses' chugging, never-ending party zone. Mani and Paul Schroeder in particular hung out with Lush.

The oldest Rose, Mani, celebrated his 29th birthday at the Bull in Monmouth. A wild night kicked off with champagne and tequila slammers with the band, the Monmouth drinking crew, Lush and their producer Mike Hedges getting out of it with the Roses' wildcard bass player. Also in attendance was Ronnie Rogers, the former guitar player with T'Pau. It all started getting bleary in the countryside.

The night ended with Mani and Lush's Emma Anderson getting a cab back to the studio where Emma was promptly sick all over the place.

Rock'n'roll – it's a crazy life, isn't it?

Meanwhile the media were again becoming worried about the Roses. Like just where were they? Where were the figureheads of the new pop revolution? They hadn't been spotted for years now, disappeared over the edge into nowhere land. There was no precedent for this sort of behaviour; bands don't just make it and then seemingly give up.

Maybe Brown's oft-quoted maxim that he hoped the band would make it and then just fade away was coming true.

In the news pages and the gossip columns the stories continued. Some of them crazy, some of them true, and all of them entertaining. The band were getting more press coverage by doing nothing than by playing the game.

It was a long time down the trail from being skinhead scooter punk mods and hanging out in south Manchester. They had been in a band for nearly ten years and released one album and had become perceived as the most important new band in the country. They were trapped in that eternal and strange bubble of youth that bands get into.

There was some vague talk from Mani about a comeback and how he thought Spike Island and Alexandra Palace were complete farces. He mentioned that the band far preferred Glasgow Green and that they might take the big tent out again for a big tour.

In December, their publicist Philip Hall, curious about what was exactly going on, travelled up to Rockfield to listen to rough mixes of the album. Hall, along with his brother Martin, was slowly beginning to build up a rock'n'roll empire (managing the likes of The Manic Street Preachers) with a combination of cool taste, a massive rock'n'roll enthusiasm, a level-headed common sense and an affability that made him very popular within the business.

He had been doing the press for years for the Roses after Evans had been given the publicist's number by a music biz insider on a train to London and had phoned him up.

Hall Or Nothing, his company, was regarded as the best in the business and Hall, an ex-*Record Mirror* journalist, had built his reputation master-minding the PR campaigns for the likes of The Pogues.

While in Wales, after being blown away by the finally recorded new material, Hall sat down with the band and, during a four-hour meeting, was asked to be their manager. He would have been a perfect choice with stacks of enthusiasm, a calm sense of what was going on and a big heart in a mean and vicious scene. He had put £45,000 of his own money, re-mortgaging his house, into The Manic Street Preachers; he had even let them live in his cramped west London flat where they had done all his washing and cleaning for him without being asked! This was a committed man.

Hall accepted the Roses' offer. It was a decision that would have put the band back on course.

Unfortunately within weeks Philip had died of cancer. A complete and utter tragedy, as one of the nicest people of the scene was taken away by the meanest of mean diseases.

The band made a rare trip to London to attend his funeral. It was a sad affair. They returned to Rockfield and again grappled with the album.

Another bizarre report in the *NME* was that the band were racing their flash advance-payrolled cars around the country roads and back lanes of

Monmouth, and that engineer Simon Dawson crashed his into a ditch but luckily crawled out unscathed. The band later denied these stories but it was a sad portent of what was to come when four years later The Charlatans' keyboard player, Rob Collins, crashed his car on the same roads – when returning from the pub to Rockfield for a session for The Charlatans.

Listening to Neil Young, the blues, Led Zeppelin (John) and hardcore underground rap and dub and Bob Marley (Ian and Mani), they were attempting to work these influences into staggering long sessions and fiddle around with their songs. It was like trying to get two entirely different qualities into a piece of music – a nigh-on impossible task which could only contribute to the nightmare of the sessions.

On the other hand there were still songs going down, some great stuff was getting recorded. It was just the time it was taking, the money it was costing, the slothful slowdown of the band, but despite all this there were tunes in the can. Friends like John Brice visited them in the studio and liked what they heard; his mate Paul Schroeder was still at the controls observing what was going on.

'The dynamic had changed because now John Squire was writing almost all the songs,' he says. 'I always thought they were very much like school kids rebelling against a teacher. As soon as you got a producer in the room they'd get themselves together and you could feel not animosity but "Let's have fun with the producer", which happened when I took over – I became the headmaster kind of thing. I could see that that kind of happened with John Squire as well. It can alienate you. I felt the same thing when I became producer. "I'm not one of you any more."

'Coming up with the ideas took fucking forever. Rockfield is a very expensive studio, it's like £1,500 a day. Reni was absent a lot during the sessions. John Squire spent a lot of his time just trying to come up with parts in his room. There are only so many vocal takes and re-doing bass takes that you can do on something you already know is pretty good. I can't stand putting vocals to unfinished songs, I find it a bit irrelevant sometimes. So a lot of the time we were just waiting for John. And also, as a producer, I was going, "You are wasting your money here, boys, you can't wait around all this time, waiting for John to come up with something. You are paying this money."'

Schroeder was working with a band at the end of its tether.

'John Squire had a fear that if we all went home that would be it. That the band might implode. I had to finish off the record, because I thought that without it they would implode, which they did afterwards. I felt there was a definite chance it might happen during the session. It didn't feel right after the first month. The American involvement didn't feel right, the American A&R guy didn't feel right. They wanted the first album so they were very much into "Ten Storey Love Song". They wanted more records like that. You know how Americans like English people to fit into a viewpoint of how they see them, of how they wanted the band to be. I thought it was completely stupid. Sometimes with the music business you fail to see that as a business they have to sell as much as possible. I know that now, having run a label for a few years. But you have to give artists their full due as well [so they can] come up with something that's going to change things.'

Despite all the problems, though, the album was finally coming together, something that Paul Schroeder takes great pride in.

'I put the end result down to John Squire actually getting it right and I put it down to the band and the mixing and the co-producer as well. Everyone that's on that record did a really good job. It was a difficult album to make; it was from sessions from five years ago with different personnel coming in and out. I don't think a record like that had been made before in that way. There was a huge amount of pressure after the first record, but I wasn't getting caught up in that side of it. I'd zenned myself out so much – I realised that their first album was probably their greatest hits, so I just wanted this next album to be their first album. Because their first album was so big, you could never make an album as big as that one. It had the zeitgeist. The Stone Roses' next album might be a signpost.'

Paul Schroeder himself didn't make it to the end of the record; he too was burned out by the endless process and the band dynamics.

'I left prior to the album being finished. As a football manager would say, I think I'd lost the dressing-room a little bit. I didn't think they could finish the record with me. Most of it was done, from hearing the record, about 95 per cent of the record was done [when] I left. But I just needed someone else to top and tail it. That doesn't undermine Simon Dawson's involvement; he did a fantastic job. It's very difficult to finish a record. All I know is they used everything I made with them and it sounded ace.'

Looking back at the album-making process Paul Schroeder feels for the pressure that John Squire was under.

'It's been well documented John was using cocaine. I know that when I've taken a lot of cocaine I get paranoid, and maybe he was getting paranoid and I wasn't giving him the comfort and direction that he thought he needed. Maybe I wasn't being sympathetic enough. Maybe he found that empathy or sympathy with Simon Dawson. They finished the record off and they did a good job.

'John is very much a dry wit, super intelligent dude. He works hard at his art. I don't think he's a naturally gifted guitarist. I think a lot of it is hard work learning those parts and making them sound effortless. He's artistic, of course, but I'd say as a guitarist he's a very good player but purely through passionate learning, trying to get his parts sounding as good as he wants them to sound and as interesting.

'I always thought John and Ian were exactly how you want your two writers to be: where one lacks, the other one takes over and vice versa. Even though people think Squire wrote all the lyrics, I definitely think that Brown had a whole lot to do with them. We'll never know; it's like Lennon and McCartney.'

The sessions were finally coming to an end and, towards Christmas, with some of the tracks shaping up, Geffen finally put their foot down and set a delivery date for the record. John Squire had finished the artwork and there was talk of a first release on Valentine's Day, 1994, of 'Love Spreads', the bluesy Old Testament infused rocker that was to be the first single.

Geffen also talked of a March release for the album. They still obviously didn't really realise what they had on their hands here.

A week before Christmas Ian made a trip down to TJs in Newport and was hassled by a reporter from the *Western Mail* for an interview, an interview which he declined: 'Speak to me as I am, not with a tape recorder' was his riposte.

The last of the wilderness years drew to a close, with a bulk of the material in the can. The band were finally putting the finishing touches to what they hoped would be the *Second Coming*.

1994

My God, There's Something Stirring

Early in 1994, with a new album looming, the Roses decided that they needed to sort out some sort of management. They knew that they had a big job afoot and they needed the right person at the helm to guide the project home. By now, though, their reputation preceded them. Because they didn't act like humble buffoons and serfs like most musicians, they had gathered a reputation for being difficult, for being a band that you just couldn't manage.

Some managers just want to hang around with the gang. They are the band's number-one super fans, caught up in the male braggadocio and bravado of the 'group as gang' thing. Some managers are wheelers and dealers – they haven't got a clue about the music business but they can cut a deal with anyone. The Stone Roses had already had one of those; they wanted someone more 'music business' this time, someone who could kick-start their career in America for them.

In January 1994 they flew to New York City to meet up with Peter Leake, who was manager of The Waterboys and The Cowboy Junkies but, again, their plans fell through.

With February looming, 'Love Spreads' slipped off the release sheets again and the schedule was put back. It was coming up to five years since *The Stone Roses* and the band had become shrouded in legend. Now this new band Oasis were happening. It was the calm before the storm – Britpop was starting to kick off big style and the heritage of the Roses was finally going to hit pay dirt, as the bands that were influenced by them and the space that they created finally got their act together and swamped the mainstream. The only band missing, was, ironically, the Roses themselves.

Paul Schroeder had left Rockfield Studios for London. Due to a prior commitment of producing his sister's band, however, he reluctantly had to leave. 'He'd have been an arsehole not to go,' says Brown. 'Family commitments are important.'

Schroeder had produced 'Breaking Into Heaven', 'Driving South' and 'Good Times', the old-school rock'n'roll tunes.

Now they promoted Simon Dawson, the son of the Rockfield owners, up to producer; their third producer. He had been in on the sessions right from the start so it was a logical move and kept the ship stable. He produced the final version of 'Love Spreads', one of the last songs to be completed early in 1994.

Geffen, obviously living on a different planet to everyone else, put the album, now officially titled *Second Coming*, into the schedules for April. It was yet another date that would be trashed.

One afternoon at the tail end of the sessions two generations of Manchester rock'n'roll collided. While in Monmouth, Ian Brown was walking out of the newsagents WH Smiths on the high street and bumped right into Noel and Liam Gallagher. The night before he had listened to Steve Lamacq on Radio 1 and had heard the two brothers in full flow playing new Oasis tracks. He was impressed, recognising a great new rock'n'roll band on the block and probably pleased that the quiet boy that used to roadie (well hang around with) the Inspiral Carpets, Noel Gallagher, was getting a big head of steam on him.

Maybe recognising that the baton was finally being handed on from the Roses to the next generation, Brown was magnanimous as ever. Most musicians would have been bitter that they were being usurped by the new breed, but not Brown.

Spotting the Gallaghers, Brown shadow boxed towards the two bemused brothers. He'd got the Muhammad Ali moves down. He was looking lean and looking good. The Gallaghers, who were at the beautiful Monnow Valley studio down the road recording *Definitely Maybe* and had probably spent most of the session discussing what the fuck the Roses were up to at Rockfield two miles away, were secretly thrilled.

'You're the guys out of Oasis, aren't you? "Cigarettes And Alcohol", fucking hell. Great song,' Brown rasped, staring with his large brown eyes.

Noel Gallagher told the *NME*, 'We were recording our album in Monnow Valley studios and The Stone Roses were two miles up the road in Rockfield. There's this little village called Monmouth right, and although me and Liam know Mani – we've never met Ian Brown, he's never seen us, even.

'Anyway me and Liam went to the shops one day and Ian Brown bounces out of WH Smiths, shadow boxing like Muhammad Ali. He knew that we were Oasis and he knew that it was about time.'

Noel was asked about the Roses album and, in true Manchester style, was supportive. 'With any luck it will get them back to the way that it was. Where all them fuckers and pure chancers and all that junk food music will be gone and there'll be loads of real bands like The Kinks, the Stones, The Beatles, The Small Faces and the Roses and everyone will go, isn't it great to be alive.'

It was a dream that was coming true fast for Noel.

Brown shadow boxing in front of the Gallaghers on Monmouth High Street. It was a classic rock'n'roll moment, the past meets the future and it comes out fighting. It was the moment when Oasis assumed the mantle and the Roses took the back seat, the master and his pupils. This was the point where Oasis got on board and the Roses stood back helpless – bogged down in the courts and in the studio while the hard-working Gallaghers roared away.

The two bands finally met each other in Monmouth whilst they were both recording in the two studios near the town, as Ian Brown remembers: 'I met them when they were doing *Definitely Maybe* and I thought they were good lads. That was the first time I met Noel. I'd seen him around Manchester because I recognised his face but it was the first time I had met Liam. I had heard a lot about Oasis off Steve Adge. I knew that he had seen them early on at the Boardwalk and said they were going to be massive and he said, "They love you lot."'

Noel Gallagher continues: 'We knew they were in the next studio up the road from us. Remember this was before mobile phones. We were not like fanboys who would knock on the fucking door of the studio but Monmouth is a small place so we knew we would bump into them.

'The next time was when me and Bonehead met John; we were shit-faced and John is a quiet character at the best of times and was a bit freaked out because we were properly drunk and out of it. Then we went down to Rockfield to meet them and some of us went out scoring drugs in deepest Wales.

'When we got there I've got this memory of Mani walking between two of the rooms dressed in a monk's habit. Nobody said anything. He was holding a candle – a proper psychedelic cat. Mani said he did that to freak people out – and I've never met Reni properly to this day.'

Ian Brown has vivid memories of that first meeting.

'Liam came down the studio with a couple of his mates, and Tony McCarroll the drummer. By that time they were massive. I was buzzing for them. I remember when we were all watching *The Chart Show* on Saturday in the studio and they came on doing "Shakermaker" and John wasn't sure at first. I was saying, "I think they are great, they are from Manny, they got bowl haircuts and it says that they love the Roses." How could we knock anyone when in Liam's first-ever interview he said his favourite living people were his mum and Ian Brown? At least they acknowledged us, unlike Blur or Suede, who had the baggy pants and the bowl haircuts. None of them came and said they loved us, plus you always support lads from your own city and the north-west in general, don't you?'

'I thought it was really funny that we were supposed to be the masters and the kids who loved us had grafted it and robbed us when we were asleep.'

For Ian the great bands are part of an ongoing tradition.

'I think us and the Mondays benefited on a lot of the work that New Order and The Smiths had done, and they benefited on work Bunnymen had done, and alternative music was getting bigger and bigger. When we first signed to Silvertone and Zomba they wouldn't dream of getting in the charts and I was like, "We will," and the album went to number 19 and they were blown away that it got in the Top Twenty. We were told, "Don't expect it, you won't get on *Top of the Pops*." There was not even a budget for a video. I knew that we were fucking doing OK because we were getting a hundred in each town. It was alternative, which they called it before they called it indie. I always hated that term "indie". "Indie" is like anaemic. The Smiths had made the independent scene bigger and there was bands that wrote their own songs and dressed themselves, styled themselves, and that's what we were.'

Midnight tractor rides in the fields around Monmouth were reported in the *NME*. Constant name-drops in the press meant that the lineage between the two groups remained strong.

The Roses reconvened again at Rockfield for another two-week spell. There were a few loose ends to finish off. The album was nearing completion and they must have been getting pretty excited about the shape of it. It was a noticeable jump forward – it was, as some pundits promptly pointed out on eventual release, like listening to the third album and missing out the second one.

That May the *NME*, fed up with waiting for the album, sent out another crack team of reporters to look for the Roses. It was the fifth anniversary of the début and they just wanted to know what the fuck was happening.

The piece, by Stuart Baillie, was great. It added to the mystery of the band – various music biz figures who had heard the album attempted to describe it. All were frothing at the mouth. Matthew Priest, the Dodgy drummer, had had a sneak preview.

'They had a huge bag of grass that they were skinning up over an Aerosmith LP, so that gives you an idea of where they were at. The stuff that we heard doesn't have any vocals. It's like Led Zep but with a trancey vibe.'

It was at Rockfield that Priest came up with the King Monkey nickname for Ian Brown.

'We were finishing our session, they were starting theirs, and they had this massive big pile of grass on the table. They're like, "Fuckin' skin up, mate." Really friendly, asking us if we were all right. It was just great, and I was so in awe – in fact I was making a dick of myself, asking all the wrong questions and that, acting a bit mad because I just couldn't quite get my head round it, you know. With the grass and that it just sent me over the fucking edge and so I had to walk out because I just couldn't handle it. Then a couple of weeks later I get the phone call from a journalist, asking all about The Stone Roses so I just came out with it. I said that Ian Brown was refusing to answer to any name apart from King Monkey but it just went a bit daft, didn't it? To tell you the truth, the first feeling I did have when I saw the interview in the *Guardian* – where she had actually printed everything I'd said word for word – was, shit, the Roses are gonna be really angry with me. I'm a massive fan and essentially I was taking the piss, not out of them but out of the whole thing. I'm thinking, they'll be like, "Who's this fucking Dodgy kid saying all this monkey stuff?" [in a put-on Manc accent], so I'm worried about it. I didn't think they'd print it, word for word as well.

'Later I heard through the grapevine that they laughed and that they loved it. In the end I went to a Primal Scream gig at the Apollo in Manchester, and later, backstage, Mani comes in, bounding over [Manchester accent], "That fuckin' Dodgy geezer, fucking laughed our fuckin' socks off, mate," which was just great.

'Then, you know, Ian Brown went on and recorded his solo album, *Unfinished Monkey Business*. It was so strange because I was such a massive fan. They were my band and I loved them and just to add something like that, something I did, or said, that actually found its way

into the mix and changed or affected something with the Roses is just
bloody bizarre...'

One phrase kept coming up in all descriptions of the band at this time –
Led Zep. It seemed that the band and John Squire in particular had been
listening to a whole heap of Jimmy Page's Brit blues band of the early
seventies and it was affecting their sound.

Led Zeppelin were certainly an awesome outfit. Their funky old blues
riffs and knack for neat songwriting, combined with John Bonham's heavy
drums, had made them a classic band, especially in the States, where they
were one of the biggest bands of all time. The fact that the media hated
them and they were always music-business mavericks who could stand on
their own two feet must have appealed to the Roses, who at this stage
must have felt so far away from the music business that they were positive
outsiders to the whole circus.

After a fortnight they were off again. John left for the south of France
to go mountain biking, probably the best cure for the studio fog that must
be filling his head now. It had been a long, hard and weary battle but the
record was finally nearly made.

It was reported in the *NME* that Reni was recovering from a debilitat-
ing illness, though the nature of the disease was not disclosed.

Geffen, feeling bolshy, started talking up the album – dropping Led
Zeppelin references. Fans were now starting to wonder just what sort of
record was getting put together out there in Wales. They were expecting
another pop-stained opus and they were getting promised Zep – there was
a distinct unease among the fan base.

John Kennedy, the band's lawyer, was promising everybody that it
really would be a *Second Coming*. The record was already so talked up that
there was an air of excitement as the mythical figures prepared for a return
to the real world.

As the summer of '94 approached, the Roses were well and truly overtaken by Oasis. For many the waiting was over and the Manc megamouth
band had returned, only this time it was fronted by the Gallaghers and
not by Ian Brown.

With Noel's brilliant songwriting, no-bullshit interviews and Liam's
simplifying of the Ian Brown stagecraft, Oasis took the Roses' model and
created the biggest British pop phenomenon since The Beatles.

Oasis had well and truly stolen the Roses' thunder. The dithering about had meant that although expectations were still really high most people knew that the crown had been stolen by another outfit. Forget the *Second Coming*, the new gods were the Burnage boys, and the Roses were, at best, Moses or John The Baptist, the old prophets coming down from mountains with dark tales of pop wars past.

During the summer, Mani was backstage at the Glastonbury Festival taking handshakes and looking very confident, basking in the brilliant hot sun of one of those golden summer days that makes old Blighty one of the best places to be in the world. He didn't look like a man panicking as Oasis rocked the *NME* stage – their first truly big stage appearance that they took with ease. He claimed that the album was nearly finished and sang its praises.

Geffen, getting tired of moving the release back and getting a tad worried about their investment, sent Tom Zutaut over to Wales more and more to check the 'progress' of the record, while the band kept on talking to Peter Leake, desperately attempting to get him to take them on.

Tom Zutaut finally got to hear the unmixed album and he was blown away. The Roses were starting to feel more confident about what they had got on their hands. They invited their radio pluggers Beer Davies over. Gareth Davies and James Chappell-Gill made the trip.

It was a strange feeling for the radio pluggers. They would be the first people outside a tightly-knit circle not only to hear the record but actually see the Roses since they mooched off the stage at Glasgow Green four years ago!

While the pluggers were making their journey over to the studio, 'a desperate, bizarre incident took place' when two fans had decided to head down to Rockfield Studios to see what was going on. They arrived in Monmouth then headed up to the studios, which were just outside the town. They wandered up the drive and asked a mysterious-looking man hanging around at the end of the road in the night darkness if this was the Rockfield Studios that those Roses were recording at. 'Yeah' replied the gaunt figure, before telling them that the album was great as well.

Justin Hammond was one of the fans. 'We were shocked to see Ian Brown just wandering about. We thought that he would be really moody and pissed off that we had just turned up but he was really made up. He was wandering around with an acoustic guitar and a Bob Marley song-book. He had been sat around learning to play the guitar. He knew a couple of chords. He said he was going into the studio to put down "Redemption Song" (you can hear his plaintive version complete with a great vocal on one of the Roses bootlegs that does the rounds...recommended). He then asked if we wanted to hear the album.'

Brown seemed out of it, otherworldly. 'He was speaking really slowly. He was slagging the *NME* off for turning up and doing those pictures of them. We went into the studio and the engineer was sat there. He was just paid to sit there all day in case one of them turned up and wanted something. We asked Ian where John Squire was and he shrugged his shoulders and said, "Probably cycling somewhere." Mani was in the main house part of the place watching the World Cup and every time someone scored he would phone up the studio. Ian got the engineer to put the album on and we sat there listening to it. It sounded great. He asked us what we thought of the record and he seemed to be really made up that we liked the tracks. He was dancing around the room clicking his fingers. It was really weird, you wouldn't think that he cared what we thought of the record. He kept saying that the record was going to prove that the Roses were one of the best two bands in the world and my mate said like The Smiths and New Order. Ian Brown just stared at him and said, "No The Beatles and The Stone Roses," totally seriously.'

Justin remembers the weird vibe around the studio. The band were in the Coach House, a seventies-styled snug studio complex on the farm. The Roses had been there a long time, long enough to etch a drawing of the devil on the door of the studio.

'It was like he [Brown] didn't want to be there really. He seemed like he was missing his kid. It didn't seem like anyone wanted to be there. He was really cool to us, though, and he seemed really quiet and intense.'

Later on the Beer Davies pluggers arrived and Ian and Reni played the album back to them. James was completely blown away. The two Mancs sat there nodding their heads.

Gareth Davies was enthralled by what he heard: '[They] played a lot of the tracks, which sounded great, and [we were] blown away. There was plenty of press trying to get in and find out what was going on [the press didn't get in] but there was these two kids in there because they were Stone Roses fans who were camping nearby; they just turned up and were welcomed in.'

Not to be overtaken in the makeshift promo stakes, Steve from Novocaine was invited to the studio and sat there with various pluggers listening to the album and was blown away. For the Roses it was the record that they had been working on for years and like all bands they now had difficulty in hearing how good or bad the record was. It seemed that the snippets that they played out to people sounded awesome. As a record that stood on its own it was indeed a great album, but with all the attendant cultural baggage it was going to have to carry with it when it finally did come out, it had a big fight on its hands.

The Roses had dug in deep with the local band scene. Always affable, they easily got on with other bands. When they first came into Rockfield they hooked up with local outfit the Blood Brothers who then split into Dub War and 60ft Dolls, two of the most successful bands who came out of the nascent Newport scene. Newport itself, being a hotbed for hardcore and left-field noise bands, always boasted a great music scene and Rockfield being only twenty miles up the road was a perfect magnet.

Ian and Mani were telling all in earshot that the record had taken so long to finish because they wanted to make something perfect and that they were bursting to get out and play live as soon as possible. The Roses were getting ready to get back to business – quite possibly not realising that the pop scene had moved a million miles away from where they were last standing when the début came out. The times were meaner, the groups were more and more brutal and the summer of love had well and truly pissed off.

In October, with yet another year running out the Roses moved the whole operation to Metropolis Studios in Chiswick to get the album's final mix fine-tuned with Bill Price. The legendary fixer had salvaged The Clash's *Combat Rock* as well as producing the same band, the Sex Pistols, Mott the Hoople and Guns N' Roses. Perhaps one of the greatest rock 'n'roll producers in the world, Price was legendary in his ability to get life out of battered tapes.

The Roses' sessions were a mess, they just needed some level of continuity. They had been recorded in so many different locations, from a 16-track Fostex machine to a full-blown 48-track setup. Some tracks were recorded in the full-on studio environment while others were tarted up rough-and-ready demos ('Tightrope', recorded in the Rockfield TV lounge using just a stereo Neumann, being the obvious example). Price tidied up the record, cleaning up the army of guitars that Squire had laid down repairing the record, getting it ready for delivery. And by the spring of 1994 the record was just about ready.

The big question now was: was the world ready for The Stone Roses again?

The tapes were now finally finished and compiled and the Roses finally had their second album ready. It must have been a strange and empty day when the final tape was put into its box.

At last they had something to play to Geffen and the band flew to LA to play the company the tapes. They got an enthusiastic thumbs up. The album's rockier feel and more Led Zeppelin touches put it perfectly into the stream for some action in the United States, more so than the first album. The Stone Roses had got something that could really kick off in the USA.

The next appointment was with Hall Or Nothing, their British press people, to work out the promo campaign for the comeback. Typically they failed to show for the projected meeting, the lackadaisical air still hanging over the band.

There was, of course, a lot of interest in the record – the amount of time they had been away had built expectations up to fever pitch. The old warriors were back from the wars but the land that they once inhabited had changed drastically – they were going to have to jostle for position with the rest of the pack.

This, of course, is something that they were not prepared to do. So a careful battle plan was going to have to be thought up.

The band insisted on a late-November release date for the single with the album to follow in the difficult Christmas market. This was complete madness. Christmas is the time when the music business goes crazy and the Mr Blobby season starts. Foul old entertainers raking in as much cash as possible with schmaltzy vile songs. It's a dull and frustrating time of year for the rock freak and there is no space for a serious act like the Roses. They would be out competing with the old dossers that always clog up the Top Ten at that time of the year.

But this was *Second Coming*! Aptly titled for Christmas release, and feeling bolshy as ever the Roses decided to go for it. It was a bold and crazy gesture and one that could have cemented them into the mainstream if they had totally pulled it off.

'Finally the album was finished and we believed in it,' says Ian Brown. 'It had not been easy. I was disappointed in John at the time. It felt like he wanted to write songs on his own. He co-wrote the songs and he did the sleeves; I was quite happy for him to get on with that – the fans knew that.

'People don't know I wrote lyrics on the album. I would change all his negatives into positives, and there were loads of negatives which weren't me. I thought I would leave him to it with this album, let him get it out of his system, let him show he can write songs.

'I felt at the time, it's only an album. I can let that go now. I regret it because I was stood with someone who was not stood with me. Now I wish I hadn't done that but at the time I was prepared to give up my side, which was to come up with the words and vocal tunes. I was thinking we'd got another three LPs left in us.

'I wasn't a negative person. I don't want to make a dark album – his idea was the first album was all sunshine and colours so the second album will be dark. I'm thinking, I don't like dark music, I love reggae and Tamla Motown, uplifting music like hip-hop and punk rock – I don't like dark music. I don't feel dark as a person. I don't feel I have a dark side. I mean I might do but I don't want to find it!'

By now Geffen UK had taken Beer Davies off the radio and TV plugging account, a fatal mistake since the company had built the band's profile up from the start. Geffen had decided to plug the record in-house, losing the crucial personal touch of the affable pluggers.

Their first plan was to exaggerate the secrecy of its release, build up the crescendo of the buzz that already resounded off the record. The track that everyone in the music business was dying to hear and yet no one could.

They sent the 'Love Spreads' single down to Radio 1 in a security van, played it to them once and left. The exclusive play was on Steve Lamacq's show on Monday 7 November. It was a corny trick but then rock'n'roll always thrived on mythology.

I heard it for the first time later that day in a van hurtling across the moors at four in the morning, played on the Claire Sturgess show. Its dirty blues undercarriage and spooked ambience were perfect for the mist-swilled night high in the hills above Manchester. It was a classic Roses Old Testament anthem. It had Ian Brown, the spiritual soothsayer, stamped all over it, but it turned out later that John Squire wrote the words!

It sounded awesome.

Four years after 'One Love' there was finally some Stone Roses vinyl out. And it was a markedly different-sounding band that was finally returning from the wilderness years

'"Love Spreads" went straight in at two and there was a sense of excitement,' remembers Ian Brown. 'We had a big world tour. The agent got out a world map and said, "Here's a pin – where do you want to go?"

'I think we did twelve dates in Japan, seven or eight different cities, which was exciting because you would normally do [just] Tokyo. After three/four weeks in Japan we went to Australia. Some of the best shows were in America, away from the main cities where it was all pressing the flesh and meeting all the Artie Puffkins...outside that it was meeting all the retailers every single night, having a game of pool with the lads from the local HMV or whatever – that's how you get on in America and we were not the sort of people who would do that. We went to a couple of them things, it was nice to meet people, but we realised that's how you do it in America. [It's] not about how great your chorus sounded but how many hands you're going to shake.'

'Love Spreads'

Described by Primal Scream's Bobby Gillespie as 'The greatest comeback song ever', 'Love Spreads', released December 1994, was a swaggering avalanche of dark-hearted blues, a proud and bold slice of great rock'n'roll that blew away any conceptions about the band being a spent force.

It was also a brave move releasing that close to Christmas and holding back 'Ten Storey Love Song', the dead-cert number one for the second single. 'Love Spreads' still hit the charts at number two. There was also a lot of curiosity out there but 'Ten Storey' would have easily nailed the number one with its classic Roses pop ooze.

Still, that takes nothing away from this song and the Roses were pushing their audience's expectations of what this band was about.

Dig deep though and there are still some of the hallmarks of the classic Roses. The biblical-imagery lyrics. Ian's hoarse stoner-prophet vocal as débuted on 'Fool's Gold' all those years back and a powerhouse groove that only the Roses among their contemporaries could deal out. Oh and Mani deals a killer bass line in among that mountain of zig-zagging guitars.

When the song came out, everyone thought it had been penned by Brown, the lyrics were so much in his style (the lyrics by Squire ponder Jesus being a black woman, and in John Squire's words are about 'the hijacking of a religion'). The 'B' side of 'Love Spreads' featured 'Your Star Will Shine', 'Breakout' and on some versions an extra track, 'Groove Harder'.

The Squire artwork is a clean break from the past as well. The Pollock cut-ups are gone, replaced by a snap of a cherub's head from the bridge in Newport town centre.

'I took that,' says John Squire. 'I drove past it in Newport, went and bought a Polaroid camera and drove back to the bridge. The fag in its mouth [on the *Second Coming* cover] is what appealed to me.'

The cherub sat over a coat of arms would be the Roses' comeback logo. Fans were travelling from all over the world, having their picture taken beneath it. Some of the more light-fingered kept stealing the cherubs – the band paying for replacements. Just another chapter in the cherub's history!

The gold shield with the upright red chevron dated back to the sixteenth century. Originally it was the shield of the Duke of Buckingham who was the Lord of the Castle and the Borough of Newport. It was incorporated into the seal of the town.

When on 17 May 1521, almost 468 years before the release of the Roses début, the Duke of Buckingham was beheaded, his lands were handed over to the crown, the colours being symbolically reversed.

Some claim that the shield was inverted under orders from Queen Victoria after the Chartist uprising of 1839 when workers attacked the Queen's soldiers at the Westage hotel back in the days when the Welsh took no shit from the English.

The elders of Newport dispute this, explaining that the shield was reversed just to make it stand out from Buckingham's shield. The coat of arms though was not officially approved by the town until 1939.

The cherub that sits on top of the shield had no explanation apart from artistic licence; its origins were a full-blown mystery but for most people now the whole piece of artwork was the cover of the Roses début comeback single.

In 1957 they decided on something more significant to the town's history and stopped using the cherub and coat of arms for the insignia, not realising that nearly forty years later some damned pop group would make the whole thing history again.

So off the bridge went the cherub's head and into the pockets of eager fans seeking a small token of Roses-inspired artwork. This really pissed the locals off and surprisingly it didn't make the band too happy either.

Ian Brown, a man not always noted for his respect for local architecture, was quoted as saying. 'People should have more respect for architecture.' His tongue was probably rammed into his cheek with that one.

The Borough Council were a bit more forthcoming. 'They were stolen once before in the past. Then they were found dumped on the riverbank and put back in place. This time it would probably be a case of using the original moulds to replace them.'

The cherub itself had already been used on artwork when Frug Records, a Newport-based independent label, had put out a compilation using the supercilious motif. They weren't happy but there was very little a tiny label could do about it.

Never has a piece of artwork caused so many ridiculous problems. Squire must have sat back and wished that he had used the usual paint splashes.

'Love Spreads' is a classic slice of kick-ass dirty rock'n'roll and quite different from anything The Stone Roses had done before. It is low-down dirty and nasty, Ian Brown's voice sounds shot and weary – and it is perfect for the song. It's a great vocal, conveying a sinister world-weariness. The vocals' very understated nature is the perfect complement to the heaps of nasty guitars piled in there by John Squire.

It seemed that the Roses were well and truly back. They had got their own vibe, a new sound, a new attitude.

The single came accompanied by a video designed to add to the enigma: lo-fi Cine 8 footage of them fooling around in the studio. It was like the Roses themselves had disappeared and gone all fuzzy at the edges and they were slowly returning from the murk.

The pop nation craned their necks like mad just to see what the band looked like – had Ian Brown turned into Demis Roussos? Had Mani gone completely mad? The smudged images showed that they had hardly changed at all. Scarily time had stood still in the Roses camp. They still looked lean and hungry – it's a Dorian Gray situation – the world had moved on and they had remained in a time-zone where, physically, it is 1989 for ever.

But their music shows that a dark angel was casting its shadow over the band – there had been some black goings on in their lives – there had been relationship turmoils, drugs and death to deal with – each personal incident scouring the band's soul.

This was a band with a heavier and darker heart oozing through a commitment to the blues that still packed a powerful melodic brew. The single crashed in at number two. The aura was still there to power them to the top end of the charts.

Are You Ready for the *Second Coming*?

In late '94 with the album weeks away from release, Steve Adge went down to Rockfield to collect the last of the tapes that had piled up since the jamming sessions started. His ansaphone message was a small child shouting 'You'll Never Take Me Alive Copper.' The phone is inundated with requests. The mystery was over and the world wanted to grab a slice of the returning band.

Geffen were going to extraordinary lengths to keep the album secret, but it was leaking out in the most unlikely of places.

A Japanese magazine printed a track list and the artwork of the album. Typically the media was rife with rumours about what the album was like. The single had cranked expectations. It was a lot better than many people had feared. Everyone now knew that the album was called *Second Coming*. Some believed the Roses could just about pull this off.

On a grey afternoon in late autumn, they stumble out of the hotel across the road from the Cornerhouse in central Manchester, on the way to a photo shoot with Pennie Smith. It was the first time that the whole band had been spotted in public for years. I run smack bang into them in the street and do an impromptu semi-interview with the band that the *Melody Maker* run on the news page the following week. Heads turn as we chat as even after five years the Roses are still legends in Manchester. The band are affable, confident and despite many people noting that they no longer hang like a gang in the photo sessions the way they did years ago, they seem to be in jovial mood. Reni is particularly talkative and Ian Brown is as friendly and forthcoming as ever.

The wraps were off. *Second Coming* was ready.

Finally It's Here: The Second Coming That Came and Went

With 'Love Spreads' at number two, The Stone Roses' biggest ever hit, Geffen's campaign seemed to be working. Now, in mid-December, it was time for the album. They were putting so much front on the release that nothing less than a number one would do. The press campaign played up the enigma. It was decided to just do an interview in the *Big Issue* (the street magazine sold by people who had fallen into the poverty trap) and skip the normal media route. The pop press were appalled that Gary Crossing at the *Big Issue* got the big exclusive and the band's relationship with the press soured. Philip Hall had come up with the idea, one of the last ideas he had before his death. It was a brilliant move.

It kept the band out of reach and it made the *Big Issue* a fortune.

The music press, though, were very pissed off. The claws were out. The Roses were going to get a kicking.

And when the reviewers finally heard the album they were confused. This was definitely not the album that anyone was expecting. There was a very mixed bag of reviews.

So where do we all stand on *Second Coming* now? The long wait and the band's status as living legends for the nu-pop generation meant that this was a record that was never going to get a normal reception.

Some people expected manna of the gods, some people expected a great pop album like the début, some people were ready for the return of the Roses, some had their knives out, some couldn't care less.

Times had moved on. The band may have been at the centre of British pop in the late eighties but the whole new scene of bands that they had unwittingly kicked off had gone and got massive. Now the Roses seemed mortal, no longer the gods; they seemed like just another band.

The talk was of Britpop and it was no longer unusual to see UK guitar bands chew up the charts with their latest single or album. In fact things had moved on much more than that – Oasis were locked into a sales spiral that would leave them with the second best-selling album of all time. In their wake came a whole slew of bands making big money.

The Roses' return was a mixture of massively heightened expectations and muted disinterest. Into this vacuum would arrive an album that wasn't playing easy to get, with a marked move away from the pretty pop and dark-heart melodies of the début. This time there was a collection of songs that were not instantly accessible melodically and were far heavier than those on *The Stone Roses*.

Even the sleeve was different. It was darker, meaner, harder to make out, murkier and hinting at something more menacing than the pop strokes of the first album. Says John, 'It wasn't supposed to be that dark, that was a mistake. I got a little carried away with the paint, I got distracted – I put it on, went for a piss and it had dried. I was hoping to wipe it off a lot more than I managed to. It was a nightmare, it took ages to make. I made the material by sewing rectangles together. I was going to make a shirt, but I got bored and dumped it. Recycled it by dipping it in wood glue and draping it over a board.'

Nothing seemed to be easy!

Christ, even the band's photos snapped in Manchester's Chinatown by legendary lenswoman Pennie Smith (whose collection of shots of The Clash ranks as the finest collection of shots of a rock'n'roll band ever) showed a group looking more pensive and less surly than the late-eighties shots, not looking that comfortable in each other's company. It was almost like they had forgotten how to pose as a gang.

Had they forgotten how to make records?

Second Coming

Give the album another listen, kid! Sure there are weak spots but there is some great rock'n'roll on this record.

Second Coming kicks off with a swathe of vicious feedback before segueing into a tape of the River Monnow, the cold Welsh river water sluicing down the mountain on its way to the Bristol Channel, captured by Ian Brown on a portable DAT player. Shades of the *Apocalypse Now* soundtrack, especially as in the background there are swathes of dark feedback. Also slashes of the FX-laden guitar noise that used to punctuate the Roses' songs way back.

The track fuses gently into Reni's drum pattern, a tribal workout that sounds almost like Fleetwood Mac's 'Tusk'. Squire kicks in and we're finally off into the album's début track, 'Breaking Into Heaven', and we are into classic-rock country. There are shades of Jimmy Page and the whole album has the much mooted Led Zep stamp on it. There are several layers of guitar – most of them forwards and some of them sliding in backwards, joining the occasional backwards snares that slurp in and out of the sound collage.

Clocking in at 11 minutes it was to be the Roses' longest-ever song.

The track was one of several jammed versions of the song. 'Breakout', the flipside of 'Love Spreads', was yet another version of the tune. The jam sessions were one of the keys to the album, as eventual producer Simon Dawson told the *Melody Maker*. At least it gave a chance for the rest of the band to feel involved!

'We spent a lot of time getting the backing tracks feeling good. They'd go in and just jam it for maybe a few days. They'd sort of play it all afternoon and maybe get bored with it and play something else and come back to the first song later with a slightly different feel. They just like playing together as a band, so that's what they wanted to try and capture. If you want to make an album that sounds live, it's as simple as that. They did spend a lot of time jamming in the studio, and a lot of different feels came out of that.'

Brown sings with a strong, nasal northern accent. It's a million miles away from the American blues tradition and puts a northern stamp all over the track. His voice is husky and rough. It sounds like a man dragged out of bed; it suits the deadly poison of the song. Reni's backing vocals on the chorus are great. It would be more than the drums that he was finally missed for.

About eight minutes into the song there is a great chord change and the song shifts a gear. 'How many times do I have to tell you that you don't have to wait to die?' Brown intones as the song builds towards a climax.

It's a fucking great song, a long way from the three-minute pop most people were waiting for but exactly where the Roses should be ten years down the line.

There is no play safe here. Most bands put on a punchy radio tune to get things going. From the off, though, you can tell that this is Squire's record. There are heaps of guitars on here, great licks, Zep guitar squalls, adept, artsy, clever rock'n'roll.

It's guitar heaven! There are piles of them dominating the band's sound, layers and layers of guitar sounds much like the way Jimmy Page piled up the six strings in his days with the Zep. His '59 Les Paul cranked through a hotwired Fender Twin. It's unfair to say that the guitars ruined the record; on tracks like this Squire's work is awesome.

Mani's Rickenbacker bass is deeper than ever before – an almost bowel-shaking tone – if only it was higher in the mix you could then fully appreciate its Jah Wobble sound that dominated Public Image's finest moments.

The album is that combination of hard rock and English folksiness that Zeppelin mastered; it's music that slots into US rock. Except that the Roses had maintained some sort of edge, a smattering of Manchester city toughness that stopped their music tipping over into rawk boredom.

Maybe this was down to Ian Brown's voice. When he finally kicks in five minutes into 'Breaking Into Heaven' he still sounds like classic Brown. Of course he 'sure can't sing', but somehow he makes his voice work with the music. It's all attitude, flat vowels, northern accent bending the US-styled rock'n'roll back to the UK and that's just the verse!

When they kick into the chorus it still has that effortless rush of all the classic Roses' choruses, especially with Reni's backing vocals.

Brown's vocals are one of the key points of the album. Sometimes sounding listless and bored and sometimes displaying a curiously emotional cracked intensity, he sounds like a man at the end of his tether and remarkably squeezes some sort of emotion in a menacing and laid-back manner out of John Squire's words.

Squire wrote nearly everything on *Second Coming*, whereas on the Roses' début the lyric-writing had been a shared thing. Ian: 'We shared writing the lyrics. "Adored" is all me, "She Bangs The Drums" is half and half, I did the verses, he did the chorus, "Waterfall" – John did most lyrics on "Waterfall", "Don't Stop" is about fifty–fifty, "Badman" about fifty–fifty, "Elizabeth My Dear" I wrote, "Made of Stone" I wrote 90 per cent, "Shoot You Down" we both wrote, "This Is The One" I wrote, "Resurrection" I wrote. So John wrote some of the lyrics, yeah. But we both wrote melodies, and the melodies and the music were made at the same time.'

It's never easy singing someone else's lyrics. Brown, when pressed on this, said that 'He was constantly writing really good stuff so there was no point in me doing anything.'

The lyrics miss the début album's homespun philosophy, dark jokes and revolutionary anger which are mixed into what are perceived as love songs.

Brown sounds all at once uninterested, dispassionate, mean and lovelorn; all this with a voice that barely rises above a hoarse whisper.

'Driving South' is twelve-bar Zep boogie driving on a mean riff.

Again the guitars totally dominate. It's as close to Zeppelin as they get, like 'Immigrant Song' crossed with 'Whole Lotta Love'; a twelve-bar boogie and the bass end is reduced to a massive mush in the battle for attention. A lot of Roses fans skip this track, the band having wandered a long way from what they love about them, but the song does have a certain kick-ass charm about it and Reni's rolling drumbeat is classic Roses.

Already the difference between the two albums is becoming apparent – on the début maybe the Roses played as a team, as a sum of their parts but now they are all plying their separate paths, all chasing those heaps of Squire guitars.

Not that Reni is panicking. His drums are effortlessly brilliant through-out, deceptively simple skip beats and great timings. This guy is a constant, totally amazing. He never even changed the skins on his kit and was still using the same drum kit from the first album. Reni was not averse to messing around with his rhythms. As Simon Dawson remembers.

'Reni is well into taking bits of something, sticking it into a sampler and re-triggering it and see what comes out, getting a groove from that. We'd go down that line for weeks sometimes.'

And just when it seems the Roses had fucked off in a totally different direction, one of the best songs they ever wrote kicks in. After 60 seconds of guitar noodle, 'Ten Storey Love Song' sounds like it is tagged on to the end of a studio jam – all drums and guitars attempting to find the song before the song itself slopes in.

And when it comes in it sends the heart soaring. Heaps of melody pile up; each change in the song is yet another great tune heaped up all the way to the stunning chorus. This is 'Made of Stone' taken up another level, it's the effortless pop Roses of old, the spiritually affirming rush that they were almost unwittingly adept at. 'Ten Storey Love Song' is the album's link to the old days, melodically and lyrically.

Brown's vocal on this is great. One of the key points of the track, all cracked and broken. It's sound is one part the fallen choirboy of old and a worn-out old soul. Squire's guitar is a simple chime and nails the melody down. Suddenly it feels like the first two tracks make sense as teasers build-ing towards this, one of the great crystalline moments of the Roses' career and one of the best songs that they ever wrote.

'Ten Storey Love Song' segues straight into 'Daybreak' which again moves along with great fractured drums. At first the song sounds disjointed, unfinished…but, fuck, it gets under your skin, it sounds like hot players really jamming good. Reni's drums are loose-limbed, you can hear the fuckers as well! His snare work is brilliant, chasing the beat all over the room; locking with that insistent bass, the guitar either hooks the funky riff or slashes all over the tune and when the Hammond crashes in at the end it sounds low down and dirty. The song also features some of the best lyrics on the album (Ian Brown back on lyric duties sees a shift from the rock mythology back to the political), being a homage to Rosa Lee Parks who refused to give up her seat on a bus in Montgomery, Alabama, to a white passenger, in the days of racial segregation – a brave move. This in turn inspired Martin Luther King to initiate the bus boycott, making Rosa Parks the 'daybreak' of the civil rights movement.

'Your Star Will Shine', already released on the 'B' side of 'Love Spreads', is a short acoustic tune that Squire wrote about missing his daughter growing up. 'Your Star Will Shine' is an acoustic workout with the added spice of the line about the bullet being aimed 'right between your daddy's eyes'.

For many fans the album's low point is Brown's one and only track, 'Straight To The Man'. But listen again. Its eccentricity, its mooching groove and its oddness give it a charm of its own. Armed with an easy shuffling groove, neat slide guitar and odd bounce, it has a sleazy swagger – a swagger that Shaun Ryder would capture with Black Grape's début months later. The Jew's harp in the track gives it an almost redneck biblical-preacher man feel.

The lyrics deal out a sharp rebuke against British colonialism – or they seem to, you can never tell with Brown whose words are sometimes left deliberately open-ended and vague.

'Begging You' sees the Roses finally cut a track that could be perceived as indie/dance. Its disturbed helter-skelter pile-driving nature is perfect for remixing and when it finally came out as a single months later it was reworked several times. The Roses worked with a lot of loops and samples, sometimes running the loops through monitors and jamming along to them building up whole new tracks.

The mood is completely switched with 'Begging You', the Roses' out and out distorted breakbeat monster that rides in on a massive groove and is complete with distorted vocals. One of the last songs that Ian and John actually wrote together, 'Begging You' is another suggested new direction for the band and was an attempt by John Squire to capture the dense dark feel that Public Image so brilliantly captured on their stunning albums.

'Tightrope's gentle almost English-folk acoustic guitar workout and plaintive heartfelt lyrical imagery makes it one of the fans' favourite tracks on the album. You can hear the band hunched around the one mic in the TV room in Rockfield, a campfire singalong!

After this the Roses switch deep into Led Zep territory; there have been hints, even close skirmishes, with the misty mountain hop of prime-time Zep throughout the album and now they really cut loose and enter the mystical world of Zeppelin. Like most of the punk generation they initially had a fear of the Zep, but by now most of the band were deep into the mythology and music that Jimmy Page was giving out in the mid-seventies (apart from Brown who you can almost see shaking his head sadly at this madness!).

'Good Times' and 'Tears' are side two's excursions into the classic Brit-rock fused with Peter Green Brit blues. 'Tears' is mid-seventies long hair; you can hear the acoustic arpeggios of 'Stairway To Heaven' dripping through the tune. The song is bolstered by Ian really pushing his voice, really singing out, a long way from the scowling prophet he naturally favours. The two songs sum up the cul-de-sac that the Roses were jamming themselves into. Of course the musicianship is awesome – it just doesn't suit them.

The two songs are so sprawling, so untypical that you almost completely miss the classic pop shakes of 'How Do You Sleep', a neat and concise return to their début-album brisk pop. The great forgotten song of the album, 'Sleep' would sit easily on the 'Lemon' album, with its brisk near-jazzy chords, sugar melodies and dark sinister lyrics from John. It's classic Roses, sweet tunes and dark haunting lyrics clashing…great chord change into the chorus as well – oh and a beautiful solo on the song's outro.

The album ends with the mystical magic of the first single culled from it. 'Love Spreads' is the zig-zag wanderer, a dirty-assed blues howl and another of the Roses' total classics and is as good as anything they ever wrote. It storms in, cutting through the acoustic mid-seventies mush much in the same way that punk did in the Roses' far-off youth.

Brown was buzzing when John Squire gave him the lyrics to 'Love Spreads'. A critical song dealing in religious imagery, as 'I Am The Resurrection' had on the first album, 'Love Spreads' contemplated the idea that Jesus should have been a black woman. A powerful idea, a twist on the patriarchal imagery of the church.

And that was it, unless you left the CD running for about ten minutes till it hit track 64, 'The Fox', when you were treated to the Roses dossing around with violins and a plinky plonk piano for a very drunken-sounding exit.

And that's it – *Second Coming* all boxed up and ready to go.

Five years of work and now it was time for release…

December 1994: *Second Coming* – What the World Is Waiting For?

When Steve Lamacq played 'Love Spreads' for the first time that November on Radio 1, the UK pop scene was singing to a very different tune than the last time the Roses had wandered the earth. The ball that they had started rolling in 1989 had really rolled. Big time! Now the charts were full of guitar bands, there was the tail end of baggy, there was Britpop, and there was Oasis – the Gallagher brothers had picked up that baton and really run with it. They were now the biggest British group since The Beatles. It was as if all Ian Brown's big talk had come to life!

The Roses were still a big deal – their legend had grown in their absence – but they were no longer the leaders. They were the prodigal sons making a return. But where would they now fit in?

And there was the interview in the *Big Issue*.

This was different. The Roses hadn't been interviewed since 1990. There had been attempts to track them down but they had managed to avoid the press for years. They had spent the nineties hogging the news pages of the rock press and now with the album ready to go it was firmly expected that they would do the usual round of press. Talk to the *NME* or *The Face* and then to *Melody Maker* before moving on to other papers – it's a well-worn road, a system to build up the hype on a band.

Nope.

The Stone Roses being stubborn old sods decided to do a Big Issue interview first. Uh?

No one did interviews with the *Big Issue* unless they were a couple of months into their 'promotional campaign'.

But in this case, people were so fascinated to find out where the band was at that they bought thousands of the magazines; it was the *Big Issue's* best-selling copy ever.

They did the interview on 21 November. The Roses, of course, were giving nothing away. So some things hadn't changed. The *Big Issue* had its biggest ever selling issue, money for the poor! Punk rock! The Clash would have been proud!

But this interview, combined with the record's endless delays and the atmosphere of secrecy around the album, only served to set the band up for a rough ride in the papers. In the weeks before Christmas *Second Coming* came in for some pretty damning reviews. The band were shellshocked.

Says Ian Brown, 'We were really surprised with the reaction to the album, we thought it a great record,' he sniffed.

It had come out to some very mixed reviews – the *NME* scratched their heads, Everett True typically went against the grain and gave the album a great review in *Melody Maker* (he also managed to capture just what made the album work). No one was very sure about it.

Under the headline 'Wonky', Danny Kelly gave it two stars in Q, adding 'the *Second Coming* is just OK, which is a disappointment', reminding readers of just how great the first album was and of how far the band had wandered into a mid-seventies mushy pop rock.

The *Big Issue* interview had done them a lot of damage. The mainstream rock press was severely pissed off that it had lost the exclusive piece on what it considered to be its band.

In media terms *Second Coming* was a brag too far and the Roses were getting a kicking – they were too far gone, too Led Zep (what is this paranoia about Zep, a fantastic band?) and more importantly…too late!

Out on the streets, of course, things were very different.

The single had crashed into the charts at number two and no one was complaining about the quality of that record. The fan base were hungry for The Stone Roses and excitement was building for the album.

And at last, after all the wait, all the hype and all the bullshit…*Second Coming* was to be released on 5 December, the worst time of the year for a rock band. From the off it would be battling with all the Christmas crackers. No time for a serious record.

On the night before the album release the city centre of Manchester was buzzing. Sunday night, at midnight, the stores opened as a neat promo stunt. I went down with Ian Tilton and we interviewed freezing kids patiently queued up in the streets. At midnight the store opened and the fans filed in to buy the album. In the background the record played on a continuous tape loop and the kids craned to hear what was going on there. If they were waiting for a series of straight pop anthems when they got home they were going to be sorely disappointed. The great *Second Coming* debate was about to kick off around the city's bedsits!

Virgin and HMV had queues of kids going round the block, seeking some pop magic. As an exercise it was highly successful; the record was soon to be number one in the midweek chart. The buzz was selling the Roses. By the weekend, though, the Christmas malaise combined with confusion over the music that was actually on the record was pushing it back down the charts. Charts which, that weekend, had the album listed at number four. Not bad for a normal band but not exactly the *Second Coming*!

In the weeks that followed, the truth kicked in. Despite being a big-selling record, its chart positions of 4, 14, 21, 14, 14, 13 and 19 were telling their own story – that even though it was charting higher than the début, the public was confused by the Roses' comeback.

It was a *Second Coming* that didn't really come.

1995

Countdown to Tour: January

1995 and now what?

Time to tour!

But how? How do you go back on the road when the last full-on tour you did was in 1989? And you've built your reputation on doing off-the-wall shows, unusual shows? In January there was talk of a series of low-key gigs that were announced only on the day of the gig on local radio. Keep it secret. Get a buzz. A touch of the warehouse gigs. Perhaps Steve Adge had come up with the plan. Still in the frame, Steve had pretty well become the Roses' manager. The Adge was holding the fort; he was quite capable of managing the band but to hook into the American market they were going to have to get some big shot in.

So just how do you go back on the road when you were the band that didn't do normal tours? The Roses had spent 1989 breaking the big audience with a run of imaginative secret gigs, or a Glastonbury headliner. Michael Eavis had asked the band if they wanted to headline the Saturday night. They seemed keen. It would be a triumphant return to the big stage. A perfect way to reinstate that damn myth!

In mid-January they went down to London to mix the 'B' sides to the next single to be pulled off the album. The talk was of it being 'Ten Storey Love Song', an obvious choice. From there they flew straight out to the States to do the pre-promotion on the *Second Coming* which was due for release over there on 16 January – the album had done 300,000 in the UK and there were high expectations that the rocked-up Roses may just be ready for America.

In an interview towards the end of the month Reni admitted, 'Personally I'm sick of underachieving.' It was an ominous remark that meant little at the time but a few months later would be put into a far firmer context. The managerial problem was seemingly closer to getting resolved with the latest unlikely addition to The Stone Roses' canon.

Doug Goldstein had cut his teeth managing since 1988, Guns N' Roses, the US metal band whose singer Axl Rose was legendary for his tantrums and keen adherence to the rock'n'roll lifestyle. Very much a US industry man, Goldstein seemed a bizarre choice as manager for the maverick Roses, but with the band getting very keen on breaking into the US, a scene that had been notoriously difficult for UK bands to break into for several years, heavyweight help was required.

The Roses were not exactly going out of their way to creep to managers. Their whole attitude to the affair was almost jocular. They had faxed Ed Bicknall, the manager of Dire Straits, with the simple and blunt message: 'The Stone Roses are auditioning managers.' He wasn't impressed!

Goldstein flew into Manchester and booked into the Charterhouse Hotel and rang up Steve Adge. It was an audacious move but it got the band interested. They went down to the hotel and hit it off with the US big shot.

A spokesman for the Roses concluded: 'The Roses didn't just want a manager, they wanted someone who could make them laugh – and Doug Goldstein does that.'

Goldstein was duly appointed but it was going to be a short and rocky ride.

February

The Roses went on a radio tour of the US to flog the album that was starting to open a few doors for the band Stateside (in its first week it was number forty-seven, selling 21,953).

At the time, before Oasis really went in there and mopped up (seven tours in two years; the Gallaghers were serious about doing good business in the States) the Roses were considered to be the spearhead of a new British band insurgence into the States. They were the first of that generation of guitar bands to break into the US top fifty.

The Americans, since the New Romantic wave of the early eighties, had been gradually getting more and more bored with British bands. The US market, dominated by hard-touring MTV-friendly outfits, found very little space for UK acts and their whingey ideas of cool. It made no sense translated across the Atlantic. In America it was all big gestures and back-slapping. The Stone Roses, obviously, would have no part in this charade but with the might of Geffen behind them they were beginning to make tiny inroads into the vast US pop scene.

America is the big one. It's the pot of gold, the biggest record market in the world – and it is also the most influential. A big success there has a huge knock on effect across the whole globe. Post grunge though, it had been looking more and more inwards, promoting its own bands. Maybe it was a sign of the times, a part of the slow US withdrawal from the world stage, or maybe it was part of the xenophobia that was going on all over the world. A xenophobia that was witnessed back home with the rise of such stupid notions as 'Britpop'…the new nationalism, it was getting scary.

The fact that there hadn't been any big British bands since The Cure, Flock Of Seagulls and Depeche Mode may, on one level, be self-explanatory, but it was getting to be a worrying vacuum.

On the January promo tour of the US Ian Brown stirred up a piece of Lydonesque controversy. On a Los Angeles radio station he urged the American army to stop killing babies, and hundreds of listeners jammed the phone lines complaining about Brown's comments. It was the sort of talk that could get a man into deep trouble among the more gung-ho sections of the US community.

America was there for the taking. The fact that the Roses would piss it all away is a mere footnote in history. They could have had it. They could have toured like fuck, put out the third album and watched it do Top Ten business but they seemed to lose total interest.

Eventually it would be Oasis, Bush and then The Chemical Brothers and The Prodigy that would mop up, the latter two being a brilliant example of what British pop was really about in the late nineties.

The Roses also claimed in another US radio interview that British bands were 'cry babies' because they couldn't break the States, adding 'a lot of bands expect to be heroes there – they play ten dates and go home and expect to be heroes. The only reason a British band hasn't cracked it is because there hasn't been any great ones recently.'

While 'Love Spreads' was chosen as the theme tune for a German quiz show, Albanian state TV were also using the track as opening music for a sports programme! It was announced that the second single from the album, 'Ten Storey Love Song', was due for release on 27 February.

In mid-February the band filmed the video for the single in London. At the same time Gareth Evans was re-emerging with his name being linked to The Ya Yas – an Oldham guitar band who had been on the local circuit for a long time without making much of an impact (they would re-surface in 2000 as the excellent Morning Star).

Gareth was reported as saying of the Ya Yas in the *Manchester Evening News*, 'I've had loads of tapes and offers but until I heard The Ya Yas I just haven't been interested. But I've got the buzz again. These guys can happen. They are more wholesome than the Roses. They actually like people. They smile.' But then that was the whole appeal of the Roses in the first place.

Evans, now forty-five, had been annoyed by his departure from the band. After being a major player in the rise of the band, his bolshy attitude, ability to talk things up and that belief in them had done them no harm in their swift rise to the top. It was Evans who had given away stacks of tickets at those early International gigs that had started to build up their following; his vision with the special big shows had been coupled with the band's talent and self-belief – and that heady mixture that had built them up fast in the late eighties.

The management deal that he struck with the band, though, was the bone of contention.

According to an *Observer* article written by Jay Rayner it was a complex situation: 'Evans claimed that the Roses and John Squire in particular insisted that all earnings must be divided equally. When the money did start coming in, Evans says the deal reverted by mutual agreement to the standard management cut of 20 per cent, a claim which will be argued over in court in March.'

Evans was talking about his contribution to the whole caboodle in the same piece. 'What I gave them was their mystique. I told them look at other bands, when they came off stage, they mix with their fans. You shouldn't do that.'

He also claimed in the same piece that his vision was long term, that the whole process was slowly building up towards something. 'Everything that we had done up to that point, the free T-shirts, the free tickets, the big gigs, all of that was aimed at the US. We put in over a hundred grand from the money that we made at the International club and took nothing back in manager's commission.'

It was more stuff to be argued about in court.

In the US the Roses video for 'Love Spreads' was rejected by MTV because it was claimed that it was of 'poor quality'. They promptly reshot the video with Steve Hanft, whom Beck had used for his 'Loser' video.

Speaking to the *Los Angeles Times* John Squire came clean about his cocaine use. 'I made this mistake of using cocaine for a while, thinking that it would make me more productive, but it made me unsure, more paranoid. For one thing it gives you endurance. A lot of what I do comes from spending time on guitar...just getting locked into a private world and turning things around, and something will grow from that.'

In the same article Squire claimed that the band eventually pulled back from the drugs that stopped them working, although in post-Roses interviews he claimed that drugs were one of the main reasons for splitting up.

So much crap is talked about drugs but nowhere near as much crap as is talked while actually on cocaine.

Cocaine hinders creativity and produces banal work which is bolstered by the feeble self-confidence and big-mouthed arrogance that the band produces.

Insiders to the Roses camp claim that one of the problems with the five-year hiatus is that 'all four members of the band were on different drugs all at once'.

Phil Smith: 'Nothing has ever been said about it since. They're a quiet bunch...things have been alluded to but you'd have to ask them. They were all doing different drugs at different times. Ian was Emperor Haile Selassie. They stopped talking but they'd never had an argument. Oasis used to split up before they'd even been in a band. It was always easy to come back from a fight. But the Roses never had a cross word, they were so tight the four of them, and once one fell out with another there was no structure in place. They just seemed to carry on not talking.

'On that last tour, we had a fucking great time, the crew...In the end, with a band, if you're not enjoying it, you don't have to do it, do you? Nobody's making you do it. It wasn't like it was. It was easy to compare it, as crew, with how it used to be, because they disappeared for three years even from us. Nobody had seen them as a unit. And obviously they weren't a unit.'

No wonder communication was difficult. You would have thought that a band as fantastically talented as this would have got the rush from just jamming – getting that amazing feeling of power that playing together at the height of your powers produces.

Squire, though, was under a lot of pressure to produce something special with *Second Coming*. Expectations were ridiculously high. When asked about the stress in the *LA Times* he replied, 'I certainly felt it. But we weren't sitting in the studio asking ourselves what the critics are thinking, or even what the fans are thinking. I wasn't caught up in thinking of us as the saviours of UK rock'n'roll or worried about too much time going by.

'The pressure was more of a result of wondering if you could live up to your own standards. I think every time you sit down and write, you worry that the last song you wrote was the last one.'

This is the constant fear of the artist. That they have captured the moment, that they have burned out, dried up, that there is nothing left to give. Some people try and fill this void or try to grab the moment again with drugs. It's a very easy trap to fall into and Squire was ensnared for a while.

The mooted small-club tour was announced and then a few days later cancelled because John Squire had pneumonia. Yet more frustration!

They did another round of press to promote the upcoming 'Ten Storey Love Song' single but this time there were only three of them doing the interviews. No Reni.

'Ten Storey Love Song'

At the end of February they finally got round to doing what most people figured they should have done in the first place and released 'Ten Storey Love Song' as a single. It was the obvious classic on the album and the track that melted most fans' hearts. Flipped with the Zep fused instrumental 'Moses' and the plum-stir crazy 'Ride On', it would just miss the Top Ten. Two months previously it would have been a number one. Most people now had bought the album, scuppering the single's chances of the big one.

'Moses' was smoking slowed-down trip-hop groove written by the band. Recorded that January it was to be the last thing all four of them recorded together in the studio. Some fans claim that they can hear a slowed-down 'Breaking Into Heaven' in the song but I haven't picked this out yet.

'Ride On' was also put down at the same sessions and again is another trip-hop mooch, perhaps a vague attempt at a new direction from the band in the form of an experimental 'B' side. This time it came complete with a vocal from Brown who was deep into some sort of preacher man mysticism and weird Dylanesque imagery. With the songwriting credit going to Brown/Squire, it was the last time the classic team would work together.

Squire's riff out of the song has been around: it started off in the sessions for 'Daybreak' and ended up on Brown's solo album, having been copped by Aziz Ibrahim for the Squire-slating 'Can't See Me'!

Bagged in the least Roses-like artwork from Squire so far ('It was 24 Michelangelo's Davids that I saw in an Oxfam shop in Stretford. I shot them up with an air pistol') the single peaked at number 11 that spring. It would have been number one if it had come out before Christmas.

Countdown To Tour: March

On 10 March 1995, with the Gareth Evans case against the Roses about to kick off at the high court in the Strand in London, Gareth received a fax from the band. They wanted to settle out of court and for a large sum of money. Gareth did just that, although the settlement was nowhere near the ten million pound mark that had been floating around the press.

Late March and there was talk of another set of small-club dates in the UK. At last the band were back on the road!

They announced a gig at Liverpool State Ballroom on 6 April. It was to be their first UK date in five years. They were also to play five gigs in mid-April, before going to Europe and Japan. The small date comeback tour of the likes of Blackwood (Manics country!), Liverpool and Ipswich was postponed and eventually blown out yet again. The leaked dates had caused too much advance publicity in the press. The secret gigs were no longer secret! The band who had been in extensive rehearsals in Manchester were frustrated yet again.

None was more frustrated than their drummer.

Reni Has Left the Building!

Looking back now you can see the cracks. The Roses drummer wasn't happy. As had always been suspected Reni was more than 'just the drummer'. Here was someone who was a great singer, a really good guitar player and had even been writing his own tunes. That February on the American radio interview tour he had hinted at his dissatisfaction and his own personal creativity.

'I've written my own stuff, my problem is finishing it. The last few years I've been learning the guitar; I'm a very basic strummer but I just can't help writing songs. In fact my drumming suffered 'cause I was always working on songs on my four-track at home. I've got a keyboard and a guitar and you can play those at home whereas you can't play drums – at least not where I live 'cause it would annoy the neighbours. I've been working on some Gang Starr loops that I've put stuff over that sound great. I could develop those ideas. If it takes us this long to record another album I'll have my solo LP out first.'

At the time no one thought much of this. Reni was hardly going to quit the Roses! This was the gang! The tightest ship in rock'n'roll. But that was from the outside. On the inside of the camp the unity had gone. The gang had fizzled out. Everyone had outgrown everyone else partly due to the use of different drugs at different times. Lob into this equation kids, mortgages, houses in different towns and what you have is the real world creeping in.

And then add on to that the fact that the Roses were turning into the John Squire Experience! Reni felt edged out. It had been bad enough years ago when the Brown/Squire songwriting credit was slapped on the songs. After all he was no average drummer – fuck, he was the first reason anyone really loved this band. 'Go and see the Roses, their drummer is amazing' is what people used to say. And now in the eternal twilight of the *Second Coming* sessions he would sit there jamming with Mani. John had his own agenda, he was talented and he was running the show, but that didn't make Reni's life any easier.

And then there was the stop/start shambles of the last few months. It seemed like an eternal state of limbo as the Roses attempted to resurrect their legend and everything seemed to conspire against it.

Ian Brown remembers: 'Reni didn't turn up for the interview with the *Big Issue*, which was our first interview when we came back…Six homeless people in Islington [got] homes off the money we raised, which was a positive thing for us, to use our position to help people. The next day we met an agent for an interview and he didn't turn up for that either. The next day we had a video and he didn't turn up for that either, then we had a cover shoot for the *NME* and he didn't turn up for that either. The writing was on the wall. 'In the meantime we had this guy, Doug Goldstein [manager of Guns N' Roses], holed up in the Midland hotel in Manchester waiting to meet. He left this message: he's not leaving town till he's met [us] and we said, "Fucking let him stay there."

'[Eventually] we went to meet him and...he was a lovely fellow, actually, but we didn't take him on in the end. And Reni didn't turn up for that as well, and Doug Goldstein said, "Look, I'm your perfect manager because what you got in your band, I've already been through." He knew exactly what he was talking about, he had worked with Guns N' Roses, and I thought, "You're a sharp fucker"...He said, "All the problems you got in your band, I can help you with. Believe me, it's nothing to me, this."

The situation with Reni was becoming untenable. There was a flash point between him and Ian.

'We had a bit of a barney and he said to me, "Right, get yourself another drummer," so I did. I heard that Robbie Maddix was a good drummer so I phoned him up and that was it.'

The situation hadn't sunk in at first. Twenty-four hours later Reni phoned up about coming down to rehearse so Ian had to tell him that he was serious and that he wasn't in the band any more.

'It was sad but we couldn't be waiting on the kid. He was getting up at eight o'clock every night. He wasn't turning up to all the important things. We can't spend our lives waiting on him. We was all 31, 32. We couldn't spend our lives waiting on someone [so] we got Robbie in and Reni never made that tour. His last gig was Glasgow Green.'

John Squire is on record as saying he now had to choose between the singer and the drummer to do the upcoming UK tour. Since this was no normal band, this was a tough choice.

On 5 April it was announced on the Jo Whiley show that Reni had quit. It came as a massive shock. The dream was over. How could they even think about carrying on without Reni, the hat boy with the fantastic drum barrage! But he was gone and the Roses were planning to continue. Since those 'B' sides they recorded in January and that American promo tour Reni had in effect quit – they had done photo sessions and interviews without him; fuck, even the video for 'Ten Storey Love Song' had a roadie with a mask on pretending to be Reni. He simply wasn't turning up any more. For that week Reni appeared all over town, uncharacteristically bouncing round bars, celebrating, the burden off his back. The negativity and cynicism of the Roses was gone. There was some life to be lived.

On 14 April Reni broke his silence about the split. 'That's it now. I've quit. I'm not drumming any more. There's other things going on, but I'm not drumming. I want to spend more time with my family – I haven't seen them for a month.' The rock'n'roll world held no more magic for the drummer, the pull of family life was stronger.

There was talk of a golden handshake. A few weeks later John spoke about the split and Reni, even hinting that some of the album delays may have been down to Reni losing interest in the whole project. 'He had very strong opinions about everything. He was very funny as well, but he was showing all the signs that he wanted to leave. I'm not trying to blame him for the delay, but it was apparent he wasn't really interested. He wasn't there a lot of the time.'

John is closest on record to admitting that the loss of Reni was pretty well the end of the Roses. 'The thing is, I don't think it'll ever be the same as it was, because part of the spirit died when he left. I think the four members of the band, at that time, meant it was greater than the sum of its parts; the fact that we'd all started from nothing and worked our way up there made it somehow special. There was that inner core, and we could all look at each other and know what we were thinking. It's bound to be different when someone new comes in, who applied for the job. You feel different about yourself too, once you're choosing people to play with. It can never be the same, because anyone new isn't going to spend time on the dole with us, waiting for buses, holding guitars ...'

The drummer's loss of interest had been noted by other members of the band. Says Ian, 'We knew he was going to leave, 'cos he said so. All the time.'

It's not as clear cut as this, though. Some say Reni left the band, some say he was bored of waiting, some say he needed to get his health back, some say he was sacked by Ian.

'Ian had a row with Reni and came into rehearsal and told me and Mani that he'd had it with Reni and that he'd never work with him again and that he wanted to see him in the gutter,' recalls John Squire. 'And we said, "Hang on a minute, we've got a tour starting in ten days," or twelve days, I think it was. But I knew from Ian's...I could see in his eyes that if it came to it Ian would walk out. In fact he said, "It's me or him." So we had no choice but to look for somebody else. I was determined to tour the album and there's no way I could have done that without the singer.'

Did you feel then that the democracy had been lost?

'Yeah, prior to that point no member of the band would have been able to make that statement. We did run the band democratically but everything changed from that point on because he held a gun to our head basically. Though strangely I know that Ian told [*Guardian* writer] Dave Simpson that it was me that had the falling-out with Reni and that was the reason he left.'

Already Reni had retreated back to his house in Whalley Range with his eight-track, and begun the patient, long, slow, work on his tunes. This time it wouldn't matter how long it would take. It was his own stuff after all!

If That Wasn't Bad Enough There Is a Tour to Do!

A Scandinavian tour at the end of April, the beginnings of a world tour, all those British gigs that had been booked and unbooked. Had the Roses bottled out of playing in Britain? Was the pressure on them just too ridiculous? Would the Roses ever hit the road? All that sort of talk. But they did have gigs. There was a return to Scandinavia at the end of the month. Fuck. How difficult was this all getting!

Obviously they needed a drummer. Auditions were set up almost 11 years to the day when Reni had burst into Decibel Studios and changed the band. They were checking out drummers. Two unnamed guys passed through the sessions but they weren't right. Not quite what they wanted. Not quite able to fill the drum stool. This was more than an average job after all!

Wasn't it Joe Strummer who once opined 'you're only as good as your drummer' when he was pressed on what The Clash were like after the monumental Topper quit? They had soldiered on but it had never been the same again.

But they only had two weeks to prepare for the upcoming gigs. Phil Smith watched the balance of the band change: 'From being a tight four-piece in a Beatles style, where all four of them were equally important, all of a sudden one of them had gone. When Reni left, they needed a drummer because the tour was booked and they couldn't pull it. So Robbie Maddix was in. I knew him vaguely but not well. I'd met him a few times.

'But Reni's a big position to fill in The Stone Roses. How do you replace Reni? He's a genius. You take one out and it's all wrong. It's about the four of them. Robbie's a good drummer but he's not the right style. There's this mystical thing the Roses had. It's a very personal thing for people of a certain age. Robbie did all right, but he wasn't Reni. If Mani had left, whoever had replaced him it wouldn't have been Mani. It doesn't matter if you try to replicate his style or do your own thing, you're not that person. The Stone Roses is the four of them and that's it.'

Despite the trauma of Reni leaving, there was no choice but to still go out on the road. The dates were booked, and to blow out now would have put unbearable pressure on the group. It was time to get out there and play. Maybe a tad too soon, with their new drummer the Roses flew out to Norway that April for the Scandinavian leg of the world tour.

So often the Viking countries seemed to be the place where they warmed up or put the band together. Never in their history can there have been a time when the pressure was like this, though. It seemed like the media was willing them to implode. Shock had followed Reni's decision to quit, followed by disbelief that they were actually going to continue without him. The knives were out at the début show on 19 April at the Oslo Rockefeller Music Hall.

Finally back on stage after years and years – they hadn't played live since Glasgow Green in the summer of 1990 – it must have been a weird experience to limber up the old bones into rock'n'roll mode after a long time out in the wilderness. Typically they managed to hit the stage months after the album was released. There was intense media speculation about the Oslo show, and it grabbed a mixed bag of reviews.

It was obvious to anyone who was at those initial dates that the Roses were just not together. All those years off the road had definitely left a few rusty edges. Eyewitnesses and fans will all attest to the drums not quite being on it, Ian's vocals being off key and even John Squire sounding sloppy on some songs. There were some moments of magic of course, some moments when the power of the Roses cut through, but there were plenty of teething problems as the band attempted to remember just who the fuck they were!

As they toured Scandinavia that late April and then Amsterdam and Brussels in early May, the band were at sixes and sevens. Their show on 9 May in Lyon, France, is considered one of the worst gigs that they have ever played, with Ian not even bothering to sing on some of the songs. It was a bizarre spectacle, a band of this size and importance displaying such a fragile and human edge. But then just when it looked like they had completely caved in, their Paris show on 11 May saw them recapturing what made the band so important in the first place.

Egged on by a rapturous crowd the Roses clicked back into gear and gave the best display of their European tour.

No wonder they had avoided England! They would have been torn to shreds! But going on the road so soon after losing Reni was a mixture of brave and plain crazy. No matter how good a drummer Maddix was, he was given one hell of a job catching up with all that distinctive drum action in ten days. Ten days when the band had obviously spent more time teaching their drummer the old songs than learning them themselves. And let's not forget that after five years of not playing, bands can totally forget what a band is meant to do.

The local press slammed them, pointing out their 'lack of stage presence', and there were mentions of 'out of key vocals'. *Melody Maker*'s Dave Simpson was sent out to the show to interview the band and to see if they could cut it after such a long gap in the schedule. 'When I got there, their reactions at the hotel seemed really mixed. They remembered me from years ago when I met them back in 1989 in Leeds. John Squire looked at me like I was shit, but that might just have been me being paranoid because he was friendly enough afterwards. At the soundcheck Mani was stood on his own on-stage, playing Love songs on his guitar. We picked him up and went around Oslo doing photographs. It was weird seeing Ian do his goldfish mouth thing again after all this time! When they finally came on-stage after all that time I missed the big entrance! What a nightmare – after all that waiting I was down the road eating when they played the first two songs, I was so pissed off!'

For Simpson, the man who had loved Reni's work years before, the sight of Robbie Maddix was really strange. 'It was odd them having a new drummer; Reni was so much part of what they did. On certain songs it didn't quite work, but he was a good drummer. It was just trying to fit in where someone had really made an impression before – that must have been really hard. After a few gigs, though, he did gel with the band.'

There was some talk of this gig being substandard. 'Well, that was really weird because it was a great gig and the crowd was really going for it. Certain sections of the media really had it in for the band. They were determined to get them. They rang up someone who worked in the bar at the club who obviously didn't like the Roses anyway, and asked them what they thought of the show. It was a weird situation,' says Simpson.

After the show he went backstage and saw the band in a situation that it hadn't experienced for a long time. 'Backstage they were literally pinned into the dressing-room by hundreds of manic Norwegian fans. They didn't seem to know what to do. It must have been really odd after all that time to have these really intense fans trying to talk to you. It seemed like they didn't know quite what to do.'

Simpson interviewed them for *Melody Maker* on the tour bus, an interview that took, unusually for the Roses, four hours. 'I asked them exactly a hundred questions. I never usually write any questions down at all but this was such an important interview for me I remember getting up to question sixty-seven, and John Squire asked me what number we were up to and groaned!'

Rebecca Goodwin was in Madrid with her boyfriend, Tom Piper, and the show blew her mind. 'That was such a great concert. There was like, 2,000 people crammed into a medium-sized hall going crazy for the Roses. It was the pure Stone Roses experience, none of the pomp or media hype of Spike Island. I went down there at the soundcheck and the band seemed to be really chuffed that there was someone from Manchester at the show. They really looked after us. Mani said that there had hardly been any Mancs out in Europe for those dates. He also said that it was the best show that they had played so far on that tour. It was one of the best nights of my life and the best that I had ever seen the Roses, and you've got to remember that I went to Blackpool as well.'

Rebecca noted that the band didn't play 'Fool's Gold' – it was the big hole in the new set and a pointer to how much that song was built up around Reni's idiosyncratic drumming. It was always going to be a nightmare to replicate.

They finished off the short, bumpy European jaunt with a date in Paris on 11 May. Three days later they would be playing their first show in the US, a début show 11 whole years into their existence.

Not So Bored with the USA!

On 14 May the American tour started in Atlanta at the unlikely Mid-Town Music Festival where they played with bands as diverse as Del Amitri and Adam Ant. Elsewhere they broke the box-office records in Toronto, selling out a 3,500-capacity venue in five minutes, while their Los Angeles gig was moved from a 1,200-capacity venue to a 3,500-capacity arena due to demand for tickets. America was starting to wake up to the band. Another couple of years, another couple of tours and it would be theirs!

Finally the Roses made it to the US. The pot of gold. The country where you have to make it to prove your rock'n'roll credentials. With the new 'American friendly' rock vibe of *Second Coming*, Geffen was fairly confident that the record would set the Roses up in the traditional British rock'n'roll pantheon of heroes like the Stones, The Who, Led Zeppelin – the world-beating British bands of the seventies who are still, decades later, the standard-bearers of great rock action.

By the nineties, though, things had changed. Really changed. Maybe after The Beatles, British bands could stomp around the world cleaning up everywhere. I mean, for fuck's sake, Herman's Hermits were the world's biggest-selling band in 1965 (bigger than The Beatles!). There was a love for all things British and pop-based. This infatuation continued into the seventies with rock giants delivering and outfits as unlikely as ELO regularly scoring number ones Stateside. It was seen almost as birthright to have a number one in the States.

Punk temporarily upset the apple cart with only The Clash having any major crossover success, but then the New Romantics had conquered MTV and the American heartland in the early eighties. Since then, though, there had been an appreciable tailing off. Bands like New Order and The Smiths had made a dent but they were not mainstream, and this new baggy thing, this 'Madchester sound', y'know, groups like the Charlatans UK and the Soup Dragons, were like cool man, but were never going to get past 200,000 sales and now there are these Stone Roses, what are they about?

The Roses' delay in getting to the States had made them, in some people's eyes, a band jumping on their own bandwagon, but as 'Love Spreads' hit number one on the college radio charts and the album scraped into the bottom end of the top fifty there was enough residual interest in the band to see them easily sell out 3,000-capacity venues across the US. In fact in some cities the tickets were positively flying out.

Five years ago they had blown out that big stadium mini-tour, a cancellation that Gareth Evans had always seen as a major blight on their career span, but now here they were, still capable of putting punters into medium-sized halls. For a first tour of the USA it was all very promising.

The band was still rough live, although they were coming together gradually. There were still mistakes, songs fell apart and band members played out of time. Despite this, there were some ecstatic responses from the US audiences, proving that the band were on the verge of something quite special Stateside. If they had managed to hold it together and return the following year after they had finally managed to get their act together, who knows?

On the road however, relations between band members were getting more and more strained. The final cracks between the two key members of the band were becoming more and more apparent.

Towards the end of the tour they started delivering shows that again promised the magic inherent in the band. The gig in San Francisco saw the band suddenly clicking together, connecting with the powerful music that was tantalisingly close to them if they could just reach out and grab it.

It's also worth noting that no matter how loose the band played, the shows all kicked off, the people loved this band, an indefinable love and respect but a powerful one between the band and its audience.

On the horizon they were being offered the chance to really kick in and set their stall again! There was the offer to headline the Saturday at Glastonbury in June. This would be the righteous return to the main stage – the moment when the Roses would headline the world's most major music festival and the gig that would put them back on top of the pile. The band was really gelling, kicking ass, ready to go.

I mean what could possibly go wrong now?

The Baddest Break in the World!

So there was John Squire on his mountain bike on 2 June, relaxing a few days after the stressful but successful 11-date tour of the US. They were taking time out before travelling to Japan and Australia. Squire was keeping fit high in the hills above San Francisco, getting a rush from cruising the rough terrain. The sheer adrenaline of tackling the mountains, man and machine; it's an exhilarating rush. Suddenly he hit a lump and was on the floor, fucking knackered, but that's the way of the bike – you get a few knocks and a few bruises.

But as time went on it started to look a lot more serious. With only three weeks to go until Glastonbury, Squire had broken his collarbone and shoulder blade, and it began to dawn on the band and their management that they would have to cancel their Glastonbury show – a disaster, as Glastonbury was to be the big UK comeback. It should have been a key moment in their *Second Coming*. But there was no way they could play with a one-armed guitarist; those were damned difficult guitar parts for a two-armed player, and a one-armed man had no chance.

The announcements of the withdrawal were made and were met with astonishment. The press thought that the band were faking, and the audience likewise. It seemed like everyone believed that the Roses had lost their bottle.

All this was going on while Squire was back in England, sitting with John McGregor, the ex-Manchester United physio, desperately trying to get his arm fixed up. A steel plate and six pins were inserted across the bone but it was to no avail.

It must have been a hell of a frustrating position to be in. There was no way the band would bottle this show intentionally, and everyone was on tenterhooks.

The Roses also had to cancel a ten-date tour of Japan – a country where they were still rock'n'roll gods! Disaster was stalking the band at every move; it was the payback.

June

Losing the chance of playing Glastonbury, and blowing the place apart and re-stating their case as the premier Britpop outfit, must have really rankled. Many fans had already bought tickets for the show and there were some dark mumblings at the grass roots.

Uncharitably for many, this was the moment when The Stone Roses blew it. It would need a remarkably good UK tour that autumn to win them back many favours.

Incidentally the Roses' blowout gave Pulp the big break. The Sheffield band, who had been bottom-of-the-bill outsiders for many years, but who were starting to break through with a run of quirky pop singles, were asked to step in at the last moment. This gave them the air of saviours and they played a great set and were perhaps the best-received band at the whole of Glastonbury that year. They had the so-called 'common people' in their pocket and Jarvis Cocker, after years on the outside looking in, was finally knighted as one of pop's key spokesmen.

By late July Squire's arm had healed up again, and the battle-scarred band were ready to resume their world tour. Where else do you go to break yourself in? They returned to Scandinavia for four dates in Sweden and Finland before flying in to Ireland on 6 August for the Feile festival in Cork, a show that half counted as a sort of homecoming show for the long-suffering fans. It might have been a foreign country but, fuck, it was near enough to count and many made the trip to Cork.

This gig was also the début of the Roses' new keyboard player, Nigel Ipinson, who was formally with Orchestral Manoeuvres In The Dark and lived in Southport. There were reports of them rehearsing out at his place by the seaside.

Fan Peter Jenkins, who was at the gig, remembers seeing Ian Brown walk out into the crowd. 'There was one band headlining or playing – I think it was Tricky or someone – and Ian Brown walked out of the backstage and out into the audience. The crowd totally freaked out and everyone ran over to where he was. There were loads of people just hanging around him. It left the front of the stage totally empty.'

Caitlin Moran, reviewing the gig for *The Times*, pointed out, 'I have seen Take That, and the hysterics of their audience was nothing like the Roses fever at Feile. As the band took the stage the crowd started piling over the crash barriers before they had even played a note.' Ian Brown would go on to say that this was one of the Roses' greatest ever gigs, an opinion shared by those who were there.

Again after despondency and disaster it seemed like the band were back at last on the right track – at any point they could be massive if only things could get into gear and stay there.

When asked about the plethora of British guitar acts that had followed the Roses' call to arms, Brown was quoted as saying, 'Nah, I never feel we've been overtaken by everyone else. All the bands that were around in 1989 – it was a great time for music, but things have gone back, not forward. There's been a lull. We're here to bring things forward, we do what we want. All these bands who want to sound like Ray Davies or Paul McCartney...that's just retro shit.'

Even now you will bump into punters who go all misty-eyed about the festival. Coach-loads had travelled over to Britain to see the Roses. This was the closest the Roses had been to Britain for five years, and even if the gig was still displaying a few of those rough edges that everyone had heard about in Europe, it was like, fucking hell! The Roses! The band that had provided the touchstone album of a baggy generation. People were here to pay their respects to the band.

So what if Ian was singing a bit flat now and then. This was the band that had changed lives, made something magical out of guitars, bass and drums, made music that transcended everything. Even without Reni's fluid dexterity they could still grab the magic out of thin air. The band was playing really well now, this was the gig when the Roses really started to remember just who the fuck they were and started to play like it as well. And the crowd was going mental…before the band had even come on stage! This was still the Roses and living fuckin' legends…And there were not too many of them stalking the Britpop landscape. There might have been some all-right bands knocking about, but not bands that really meant something.

People loved the Roses.

There was talk of a British tour that autumn. And despite all the negativity of the past year, even weary cynics were buzzing with excitement. If only the band would get on the road, finally return to the British circuit that had made them.

After two weeks off they played a 'secret gig', their first British gig since that 1990 show at Glasgow Green, five bleedin' years ago. On 1 September finally it was touchdown in Britain.

As an apology to Michael Eavis and the Glastonbury people, The Stone Roses played on Pilton village green. The show was an annual event with the money going to the village nearest the Glastonbury festival that gets disrupted every year by it. Support came from Dodgy, a fruit-and-veg contest and a competition for local pets.

A crowd of about 1,500 made their way down for the show. Dodgy were totally thrilled; the Roses were their heroes and they were getting the support at the legendary homecoming of the first British dates since Glasgow Green, a whole pop generation ago.

The Roses turned in a killer set. The touring was paying off, and they were a band getting well into gear now.

As he left the stage Ian Brown realised it was time for one of his weird one-liners. 'You're the trip, see you in November,' he muttered.

The pop aristocracy was there to check them out, Noel and Liam as well as Bobby Gillespie from Primal Scream – all the different generations of Roses-style pop checking the show.

The Bristol listings mag *Venue* was there and thought the show was great, calling it the gig of the year. 'All through those five dark years of law suits, rumours, cancellations and disappointments, you knew that The Stone Roses had one perfect gig lurking deep inside them. This was the show. Stone me, what a night.'

The scene was now set for a great tour. Perhaps now after all those false starts and disappointments, the *Second Coming* could finally take place.

A couple of days after the Pilton show they travelled just up the road and back to Rockfield Studios to re-record 'Love Spreads' for the Warchild charity album for the war orphans of the fucked-up situation in the Balkans. The record already has a sleeve artwork donated by John Squire. The band, as if to disprove their slothful image, did the track in one day.

To promote the Warchild record Ian and Robbie had to do a round of interviews. Brown's hair is noted for returning to the classic baggy mop of yore, replacing the intermittent skinhead and one-inch crop he had been sporting most of the year. 'It's always the same. I grow my hair quite long, and then I get it cut off really short. I just happened to have a crop when the album was released – I didn't grow it out because I thought it was a mistake. I'll do the same – get it cut when it gets longer.'

And then, on 7 September, it was finally off to play the Japanese leg of their world tour, the date which had been postponed after John broke his collarbone. The Roses were ecstatically received by their big Japanese audience, the band still bonding tight.

Before they left they announced the British tour dates, and the tickets flew out, selling in a couple of hours, with queues around the block. The band was coming home and the fans were hungry.

Ian Brown was feeling under the weather after being spat on by a drunken Australian tourist in a Tokyo bar a few days previously. It was a bizarre incident that saw the removal of two of Ian's teeth in an unprovoked attack, meaning he needed a trip to the dentist to get some more gnashers put in.

Speaking about the incident at Sydney's JJJ studios a week later, at the commencement of the Australian leg of the tour, Brown said, 'I wanted to bottle him but I didn't,' as he sat there with a swollen mouth and a black eye. 'He threw his drink on me, so I threw one back. Then he punched me so I've been in pain since I got here, been on painkillers and shit. Every day I get toothache. It's wearing me out. I just come here to do the shows. Every show we've done in Australia there's been a sea of smiling faces with their arms up in the air,' he explained to *Melody Maker*.

In the same interview Mani was in a belligerent mood, talking up the British tour: 'We put tickets on sale and they all went in two hours. *NME* will tell you that we're finished; the people on the street will tell you that we're definitely fucking not, mate. England's waiting for us still, we ain't gonna let 'em down.'

They played four shows in Australia that were rapturously received. 'We're at the start of our career,' Mani told local radio prior to the Melbourne show on 5 October. 'After all, we've only done two albums,' he cheekily said. *Mojo* magazine was there and described a packed 2,000 crowd digging the Roses. The talk was that they could have done four or five nights as the tickets sold out so fast.

The Roses played the usual show but were plagued with sound problems. Brown was subdued, probably due to having a swollen gob.

That night they stormed through 'Breaking Into Heaven', 'I Wanna Be Adored', 'She Bangs The Drums', 'Waterfall', 'Ten Storey Love Song', 'Daybreak', 'Tightrope', 'Your Star Will Shine', 'Tears', 'Good Times', 'Made of Stone', 'Driving South' and 'I Am The Resurrection'.

The band left Melbourne on 10 October feeling confident. A reviewer reckoned that they could play in Australia for years. In fact they would never return.

They ended the tour with dates in Perth and Adelaide on 8 October. Now it was to be Britain's turn. The tour was turning into one of the highlights of the autumn season, if not the tour.

The time was right, the stage was set, at last it was the grand return.

'Begging You'

Previewing their upcoming tour, the Roses released on 30 October the track, 'Begging You', off the album. The single was multi-formatted and was a value-for-money thirty minutes with five mixes, including one from Robbie Jay Maddix, as well as by the Stone Corporation who tripped into handbag territory, the Chic mix and the Young American Primitive remix, which was distinctive with its helicopters, plus also a mix by Carl Cox. 'Begging You' was the closest the Roses ever got to a so-called indie/dance record.

'Begging You' was also maybe the Roses' best track for remixing. The band have never really sounded that convincing when they get remixed, perhaps because Reni's drums were too damn good to get messed with. The pointless money-raking cash-ins have all testified to this fact, that some bands' material is better left alone.

'Begging You' was to be the band's last proper single release and charted at number 15. It came bagged up in another John Squire sleeve, a sleeve that tells a part of the story of the creation of the tune. Says John, 'I got hooked on Public Enemy's "Fear of a Black Planet", and I wanted to make music like that, deconstruct it and reassemble it – so a guy called Si Crompton was showing me how to use the sequencers and samplers. But it wasn't for me. Too much like a science lesson. So I ripped up the floppy disks I had used and set them in plaster. I pinched all the colours from a Degas painting.'

It was released the same week as Oasis released 'Wonderwall', the cut that would take them away from all of this and into the stratosphere. 'Begging You' was a great twisting slice of techno-fused rock weirdness, but you couldn't sing it on the terraces and there would be no catching up with Oasis now; no one, not even The Beatles, would get in their way.

Early in November *The Complete Stone Roses* video compilation was released. It was directed by Douglas Hart, who had been making pop promos for years, since his days as the bass player in The Jesus And Mary Chain, one of the few bands that the Roses really admired back when they started in this whole rock'n'roll malarkey.

The video's début screening was at the Yo Yo club in Ricos, Greenock. The promoter there was Andrew McDermid, a Roses fanatic who would eventually promote John Squire's second comeback show, and who, as manager of Roses fans Whiteout, had given Oasis their first support tour of the UK.

Sod the World, it's Touring Home That Counts

At last, at bleedin' last, the band had rediscovered their chops, they had been all around the world trying to recapture the genie and shove it back into the bottle, they had coasted on the love of the fans, they still had the charisma to retain the legend and they still had the songs to rock the crowds but sometimes each one of them (apart from Mani!) had let the side down.

But now back in the UK they were hitting that groove and, fucking hell, the shows were the Roses playing like they did in 1990. Leicester de Montford Hall on 9 December is numbered as one of the greatest Roses shows ever! Check the bootleg – it oozes class, it's worth listening to just to hear how beautiful Ian's voice can be when he gives out. The belligerent stoned Ian giving way to the fallen-angel voice that was, at the end of the day, the key component of the Roses sound. When Ian sings like this the Roses are untouchable. The best band of their ilk. And when the band take off like they do on this set they really do break into heaven. They could easily coast on the charisma, the legend, the awesome records, every damn thing, but when they bring the music along to the party as well, then it's a shame that it all fell apart.

Finally, yeah finally, the Roses were back prowling the UK stages. On 28 November they played the tour's first show at Bridlington Spa, and the local papers were full of stories of fans queuing for the last few tickets released just before the show. This was their first big UK show since Glasgow Green.

Despite the excitement there was a definite scepticism in the air too. They had blown too many chances, and stretched their credibility point just a little bit too far. People weren't believing in them in the same way any more. Even people like Damon Albarn from Blur, a band whose first break had come with 'There's No Other Way', a hit single that made no bones about cashing in on the Roses' success half a decade or so back. With its wah-wah guitar, light tune and video with the band suitably baggied up, Blur were arch manipulators of pop. Albarn was putting the boot in: 'It ain't over until the flat laddie sings,' he quipped.

Not that the Roses cared about any of this piffle. 'Did you miss us?' said Brown, as the band took the stage in front of the sell-out audience. The five years seemed to have had very little effect on the size of the Roses as a live draw. A whole new audience was suckered into their pure pop. They were by now widely looked on as the saviours, the band that kick-started the whole Britpop thing, and everyone was in to pay their dues. The unlikely Humberside town of Bridlington was the focal point of the pop media that week and fans were scurrying up to this little-visited corner of the UK to see if the Roses could still cut it.

Taylor Parkes from *Melody Maker* was a man who never exactly minced his words. 'I like them but I've never believed in them. Belief is such a fucked-up condition. This idea that you get a certain number of men and, yes, it's always men, ensure they are sufficiently straightforward, play very old fashioned music and the end result is a band you can believe in,' he astutely pointed out, before going to stand aghast at the opening three songs. 'They play the opening three songs off the début album in order after all this time!'

Parkes was shocked by Ian Brown's voice (comparing it, hilariously, to Arthur Mullard), talking about his 'doped doleful drone', and found the whole show, although entertaining, hardly transcendental.

With the Roses now the fans were expecting something ridiculously unattainable. Such was the power of the myth that when they were merely mortal they were in deep trouble.

The new set was a neat blend of the first album and *Second Coming*, the songs fitting together far better live than the differing styles of the two albums would suggest.

With maybe a nod to some sort of maturity, the Roses even slotted in a mid-set acoustic spot with the house lights on.

The show was also the début of Ian Brown's knitted ski-hat.

The following night they were at the Civic Hall in Wolverhampton, and the local press's write-ups were ecstatic – 'There is something strangely magical and unique about The Stone Roses' hit it on the nail, even if Oasis were by far outselling them and were waltzing their way through much bigger gigs on a road that would lead to Knebworth, one of the biggest gigs of all time.

The Roses still possessed something that none of their rivals had; they had a strange and powerful magic which transcended everything.

This last British tour was a run of odd gigs with strange atmospheres. They weren't like normal gigs. They were events beyond rock'n'roll… emotional, exciting celebrations, played by a band that looked like it was coming apart at the seams on the stage. Careful observers remarked that group members seemed distant from each other and that there was hardly any rapport between the musicians.

On-stage there was a weird tension about the group. Ian Brown mainly stood there aloof, out of it, like he wasn't really there. John Squire detached himself from the rest of the band, and Mani, his hair scraped back into a pigtail, looked thrilled to be back on-stage. And Maddix was just about holding on. A good drummer in his own right, he was filling the biggest shoes of the times; Reni was no easy act to follow, and if there was one obvious hole in the band's sound it was the missing Reni. There was no one who could make up for him, not even Maddix.

Most of the audience seemed shocked that they could actually see the band, having got used to the idea that the legendary outfit had disappeared for ever. It was an added bonus to actually have them back. Although the expectations for the gigs were high and for the most part they delivered, for many fans the tour itself pissed all over the album. It was where the band really delivered those new songs.

One thing the tour proved was that, despite the obvious tensions, The Stone Roses were still a great live band.

On 1 December they checked into the Corn Exchange in Cambridge, before returning to Brighton for the first time since a handful of bored people stood watching them at the Richmond. This time they were at the huge Brighton Centre.

Coasting into Brighton, the town with a deep history of pop culture from mods and rockers onwards, the Roses were now on a roll. The town was buzzing, as fans from London and the south-east made the trip. The words was out; the Roses were on top form. This wasn't a limp nostalgic show but a band that was kicking ass. The show itself nearly didn't take place, though, because Ian Brown's child had fallen over at home and was rushed to hospital with a suspected head wound – no X-rays could be taken because he was under two years old. Brown was naturally worried as fuck and wanted to pull the show and go home, but with assurances that things weren't as serious as first thought the gig went ahead. He hurried home the next day.

If anything typified the band's comeback trail it was these teething problems. With families to look after and new responsibilities, the Roses were no longer a few yobs in a van trailing up and down the country. Things could and would go wrong. They were an extended family now and the gods weren't always smiling upon them.

Backstage, the band were noted to be standing in opposite corners of the room – the old gang spirit still hadn't returned. The only party animal now was Mani, as ever the rogue Rose, who at one forty-five in the morning tried to get into the Zap club and was thwarted.

A few days later on 4 December the tour resumed at the Newport Centre in South Wales. The gig was as close to a riot as the Roses' gigs ever got.

Ian Brown, never a big man for football, almost started off a ruck by putting on a Cardiff City shirt at the Newport gig. A football fan would have known that there was a massive tension between Cardiff and Swansea fans, Cardiff having a reputation for having some of the worst hooligans in Britain, with the core thugs calling themselves the Soul Crew, leaving calling cards with, 'If you like a lot of fighting at your football, join our crew.'

Brown's shirt was a red rag to a bull. Cardiff fans started chanting 'Bluebirds', their nickname, and sporadic fighting kicked off.

The band had spent a lot of the year on the road and were reaching the peak of their powers. The all-nighter at Brixton Academy is looked upon as the best show of the whole tour. They played one of their classic shows, of which Karen Black was a witness: 'I don't even like them that much and I went down that night because someone blagged me a free ticket. The atmosphere was amazing and when the Roses played they were completely brilliant. They really blew me away – it was one of those classic gigs.'

It was a memory that tallied with many others at every show on the tour.

On 13 December they played Leeds Town and Country Club, and the show was recorded live for BBC Radio One and broadcast the following March.

Journalist Dave Simpson was there and noticed that something was amiss. 'John seemed to be stood there in his own little world. I'd interviewed him three weeks before and he sounded really unhappy. There seemed to be something going wrong. He mentioned Reni leaving and how it wasn't the same any more. He said that the band weren't really speaking to each other, that it was like a marriage – just passing each other in the corridor – but no one thinks of doing anything about it. I thought nothing of what he was saying really. At the time it just seemed like a temporary thing.'

They played Liverpool's Royal Court on 15 December. Ian swapped the knitted hat for a Santa Claus hat; reviewers called the show 'the greatest gig of the decade'.

Manchester, England!

The Apollo is burning up. It's a special Manchester evening. The atmosphere is righteous, wild. The Roses haven't been in town on-stage for years. This is a special occasion and everyone is out for it. It's the hottest ticket in town. A rock'n'roll Christmas present for the faithful. People can't quite believe it. The band that kick-started the party is back in town. There is, of course, no support. The whole tour is typified by the Roses playing alone and plenty of DJing action building up to their big entrance.

The rain lashes down outside and Reni isn't going to be here (although there are rumours that he will get on-stage for the encore – rumours that turn out to be untrue).

The stage has a great set, with long strips of gold hanging from the ceiling and strip lights combining. It's sombre, almost requiem-like.

The Roses hit the stage late. The atmosphere is highly cranked and when the bass line to 'I Wanna Be Adored' lopes from the stage the place goes wild. It's a great night; they have really got a set together that works. Even the acoustic section is cool. Standouts are 'Made of Stone', which still sends shivers down the spine, and 'Love Spreads', a huge zig-zagging crazy beast.

John Squire is now the complete virtuoso, standing slightly aloof stage left – playing an amazing slew of riffs. Mani is yelling at the crowd. New man Nigel Ipinson is pushing his keyboards up, adding a funky chop house-piano break to 'Love Spreads', and putting new Hammond parts in where he could, as well as filling in the backing vocals. Robbie Maddix holds down the beat tight and hard, but lacks that bounce, that indefinable extra that Reni provided. It would take a hell of a drummer to replace the man and Maddix is working hard against the tide of history.

Ian Brown is ice cool, wearing a Puffa jacket with the hood pulled over his head; he doesn't seem to sweat a drop. He moves little on-stage, stares impassively at the crowd and lays out his vocals, which are cranked through a freezing reverb.

The neatest moment of the show was during 'Daybreak', when a banner that read 'Reni Lives' was getting waved at the band. It caught Ian Brown's attention, and there was a moment of tension when he pointed at it asking for it to be put on to the stage. The crowd sensed that there could be trouble but Brown completely swerved expectations and held the banner aloft for the whole of the next song in a weird tribute to the missing soul of the band.

At the after-show party Brown sauntered around still ensconced in the swollen jacket and still not sweating a drop.

Noel Gallagher was buzzing about just what the Roses were capable of, in fact everyone was. Those two shows are perhaps two of the best Roses gigs I have been to, and although you really missed Reni, the band had started to gel, had started to turn into something else, a Roses Mark 2 maybe? John Squire's guitar playing was awesome. It's hard to believe one person could make those many notes! 'Soloing like a bastard,' as Noel typically and succinctly put it.

The crowd was ecstatic, so buzzed up on the Roses that even Liam Gallagher was pretty well left alone to watch the show in peace. There's always something quite powerful about the bond between The Stone Roses and Manchester and it seemed quite fitting that these two, virtually the last two proper gigs they ever played, would be here, in the town that sent them on their way.

On 28 December they played the massive Sheffield Arena. The gig wasn't as good as the Manc shows. It couldn't be, but it really underlined their pulling power and set them up for the Wembley Arena gig the next day.

Now it was time for London, and in 1990s pop terms this was an historical gig. It was the Roses' last stand with John Squire, as well as the Manics' first big show without Richey Edwards (their guitarist) who had disappeared months before after apparently committing suicide. It was the moment when the Roses fizzled out and the Manics started to really move into the mainstream.

This was the big one; Wembley Arena is a cold, hungry aircraft hangar where things like atmosphere are banished by the draughty hall.

It's functional, chilly and unfriendly – hardly the communal celebration that rock bands seek. First on were the Manics with their comeback gig, an initial arduous task on a road that would see them, the most unlikely band of their generation, end up being vindicated as one of the great British rock bands of the 1990s.

The Roses' final stand saw them still grabbing critical plaudits to the last – in *Melody Maker* Everett True went berserk and astutely pointed out that John Squire had reinvented the guitar hero as someone without leather trousers or 'a Mars bar stuck down their pants'.

The show – their longest ever at 85 minutes! – was a vindication and further proof that, despite the odds, the Roses, even without the magnificent Reni, were on burning spectral form. They had played a spellbinding British tour.

1996

Exit John Squire

That Xmas as they left the stage at Wembley there were no set plans for the band. They went their separate ways for the new year.

The UK tour had been a result! The fans were ecstatic, even most of the reviews were pretty good. But the tour only clouded over the actual picture. The band were still managerless. Says John at the time, 'It's hard to get a unanimous decision out of this band.'

Perhaps jumpy after their experiences with Gareth and Goldstein, the Roses were not making any decisions at all. They were a rudderless ship. If they had managed to get a manager years back this whole fragmentation could have been avoided. But as 1996 continued the band were in limbo. Drifting.

In early '96, as the whole band apart from John reconvened to write some tunes, occasionally the band would bump into John down at Old Trafford, where Mani and John would watch United. The pair of them were even talking football with the *Red Issue* fanzine, an interview which is the last-ever interview that John did as a Stone Rose.

In that interview John claims that there were eight or nine new Roses songs and some half-finished bits and pieces for the band to jam on (one of which, 'Standing On Your Head', he would use later on). It's not clear if he's including the six songs the rest of the band claim to have written – six songs that include 'Ice Cold Cube' and 'High Times'.

In March 1996 John received a letter from a lawyer representing the other three members of the band. It started 'Positive noises are being made about the group going into the studio ...'

John, who had been considering quitting for months, stalling the inevitable, wondering what to do, was stunned by the letter. Was this where the band stood now? Letters from lawyers? How far apart was the much touted gang now?

On 21 March he phoned the other three members of the band. He was leaving. On the last tour he'd felt like a phony and couldn't do it any more. When Ian asked what 'it' was he replied shakily, 'play guitar'.

And with that brief flurry of phone calls, John Squire had quit the band that he had helped to form twelve years previously.

No longer would we see Squire's sunburst '59 Gibson Les Paul Standard on-stage with the Roses. Almost exactly a year after Reni left the band, The Stone Roses were dealt the mortal blow – John Squire had left.

The split had been a long time coming. Maybe carrying the baggage of the Roses legend had proved too much or maybe the band had grown too far apart. Anyone who watched this last tour could see that this was no longer a tight gang unit.

Squire told *Q* magazine that his decision to leave the group had come when he realised just how far they had all drifted apart.

'I got a letter from the group's lawyer saying that positive noises were being made about going into the studio, which is indicative of the dysfunction of the group. The fact that it had come to that. I just thought that it was…fair. I wouldn't have scuppered a tour or an album, but as we were in a rest period, that was the time to do it. And I feel a lot better for it.'

Time had taken its toll on the band. 'I just wasn't in the band that I had joined. I don't think any of us were. All that kept us together during the break was the name. We saw very little of each other. We just…drifted apart. Crumbled.'

The split was announced nationally on 25 March on the Jo Whiley show on Radio 1. Even while the announcement was being made there was a flurry of activity as the band vainly attempted to patch up the situation.

The remains of the band were shellshocked. For the first time for a long time there were phone calls between band members and at an eventual meeting at their lawyer John Kennedy's office, the other four tried to persuade Squire to remain and work on the third album. It must have been a tense meeting, the first time they had actually all been together since the Wembley show the previous December. Squire, though, had made up his mind – he was off. He was adamant that that was that – the band had drifted too far apart, it just wasn't the same without Reni. He missed his drumming and his camaraderie. The lack of communication between band members became apparent in the terse statements that followed the split.

Says John, 'When I told Ian I was leaving it was, like, the first time I'd spoken to him for a good few years. I don't really know who he is now.' He added, 'People change, relationships change, hair styles change, that's life isn't it?'

Q cheekily asked Squire if he had left because of Brown's singing. His answer was honourable. 'No, I knew that he was doing his best. It wasn't sabotage. We all started out from the same amateur level. None of us were any good apart from Reni. He was the only natural, I'll deny any attempt to say that I left because of Ian's voice. This thing is all very difficult to talk about. I do feel this obligation: to the gang. It does feel dishonourable to discuss the band without them being present.'

Ian Brown looks back on the split: '[The] world tour was mega fantastic. It went so well that at the end we were playing Sheffield Arena and Wembley Arena. Wembley was our last gig then John leaves. As we left Wembley Arena that night, I [saw] him waving from the window of the bus. It was March '96. He left three months later...'

The cracks were already apparent to Ian Brown.

'On tour there was a distance between us because he didn't smoke weed and I didn't take coke. This new drummer Robbie and his mate Nigel on keyboards, they smoked weed like I did, which was all day and all night. John had his own crew and they were into different things and I had the security guy and the DJ called Sexton and we were the weed smokers. We were travelling on separate buses. We play[ed] that track by Genius/GZA, "Liquid Swords" [which is about coke]. We were all laughing at this and they were all wired and didn't get it. We felt we were with the kids out there and every night I didn't know how long the solos were going to last. [I've] got a Brixton tape, it's 18 minutes long, breaking into [the] "Heaven" solo. We had turned into what we had set out to destroy in the punk days, all those old dinosaurs with their cocaine. We had become that.'

Different drugs, different friends, different music tastes, the band was at a full stop.

'I was playing *Songs in the Key of Life* and I was into hip-hop as well and they didn't like it. We had a lot of arguments about "Driving South", which was a Zeppelin riff. The key of it was a lot higher and I wouldn't sing it high like Led Zeppelin. I was saying I wouldn't sing it if it was like I was in a heavy metal band and I said, "You fucking sing it," and John went green at the prospect. At that time he never dreamt of singing. He reluctantly let me sing it the way I wanted.

'The Seahorses' song, "Love Is The Law", was going to be on *Second Coming*. We demoed it; it's better than their version, the singing was better [laughs]. Reni just plays an acoustic on it and so does John. It's a good song. I was dead keen to get it on the album but John wasn't into it.'

The remaining three Roses elected to carry on in the face of a barrage of hostile criticism from the media. It was assumed that post-Squire this really was a dead band. They swiftly announced that they would be playing Reading Festival, but in what form? How could they replace John? Names like Bernard Butler were put forward as well as, bizarrely, the former guitar player from Girlschool. It seemed like this was a band clutching at straws.

They released a tense press release; they had decided to come out fighting. 'We feel as cheated as everyone else who has heard the news. We were in the middle of recording the next LP. We're disgusted, yet feeling stronger and more optimistic than ever.'

John Squire's press release was, inevitably, more balanced. 'After lengthy deliberation, it is with great regret that I feel compelled to announce my decision to leave. I believe that all concerned will benefit from a parting of the ways at this point and I see this as the inevitable conclusion to the gradual social and musical separation we have undergone in the past few years. I wish them every success and hope they go on to greater things. My intentions are to continue writing while looking for partners in a new band and to begin working again as soon as possible. Thanks for everything, John Squire.'

The Last Stand: Reading Festival

Reading Festival 1996. The winds were howling and the rain poured down. The hardy pitched their tents in the wild summer squalls. It was a freezing first night and a miserable one for the late arrivals in the field around the rock'n'roll electric amphitheatre.

Reading 1996 was a watershed for the Manchester prime movers of the late 1980s: on the Saturday Black Grape played a shambolic show that was still a triumph – no matter how sloppy Shaun and Kermit and their crew got, their congenial party vibe was perfect for a crowd that was willing to match them for chemical excess.

All through the weekend, though, the talk was of the Roses. Could Ian Brown really pull it off again? Now the chips really were down would the enormous pressure that the band was under make them collapse? Would the expectations finally crush them?

A couple of weeks before, they had played the Benicassim festival near Madrid, and varying reports filtered back – some went on about a 'dancing girl' and some mentioned the début of new guitar player Aziz Ibrahim, another Manc from Burnage with the unlikely background of Simply Red and prog rockers Asia.

Aziz had been on the music scene for years playing his guitar. He also had a history that entwined with the Roses.

Aziz, a brilliant guitar player, had seemingly learned all the John Squire parts in a fortnight. It was going to be one of the hardest jobs in rock. If he wasn't nervous before going on-stage at Reading he must have had nerves of steel and a hide of leather.

Have Guitar, Will Travel: Aziz Ibrahim

Of Pakistani roots, the dapper, urbane, seemingly egoless Aziz Ibrahim was born, bred and lived his whole life in Longsight, Manchester.

'I went to Burnage High School for my secondary school education. There were four top classes that did GCSE/O levels (as they were known then) called Alpha 1, 2, 3 and 4,' he says.

'There was a Gothy-looking guy, who was Pete Garner (I think his hair was pretty long then), in one of them and I was in another. Then we wore Kickers and Fred Perrys but he wore winklepickers and drainpipes with a black trench coat. We used to get on well as we both were into art and had a talent for painting and drawing. He was also best mates with the tallest player of the basketball team through whom we probably first met. He was pretty cool for school…'

The classic 'have guitar will travel' sideman, Ibrahim had spent the last decade in a confusing sprawl of bands learning his craft.

At first the idea of the Roses having a session guitar player in their line-up and one who had played in Asia and Simply Red seemed bizarre, not something that the Roses was about. But Aziz had roots in the city's music scene and the knowledge of far better musics than his CV was owning up to.

Aziz came from a strict religious background where even 'wearing jeans was considered rebellious!' He got into guitar at an early age and quickly became the kid at school who was always carrying a guitar.

His range of influences was breathtakingly eclectic.

'I sneakily listened to everything, rockabilly, punk, blues, rock...I was into all kinds of music, Bollywood stuff. And my roots are Pakistani traditional music...I'm second generation. When I was a kid I was not allowed to listen to western music.'

When you listen to Aziz playing you can hear the eastern flavours. He may have learned John Squire's music note for note, he may have slotted into the background of Simply Red, but his real sound is a mixture of his roots, the western rock roots mixed with traditional ancient guitar scales, an interesting fusion of guitar action.

Says Aziz, 'I became a session player by accident. I never intended music as a career, let alone session. I was playing reggae in 4th Generation, that's where I cut my teeth, Simply Red came from that. Word got out that Hucknall was looking for someone who understood his reggae and jazz vibes. I'd done some work for a band whose manager worked at their office and that's how that came about in the early eighties...'

Simply Red was an experience he doesn't have the fondest memories of. 'I was a sideman, just playing what I was told to play. It was a weird experience. After Simply Red ended most people thought I wanted too much money and that I'd broken away from the local scene, so I did more session work with Rebel MC, Dennis Brown, Barrington Levi, Freddy MacGregor, Ruby Turner and Errol Brown's Hot Chocolate and PM Dawn. I joined Asia for some time and left because it had run its course, I didn't fancy wearing sky blue jewellery any longer!'

A few months, in early 1996, later the call came from the Roses who although ostensibly were still in existence needed a guitar player to help them on some demos they were putting together.

'I didn't know the Roses personally then. The first I'd heard of them was years ago when Gareth Evans was asking me what I reckoned to this band that he was starting to manage. I said, "What do I know"!'

Aziz ended up getting the call-up for the Roses from knowing Robbie Jay Maddix.

'We were old-time friends and had played in the same bands previously. We were in probably the first black rock group from Manchester called Gina Gina. It wasn't exactly Living Colour, more like Prince. In the band was yours truly, Robbie Jay, Jonathan Beckford, Barrington and Lawrence Stewart. We sat at the table with Chris Blackwell and nearly signed to Island Records. It could have been different for us but it wasn't to be.

'We knew the Roses from before when we were recording up at Coconut Grove, so there was already a connection. And I knew Gareth and Matthew from the International – I was always in there. It was only walking distance from my house on the Anson estate in Longsight. Gareth always used to ask me, "What do you think?", but I'd be like, "What do I know, mate? I play in Simply Red." [laughs] I was never keen on Simply Red but it was my first big gig.

'[The Roses] were a bunch of lads, mates, in a band together and at the time I saw them as the definitive scenario that I wanted to be in – a band with mates. As you might know they were writing the Third Coming, as I call it, for lack of a title, and at that time they couldn't get in touch with John and they wanted to get their demos together, asking me if I wanted to do some guitars for them so the tunes sounded complete.'

He went down to meet the band. Aziz quickly hit it off with Ian Brown. 'The first time I met Ian we were chatting for ages. I was teaching guitar at the time and I taught Ian a couple of tunes! He was heavily into the Hendrix chord…E7 sharp!…Ian is a really spiritual guy. He's read a fair amount of the Koran, he was intrigued with me being involved in rock'n'roll and also being a Muslim…And I am without a doubt. I don't believe this world exists without help from above. I was helping out on demos they were putting together, then news broke that John didn't want to do it no more. A few weeks later I got the call from Robbie. They'd been to see John Squire and it wasn't happening. I was jumping up and down with excitement. There is nothing like being in a band, a proper band.'

The new line-up started rehearsing over at Ipinson's place in Southport. 'We started rehearsing in Southport. But word got out and everyone was queuing outside the doors. We then moved to this other rehearsal room in Salford behind Renaissance gym. Robbie knew the owner.'

Before they hit Reading there were a few festivals in Europe to play. The new line-up were going to début in the rawest environment; the no soundcheck, big crowd outdoor scenario. The handful of shows were typified by the Benicassim festival, where some of the tightness problems that had dogged the band in 1995 were still apparent. Aziz held down the guitar parts well, although it was impossible for him to get the feel that John Squire had brought to the band. The audience was confused but attempted to stay with the band and the appearance of the partially clothed dancing girl gyrating through the set was ridiculously out of place.

It was a hotch-potch Roses that was staggering across Europe. Fans who were reporting back were scratching their heads. It wasn't like the band was awful – they were playing OK and Ian's singing was fine. It just wasn't really the Roses up there. It was obvious to everyone that they had lost one too many members.

The last Euro date was in Portugal and the band headed back to play the Sunday night headline slot at Reading Festival, ironically their first-ever British festival appearance (that they actually managed to play).

They still rehearsed on the edge of Salford, as one of the other bands rehearsing in there remembers: 'This band moved in the room upstairs. We thought that they were a Roses covers band. They sounded really un-together. One day we went out in the corridor and there was loads of gear out there, far too much for a covers band, and we thought, fucking hell, it is The Stone Roses!'

The day before their set at Reading, Brown popped up backstage at the festival, hanging out with old cronies like Cressa or just standing around on his own – an out-of-sorts figure, looking too famous to be mingling backstage at the village-fete-like atmosphere of the festival.

Brown also wandered out into the crowd, a detached figure in rock-star fatigues – all velvets, loose trousers and shirts…stoned, immaculate, the lost prophet of Britpop, limbering up for what couldn't help but be the last stand.

Mani was in a far more down-to-earth mood, with finger-snapping handshakes and buoyant confidence. 'We're having it large,' he steamed backstage.

'They'll pull it off,' the rump guard of the Roses' believers shouted in the heated backstage arguments. The Sunday night would be the last chance for the much-damaged outfit, now patched up with an oddball collection of session players – ex-OMD members and guitar players like Aziz, who, despite awesome technical ability, just didn't feel right. The beauty of the Roses had been that gang, the crew, the bunch of lads who had bust out and made good. All the great British rock'n'roll bands had been like that for years.

The moment when it seemed like things were getting desperate was at the press conference. Unlike the pre-Spike-Island press conference, when the band's cold indifference to the bemused press pack had actually worked, their rabbit-caught-in-the-headlights of the hostile press at Reading was a disaster.

Mani shot his mouth off about John Squire, making comments that he would later regret, while Ian Brown was cutting and cruel. Squire had been dignified on his departure, but this bickering was out of character for the band who had always held a united front even at times of crisis.

But then, like the marriages and close affairs that bands seem to cruelly resemble, the hatred was a natural reaction to the deep hurt caused by the departure of one of their best friends.

The Roses were on death row and even they were sensing it now.

As the day drew on and Sonic Youth played one of their mind-blowing sets, the Roses were looking like they were on a hiding to nothing. On the *NME* stage the newly triumphant Underworld were limbering up for what would be a victorious exit from Reading Festival; it had been a great year for them, topped by 'Born Slippy', their surprise smash hit from the *Trainspotting* soundtrack. The fact that the Stone Roses were playing directly against the hot new dance act could only add to their problems.

Still, this was the fucking Roses! Ian Brown had never let anyone down before and for a lot of the audience they were a legend – the band that started the whole damn 1990s Britpop thing, and here they were at last live on-stage at a huge festival.

And there was Mani, boisterous as ever and having it large, the familiar rumble of the bass, so often the signifier to the great pop moment, and 'I Wanna Be Adored' burst out. There was an appreciable sigh of relief from the crowd – could the Roses be about to pull the whole damn thing off? The guitar was swirling around a bit oddly but then the familiar figure kicked in, followed by the 4/4 thump of the bass drum; the crowd chugged along, ready for the revival. There was a genuine feeling that the band could pull it off at this stage.

Ian Brown sauntered on-stage, and some young fans were heard to gasp, 'It's Liam Gallagher' – the toll of the time out of the limelight was beginning to tell. Oasis had recently packed out Maine Road football ground for two nights; they were now massive legends well on the way to being bigger than the fucking Beatles, and yet here was the band that set the blueprint and built the foundations.

Brown looked good, limbering up, doing some boxing moves; and then he started singing, skidding around the tune, 'I don't have to sell my soul.' It was OK, but a bit cracked, a bit nervous.

As the set went on Brown's vocal sounded not just flat, which was never a major concern, but bored, disconsolate, detached – it wasn't like the

Brown of old, the exuberant positive pop messiah, late-1980s generation. This was a shell of that man.

Martin Audioweb remembers: 'I went to the Reading gig and Ian [was] walking round the site. People [were] coming up non-stop , saying, "Fucking hell, it's Ian Brown , he's walking around." He had no sleep; when they played I wish to God I could have plucked out my voice and given [it] to him for that gig. You can't stay up all night if you're a singer...'

They played two new songs. One, 'Ice Cold Cube', a mundane twelve-bar with a title that was reputed to be a band nickname for John Squire, was rattled out with a perfunctory chunder. This was a band that lacked the majesty of the old days; the sheer inspirational euphoria that had been their calling card had gone. Ian Brown stood there just going through the motions. It wasn't John Squire's absence that nobbled The Stone Roses that day: it was Ian Brown's – a victim to 24 hours staying up.

Aziz was holding the guitar down well – he had learned Squire's licks fast, a major achievement considering just how good Squire was. But there was no soul, apart from Mani, who was virtually carrying the gig, trying to hold a massive legend upon his shoulders; he wouldn't cave in, even to the bitter end. The man on the streets, Mani knew what the legend looked like from the outside. At least it couldn't get any worse.

It couldn't get any worse? Suddenly a dancing girl was on the podium gyrating to the Roses' music. It was all wrong – the Roses were always aloof and they never had things like dancing girls. The last straw was someone shouting, 'C'mon, put your hands together.' The spell was broken. It was all wrong; the diehards walked away, people were laughing or groaning and leaving in droves, faces from the old days shook their heads in shame. To be fair, very young fans who had never seen the band before were still caught up in the remnants of the legend and the songs which were still classics.

'I'd never been to a festival before and The Stone Roses were the best band on all weekend,' remembers Jane Scott, who was 17 at the time. 'I couldn't understand why everyone slagged them off afterwards.'

Backstage Cressa was fuming. 'It's a nightmare, it's awful,' he snarled, staring at the floor. 'Get backstage and tell him, just tell him how crap it was, tell him to finish it, it's a travesty.'

'You tell him, he's your mate,' everyone replied.

Cressa turned on his heels and disappeared into the throng backstage.

This was the band that had inspired the formation of nearly every guitar pop band in Britain in a brilliant 18-month period when they were untouchable. When you've been that good, meant that much, you simply can't let people down. You are just far too important.

Initially Ian Brown had been optimistic about the split. 'I honestly thought after John left, "Great, this is a brand new start. We can call ourselves The Brand New Stone Roses", "The New New Stone Roses". I naively thought it wouldn't matter, that we could just carry on as "The New Stories" or "Mark 2" or "Mark 3" or whatever…'

There had been some unlikely offers to help the band.

'Slash offered to play at Reading with us. "Tell him and his boa constrictor to fuck off!" we said. At the time we thought he was an LA twat but [we] were wrong; it would have been really fucking amazing. Thing is, we were ridiculed for that gig but I saw thousands of arms in the air at the gig. I've heard the tapes and I know I was singing in a different key to the band for most of the tunes. At the time I didn't see this mass exodus of people crying and people's worlds caving in. I just saw 60,000 arms in the air when we walked off the stage. As I come off stage there's our man again, Cressa…Cressa was there [and he said], "You got to end it, you got to end it. It's just a debacle." Shit, I didn't realise that I was singing out of tune and he had a cassette which I heard the next day, so I didn't really know where he was coming from at first.'

The gig was, in some ways, the perfect end to the band's career.

'It was punk rock to play the big show and blow it. Not many do…I did hear a story a week later that the *NME* had a meeting on the first day [of the festival] and they said, "Look, we're going to bury the Roses on the Sunday'…According to this girl that I knew, they'd always been against us…We were the first band to get on the cover that got slagged off inside; for some reason they had it in for us [so] we were up against the wall.'

The press had a field day slamming the band. Aziz came in for a lot of the negative reviews that he attempts to rationalise.

'I could speculate but maybe it was a culmination of a few things,' he says. 'Perhaps it was the fact two members had gone and that was, like, enough's enough for some people. Or we can handle one person going but this is just too much…

'The criticisms weren't just about Reading. They were about replacing some awesome musicians, their songwriting, the chemistry they shared and their world influence on so many different levels. I can see that – I'm not stupid…I can appreciate that John and Reni leaving was a great loss and nothing was ever going to replace that. Whatever was going to come in next was going to be different. It's the fact it wasn't really given a chance and really the finger's got to be pointed at the press, magazines like the *NME*, *Q* and *Vox* and other writers. There were papers out there that know they were jumping on the bandwagon.

'We know we played badly or sounded bad at Reading, but it happens to all musicians all the time. No one has a perfect track record, especially musicians, but compare the Reading performance to earlier Roses gigs. Were they all perfect? It was just another unpredictable night of the Roses but the press had already written the story before the gig so it had to follow the storyline. I guarantee it.

'It's like the comment about "people who left in droves". There's plenty of videos around of Reading '96 and whether it was good or bad, the videos speak for themselves. The crowd that were there were still there at the end of it. So [it's] very poetic but not the truth.

'Don't get me wrong, musically it lacked in certain areas. [There were] things that we needed to work on, but it was early, you know; we'd done a few festivals around Europe then gone into Reading.

'Noel Gallagher said, "It was the hardest job in the world to fill the shoes of John Squire," and he's right! I can't be John Squire but John Squire can't be Aziz Ibrahim. Maybe the external antagonism led towards Mani joining Primal Scream or Ian saying he didn't want to carry on with it. I think they were all factors.

'Like I said, the truth of it is that some things went wrong and there were bad decisions made…but it would have just got better.'

Aziz made some comments about John Squire that were off the cuff and out of character for the talented and amiable guitarist that he didn't really mean and that he instantly regretted.

'What I actually said, and I can't believe I said it – "I'm so excited to be in this band and I've always felt that this was my band but some joker was there before me" – but I wasn't even thinking of John Squire. I was oblivious that I was insulting or hurting John or Roses fans…

'I can only go on to apologise to John. It was never my intention or a personal thing against him. It was just me being excited about a job and to me it didn't matter who was there before me, but I was just happy to be there.

'So I apologise for that and to The Stone Roses fans who took it as a personal insult. I disrespected somebody who's created my livelihood and also put me on the map and set me on my own path. That's how I see it.'

After the band Aziz maintained his relationship with Ian Brown and initially worked with him on his solo albums.

'Musically speaking I felt it was a shame that it didn't go on to where I wanted it to go, i.e. guitar-based songs, but Ian went on to make several great albums with some genius choices of direction like brass or strings.

'Personally, I'll always remember the best times of us writing and recording *Unfinished Monkey Business*. Being stuck behind a bus and on its derriere, an ad for "My Star" (my first co-write with Ian) staring at me all the way through a traffic jam! The closest collaboration of them all was "Corpses". Back and forth it went until we nailed it.'

The band were, to all intents and purposes, now finished. Most pundits thought that this was definitely the last stand, the final moment. As the closing chords reverberated out of their amps the legend of The Stone Roses would ebb away with the sound.

No one bothered to tell the Roses that, though.

Ian was later to comment, 'I didn't go to bed the night before, like a dick. We'd done five shows in Europe, and we'd been getting better each one. I saw Cressa the night before Reading and I partied with him. Smoking weed all night. I was so excited. Normally I don't drink. No powder, no. I haven't touched powder since 1990. But I must have fucked me voice. At the time, on stage, I didn't realise it was all going wrong. From the stage, I couldn't see anyone crying or leaving. But later, when I heard the tape, I knew I sounded terrible. It was a cabaret version.'

The Legacy

The band spent all their money from the Reading Festival on buying up Square One studios in Bury and renaming it 'The Rose Garden'. They had planned to put the third album together in their own studio, on their own terms. Geffen was now showing very little interest in putting the record out, so it looked like they were on a hiding to nothing.

If this was a normal band then that would be that. But the Roses touched far more people in bigger ways than all this would suggest. They changed the whole soundscape of British pop, inspired bands, fired up people. Mistakenly Suede get the credit for inventing Britpop, but you can't rewrite history for ever – the key band was The Stone Roses. The musicians know, the people understand, the Roses' name is still talked about in hushed adoring whispers, and their albums still float around the bottom end of the charts years later.

The Roses made indie guitar, white-boy pop music sexy again, and they smashed down the doors of the charts; before then the closest anyone got was with The Jesus And Mary Chain and they always seemed to get stalled at number forty-one.

Now, when a teen-band's hearts break when they don't get on *Top of the Pops* with the first single, the Roses' achievements seem smaller. But The Stone Roses changed the notion of what a pop band was allowed to do. Before, in the righteous schedule of post-punk, bands tried to smash rock'n'roll to pieces; this was great in some cases, as some truly startling genius music was made, but it also doomed a lot of bands to failure.

The Roses and the Mondays were the most inspirational bands since punk rock. How many bands were inspired by 1980s rock gods like U2 or Simple Minds? Erm, about none at all.

Some bands like The Bluetones took the Roses' blueprint all the way and seemed to model themselves on the band, while others like The Manic Street Preachers used them as something to measure themselves against while admitting a secret respect for the band.

Others such as Ride saw the Roses live in 1989 and formed a band instantly; some like Liam Gallagher saw the Roses play and just knew what to do with their lives; some people saw the Roses and became journalists or superfans who eventually worked within the music industry.

They were a clean broom, a new way of doing the same old thing. Ian Brown, unlike most of the twerps in bands in the 1980s, was a folk hero, something that people like Bono would die for but never achieve. John Squire made musicianship hip again, and their songs soundtracked a generation growing up with ecstasy and acid house, and the new hope and optimism of the late 1980s.

Primal Scream managed to resurrect their career in the space provided by the Roses, and a whole host of lesser imitators carved out short careers in their fallout. A slew of Manchester bands had their five minutes of fame and then got burned.

The Charlatans, a band hugely inspired by the Roses – even supporting them at many early gigs – gradually got taken more and more seriously, and bypassed desperate tragedy to become one of the great British rock bands of the 1990s. Even now, though, there are echoes of Ian Brown in Tim Burgess's stagecraft and his singing voice – that husky whisper and studied cool reflect the Roses' frontman at his peak. The stoned nonchalance and stone-dead stare that turned on a generation are still there in every gangling sub-Liam-Gallagher frontman mooching about in the UK's rehearsal rooms.

The Inspiral Carpets arrived stage left and exited stage right with a heap of under-rated singles. The Stranglers of the 1990s, they were never hip but were consistent enough to be respected by a huge fan base. The Roses' fans drifted into dance or back to where they had come from. They had been a part of a time when pop went mad and elected fresh heroes, new fucked-up leaders and flawed bands.

Never career animals, the Roses were at one time the tightest and toughest gang on the block.

They ripped themselves apart, but their legacy lives on, and now British pop has been well and truly resurrected.

Just a few days after the Reading appearance Ian Brown bounded into press agents Hall Or Nothing's London office as if it was business as usual.

It was as if the gig was not a disaster or a temporary blip or even a fuck-up. Brown was buzzing, upbeat.

Reading had been a pricking of the myth. A deflating of the legend and that was perhaps all that was great about the show. Mani, who had stayed loyal to the end, finally took the Primal Scream job that he had been offered months earlier. John was rumoured to be putting a band together and Reni was still working up tunes on his eight-track.

Ian Brown knew the game was up and offered the following press statement on 29 October and then fucked off to Morocco to get his head and his life back together.

'Having spent the last ten years in the filthiest business in the universe it's a pleasure to announce the end of The Stone Roses. May God bless all who gave us their love and supported us throughout this time. Special thanks to the people of Manchester who sent us on our way. Peace be upon you.'

And that was it. The Roses was finally over.

Ian Brown got on a plane and went on holiday to Morocco. It looked like it was the last time the world was going to see the King Monkey in action. All that was left for Roses fans was this new band that John Squire was putting together.

THE SOLO YEARS

Apocalypse Now! Squire Leaves the Roses and Gets Reborn as a Seahorse!

That final phone call hadn't been easy to make. But John Squire, like Reni the year before, was owning up to the truth. The Stone Roses only really existed in name. The band as that mythic gang had gone years ago had grown up. Changed. They were all in a different place now. They had married, divorced, had kids, got mortgages, got lost and found in drugs, got into very different music, that's the way. You change. The soundtrack changes. Who hangs around with childhood friends when they hit their mid-thirties?

Making *Second Coming* had been a strain.

There were no wrong or right parties. John had cut himself off from the band, writing in his room, drained from the responsibility, exhausted from the pressure, self-confidence propped up by drugs. The pressures of creativity – creating something magical from thin air – will get everyone in the end. He had salvaged the second album, done great work in the hardest of conditions, but the band had been put under strain.

John Squire had watched the creative process ebb away. 'In the early days with songwriting there wasn't a catalyst,' he told the UCD college newspaper. 'The ideas usually came from me, because Ian didn't play an instrument. So I'd be roughing out the songs and we'd fine tune them together. But somewhere in that period, after writing and recording the first album, we weren't working at each other's homes because we had children. So we'd go away and rent a house somewhere for a week or two weeks and try and write. Very little came of it.'

Putting it out and touring had been worse. Everything possible had gone wrong. They were not really getting on. There was a distance. Only bands that were once so close could get so far apart. The golden partnership between Squire and Brown had broken down. 'I could no longer relate to Ian...didn't know who he was any more. It developed in the studio while we were recording the second album.'

In the end, John made that phone call to Ian Brown from York where he was hanging out with his guitar tech Martin. Of course it was a difficult call. But when he had done it he felt strangely relieved. He no longer had to carry the burden, the burden of ridiculous expectation that The Stone Roses had become.

To celebrate he went out on the town with Martin and got plastered. They stumbled round the tight-knit pubs in York's carefully maintained medieval tourist-trap centre. In one pub there was a band blasting through a James Brown cover in the back room. Naturally they sat down and checked them out. It's irresistible when you're a player, you have to keep listening. The band were busily getting pissed blasting out tunes, having a whale of a time. They ended their set with a Chuck Berry cover. The band was The Blueflies, a classic bar band, good time beer and fags music, a few quid for a few covers.

John was struck by the young bass player in the band, just how good he was, how he'd be great to play with. Maybe, ridiculously, he could grab the bass player and start a new band now. Just get going again. Already.

It was a lucky break for the 20-year-old Stuart Fletcher who was approached by the legendary guitar player after the gig. He was only standing in that night because the band's normal bass player had RSI and couldn't make the gig. He'd been playing bass since he was 11 and had even passed through one of the earlier line-ups of local heroes Shed 7.

As he stood there getting pissed at the bar with these two older guys, talking about his bass playing and this band that they were putting together, he had no idea that it was John Squire from The Stone Roses. He was, of course, bemused…But what the fuck, it was a gig!

As he left the pub, according to *Guitar* magazine, John Squire banged his head on a fibreglass sea horse that was hanging on the door.

Now he knew his new band would be called: the Headbangers! (Just joking…)

John had been too drunk to take Stuart's phone number. Luckily Martin was together enough to grab the goateed bass player's number. A quick phone call was made the next day and he went over and met the pair again.

Of course, in the cold sober light of day, Fletcher realised exactly what was going on. This was John Squire and he'd left the fucking Roses and he wanted him to be in his new band. And he hadn't even realised the Roses had split. But then it hadn't even been announced yet!

John played him some of his Portastudio demos of the new songs that he had – 'Happiness Is Egg Shaped' and 'Standing On Your Head' – songs that could have been the backbone of a third Roses album. The only condition for joining the band, he was told, was to be 'independent and flexible'.

It seemed an easy enough ticket and he was in. 'Meeting Stuart just hours after I'd left The Stone Roses can't be just coincidence,' Squire offers quietly. 'It was fate.'

Squire had the kernel of a group. Now all he had to do was get a frontman!

A mate of John's was walking down York high street when he spotted a busker. The shaggy-haired young man singing his heart out might be interesting. He put a call through to Squire who was equally taken aback. Good job he went to York! The place seemed to be teeming with band members.

The 25-year-old Chris Helme had just returned from a busking tour of France in his own outfit, Chutzpah. Returning from the tour he had lived in a squat in Brighton with his girlfriend, an existence so meagre that he went back to York at the first opportunity.

'We had the usual influences like the Rolling Stones and The Beatles, but we also had a drum and bass thing going on, which made for some interesting music (ha ha). I was 23 when we went to the south of France on tour. We had a good laugh but five young lads cooped up in a van on the road, the inevitable happened and there were arguments and what not. We came back to York and I went to live in Brighton for a bit. I came back to York because I was broke and started busking, plus I started writing quite a lot as well. I was also working at [York venue] Fibbers and playing there and busking.'

Picking his spot outside Woolworths on Sunday afternoons it was a particularly exuberant version of the Stones' 'No Expectations' that caught the ear of the drunken mate of Squire's staggering past. He told Helme that Squire was looking for people and told him to send a demo tape and passport to this address.

'This is around the time I passed a tape on to a friend of John Squire,' Helme recalls.

John was, apparently, not that knocked out with the tape but still intrigued enough to go and check Helme out singing in Fibbers, the main circuit venue in York. Of course with so much riding on the 'audition' everything went badly wrong: the strings flew off his guitar, snapped by heavy-handed nervous strumming, he was well drunk and by the time he crashed into 'No Expectations' his eyes were screwed shut with the nerves.

Squire looked at the singer on the stage. Did he look right? After all, he was going to be the public face of The Seahorses, this was going to be the person who was going to personify the songs that John was writing. Helme looked like a busker, shaggy-haired, folky even, but then maybe that was what John was after, something away from the street hip that had been the Roses' ticket. Something more traditional.

Says Helme, 'At the time John Squire was looking to do his own thing after The Stone Roses and it was a guy called Dennis, a friend of John's guitar tech, who heard me and asked, "Have you got a tape?" So I handed it over and later on I played a set at Fibbers for John and his guitar tech, Marin Herbert. It was obviously a big deal to me and I'd had a few drinks to calm the nerves. I went through the tunes and played my set but I really thought I cooked my goose because after it I drift up to John and say, 'Well, what do ya think, did you like it?", and he said, "Yeah, you were good, mate." But I did this a couple of times, walking up to John with Newky Brown in hand, more than a little drunk, and asking him what he thought. After a few times he just said, "For fuck's sake. I've told ya once, you were all right!"

About a week later I did another gig at the same venue and John, Steve "Adge" Atherton and Simon Moran were in attendance. At the time John was actually looking at the singer of The Steamboat Band to set up his new band with. As far as I was concerned, the thing with Squire wasn't happening after my earlier boozy display so I got up there and played with the reins off. I just thought, "Fuck it, nothing to lose," and went through my set with a more confident performance, and it was that night John came up to me and said he was well impressed and had really enjoyed the gig.'

Chris was given another chance to audition.

'He then set me up a gig at The Roadhouse in Manchester, which was the first solo gig I'd ever played that wasn't in cosy old York,' he says. 'They put me on in the middle of three rock bands, but I came away unscathed and the audience were pretty warm towards me. John came up at the end and said, "Do you wanna join a band then?"'

The Roadhouse audition went well and The Seahorses were now three. They retreated to Coniston in the Lake District to a cottage up in the hills and during that long hot summer of '96 started piecing together the début album.

While the rump of the Roses were self-destructing at Reading Festival, The Seahorses were putting the finishing touches to the tunes that would form the backbone of the album. John refutes claims that The Seahorses was somehow pre-planned during the final days of the Roses, as he explained to the UCD magazine.

'There's only one song on *Do It Yourself*, 'Standing On Your Head', that was completed before I left The Stone Roses – but I didn't write it with the intention of it being the start of a secret store of songs that I could use for any solo project. It was just something I held back from *Second Coming* because I felt we had enough to work on at that time. Things were going so slowly I just didn't want to add another song to the pot. But looking back on it, it does seem strange that The Seahorses came together so quickly.'

The endless summer in the idyllic countryside was broken by just one appearance. The now legendary Oasis show at Knebworth – the biggest ever rock gig by one band in the UK. The Roses' understudies had, by the summer of 1996, gone so ridiculously massive even they couldn't believe it. And here was John Squire as special guest during the spiralling psychedelic freak-out encores of 'Champagne Supernova' and 'I Am The Walrus'.

It was an honour for the Gallaghers to have the Roses guitarist on stage with them, as Noel explains.

'I remember being on the tour bus somewhere and we were saying if Spike Island had 35,000 people, we have to have 36,000. We have to take it to another level and it was only five times as big in the end!

'I love John and he graciously agreed to do the gig. Paul Weller had played the solo on "Champagne Supernova" when we recorded it and I knew he wouldn't do it live. I wouldn't ask him, anyway, so I thought, let's ask John as a tribute to the Roses. There was always something between the Manchester bands. We were all from the same streets regardless of what we think of each other musically; we went to the same nightclubs, we went to the same football stadiums, drank in the same pubs, know each other's back stories as they say in America. Loads of people said to us that we had outdone The Stone Roses but we outdid The Beatles as well! Ian was always respectful of us in interviews; when the *NME* were saying what about this mob, he said, "They are real as fuck, they are bollocks," and I remember being pleased about that.'

When John Squire entered the stage at Knebworth, it was quite a moment.

'Here's John Squire…with Oasis,' an unbelieving Liam Gallagher grinned, still at heart the kid at the International 2 Stone Roses gig, as Squire leaned back and broke out into a massive explosion of guitar notes. The crowd went wild. What a perfect moment – two generations of Manchester colliding at this, the high water mark of the city's musical popularity.

Noel was equally impressed, 'He's playing all this mad Jimmy Page stuff and I'm thinking this is a moment in my life. We had done the gig at Knebworth as our Spike Island, but it had to be bigger than Spike Island – but we never thought it was going to get that big!'

Doing It Himself: Squire Completes The Seahorses

The Seahorses also now had a drummer. Andy Watts was again pulled in from the fog of the York pub scene, a bespectacled, much travelled Londoner who could sing as well as play drums. He was quickly assimilated into the line-up which was soon ready to play its first gigs.

They had announced their name to the press, attracting the attention of a band from Liverpool who had been going for years with the same name. There was a row and some sort of legal squaring up.

And finally. They were ready to go public.

How do you start again? From scratch? Well, you start from the bottom and work up.

Interest in The Seahorses was of course, high. But going out on a fully blown tour was not Squire style. Break it in from the grass roots. Work up.

Their first show was in North Wales at the Buckley Tivoli, the ornate hall that had been a circuit gig for many indie bands on the verge of the breakthrough. The gig showcased a band that was quite definitely trad rock, but the warmth of the melodies and the exquisite guitar work transcended any retro accusations. All the mid-seventies hallmarks were there, the sort of music that punk had blown away rediscovered and updated. For John it was his natural terrain anyway, the melodic guitar-hero-based music of his youth.

The next gig was in Greenock at Ricos, the gig booked by the talkative Roses fan Andrew McDermid who was also managing Whiteout at the time. Greenock, like nearby Glasgow, was staunch Roses country, and the gig, of course, was a hot sweaty affair. Andrew was quickly on the phone buzzing about the show, about Squire's guitar playing, about how good The Seahorses were. The young crowd at Ricos reared on the Roses' legend had no uneasiness about the guitar player's new direction; this generation was into their trad rock – especially this well executed – where else could the bands go after Britpop?

Late that autumn of 1996 the band relocated to Los Angeles to record *Do It Yourself* with Tony Visconti, the man who had brilliantly produced T-Rex and Bowie and a whole plethora of classic-sounding seventies glam records.

'Tony was one of Geffen's suggestions,' Squire explains. 'I actually wanted to get Steve Albini but I was told they couldn't track him down.'

Albini had made his name on the US underground recording loud, raw powerful records. Recently he had burst into the mainstream with Nirvana's *In Utero*, a raw, dark and uncompromisingly powerful record with a massive thumping drum sound that recalled the great John Bonham's primal explosive drums. Despite what people say, Albini's recording really caught the band perfectly.

With Albini you got what you played, you felt you were standing right in the room with the band. His recording techniques, utilising suitcases of vintage mics he brought to the sessions and an ear for uncompromising sound, would have been perfect for The Seahorses – an unlikely marriage that would have pulled them away from being 'too safe.' But unfortunately it wasn't to happen.

Meanwhile Squire enjoyed working with Visconti, as he told *Guitar* magazine.

'Tony flew over to Manchester Airport and when we met him he was just a really nice bloke, none of the attitude problems you'd think you might get from a guy who's worked with Bowie and what have you. Because he was so down to earth I thought he'd be really good for the rest of the band, as they'd obviously not worked at that sort of level before.

'Tony was great in the studio. He's a musician himself and plays all sorts of instruments; the producers I've worked with in the past all came through engineering and didn't have a musical background, whereas Tony could converse in that language. There were no situations where, when a song comes off the rails, the producer just says: "It's not 'right'; can you do it again?" And again, and again...there were no abstract terms like that. Tony also had great organisational sense; he got us all in on time, basically. A lot of the mood aspect of the recording can be attributed to Tony.'

The resulting album, *Do It Yourself*, was a move away from the Roses' legacy as Squire pointed out to *Guitar* magazine: 'I was very conscious of that time away. There was a philosophy with *Do It Yourself* of taking it back to basics. I didn't want this record to sound like a continuation of the Roses, a sequel to *Second Coming*; I wanted it to sound like a début album, so we contrived to capture the live sound and not spend too much time slicking it up and layering. *Second Coming* was just overworked...on the basis of the fact that we weren't a cohesive unit and we were spending just too long in the studio. The luxury of endless hours and endless overdubs meant the freshness was lost. Some songs on *Second Coming* were the third or even fourth recorded versions; things were lying around on master tapes from the first week of recording – there was no drive there, no immediacy.'

The resulting album was a set of catchy guitar rock songs that sat somewhere between The Beatles and Led Zep. It flew to the top of the album charts where it ended up at number two in the UK and number eight in the USA – the highest chart placing of any Roses member.

Critics point out its safe trad nature but like The Stone Roses the whole schtick was to make the familiar sound new, the traditional sound contemporary. Squire, a gifted songwriter, was following his muse and the guitar playing and melodies on the album are perfect. There were some good songs on there like the anthemic 'Love Is The Law', which has a great twisting chorus.

In many ways the album is an escape from the dark heart of *Second Coming*. There are daft lyrics about weetabix and giant squid, replacing the pessimistic twists that had underlined so many of John's words on the Roses' two albums; the tone was lighter, more poppy, more song-based. The album was a well-worked set of melodic guitar action. The post-Britpop kids adored it. Here was the man who'd kicked off their scene and he was back and he was making music that slotted neatly into the modern/retro nature of the mid-nineties Britpop scene.

It was harking back to a time when rock ruled the earth and the guitar hero was the main conduit of rock'n'roll.

Squire had escaped from the Roses' legacy.

*

'Love Is The Law' was The Seahorses' début single, released on 28 April 1997, flipped with Chris Helme's Beatles-tinged 'Dreamer' and Squire's own 'Sale Of The Century'. The single entered the UK charts at number three – it was Squire's highest chart position so far other than 'Love Spreads'. The Seahorses were top five and John Squire was back in business. The song was as good as anything he had written in his career with its great uplifting chorus.

The band was going well. They toured the UK, the big halls, like Manchester Academy. I caught up with them there and the venue was rammed full and the atmosphere was pretty magic, as magic as it would be for the Ian Brown shows. The Roses' aura would cloak any of the ex-members and was not just the exclusive preserve of Ian Brown.

The gig was typified by John unleashing huge guitar breaks, moving on-stage slightly, delicately, just like his idol Jimmy Page had done in Zep all those years ago. Chris Helme walked on to the stage to screams. He was considered a bit of a bohemian pin-up at the time!

The *Do It Yourself* album followed on 27 May. The reviews were a mixed bag, but then for every Squire record from The Stone Roses onwards that has been the case. The record entered the album charts at number two, with only Gary Barlow out-selling it.

The full track-listing for *Do It Yourself* was 'I Want You To Know', 'Blinded By The Sun', 'Suicide Drive', 'The Boy In The Picture', 'Love Is The Law', 'Happiness Is Eggshaped', 'Love Me And Leave Me', 'Round The Universe', '1999', 'Standing On Your Head' and 'Hello', songs that continued in the Hendrix/Zep flavour that had so dominated John's late Roses work.

'Love Me And Leave Me' was co-written by Liam Gallagher of Oasis, the frontman's first-ever songwriting credit. The second single from *Do It Yourself* was 'Blinded By The Sun'. Released in the UK on 14 July and hitting the charts at number seven it was the first ever 'A' side of any band that involved John but was not actually written by him. 'Blinded By The Sun' was written by Chris Helme and backed with Squire's 'Kill Pussycat Kill', and Chris's 'Movin' On'.

For Chris Helme it must have been a moment. 'Well, I was overwhelmed at first, getting to do what I've always loved doing – playing music 24/7 and obviously playing with John. I was eager to please, maybe a bit too eager for his tastes, but at the time he was the most focused musician I'd ever encountered, and as far as the album went,

John seemed to have a pretty pre-ordained idea of what he wanted. He was very particular about things. I imagine that's how he approached his work in the Roses. I would be into the feel of it more than repeating a structure, but John was quite adamant about a lot of things, like the way I sang, my accent, things like that. I wanted to get more of my work in there with the band, so I managed to squeeze in "Moving On", and wrote "Hello" and "I Want You To Know". The rest were John's babies. My songs [before The Seahorses] were never published. I didn't even know what a publishing deal was, never mind anything else. I had a stack of tunes but I thought they'd never get a look in. I was sensitive to the fact that John wasn't going to air his opinion either way, cards close to his chest and all that.

'The only tune that seemed to prick his ears was 'Blinded By The Sun'. Originally it was slightly faster than the finished version. Like most things, John would work on his own so when we heard the guitar lines I was real pleased with it, but I had about another 30 or 40 tunes that I had wrote and was willing to work on.'

The next single, the 'Liam Gallagher one', pulled off the album caught the attention of the over-zealous self-righteous censors at MTV America, meaning a trip back to the studio to change a line. Originally 'Don't believe in Jesus' – a line borrowed from John Lennon's stark and confessional 'God', it was now wittily re-recorded as 'Don't believe in censors'. But that poleaxed the original meaning of the song as explained by Liam Gallagher in the middle of a particularly funny rant in *GQ* magazine (the one where he went on about fighting sixties popstars in the middle of Primrose Hill).

'John Squire come round me house one night for some aspirin and we ended up having a rant – a bit of this, a bit of that – and the paracetamol was a bit too strong for him, so we wrote that song. I've had this thing in me head for ages – I don't believe in Jesus, I don't believe in Jah – I don't believe in religion basically. I was brought up going to church and after circumstances in my life changed, I thought – f*** Jesus, f*** 'em all. It was because of me Mam and her divorce, how she couldn't take the Body of Christ any more. They're telling her it's a big sin, she can't go to heaven and all that bollocks. She's put her whole faith in the church, but where's their faith in her?'

The song was the best on the album, a lush Beatlesque melody with the descending 'Dear Prudence' guitar line and a very Liam rasping vocal.

Not as big a hit as the first two singles, the record peaked at number 15 in the charts; the album meanwhile was selling strongly. Squire was now well established outside the Roses.

Four big singles and one big album in one year. The Seahorses were well on their way to becoming one of the mid-nineties' major bands – not loved like the Roses, but capable of 'doing good business'.

But then it all started to fall apart.

John Squire ponders over the split: 'The drummer and bassist walked out and the singer persuaded them to come back. But I decided that if they were going to be that flaky, I didn't want to continue.'

The lop-sided nature of the band with the superstar guitar player and the three York boys was always going to make it difficult to function. Watts was the first to go. He left for the over-subscribed 'musical differences' or for 'excessive behaviour' on tour depending on who you believe.

In 1998, the band began their second album with new drummer Mark Heaney. They played new songs on a series of secret gigs that were described as 'pretty bluesy' especially at their T in the Park performance. More new song titles were revealed as 'Tomb Raid', 'City In The Sky' and 'One In A Million'. There were two new Helme songs, 'Won't Let You Fall' and 'Moth'.

The band then entered Olympic Studios with producer David Bottrill in January 1999 to record the follow-up album, with the working titles of 'Minus Blue' and 'Motocade'. The recordings ended when John Squire walked out of the studio.

A spokesman for the band later informed the *NME* that Squire had 'become increasingly dissatisfied with the material being produced by Helme until it reached a point where their partnership was no longer possible'.

For Chris Helme it was a difficult situation to be in – the singer in a big-name guitar player's band. He got a few songs in there, but he was trying to get the songs past John Squire, someone with their own mega track record of success.

As Helme himself explained at the time, 'I was having to sing lyrics I did not want to sing. I didn't like his melodies, either, so the whole thing was unsatisfying. I started on the second album and didn't like any of it. I could see from a mile off it wasn't going to work. He's a good bloke, but we didn't see eye to eye musically.

'We had got together for the rehearsals for the next album but the sessions were really strained, and John was becoming more and more irritated with me. We'd been touring non-stop since we'd met and I was drinking heavily and turning up hungover and stinking. John's new material was starting to become something I didn't like, just loads of loud guitar riffing and lyrics that I had nothing in common with. He was too strict with the melodies and it was all a bit stiff and laboured. The publishers weren't into John's new stuff much either and even the roadies around us were pulling faces and saying it was below standard. Me and Stu started to feel like we were just session men and there just to finish his songs off with him picking up all the publishing and that. It didn't feel right. By then me and John were going two different ways, with me being more acoustic and him and his loudness. I started to express my opinions and John wasn't used to that, but I stuck to my guns. It became apparent that none of us were happy with where we were heading, and I suppose we were just tired, frustrated and getting really down about stuff.

'I remember we were playing a gig in the run up to Christmas, at Glasgow Barrowlands. It was the last gig we ever played before we started work on the second album and we put in a really good performance. After John said, "That was great, Chris, you're a fucking star!" That really meant a lot to me, but then I realised that we'd been together for three years and it was the first time John had ever given me any really positive encouragement. After the gig I came back to York and it felt very strange. I didn't feel like I was home at all and with other personal things going on in my life, I tried to get my priorities in order but just started drinking instead. My head was done in. Then the dissatisfaction of the second album sessions and more touring...a band meeting, the band split.'

Perhaps the band dynamic wasn't helped by a big age and experience range. 'Yeah, well, that's it. John was older than us. Stuart Fletcher [bass player] was 20, I was 26 and John was 36. That's quite a spread and I found myself in the middle of that in a way; I would be telling Stu to chill out because he would be doing my nut in, like you do when you're 20. John would be telling me to chill out and so it went like that, but nothing too heated. Plus John had obviously lived a bit more than the rest of us, he had been through all that with the Roses, the court case, the highly publicised break-up of the band and so on.

'On a personal level me and John got on all right. It was me and John who would do the press for the band, so I probably spent more time with him than the others, but it's not like we hung out a lot. We weren't the chattiest of fellas. I got the impression it was best not to ask too many questions about stuff like the Roses, or other personal stuff. It was nothing to do with me. However, later on when I did have the right to ask questions relating to band business dealings, I think that was when trust issues started to develop due to nothing being out in the open. This wasn't so much John, and don't get me wrong, none of us were done badly, but too many questions seemed to piss certain people off. All that niggling shite aside, being in The Seahorses was amazing. I loved the travelling, meeting people, playing to huge crowds – lucky as fuck.'

Chris Helme had tried to keep going after he had left The Seahorses. There was a low-key gig in London, a set of demos, but outside Planet Squire he was back down to earth with a bump. There were a few bitter exchanges in the music press between Helme and his former band mates. Noticeably, John Squire was absent from this debate. Helme explained to *NME*.com, 'I've been listening to Jackson Browne and early Van Morrison a lot, so there's no muso wanking like on Seahorses. I've got enough for two albums at the minute. It's confessional stuff.' Helme was hawking his demos around but there was still no record deal. He pointed out that it was because he was still tied in to his old management deal. 'It's tough when your career's in someone else's hands. But that's sorted now. I'm not desperately seeking a new deal, but I've been talking to a few people who seem to like what they've heard.'

He also clarified, to some extent, the split. 'There was a personality clash during rehearsals. When John came up with new stuff I didn't like his lyrics or tunes. I could have gone with it and made quite a lot of money, but I wasn't interested.'

The Seahorses' mailing list added an interesting adjoiner to this story with John Fletcher, father of Stuart Fletcher (bassist in The Seahorses), responding, 'I think it's a shame for Chris to slag off John Squire in the music press. Chris owes JS a lot – regardless of the fact that he wasn't keen on John's lyrics or tunes. However, it was these very things that turned Chris into a household name, and to broadcast their differences just smacks of sour grapes. My personal opinion is that Chris should have recorded the second album, having come so far with it, and then cited musical differences and left the band. I don't care what he says – the Horses were a great band, and to give the impression that he hated every minute does him no credit at all.'

Chris Helme himself has mixed emotions about his time with the band. ''I thought we put on decent shows and playing live was great. For me, seeing how the other half lived, or rather toured, was an eye-opener. Like the gig at Murrayfield supporting U2 on the Pop Mart tour; getting in the dressing room and finding crates of Guinness and bottles of champagne left for us with a note attached from Bono, though I doubt he actually wrote it himself. I remember looking out of the dressing-room window and seeing presidential-type security men with shades and earpieces ushering U2 into the stadium and getting told to get back in as "no one gets to watch the band come in".

'These were things that John had already been through but we were just taking it all in.

'I was like "more of that, please", but John had other plans for the second album, and I don't think a mellow acoustic vibe was it. He liked it loud. John was very loud on stage. You know, it's been said that Ian Brown would sometimes struggle singing live but I've heard Ian sing live a few times and that guy can definitely sing. I actually think he had the same problem I did, just finding it hard to hear yourself over John's guitar!

'Of course John gave me my chance and I took it. I realised the opportunity he gave me was a big one and like I said I wanted to please, wanted to get it right, and regardless of how it finished, it was one of the greatest times of my life.'

The e-mail from John Fletcher came only a few months after the split so the wounds were still pretty raw. The bad feeling spilling out into the press underlined one thing. The Seahorses was quite definitely over.

And John Squire's musical career had ground to a halt.

Back To the Drawing Board (Squire Starts Again!)

Groundhog Day! Squire was starting from scratch with yet another band. Just like The Patrol, The Waterfront, the Roses, The Seahorses: time to find another singer to join Andy Couzens, Kaiser, Ian Brown and Chris Helme as the vessel for his songs, the mouthpiece for his lyrics.

John the instigator was left to pull the strands back together. And midsummer 1999, the ever-industrious guitar player acted swiftly.

He still had his deal with Geffen – no wonder with those record sales! The next couple of years Squire went to ground, prompting plenty of rumours, plenty of false trails.

At first there were rumours of the band being called Reluctance. In October ex-Verve bass player Simon Jones was working with John writing new material in a Manchester rehearsal room. The rhythm section was completed by ex-Seahorses drummer Mark Heaney. The name Reluctance seems to have been replaced by Skunk Works, named after a Californian weapons system plant where the U2 spy plane was developed for the American government, although this was just loose talk as it also seems that they never really decided on a name.

Oh well, there is still the Angry Young Teddy Bears!

An insider told the *NME*: 'It's all going really well apparently. Simon [Jones] is excited about it and it takes something special for him to get excited.'

There was talk that the new band were still working on some of the leftover Seahorses songs but that didn't seem that likely with the guitarist's avowed mission to keep moving forward.

Late August John Squire and Mani were spotted chatting backstage at an Oasis party. John was still sporting the Jimmy Page-style beard that had sprouted in May. There was also a grass-roots rumour from a band in the same rehearsal rooms as Squire that they had overheard the new outfit rehearsing a version of Arthur Brown's 'Fire' and other songs which sounded like *Second Coming*-era Stone Roses. Rumours, rumours, rumours...just like the *Second Coming* days!

For John, that summer was one step forwards and two steps backwards – first he finally found a new singer in ex-model Duncan Baxter, but then in August Jones and Heaney quit the project. Simon Jones's heart 'wasn't into it any more'.

The pair of them continued to work on the project. Speaking to sources very close to the 'band', I was told that the music was returning to the pure pop of the earlier Roses and was veering away from the heavyweight guitar workouts that had dominated Squire's works for the past decade. Good job, as in December there was talk that Geffen had dropped Squire from its rosta, although, typically this was unconfirmed.

As 1999 rolled into 2000 John Squire disappeared further and further from view. There were occasional snippets of information round town about what John Squire was up to.

In February 2000, in an interview with the *Guardian* newspaper, Ian Brown revealed that John Squire sent him some Maltesers with a note saying, 'I still love you' while he was in prison for the 'air rage' incident. Apparently when they were kids they used to give each other a box of Maltesers for Christmas.

2001 and John Squire was back out there in the mythic hills, growing beards and having kids and painting his great paintings.

In 2002 he suddenly reappeared for a surprise solo album. The biggest shock was that he was singing. Hardly anyone had ever heard him speak, let alone sing. His voice had a rasping, emotional, Dylanesque drawl with a touch of Bowie to it and was pretty effective over the music that was classic John Squire – all tumbling guitars and warm melodies. Of course it was not the first time he had ever sung in his life – there were all those Portastudio vocals as he laid down the melodies of The Stone Roses' tracks over the years, but these were the first public outings.

The début album, *Time Changes Everything,* doesn't sound like it was meant to be the big statement. More like pages of a diary pulled out for anyone who was interested, it had many allusions to The Stone Roses, from the Pollock-style paint-spattered goat skull on the cover to lyrics that hinted of the past and the fallout with Ian Brown. The song 'I Miss You' could be either a song of lost love or possibly about wanting to end his feud with Ian Brown. The title track had a real Roses flavour to it with hints of the outro of 'Resurrection' in its guitars.

Released on his own North Country Records, the album reached number 17 in the charts.

In February 2003 John Squire toured his solo stuff and played a solo show at Manchester Ritz. The gig had an emotional edge to it because of the recent death of Joe Strummer, John's hero from his teenage years. He went on stage with a Clash-style stencilled shirt with 'Screw The Government' on the front.

I was there to review the gig for *Drowned In Sound* website: 'These are desperate times. Every politician in the world is cranking up the lie machine. Scum weapons seem to be everywhere and there is some dumb muscle flexing going on. *"Gimme some truth"* as someone once sang.

'So John Squire's stencilled "Screw The Government" shirt looks pretty damn apt. It's a fucking bang-on slogan and The Clash-style graphic is a neat nod to Squire's youth when the skinny south Manc kid was The

Clash fanatic of a motley crew of punks and scooter boys that eventually coalesced into The Stone Roses.

'And roots is what it's all about tonight.

'The John Squire show hits Manchester on the back of a solo album that seemed to be dealing with the great rift with Ian Brown and the collapse of potentially one of the biggest bands of the past ten years. Squire seemed to be saying, "Let's patch it up, here's the olive branch." In the meantime, before The Stone Roses eventually hit the road again (and the rumour mill never stops with this great band – latest talk is 2004 – but we need them now, a bolshy British rock'n'roll band that is smart and has the power to uplift the people), Squire is working the golden back catalogue and there are plenty of Roses songs tonight – "Made Of Stone" and "She Bangs The Drums" are still spine-tinglingly awesome with Squire's rasping voice giving the songs a different spin.

'"Waterfall" is still a gem – it's great to hear those timeless guitar licks. The Roses tunes slot in neatly with Squire's current tunes, which sit back deeper into the Dylanesque songbook so beloved by the elder rock states-men of the baggy generation.

'John's voice sits somewhere between Bowie and Dylan and while it's odd hearing the quietest man in rock'n'roll sing, he actually has a strong voice and is a great frontman, as he leans back with his trusty Les Paul, stick thin, cool-as-fuck, looking from underneath his fringe.

'And then at the end he dedicates the last encore to Joe Strummer and the band rattle through the wholly apt and superb version of "I'm So Bored Of The USA". It's a brilliant song done with total conviction. Squire's voice is surprisingly powerful in a punk rock kinda way. There's not a dry eye in the house. The Clash and The Stone Roses: two bands who meant the same to their twin generations, rock'n'roll heroes who understood the swagger and the outlaw status of great R'n'R. And that's why years later, even on a low-key tour, John Squire can ram out a concert in Manchester and the crowd give him a wall of affection and test out their "John Squire" football singalongs.

'Now we just need to get the other three back up there with him again.'

In 2004 Squire released the follow-up album *Marshall's House*, which came with a painting on the sleeve with the intriguing title of 'Swimming through holes of dead American painters'. The title track was the best thing he had done since the Roses, a croaking, tripped- out *White Album-* period Beatles trip of a song that had its own unique atmosphere.

The album continued the musical theme of the début but didn't chart, maybe because its creator was keeping things low key, and Squire hung up his guitar to become a painter with several successful shows and that rarest of things, a musician who had a great rep in the art world.

Mani: Having It Larger than Large – The Rogue Rose Joining Primal Scream, Know What I Mean!

Perhaps the greatest free transfer in the history of rock'n'roll, Mani's move to Primal Scream was so perfect, so right, that it couldn't have been planned any better.

I mean, what other band in the UK had punk-rock roots, working-class righteousness, a psychedelic pop edge, a huge vested interest in the house scene and a completely ramshackle anarchic mode of operation! No sir, the Primals were perfect for the mighty bassman and after a series of phone calls put in place even before the infamous last stand at Reading, he was planning his move.

Not that Mani would ever let his old muckers down. To the end he was still firing on full Roses cylinders at Reading, giving it his usual 100 per cent, thrusting his bass at the crowd.

In the weeks after the show he made his mind up fast. It was obvious that the Roses game was up so he jumped ship and moved to the only other band that would accommodate his punk-funk bass and wild-ass lifestyle. He announced, 'After much speculation I've decided, along with Ian Brown, that it's time to end the Roses saga. I will be joining Primal Scream, who are one of only three other bands I would ever consider joining. I'm absolutely delighted and am relishing the opportunity of playing with Bobby and friends.'

It seemed like the most natural thing in the world. Mani had arrived, and with him a new leash of life for Primal Scream.

Mani had been noting the Scream's progress throughout the years. 'I'd always been aware of the Scream. Just from the fact we're all music lovers. We were always listening and conscious of what was going on around us. There were a lot of parallels between The Stone Roses and Primal Scream, quite similar backgrounds musically and culturally. It's kismet that I ended up with them.'

The first meeting between the two godheads of British acid rock'n'roll punk rock was in Brighton way back in 1988.

'I probably first met them in an ecstasy haze, probably in the Hacienda. I can remember when we went down to play in Brighton at the Richmond in 1989 – just before the Blackpool gig and someone had forgotten my bass amp and all my equipment, and there were about thirty people at the gig – a large contingent of which were the Scream mob. I think we did something like four songs and just went "Fuck it, we can't be arsed" and steamed off. Bob remembers that gig as a blinder, full of attitude.'

And when the call came from the Scream camp for Mani, at the tail end of the Roses, his exuberant spirit was just what the group needed.

Gillespie, Innes, Young and Duffy had just put together an eight-track studio near Creation's office in north London and were getting together ideas for a new album.

It was difficult, slow going. Alex Nightingale, manager of Primal Scream at the time, pointed out. 'A lot of people had written them off and eventually they started saying "Fuck it, we'll come out fighting." Then there was Mani – a godsend. The best signing since Cantona.'

'When Mani joined us, it seemed like a band again,' agrees Bobby Gillespie. 'I think if Mani hadn't joined I would never have played live again. He was like a nuclear fucking explosion. He saved our lives.'

At that point in time Primal Scream needed the energy of Mani.

And what better band could he join.

Their career had run in parallel with the Roses with ups and downs, punk roots, creative highs and lows, acid house, post acid house, rejuven-ated guitar music, a political edge; uncompromising hard-ass bands with soft melodic songs, intelligent scowling presences on *Top of the Pops*.

Fuck, where else could Mani go?

After their ground-breaking *Screamadelica* set of 1991 when they seemed to be setting the agenda with the Roses and the Mondays, the Primals had seemed to hit the same sort of slowdown. There had been *Give Out But Don't Give Up*, a far rockier affair, a record pasted by most reviewers who labelled the band 'dance traitors,' but one that stands up really well listening to it years later.

'Rocks' is still one great shit-kicking slice of rock'n'roll and the term 'dance traitors' has to be considered a bit of a joke when you hear this track live in a club electrifying the dancefloor. It does open the debate of what dance music was anyway. Dance is not just acid house. Let's not forget the Rolling Stones are probably the world's biggest dance band! Add on to this 'Jailbird' and a few other choice cuts and you ignore a record that is far better than most people seem to remember.

The only problem is that as good as the Primals' rock music is, the expectations are for something more, something darker and more dangerous, more off-the-wall. If *Screamadelica* had been the blissed-out soundtrack to the summers of love, who would dare soundtrack the comedown, the hangover?

After all, this is a band that was formed by singer Bobby Gillespie wacking dustbins in a liftshaft in a vague approximation of German noise avant-gardists Einstürzende Neubauten. And the fevered mind of reticent guitar player Andrew Innes, who even then was learning how to fuck with the controls in the studio.

Throw into this mix a bass player free of the constraints of his beloved band and hungry to create some new space for himself and you've got a hot mix.

All through Mani's Roses stint there had been hints of something a bit darker and more twisted, a bit more underground than the Roses pop template allowed. Hints of Can would occasionally bubble up to the surface in 'Fool's Gold' or 'Something's Burning'.

Unleashed in Primal Scream and allowed to run amok in their seemingly impossible agenda of criss-crossing the greats from *Bitches Brew* Davis to Can, to PIL, to the MC5, and Mani was very much in his element.

Now that the Primals had decided to throw off the yoke of 'classic songwriting' and go back to their post-punk roots of fucking with the form they suddenly opened up a wasps' nests of sound.

The first single from this new line-up was the stunning 'Kowalski', a piece of sound driven by one killer Mani bass line. Gillespie's whispered vocal hints of paranoia and the hook 'soul on ice' a quote from Eldridge Cleaver's biography of Marcus Garvey.

The fact that the single was a Top Ten hit proved the strength of Primal Scream's following and the hunger for some brave music out there. When the 1997 Creation Records-released *Vanishing Point* album followed, it blew open the Primal Scream debate. Written as an alternative soundtrack to the road movie, this was the sound of a band finding its sound, mashing up the rebel musics of rock'n'roll and acid house.

No longer considered a burned-out bunch of lost indie rockers who had delivered their classic, Primal Scream were now entering new territory. For some it was their hangover album, the comedown from the acid house high to the smack- and filth-infested mid-nineties hellhole – the post-euphoric world, the necessary kickback after all those highs. A bleak, freaked record, it was electric soundscapes and dark, dank paranoias, like PIL's incredible *Metal Box* from 1979. This was the record that came out after the party but was somehow still made with enough resolute strength to capture the strange dark hue of the period.

For such a non-conformist, dark-hearted howl of a record to go to number eight was fantastic.

Of course, being in Primal Scream, life was never easy. There were bizarre, untogether gigs with a drum machine, a dark descent into a chemical hell and messed-up lives. Post *Vanishing Point* was a bumpy ride but they eventually got their live show together and harnessed those demons.

How the fuck they managed to regroup and record the amazing follow-up, 2000's *XTRMNTR*, released by Creation, is a testament to their inner strength. The album is perhaps the key British release of the period. They sound like the only major league rock'n'roll band that seems to be in touch with the modern world – no fucking Beatles, or fucking Gerry And The Pacemakers, a tuff-as-nails V-sign to the establishment – political and musical. It's an anti-corporation album that predicted the future and made music that was a direct descendant of post-punk.

Their 2001 tour saw some awesome gigs – Bobby hunched up waif-like on the mic like John Lydon when he was cool; the added figure of My Bloody Valentine's Kevin Shields adding his warped guitar noise over the top like he had done on the recent album, just added to the insanity. Soundchecks with punk covers, gigs that reached at all points of the rebel music universe, how fucking good could a band get. And Mani, the garrulous king of the bass virtually fronting the show!

So what if they had lost all their money due to some problems with their book-keeping, that they had to sack their manager, that their long-term record label Creation didn't exist any more. Primal Scream seem to thrive in a crisis.

And through it all is the bass player, swinging the bass around, driving the songs, practically fronting the band, shouting good times at the crowd, living the rock'n'roll life to the hilt and playing some great bass at the same time.

Off-stage he is still Mani popping up all over town. Good times. Good tunes. Now and then he will issue a rallying call to the rest of the Roses to get together for some festival, go out on a high note, bury the hatchet, show 'em who's the best .

2002's *Evil Heat* was the third part of this stark trilogy of albums, another ground-breaking collision of Krautrock, electro, industrial and indie rock'n'roll.

Four years later the band reverted to their rock'n'roll roots with 2006's *Riot City Blues*. The album brought in a whole flux of guests, fellow travellers in rock'n'roll like Will Sergeant (Echo And The Bunnymen) on 'When The Bomb Drops', Warren Ellis (Nick Cave And The Bad Seeds, Dirty Three) on 'Hell's Coming Down' and Alison Mosshart (The Kills) performing backing vocals on 'Dolls (Sweet Rock And Roll)'. The first hint that the band had exhausted the dark soundscapes of the hangover trilogy was the 'Country Girl' single, a Stonesy country rock romp that proved that their guitar rock'n'roll pop touch had not deserted them. The single charted at number five, the band's biggest hit so far.

2008's *Beautiful Future* was a mixture of all the Primal Screams, the many styles that they had toyed with over the years. The band was settling into a groove; they were festival headliners and had a strong fan base. They could always be relied on to do something with a twist, to make another album that sounded like the result of being the professors of rock'n'roll that they were – huge record collections of archived underground and classic black and white music mashed together and given their own idiosyncratic twist.

It was a long way from the 'Velocity Girl' tune that had so influenced The Stone Roses all those years ago.

Reni: 'John the Baptist' – The Beard Years

In 1993 wandering through town I bumped into Reni. The cheeky scamp was mooching down Oxford Road unrecognised by the passing pop kids. Kicking his heels in a pair of baggy jeans and deck shoes. It had been a few years since I'd seen him, in fact it seemed like another pop lifetime since anyone had seen the Roses.

They had disappeared deep into Wales to write and record and then, er, nothing.

We walked down Oxford Road and towards the Salutation in Hulme where the penniless drummer scabbed a drink off me and, sat out in the sun, Reni talked about the album and how he was not even going to drum on it. 'I'm into programming now,' he explained. 'I don't need to have my drums on the record,' he added, perhaps sarcastically, as I wondered why it was taking so long to make the record. Reni revealed that he was taking his drums off the already recorded songs and replacing them, and that the band was going to go 'in a 'Fool's Gold' direction.

Two years later the album finally came out and after a brief promotional tour Reni quit the band.

In the years after he left the Roses Reni had disappeared into a mythic rock'n'roll half-life. Rumours preceded the drummer, who was actually living quietly in Whalley Range bringing up his kids and getting his own music together. Everyone wondered why he quit – was it drugs? Was it money? Was it a personality clash?

There has never been any kind of explanation. Just a fistful of myths.

And so to Whalley Range where in the mid-nineties he started work on his music in his upstairs studio, working on tunes. A whole mountain of songs had been piled up, with Reni singing and playing guitar in the outfit.

'You've got to remember that Reni was always a brilliant guitar player,' points out Pete Garner who was actually playing bass with Reni and was, as he jokingly laughs, his 'spiritual advisor' .

They had hooked up a rehearsal room and started putting a band together properly. Rumoured to be trading under the name of Hunkpapa for a few months, it looked like Reni was ready to emerge from the shadows again.

'But Reni is so meticulous,' points out a friend. 'He wants to get everything completely note perfect before he lets it out. The stuff I heard sounded spot on but he still wasn't happy with it.'

The band continued to rehearse into 1998 but then Pete left...and rejoined...and left again! It seemed like a weekly occurrence. Pete and Reni – the old rhythm section was not going to happen. Pete didn't want to play bass in a band all those years ago and was just helping out a mate.

Eventually Pete left for good, happier just to be mates with Reni than play in the same band as him.

Reni carried on working with the new drummer and retreated back to his bedroom eight-track polishing those songs up. There was even a demo tape floating around…

During the late nineties Reni would pop up now and then. Bizarrely he and Pete appeared on a local Granada TV programme for a short interview. Reni was long-haired and big-bearded, looking like a wildman from the mountains and certainly filling the part of the long lost musician, half returning from some sort of self-imposed exile. Soon after Pete left again, although there was no real fall-out, and they were still mates. Reni recruited local sound engineer Tom Evans to play bass with him but has yet to get a full line-up.

Ian Brown noted Reni's drastic change of appearance at the time. 'He's got big hair and a beard and I call him John The Baptist.' Ian also pointed out. 'There's every possibility that we'll play together. I was jamming with Reni last week. He's now singing, playing guitar.' There was low-level talk that Reni may be joining Brown in some sort of capacity, either live or in the studio.

At the time there was a bootleg of Reni's unnamed band floating around, featuring tight melodic songs, touches of The Police, the powerful melodies of Love, clever songs, a blues rock, like Led Zeppelin in their non-metal moments. It was full of songs called things like 'Kaleida', 'Soul Full' and 'Savvy'. There was even talk of a single called 'Selective Indignation' that never materialized.

Six years in the making, finally Reni was ready. His band the Rub were out on the circuit. A bunch of dates in the spring of 1991 met with a mixed response. Finally the last Rose had emerged from the mod shadows.

Like Dave Grohl, the drummer had stepped out from behind his kit. Reni was fronting his new outfit, proving those rumours of guitar skills and vocal ability were more than mere chit chat.

Phil Smith didn't see Reni for years: 'I was sat at home one night when I was living at Mani's and the phone went. I answered it and someone asked for Mani and I said he was out. The voice said, "Who's that?" I said, "It's Phil Smith," and the voice said, "It's Reni!" I hadn't spoken to him or seen him since he'd left the Roses. He said, "I've got this band together and I've got them rehearsing in the attic in my house, and I was going to ask Mani to come down and give them the once over. I want someone outside of it to watch them. Do you fancy doing it?" I said, "Yeah, all right."'

Intrigued, Phil went across Manchester to Reni's place.

'So the next thing I'm in his house. He looked great as well. You've heard the stories but he just looked exactly like Reni. He had this guy from Scotland drumming. After a while, he wasn't criticising his drumming, but he said, "I want it to be more like this." He just had a three-piece kit, and he got rid of the kit apart from the snare and says, "This is what I want you to do," and he just started drumming on the snare. He was mega. He was as good as he'd ever been. He didn't seem any different.'

On the tour I saw the Rub in Manchester at what is now the Academy 3. The tightly packed room was electric with anticipation. A floppy haired lunatic had got the microphone and was shouting 'give it up for Reni' and generally larging it about on stage like he does this sort of thing for a living…'Fuckin' hell it's Mani!!' correctly observes the geezer next to me and indeed it was the other half of that legendary Roses rhythm section doing the compere bit, bigging up his former sticksman.

The Rub shuffled on-stage and started picking out some sort of groove and there he was, Reni, looking good for his 35 odd years – fag in gob, the trademark smirk, cockiness intact, picking out the incessant groove of the Rub's very rhythmic muse.

The crowd, of course, were with him, hoping for the third coming. This was Manchester and Manchester had always loved the Roses (whether they are written out of the *24 Hour Party People* film or not). The Roses inspired a special bond with their fans and a decade later they are still there willing them on.

No one knows the new tunes and to be fair it's hard to pick them out at first. There's a couple of shimmering pop moments that could be early Roses, like pop thrills, but most of the rest of the stuff sounds like jammed-out workouts, a band feeling its way round riffs. In these hands it works a lot better than that sounds, there's a tightness about the music and a hypnotic adherence to the first rule of groove – a groove that was less funk than rhythm guitar, chopping onto the snare-tuff backbeat of prime-time power pop. Some of the songs are pure guitar pop rushes that have that sliver of magic like Reni's beloved Love. Listening to the songs now, they sound great, as melodic and magical as those classic Roses tunes. I wonder what will become of them.

Reni's vocals sound great – anyone who listened to the Roses already knew that – and you can hear that sweet croon that underpinned the Roses' classiest moments picking out what tunes there are.

For some reason Reni stands on the side of the stage, not in the middle, whilst in the background lurks Pete Garner, the Roses' first bass player, shaking maracas. It's the first time he and Reni have shared stage space since the Manchester International way back in 1987, but then Pete was a mate and he nearly played bass in the Rub.

Keeping it in the family, Roses style.

Reni was back, but where this one was going to go was anyone's guess.

But no matter how great this project could get, how effortlessly good his guitar playing and vocals are, there was the nagging feeling that you want to see him behind his drums, the man with a god-given gift...

And therein, ha! ha! lies the rub!

The rest of the tour brought many different reactions...fans looking for the neat melodic touches and the effortless grooves of the prime-time Roses were left feeling baffled, whilst some were prepared to embrace whatever direction Reni was choosing to take and all were waiting for the first recorded stuff, which never appeared.

Reni, the perfectionist, was working on the project every day but nothing ever came out.

The next time we saw him in public he was bounding into a room in a hotel in Soho and about to engage the world's media with the rest of the Roses.

Stone Alone! Ian Brown

The Seahorses were in full flow, Mani was rocking out with the Primals but where was Ian Brown?

The icon of baggy, the touchstone of that generation seemed to have disappeared. The whole messy demise of the Roses in 1996 seemed to have crushed his will to make music.

Of all four Roses Brown had the easiest and yet perversely most difficult set of choices in front of him. As the frontman he could easily gather up a band and get back out there again and yet as the only non-musician in the Roses he would find it difficult to make music.

If he wanted to make music at all.

He had last been spotted heading to Morocco, where his head was turned. His spiritual side strengthened in the Muslim country and his disdain for the decadent rock'n'roll lifestyle was further bolstered by the way Morocco had been treated by hipsters in the last few years.

He witnessed the muezzin call to prayer – a powerful sound that cuts through daily life, people singing without any commercial purpose, purely spiritual, a pure expression of Islam. Stuff like that can affect you.

'It lifted me off my feet, like a Saturday afternoon when I was fourteen – it was so rough and raw, echoing off the walls. The most uplifting thing I've heard for a long time.'

A million miles away from the empty world of rock'n'roll. The new Brown was now fracturing into a myriad contradictory parts; there was the spiritual Brown, the Koran-reading, righteous anti-drugs and booze rock'n'roll street preacher who still had one foot inside the world of rock 'n'roll; there was still the political animal now with an added Old Testament edge; and there was a commitment to speaking his mind, speaking the truth no matter who it might offend; a personal truth, his truth whatever it may be.

Less accepting of the bohemian types who have used North Africa to indulge their sensual whims, Ian comments, 'There used to be a thousand brothels in Tangiers. Westerners used to go to get smashed out of their faces, to pick up women and kids. '60s intellectuals and pop stars – they all went over there to abuse the people. William Burroughs, he was another bum. He abused his life and he wrote a book about it. There's nothing more boring than hearing someone else's drug stories. But he's held up as some kind of literary great. For me, he was just a bum.'

Then there were reports of Ian returning to England. Going to ground. There were rumours of beards and biblical-style forty days and forty nights soul searching, reading the Bible. Says Ian, 'I know about the lies and the abuse that goes on in organised religions. But yes, I've read the Koran. Me sister bought me it in 1991. It's a beautiful book.'

Ian spent months reading religious wisdom and smoking sensi (the strongest draw) with a Rastaman righteousness and the deep spiritual vibe that burns from classic Jamaican music – from dub, to ska, to reggae, to dancehall, to ragga. Y'know that biblical righteousness combined with the anger of Babylon, the cry for freedom tempered with occasional sexism and homophobia. A weird and wild mass of contradictions, like the Bible itself. How far Ian Brown was into this trip was open to speculation. He had certainly picked up on the anti-decadence schtick, the anti-rock'n'roll lifestyle arrogance. There was even talk of him becoming a gardener! Of giving rock'n'roll up completely.

'I'd seriously considered gardening. Fuck it, everything I'd believed in was finished. John had left me. Me best mates were robbing money off me. I had summonses up to here. I didn't want to know any of it. Fuck it, I'll do gardening for old people. But then I'm going out and kids are coming up saying "When are you going to do something?" In the end, I thought I probably should.'

Manchester has produced its fair share of musical mavericks over the years. Unconventional musicians who bludgeon their own way through the rule book and end up with their own style of music. Post-Roses Ian Brown wasn't about to change this.

Brown was caught between two stools. It was pretty inevitable; being the virtual spokesman of a baggy generation and a turn-of-the-decade icon, he was pretty well placed to get some sort of solo career off the ground. On the other hand the near-mythic status that he had accrued since The Stone Roses was going to be a huge burden on him.

Expectations had been too high for the second Roses album, expectations that had only resulted in disappointment.

Burned out, Ian Brown retreated to Lymm and grew a beard.

He had no plans to re-enter the filthiest business and is still bemused by an unlikely meeting. 'I looked out my window; it was after the Roses had finished. I didn't have any money and I was skint. I was living at my ma's, which was pretty devastating for me, then I got a cheque for eight grand which I put on a council house in Lymm. I thought Lymm, a quiet little spot, and I'll be able to live there without all the grief. At that time I had split with the mother of my two eldest kids – within three weeks everything went tits up and I was happy that I had a roof over my head. At that time Gareth turned up on my doorstep...I saw his car outside and I found out later that he had been at the newsagents at the end of the road saying, "Where does Ian Brown live? I'm his brother. I've been out of the country for 20 years, I need to see him." The woman in the shop says, "Oh, Ian, he lives down there."

'I looked down and I could see him looking, and instead of saying, "You fucker, you owe me 30 grand," I was like, "All right, Gareth," and shaking his hand. He was shocked that I was being nice. He said, "What you up to? Why are you living here?" I could see him thinking, "How's he ended up here?" I could see he was shocked because I didn't call him a cunt. I don't know why he came round. He didn't get out of his car, we just chatted for ten minutes. Coming round like – Gareth wasn't scared of anything. He run a nightclub, was totally brazen.'

Despite everything, Gareth Evans was still an intriguing character.

'We did like him. I tell you why we liked him: because everyone else round town thought he was a cunt. He was the worst dressed guy, he wasn't cool, was he! And we loved that because it used to make us sick the way everyone thought they were really cool like you got to have the right jeans and the fifty quid Italian shirt. We still had mates who had to buy their gear off the market. Just because you didn't have the right train-ers on didn't mean you were not cool! Just because you got your dad's wellies on because you got no money made no difference to us. Gareth didn't try and be cool like that; he didn't have a clue about clothes. Every-one thought they were so cool, you had to have the right record collection, the right haircut, the right wardrobe, and he had none of that. He didn't give a fuck about that. Everywhere we went in town, people were saying, "Your manager is a dick, what have you got him for? Every-one hates him. Everyone thinks he's a twat," and we were saying, "That's great, we want a guy like that. He's fearless, he doesn't give a fuck." He grafted 24/7, he wasn't scared of no one. He wasn't in awe of someone because they were a bigwig at a company or wrote for the *NME* – he would get on the phone and didn't give a fuck and that's why we kept him, and seeing him there a few years after we sacked him made me remember all that.'

The unpleasant end of The Stone Roses had left a foul taste in Ian's mouth. He was thirty-four, an unemployed icon, no record deal and a fistful of boring business problems.

It was a good time for some sunshine. Time to bail out. As Ian told *Record Collector*: 'After the split I went to Morocco. I felt great while I was there. I was away from the West…I could sit back and look at what the Roses did; I was always looking forward, I never looked back during the Roses, and I could now look back on Spike Island or when we played in New York or whatever. That cleansed me. And then I came back. I said to myself, okay, I've done my bit, John doesn't want to continue, I finish it – No, sorry, that came after Reading. Cressa, who used to dance with us, he said to me, people say it's not the Roses any more, you have to finish it. So I went to Morocco, came back and it was winter '96.'

And the music just started to seep out...

'I was ready to sign on, I was really skint. I sold my Portastudio for four hundred quid and I thought I got to make this four hundred quid last as long as possible and then I got the cheque for eight grand, which was my cut of the publishing due from the *Second Coming*. I had given up music, thinking, "What's it all about?" When I moved back to my mum's it was the first time I'd been in my bedroom since I had left all those years ago. What's it all about? I'd not got a pot to piss in, I got no band and two of my best mates have gone.'

A few months after Reading, Aziz decided to go and see Ian. 'After Reading there was a nothingness. Everybody vanished. Nobody could be contacted. All there was was this bad press. That was all I ever heard. Mani was first to jump ship...He was always planning this anyway. He already had a meeting with Primal Scream manager Alex Nightingale before Reading. I couldn't get in touch with anyone after Reading. I called round at his [Ian's] house. The first time I'd seen him for ages and he said that he wasn't doing it no more, he'd had enough. After that I called round as a mate. I'd have a guitar with me like always and showed him some tunes, some chords. Pretty soon we were writing tunes, jamming. I had a couple of things like the "My Star" riff and the bits of things that became "Corpses" and he had got the lyrics for "Corpses" and "My Star".'

Ian Brown was now spurred into creative action as he remembers: 'Aziz had come round to my house one day and knocked on the door and said, "Let's do some tunes." So we started writing. We wanted Mani to join us but we couldn't find him. At the time he had gone a bit wild and we tried to track him down. We would go round to his house in Moston but he was never there. Then one day he phoned me and said he had been asked to join Primal Scream and could he have my blessing and I said of course. I was always touched that he rang me up about it. So I continued writing with Aziz and we were thinking of calling the band The Brown. We were going to call the band The Brown and then the others said why don't I go solo. It was a bit like when Geno Washington had told me I was a star all those years ago.

'And I felt like, I'm gonna stick in me room, put carpet upon the walls and I won't go out until I've got at least ten or twelve songs together. And that's what I did. I booked into a studio and started to record it.'

Ian started messing about on his roughly constructed studio. Buying bits of equipment. Playing about with gear and bits of tunes. He set everything up, read the manuals and started to make some music. Never the musician in the Roses, Brown was obviously in the most difficult position to kick-start a solo career from scratch.

He had spent some time during *Second Coming* learning the guitar. Some rudimentary chords plucked from Bob Marley' *Chord Song Book*, chords to get by with, something to build songs on to.

He was working at his own pace, letting the creativity come naturally. He'd been dropped by Geffen but that was cool – no more schedules, no more stupid concessions to industry standards. Just making your own music at your own pace.

Aziz and Ian quickly got working upstairs in Brown's mini studio. Says Aziz, 'He'd got a little set-up in his bedroom. Got all the gear together, working out how to use it. I'd help out with programming. Get him going. He'd switch on the eight-track and a couple days later he'd come up with the finished lyrics for the songs. They were great lyrics, really made the songs. I went back to my house on my Portastudio and finished the music to "My Star". I took it back to Ian's and we worked a bit more on it there. Later on in the proper studio we added overdubs, like the NASA loops and military drums. We'd go to the house to do his stuff, four-tracks of vocals and harmonica.'

It was the first time that Ian Brown had written with anyone else apart from John Squire. Now he was out on his own writing by himself or collaborating with Aziz or whoever was on hand, learning as he went along. Stumbling along, creating a record from scratch. These were all factors that helped to give the songs that were coming together their idiosyncratic flavour.

Almost as a reaction to the years of polish and hanging about that had gone into *Second Coming*, this record was coming together fast. A record that was reflecting exactly where he was at.

Against this burst of creativity John Squire was achieving take-off with The Seahorses – selling out tours and records, playing onstage with Oasis at their record-breaking 1996 Knebworth gig, carrying their guitar flag that he had unfurled for *Second Coming*, leading the post-Roses breakout.

And while John was out there succeeding Ian's songs were nearing completion and studio time was booked. The record gradually gained its own momentum.

It was clear that Ian Brown was operating on his own agenda. This was not a band thing. An ad hoc series of musicians passed through the sessions. Some of the tracks were worked out by Brown utilising his rudimentary guitar skills, scrubbing basic chords out of his acoustic guitars, some were brought to the party by Aziz, the master session player with a heap of unused licks from his frustrating sideman years; some were brought in by Robbie Maddix and Nigel Ipinson; some parts even came from a Roses jam between Reni and Mani from the *Second Coming* sessions. Scraps of music, bits of sound, anything that caught Brown's attention and needed turning into a song …

The deal was done with Polydor. They knew how to handle this situation – just leave the man alone. Brown delivered the album. Most labels would have scoffed at the raw music handed over, but Polydor knew that they were on to something good. After all, the Roses' mystique had grown stronger in the years since the final collapse. Many in the music business had considered Brown burned out, a relic from the past, while John Squire was getting looked on as the true torch bearer of the spirit of '89. But when the former frontman released his debut single, 'My Star', it flew into the top five.

Ian Brown talks about how he got the record deal: 'I was really made up with "My Star" [going] straight in at number five. That was a fucking big achievement. John Kennedy, the solicitor who was the solicitor when we were doing the Geffen thing in court, was made head of PolyGram, as it was at the time, and when the Roses finished we all had to sign everything off. He said, "If you ever want to do anything in music now, get in touch." I said, "Naah I've had enough," but he said, "If you ever do, let me know." That was the summer of '96 and a year later I'd done all the record and it cost me eleven grand so I went to see him in that building near the Westway in Hammersmith and I went in there and I played him "My Star" and he said "I love it" and I played him the second track, "Can't See Me", and he said, "I love it. Which label do you want to go to? I got Polydor, Island, Mercury, Go! Discs." All my life my dad told me, "It's not what you know, it's who you know," and I thought, "I don't know anyone – that's why it took me years to get anywhere!"

'And all of a sudden it was coming true. I said [I wanted] Island because I wanted the palm tree on the label of the record, but they were not right and then there was this guy Paul Adam at Polydor who got in touch.

'So Paul came up to see me and I went out for a drink with him. He was a really nice guy so I went down to London with him and I met them

THE STONE ROSES • 457

all and the people in the office were really nice. They didn't seem like cokeheads.

'I was buzzing anyway because Polydor was Slade, Jimi Hendrix and James Brown. I said, "I want that logo – the red one with the black thing on it." That was important to me.

'It was through knowing John Kennedy, that got me through the door. So they took that album off me and put it out as what it is. I wanted the Dust Brothers in America to mix it, they had done the Beastie Boys, but I would have to wait six weeks for them and that seemed like an eternity at the time and I was like, "Fuck it, I want it out now."'

The rumours of the record deal and the upcoming releases sent a buzz of excitement round.

Ian Brown was going to be back in business but what, exactly, was he going to sound like?

It was easy to work out what John Squire would be doing but no one knew what sort of songs Ian Brown wrote. This record could go anywhere.

And when they started playing the 'My Star' single on the radio you could feel the relief. It sounded like the Roses, all guitars and husky vocals and a great melody to boot.

'My Star'

The release of 'My Star' in January 1998, three years after *Second Coming*, broke a long silence for Brown. As the pre-release tapes floated round eyebrows were raised. For a start it was a fantastic slice of guitar music. Built around Aziz's descending guitar shape borrowed maybe from The Beatles' often-raided 'Dear Prudence', it was a slice of guitar pop easily the equal of anything that the Roses themselves had recorded and fitted easily into their canon of sombre, majestic guitar pop.

The dark-hearted tune was underlined by Brown's convincing vocal. It was swiftly noted that this was a deeper darker voice, a new voice, much less the angelic rush of yore, the fallen choirboy that had soundtracked the kings of the baggy blitz. Brown sounded more mature; he also sounded smokier, lived-in.

On 'My Star' Brown was picking up the political baton put down at some point during the long months in between the two Roses albums.

'I see it more as social comment than politics. I've always been principled. I was brought up that way. The song's just pointing out that we have these wonderful space programmes, but they're mainly used for military purposes. It's vitriolic, but positive as well. I'm interested in the fact that two-thirds of people on the earth don't have enough to eat, but that billions are spent on rockets and bombs.'

From the release of the single, Ian Brown set out on a non-stop round of interviews. This was a very different plan of attack than in the Roses days. Instead of the guarded interviews, Brown seemed like a man who wanted to get a few things off his chest.

In the two years since the Roses had imploded at Reading Festival, the musical landscape had shifted somewhat. The Britpop/baggy whatever-you-want-to-call-it scene was fast coming off the rails. Boy bands were beginning their never-ending dominance of the charts, the Oasis hangover was still in full effect and The Verve, fronted by former Roses fan Richard Ashcroft (who had been a regular face on the '89 Roses breakthrough tour) were the biggest outfit in the so-called 'indie' genre. Their hit 'Bitter Sweet Symphony' became the anthem of the year.

In interviews Brown was talking in a deeper, more clipped, hoarse voice, talking about the Bible, the spiritual tip. Ian Brown in the late nineties was Old Testament spiritual mystical, like a dub prophet...

His musical taste was now a long way away from Brit white-boy indie and in interviews it showed! Brown was slating every other band on the scene. The bands that had been inspired by the Roses were getting the sharp edge of his tongue. He was openly bemused at Tim Burgess, scornful of Oasis and damning of indie music in general. He was shouting up hip-hop and ragga.

The interviews also showed a very human side to Brown. Obviously still feeling the hurt from the exit of his former best mate John Squire from The Stone Roses, he was laying into his former partner.

It's always difficult for any fan of any band to watch their former heroes tear each other apart in the press. For many long-time Roses followers, the vicious digs at Squire seemed to be very out of character – after all the band had presented a united front, they were the ultimate pop gang, close-knit, us-versus-them, 'the-band-against-the-world' type of outfit. For the press it's great copy and even for the disinterested it makes great visceral reading.

The Roses' long, slow split had left its scars and Brown was displaying them in public. Obviously very pissed off by the manner of John's departure Ian Brown was giving no mercy. Another feature of the new Brown was an anti-drug stance. He still may have smoked draw but it was the man-made drugs he railed against and cocaine especially. Cocaine was by 1998 enjoying a fast rise in hipness; London was caught in a snow storm, people who never used to take drugs were hogging the toilets at parties, cocaine was greasing the wheels of the music industry.

His anti-drug stance goes right back to the late seventies, when the Pistols drew a line between themselves and the previous hippie generation with their anti-drug attitude. It left a spark in the minds of a new generation.

At first the Roses didn't even drink, but were, in classic punk style, speed freaks. This was reflected in their wired, intense performances and Brown's wild stage antics. When they switched to marijuana their whole schtick slowed down, the music was tinged with psychedelic edges and the band were motionless on stage.

Too Much Monkey Business!

Released in March 1998, *Unfinished Monkey Business* came as a surprise. Wrong-footed by the tumbling-arpeggio near-Roses pop of 'My Star', some people seemed to be expecting a third coming, a guitar-laden series of obvious songs. Some people were going to be very surprised.

Says Ian, 'It was important that my solo début sounded like that after the *Second Coming* being 48 tracks and Bill Price mastering. I had to take it back down and make it real. There's good parts on *Second Coming* – my singing stops it being like a heavy rock band. Jarvis Cocker said that "Ten Storey Love Song' is great. I do like it – the music is brilliant. "Breaking Into Heaven" is a great song, "Begging You", "Straight To The Man" is good.

'The first Roses album was about the light colours, whilst the second one was deliberately dark. We set out to do that. I never play it; it reminds me of the days we were falling apart and lost it.'

Brown may have been the Roses' frontman but no one was sure if he was a songwriter as such. He may have lugged that keyboard over to John Squire's house to work on vocal melodies in the old days, but did he actually write songs or just vocal melodies?

Unfinished Monkey Business, with its raw production, open-hearted vitriol and anger, questioning songs and truth-attack honesty came on like John Lennon's first couple of post-Beatles albums. The hurt of the Roses' collapse was there for all to see. Truth and plain honesty were the order of the day. The music was a mixture of the Roses' guitar shimmers and the stripped electronic post-acid house daze that Brown was hooked into and would make his signature.

Ian Brown was buzzing over his new-found solo success: 'It was number one all week before it ended up at number four. It was the Saturday morning Woolworth sales that knocked it off number one – so I was like on fucking cloud nine then, because suddenly I was back in the music and I signed for five albums.

'I was in a unique position. I'd been in this loved band and had gone solo. If no one wanted to put the album out I could have pressed up the albums and done the sale and return myself, taken a hundred copies into HMV in every town, but in the end I just wanted it done properly and signed the deal.'

The album cover was a picture from Barcelona zoo.

Ian Brown: 'There was a white gorilla, he's died now. He was a bit angry and sad looking and I got my girl to take the picture of me doing an impression. It was just me pulling that face, looking like the gorilla's sad face. It's not right that he was there; his missus was sat there just chucking bits of mud about and he was sat there, poor fucker. It was one of our holiday snaps and I thought I'd use that for the album cover. It looks ace blown up on a poster. Polydor had that genius move when they got it on the back of buses; it was there for months and months, that picture.

'The album title is from the *Guardian* thing when they rang Rockfield trying to find out what the Roses were up to and him out of Dodgy was saying, "Ian Brown only answers to the name King Monkey," which was fucking brilliant. [laughs] He said that "Ian Brown is so up his own arse that he only answers to the name King Monkey" – brilliant.'

Free from the confines of being in a band, Ian Brown was in creative hyperdrive.

'As far as I care I had already made the ultimate record with the Roses so it was great to be making some stuff on my own. I could never be in another band like that again. There was no point in even trying it. I didn't have any ambitions to do it again. I was happy to get the album released and then I got an offer to play the Vs and then an offer to play

Glastonbury. I was like, "Well, wow, all right. I'll put a band together." I did a few small gigs in places like Buckley and Gloucester – I think I did the Roadhouse here in Manchester. I did a few little shows and then I got a letter from Inder Goldfinger and it made me laugh: it had a rubber stamp and cartoon of his own head with a big beard and a turban saying he had been in group called Fun-Da-Mental. I knew Aki, the band's main guy, from the punk days – he was a good kid, and it said, "If you ever want to play music again, I'm your man."

Intrigued, Ian contacted Inder.

'I invited him down to rehearsal. There was me and Aziz and this guy Simon Moore, the drummer, and I got Sylvan Richardson on bass because there was a rumour in the *Evening News* that Sylvan was going to replace John Squire. I phoned Sylvan up and he said, "Ooh, guess what? Me and you are both born on the same day, February 20 1963, and I think that means we are going to make some music together."

'It had been rumoured in the paper that he was going to be the next Roses guitarist when in fact we had got Aziz, so I thought it would be a cool band if we got him.

'Inder is a really lovely person – says it takes all sorts to make the world. He's always looking for excuses for people even when they were wrong 'uns. He would have fitted in the Roses. I wish I had met him years ago.'

The album has aged well. Its stripped down and lo-fi dynamics give it an experimental feel and the unconventional sounds and electronics mix well with Aziz's great guitar playing over the infectious breakbeats and grooves. Far from a conventional album, Ian Brown had cut a piece of experimental music that would have sat in the post-punk canon. This was a brave and bold work. Despite selling really well, it has never been appreciated as the ground-breaking piece of music that it is.

The subject matter on the songs was brazen and heart-on-the-sleeve; there were songs that might have been about former bandmates.

'Ice Cold Cube' was a reworking of the song that featured at those last Roses shows in '96, the song title a nickname that Reni may have had for John. But the song is not about John; the lyrics are a personal dig at the attitudes of coke-snorting associates, but not at John Squire. The only song about John Squire seems to be 'What Happened To Ya' co-written by Nigel Ipinson and Robbie Maddix. Tracks like 'Can't See Me' and 'What Happened To Ya' had that slinky Roses groove that hinted at the great lost Roses album that could have been made around the time of 'Fool's Gold'.

The record was very much Ian Brown. There were teasing touches of pop brilliance on 'Corpses In Their Mouths' and 'My Star', the incessant hook of 'Nah Nah', wandering drum machine-driven workouts like 'Lions' and a set of lyrics that seem to strike out in many different directions.

Some thought 'Corpses' was another Brown put-down of John Squire. The vitriolic attack on cocaine was considered by some a continuation of his interviews when he discussed his alleged accusations of John Squire's drug intake but again he denied this. Says Ian, 'I didn't write that one… that's about girls who hang round people in bands for cocaine.'

Mani and Reni provided a link with the Roses, with their jammed grooves from Rockfield sessions for *Second Coming* getting a reprise.

About 'Can't See Me', Brown says: 'It's a DAT that I had from '95 of Mani and Reni. I play bass over the top of it. I phoned them up and said "Can I use it?" – and they were cool. There's every possibility that we'll play together. I was jamming with Reni last week. He's now singing, playing guitar. In '95, me and him were in New York and we saw this kid playing drums in Times Square. Reni was looking at this kid and he knew the kid was better than him. It gutted him. He didn't pick up his sticks for a year. But now he's playing drums better than ever. "Can't See Me" is my favourite, yeah. Very fresh. We never followed up "Fool's Gold" because John never rated it! He felt embarrassed to play the funk.'

The track sees Ian Brown the righteous soul surrounded by corruption and careerism. Brown drawls in his husky Manc take on patois: 'All Babylon all around. And those that are close, you can't see who you are, and what you're doing. There's more to life than your own selfish ambition.'

Brown himself played on several tracks. 'I spent the winter of 1997 holed up with a bass, an acoustic guitar and a drum machine, learning audio techniques to add to the things I'd picked up over the years. The first song I came up with was "Lions" on the acoustic. I thought, "I can do this".'

'Lions', built around an incessant chanted hook and featuring Denise Johnson's typically great counterpoint vocal, was the longest track on the album. Its meandering structure makes it appealingly non-musical, a V-sign to the tight structures and trad middle eight 'classic' songwriting of The Beatles-loving Britpop bores. There was method to the madness and, built into the story, a typically Brown lyrical idea.

'I got the idea from the England–Germany game. I thought it was pathetic, grown men crying. Years ago there was a religious programme on BBC2, and they had a dread answering questions about his faith. And, as the credits went up, this dread's beating his staff going "There are no lions in England. Why do they have lions in Trafalgar Square and on the England shirt? There's never been any lions here."'

'Deep Pile Dreams' sneers at the dumb rock-star lifestyle, the temptations of luxury and powders and there's even a personal remonstration here. Says Ian, 'I think my mind had fallen into that category, definitely. We'd been given too much love; too many people believed in us.'

But Brown was a smoker – surely that was as mind altering as cocaine? 'No. I smoke weed. You can't ban a plant. It's a natural thing – it comes from the earth. Whoever heard of banning a plant? I've got a friend who was taken to court for growing it, and he refused to plead unless they changed the charge from growing marijuana on common land to growing marijuana on God's earth.'

The album came as a shock. The looseness, the toughness, the growing-up-in-public sound – it sounded unfinished but that made it sound defiant. Its neo-demo quality is what made it work. Why should music not be made like this? Overproduction is what has choked the life of most music in the modern age.

Compared to the over-produced *Second Coming*, it was a turn in a very different direction. Brown seemed almost determined to make this record his and if that meant ditching those tedious long hours of sitting around doing fuck all in the middle of the Welsh countryside, then all the better for it. Ian told *Hot Press* in an excellent 1998 interview, 'I didn't know if I could make anything musical. I didn't want it to sound like punk. But I wanted to destroy the mystery of sound production and the pretentiousness of musicians. That's what I was after. Where's this singer who can't sing? Now he's playing all the instruments.'

Gathering up an ad hoc collection of players from his current inner circle and learning as he went along Brown was wearing a lot of hats on this record. Songwriter, musician, producer...it would have been easy for Brown to have grabbed a bunch of cold session faces and put together a slick bunch of tunes.

He could have also bluffed his way through on his own and done it all himself. But with Aziz knocking on the door and other willing players a phone call away, a mixture of faces could only benefit these ideas.

Ian explained his set-up to *Record Collector*, 'I couldn't have done it all myself. I'm not a virtuoso. But I play bass, acoustic guitar, keyboards, drums, harmonica, and a trumpet! Then there's Reni, Mani, Simon Moore – a brilliant drummer, Aziz, Nigel Ipinson, keyboardist with the 1995–96 Roses. I've got the buzz now, I am writing all the time.'

Brown himself also continued to learn how to play guitar and a whole pile of other instruments. Although he is still a pretty rudimentary guitar player, having Aziz on board opened up a lot of possibilities. Brown himself was buzzing on working with Aziz. 'Aziz plays on six tracks, he's co-written four. He's perfect for me because he doesn't drink and he doesn't take drugs. And he'll chat.'

Post Roses his musical crash course continued. As he went along he started writing songs. Picking up scraps of melody from this rudimentary guitar playing, finding his way through songs, creating his own pile of tunes.

But this was a very personal effort with a loose ragbag of musicians and mates and with a lot of the programming and playing done by himself (including a return to the bass guitar on a couple of tracks, the instrument he had first picked up a couple of decades earlier in The Patrol). The album had a home-made feel to it, kinda like McCartney's or Lennon's débuts.

The sessions had started soon after the Roses' final, bitter fall-out. Muddling around on his home four-track, then getting help from Aziz and from four-track to four-track, bedroom to bedroom, they worked up the tunes.

The project was then moved to Forge Studios in Oswestry, a studio chosen because Aziz knew someone who worked there, and from there the final recording and mixdown were put together in the valve studios of Chiswick Reach.

Meticulously assembled with valve equipment, Chiswick Reach was perfect for capturing the 'warm' end of the classic guitar bass and drums line-up. It was picked because most of the Trojan singles were recorded there. It could even be used to warm up the dry hard sound of technology and sample-based tracks. It may have seemed like an odd choice of studio for a key comeback album, being more used to wilful eccentrics and lovers of the pure sound that its equipment gave to recordings. The sort of musicians who went there to make records had little or no interest in any kind of chart action.

Says Aziz, 'Ian's philosophy was to use valve gear and record on to tape not DAT...We transferred what we had on to two inch and added things.'

Take it or leave it. How Manc!

Crashing in at number two, the album sold 300,000 copies. The King Monkey had now regained his throne!

... And Down Again!

And then in one single *Melody Maker* review Ian Brown well and truly blew his whole 'good relationship' with the press.

The off-the-cuff comment about homosexuality touched a raw pop nerve and had a whole legion of commentators out for Brown's blood. Just when it seemed that the whole pop scene had slumped to an apolitical disinterested party mode, Brown had kicked off a pop political debate.

The *Melody Maker* would invite some pop star of the day in to talk about that week's singles. Something to alleviate the boredom of doing the singles. Brown dutifully made Audioweb the single of the week and hated Prolapse the most and put it in the dumper. But that's not what that week's singles will be remembered for.

In the pile of singles was Divine Comedy, the earnestly ironic Irish outfit who were having a few mini hit singles at the time with their foppish Noël Coward-lite pop. It set Brown off on a rant, the gist of which, as remembered by Brown in *Select*, is as follows:

'Julius Caesar was known as every man's wife. Romans were homosexuals. The top Nazis were homosexuals. Greece was homosexual. Most of the things that we had to suffer, the teachings of the Greeks, the philosophers – they're homosexual men. Now when they opened the gymnasiums and stripped the young boys, these were homosexual practices. I'm sayin' that that's what the West has been built on. It seems like the biggest heroes in Britain are homosexuals. Elton John, Danny la Rue, Noël Coward, whether you're from working-class people or whether you're the Queen Mother, you're looking up to these guys who're dressing up as women...'

Brown then added, 'You know what I'm saying, I'm not saying it's a bad thing. I'm just saying that's the way it is...'

And then the shit hit the fan.

The letters page was deluged with complaints. Brown had stirred up a hornet's nest of controversy.

Whatever was trying to get said, and Brown is not homophobic, it ended up being boiled down to 'Ian Brown is homophobic' and it did his reputation no good at all. This was the man who had marched against clause 28. The comments were strong but they were not directly homophobic, more an off-the-cuff comment taken out of context. That's one of the pitfalls of modern media.

The rest of 1998 seemed to see the tide of goodwill turn against Ian Brown. Reviews seemed to get sour, his image was suffering even if his record sales were still good. His 'truth attacks' in the press had stung; the Britpop bands, the Manc bands, the baggy bands he had ostracised were sniping back. The music scene didn't like what they were hearing.

The people, though, were still enthralled and he was playing to packed houses of devoted fans, many of whom would have been too young to have been into the Roses in the first place.

Too Much Monkey Business, Part Two: From Air Rage to 'B' Wing

The summer had been spent touring. Brown had a cool band together, a touring band that featured Aziz on guitar alongside Inder Mathura (GoldFinger) (percussion), Simon Moore (drums) and Sylvan Richardson (bass). Ian played a five-date secret club tour, followed by impressive appearances at the 1998 Glastonbury Festival and V98.

But there were shadows. Another problem collected earlier in the year was going to rear its ugly head that autumn.

If Ian Brown had thought the reaction to the *Select* article had been strong then what happened on flight BA 1611 from Charles de Gaulle Airport on 13 February was going to really blow up! The case had hung around for months, forgotten by the take-off of the album, at the back of minds during the press controversy and then starting to loom again that autumn.

And when the details emerged in court it was obvious that things were not going to go well for Brown.

There they were, Brown and band, flying rock-star class, all up front. There was a bit of gesticulating, a stand-off and an arrest. Of course both sides have their own story to tell. In court the prosecution claims that the cabin attendant Christine Cooper approached Ian Brown and his band thinking that he'd gestured for her attention. When she got there she realised they hadn't called for her attention and motioned with her hand apologetically. Ian was allegedly abusive.

As he was led away from the scene by guards, Brown said: 'The captain told lies. The captain is a magistrate. I did not defend myself because I did not do it. I never did it.'

Coming after a few months of various so-called 'air rage' incidents, he didn't stand a chance in court. It was time to make an example of someone and Brown copped the rap.

Magistrates heard how Brown approached the door of the flight deck when the seatbelt signs were on and the plane was coming in to land, and knocked repeatedly for twenty or thirty seconds. Captain Drake radioed for police help after becoming concerned that someone was 'potentially attempting to break into the flight deck'.

Brown, who had denied the charges, asked magistrates to suspend the sentence for the sake of his two children, but was immediately taken into custody.

He went down for four months. There was an appeal, but the appeal court judge said Brown was guilty of 'disgraceful and loutish behaviour' and upheld the conviction.

Aziz Ibrahim is still bemused by the series of events: 'There were events that completely shook the foundations, like Ian being sent down…the knock-on effect [was that] Ian came out changed. A different focus. He had new songs, lyrics and stuff, but it was also the beginning of the end for me, as in the writing thing. He had plans but it didn't include a lot of guitars. He wanted to pursue new directions but I was still submitting music he liked, "Getting High, Longsight M13", "One-Way Ticket To Paradise" and other stuff on the *Solarized* album, which was later on. I was in and out at different points but the last time was on *The Greatest* tour with Noel Gallagher and myself as special guests.

'But we've always been friends regardless. Like all friendships, they have their ups and their downs, they have good times and bad times but at the end of the day friendship prevails and that's just a continual saga of our relationship and the Roses today.'

468 • JOHN ROBB

He Fought the Law and the Law Won: Brown Goes Down

'A hundred and ninety-eight...199...200.'

Prisoner number B9311 was doing his sit-ups. His feet jammed under the metal rim of the bed, keeping in shape with the same relentless discipline that had pushed him through his karate in his youth.

It was November 1998 and Ian Brown was in Strangeways, the renovated and world-famous prison that glowers just to the north of Manchester City centre.

Strangeways had hit the headlines back in the baggy days with the thirty-day sit-in on the roof bang smack in the middle of the Manchester E party. The party spirit of Manchester even in that fuckin' jail! The whole city was going mad.

And who was that in his cell doing his press-ups? It was none other than Ian Brown, one of the prime motivators of that long-gone era.

Now instead of writing anthems for the flared generation, he was getting knocked up at 7.30 am, going down for his breakfast, and then spending the rest of the day in his cell doing sit-ups and press-ups followed by half an hour wandering round the yard, 'exercise time' and then half an hour 'association time' where the choice was a shower, watching TV or playing pool.

It's all a part of the dehumanisation, prison life. A tough regime.

And then it's back in the cell for hours a day. Long hours. Long empty hours which Brown fills in by lyric-writing, reading books like Eldrige Cleaver's *Soul On Ice*, the biography of black activist Marcus Garvey. Grabbing information, keeping his mind alert, avoiding his mind turning to mush.

Lights out at 8.00 pm.

Is this how 1998 is to end? He'd gone from outsider to critically acclaimed hero. Then it was the bitter enemy of the rock'n'roll business, the man who hated all he had spawned and had fallen out bitterly with ex-band mates; the positives were fast turning into negatives. He was now, in the media's eyes, the maligned 'homophobe', the bitter outsider, the press enemy, and, finally, prisoner B9311.

What a bizarre see-saw of a year.

There was plenty of time to reflect on this in prison.

He'd been banged up since the end of the trial on 23 October, and then in the van en route to Risley he had heard the story of his own incarceration being read out on the news. A surreal situation. After a weekend in the notorious Risley he was moved to the more laid-back environment of Kirkham Prison. The last time he'd gone up the M55 was for Blackpool in '89. Now he was near Blackpool for some very different business.

Being the pop star in prison had its own problems. Sitting down for his first meal, a scouser had made a sneering threat, only to be shouted down by a Manchester ecstasy dealer that Ian knew back from '88, guaranteeing Brown a certain passage of safety.

Brown was still hopeful. The appeal was in a week and he was bound to get out, the charge was ridiculous. Whoever heard of anyone getting four months for a bit of a stand-off on a plane?

But the appeal was thrown out and Brown was on his way to the grim Victoriana of Strangeways. Shunted from wing to wing, he even had a job putting screws into electrical components for cookers.

The governor of Strangeways confessed that his son was a fan and gave him a pen and told him to write some songs. So Brown came up with the words for 'Free My Way', 'So Many Soldiers' and 'Set My Baby Free', the eventual backbone for the album that he was planning for '99. The songs gave the album its flavour.

In the end he was put on B-wing and allowed out of his cell for twelve hours a day, wandering about, semi-free, signing autographs for fellow inmates.

But the last two weeks had been mostly a laugh. Says Ian, 'It was like school dinnertime.'

And then halfway through the four-month sentence, he was up for parole, released and free to go home for Christmas. The prison was buzzing. Ian is still clearly moved by the experience. 'Kids were running up to me, giving me hugs, risking twenty-one more days in there. The love I got on that last night was equal to Spike Island.'

On the morning of Christmas Eve of the most chaotic year of his life, Ian Brown walked out of Strangeways, out of the prison gates then down past the run-down shops, past Victoria Station and then down Deansgate, Manchester's posh shopping street, unnoticed in the last-minute

Christmas rush. He walked the length of Deansgate till his feet were sore, soft from eight weeks of sitting around in prison. He walked past Atlas Bar and then into Deansgate Station and got the train back to his parents' house, back to the south of the city.

Four days later he was with his Mexican then-girlfriend and future ex-wife Fabiola Quiroz, lying on a hot beach smoking a spliff, grinning his Cheshire-cat grin.

A free man.

Golden Greats for a New Millennium

Washing those prison blues right out of his hair, Brown was swiftly in the studio putting together the second album.

The plan was to move on from the début solo outing, get some bigger production on board, move further away from guitars, pull in some of those acid house and electronic music flavours, make a record for the 21st century.

The result, *Golden Greats*, released 1999, was a resounding success. A new direction.

Never one to rest on his laurels, Brown had started work virtually on his release from Strangeways and early in 1999, he was booked into Metropolis studios for sixty days, a very different recording environment than the first album, a lush environment that is reflected in the record. The second Brown album was a big departure from his début. Indeed it was a reaction to the near lo-fi flavour of that record.

Richly produced by Brown himself and engineered by Tim Willis, the record left any kind of indie roots far far behind.

Not that this was an attempt to make a smooth record for the mainstream. *Golden Greats* resonates with darkness and reeks of claustrophobia, of prison and paranoia, haunted by iron bars and an increasingly vitriolic music press who were now viewing Brown very differently than during his comeback.

The closest kind of atmosphere to the record would be Joy Division's later work when they took on a more electronic flavour which captured their stormy atmospherics.

Golden Greats took Ian Brown in a very different direction. The first noticeable change was the album's electronic nature.

His disdain for most of the post-Roses bands and indie music in general was obvious. The sort of music he was talking about was ragga and electronic and and although the record was never a straight acid record, it was very different. Moody, dank, dark soundscapes suiting his voice.

Not that the record was purely electronic soundscapes. The guitar was not dead yet. Says Aziz, 'The most guitars on the record are on the opening track "Getting High". It's a Free/Bad Company riff! A classic rock riff! Again like the first album we did it on the Portastudio at home.'

Aziz also points out that both albums have parts of the same song meshed into them, I have this track, "Morassi", a Chinese instrumental sort of thing and Ian really liked it. He took sections out of it for both the albums. It's that little snippet before "Getting High" and it's also in "Underneath The Paving Stones" on the first album. It's part of that sound-collage with kids talking...on both albums...I'm really proud of that song. It's a beautiful little journey this tune...I want everybody to have it...'

But this was no dance record. Instead of the fractured ragga beats or the dancehall vibes of contemporary Jamaican musics that Ian was giving props to in interviews, it was actually closer to the dark side, the left-field underground of post-punk Manchester.

Ian Brown explains the music's development: 'After *Monkey Business* I realised how you had to tighten up the programming. I got a proper contract now and I want to go in a proper studio. I got in that SARM West. I go down there and phone the engineer and I said, "I want a programmer," and he said, "There's this young kid in town called Dave McCracken." I said, "Can you get him for me?" And he did and I got on with him like a house on fire.'

The pair started working on Brown's new songs.

'I got some tunes on an eight-track and I didn't have bass lines so I went to do "Dolphins Were Monkeys" and I had a beat I done myself, a few bass notes, and I was singing lyrics and the melody. I needed guitar and keyboards, and this kid comes up with something on the keyboard and I put that line over my beat...it sounded ace. He said, "That's what I do, I'm a programmer," and I said, "That's composing," and he said, "I just worked for All Saints and I did the same for them and I got money for programming only." I said, "I'm not getting 100 per cent of songwriting and lying awake at night knowing you came up with the tune, and I'm not arguing, half that tune is yours now." "Golden Gaze" was a similar thing. Si Wolstencroft, who was with me from the early Roses days, had the beat and we chopped it up. Si had been our mate from years ago, from school.'

Si Wolstencroft was back with Ian Brown after his initial group of musicians had a falling out.

'Si Moore, Aziz and Sylvan weren't getting on and I got sick of it, so Sylvan and Si Moore had to go and that's why I got Si Wolstencroft back. The album is the same as *Unfinished Monkey Business* but tighter, more cohesive and more professional sounding. Dave had some ideas he had written and I said, "Brilliant, I got the lyrics to go with it." I said, "You write the music and I'll write over that." Every couple of days we would go to his house and get some new tunes and take them to my house and add lyrics and then chop them up or double a bit here. I said, "I'm not arsed, I got my name all over the cover anyway, why don't we say you co-produced the album. I spent six months in his front room and he had his wife and kids in the bedroom or watching the telly while we had the mixing desk and all the gear in his front room. I said, "I blew it last time because I didn't get the Dust Brothers in to produce it and I'm not sure if I got the best ears in the world. I want it to sound good on a window cleaner's radio and on a five grand stereo, or on a car radio."'

Ostensibly still a pop record, the second album's songs' sparse electronic backdrops and off-the-wall structures were more the result of the singer's lack of experience in writing songs in the so-called 'classic' songwriting mode. Put this against a post-Oasis backdrop of the so-called 'Dadrock' scene when every band in Britain seemed to be in thrall to The Beatles and the Stones and the whole damn encyclopaedia of rock and it makes the record seem a far braver and more individual thing.

Aziz's oriental-flavoured instrumental at the top of the album gives a false impression. Within a minute the mood has switched.

The first salvos of a big rawk riff kick in. Built around a hypnotic loop 'Gettin' High' is the closest to straight rock that Brown has ever got.

'Aziz played me this riff,' says Ian. 'It was the classic rock'n'roll riff like Free's "All Right Now". It's the first track, I wanted it to sound definitive.'

Next is the single, 'Love Like A Fountain', the shuffling rhythm and the hypnotic melody riding over the bubbling old-skool house synths. It's one of the best songs Brown has ever been involved with and is the first indication of the stylistic switch in the album. Guitars are down, rhythms are up, the space suits Brown's voice – there's plenty of room for it. The record sounds like the sort of post-acid house non-trad guitar record that Brown had been talking up for years.

Of course it's not hip-hop, but it has the same kind of structure, the same kind of space. If hip-hop is a very American form, maybe it's more honest for the British with their different roots, different lives, to bring a different flavour to the most influential music form of the nineties.

Now things get really moody with 'Free My Way', one of the three sets of lyrics that Brown had written in jail. With its jangling key intro (a nod to the Stones' 'We Love You'?) dark vibes, prison lyrics and scowling synth strings, the song switches from sonorous undertones to James Brown's 'It's A Man's World' plucked sections. The vocal is at once belligerent and doleful as it intones the dark mood of jail life.

Brown's favourite track on the album, 'Set My Baby Free', was built around a distorted funky chop keyboard loop he was given by Anif Akinola, who had worked with the classic Guy Called Gerald 'Voodoo Ray' track, one of the best tracks to come out of the acid house thing, a song that is so evocative of that era that it is pretty well a signature song of the Madchester period. 'Voodoo Ray' still sounds as strong today as when it was originally released in the late eighties. The song is stark, simple and powerful and melodic in its sombre vibe.

'So Many Soldiers' is another jail lyric. The title came from a letter that Brown had been sent in prison by Fabiola. The song continues the spooked darkness that haunts the record as Brown, in a strong northern accent, switches the subject from his personal jail experiences to an anti-war tirade over a sparse trip-hop workout.

Coming in with castanets and a Spanish neo-flamenco acoustic that hints at Love circa *Forever Changes*, 'Golden Gaze' at first alludes to Brown's avowed attempts to learn Spanish before switching to a crunching riff as the singer states the simple transcendental pleasure of life. The semi-stoned ooze of 'Golden Gaze' caught a perfect moment a million miles away from the claustrophobic grimness of prison.

'It came from a visit to Jamaica, sitting in a straw hut on the beach, with the sun rays pouring through the roof. All I could see was gold,' explained Ian.

The coolest thing about this tune is the way it is completely unmusical. The maverick spirit reading the manual and playing one-fingered keyboard still lurks in this album, only this time there is some added polish and some expertise from engineer Tim Willis and programmer Dave McCracken.

The number of songs written about monkeys returning to the ocean to evolve into dolphins can probably get counted on one finger let alone one flipper. 'Dolphins Were Monkeys', released as a single, arrives bouncing around on a phat funky keyboard chop and more of those bubbling old-skool acid squelches, picks the pace up. The song comes complete with a great vocal.

'Neptune' brings the pace back down again – an ambient wash, a relaxing stoned chill-out, while 'First World' is Brown digging at the cultural imperialism and empirical arrogance of the world's major powers, still crushing the so-called 'Third World'.

The album ends with 'Babasonics', a lilting chiming guitar thing provided by an Argentinian group of the same name. Ian liked the track so much that he took it and made his own song from it, running the track in the studio, adding a shuffling drum loop behind it and a resigned sounding vocal over the top. It sounds like a lazy ending to the record but its sheer oddness works.

Golden Greats is Brown finally breaking free from the shackles of the Roses. There are no songs referring to the band or John Squire. The music is a million miles away from the Roses. The stark samples and dark moods dripping from the album make it a great listen. The scope of sounds and the broad vision mark it out as one of the best records of 1999.

It was bagged in a striking painting of Brown. 'The cover happened after this guy sent me a picture he'd done of Mike Tyson in orange and green and yellow. He said he wanted to paint me, so I sent him a photo. He's called Ian Wright. He's a really talented artist. In an interview with some magazine, Jarvis Cocker said, "Ian Brown, he's no oil painting." Well he is now!'

Golden Greats in one fell swoop re-established the singer as a creative force and was greeted with some rave reviews.

Brown was back in business.

A Stone Alone: Brown Greets the New Millennium

1999 ended with the triumphant return to Manchester Apollo. As usual the atmosphere was intense and Ian made the most of the night, delivering a faultless show. The stripped down band, the simplicity of the songs, made a powerful base for his vocals which were bang on.

All that was missing was Aziz's guitar for tunes like 'My Star' and 'Corpses', a fact that the genial Aziz would only grin about when I asked him at the gig as we hung around at the back of the Apollo. Perhaps the best gig of his solo career so far, Ian Brown was leaving 1999 on a high note, no jail, no major bust-ups, a great cutting-edge record, a good slab of UK sales and some critical acclaim.

The year ended at the millennium show at the Castlefield Basin in Manchester where I trooped down with another 10,000-plus partygoers to check out Brown, the main attraction to the end of the millennium in a classic Manchester drizzle, the best thing in a huge non-event of a night.

2000 was a fairly quiet year. There was a spate of festivals and a bunch of shows with Aziz back on guitar. I caught up with Ian Brown at Reading Festival where he blew the roof off the tent with the best show yet. The constantly evolving band of the past two years was pretty well honed to perfection, Si Wolstencroft looking ageless and razor sharp as ever laying down the backbeat twenty fucking years after playing with Ian in The Patrol! And Aziz was back on guitar, filling the gaps in the early period solo stuff and being a good foil to the stark, cold electronics. The atmosphere in the tent was of course outrageous but now, instead of coasting along on the past, Ian Brown was looking to the future, still looking for the cutting edge, still changing his music. Affable backstage and easy-going on stage, it seems that Ian Brown has finally found an even keel, a groove.

2001

'Music of the Spheres'

If *Unfinished Monkey Business* was Brown working out how to use a studio, its very charm being its fumbling nature, the lack of technical knowledge adding to the songs' DIY feel, *Golden Greats* had been a more disciplined affair. The new album was even more lush and rounded.

The album's classic was 'F.E.A.R.', where the first letter of each word in a line spell out the song's title. 'F.E.A.R' was brooding and stark and full of new millennium darkness. It was a long way from the guitar-oriented music of The Stone Roses. Brown was very much on his own tangent and making highly original music.

Perhaps most apparent is the influence of his Mexican wife with the Spanish vocals on 'El Mundo Pequeño'. The album's bold and stark stripped-down nature is underlined by 'Hear No See No', where the electronic pulse is added to by Brown whispering the song's lyrics. 'Stardust' and 'Shadow Of A Saint' are the album's other standouts, and it's a bold and confident work of highly original music, again with Dave McCracken playing a vital role in the songwriting and programming.

In 2004 Ian Brown released his fourth album, *Solarized*, which combined strings with slick beats. 'For the fourth one I wanted to get my hands dirty again and work out some bass lines,' he says. 'I love the freedom of not being in a band. I can work with who I want. If I want a track with only keyboards on it then I can. With the Roses we would always pull the voice down because it always made the music sound too weak but now because it's solo and got my name on it I can turn the vocals up a little bit, I can have the voice a bit louder, there's more space with the beats. I think the albums are improvements, one after the other. The first one was almost like a demo; the last one, slick beats and full-on orchestra – way over budget! I spent far too much on it but you may never make another one; you never know if it's your last one.

'I thought whilst I got the opportunity to get the money I may as well spend it and make the strings as big as I can and put them to slick beats.

'Gary Aspden, who's my mate who works for Adidas, met this guy at Universal who had a mate who made hip-hop beats and wanted to work with some different people. He sent me some beats – that's the way I work now. It's always got to be new; it's gone full circle for me. I'm not looking to change music, I [just] want 12 great songs.'

The album was another major UK hit and saw Brown firmly established as a solo star, a process continued by his next album, 2007's *The World is Yours*.

The album lead-off single 'Illegal Attacks', with Sinead O'Connor ,was a plaintive work of guitar arpeggios and cello, and culminates with Ian Brown pleading earnestly for the return of British soldiers to their homeland – one of the most directly political songs of his career.

The album also was a Mancunian homecoming of sorts with the Manc bass titans Andy Rourke and Paul Ryder being involved. Brown had also asked Paul McCartney but the ex-Beatle was not available.

There were more special guests on 'Me And You Forever', which was a particular thrill for Brown as it features Steve Jones and Paul Cook from his beloved Sex Pistols.

His last solo album before the Roses reunion was his sixth, 2009's *My Way*. The album featured one his best songs, the jaunty piano-driven 'Stellify', which was never as big a hit as it should have been but which has become one of those songs you hear everywhere.

The album sounded like the end of an era. A near-autobiographical work that visited some of the musics of his youth, its very titles pretty well summed up Ian Brown. Brown took the opportunity to reference his former band and his life with songs that are littered with clues about the Roses, friends and foes from a turbulent few decades at the frontline of British pop culture.

My Way was also a neat reference to one of Ian Brown's favourite groups, the Sex Pistols, with iconic Pistols bassist Sid Vicious's genius destruction of the classic song being one of the cool situationist punk-rock moments. It's that kind of maverick Pistols approach to music that Brown still invokes. That full-on attitude and swagger that for a brief period the Pistols had, Brown has maintained for years.

The album was a statement of intent. Brown had never compromised his vision; he had made pop on his own terms and never by the rules. His lack of muso knowledge was his strength; this is a purely instinctive music that follows its own nose and somehow works. Unconventional and yet accessible – that's a cool trick to pull off.

My Way was the latest instalment in his idiosyncratic canon, with songs that musically and lyrically touched on key moments in Brown's life. The feel is upbeat, and the album was his most varied – and perhaps his most commercial – yet with some sublime pop.

Again working with key collaborator Dave McCracken, Brown explored many different facets of pop. The album took the strong points of each of the preceding albums and combined them into one almighty whole. It was his strongest work yet.

Opening track and single 'Stellify' bounces in on a piano motif that sounds almost seventies, hooky as fuck – this is the first of many potential singles on the album. Brown's voice sounds strong with that fallen-angel innocence about it that underlined all the great Roses songs. There's a great horn break on the track; it's piano-driven, bouncing, upbeat, super-hip, modern urban pop.

The mood switches with the dark, melancholic, electronic pulses of 'The Crowning Of The Poor', which is so typically Brown – few British artists in this period get as dark as this and make it work. The song shows that the political side hasn't left the singer after all these years. He sneers at the millionaires on their yachts, pointing out that they have the money, but they haven't got the heart and soul of the poor. Brown has been working towards this moment through all his albums. Each time it's worked but this time the dark track has bloomed into something else quite extraordinary and original.

In comparison 'Just Like You' is almost jaunty. It still retains that pure melancholy, but also packs a crystalline pop chorus – the kind of chorus New Order were knocking out at their prime. The breathless vocals trip over themselves in a rush to get the message home. This is another hit single and radio smash in waiting. It makes you think of the Hacienda at its peak, those big songs echoing around the E-drenched room. Good times. Twenty-four-hour party people, moving on.

Swerving away from the death disco of the last two tracks, Ian opted for a cover of Zager and Evans' 'In The Year 2525'. Brown had done off-the-wall covers before – there was that brace of Michael Jackson workouts. In Brown's hands 'In The Year 2525' sounds like some kind of political anthem. There is the welcome return of the mariachi trumpet, which is such a part of the Brown sound, adding a levity to the music and also referencing his then-wife's Mexican background. 'In The Year 2525' brings back memories of the Roses classic 'Made Of Stone', with the same descending chord structure and anthemic darkness in its brooding power, and there's plenty of those dread biblical references in there, which Brown is always so adept at delivering.

Could 'Always Remember Me' have been referencing the Roses? Who exactly was 'throwing it all away'? The song has a wistfulness, a sense of regret not always apparent in Brown's iconic, upbeat presence. It's a sensitivity that has always been there, from day one. It's in the voice, which packs attitude and humanity in its now-husky intensity, sung over the deep, dark echo-drenched sound that hints at mid-eighties feedback-drenched indie underground and those sun-kissed Spectorish ballads that sound so timeless. Ian sings a vocal melody that is reminiscent of early Roses. The backwards guitar loop is magical as the song oozes to its stormy climax.

Was 'Vanity Kills' a precautionary tale for pop scenesters in a world where we all have to get old? The song sounds like a film soundtrack, a brooding, atmospheric piece that looked at the dark underbelly of love or pop stardom. The Roses may have collapsed spectacularly but Brown unpicks the dark side of the fall-out and leaves the wreckage, walking tall. Having any kind of sanity left in the fractured world of rock'n'roll is some kind of achievement.

'For The Glory' is another great vocal, full of biblical references and defiant swagger. Brown cryptically intones. Could he be making a stand for the Roses? For his solo output? 'He didn't do it for the glory' he sings and we believe him. As the song continues the Roses references come thick and fast – he even sings 'bang the drums' at one point. Could this song be putting the Roses legend to rest after all these years?

The pace picks up for 'Marathon Man', which sounds like nothing you've heard before, with stripped-down electronics and scorched-earth rhythms that built up to a hooky chorus.

This was a song about reasserting yourself, and that legendary Brown confidence and self-belief that powered Generation E. The swagger of that vibed generation, that total self-belief that made people feel ten feet tall, that non-blinking stare back at the establishment; it's all in here.

'Own Brain' sees the author standing up for individuality in a world where following the herd has become the norm. There's seemingly no space for mavericks in the twenty-first century, with the outsiders and the originals brushed aside. But somehow they still squeeze through and are always given a heroes' welcome. That explains Brown – one part everyman, one part English eccentric. He doesn't fit into the pop machine and that's his strength. 'Own Brain' is the manifesto for his attitude and is also an anagram of Ian Brown...

'Laugh Now', intoned over a chiming keyboard, is a moral tale, a nursery rhyme oozing wisdom, whilst 'By All Means' is savage, trying to find mercy for someone who has done Brown wrong. But he's having difficulty in dispensing that mercy and wishes the perpetrator to hell – it's the demonic preacher man rearing his head again...dark stuff over a backing track that again invokes big filmic themes, like Morricone on a digital keyboard with big 3D soundscapes.

'So High' is a great last track, almost a singalong with a whirling Hammond neo-soul melting pot of sound that creates a fantastic atmosphere for Brown to clear the slate. This track waves goodbye to all the mercenaries who attempted to leave Brown behind. It's a rocky road that musicians have to travel and with all the relationships that make or break careers, the mercenaries could be anyone – they could be lawyers or fellow travellers or managers, Brown doesn't specify, but you can feel the sense of injustice in this sardonic classic.

Original, autobiographical and self-reliant, perhaps Brown's best album, *My Way* is Brown's aptly named masterpiece.

Moulded by punk, Brown had carved his own swaggering path. A uniquely English presence existing on his own terms, he had become a northern folk hero and icon. In the meantime he had created a series of great records in an idiosyncratic and ground-breaking solo career. The live atmosphere at one of his solo gigs is unlike anything you'd experience at any other gig in the UK – the intense support for a folk hero, an icon who never seems to back down, a Bruce Lee of indie – a musical maverick who shadow boxes his songs like a youthful Ali, holding up his chin and taunting the enemy.

Brown's career has been the story of a generation – from the initial teenage thrill of punk, the mish-mash of mid-eighties culture, mods, scooter boys, skins and punks, Creation Records, paisley shirt psychedelia. Drifting in and out of bands, cheap drugs, wild nights, pretty girls, great records, and then finally finding a band that everyone would soon call their own and a band that still means so much to so many people – The Stone Roses.

Whither the Roses?

In the new millennium everything is so, so different. Manchester has changed beyond recognition.

The Hacienda is a pile of rubble. Another block of over-priced yuppie flats is in its place. Manchester city centre is full of designer wine bars. The clubs are stuck in a limbo. The music scene has revived, moved away from the so called 'baggy' boom. There are arguments about it being trapped in its past, but this ignores the endless new talent coming out of the city. At the time of writing, Wu Lyf had recently released an amazing début album and young bands like Frazer King, Deadbeat Echoes, Janice Graham Band and many others were poised to take music in their own diverse directions.

A different mood, a different music…

The ex-Roses still made headlines. There were solo careers, big festivals, gigs. They were carving out their own paths in the post-Roses landscape.

Ian Brown had the highest visibility; his solo career had really taken off. John Squire was a respected artist, Mani was the bass king and Reni? Where the fuck was Reni?

But there was always that feeling of unfinished business, that the Roses had ended with a comma rather than a full stop. Ian Brown was playing Roses songs in his set and the crowd was going crazy. Over the past 20 years the tunes had seeped into the public consciousness and the band had become iconic.

People were asking what would you give for one last throw of the dice? One last chance to see that amazing rhythm section just go off on one? John Squire's guitar get all crystalline and pure pop before soaring off into some solo that actually made you feel something, and that pimp roll executed properly by the King Monkey himself? What would you give for one last resurrection of this great British rock'n'roll band…THE third coming?'

2011

'I'd love to see Reni play again. I think what it is with Reni is the fact that he doesn't think he can do better than he has done before. I can see his view on that in a way but I'd fucking pay money to see him play the drums again. He's got a style unlike anything I have seen. You know, Keith Moon and John Bonham is in there but it's more – he had the swing, the rock and the roll and he was a proper showman and he had more styles of drumming.' Mani, 2008

All summer 2011 there had been whispers of the return of The Stone Roses. Rumours had already been refuted. Gossip laid to rest. The talk had needlessly flared up in the spring after Ian Brown and John Squire finally met up at Mani's mother's funeral. Instead of leaving the bass player to grieve, the tabloids had run with a reformation story and whilst it was true that three of the band had met for the first time since that last Wembley gig on 29 December 1995, they hadn't reformed. Yet.

That sad day, though, had rekindled a friendship and Ian Brown and John Squire realised that they still had so much in common. The weeks that followed saw phone calls and then meetings and eventually music as new songs began to form. They texted Reni and asked him if he wanted to listen to what they were doing and were surprised that he was keen. They went round to his house and Reni was blown away with what he heard. With Mani back on board, having resolved the emotional decision as to whether to leave Primal Scream, the full band was rehearsing again in Manchester over the summer of 2011.

That first rehearsal had been a blast. There they all were: back in the room together again. Face to face. Amps buzzing, drums rattling. The first song they played together after all this time was 'Shoot You Down', its loping beat and trickle of melodic guitar gently coaxing the band back into gear. From the start the buzz was there.

Somehow their new manager Simon Moran had booked the 75,000-capacity Heaton Park in north Manchester for June 2012 without anyone noticing. Everything was in place. Summer turned to autumn and the band waited. Patience was always part of the Roses' story. This was the band that took five years of poverty to write its first album and then sloped off from the limelight for a similar amount of time to write the second. What's 15 years between friends?

In early October I got an email about a press conference in London. 'You have to be there!' said the band's press agent, Murray Chalmers. How odd. It didn't say who it was for.

'You know the band…' it continued. Could it be the Roses? There had been that niggle, that talk. Ian Brown had been very quiet all year.

In town someone else said you have to be at this press conference. It was all falling into place. Something was going on and there was only one story left big enough to justify these kind of whispers.

Clash magazine flashed it up on their website. Another Roses' reform story. I texted Ian Brown and he texted me back.

It was happening. I confirmed the rumour on my *Louder Than War* music website: 'It's On' was the message and the website crashed from the amount of people reading the story. The secret press conference for the next Tuesday was The Stone Roses announcing their reformation. This was the big one.

There were curveballs, of course. Reni released a cryptic statement: 'Not before 9T will I wear the hat 4 the Roses again'.

What did this mean? Was he not coming to the party? There was panic on the internet. And all the way till the day before the conference there was doubt that the drummer was going to make the show.

Press conferences are part of the theatre of rock'n'roll. A good press conference is a pop cultural moment. The Roses had been here before: the press conference the night before Spike Island was a media stand-off with the band psyching out the world press. What would this be like?

There was some media cynicism. Comebacks are commonplace in music these days. In 2011 it was Pulp, and Pixies have been flogging their back catalogue for years. These bands are above criticism, so where do the Roses stand?

Soho, on that murky but strangely warm late morning on 18 October, is dotted with Manchester veterans down for the crack. I take refuge in a cafe and spot Ian Brown walking down the street. He pops in and we hug like husky-voiced music veterans of the north. Ian is bouncing, proper bouncing; this is actually all rather exciting.

We go back a long way and I understand why this return really matters. Rock'n'roll needs a romantic narrative – real life can be very grey and people need folk heroes. The Stone Roses made great records that em-powered people, an empowerment that made a generation of kids like the Gallaghers or The Verve or any British band in the nineties say, 'Fuck you, I'm not a nobody. I'm going to make my own art.'

And that's why we are all here at this press conference, well, why me and Ian are sat in a cafe a couple of hundred yards from the Soho hotel where the conference is about to take place. Ian can't sit still. He's on the tips of his heels with a non-stop grin on his face. We talk of the return and getting to see Reni play drums again. We agree that if you set him up on his own with his stripped-down drum kit in Manchester Apollo we'd both pay just to watch him play for hours. 'I'm lucky,' smiles Ian. 'I get to watch him play in the rehearsal room.'

Today Ian Brown has the air of a man whose destiny has been fulfilled and all that talk of unfinished (monkey?) business can finally be put to rest. There are new songs, he says, psychedelic pop music, and it's going to be massive.

Press conferences are normally stale things. Bands mumbling answers like robots from some kind of autocue. The Stone Roses, though, do things differently. The event is in Soho House, a posh London drinking club full of suits and non-famous celebrities. The northern contingent look out of place but in control. The conference room is packed and when the band mooch in it's to a big cheer.

The press has been preparing tough questions. Everyone is cynical about comebacks but as soon as the band has sloped into the room they get a standing ovation. I've never seen that before. Their magic remains intact despite all the years and the wrong turns.

'It was great to walk in to claps and cheers. I thought we might be facing a firing squad in light of all our previous reformation comments so to feel the love when we walked in was great,' Ian Brown says later.

The band sit back, everyone takes a deep breath and then Mani shouts, 'We are here to announce we are splitting up,' and everyone laughs.

I get to ask the first question about whether there will be new songs and we're off. This is very off-the-cuff, very northern; very straight answers, bits of piss-taking. Fans will spend the next few weeks looking at YouTube and wondering what it all means. The band's personalities are intact from the old days. Mani is no-bullshit northern funny. Ian Brown skilfully bats back tricky questions – putting down the *Daily Mail* with the

'What does it feel like to write for a newspaper that used to support Adolf Hitler?' comment. John Squire says everything by saying very little and Reni is hilarious as they announce Heaton Park as he wonders aloud if he has the energy to do it.

Afterwards we retire to the bar and the band are affable. Ian Brown is still beaming. It's good to see Reni after all this time. He is still worrying about having the stamina to play these high-profile gigs but we know he will deliver. It must be strange to be thrust back into the limelight after all those years of living in the real world.

A few days later Alan McGee, the former Creation boss, is still laughing at the audacity of it all. 'You're right, there's nothing more rock'n'roll than a good press conference. The *Daily Mail* guy gets slaughtered by Ian Brown – how cool was that! "What does it feel like to write for a paper that supported Adolf Hitler?" – hilarious. The Stone Roses were as cool as the Pistols were at their press conference when they announced their comeback a few years ago. That was different, though, really antagonistic – everyone was trying to put them down but Johnny was slaughtering them, killing them, knocking them out of the park when everyone was trying to have a go. This was good but in a different way.

'How did they keep the reformation off the internet? How did they rehearse all summer without anyone knowing? How did they do that? I didn't know they were rehearsing. I had heard rumours from a very unlikely source about them reforming, but I had heard them before. I kind of tended to believe this one though because it came from close to the band, but till it was announced I didn't quite believe it. I loved that quote from Ian Brown when he said that he wanted to announce the reformation the day after the riots. I fucking love him for that, it's so Ian Brown. I'm not sure how many people get that. The Stone Roses give people hope. Most people reform for the money. But the record deal and the plans for a new album mean that it's more than a bank job. If the record is not good people will kill them! They have lots to lose. They have to make a good record.'

McGee looks up and adds, 'The media was trying to get me to take a pop at the Roses for reforming but I said "great". They asked why, and I said people have got nothing at the moment, nothing to believe in. They are making a new record, not only giving people hope but putting their balls on the line. Like the Primals, they are defying gravity, which is good.

When you get older than 50 the chance to make records for 25-year-olds to understand is very difficult but they can do it. They have sold loads of tickets. It's great for Mani, after all these years – he will be rich – and Reni as well! These people actually deserve it. I think of all the cunts that have come through music and done well and not even had an inch of talent. Everyone took their act. Oasis were amazing; they were influenced by the Roses and they got paid. The Roses never got paid. I don't even know what Reni did for the last 20 years. They met up at the funeral. They talked. They decided to do something. It worked. It's not that cynical.'

John Brice: 'I heard about the reformation on the Thursday or Friday. I bumped into someone who said, "Have you heard the news? The Roses have reformed." I said, "Mani has been saying that for years," and then there it was, the press conference.

'John Squire came out with the same haircut and looked cool, the classic guitar player haircut. Reni was the funniest one, I forgot that until the press conference. He was always the funniest; I remember how quiet the rest of them could be.'

The Stone Roses had returned looking older, looking wiser. The press conference was pure pop theatre. There were no slick promises from the band. They hinted that it could all collapse at any moment. What will happen next is anyone's guess. Ian Brown told me of the great new 'psychedelic pop songs' they were writing. The gigs sold out in minutes and everything was set up for the most unlikely of all comebacks...

'I'm taking a year off and going to every gig,' a thrilled Liam Gallagher told me.

The rehearsals were going well, onlookers talked of a band at the top of their form, the perfect arrogance of the past tempered by all life had thrown at them, the unique chemistry flowing again. This was a band that should have taken the world and which was now reclaiming its rightful place, a band that could have been as big as U2, but who seemed to have been resigned to cult status, suddenly re-emerging, a band that paved the way for Britpop, Blur and Oasis, suddenly reappearing from nowhere and grabbing their rightful crown as the biggest band in the UK.

The four of them had been through so much. Thirty years down the line, the band that had meant so much and had seemed to be the ultimate in what ifs, had come back as the biggest band in the UK.

They had seen all the highs and the lows, the triumphs and the mistakes; they had promised so much and snatched defeat from the jaws of victory; they had an astonishing self-belief and a pure talent. They had been the closest band – a tight-knit crew that had torn itself apart.

They had enjoyed the euphoric rush of when they were the most important band in the country that had changed everything. They could have been the biggest band in the world but they fell apart amongst bickering and bitterness. For the fans it was heartbreaking to see where it had ended up and be left with unfinished business. The years following the split they seemed, like The Beatles, beyond reforming, and yet somehow when they finally met the pull of that friendship between Ian Brown and John Squire that had gone back decades was too much; the perfect partnership that had complemented each other perfectly was rekindled. Within minutes of the announcement they had reclaimed their crown from all the bands who were so influenced by them. The press conference was a triumph; the tickets were flying out. There was a massive new record deal and the most unlikely comeback was going better than anyone could have dreamed.

Justice Tonight

Eight weeks later and the press conference is already part of pop culture history. The *NME* ran two consecutive front covers on the band for the first time in their history and it was all over national TV.

The tickets for the three Heaton Park gigs in Manchester for 75,000 people a night sold in 40 minutes and the band have gone to ground again. It's December and I'm the compere on a remarkable tour with Mick Jones from The Clash, playing a set of Clash songs (for the first time in 30 years), along with The Farm and Pete Wylie, in support of the 'Justice for the 96' campaign for the Liverpool fans who lost their lives at Hillsborough on 15 April 1989.

The first night in Cardiff on 1 December is a stunning gig; special guest James Dean Bradfield from The Manic Street Preachers delivers a really great version of The Clash's 'Clampdown' but all the talk backstage is of the special guests who will be playing Manchester tomorrow – John Squire and Ian Brown are going to turn up and show their support for the cause! This has to be kept quiet – The Clash and the Roses sharing a stage is quite something.

Manchester Ritz had been many people's favourite Manchester venue for years. Built in the 1920s, it retains the proper dusky music-hall feel that suits great rock'n'roll. It's seen its fair share of history – The Smiths played their first-ever gig there on 4 October 1982 and the Roses themselves played a gig there on 7 July 1986.

I arrive at five o'clock and there is an ad hoc band soundchecking. It's Ian Brown and John Squire playing in semi-public for the first time since the reformation. About ten people mill around in the room as they run through Clash classic 'Bankrobber' with, bizarrely, Simon Wolstencroft: school friend, Manchester drumming legend and the drummer in their first teenage band, The Patrol.

They had got there early, wanted to run through the songs, needed a drummer and Si was there. It's the first of several circles that get closed tonight. It's not The Stone Roses who have reformed at this soundcheck but The Patrol! Afterwards Si explains how strange it was to be playing with them for that brief moment after all this time. 'I just got up and it felt like all those years ago. John nodding at me as we were playing. That was great. John was dead cool and sat down at soundcheck and we chatted. I'd not seen him since 1996. He was there with his guitar and with a big smile on his face doing in-jokes from the school days. It cracked me up right away like Ian always does when I see him and he does jokes about the old teachers from them days.'

'Bankrobber' is the perfect choice because it comes with its own great Roses story. In 1980 The Clash took a day off from their UK tour and recorded the song in Manchester with two teenagers hanging out in the studio – Ian Brown and Pete Garner, The Stone Roses' first bass player. After the soundcheck Ian and I phone Pete up and get him to come down to the gig. He turns up and another great circle is closed.

The gig itself is already special. The Clash songs have grown men in tears and it's an emotionally charged event. At the end of the mini Clash set the band walk off as the crowd hope for an encore. No one really knows what's going to happen next. There had been some Twitter action but very few people in the venue have any idea of what's about to happen. The lights dim and two figures shuffle onto the stage. For about 30 seconds no one seems to notice them...

Then, wooosh – fuck me, it's The Stone Roses!

Ian Brown and John Squire have chosen this tour, this cause, to make their post-reformation live début, to make their statement. It's the perfect way to ease back into the spotlight. None of the big showbiz bullshit, but an important gig on an important tour and a chance to tie up a lot of loose ends, all at once.

There's something quite moving and important about big Manchester United fans like John Squire and Ian Brown making this statement of solidarity with Liverpool fans over this call for justice – but then they know that this is a bigger story than one of rival clubs.

They know that the demand for justice on this tour is universal and not just about one team. Like Mick Jones – who's a big QPR fan – this is about the bigger picture, this is about the way that people died that horrible afternoon and about the way that football and rock'n'roll integrate in our culture and resound so strongly with us. It's about the way that the people's music is the perfect match for the people's game and it's about that ancient cry of justice that is so part and parcel of all great rock'n'roll.

For John Squire this must be a big moment. He may be in what has to be the biggest band of the moment in the UK but in his youth The Clash were everything to him. He had a Clash mural painted on his wall and the story goes that he had guitar strings used as laces on his brothel creepers the way Joe Strummer apparently once did. After all, he was a 14-year-old kid besotted with one of the greatest rock'n'roll bands of all time – what a cool way to start his long musical journey.

John stands there on stage looking cool as fuck, tousled hair, guitar slung, ready to go. The already-electric atmosphere is now cranked up a lot of notches. Everyone realises that this is a moment of pop culture history, the return of the Roses.

Mick has asked them to play 'Elizabeth My Dear', the very direct anti-monarchist song off their classic début album. What a perfect moment; a strong political statement and not one of the obvious hits.

It's just like the comeback for *Second Coming* when they ignored the mainstream and only gave the *Big Issue* an interview, a statement of where they are coming from, using their power in a good way and never taking the easy, obvious route.

The song starts with John playing the guitar line with an effect on it that gives it an almost sitar-like drone and then Ian intones the words and the 'Scarborough Fair' melody. He sings in that great nasal, almost folk English voice of his that adds to the ballad's English folksiness, giving it an ancient air. It could have been written hundreds of years ago and makes you think about the power of song and the way that protest songs have been so much part of our culture for such a long time.

Then Mick Jones, Pete Wylie and The Farm join the pair on stage and they run through 'Bankrobber' with Ian Brown singing and then The Clash version of the Willie Williams' 1978 reggae classic 'Armageddon Time'. It sounds great, and the Roses pair are on form. Ian Brown does his Ali shuffle to break the ice while John Squire trades smiles and guitar licks with Mick Jones, who is grinning like a Cheshire cat. After the show Mick says Squire is a real joy to play with. 'He's so intuitive, the way he plays around you, an amazing guitarist.' Even with only half the band on the stage, The Stone Roses are back in business. The story isn't over yet.

ACKNOWLEDGEMENTS

I would like to thank the following people: Ann Marie Hayes, Louise Cuzner, Gillian Gaar, Marije Tintin, Andrea McGowan, David Fisher, Carl Stanley, Craig McAllister, Eva Seljan

ABOUT THE AUTHOR

John Robb first met an embryonic Stone Roses in the post-punk fallout of the early eighties when his band used to rehearse next door to theirs. As a result he was the first journalist to document their remarkable rise to the top in a series of articles for the national music press, and attended show after classic show that saw them change the face of British music. In 2011, he launched an online rock music and pop culture magazine/blog www.louderthanwar.com.